Technology, the Environment, and Social Change

SALALM Secretariat
General Library
University of New Mexico

Technology, the Environment, and Social Change

Papers of the Thirty-Eighth Annual Meeting of the
SEMINAR ON THE ACQUISITION OF
LATIN AMERICAN LIBRARY MATERIALS

Instituto de Bibliotecas de la
Universidad de Guadalajara
Feria Internacional del Libro
de Guadalajara

Guadalajara, Jalisco, Mexico
May 15-20, 1993

Patricia Noble
Editor

SALALM SECRETARIAT
General Library, University of New Mexico

ISBN: 0-917617-49-5

Printed in the United States of America

Contents

Preface

The theme of the thirty-eighth meeting of SALALM was to some extent conceived as a follow-up to the United Nations Conference on Environment and Development which had met in Rio de Janeiro in June 1992. Also known as the Earth Summit, the meeting was an important milestone in the development of international concern over the increasing degradation of the environment by human activity and technological processes. Some of the most catastrophic effects of this destruction are to be seen in the Americas. By an ironic coincidence, 1992 was also the five hundredth anniversary of the first encounter between the peoples of the Americas and Europe, the outcome and consequences of which were to a significant extent determined by the technological superiority in decisive areas of the invaders. In recent years, however, Latin American organizations and institutions have begun to explore the possibilities of innovative uses of electronically based technologies such as video and computers, particularly in the fields of popular communication and the dissemination of information. "The Impact of Science and Technology on Human Communities and the Environment in Latin America and the Caribbean" seemed therefore an appropriate and timely theme for SALALM's 1993 meeting.

The papers in this volume are arranged in two principal sections: the first contains papers directly inspired by the conference theme; the second, papers read at sessions dedicated to non-theme topics. The conference also included demonstrations of some new technologies. A hands-on workshop on computer databases produced in Latin America itself, or relevant to Latin American studies, was organized with the assistance of our hosts at the University of Guadalajara in collaboration with the Latin American Database Interest Group (LADIG) and the Latin American Scholarship Program of American Universities (LASPAU). A session on independent video production included the showing of extracts from videos made by Peruvian and Brazilian community groups. Bibliographies and resource guides which were distributed at these events are included here.

The volume closes with a essay on the Chilean scholar, José Toribio Medina, in whose name SALALM awards an annual prize for bibliography; this is the first in a projected series of studies of outstanding figures in the world of Latin American bibliography and librarianship.

As always, however, it should be noted that the papers published here represent only the more publicly prominent aspect of SALALM's activities and achievements; the organization is much more than an annual conference. Meetings of the SALALM committees listed in the backmatter occupy the first day and a half of each conference, and committees often continue their discussions during the next few days. Reports of these proceedings are not included here, although brief summaries were published in the *SALALM Newsletter* (vol. 21, no. 4, February 1994), and audiotapes are stored in the SALALM Archive at the Benson Latin American Collection at the University of Texas.

The work of these committees provides, however, the true raison d'être of SALALM, whose main purpose is the promotion and coordination of research provision for Latin American area studies in the Americas and beyond. To this end it works on long-term projects, often in cooperation with organizations such as the Association of Research Libraries and the Mellon Foundation, while also maintaining its own major publishing program of bibliographies and reference works. These activities are sustained between conferences by individual members working within this committee structure. Their willingness to commit their talent, energy, and often a great deal of their personal time in this way is the primary source of SALALM's continuing strength and vitality.

P.N.

Acknowledgments

The Executive Secretary of SALALM, Sharon Moynahan, and her assistants, Nikki Gaedeke and Christine M. Schooley, labored heroically throughout the year leading up to this meeting, acting as liaison with our hosts and with the hotel management, acting as a transit point for communications between the U.K. and Mexico, compiling, editing, and designing the conference program, and coordinating and organizing registration at the conference itself, and always with unfailing energy and patience. I owe each of them personal and heartfelt gratitude.

Grateful thanks are also very much due to the organizations and the many individuals who made this meeting possible. The conference was hosted by the Instituto de Bibliotecas of the University of Guadalajara and the Feria Internacional del Libro of Guadalajara (FIL). We owe warm appreciation particularly to Lic. Irma Pellicer, director of the Instituto de Bibliotecas, for her support, administrative, financial, as well as personal, her assistance in enabling the participation of our three Cuban colleagues, and in providing computer and video equipment, together with technical support, for the database and video workshops. We are also deeply indebted to Maricarmen Canales, director of the FIL, and her staff, who were responsible for publicity, promotion, liaison with bookdealers, and the most attractive conference site; to Carlos Andrade and the staff of Viajes Copenhagen, who handled the hotel and travel bookings with great aplomb; and to the management and staff of the Holiday Inn, Crowne Plaza, for their efficiency and helpfulness.

Finally, but not least, I know I speak for all those who attended the thirty-eighth SALALM in expressing our most sincere gratitude to our bookdealer colleagues and friends, the SALALM libreros, for the reception on the final evening of the conference in what has become a tradition of generous hospitality.

The Historical Background

1. Beyond Crosby: Recent Historiography on the Columbian Exchange

Peter Stern

The quincentenary of the discovery and conquest of America began as a celebration, and ended as a wake. Almost lost in the revisionism and Western flagellation was an appreciation for the degree of change both Old and New Worlds have undergone as a result of what was termed "The Encounter." The work of cultural geographers, anthropologists, and paleontologists provided evidence which scholars in the "softer" social sciences have employed in a variety of ideological positions.[1] The physical scientists have provided ammunition for their brethren in the great ongoing polemic over the meaning of 1492, a debate which began with the promulgation of the *leyenda negra* in the sixteenth century and continues unabated to the present day. I propose to examine both the literature and some of the ramifications of the Columbian Exchange; in doing so I will touch unavoidably upon the Great Polemic itself.

Although the muse Clio has had to prostrate herself more and more in the last decade before the holy trinity of race, class, and gender, there are those who have not forgotten that hard agricultural, parasitological, immunological, hydrological, and meteorological realities still rule the world with an iron hand, and that these realities have shaped, and continue to shape, our lives even in the postmodern era in which we consider ourselves to be living. Germs, plants, seeds, animals large and small, insects, the abundance or scarcity of water, topography, wind, soil composition—these and other factors have influenced the course of history. Physical and cultural geography have taken a backseat to more fashionable "-isms" in our present intellectual Zeitgeist as agents of societal development, but we would do well to remember them.

Let us consider the following for a moment. Who could ever have predicted twenty years ago that a retrovirus, one perhaps living dormant and nonparasitically among populations for centuries, could profoundly alter the course of human society, would infect and kill millions all over the world, decimate an entire generation of creative artists, exacerbate fear and intolerance in our supposedly enlightened society, retard the social liberation of a repressed minority, and bring to a screeching halt the most profound changes in human sexual behavior (made possible by the development of effective birth control) in centuries? HIV and AIDS have brought a degree of humility to our egotistical dreams of total control over our environment. They remind us that the realm of the physical intrudes into the theoretical world in which the humanist and social scientist dwell. The past decades have seen the development of historical philosophies rooted in theoretical frameworks encompassing such factors as economics, sexual preference, gender, race, class, Marxism, deconstructionism, intertextuality, and a hundred other "-isms"; these epistemologies have proliferated to the point where the physical world which encompasses these conceptual universes is made irrelevant. Let us remember that the metaphysician may propose, but biology has a nasty tendency to dispose.

The appearance two decades ago of Alfred W. Crosby Jr.'s *The Columbian Exchange: Biological and Cultural Consequences of 1492* was a milestone in the historiography of New World cultural geography. More synthesis than primary research, Crosby's book nevertheless drew together a disparate body of work by historians, physiologists, biologists, and geographers to explore the macro-effects of European contact with the Americas. His own article of 1967 in the *Hispanic American Historical Review*, titled "*Conquistador y pestilencia:* The First New World Pandemic and the Fall of the Great Indian Empires," served both to underline the Cook-Borah thesis of large indigenous populations in the Caribbean and Mesoamerica prior to contact, and to deflate the infamous European "Black Legend" by establishing the crucial role of epidemic disease in the destruction of the New World's indigenous empires. Crosby's work was amplified a few years later, when William McNeill published *Plagues and Peoples* in 1976. Here the entire globe and its history were examined for the effects of disease upon the development of societies. McNeill in his forward credited his puzzlement over the relative ease of the Spanish conquest of the Aztecs with spurring him into examining the role of epidemic disease in history.

The isolation of Amerindians for millennia provided fertile ground for the diseases which the Spaniards and Portuguese brought with them: pandemics of smallpox, measles, typhus, scarlet fever, chicken pox, diphtheria, whooping cough, scarlet fever, and influenza swept through the Caribbean, Mesoamerica, the Andes, and Brazil in the decades which followed first contact. Mexico, for example, was swept by successive waves of epidemic disease in 1520, 1548, 1576, and 1595. Isolation as a factor in the spread of disease vectors was aided by other conditions: the Americas were incapable of supporting infectious chains of organisms which would have encouraged the spread of epidemic disease. Although they had more than adequate numbers in terms of population, they lacked the necessary numbers of domesticated animals which would have passed parasitic organisms from animal to human host.[2] In the case of the Americas, it was human and animal carriers from Europe which were the disease vectors. These diseases led not to total destruction of the aboriginal populations, but to extremely sharp reductions followed by gradual recovery. Cook and Borah calculated that a disease vector among an untouched population brought a mortality rate of up to 90 percent.[3] After that, in Crosby's words, the hardy survivors interbred among themselves and with the new European immigrants, which led not only to better resistance to disease, but also to the beginning of population recovery.[4]

But the cold statistical calculations of immunologists and physiologists cannot capture the anguish and loss of Indian society; Crosby reproduces the famous lament from the book of *Chilam Balam*: before the advent of the Europeans,

> Then there was no sickness; they had no aching bones; they had then no high fever; they had then no smallpox; they had then no burning chest; they had then no abdominal pain; they had then no consumption; they had then no headache. At that time the course of humanity was orderly. The foreigners made it otherwise when they arrived here.[5]

One of the main points of Crosby's discussion is that the deadly epidemics resulted not merely in high mortality, but also in the complete disruption of political, military, social, and economic institutions. Smallpox destroyed the ability of the Aztecs to fight back effectively during the siege of Tenochtitlan; it also very probably killed off the Inca Huayna Capac, his son and heir, and many other prominent governors and military leaders. These Andean losses were sustained some years before the Spaniards even set foot in the lands of the Incas, as their germs traveled before them, borne by refugees from the Mesoamerican holocaust. The enormous demographic catastrophe of native Americans engendered an equally devastating psychological blow to native cosmology. The immunity of the invaders to the many sicknesses ravaging the land reinforced in Indian minds the superiority of the Europeans and their one god, and the overthrow of the native deities. Little wonder then that the Cakchiquel Mayans lamented, "We were born to die!"

But not all of them died; those who survived lived in a world increasingly altered by the less lethal agents of biological change which the Europeans brought. Crosby cataloged the impact of Old World plants and animals in what he termed the "Europeanization" of flora and fauna. Much of this Europeanization proceeded from the cultural insularity of the Europeans: when not absolutely necessary, they preferred not to have to eat maize, manioc, or potatoes, and so imported wheat (which did not thrive in many tropical and semitropical areas). Because the New World was in their eyes not overprovided with protein-rich animals, they brought pigs, chickens, and cattle. The horse was their symbol of military and cultural superiority, and natives were forbidden to possess or ride this animal. As time went on and Spaniards tried to recreate insofar as possible their home environment, other fruits and vegetables, most notably olive trees (for their oil) and vine cuttings (for sacramental and nonsacramental wine), were transported and planted.

This widespread invasion of foreign organisms was very much a mixed blessing for the Americas. Each importation had a cultural as well as a biological impact, often an unfortunate one. While the Spaniards turned their noses up at the meager native choices for meat, which included dog, turkey, duck, llama, and guinea pig, the Indians immediately loved chickens, cattle, and, above all, pigs. But the Spaniards' cattle trampled their milpas, occasioning endless lawsuits in the courts, and pigs ran wild in enormous numbers, eating up Indian gardens. This may have been a small price to pay in exchange for the tremendous gain for the Indian diet, which for non-elites had been usually poor in protein. But for every gain there was some loss. In exchange for clothing of cotton or agave fiber (insufficient for the cooler temperatures of the valley of Mexico), the natives received wool, and sheep raising became an integral part of the Mexican and Peruvian economies. But llama and alpaca populations in the Andes diminished as the European animals transmitted animal diseases, and the colonial *obraje* or textile mill followed the introduction of sheep as the capitalist component of the exchange. *Obrajes* were often little more than sweatshops, and a common destination of criminals who would work out their sentences locked in a textile mill.

So for culinary gain there was concomitant cultural loss. Crosby notes that Indians who lived in areas controlled by the Europeans lost out in biological competition with newly imported livestock, but that natives living beyond the boundaries of European settlement received horses, cattle, sheep, and goats not as rivals but as valuable additions to their sources of food, clothing, and energy.[6] It is true that the Chichimecs, Apaches, Comanches, and other nomads of the northern Mexican borderlands, the Tehuelche of the Argentine pampas, and the Araucanians of Chile gained immeasurably (if briefly) from the biological exchange, but for the greater mass of sedentary natives in Peru and Mesoamerica, the imports of the conquerors were a mixed blessing. Indians did not like growing wheat, for example, because of its expense and trouble. Maize needed but slash-and-burn preparation and a *coa,* or digging stick; wheat required flatter land, renting or purchasing oxen, and a plow. In addition, tribute to an encomendero was usually paid in maize, but tithes had to be paid on wheat or any other European crops the Indians raised. (In the some areas, Spaniards who desired bread simply made wheat a part of Indian tributary quotas, leaving the natives no choice.)[7] In other areas, the decline in native population brought increased animal husbandry; the animals supplied more calories with less human labor than sowing crops. As villages were all but wiped out, there were fewer and fewer people left to preserve traditional agricultural practices, especially where agriculture was communal.[8]

There is no denying that European imports like sugar and coffee totally transformed certain sectors of colonial society. In fact, "the economic underpinnings of most of the important European settlements in the tropical and semitropical zones of America historically have been the raising of a certain few crops on large plantations for export to Europe."[9] Sugar turned the depopulated Caribbean into the greatest market for slave labor the world has ever known; the cost of that human diaspora from Africa is one that is still being paid by U.S. society today. The capitalist plantation complex, with its concomitant labor, economic, and societal patterns, shaped the emerging Caribbean, Brazil, and states in the U.S. south into distinct societies; even as spectacular crops of cotton, sugar, coffee, rice, and indigo were being shipped to Europe, the seeds of future turmoil were being planted.

But Crosby's greatest contribution was to remind us that the Columbian Exchange was a two-way street: the impact of New World crops on Old World demography was nothing less than revolutionary. Crosby proposes that the spectacular rise in world population can be traced to the Encounter; in his words: "Rapid worldwide human population growth probably occurred only twice before in all history: once when man, or proto-man, first developed tools and again when man invented agriculture. And then it happened again, after the century in which Europeans made highways of the oceans."[10] Nothing, he states, but increased food production can account for the doubling of human population between 1650 and 1900, especially since significant advances in medical science and hygiene did not take hold until the end of the last century. Maize, potatoes, sweet potatoes, beans, and manioc have increased the number of basic cereals upon which humankind has survived, and they offer some advantages over traditional European grains. Maize, for example, will prosper in areas too dry for rice and too wet for wheat; its yield per acre is roughly double that of wheat, and its growing period is shorter. Potatoes can be cultivated from sea level to over 10,000 feet and need no sophisticated equipment to grow or harvest. Sweet potatoes yield 3-4 times the crop of rice per unit of land and are very resistant to drought and tolerant of poor soils. Beans, including French, kidney, navy, haricot, snap, string, lima, butter, and frijole are all American, and especially high in protein, oils and carbohydrates.[11] New World quantity is equaled by quality: only rice can match American cereals in terms of millions of calories produced per hectare; potatoes, sweet potatoes, and manioc are far more calorie-intensive than wheat, barley, and oats.[12]

Crosby's principal point was that American foodstuffs were not necessarily superior to Old World foods, and complemented rather than replaced them. Their greatest advantage is that their demands upon soil, weather, and cultivation technique differed from Old World foods; by and large they were easier to grow and demanded less labor than traditional European grains. But overdependence upon new foodstuffs could result in tragedy. The potato seemed to be a gift from God for Irish peasants of the eighteenth century: one and a half acres could produce enough tubers to feed a family for a year. Demography, soil, and weather conspired to make the Irish dependent upon their potato plots, and their population more than doubled between 1754 and 1845. When blight wiped out the crop in mid-decade, one of the worst famines of modern times occurred; as many as a million people died, and several millions more emigrated. The impact of the potato upon the rest of Europe (especially Russia), of maize upon Africa, and of sweet potatoes, peanuts, and manioc upon certain areas of East Asia has been profound, if less dramatic and traumatic than that notorious episode.

In sum, Crosby concluded that the Old World came off the winner in the Columbian Exchange. Europe, Africa, and Asia gained invaluable foodstuffs and commercial plants, while the Native Americans who survived the greatest demographic catastrophe in human history can console themselves on their miserable remnants of sovereign land with the thought that their diet is richer (they die from all the ailments of "modern" man), and the Renaissance. The results, says Crosby, of the biological transfers from eastern to western hemispheres have been, at best, mixed. The ecology of vast areas of the Americas has been altered by the propagation of Old World life forms, from large animals like cattle and horses, to plants and microorganisms. Indigenous plants have been either eliminated or restricted to small, uncultivated areas in thousands of square miles. Native animals have been outgrazed and outprocreated by hardier, more aggressive European immigrants. The positive results have been an enormous increase in food production and, thereby, in human population (optimistic words for 1972). The negative results have been the "destruction of ecological stability over enormous areas and an increase of erosion that is so great that it amounts to a crime against posterity."[13] While subsequent historiography may have deepened our understanding of the ramifications of the Columbian Exchange, nothing in the two decades since Crosby penned those words has softened his judgment or censure.

In fact, fourteen years later Crosby revisited the subject on a wider scale. In his *Ecological Imperialism: The Biological Expansion of Europe,*

900-1900 (1986), the stage upon which the interchange of Old and New World flora, fauna, and microbe impact is measured is the entire world. "Ecological imperialism" is Crosby's unsubtle way of characterizing events after 1492. Crosby summarizes all of biological history, from the breakup of Pangaea (the proto-continent) to the present, as a relentless drive of life forces to fill vacuums, to escape from competition. He credits first the great migration from Africa, and later the invention of agriculture, to overpopulation and competition for natural resources. Everywhere man goes, he proposes, he tries to adapt nature to his own ends, almost always with unfortunate results. Crosby dots his eclectic history with melancholy examples. The Norsemen sailed west to Vineland (America) not out of a sense of adventure, but because Greenland was too inhospitable, and Iceland had been deforested and eroded through overpopulation and ruinous agricultural practices.

In another example, the Portuguese arrived in the Madeiras, and "set to work to rationalize landscape, flora, and fauna previously unaffected by anything but the blind forces of nature."[14] The settlers almost inadvertently introduced rabbits into the islands; with natural predators lacking, they soon exploded in numbers, eating the natural vegetation to the ground. Wind and rain erosion followed, and the "empty econiches" were occupied by weeds and animals from the continent. Crosby notes that this same mistake was made over and over again, with burros in the Canaries, rats in Virginia, and rabbits again in Australia. Madeira was thickly forested when first sighted, hence its name. The Portuguese promptly began burning down the forests to clear cropland; the resulting conflagration almost burned them off the island. Since Madeira's own biota contained little of commercial value, they set about to transform it with plants and animals which were valuable. Pigs, cattle, grapevines, and wheat were imported both to give them their accustomed diet and to provide for cash crops. Sugar, the ultimate capitalist crop of the period, was a resounding success. But to achieve that success the Portuguese built an elaborate irrigation system at the cost of back-breaking labor (not their backs). They also imported slaves—not black Africans, but the Guanches of the islands, and probably Berbers from North Africa, suspect Portuguese who were either too Moorish or too Jewish for their own good, and criminals.

So even before 1492, the year from which we like to date the Great European Rape of the World, patterns which will be repeated over and over again in the centuries to come are discernable. Man is disposed to transform the unfamiliar into an environment more to his liking and, increasingly, to his profit. Native plants and animals are inadequate or unsuitable, and so nonnative species are introduced. Human agricultural practices are usually shortsighted and destructive. Profitable foods or other substances almost always require nonbenign growing or harvesting techniques and a coerced labor force. The results are usually the same: erosion, unforeseen ecological imbalance, overpopulation, and genocide of the nondominant native ethnic group.

In subsequent chapters on "winds," "weeds," "animals," and "ills," Crosby expands upon the ideas of biological cause and effect in world history. He points out that the Europeans created a whole series of what he calls "neo-Europes" all over the world: in North America, Australia, and New Zealand; in certain parts of Africa and Latin America. By neo-Europes he means that the descendants of the immigrants from the 1400s on may be geographically scattered, but they are to be found in similar latitudes, in the temperate zones of the northern and southern hemisphere, with roughly similar climates. The plants and animals upon which they have depended for food, fiber, power, leather, bone, and manure all prosper in warm to cool climates with a certain amount of rainfall. While the native biotas of all these areas were radically different from northern Eurasia, today these regions export more foodstuffs of European origin—grains and meat—than any other countries on earth. Five hundred years ago they had no wheat, barley, rye, cattle, pigs, sheep, or goats whatsoever.[15] The export on a massive scale of wheat, cattle, and wool from Canada, the United States, Argentina, Australia, and New Zealand testifies to the success of the neo-Europeans.

Crosby's thesis is simply that these neo-Europes were created through biological imperialism. Political and military imperialism helped out as well, but attempts to create neo-Europes in almost all tropical areas in Asia and Africa failed. Heat, humidity, and microbes defeated the invaders and colonizers. They had a little more success in the Northern and Southern American tropics, but generally failed to create neo-Europes; rather, plantation colonies peopled and worked by non-European peons, slaves, and contract workers were the rule.

Years of isolation, 10,000, 20,000, perhaps 30,000, from Eurasian pathogens made the aborigines of the Americas, as well as those of the Pacific and Australasia, essentially defenseless. The Ice Ages finished off the largest land mammals of the continent; accordingly, the large animals the Europeans introduced had fewer and less dangerous predators with which to contend. With their immunity to the diseases they brought and their technology, the human invaders had vast advantages on their side. Their flora and fauna, animals, and microbes were the shock troops of European biological imperialism in the greatest sustained campaign of conquest in history. Behind this first wave came the second, what Crosby terms a "Caucasian tsunami," a mass migration of Europeans from the Old World to the neo-Europes around the globe, impelled not so much by a hunger for freedom as by sheer hunger itself. In the empty lands of the neo-Europes (conveniently emptied in some places by invading pathogens) they brought reassuring and familiar plants, animals, and foods with which to recreate, or improve upon, the societies they had left. Considering the agricultural bounties of the neo-Europes, Crosby opines that the Americas and Australasia have provided windfalls for the rest of humanity, although at extremely high human cost.

Both the windfall and the high price that was paid to obtain it have been prominent in the literature which the quincentenary of what was euphemistically termed "the encounter" has seen written in the past few years. Although the Great Voyage of 1492 also engendered the Great Polemic of 1992, that debate itself is only peripheral to this discussion of the Columbian Exchange. It is merely sufficient to note that rarely has the muse Clio witnessed so thorough, complete, and damning a case of historical revisionism. From cultural icon to racist architect of genocide in a few short years must surely be some sort of record. Indeed, one critic wrote, Columbus was mugged on the way to his own party,[16] beginning with what was termed a preemptive strike by Kirkpatrick Sale (*The Conquest of Paradise*).

Typical of the new historiography is David Stannard's *American Holocaust: Columbus and the Conquest of the New World* (Oxford University Press, 1992). The stirring tapestry of westward expansion has here been replaced by a mantle of the deepest, blackest guilt: Stannard quotes Richard Slotkin to the effect that the heraldry most appropriate to the European settlement of America would be neither heroic nor romantic, but an emblem of a pyramid of skulls.[17] More significant than the 280 pages of criminality and culpability which follow is Stannard's unquestioning acceptance of Woodrow Borah and Sherburne Cook's estimate that two decades of Spanish colonization of the island of Hispaniola resulted in the death of some eight million people,[18] a process which Stannard likens to the equivalent of fifty Hiroshimas. And Hispaniola, he intones, was only the beginning.[19] American historians, in accepting the theory that the precontact native population of the Americas was reduced by an average of 95 percent, have not merely accepted the Borah-Cook thesis but they have embraced it; indeed, they seem determined to wallow in guilt. Latin American historians, having passed through the Great Population Debate some thirty years ago, are on the whole more inclined to leave recriminations behind for more productive discussions of acculturation and interchange.

Fortunately, a by-product of the Great Controversy (during which legions of shocked American historians discovered facts familiar to Latin Americanists for decades) has been considerable scholarly and popular discussion of biological and cultural interchange. Both the impact of epidemic disease and the contributions of New World plants to world culture have occupied prominent places in those discussions. High precontact aboriginal population counts, the complexity and sophistication of Amerindian societies, the devastating impact of European technology, pathogens, and culture, and the complicated ramifications of European-American acculturation have been finally incorporated both into the public consciousness and into the historical canon.

Kenneth Maxwell, in an essay in the *New York Review of Books*, notes that the first great contribution of recent Encounter scholarship has been to delineate the oceanic system of European commerce and navigation which begat the Columbus voyages; the second has been to explore the consequences of the arrival of the Europeans in the New World. The train of historical investigation which originated with the work of the "Berkeley school" of Carl Sauer, Sherburne Cook, and Woodrow Borah in the 1950s and 1960s[20] and which led to Henry Dobyns, William Denevan, and others in the 1970s and 1980s[21] is evident in recent Encounter literature. The Smithsonian Institution produced two outstanding volumes in 1992 to commemorate the Encounter: *Seeds of Change* and *Disease and Demography in the Americas*. The latter represents the very latest scholarship in the demography debate which began more than fifty years ago. It examines population and disease before contact and after 1492 in various areas of both North and South America. Conclusions for each cultural and geographical area vary, but scholars agree that the grounds of the debate have shifted enormously. The great American anthropologist Alfred L. Kroeber offered the meager guess of some 8.4 million inhabitants for all the Americas. By the 1960s Cook and Borah had raised the lowest estimates to triple that figure for Mesoamerica alone. The leader in the numbers game is definitely Henry Dobyns, whose guesstimate that Indian populations in any given area were 20-25 times their lowest number after the "population crash" places him far ahead of any other scholar. Dobyns offered an estimate of 90-112 million for the New World in 1492, a figure that has engendered much debate, much of it rancorous.[22] Crosby, in summarizing the state of the debate, looks forward to the day when the hemispheric estimate will be accurate to a tolerance of plus or minus 30 to 50 percent.[23] The volume's conclusions were rather tentative; hedging their bets like good social scientists, the editors called for more work between and among scholars in history, physical anthropology, demography, ecology, paleopathology, and related disciplines.

An excellent synthesis of much of the post-Crosby scholarship of native depopulation is W. George Lovell's "'Heavy Shadows and Black Night': Disease and Depopulation in Colonial Spanish America," published in the special "1492" issue of the *Annals of the Association of American Geographers*. Reviewing population data for Hispaniola, central Mexico, northwestern New Spain, Guatemala, and the central Andes, Lovell concludes that the magnitude of demographic collapse continues to spark debate, but that consensus now prevails on the reason behind the precipitous decline—epidemic disease. We take this for granted, but Lovell reminds us that as late as the 1980s, some scholars preferred to blame Spanish cruelty rather than virus for depopulation.[24] On the other hand, there are those who prefer to let the viruses and germs take the whole rap; some scholars' near-exclusive focus on epidemiology and biological inequality has "white-washed" what Lovell says cannot be denied: "barbarous heavy-handedness on the part of the conqueror, from which Indians suffered dreadfully and against which individuals like Las Casas fought and lobbied nobly."[25] To say that "the American Indian was victimized by sickness, not by Spaniards"[26] is to build an epidemiological *leyenda blanca* which serves history as poorly as did *la negra*.

One interesting conclusion which most geographers have reached is that the idea of America as a disease-free Eden before contact is illusory. Evidence indicates that many areas of the New World experienced significant levels of morbidity and mortality owing to problems of population density, diet, sanitation, and war. While not lessening the shattering impact of epidemic disease imported by the Europeans, the evidence shows that the "earthy paradise" reported by Columbus was plagued by endemic disease, warfare, overpopulation, and environmental degradation varying from location to location. Generally relegated to the science sections of newspapers or scientific journals,[27] such reports of high rates of soil erosion in central Mexico and Guatemala confirm the work of early geographers like Carl Sauer.

The idea that prehistoric man's agricultural practices were invariably environmentally friendly is as much of an illusion as the aboriginal Eden. Kirkpatrick Sale, in *The Conquest of Paradise*, claimed that New World peoples lived in harmony with nature and refrained from altering their environments, maintaining an idyllic ecological equilibrium. He contrasted this with an alleged European ruthless land ethic, driven only by materialistic goals, which introduced a harmful agrosystem whose end result was environmental destruction of apocalyptic proportions.[28] William Denevan, in an article titled "The Pristine Myth" published in the *Annals of the Association of American Geographers*, reviews the substantial evidence that much of the Americas was a humanized landscape. Agricultural burning and clearing converted much forest into grassy savanna. Other forests were composed of secondary, not primary, growth, in which the composition of the trees was altered from single to mixed stands. Although controversial, the thesis that great grasslands and savannas in certain areas of the New World were created by fire, not nature, is accepted by many geographers.[29] Human population increase had severely reduced the number of animals in Central Mexico; on the other hand, forest disturbance and burning had created ideal habitats for large numbers of game animals in eastern North America. Extensive mounds, terraces, and raised agricultural levies in the United States, Mesoamerica, and the Andes point to advanced agricultural techniques.[30]

It is generally accepted that erosion in Mesoamerica and salinity in coastal Peru were serious problems; indeed it has been proposed that central Mexico actually stood poised on the brink of ecological collapse in 1519 as population growth outstripped the capacity of the land to sustain Mesoamerican society.[31] The collapse of the Mayan city-states and the mysterious abandonment of Teotihuacán at the end of the "classical" Mesoamerican period have long pointed to soil exhaustion and over-population as periodic problems; in fact, scientists now believe that there were at least three distinct periods of soil erosion in Mexico before 1519.[32]

Still, even though the balance between food and people had tipped toward disaster several times prior to contact, the ideological imperative of our politically correct times requires a minimalization of pre-Hispanic troubles and an emphasis on postcontact disaster. Much of the literature of the past two years proceeds from this point of view.

One notable exception was *Seeds of Change*, first a popular exhibit at the Smithsonian and later a handsome and informative volume on the biological and cultural exchange. In chapters on disease, New World foods and their impact upon the Old World, the development of plantation societies based upon coerced labor, and the African presence in the New World (culturally and physically), the authors strike on the whole a judicious and balanced note. Either from its choice of scholars or because it proceeded from a museum exhibit (and was therefore inclined to avoid controversy), *Seeds of Change*, exhibit and book, analyzed and explained rather than condemned. (In fact, a book review at the end of the special issue of the *Annals of the Association of American Geographers* managed only feeble praise for what the reveiwer called too timid and compromised an approach to certain potentially controversial areas such as Native American religions.)[33]

In an essay on health and disease in the pre-Columbian world, John Verano and Douglas Ubelaker theorize that the Americas were relatively disease-free because of several factors. The long and arduous trek across the Bering Strait, through cold Arctic steppe and in small bands, probably limited the parasitic and infectious diseases brought from Eurasia; indeed one anthropologist has proposed that the steppe acted as a "cold filter," discouraging the survival and propagation of infectious organisms and parasites.[34] In the New World itself, Native Americans did not engage in the large-scale, continuous mass emigration which characterized Eurasia for millennia, mass movements which encouraged the spread of disease and eventual immunity from it. Verano and Ubelaker review the evidence for routine illness in the Americas. Unfortunately, without a written language, pictorial remains are inadequate to document the scale of disease in society, and skeletal remains, while useful, are limited for purposes of documentation. Acute infectious diseases which kill quickly, like smallpox, influenza, typhoid, and measles, do not leave their signature on human skeletons. Long-term illnesses like arthritis, chronic infections, and some dietary ailments do leave traces which anthropologists can "read."[35] Furthermore, in some areas, such as the American Southwest and the west coast of South America, naturally and artificially mummified remains have been found at archaeological sites, and they have provided the scientists with conclusive proof of the presence of diseases such as tuberculosis and pneumonia. Fossilized fecal material, called coprolites, from archaeological sites shows evidence of parasitic infestations.[36] Still, the authors compare favorably the medical beliefs and practices of America with those common in sixteenth-century Europe. Both depended heavily upon herbal medicines, and both practiced trephination. But while in Europe about 10 percent of the patients survived the surgery, in the Andean areas success rates seem to have averaged between 50 and 60 percent, even in cases of severe skull fractures.[37]

In a charming and amusing sidebar, the "health profiles" of an Aztec warrior and a Spanish conquistador are compared. The cleanliness of the Aztecs and their habit of frequent baths, sweat and otherwise, are noted, as is the fact that Spanish conquistadors often sought out Aztec medicine men after the conquest, in preference to consulting their own barber surgeons.

The most enduring legacy of the Columbian Exchange remains the large-scale transfer of plants between hemispheres. No less than three impressive new sources examine the impact of American foods on the world: *Seeds of Change*, *From Chilies to Chocolate: Food the Americas Gave the World*, and *Intercambio y difusión de plantas de consumo entre el nuevo y el viejo mundo*.[38] The last, by Spanish historian Julia García Paris, is a handsome volume that traces the history of American foods (including maize, cacao, potatoes, tobacco, tomatoes, avocado, pineapples, and others) brought to Europe and European foods (including wheat, sugarcane, rice, coffee, olives, melons, and citrus fruits) which made the reciprocal voyage. Color photographs and extensive historical research embellish each plant or food chapter. Paris observes that large-scale dietary changes were as reciprocal as the exchange of foodstuffs. The diets of Ireland and Central

Europe may have been revolutionized by the introduction of the potato, but, she points out, rice constitutes the principal source of calories in the Dominican Republic, Costa Rica, Panama, Colombia, and Brazil today, while rice, wheat, sugar, coffee, and wine (all Eurasian foods) dominate the daily diet of a typical Europeanized Latin country such as Uruguay.[39]

From Chilies to Chocolate is the result of a 1988 public symposium at the California Academy of Sciences. The participants were a curious mix of biologists, anthropologists, and food enthusiasts, which accounts perhaps for such quirky chapters as "Vanilla: Nectar of the Gods" and "Native Crops of the Americas: Passing Novelties or Lasting Contributions to Diversity?". Nevertheless, the eclectic backgrounds of the participants brought new insights to familiar territory. World cuisine, we need reminding, was enriched even as empty stomachs were better filled by the new plants. The American berry—the tomato—enlivened Italian foods; the hot chili pepper transformed Korean, Chinese, East Indian, and Hungarian cooking; peanuts took root in the Southeast Asian diet. The cacao bean, transformed into chocolate, has had an enduring impact.

The reaction in Europe, however, to new plants which the explorers brought back from their voyages was not universal glee. It took considerable time for a conservative public to accept most of these foods. Those which most easily won a place in the European diet had analogues in the Old World to which people could relate. Beans, for example, were widely eaten in Europe, and so New World beans quickly won acceptance. Similarly, maize caught on right away, particularly in the Middle East; hence its early nomenclature as "Turkey wheat." Chocolate was analogous to coffee, but for a long time was classified as a luxury, almost a medicinal beverage, with stimulating qualities, and therefore cost a high price. Its widespread acceptance had to wait until the seventeenth century. Pineapple was treated as a botanical curiosity (because of its unusual appearance) and did not appear in a recipe in English until 1732.[40] Spices were adopted quickly, particularly peppers, while tropical root vegetables which required extensive treatment to be rendered safe (manioc) never quite caught on.

Tomatoes were fruits, but acidic fruits, which puzzled people. The tomato was long regarded as a kind of eggplant (to which it is related); one linguistic theory is that since the eggplant was called *pomme des Mours*, fruit of the Moors, the tomato acquired the name *pomme d'amour*, or love apple. It was not until the publication of José de Acosta's *Historia natural y moral de las Indias* in 1590 that Spaniards learned that the tomato was primarily used in sauces. Unfortunately, its reputed powers as an aphrodisiac proved totally unfounded.

The potato was the first vegetable the Europeans had seen which was grown from tubers rather than from seed; the flesh-colored nodules were likened to leprous growths. Its resemblance to the deadly nightshade (of the family Solanacae) did not help its acceptance, and it was widely regarded as poisonous for a long time. Its acceptance in Europe moved from west to east; it first became popular among one of the most wretched peasant peoples in Europe, the Irish. Potatoes are a nearly perfect food; combined with milk, a diet of potatoes will keep a person alive and well indefinitely. The adoption of the potato was motivated either by desperation or by government edict. After it had conquered the British Isles, Frederick the Great ordered it cultivated, and in Hungary the government also ordered it grown after a famine in 1772. In general the potato needed some catalyst in order to become popular. It tended to establish itself after a famine, because no other food furnished so many calories from such small plots of land with minimal care.[41] But the authors stressed that luck and happenstance played a large role in the adoption of American foods in Europe; prejudice, fear, and ignorance prevented rapid adoption of many foods.

Other New World foods still were never eaten at all, by either Spaniards in America or Europeans in the Old World. Several chapters of *From Chilies to Chocolate* as well as articles in the popular press deal with "lost" crops of the Americas.[42] Fruits like *cherimoya* and *pepino dulce*, roots like *arracacna*, and beans like *nuñas* are still eaten in the Andes. Unfortunately, amaranth and quinoa, grains from Mesoamerica and the Andes, are relegated to health food stores, although both are exceptionally nutritious. Amaranth seed contains about 16 percent protein, more than wheat, rice, or maize. Like maize, millet, and sugarcane, it is an efficient converter of solar energy, is fast-growing, and resists drought. Quinoa is a pseudo-cereal because it belongs to the grass family (as wheat, oats, and most grains do). Like amaranth, it is a leafy grain; its seed contains a nearly perfect balance of essential amino acids, including lysine. Its protein level averages about 16 percent, but can be as high as 22 percent. Both grains are grown and consumed mainly by peasants; middle classes and elites reject them as "Indian" food.[43] Anthropologists and nutritionists are helping in the "recovery" of foods which could play a significant role in future world diets.

In the end we have come full circle back again to McNeill, and Crosby, to whom we shall give the last word on the benefits and tragedies of the Columbian Exchange. In *Seeds of Change* it is McNeill who muses upon the impact of New World foods upon the society of the Old. Of the four chief staples of the world human diet—wheat, rice, maize, and potatoes—the two American crops account for 78 percent of the wheat and rice crop. McNeill asks why peasant farmers, normally the most conservative of peoples, gave up familiar crops for new ones? While familiar foods were available in sufficient quantity, and enough land was available for cultivation, there was little incentive to try new crops. But crop failures, destructive weather, and war meant hunger and famine, and population growth put pressure on available cropland. We have already seen that both maize and potatoes produce more calories per acre than traditional European grains. In the northern European plain, extending from the North Sea to the Ural mountains, rye was the only grain that could be depended on to ripen in the short and often rainy summers customary there. But potatoes thrived in such a climate and produced four times more calories per acre than rye. More people could live on potatoes than on rye bread.[44]

Potatoes had even more advantages over grain. They could be planted in fields which had to lie fallow between crops. They needed only hoeing to destroy weeds, although hoeing required more labor than tending grains. But there was an even more important, although subtle, advantage to potatoes. Ripe grain had to be harvested and stored in a barn or silo. Here it could attract the unwelcome attention of tax and rent collectors, or of marauding armies on the march which foraged from hapless peasants for their food. Wartime requisitioning often meant nothing less than starvation for peasants. Potatoes could be left in the ground through the winter and only dug as needed for daily consumption. Soldiers stealing food on the march was a common scene in wartime; soldiers stopping to dig for potatoes was less common. Potatoes therefore served as wartime insurance for European peasants.[45] Potatoes probably reached Europe via the families of Basque sailors along the Biscay coast of northern Spain; very possibly those same Basque sailors brought potatoes to the Irish fishing off the Irish coast. From there, as we have seen, they spread to the east, speeded along their way no doubt by war and famine. Since the Columbian Exchange has never ceased in the five centuries since it began, it should not surprise us that the fungus that blighted the potato crop and plunged Ireland into famine arrived from America, on fast, new steamships.

McNeill credits the potato with foiling, or at least retarding, the colonial schemes the English had in mind for Ireland. Oliver Cromwell intended to drive Irishmen into the rainy western portion of the island, settling the best farmlands with Protestant soldiers from England. The potato enabled the Irish to repel this forced resettlement; since one acre could support an entire family, they could undercut the army veterans and work for English landlords for lower wages than the Protestants, who insisted upon eating their familiar wheat bread. Thus the Irish survived, at the cost of abject poverty and dependence upon a single food crop. The rest is sad history.[46]

Elsewhere in Europe the potato became a supplementary rather than a dominant food crop for peasants, but it eventually became the principal food of the poor in the nineteenth and twentieth centuries. McNeill credits it with allowing, for example, Germany to industrialize on the basis of domestic food supplies. German farms could feed German cities on potatoes, which they could not do with wheat. By the 1880s railroads and steamships brought cheap American grain to Europe, but by then German population growth and industrialization were well established. The swift rise of industrial Germany led eventually to two world wars. McNeill writes:

> If one looks for a measure of the importance of American food crops in Old World history, this is it. The surge of population and spread of industrialization in northern Europe, with shifting results of power since 1750, simply could not have followed their actual course without the nourishment provided by expanding fields of potatoes. No other single American crop played such a decisive role on the world stage; but maize in southern Europe and in Africa, together with sweet potatoes in China, also transformed the lives of millions of people.[47]

In the same manner maize enabled the Greeks, Serbs, and Vlachs of southeastern Europe to live all year round in high mountain valleys, where they could avoid both malaria and the Turks, who ruled the Balkans. As the political and economic balance of the Balkans shifted, Greek and Serbian nationalism was born:

> Thus one might say that what potatoes did for Germany and Russia between 1700 and 1914, maize did for mountain Greeks and Serbs in the same period of time. In each case, a new and far more productive food resource allowed population to surpass older limits, and larger populations in turn provided the basis for the enhanced political and military power attained by the four peoples involved.[48]

Although a combination of political, economic, and technological development had fueled the expansion of European power since well before 1492, McNeill credits American foods with sustaining larger European populations and urban, capitalist development.

We return, finally, to Crosby. In his essay "Metamorphosis of the New World," Crosby imagines what Lord Ahuitzotl, ruler of the Aztecs in the year 13-Flint and builder of the great pyramid consecrated to Huitzilopochtli and Tezcatlipoca, would have seen had he returned in the year 3-House, or 1521. The year 3-House was not just the worst discrete year in all of Mexica history, but the beginning of the worst century the Mesoamericans had ever known. In Crosby's words, "their civilization suffered massive amputations and survived at the root only by accepting alien graftings in the branch, as the conquistadores and the friars replaced their ancient noble and priestly classes."[49] There were advantages that came with defeat: the alphabet to replace their logo-syllabic writing system, the true arch to replace the corbel arch, tools with iron edges to replace obsidian chips. But the very biota of Mexico, life itself, was about to undergo a thorough transformation.

One hundred years later Lord Ahuitzotl would have returned to recognize much in his homeland. The mountains were the same, as were the plants and birds. The holy food of the people was still maize. But alien plants and animals would have surrounded him. Peach, pear, orange and lemon trees, chickpeas, grapevines, melons, onions, radishes, wheat, oats, barley—all these were new. European clover was now so widespread that the Aztecs had their own word for it. Pigs, goats, sheep, burros swarmed in the streets of Mexico City, and cattle and horses in the fields outside it. During Lord Ahuitzotl's lifetime the best way to transport four hundred ears of maize was to load it on the back of a carrier, a *tameme*. Now the bent man loaded the same amount of corn into a wheeled cart hauled by a mule.[50] But what would have truly shocked and dismayed the Aztec lord was how few of his people he would have seen. War, brutality, exploitation, hunger, social and family disarray, loss of farmlands to the invaders took their toll, but disease was the worst enemy; the *hueyzahuatl* of 1520-1521 and the *cocolitzi* of 1545-1548, the bleeding from the nose and eyes left but one person in ten of the population of Central Mexico in the year 3-House. The survivors were pockmarked on their faces, and many of them were mestizos, the children of Spanish men and Indian women. Crosby writes:

> The mestizo, with his Indian skin and Visigothic eyes, proffering a cup of cocoa, a mixture of *chocolatl* and Old World sugar; the wild Chichimec on his Berber mare; the Zapotec herder with his sheep; the Aztec, perhaps the last of the line of Ahuitzotl, receiving the final rites of the Christian faith as he slipped into the terminal coma of an infection newly-arrived from Seville—in so many ways New Spain was *new*, a combination, crossing, and concoction of entities that had never before existed on the same continent.[51]

And Crosby points out that biology did not stop functioning after the first period of transformation; the Columbian Exchange is an ongoing process. Alaskan, Canadian, and Amazonian Indians continue to die of European diseases. Japanese beetles, Dutch elm disease, kudzu, flying Asian cockroaches, and aggressive African "killer bees" are some notorious recent imports. The virus that causes AIDS shows that viruses can still travel from continent to continent, wreaking havoc among diverse societies. "By sea and by air, by mammoth container ship and by jet aircraft, by diplomatic pouch and by impromptu encounter, the homogenizing process accelerates."[52]

Although native Americans often object to the term "the New World," pointing out that what was novel to Europeans was familiar to them before the invaders came, Crosby believes that it is an apt phrase. Columbus's voyage did not merely signal the expansion of Europe, but in fact the creation of a new world. The Old and New Worlds had markedly different flora and fauna, the product of isolated and independent evolutions. Since 1492 both have been significantly altered by biological interchange.

Contemplating the legacy of Columbus and the Columbian era, one might well consider Crosby's final words: "The great Genoese navigated, administered, crusaded, enslaved, but above all he mixed, mingled, jumbled, and homogenized the biota of our planet."[53]

NOTES

1. Two extensive reviews of quincentenary literature are David Block, "Quincentenary Publishing: An Ocean of Print" (unpublished ms), and Allan Metz, "Christopher Columbus: A Selective Guide to Literature, 1970-1989," *Reference Services Review* 19:4 (1991), 21-44.

2. William McNeill, *Plagues and Peoples* (Garden City, NY: Anchor Books, 1976), p. 178.

3. Sherburne F. Cook and Woodrow Borah, *Essays in Population History: Mexico and the Caribbean*, 3 vols. (Berkeley: University of California Press, 1971-1979), vol. 1, p. viii.

4. Alfred W. Crosby Jr., *The Columbian Exchange: Biological and Cultural Consequences of 1492* (Westport, CT: Greenwood Press, 1972), p. 39.

5. *The Book of Chilam Balam of Chumayel*, edited and translated by Ralph W. Roy (Washington, DC: Carnegie Institution of Washington, 1933), p. 83; reproduced in Crosby, *The Columbian Exchange*, p. 36.

6. Crosby, *The Columbian Exchange*, p. 99.

7. See Daniel W. Gade, "Landscape, System, and Identity in the Post-Conquest Andes," *Annals of the Association of American Geographers* 82:3 (September 1992), 460-477.

8. Ibid, p. 467.

9. Crosby, *The Columbian Exchange*, p. 68.

10. Ibid., pp. 165-166.

11. Ibid., pp. 171-172.

12. Crosby obtained these figures by multiplying yield statistics in kilograms in the *FAO Production Yearbook* for 1963 by the caloric value statistics in the *FAO Food Composition Tables for International Use*. See Crosby, *The Columbian Exchange*, pp. 175, 203. Advances from the "Green Revolution" and genetic engineering may have diminished the caloric advantages of American grains.

13. Ibid., p. 211.

14. Alfred W. Crosby, *Ecological Imperialism: The Biological Expansion of Europe, 900-1900* (Cambridge: Cambridge University Press, 1986), p. 75.

15. Ibid., pp. 6-7.

16. Kenneth Maxwell, "¡Adios Columbus!," *The New York Review of Books* 40:3 (January 28, 1993), 38.

17. Richard Slotkin, *Regeneration Through Violence: The Mythology of the American Frontier, 1600-1860* (Middletown, CT: Wesleyan University Press, 1973), p. 565; quoted in David E. Stannard, *American Holocaust: Columbus and the Conquest of the New World* (New York, NY: Oxford University Press, 1992), p. x.

18. See Sherburne F. Cook and Woodrow Borah, "The Aboriginal Population of Hispaniola," in Cook and Borah, *Essays in Population History*, vol. 1, pp. 376-410.

19. Stannard, *American Holocaust*, p. x.

20. One of the earliest works of what the admiring French called *l'école de Berkeley* was Sherburne F. Cook, "The Incidence and Significance of Disease Among the Aztecs and Related Tribes," *Hispanic American Historical Review* 26 (August 1946), 320-325. This article was followed in the early 1960s by several collaborative efforts, most notably Sherburne F. Cook and Woodrow Borah, *The Indian Population of Central Mexico, 1531-1610* (Berkeley: University of California Press, 1960), and their *The Aboriginal Population of Central Mexico on the Eve of the Spanish Conquest* (Berkeley: University of California Press, 1963). A few years later their close colleague Carl Sauer published his *The Early Spanish Main* (Berkeley: University of California Press, 1966), which established large precontact native populations and near-total postcontact depopulation in the Caribbean. Other significant early contributions include Henry F. Dobyns, "An Outline of Andean Epidemic History to 1720," *Bulletin of the History of Medicine* 37 (November-December 1963), 492-515, and Jehan Vellard, "Causas biológicas de la desaparición de los indios americanos," *Boletín del Instituto Riva-Agüero* (Pontificia Universidad Católica del Perú), no. 2 (1956), 77-93.

21. Most notably the collection of essays edited by William M. Denevan, *The Native Population of the Americas in 1492* (Madison: University of Wisconsin Press, 1976; second edition, 1992).

22. Alfred W. Crosby, "Summary on Population Size before and after Contact," in John W. Verano and Douglas H. Ubelaker, eds., *Disease and Demography in the Americas* (Washington, DC: Smithsonian Institution Press, 1992), pp. 277-278.

23. Ibid., p. 278.

24. See, for example, J. Friede, "Demographic Changes in the Mining Community of Muzo After the Plague of 1629," *Hispanic American Historical Review* 47 (1967), 338-343, and C. Sempart Assadourian, "La crisis demográfica del siglo XVI y la transición del Tawantinsuyu al sistema mercantil colonial," in N. Sánchez Albornoz, ed., *Población y mano de obra en América Latina* (Madrid: Alianza Editorial, 1985), pp. 69-93; both cited in W. George Lovell's "'Heavy Shadows and Black Night': Disease and Depopulation in Colonial Spanish America," *Annals of the Association of American Geographers* 82:3 (September 1992), 426-443.

25. Lovell, "Heavy Shadows," p. 438.

26. F. Guerra, "El efecto demográfico de las epidemias trás el descubrimiento de América," *Revista de Indias* 46 (1986), 41-58; quoted in Lovell, "Heavy Shadows," p. 438.

27. See William K. Stevens, "An Eden in Ancient America? Not Really," *The New York Times*, March 30, 1993, pp. C1, C9.

28. Kirkpatrick Sale, *The Conquest of Paradise: Christopher Columbus and the Columbian Legacy* (New York, NY: Knopf, 1990); Sale is here summarized and criticized by Karl W. Butzer, "The Americas Before and After 1492: An Introduction to Current Geographical Research," *Annals of the Association of American Geographers* 82:3 (1992), 345-368.

29. See William Denevan, "The Pristine Myth: The Landscape of the Americas in 1492," *Annals of the Association of American Geographers* 82:3 (September 1992), 369-385. Denevan's article contains an excellent bibliography.

30. Ibid.

31. McNeill, *Plagues and Peoples*, p. 179.

32. Stevens, "An Eden in Ancient America," p. C9.

33. Herman J. Viola and Carolyn Margolis, eds., *Seeds of Change: A Quincentennial Commemoration* (Washington, DC: Smithsonian Institution Press, 1991); reviewed by Stephen C. Jett and Joseph S. Wood in *Annals of the Association of American Geographers* 82:3 (September 1992), 566-568.

34. See T. D. Stewart, "Stone Age Skull Surgery: A General Review, with Emphasis on the New World," in *Annual Report of the Smithsonian Institution* (Washington, DC: Smithsonian Institution Press, 1957), pp. 469-491; cited in John W. Verano and Douglas H. Ubelaker, "Health and Disease in the Pre-Columbian World," in *Seeds of Change*, pp. 209-224.

35. Verano and Ubelaker, "Health and Disease," p. 213.

36. Ibid., p. 213.

37. Ibid., p. 217.

38. *Seeds of Change*; Nelson Foster and Linda S. Cordell, eds., *Chilies to Chocolate: Food the Americas Gave the World* (Tucson: University of Arizona Press, 1992); and Julia García Paris, *Intercambio y difusión de plantas de consumo entre el nuevo y el viejo mundo* (Madrid: Servicio de Extensión Agraria, Ministerio de Agricultura, Pesca y Alimentación, 1991).

39. See Paris, "Introducción," *Intercambio*, p. 11.

40. Alan Davidson, "Europeans' Wary Encounter with Tomatoes, Potatoes, and Other New World Foods," in Foster and Cordell, eds., *Chilies to Chocolate*, pp. 3-4.

41. Ibid., pp. 13-14.

42. See William K. Stevens, "Rediscovering the Lost Crops of the Incas," *New York Times*, October 31, 1989, p. C1.

43. See Daniel K. Early, "The Renaissance of Amaranth," pp. 15-33, and John F. McCamant, "Quinoa's Roundabout Journey to World Use," pp. 123-141, in *Chilies to Chocolate*.

44. Robert McNeill, "American Food Crops in the Old World," in *Seeds of Change*, p. 45.

45. Ibid., pp. 46-47.

46. Ibid., pp. 49-50.

47. Ibid., p. 51.

48. Ibid., p. 52.

49. Alfred Crosby, "Metamorphosis of the Americas," in *Seeds of Change*, p. 73.

50. Ibid., pp. 73-74.

51. Ibid., p. 74.

52. Ibid., p. 89.

53. Ibid, p. 89.

2. The Humboldt Current: Northern European Naturalists in Latin America: A Bibliographical Survey, 1799–1859

Robert A. McNeil

The Humboldt Current, also known as the Peru or Peruvian Current, carries cold water from the Antarctic along the Pacific coast of South America to the Ecuadorean border, where it turns west into the ocean. Its effects are generally beneficial, creating an equable climate along the coasts and bringing plankton to feed the sea-birds that produce the guano deposits of northern Chile. The Humboldt current I shall be discussing here, on the other hand, was the result of an attraction exerted for more than half a century by one man, carrying naturalists from the cold climate of northern Europe to the tropical and subtropical regions of Central and South America. From 1799, when Humboldt and Bonpland first set foot in the New World, to the mid-century and beyond, European scientists made vast strides in the description and classification of the natural phenomena of Latin America, now more open to them than ever before. On the Amazon vast tracts of virgin forest offered to zoologists and botanists the prospect of innumerable unrecorded animal and plant species, while in the 1820s and 1830s Patagonia began to yield up skeletons of fossil monsters for the study of geologists and palaeontologists. It was left to Darwin, who had surveyed the coasts of Chile and the Argentine, and Alfred Russel Wallace, who had hunted insects in the Brazilian rain forests, to provide an interpretation of the new data in their theory of natural selection. *The Origin of Species* was published in 1859, which was also the year of Humboldt's death.

The purpose of this paper is to illustrate the strength and depth of the Humboldt current by describing the achievement of Humboldt himself and of nine of his European disciples: where they went, what they found out, and how they made their findings available. The bibliography lists the primary publications that resulted from each of the expeditions described. My choice of Humboldtians is, I hope, representative, though I am conscious that it is also an arbitrary one: I have concentrated on three Englishmen, three Frenchmen, two Bavarians, and three Prussians—one of whom adopted British nationality.

Of course, while concentrating on the work of foreign scientists it is important not to forget the flourishing condition of science in Latin America itself at the close of the eighteenth century. Military and naval geographers were producing accurate maps of the region, and the eighteenth-century scientific expeditions had led to the establishment of many centres of learning in the Spanish colonies. In the field of botany alone, the Linnaean system of classification was being taught at the University of San Marcos in Lima as early as 1780; a botanical garden and chair of botany were established in Mexico City in 1788; while in Brazil José Maria de Vellozo had collected a large herbarium and described many new plant species. It seems that scientists in Lima, Mexico, and Bogotá were purchasing their books and equipment directly from Paris and London: certainly when Humboldt visited José Celestino Mutis in Bogotá in 1801, he found a herbarium for 20,000 collected plants and a botanical library which he ranked second only to that of Joseph Banks, director of Kew Gardens in London.[1]

Many of the enlightened creoles in the Spanish colonies were followers and admirers of Benjamin Franklin, both as an experimental natural philosopher and as a political revolutionary. As a result, when the wars of independence broke out in the early nineteenth century, science was among the earliest casualties: those Americans whose interest in nature was greatest soon became the political leaders, the champions of liberalism and independence, and thus the targets of the forces of reaction. Many scientific institutions did not survive into the independence period, and those that did found themselves feeble and impoverished. It was this gap that the followers of Humboldt were, in some degree, able to fill: they helped to keep alive the world's interest in the flora and fauna of the new continent. This was an important contribution, and it was recognised as such by several Latin American governments later in the century: Claude Gay was rewarded for his *Historia física y política de Chile* with honorary Chilean nationality, while Humboldt himself was respected and honoured all over the region. And several of the works of the European naturalists I shall be discussing currently remain in print only in Latin America, in Spanish or Portuguese editions.

Humboldt and Bonpland

Friedrich Wilhelm Karl Heinrich Alexander, Freiherr von Humboldt—sometimes described as the last great universal man—was born in Berlin in 1769. He was educated as became a Prussian aristocrat, but early showed the interest in natural history that was to last all his life: as a child he collected flowers, butterflies, beetles, shells, and stones. While he was at the University of Göttingen he became friendly with Georg Foster, who had accompanied Captain Cook on his 1772 circumnavigation; this helped to strengthen Humboldt's interest in scientific exploration. He spent five years in the Prussian Department of Mines and became an authority on mineralogy, in addition to pursuing studies in galvanism and natural science. At last, on the death of his mother, he felt free to give up his job and embark on the career of an explorer-naturalist.

But where to explore? America was by no means a foregone conclusion. Humboldt's first idea was to study volcanoes in Italy, his second to join an expedition up the Nile at the invitation of the eccentric Earl of Bristol, the freethinking Bishop of Derry. But Napoleon's armies were in Italy and Egypt, and Humboldt decided to head for Paris and join the scientific community there. He met Bougainville, the celebrated explorer of the Pacific, and through his agency was invited to join a planned French circumnavigation of the globe, visiting South America, the Californias, the South Pole, Madagascar, and West Africa. The escalating war in Europe forced the postponement of this expedition, however, and once again denied access to Egypt, Humboldt finally set off for Spain, accompanied by the 25-year-old botanist Aimé Bonpland.

In Madrid, the two profited from Humboldt's diplomatic connections in securing introductions, first to the prime minister, and then to the King of Spain himself, to whom Humboldt presented a hastily prepared memorandum on the advantages of a scientific expedition to the American colonies. The King was impressed and intrigued; passports were issued to Humboldt and Bonpland under the royal seal, and suddenly the New World was open to them. As Humboldt subsequently wrote, never before had a traveller been granted such unlimited permission, and never before had a foreigner been honoured by such marks of confidence from the Spanish government.

I have spent some time on the antecedents to Humboldt's trip to show how fortuitous it was that South America was chosen as the object of his researches. He might have gone to Italy; he might have gone to Egypt; he might have gone to California and the South Pole. Latin Americanists have reason to be grateful to Napoleon Bonaparte and the King of Spain.

Humboldt's great expedition to South America falls neatly into three stages. The first, from November 1799 to November 1800, was spent in Venezuela, principally on the exploration of the upper Orinoco river and the unknown region of the Casiquiare canal, finally established as the link between the Orinoco and the Rio Negro which flowed into the Amazon. The second stage, from November 1800 to February 1803, took in Cuba and New Granada, and culminated in the ascent of mount Chimborazo in June 1802, when Humboldt reached a height of 19,286 feet—the greatest altitude attained by any human being in history up to that time. It was this achievement that captured the imagination of the public when it was reported (many months later) in the Paris journals and established the enormous reputation that Humboldt was to maintain in Europe for more than fifty years.[2] Finally, from February 1803 to April 1804 Humboldt and Bonpland were travelling in New Spain, the most developed of the Spanish American possessions, and spending as much time in libraries and offices as they did in the field. A short visit to Washington enabled Humboldt to make the acquaintance of President Jefferson, and by August 1804 he was back in France, never to cross the Atlantic again.

A large proportion of the remainder of Humboldt's long life was spent in preparing for publication the documentary results of his American travels.[3] He based himself in Paris, where he was said to be the most famous man in Europe (with the single exception of the Emperor Napoleon), and where virtually all of his monumental work was to be published. Thirty volumes appeared in thirty years, under the general title *Voyage aux régions équinoxiales du nouveau continent fait en 1799-1804 par A. de Humboldt et A. Bonpland* [1, 3-18];[4] the first to appear was *Essai sur la géographie des plantes* in 1805 or, as the title page insisted, year XIII of the Revolution [12]; the last, the final part of the *Examen critique de l'histoire de la géographie du nouveau continent* in 1834, two revolutions later [5]. The volumes fall roughly into three categories. The scientific results, consisting of the botanical, zoological, meteorological, astronomical, and geological data, were produced with the help of experts in the different subjects. The other two categories were written entirely by Humboldt; these were the treatises on the political economy of Cuba and Mexico, and the (incomplete) narrative account of the travels, with the atlas-volume of views and native American artefacts and the account of previous explorations. It is notable how many later travellers followed a similar plan when they produced their own travel accounts. Humboldt's narrative suffers from a leaden prose style and the author's congenital inability to leave anything out; modern readers find it heavy going, but in its time it became an instant classic, with translations into all major European languages.

Bonpland did not long share Humboldt's celebrity. Despite his assiduity as a botanical collector (he had returned from America with some 60,000 specimens representing 6,000 species, more than half of which were unknown to science), he proved to be incompetent as an author, and the volumes he took responsibility for were severely criticised for their errors of classification. He returned to South America, where he spent nine years in a Paraguayan jail at the behest of the dictator José Gaspar Rodríguez de Francia; freed at last, he passed the remainder of his eighty-five years living in poverty in a remote hut on the Uruguayan pampas, surrounded by the children he had fathered on an Indian woman.

Prince Max of Wied

Prinz Maximilian von Wied-Neuwied was the first of Humboldt's great German followers. Born in Neuwied in 1782 (when Humboldt was still only thirteen) he joined the Prussian army at a very early age and soldiered through the Napoleonic Wars. Retiring in 1815 with the rank of major-general, he devoted the rest of his life to the study of geography and the natural sciences. Almost immediately he set off for Brazil, where he spent two years. His travels took him through the sertões north from Cabo Frio to Ilheus; then inland to the borders of the captaincy of Minas Gerais; and finally north again, crossing the Iquiricá and Jaguaripe rivers, to Bahia. His account of the trip, published in two volumes in Frankfurt in 1820-1821 [21], was almost immediately translated into English. There was good reason for this: despite his military background, Max took an almost poetic interest in the things around him, and was able to communicate his interest to the reader: palm trees, birds, Indian customs, styles of building. He was particularly fascinated by the Brazilian Indians (especially the savage Botocudos) and his book includes word-lists of several of their languages and coloured illustrations of their artefacts. Like Humboldt, he published some more specialised volumes on his observations and collections: the *Beitrag zur Flora Brasiliens* [24] appeared in Bonn in two parts (1823-1824) and the *Beiträge zur Naturgeschichte von Brasilien* [25], with its accompanying volume of plates, was published in Weimar from 1825 to 1833. Maximilian was an assiduous naturalist throughout his life: in 1832 he crossed the Atlantic again to make a tour of the United States, and published another very successful volume of travel-literature.

Spix and Martius

In 1817 Leopoldina, Archduchess of Austria, sailed to Rio de Janeiro in order to marry Pedro, then Crown Prince of Portugal and later Emperor of Brazil. With the bridal party travelled two scientists from the Academy of Sciences in Munich, with a commission from Maximilian I of Bavaria to carry out a scientific exploration of Brazil. Johann Baptist von Spix, a zoologist, and Carl Friedrich Philipp von Martius, a botanist, travelled widely for three years. From Rio they went west to São Paulo, then up through the Brazilian highlands to Bahia, and across to Maranhão and Belém. On 21 August 1819 they set out up the Rio Pará and thence along the Amazon, splitting up to explore the northern tributary rivers: Martius followed the Japura river well into what is now Colombia, while Spix ascended the Amazon proper to the Peruvian border and subsequently followed the Rio Negro as far as Barcelós. In 1820 they sailed home to Munich and general acclaim, carrying with them so many specimens, zoological, botanical, and mineralogical, that a new gallery was opened for them by order of the King of Bavaria.

Unlike Humboldt (who published most of his findings in French), Spix and Martius recorded their collections in Latin, still regarded by some as the language of international scholarship. Martius produced a comprehensive collection of all the new specimens of plants he had collected in three volumes from 1823 to 1831 under the title *Nova genera et species plantarum* [37]. Perhaps more than any other botanist, Martius set his mark on the study of Brazilian plant life: he produced books on the country's ferns and palms and began the monumental *Flora Brasiliensis* [41], which was not completed until 1906, thirty-eight years after his death. He also found time to write copiously on the Brazilian Indian tribes and their languages, particularly the Tupi.

Spix was less fortunate: though he was able to prepare volumes on the new species of monkeys, bats [31], and reptiles [33] he discovered, in addition to a finely illustrated collection of previously unknown birds [34], his early death in 1826 left much of the zoological work incomplete. The indefatigable Martius completed it, with the aid of other specialists, including Louis Agassiz. Spix was also able to contribute only to the first volume of the general account of their travels [27] (much more readable than that of Humboldt) which appeared in Munich in 1823 (and in English by 1824); subsequent volumes by Martius alone were published in 1828 and 1831.

Orbigny

Alcide Dessalines d'Orbigny was born in 1802, eleven weeks after Humboldt had reached the summit of Chimborazo. Orbigny grew up in a scientific family, and at the age of only twenty-three became a travelling naturalist for the Museum of Natural History in Paris. In preparation for his trip to South America he called upon Humboldt, still living in Paris and overseeing the publication of his American works. The old scientist gave advice on equipment and an itinerary, as well as providing letters of recommendation. Orbigny set out on 31 July 1826 for an eight-year trek through Latin America: starting (like Spix and Martius) in Rio, he journeyed through Uruguay to Montevideo and Buenos Aires. He then conducted a detailed survey of the Argentine Republic, first travelling up the Parana river to Corrientes and Misiones, visiting the Paraguayan Chaco, then down to Bahía Blanca and part of Patagonia. Back in Montevideo he took ship and rounded the Horn to Valparaíso, then on to Bolivia, where he carried out another intensive survey, and eventually to Peru. Finally back in Paris in 1834 he set about the organization of his observations, which saw the light from 1839 to 1842 as *Voyage dans l'Amérique Méridionale* [44]. In nine volumes, with around 500 coloured plates, the work includes descriptions of animals, birds, insects, and molluscs (Orbigny's special interest) and marks a significant advance in the study of ethnography, geology, and palaeontology. Significantly, the work is dedicated to Alexander von Humboldt.

Though Orbigny started the voyage as a general naturalist, his interest in molluscs led him to realise the importance of the fossil record of South America, a study which eventually earned him a special chair in palaeontology at the Museum of Natural History. From 1840 he began to publish the monumental *Paléontologie française*,[5] and he is now considered the father of the study. For his contemporaries, however, the mark of his stature can be found in the *Voyage pittoresque dans les deux Amériques* [45], a composite account of the whole American continent published in 1836 "sous le direction de M. Alcide d'Orbigny." The frontispiece shows the four leading interpreters of the New World: Columbus, William Penn, Humboldt, and Alcide Dessalines d'Orbigny.

Gay

Claude (later Claudio) Gay was born in Provence in 1800, while Humboldt was crossing the llanos of Venezuela. Educated in Paris, he soon abandoned the medical career he had been destined for and became engrossed in the study of botany; by the age of twenty he had already been on plant-collecting expeditions to the Alps. In 1828 he went to Chile to study the previously undescribed fauna and flora of the country while making a living teaching general sciences at a newly established private school. By 1830 he felt ready to write to the Vice-President of the Republic, offering his services to carry out a scientific survey of the Chile, describing the geography, geology, and natural history of the new nation. The Vice-President agreed, and a contract was signed with the Department of the Interior on 14 September 1830.

For most of the next eleven years Gay studied Chile, province by province. There were initial setbacks: on his first excursion to the Atacama desert, for example, an extreme dry season had virtually wiped out the vegetation he was hoping to collect. He took a year off in France, taking with him a collection of plants, fossils, and a live condor, and returned with some scientific equipment and a new bride. The work went on: he surveyed the Santiago region, then turned his attention south to Valdivia and Chiloé; he climbed the Andes, visited Peru, and made a second, more successful attempt on the Atacama desert. At some point he was persuaded to add a political history of the Chilean people to his plans; when in Lima (in the aftermath of the war between Chile and the Peru-Bolivian Confederation) he was able to examine the archives of the Viceroyalty and talk with Bernardo O'Higgins.

His work was finally approaching completion, and it was decided to publish it, like Humboldt's, in Paris. Gay returned to his native land to see it through the press—an effort which cost him almost as much trouble as the collection of materials, and caused the breakup of his marriage. Working twelve hours a day, Gay succeeded in producing the magnum opus in thirty volumes from 1844 to 1871: *Historia física y política de Chile* [47], consisting of eight volumes of *Historia* (with two of accompanying documents), eight volumes of *Botánica*, eight of *Zoológica*, two of *Agricultura* and a two-volume atlas containing plates and illustrations. Although Gay was rewarded with Chilean nationality, he returned only once to his adopted country, and died in 1873 in his native Provence.[6]

Darwin

There can be little doubt that the most significant scientific expedition to Latin America in the nineteenth century was that which carried Charles Darwin to Patagonia, Chile, and the Galapagos. To do justice to Darwin's achievement would need rather more space, and much more scientific knowledge, than is available to me, so I shall be brief. He was born in 1809 and, despite an early fascination with natural history, was destined for the Church as a profession. Of all the naturalists I have been discussing, Darwin was probably the most convinced Humboldtian—the *Personal Narrative* had long been his favourite reading, and Humboldt was always, for Darwin, "the greatest scientific traveller who ever lived."

In 1831, to the despair of his father, Darwin accepted an invitation to join HMS Beagle as ship's naturalist on what was intended primarily as a coastal survey voyage to Tierra del Fuego. With Captain FitzRoy and his crew he visited the Brazilian forests, the Uruguayan pampas, the Argentina of Rosas; he marvelled at the fossil record of Patagonia, threaded the Beagle Channel, geologized in the Chilean Andes and, most memorably, recorded the strange species of animal life in the Galapagos Islands. He returned to England in 1836 with a large number of specimens, geological, zoological, and fossil. While FitzRoy prepared a full account of the Beagle's voyages ([49], published in 1839, with Darwin's famous journal occupying the third volume), Darwin was working on a five-volume conspectus of his findings, with full descriptions and coloured illustrations. *The zoology of HMS Beagle* [55] was published from 1840 to 1843, each volume prepared, under Darwin's editorship, by a specialist in the field which it covered. In addition, from 1842 to 1846 Darwin published three monographs on the geology of South America [51-53], and in 1845 reissued his journal under the title *Journal of researches into the natural history and geology of the countries visited during the voyage of HMS Beagle* [54]. The theory of natural selection, implanted by the Beagle voyage, was to grow in his mind for more than twenty years, and was not promulgated until he was stimulated by the ideas of another great Humboldtian, Alfred Russel Wallace.[7]

Schomburgk

Robert Hermann Schomburgk was born in Freiburg in 1804, the day after Humboldt had lunched with President Jefferson in the White House. He soon fell victim to Humboldtian fever: in the United States on business in his mid-twenties he determined, at his own expense, to carry out a coastal survey of Anegada, one of the British Virgin Islands. He sent the results to the Royal Geographical Society in London, which in turn entrusted him with the conduct of an exploring expedition to what was then British Guiana. Between 1835 and 1839, with two companions, he explored the Guianan rivers, following the Essequibo and the Rupunini through to the Rio Negro and eventually to the headwaters of the Orinoco—Humboldt territory—as well as investigating in detail the resources and capabilities of the colony. The action that brought him most celebrity, however, was the discovery of the giant water lily which he named the Victoria Regia in honour of the new queen.

On his return to England in 1840 he received the gold medal of the Royal Geographical Society and was promptly appointed a boundary commissioner for Guiana, with the responsibility of surveying the frontier with Venezuela. He had time to publish *A description of British Guiana, geographical and statistical* [58] (1840) and write the commentary to a spectacular volume, *Twelve views in the interior of Guiana* [61] (1841), based on sketches made during his expedition. It is interesting to note, however, that the full account of his expedition appeared only in German: *Reisen in Guiana und am Orinoko während der Jahre 1835-1839* [59] (Leipzig, 1841), with an introduction by Alexander von Humboldt; it was not translated into English until 1931. Schomburgk also produced a richly illustrated monograph, *The natural history of the fishes of Guiana* [62] (1843); by the time it appeared he was back in South America, plotting the once-celebrated Schomburgk Line, intended as a boundary between Guiana and Venezuela but never in fact recognized by either party. Knighted for his services in 1844, he became for a while British consul in Santo Domingo, and then left Latin America for good when he was moved to the consulate in Bangkok. He continued his scientific activities in his new post, and died in Berlin in 1865.[8]

Bates and Wallace

Henry Walter Bates and Alfred Russel Wallace were nineteen and twenty-one respectively when they met in 1844. Bates was apprenticed to a hosiery manufacturer in Leicester, where Wallace taught English at a local school, and the two were brought together by their interest in natural history and, more specifically, by a common enjoyment of the works of Humboldt. After discussing several schemes for scientific exploration, they set out together in 1848 for the river Amazon. Neither had much money: they intended to sell the specimens they hoped to collect in order to defray their expenses. Bates's particular interest was in entomology, an enthusiasm he communicated to Wallace, and both were overwhelmed by the variety of insect life they found in Brazil. Together, they explored the Amazon river system from Pará to Manaus, where they parted company in 1850. Wallace continued along the Rio Negro and the Orinoco (Humboldt territory again) until 1852, when he returned to England. On the return voyage his ship was destroyed by fire and all the specimens he had collected were lost. Undaunted, in 1853 he published *Palm trees of the Amazon* [66] and *A narrative of travels on the Amazon and Rio Negro* [65], which combines a detailed account of his expedition with chapters on the geology, vegetation, zoology, and inhabitants of the Amazon basin. In 1854 he was off again on further explorations, this time in the Malay Peninsula, where he spent the next few years developing and refining the theory of natural selection which he and Darwin were to promulgate jointly in 1858.[9]

Bates remained in Brazil for eleven years, exploring the Amazon and the Tapajos. He made his headquarters at Ega on the upper Amazon (where he discovered 550 new and distinct species of butterfly). When he returned to England, his health seriously affected, he had collected no fewer than 14,712 specimens, of which some 8,000 were species new to science, and on which, incidentally, he made a profit of some £800. He published numerous papers in entomological journals, but only one book—*The naturalist on the river Amazons* [68] (1863)—one of the most delightful books of travel in the English language. In the words of the *Dictionary of National Biography*, "the narrative grips the reader at once, and inspires him with an intense desire to visit the regions described."[10] Which was, of course, precisely what Humboldt's writings had already done for a whole generation of European naturalists.

With hindsight, the year 1859 seems to mark the end of an era. On 6 May Humboldt died at his home in Berlin; on 2 June Bates sailed from Brazil for the last time; on 24 November Darwin published his long-awaited monograph *On the origin of species by means of natural selection, or the preservation of favoured races in the struggle for life* [56]. The work of observing and recording nature in Latin America was rapidly being completed.

Eurocentric writers on the great nineteenth-century scientific travellers have talked of a "rediscovery" of Latin America and written of the scientists as the "new conquistadors." Though this is ludicrously overstating the case, one parallel holds good: in the early nineteenth century, as in the sixteenth, Latin America was again seen by Europeans as a treasure-house overflowing with undiscovered riches. This time, though, the wealth was in nature and natural history rather than in precious metals. Instead of gold, the new explorers brought back case upon case of scientific specimens—plants, rocks, fossils, animals alive and dead—which were exhibited and described in print all over the Old World. Bernal Díaz famously reported that the first conquistadors went to America "to serve God and the King, and also to get rich." Their nineteenth-century followers went to serve knowledge, science, and nature, and also to get published.

NOTES

1. For more information, see Thomas F. Glick, "Science in Latin America," in *The Cambridge Encyclopedia of Latin America and the Caribbean* (Cambridge, New York: Cambridge University Press, 1985), pp. 421-427.

2. It is perhaps salutory to remember the extent of Humboldt's indebtedness, in his explorations, to the help and advice of the colonial authorities and local inhabitants. The royal passport and the hospitality of missionary fathers were to smooth his way everywhere. In his exploration of the upper Orinoco, for example, he was accompanied and aided by Nicolas de Soto, brother-in-law of the local governor, and Father Bernardo Zea, who had spent years among the Indians; even at the mysterious Casiquiare canal he found a mission-station, where he was told that the link between the Orinoco and Rio Negro had been an established fact for fifty years. In Quito he was welcomed and assisted by the Marques de Selvalegre, the provincial governor, whose son accompanied Humboldt in his ascent of Chimborazo. On the famous ascent, Selvalegre's son, Aimé Bonpland, and an Indian from a neighbouring village climbed just as high as Humboldt without sharing his glory. Of course, this in no way detracts from Humboldt's own achievement.

3. The standard biography of Humboldt is Hanno Beck, *Alexander von Humboldt*, in two volumes (Wiesbaden: Steiner, 1959-1961). A shorter, illustrated text for English readers is Douglas Botting, *Humboldt and the Cosmos* (London: M. Joseph, 1973).

4. The bracketed numbers following the title of a published work indicate the number of the work in the bibliography below.

5. Alcide Dessalines d'Orbigny, *Paléontologie française: description zoologique et géologique de tous les animaux, mollusques et rayonnes fosiles de France,* 23 vols. (Paris: Chez l'auteur, 1840-1894).

6. Gay's life is best approached through the collection of documents edited by Carlos Stuardo Ortiz (no. 48 in the bibliography below).

7. The standard source for Darwin's life is *The Life and Letters of Charles Darwin, Including an Autobiographical Chapter,* edited by his son Francis Darwin in three volumes (London: J. Murray, 1887). There are also recent biographies by John Bowlby (1990) and Adrian Desmond and James Moore (1991).

8. There is currently no full-length biography of Schomburgk, though one is in preparation by Peter Rivière.

9. For more on Wallace's life and thought see H. Lewis McKinney, *Wallace and Natural Selection* (New Haven, CT: Yale University Press, 1972).

10. *The Dictionary of National Biography, vol. 22: Supplement* (London: Oxford University Press, 1922), p. 143. For more on Bates, see George Woodcock, *Henry Walter Bates, Naturalist of the Amazons* (London: Faber, 1969).

BIBLIOGRAPHY

I. Publications of the Humboldt/Bonpland Expedition

General

1. Humboldt, Alexander von. *Relation historique du Voyage aux régions équinoxiales du nouveau continent, fait en 1799, 1800, 1801, 1802, 1803 et 1804 par Al. de Humboldt et A. Bonpland.* Rédigé par Alexandre de Humboldt. 3 vols. Voyage de Humboldt et Bonpland, pt. 1. Paris: Schoell, 1814-1834.

Includes the political essay on the island of Cuba. A fourth volume which was to complete the narrative was never published, though Humboldt's notes (in French and German) on the remainder of the trip have been edited by Margot Faak as vols. 7 and 9 of the Beiträge zur Alexander-von-Humboldt-Forschung (*Reise auf dem Río Magdalena, durch die Anden und Mexico.* Berlin: Akademie-Verlag, 1986-1990).

2. Humboldt, Alexander von. *Personal narrative of travels to the equinoctial regions of the new continent during the years 1799-1804*, by Alexander de Humboldt and Aimé Bonpland. Translated into English by Helen Maria Williams. 7 vols. London: Longman, Hurst, Rees, Orme and Browne, 1814-1829.

The first English version of [1], above. Another, better, translation by Thomasina Ross was published in three volumes in Bohn's Scientific Library (London: Bohn, 1852-1853).

3. Humboldt, Alexander von. *Vues des cordillères, et monumens des peuples indigènes de l'Amérique.* Paris: Schoell, 1810

The plates to go with [1] above.

4. Humboldt, Alexander von. *Atlas géographique et physique des régions équinoxiales du nouveau continent, fondé sur des observations astronomiques, des mesures trigonométriques et des nivellemens barométriques.* Voyage de Humboldt et Bonpland, pt. 1. Paris: Schoell, 1814.

5. Humboldt, Alexander von. *Examen critique de l'histoire de la géographie du nouveau continent, et des progrès de l'astronomie nautique aux quinzième et seizième siecles. Analyse de l'atlas géographique et physique.* Voyage de Humboldt et Bonpland, pt. 1. Paris: Gide, 1814-1834.

Zoology

6. Humboldt, Alexander von. *Recueil d'observations de zoologie et d'anatomie comparée, faites dans l'Océan Atlantique, dans l'intérieur du nouveau continent et dans la Mer du Sud, pendant les années 1799, 1800, 1801, 1802 et 1803*. 2 vols. Voyage de Humboldt et Bonpland, pt. 2. Paris: Schoell, 1811-1833.

Politics

7. Humboldt, Alexander von. *Essai politique sur le royaume de la Nouvelle Espagne*. 2 vols. Voyage de Humboldt et Bonpland, pt. 3. Paris: Schoell, 1811-1812.

8. Humboldt, Alexander von. *Atlas géographique et physique du Royaume de la Nouvelle Espagne, fondé sur des observations astronomiques, des mesures trigonométriques et des nivellemens barométriques*. Voyage de Humboldt et Bonpland, pt. 3. Paris: Schoell, 1811.

Geodesics

9. Humboldt, Alexander von. *Conspectus longitudinum et latitudinum geographicarum per decursum annorum 1799 ad 1804 in plaga aequinoctiali ab Alexandro de Humboldt astronomice observatarum*. Calculo subjecit Jabbo Oltmanns. Lutetiae Parisorum: Schoell, 1808.

10. Humboldt, Alexander von. *Nivellement barométrique fait dans les régions équinoxiales du nouveau continent en 1799, 1800, 1801, 1802, 1803 et 1804*. Toutes les hauteurs ont été calculées par M. Oltmanns, d'après la formule de M. Laplace et le coefficient barométrique de M. Raymond. Paris: Tubingue, 1809.

11. Humboldt, Alexander von. *Recueil d'observations astronomiques, d'opérations trigonométriques et de mesures barométriques, faites pendant le cours d'un voyage aux régions équinoxiales du nouveau continent, depuis 1799 jusqu'en 1803*. Rédigées et calculées, d'après les tables les plus exactes, par Jabbo Oltmanns. Ouvrage auquel on a joint des recherches historiques sur la position de plusieurs points importans pour les navigateurs et pour les géographes. 2 vol. Voyage de Humboldt et Bonpland, pt. 4. Paris: Schoell, 1810.

Plant Geography

12. Humboldt, Alexander von. *Essai sur la géographie des plantes, accompagné d'un tableau physique des régions équinoxiales, fondé sur des mesures executées, depuis le dixième degré de latitude boréale jusqu'au dixième degre de latitude australe, pendant les années 1799, 1800, 1801, 1802 et 1803 par Al. de Humboldt et A. Bonpland*. Voyage de Humbolt et Bonpland, pt. 5. Paris: Schoell, an XIII (1805).

13. Humboldt, Alexander von. *Tableau physique des Andes et pays voisins, dressé d'après des observations en 1799-1803*. (Géographie des plantes équinoxiales). Paris: Schoell, 1808.

One large folding map.

Botany

14. Bonpland, Aime. *Nova genera et species plantarum quas in peregrinatione ad plagam aequinoctialem Orbis Novi collegerunt, descripserunt, partim adumbraverunt Amat. Bonpland et Alex. de Humboldt*. Ex schedis autographis Amati Bonplandi in ordinem digessit Carol. Sigismund. Kunth. Accedunt tabuli aeri incisi, et Alexandri de Humboldt notationes ad geographia plantarum spectantes. 7 vols. Voyage de Humboldt et Bonpland, pt. 6. Lutetiae Parisiorum: Librairie Graeco-Latino-Germanicae, 1815-1825.

15. Humboldt, Alexander von. *Monographie des Melastomacées, comprenant toutes les plantes de cet ordre recueillies jusqu'à ce jour, et notamment au Mexique, dans l'île de Cuba, dans les provinces de Caracas, de Cumaná et de Barcelone, aux Andes de la Nouvelle-Grenade, de Quito et du Pérou, et sur les bords du Rio-Negro, de l'Orénoque et de la rivière des Amazones*. Mise en ordre par A. Bonpland. 2 vols. Voyage de Humboldt et Bonpland, pt. 6. Paris: Librairie Grecque-Latine-Allemande, 1816-1823.

16. Humboldt, Alexander von. *Plantes équinoxiales, recueillies au Mexique, dans l'île de Cuba, dans les provinces de Caracas, de Cumaná et de Barcelone, aux Andes de la Nouvelle-Grenade, de Quito et du Pérou, et sur les bords du Rio-Negro, de l'Orénoque et de la rivière des Amazones*. Ouvrage rédigé par A. Bonpland. 2 vols. Voyage de Humboldt et Bonpland, pt. 6. Paris: Schoell, 1808-1809.

17. Kunth, Karl Sigismund. *Monographie des Mimoses et autres plantes légumineuses du nouveau continent, recueillies par Mm. de Humboldt et Bonpland*. Voyage de Humboldt et Bonpland, pt. 6. Paris, Librairie Greque-Latine-Allemande, 1819.

18. Kunth, Karl Sigismund. *Révision des Graminées publiées dans les Nova genera et species plantarum de Humboldt et Bonpland, précédée d'un travail général sur la famille des Graminées*. 3 vols. Voyage de Humboldt et Bonpland, pt. 6. Paris: Gide, 1829-1834.

II. Other Publications Relevant to the Humboldt Expedition

19. Bonpland, Aimé. *Archives inédites de Aimé Bonpland*. 2 vols. Trabajos del Instituto de Botánica y Farmacología, 31, 42. Buenos Aires, Instituto de Botánica y Farmacología, 1914-1924.

20. Humboldt, Alexander von. *Lettres américaines d'Alexandre de Humboldt (1798-1807)*. Précédées d'une notice de J.-C. Delamétherie et suivies d'un choix de documents en partie inédits. Publiées avec une introduction et des notes par E.T. Hamy. Paris: Guilmoto, 1905.

III. Prince Maximilian von Wied

21. Wied, Maximilian, Prinz von. *Reise nach Brasilien in den Jahren 1815 bis 1817*. Mit zwei und zwanzig Küpfern, neunzehn Vignetten und drei Karten. 2 vols. Frankfurt am Main: Bronner, 1820-1821.

22. Wied, Maximilian, Prinz von. *Travels in Brazil in the years 1815, 1816, 1817*. Illustrated with plates. London: Colburn, 1820.

A translation of vol. 1 of [21], above.

23. Wied, Maximilian, Prinz von, ed. *Abbildungen zur Naturgeschichte Brasiliens*. Weimar: Landes-Industrie-Comptoirs, 1822-1831.

Issued in 15 parts.

24. Wied, Maximilian, Prinz von. *Beitrag zur Flora Brasiliens*. Mit Beschreibungen von Nees von Esenbeck, und von Martius. 2 pt. Nova acta physico-medica, vol. 3. Bonnae, 1823-1824.

25. Wied, Maximilian, Prinz von. *Beiträge zur Naturgeschichte von Brasilien*. 4 vols. in 6. Weimar: Landes-Industrie-Comptoirs, 1825-1833.

26. Wied, Maximilian, Prinz von. *Brasilien: Nachträge, berichtigungen und zusätze zu der beschreibung meiner Reise im östlichen Brasilien*. Frankfurt am Main: Bronner, 1850.

IV. Spix and Martius

27. Spix, Johann Baptist von and Carl Philipp Friedrich von Martius. *Reise in Brasilien auf befehl Sr. Majestät Maximilian Joseph I, Königs von Baiern, in den jahren 1817 bis 1820 gemacht und beschrieben von Joh. Bapt. von Spix und Carl Friedr. Phil. von Martius*. 3 vols. + atlas. München: Lindauer, 1823-1831.

Vols. 2-3 by Martius alone.

28. Spix, Johann Baptist von and Carl Friedrich Philipp von Martius. *Travels in Brazil in the years 1817-1820, undertaken by command of His Majesty the King of Bavaria by Joh. Bapt. von Spix and C.F. Phil. von Martius*. 2 vols. in 1. London: Longman, Hurst, Rees, Orme, Brown and Green, 1824.

Vol. 1 of [27] above, translated by H.E. Lloyd.

29. Martius, Carl Friedrich Philipp von. *Die Pflanzen und Thiere des tropischen Amerika: ein Naturgemalde*. München, 1831.

Appendix to vol. 3 of the *Reise in Brasilien* [27].

30. Spix, Johann Baptist von. *Brasilien in seiner Entwicklung seit der entdeckung bis auf unsere Zeit.* München: Lindauer, 1821.

31. Spix, Johann Baptist von. *Simiarum et vespertilionum brasiliensum species novae, ou Histoire naturelle des espèces nouvelles des singes et de chauves-souris, observées et recueillies pendant le voyage dans l'intérieur du Brésil.* Monachii: Hubschmann, 1823.

32. Martius, Carl Friedrich Philipp von. *Historia naturalis palmarum: opus tripartium, cuius volumen primum palmas singulatim tractat; volumen secundum Brasiliae palmas singulatim descriptione et icone illustrat; volumen tertium ordinis, familiarum, generum characteres recenset species selectas describit et figuris adumbrat adiecta omnium synopsi. Accedunt tabulas CCXLV.* 3 vols. Lipsiae: Weigel, 1823-1850.

33. Spix, Johann Baptist von. *Animalia nova, sive, Species novae testudinum et ranarum quas in itinere per Brasiliam annis MDCCCXVII-MDCCCXX jussu et auspiciis Maximiliani Josephi I Bavariae regis suscepto collegit et descripsit J.B. de Spix.* Monachii: Hübschmann, 1824.

34. Spix, Johann Baptist von. *Avium species novae quas in itinere per Brasiliam annis MDCCCXVII-MDCCCXX jussu et auspiciis Maximiliani Josephi I Bavariae regis suscepto collegit et descripsit J.B. de Spix.* Monachii: Hübschmann, 1824.

35. Spix, Johann Baptist von. *Serpentum Brasiliensium species novae, ou, Histoire naturelle des espèces nouvelles de serpens, recueillies et observées pendant le voyage dans l'intérieur du Brésil dans les années 1817, 1818, 1819, 1820.* Ecrite d'après les notes du voyageur par Jean Wagler. Monachii: Hübschmann, 1824.

36. Martius, Carl Friedrich Phillipp von. *Specimen materiae medicae Brasiliensis exhibens plantas medicinales quas in itinere per Brasiliam annis 1817-1820 jussu et auspiciis Maximiliani Josephii I Bavariae regis suscepto observavit Dr. C.F.P. de Martius.* Monacens: Seidel, 1824.

37. Martius, Carl Friedrich Phillipp von. *Nova genera et species plantarum quas in itinere per Brasiliam annis MDCCCXVII-MDCCCXX jussu et auspiciis Maximiliani Joseph I Bavariae regis suscepto collegit et descripsit Dr. C.F.P. de Martius.* Pingendas curavit et secundum auctoris schedulas digessit Dr. J. G. Zuccarini. 3 vols. Monachii: Lindauer, 1824-1831.

38. Wagner, Andreas Johann. *Testacea fluviatilia quae in itinere per Brasiliam annis MDCCXVII-MDCCXX jussu et auspiciis Maximiliani Josephi I Bavariae regis collegit et pingenda curavit Dr. J. B. de Spix.* Digessit, descripsit et observationibus illustravit Dr. J. A. Wagner ; ediderunt F. A. Paula de Schrank et C.F.P. de Martius. Lipsiae: Weigel, [1827?].

39. Spix, Johann Baptist von. *Selecta genera et species piscium, quos in itinere per Brasiliam annis MDCCCXVII-MDCCCXX jussu et auspiciis Maximiliani Josephi I Bavariae regis peracto collegit et pingendos curavit Dr. J. B. de Spix.* Digessit, descripsit et observationibus anatomicis illustravit L. Agassiz; praefatus est et edidit itineris socius F. C. Ph. de Martius. Monachii: Wolf, 1829-1831.

40. Martius, Carl Friedrich Philipp von. *Von dem Rechtszustände unter den Ureinwohnern Brasiliens: eine Abhandlung.* München: Fleischer, 1832.

41. Martius, Carl Friedrich Philipp von. *Flora brasiliensis: enumeratio plantarum in Brasilia hactenus detectarum quas suis aliorumque botanicorum studiis descriptas et methodo naturali digestas partim icone illustratas ediderunt Carolus Fridericus Philippus de Martius et Augustus Guilielmus Eichler iisque defunctis successor Ignatius Urban.* 15 vol. in 40. Monachii: Oldenbourg, 1840-1906.

Issued in 130 fascicles.

42. Martius, Carl Friedrich Philipp von. *Glossaria linguarum brasiliensium = Glossários de diversas lingoas e dialectos, que fallão os índios no Império do Brazil = Wörtersammlung brasilianischer sprachen.* Beiträge zur Ethnographie und Sprachenkunde Brasiliens, vol. 2. Erlangen: Junge, 1863.

43. Martius, Carl Friedrich Philipp von. *Beiträge zur Ethnographie und Sprachenkunde Amerika's zumal Brasiliens.* 2 vols. Leipzig: Fleischer, 1867.

V. Orbigny

44. Orbigny, Alcide Dessalines d'. *Voyage dans l'Amérique Méridionale (le Brésil, la République Orientale de l'Uruguay, la République Argentine, la Patagonie, la République du Chili, la République de Bolivia, la République du Pérou), exécuté pendant les années 1826, 1827, 1828, 1829, 1830, 1831, 1832, et 1833 par Alcide d'Orbigny.* 9 vols. Paris: Pitois-Levrault, 1835-1847.

45. *Voyage pittoresque dans les deux Amériques: résumé général de tous les voyages de Colomb, Las-Casas, Oviedo, Gomara, Garcilazo de la Vega, Acosta, Dutertre, Labat, Stedman, La Condamine, Ulloa, Humboldt, Hamilton, Cochrane, Mawe, Auguste de Saint-Hilaire, Max. de Neuwied, Spix et Martius, Rengger et Longchamp, Azara, Frésier, Molina, Miers, Poeppig, Antonio del Rio, Beltrami, Pike, Long, Adair, Chastellux, Bartram, Collot, Lewis et Clarke, Bradbury, Ellis, Mackenzie, Franklin, Parry, Back, Phipps, etc.* Par les rédacteurs du Voyage pittoresque autour du monde; publié sous la direction de M. Alcide d'Orbigny. Accompagné de cartes et de nombreuses gravures d'après les dessins de MM. de Sainson et Jules Boilly. Paris: Tenré, 1836.

46. Orbigny, Alcide Dessalines d'. *L'homme américain (de l'Amérique Méridionale), considéré sous ses rapports physiologiques et moraux.* 2 vols. Paris: Pitois-Levrault, 1839.

With atlas (15 leaves of plates).

VI. Gay

47. Gay, Claudio. *Historia física y política de Chile, según documentos adquiridos en esta república durante doce anos de residencia en ella y publicada bajo los auspicios del Supremo Gobierno.* 30 vols. París, En casa del autor, 1844-1871.

Contains: Historia (8 vols., 1844-1871). Documentos sobre la historia, la estadística y la geografía (2 vols., 1846-1852). Botánica (8 vols., 1845-1853). Zoología (8 vols., 1847-1854). Agricultura (2 vols., 1862-1865). Atlas (2 vols., 1854).

48. Ortiz, Carlos Stuardo. *Vida de Claudio Gay, 1800-1873, seguida de los escritos del naturalista e historiador, de otros concernientes a su labor y de diversos documentos relativos a su persona.* Con un escrito sobre Gay através de su correspondencia de Guillermo Feliu Cruz. 2 vols. Santiago de Chile: Nascimento, 1973.

VII. Darwin

49. Fitzroy, Robert, ed. *Narrative of the surveying voyages of His Majesty's ships Adventure and Beagle between the years 1826 and 1836: describing their examination of the southern shores of South America, and the Beagle's circumnavigation of the globe.* 3 vols. [in 4]. London: Colburn, 1839.

Contains: vol. 1. Proceedings of the first expedition, 1826-1830, under the command of Captain P. Parker King—vol. 2. Proceedings of the second expedition, 1831-1836, under the command of Captain Robert Fitz-Roy—vol. 3. Journal and remarks, 1832-1836, by Charles Darwin—Appendix to vol. 2.

50. Darwin, Charles. *Journal of researches into the geology and natural history of the various countries visited by H.M.S. Beagle, under the command of Captain FitzRoy, R.N., from 1832 to 1836.* London: Colburn, 1839.

Vol. 3 of the [49] above, published separately. A revised edition followed in 1845 (see [54] below).

51. Darwin, Charles. *The structure and distribution of coral reefs: being the first part of the geology of the voyage of the Beagle, under the command of Capt. Fitzroy, R.N., during the years 1832 to 1836.* London: Smith, Elder, 1842.

52. Darwin, Charles. *Geological observations on the volcanic islands, visited during the voyage of H.M.S. Beagle, together with some brief notices on the geology of Australia and the Cape of Good Hope: being the second part of*

the geology of the voyage of the Beagle under the command of Capt. Fitzroy, R.N., during the years 1832 to 1836. London: Smith, Elder, 1844.

53. Darwin, Charles. *Geological observations on South America: being the third part of the geology of the voyage of the Beagle, under the command of Capt. Fitzroy, R.N., during the years 1832 to 1836.* London: Smith, Elder, 1846.

54. Darwin, Charles. *Journal of researches into the natural history and geology of the countries visited during the voyage of H.M.S. Beagle round the world, under the command of Capt. Fitzroy.* 2nd ed., with additions. London: J. Murray, 1845.

    A revision of [50], above.

55. Darwin, Charles, ed. *The zoology of the voyage of H.M.S. Beagle, under the command of Captain Fitzroy, R.N., during the years 1832 to 1836.* Published with the approval of the Lords Commissioners of Her Majesty's Treasury. Edited and superintended by Charles Darwin. 5 vols. London: Smith, Elder, 1839-1843.

    Contains: Pt. 1. Fossil mammalia, described by Richard Owen; Pt. 2. Mammalia, described by George R. Waterhouse; Pt. 3. Birds, described by John Gould; Pt. 4. Fish, described by the Leonard Jenyns; Pt. 5. Reptilia, described by Thomas Bell.

56. Darwin, Charles. *On the origin of the species by means of natural selection; or, The preservation of favoured races in the struggle for life.* London: J. Murray, 1859.

VIII. Schomburgk

57. Schomburgk, Sir Robert Hermann. *Report of the third expedition into the interior of Guayana, comprising the journey to the sources of the Essequibo, to the Caruma Mountains and to Fort San Joaquin, on the Rio Branco, in 1837-8.* London, Churchill, 1839.

    From the London Geographical Journal, May, 1839.

58. Schomburgk, Sir Robert Hermann. *A description of British Guiana, geographical and statistical: exhibiting its resources and capabilities, together with the present and future condition and prospects of the colony.* London: Simpkin, Marshall, 1840.

59. Schomburgk, Sir Robert Hermann. *Reisen in Guiana und am Orinoko während der Jahre 1835-1839.* Nach seinen Berichten und Mittheilungen an die Geographische Gesellschaft in London herausgegeben von O. A. Schomburgk. Mit einem Vorwort von Alexander von Humboldt und dessen Abhandlung uber einige wichtige astronomische Positionen Guiana's. Leipzig: Wigand, 1841.

60. Schomburgk, Sir Robert Hermann. *Robert Hermann Schomburgk's Travels in Guiana and on the Orinoco during the years 1835-1839, according to his reports and communications to the Geographical Society of London*. Edited by O. A. Schomburgk; with a preface by Alexander von Humboldt, together with his Essay on some important astronomical positions in Guiana. Translated by Walter E. Roth. Georgetown, British Guiana: "The Argosy" Co., 1931.

    A translation of [59], above.

61. Schomburgk, Sir Robert Hermann. *Twelve views in the interior of Guiana, from drawings executed by Charles Bentley, after sketches taken during the expedition carried on in the years 1835 to 1839, under the direction of the Royal Geographical Society of London and aided by Her Majesty's government*. With descriptive letter-press by Robert H. Schomburgk. London: Ackermann, 1841.

62. Schomburgk, Sir Robert Hermann. *The natural history of the fishes of Guiana*. The naturalist's library, vol. 3, 5. 2 vol. Edinburgh: Lizars, 1841-1843.

63. Schomburgk, Sir Robert Hermann. *Journal of an expedition from Pirara to the upper Corentyne, and from thence to Demerara*. London: John Murray, [1845].

64. Schomburgk, Sir Robert Hermann. *The history of Barbados: comprising a geographical and statistical description of the island, a sketch of the historical events since the settlement and an account of its geology and natural productions*. London: Longman, Brown, Green and Longmans, 1848.

IX. Bates and Wallace

65. Wallace, Alfred Russel. *A narrative of travels on the Amazon and Rio Negro, with an account of the native tribes, and observations on the climate, geology, and natural history of the Amazon Valley*. London: Reeve, 1853.

66. Wallace, Alfred Russel. *Palm trees of the Amazon and their uses*. London: J. Van Voorst, 1853.

67. Bates, Henry Walter. *Contributions to an insect fauna of the Amazon Valley: Coleoptera--Longicornes. Part I, Lamiares*. London: Taylor and Francis, 1861-1866.

    Originally published in the Annals and Magazine of Natural History, ser. 3, vol. 8-9, 12-17 (1861-1866).

68. Bates, Henry Walter. *The naturalist on the River Amazons: a record of adventures, habits of animals, sketches of Brazilian and Indian life and aspects of nature under the Equator during eleven years of travel*. 2 vols. London: J. Murray, 1863.

69. Wallace, Alfred Russel. *Contributions to the theory of natural selection: a series of essays*. London, New York: Macmillan, 1870.

70. Wallace, Alfred Russel. *Tropical nature, and other essays*. London, New York: Macmillan, 1878.

Includes more of Wallace's thoughts on natural selection.

3. La financiación de las ciencias y las expediciones científicas en Hispanoamérica bajo los Borbones

Rafael E. Tarragó

La financiación de las ciencias por el estado no es un fenómeno del siglo XX. Es bien conocida la leyenda de la escuela de navegación del Príncipe Enrique de Portugal en Sagrés en el siglo XV. En el siglo XVI, Felipe II de las Españas y las Indias envió a su médico Francisco Hernández al reino de Nueva España con el encargo de informarse sobre las plantas y métodos de curación de los médicos indígenas en este.[1] En el siglo XVII, el registra Luis XIV de Francia financió el desarrollo de la Academia de Ciencias de París. El mecenazgo de reyes y príncipes era parcialmente una cuestión de prestigio. Esta actitud se agudizó en el siglo XVIII, llamado la Ilustración en el mundo occidental. Un soberano que apoyaba las ciencias y las artes era un soberano ilustrado. Pero muchas veces este mecenazgo tuvo fines económicos y políticos.

Los cambios ocurridos en las ciencias durante el siglo XVII, a la vez que independizaron a estas de la filosofía y la teología, las involucraron más con su medio. La ciencia dejó de ser una actividad de gabinete para interesarse por los problemas concretos que plantean el desarrollo económico y social. Ello exigía forzar la transición desde una razón meramente contemplativa y sistematizadora a otra más activa y de dominación.[2] Las Academias Nacionales de Ciencias se convirtieron en una especie de órganos asesores de gobernantes, entre cuyas funciones no serán las menos importantes las destinadas a consagrar la obra de algunos hombres de ciencias y proporcionar el brillo que prestigiaba y legitimizaba la acción política del estado.

En el siglo XVIII, al heredar los reinos de España e Indias un príncipe de la dinastía francesa de Borbón, la influencia francesa se hizo sentir no solamente en la política, sino también en las ideas de estos. La influencia francesa fue general durante el siglo XVIII en Europa y los dominios americanos de reyes europeos, pero en el caso de España e Indias esta fue más directa. La primera expedición científica en que los Borbones españoles invirtieron fue una expedición ideada y organizada (aunque mal subvencionada) por la Academia de Ciencias de París y el rey de Francia.[3]

La política económica mercantilista inaugurada en España por los Borbones (el sistema de restricción de comercio de los reyes de la Casa de

Austria no merece llamarse mercantilista, habiendo sido meramente una política monopolística diseñada para tasar más fácilmente el comercio) tenía inspiración francesa.[4] El interés por el conocimiento de las ciencias útiles que se extendió en España y los reinos de Indias bajo los Borbones fue también resultado de la influencia francesa.[5]

Además del interés en participar en el espíritu de la Ilustración representada por Francia en la Europa del siglo XVIII, la Corona y los patriotas españoles apoyaron el desarrollo de las ciencias y la tecnología porque comprendían la importancia de estas para el desarrollo económico de España y los reinos de Indias. Querían una España que fuese respetada por su poder militar y por su riqueza, y por ello apoyaron no solamente la mineralogía y la geografía, sino también la botánica, como medios para convertir los dominios de la Corona en prósperas fuentes de recursos económicos. Las expediciones científicas financiadas por la Corona no ocultarían sus dimensiones militares y comerciales afines con las ideas expresadas por Don Pedro Rodríguez de Campomanes en sus *Reflexiones sobre el comercio español a Indias* (Madrid, 1762), ensayo en el que propone para España un sistema colonial puro, basado en las ideas del mercantilismo liberal inglés, donde los reinos de Indias pasarían a ser "colonias" productoras de materias primas para abastecer a España y el comercio entre estas dejaría de basarse casi únicamente en los metales preciosos y se diversificaría.[6]

En la segunda mitad del siglo XVIII se formaron en varias ciudades españolas e hispanoamericanas Sociedades Patrióticas de Amigos del País, para promover el estudio de las cosas útiles y la economía, en las cuales se discutían las ideas de autores españoles e ingleses, pero sobre todo las de los franceses, y las popularización.[7] Las Sociedades Patrióticas hicieron una gran obra de divulgación de las ideas nuevas, llevándolas más allá de grupos limitados de cortesanos y aristócratas y despertando en las clases pudientes y los letrados de provincia un espíritu cívico e interés en las economías regionales. La primera de estas sociedades en España fue la vascongada, fundada en 1763. Las Sociedades Patrióticas hispanoamericanas surgieron a raíz de una Real Cédula del rey Don Carlos III, formándose varias —entre ellas las de Santiago de Cuba (1787), Quito (1791), La Habana (1791), Lima (1793) y Guatemala (1795). Algunas ideas expresadas en estas sociedades eran avanzadas para su tiempo, como las del santiaguero Pedro Valiente, quien escribió en un memorial de 1787 a la Sociedad Patriótica de su ciudad natal que un país con una economía totalmente agraria estaba condenado a la pobreza.[8] Varias de la expediciones científicas enviadas por la Corona a Hispanoamérica fueron apoyadas por las Sociedades Patrióticas.[9]

La primera expedición científica de la Corona de España a Hispanoamérica fue la expedición franco-española para medir el meridiano en el Ecuador y comprobar que la Tierra es achatada por los políticos, enviada al Reino de Quito en 1735, y la última fue la expedición arqueológica a Nueva España de 1805. En su artículo "Las expediciones ilustradas y el estado español", Fermín del Pino Díaz y Angel Guirao de Vierna incluyen una lista de 41 expediciones, sin contar las expediciones para introducir el sistema de beneficio de la plata por amalgamación del Barón Born en el Perú, Nueva Granada y Nueva España.[10] No todas las expediciones incluidas en esa lista fueron diseñadas como científicas, pero con la excepción de la expedición arqueológica de 1805 (la cual produjo un mayor y más detallado conocimiento de las ruinas de Palenque y Xochicalco y la descripción de otras muchas) todas estas expediciones tuvieron componentes de interés económico y práctico.[11]

La más ambiciosa de las reales expediciones fue la dirigida por Alejandro de Malaspina. Originalmente diseñada para darle la vuelta al mundo, tenía como fin obtener información sobre Hispanoamérica para enriquecer las ciencias, dibujar mapas y obtener información política de los dominios ultramarinos de la Corona española, para que esta pudiese gobernarlos y explotarlos mejor.[12] En el *Plan para escribir su viaje* que Malaspina entregó al P. Gil, con el fin de llevar a cabo una narración conjunta y unitaria de todos los datos recogidos por la expedición, la sistemática influye la descripción física (geografía, demografía, recursos económicos y etnografía, todo ello en relación a la naturaleza física) y el examen político (en lo que hace referencia a la jurisprudencia natural, a la economía y a la política). En pocas palabras, Malaspina concluyó que la reorganización política depende de la social, en el sentido de tenerse que resolver como condición previa "El choque continuo de miras, de intereses y de la fuerza parcial de cada uno".[13]

Desafortunadamente para Malaspina, su actitud crítica hacia la política de Manuel Godoy, favorito del rey Don Carlos IV y de su mujer la reina María Luisa de Parma, le acarreó la enemistad de este, su arresto, juicio y condena a diez años de prisión por traición. De los trabajos escritos durante su expedición solamente la *Relación del viaje hecho por las goletas "Sutil" y "Mexicana" en el año 1792* (Madrid, 1802), por Dionisio Alcalá Galiano y Cayetano Valdés fue publicada durante su vida. Sus trabajos no fueron publicados hasta casi cien años después de su expedición por Pedro de Novo y Colson (Madrid, 1888).[14]

En este ensayo sobre expediciones científicas me voy a limitar a analizar tres de las expediciones botánicas, las tecnológicas para introducir el sistema de amalgamación de Born y la expedición de vacunación de 1804.

Las expediciones botánicas

Me atrevo a decir que de todas las expediciones botánicas financiadas por la Corona española en el siglo XVIII las más importantes fueron la de Ruiz y Pavón al Perú, la de Mutis en Nueva Granada, y la de Sessé y Mociño en Nueva España. La expedición al Perú se originó de una petición del gobierno francés a Carlos III de España para que le permitiese a un naturalista de la Academia de Ciencias de París visitar Perú para rescatar los papeles abandonados en Lima por Joseph de Jussieu, uno de los expedicionarios franceses en la expedición que midió el meridiano en el Ecuador.[15] La expedición de Nueva Granada (Colombia), se originó de una petición al rey del virrey-arzobispo Caballero y Góngora y fue organizada por el médico J. C. Mutis, residente de Santa Fe de Bogotá, y todo su personal fue americano.[16] La expedición de Nueva España (México) se originó de una idea del Dr. Sessé, un médico español radicado en Ciudad México.[17]

La historia de la real expedición botánica al Perú ha sido narrada y analizada magistralmente por Arthur Robert Steele en su estudio *Flowers for the King: The Expedition of Ruiz and Pavón and the Flora of Peru*. Esta obra tiene una introducción histórico-científica que le permite al lector ver la expedición en su contexto histórico y dentro de los conceptos de la ciencia de su tiempo. Según la historia de Steele, en la época en que el gobierno francés pidió al rey de España permiso para enviar al botánico francés Joseph Dombey al Perú comenzaba en España un gran interés por la botánica como conocimiento útil. En 1774 Don Pedro Rodríguez de Campomanes publicó su *Discurso sobre el fomento de la industria popular*, en el que sugiere el fomento del estudio de las ciencias naturales y la recompensa de aquellos que descubran plantas útiles para las manufacturas. Las Sociedades Patrióticas apoyaron también el estudio de la botánica en su relación con la agricultura, la industria y el comercio. A fines de febrero de 1776 el gobierno francés recibió la respuesta del gobierno español a su petición de permitirle a un botánico francés ir al Perú. Este le concedía permiso al botánico Dombey para ir al Perú como botánico-naturalista acompañante de los botánicos Hipólito Ruiz y José Pavón, bajo condición de que dejaría en España duplicados de todos sus descubrimientos y que no publicara ninguno antes que sus colegas españoles.[18]

A principios de 1777, el año en que salió la expedición al Perú, el Director del Jardín Botánico de Madrid, Don Casimiro Gómez de Ortega, le había dicho a Don José de Gálvez, Secretario de Indias: "si el rey manda examinar las producciones naturales de España y sus vastos dominios ultramarinos a doce naturalistas con otros tantos químicos o mineralogistas esparcidos por sus estados, estos producirán por medio de sus peregrinaciones una utilidad incomparablemente mayor que cien mil hombres combatiendo por añadir algunas provincias al Imperio, cuyos productos hayan de sepultarse en el olvido; como lo están por la mayor parte los que cría la Naturaleza en los que ya se poseen."[19] Gómez Ortega confiaba en encontrar las plantas adecuadas para ser introducidas en el comercio, y con este objeto escribió su *Instrucción sobre el modo más seguro y económico de transportar plantas vivas por mar y tierra a los países más distantes . . .* (Madrid, 1779), la cual fue enviada a los virreyes de Nueva España, Nueva Granada y Perú, a los gobernadores de Puerto Rico, La Habana, Santo Domingo, Yucatán y Luisiana, y a los intendentes de Caracas y La Habana.

Ruiz y Pavón fueron verdaderos "cazadores de plantes", coleccionistas y clasificadores, siempre atentos a los posibles usos comerciales y medicinales de las plantas que encontraban. Según los planes originales, la expedición iba a durar cuatro años, pero la cantidad de material que se presentó ante los expedicionarios al llegar a América, además de las distancias y las dificultades de transporte, prolongaron su duración de 1777 a 1787. La Corona pagó a sus botánicos un salario anual de 1000 pesos, duplicados durante el tiempo que hiciesen labor de campo. El gobierno francés le pagaba 600 pesos a su botánico, pero cuando se enteró de cuanto recibían los españoles le doblaron el sueldo. Además de un salario, la Corona le pagaba a los botánicos sus gastos en libros, instrumentos científicos y otros materiales de trabajo. Además, los españoles contaban con un fondo anual de 3000 pesos para gastos imprevistos.[20]

Los expedicionarios Hipólito Ruiz, José Pavón y Joseph Dombey pasaron su primer año en el Perú en Lima, donde fueron bien recibidos por los sabios limeños Cosme Bueno e Hipólito Unanué. Como los expedicionarios de 1735 en Quito se habían asombrado de encontrar que las ideas de Descartes, Leibnitz y Newton eran conocidas ya en ese reino perdido en medio de los Andes, así los expedicionarios de 1777 en Perú se asombraron de encontrar que el método de clasificación de plantas de Linneo no solamente era conocido, sino también la causa de disputas científicas, y de que el interés en la botánica estaba tan generalizado entre las élites de la remota Lima como entre las de París y Madrid.[21]

En mayo de 1779 los expedicionarios pasaron al territorio de Tarma, a 120 millas de Lima, en donde establecieron su centro de operaciones.[22] En el área de Huánuco encontraron varias quinas —las Cinchonas purpúrea, nítida y magnifolia— y en Cuchero observaron el proceso de extracción de la quinina. El 21 de diciembre de 1781 los tres botánicos y sus dibujantes zarparon del Callao para Talcahuano y en marzo de 1782 establecieron un centro de operaciones en Concepción. En Chile quedaron impresionados con el "pino chileno" *(Araucaria araucaria)*, en el cual creyeron haber encontrado una nueva especie del genus *Pinus* de Linneo. Después de un año en Chile partieron de Valparaíso para Lima el 15 de octubre de 1783.[23]

Joseph Dombey salió del Perú para Europa el 14 de abril de 1784 con 73 cajas de especímenes y sus notas y dibujos. Los españoles se quedaron explorando por Real Orden de 10 de septiembre de 1783, pero antes de continuar sus exploraciones enviaron a España lo que habían coleccionado hasta entonces. En mayo de 1784 ya habían enviado 55 cajas con plantas disecadas, semillas, maderas, muestras de minerales y artefactos y vestimentas usados por los indígenas.[24] Completa esta misión, los españoles tomaron camino para Huánuco el 12 de mayo de 1784, pero siguieron hasta Pozuzo, 45 millas este-sureste de Huánuco. Para el 27 de septiembre, cuando regresaron a Huánuco, habían descrito 400 plantas y corregido 250 descripciones hechas en otros lados.

La Corona extendió indefinidamente la duración oficial de la expedición en junio de 1785, pero dos años más tarde, le ordenó a Ruiz y a Pavón que regresaran a España y que dejasen a aquellos a quienes habían instruido en botánica en el Perú el encargo de continuar clasificando y haciendo dibujos botánicos de las plantas que descubriesen.[25] Antes de regresar a España los botánicos exploraron Muna, 24 leguas al este de Huánuco, en donde encontraron dos especies más de Cinchonas *(Cinchona ovata* y *Cinchona lanceolata).* En enero de 1787 enviaron a España 73 cajas de plantas disecadas, 18 recipientes con plantas vivas y 586 dibujos. También exploraron Pillar, 12 leguas al nordeste de Huánuco, y Chacahuassi, a tres días de Pillar. Cuando el rey envió otra orden requiriendo su regreso a España los botánicos se embarcaron, dejando al agregado Juan José Tafalla a cargo de la continuación de los trabajos de la expedición y recomendado para la dirección del Jardín Botánico de Lima, cuya erección acababa de ser aprobada por la Corona. Ruiz y Pavón regresaron a España con 29 cajas de especímenes, 589 dibujos botánicos y 24 recipientes de plantas el 1° de abril de 1788.[28]

El rey demandaba el regreso inmediato de los botánicos para que comenzasen a preparar los trabajos de la expedición para su publicación. En 1798 vio la luz el primer volumen de una colosal aventura editorial: la *Flora peruviana et chilensis*. De esta salieron solamente el *Prodomus* (1792), *Systema vegetalium* (1798) y los tres primeros tomos de cinco con los resultados de sus observaciones preparados entre 1798 y 1802, a pesar de la ayuda económica que la Corona recibió de los reinos de Indias para la culminación del proyecto. Según A. González Bueno, un estudio cuantitativo de las utilidades asignadas a las plantas en esos textos florísticos de Ruiz y Pavón muestra el predominio de las de acción medicinal (16.2%), seguidas muy de lejos por las de uso industrial (6.9%) y alimentación (6.1%).[27]

El médico gaditano José Celestino Mutis llegó a Nueva Granada (Colombia) como facultativo del nuevo virrey en 1760. Como tenía interés en la botánica comenzó una correspondencia con el botánico sueco Linneo, y a fines de 1763 le escribió al rey Don Carlos III, proponiéndole una expedición botánica subvencionada por la Corona bajo su dirección. Como el rey no le contestó, Mutis continuó haciendo observaciones por su cuenta, y en 1767 le envió a Linneo especímenes de una quina que había recibido de Loja, por medio de los cuales este corrigió observaciones hechas sobre esa planta. La corteza de la quina tiene propiedades febrífugas y curativas de la malaria que la hacían muy valiosa. Ocho años más tarde Mutis descubrió una especie de quina cerca de Santa Fé de Bogotá que pronto comenzó a exportarse por Cartagena de Indias.[28]

Cuando fue hecho virrey de Nueva Granada el arzobispo Caballero y Góngora, J.C. Mutis le comunicó su proyecto para una expedición botánica, y el virrey-arzobispo le envió una petición al rey para que la aprobase. El rey se mostró favorable al proyecto de Mutis cuando lo recibió del virrey de Nueva Granada y le dio su aprobación en 1783. El virrey-arzobispo comenzó la expedición en 1782, antes de recibir la aprobación del rey, y le asignó a Mutis y sus compañeros la suma de 3000 pesos de su propio pecunio. Mutis comenzó sus trabajos con Don Eloy Valenzuela como segundo y Salvador Rizo como pintor. El proyecto de esta expedición incluía un plan de observaciones astronómicas, geográficas y físicas para formar un mapa completa de Nueva Granada, además del estudio de la flora y la fauna de ese reino.[29]

Don Carlos III dotó la expedición botánica de Nueva Granada con instrumentos científicos, una biblioteca excepcional y un laboratorio astronómico ideado por Mutis y construido por Fray Domingo Retrés. Más que una expedición botánica en Nueva Granada se montó un proyecto científico que propagó las ciencias físicas y naturales en ese reino y sirvió de centro a los ingenios neogranadinos. Francisco José de Caldas encontró en ella apoyo y los medios para hacer sus investigaciones geográficas y astronómicas, en tanto que los estudios zoológicos se encomendaron a Jorge Tadeo Lozano. El que en abril de 1801 el joven naturalista alemán Alejandro Baron von Humboldt y su compañero Amadeo Bonpland subieran el río Magdalena para conocer al Dr. Mutis en Santa Fé y aprovechar sus experiencias sugiere que en ese primer año del siglo XIX las actividades científicas en Nueva Granada ya eran conocidas más allá del cotarro local.[30]

Don José Celestino Mutis y el grupo de hombres que se formó intelectualmente a su lado o bajo su influencia hicieron el primer esfuerzo para constituir una ciencia y una literatura propias por la contemplación y el estudio de la naturaleza nativa. En ese grupo se distinguió Francisco José de Caldas. Según Thomas F. Glick en su ensayo "Science and Independence in Latin America", este joven naturalista natural de la ciudad de Popayán propuso la fundación de una ciencia americana independiente de la europea.

Esta actitud se ve ejemplificada en su defensa del sistema de clasificación de las plantas usado por los indígenas del Perú, según Caldas, "siempre exacto y cuidadoso, dando a las plantas nombres derivados de sus propiedades y virtudes."[31] En Nueva Granada se dio la ironía de que la munificencia de la Corona española a favor de la difusión de las ciencias no solamente produjo la formación de un grupo científico capaz de asesorar a las autoridades realistas con sus conocimientos de los recursos naturales y la topografía del reino, sino también un sentimiento de alienación y rebeldía entre los científicos jóvenes, quienes se sintieron achicados al expandir sus conocimientos de la ciencia europea y la imposición de sus métodos y el desprecio de los hispanoamericanos y España de científicos europeos.[32]

La expedición botánica en Nueva Granada terminó oficialmente en 1817, durante la represión del General Morillo. Varios científicos en ella, incluyendo el gran Caldas, participaron en el movimiento independentista y fueron condenados a muerte por sus actividades políticas. Cuando en ese mismo año el General Morillo ordenó el envío a España de los textos y dibujos recopilados por la expedición, la *Flora Neogranadina*, empezada veinticinco años antes, era una obra voluminosa que registraba gran parte de la vegetación del Ecuador y de los estados de Cundinamarca, Boyacá, Santander y Cauca en lo que es hoy en día la República de Colombia.[33]

El 10 de agosto de 1785, el Dr. Martín Sessé le propuso al virrey de Nueva España Conde de Gálvez la organización de una real expedición botánica para continuar la obra del Dr. Hernández, enviado por Felipe II a estudiar las plantas medicinales del reino.

Entre otros integraron la expedición originalmente el Dr. Sessé (director), Vicente Cervantes (catedrático), Juan del Castillo, Jaime Sensevé y José Longinos Martínez. En conexión con la expedición se creó el Jardín Botánico de México y la cátedra de botánica linneana anexa al mismo, dictada por Cervantes, la cual debía facilitar la instrucción de todos los que hubieran de presentarse a examen de cirujanos, médicos y farmacéuticos. Los dos mexicanos que posteriormente se incorporaran a la expedición fueron discípulos destadados del profesor Cervantes: el médico José Mariano Mociño y José Maldonado.[34] La duración de esta expedición se extendió de 1788 hasta 1802 y la extensión recorrida por los expedicionarios abarcó más de 4000 leguas, que cubren prácticamente desde Nicaragua hasta el Golfo de California. Se realizaron tres excursiones iniciales de 1788 a 1791, y luego otras a cargo de distintos grupos que se destinaron a zonas diversas. Los posibles usos de las plantas descubiertas fue un factor importante en esta expedición, pero más que en las otras hubo en esta curiosidad científica y una verdadera pasión por el estudio de la naturaleza. Como en las otras expediciones, la expedición en Nueva España incluyó dibujantes, entre los que se destacó Atanasio Echeverría.

Además de las excursiones al Valle de México, Guatemala y las Antillas, miembros de la expedición en Nueva España colaboraron con participantes en la expedición de Malaspina durante su trayecto novohispano y participaron en la expedición de límites a Nutka bajo Bodega y Quadra. Hay varios libros sobre esta expedición y entre ellos sobresalen *Las expediciones científicas españolas durante el siglo XVIII: la expedición a Nueva España* de Juan Carlos Arias Divito, *Plantas y luces en México* de Xavier Lozoya y *Spanish Scientists in the New World: The 18th Century Expeditions* de Iris H. W. Engstrand.

En 1792 el naturalista José Longinos Martínez exploró las Californias, llevando un diario en el que incluyó descripciones de plantas, animales, fenómenos naturales y de las costumbres de los indígenas que encontró en su viaje.[35] Ese mismo año el médico mexicano José Mariano Mociño y otros dos expedicionarios se incorporaran a Juan Francisco de la Bodega y Quadra, cuando este fue a encontrarse con el inglés Vancouver en la región de Nutka, para establecer los límites entre los dominios ingleses y los de la Corona española en América del Norte. Bodega y Quadra no pudo ponerse de acuerdo con Vancouver sobre la frontera angloespañola, pero Mociño tomó perspicaces notas etnográficas que a su regreso a México en 1793 plasmó en el estudio *Noticias de Nutka* y un pequeño diccionario de la lengua de los nutkenses.[36] Las *Noticias de Nutka* fueron publicadas en forma seriada en los volúmenes 7 y 8 (1803 y 1804) de *La Gazeta de Guatemala*.[37]

Mociño y Longinos fueron a explorar juntos el sur de Nueva España y el Reino de Guatemala (Centroamérica) en 1795. Los expedicionarios llegaron a Ciudad Guatemala en el verano de 1796 y poco después Longinos estableció un museo de historia natural con el apoyo del Intendente Jacobo de villaurrutia, director de la Sociedad Patriótica de Amigos del País de Guatemala. Longinos se quedó en Guatemala hasta 1803, año en el que murió camino de regreso a Ciudad México.[38] La labor de Mociño en Guatemala quedó concretada en la Flora de Guatemala, cuyo manuscrito se conserva en la Biblioteca de Botánica del Instituto de Biología de la Universidad Nacional Autónoma de México. Mientras Mociño y Longinos exploraban en Guatemala, el Dr. Sessé se iba a explorar las Antillas españolas, pero debido a la sesión de Santo Domingo a Francia en 1796 y a la rebelión de esclavos en la antigua sección francesa de la Isla Española, sus exploraciones debieron limitarse a Puerto Rico (1796) y Cuba (1797).

El Dr. Sessé regresó a Ciudad México a preparar la partida de la expedición para España. El catedrático Cervantes decidió quedarse en México como director del Jardín Botánico, pero el Dr. Sessé, José Mariano Mociño y Jaime Sensevé llegaron a España en 1803.[39] Una vez en Madrid, los expedicionarios entregaron los manuscritos y los dibujos de la expedición a Hipólito Ruiz con la idea de que fuesen incluidos en una compilación de las plantas de los reinos de la Corona española, pero más tarde el Dr. Sessé pidió que se los devolvieran y comenzó con José Mariano Mociño la tarea de organizarlos. En eso estaban cuando el Dr. Sessé murió, en 1808. Ese mismo año los franceses entraron en España y Napoleón Bonaparte hizo rey de España a su hermano José. Mociño recibió la protección del rey José, quien le hizo director del Museo de Historia Natural de Madrid. Esta protección le costó cara cuando los franceses se retiraron de España en 1812 y Mociño tuvo que huir a Francia, llevándose los papeles y los dibujos de la expedición novohispana. En Francia Mociño le dio estos papeles a un científico suizo, Augustin Pyramus de Candle, quien se los llevó a Ginebra, pero se los pidió de vuelta cuando recibió permiso para volver a España. Mociño murió en Barcelona en 1820, camino a Madrid con sus papeles y dibujos, los cuales fueron incorporados al Jardín Botánico de Madrid. Estos fueron publicados años más tarde por la Sociedad Mexicana de Historia Natural en dos volúmenes: *Flora mexicana* (1888) y *Plantae Novae Hispanae* (1989).[40]

Los hallazgos de nuevos remedios medicinales en los dominios de la Corona española en América y Asia como resultado de las expediciones botánicas que en parte se financiaron en su búsqueda fueron menos de los que se esperaban. No se consiguió que la farmacopea española volviese a ser el espejo en el que debían mirar los códigos oficiales europeos, pero el esfuerzo no quedó baldío. La vinculación entre los esfuerzos de los expedicionarios y la inclusión de remedios en las diferentes ediciones de las *Farmacopeas* españolas se ven en las aportaciones en la determinación taxonómica de algunas drogas de uso tradicional en España, la introducción de nuevos remedios medicinales en las *Farmacopeas* de 1803 y 1817, y un mejor conocimiento en las áreas de distribución de los vegetales medicinales americanos.[41]

Contribución tecnológica de las expediciones

Según Marcel Roche en su breve pero informativo artículo "Early History of Science in Spanish America", el método de beneficio de la plata por amalgamación con azogue en gran escala ha sido la única contribución tecnológica original de Hispanoamérica con influencia más allá del cotarro local. Este autor dice que el primero en usarlo fue el sevillano Bartolomé de Medina, en Zacatecas, por el año 1555. Su método de amalgamación se introdujo en Perú en 1571 o 1572, y fue objeto de modificaciones en los tres siglos siguientes —la más famosa de ellas siendo el método "de cazo" explicado por el Padre Barba en su manual *El arte de los metales*, escrito en Potosí, pero publicado en Madrid en 1639.[42] Todavía el estudio clásico en inglés sobre la tecnología relacionada con la producción de plata en Hispanoamérica en el tiempo de España es *Mexican Silver and the Enlightenment*, de Clement G. Motten, en el cual este autor describe el método de beneficio por amalgamación con azogue llamado "de patio" (porque consistía en triturar el mineral y unirlo con ciertas sustancias químicas, y luego añadirle azogue y revolver la masa formada en una especie de patio pavimentado, con un drenaje).

Este método cuya descripción presenta como crudo y sin ciencia recuperaba como plata pura hasta 75% del mineral, casi el doble que lo que el método de fundición lograba en aquellos siglos, y a él se debe el que los reinos de Indias produjeran tanta plata como para inundar el mercado europeo y causar una inflación mundial.

Poco después de su llegada a Nueva Granada en 1760, el sabio Mutis se interesó en la minería y llegó a la conclusión de que la minería en América no tenía método ni ciencia y era incapaz de reducir a reglas científicas sus operaciones.[43] Mutis era contrario al método de amalgamación y favorecía al de fundición, como se practicaba en las minas pobres de Suecia y Alemania. Para esa época el beneficio de fundición comenzaba a practicarse en Nueva España y los mineros del Perú querían establecerlo en sus empresas. Cuando el virrey-arzobispo de Nueva Granada, Caballero y Góngora, formó una junta para estudiar los métodos más convenientes de beneficiar las minas de ese reino y de ella formó parte Mutis, quien propuso que se contratasen dos técnicos europeos competentes que enseñaran el sistema de fundición en Nueva Granada.[44]

El sistema de amalgamación de patio requería grandes cantidades de azogue y su rápida expansión en Hispanoamérica coincidió con el descubrimiento de las minas de azogue de Huancavelica en Perú y la gran producción de azogue de las minas de Almadén, en España, las cuales suplían a Nueva España. En la segunda mitad del siglo XVIII la producción de azogue en Huancavelica bajó y las minas de Almadén comenzaron a tener problemas. En agosto de 1785 la Corona española hizo un tratado comercial con los Habsburgo de Austria, quienes se comprometieron a enviar a España azogue de las minas en sus dominios de Istria.[45]

En la segunda mitad del siglo XVIII los Habsburgo estaban teniendo problemas de producción en las minas de plata de sus dominios de Eslovaquia. Cuando la calidad del mineral en esas minas comenzó a bajar trataron el beneficio de plata por amalgamación con azogue hispanoamericano por su eficiencia en la recuperación del metal, pero encontraron problemático el tiempo que tomaba. Esto fue lo que llevó al Barón Born, Consejero áulico en la corte imperial de Viena, a estudiar papeles sobre el beneficio de la plata por amalgamación, leyendo una propuesta presentada en 1588 por Juan de Córdoba para la adopción del beneficio por amalgamación con azogue como se usaba en Nueva España por los Habsburgo en Centroeuropa, y su refutación por Lázaro Ercker, Director de Minas de Bohemia. El Barón Born comparó las objeciones de Ercker con lo que el Padre Acosta dice sobre el tema en su *Historia Natural* (1590), con el manual del Padre Barba (1637) y con la información que tenía de los resultados de esta en Hispanoamérica.[46]

Hacia 1785 el Barón Born inventó una máquina de amalgamación en barriles que prometía ventajas sobre el método de patio. Esta máquina ahorraba tiempo, mano de obra y azogue. Antes de someter el mineral triturado a la amalgamación con azogue, el Barón Born lo calcinaba, y por lo tanto su método requería gran cantidad de combustible y la construcción de hornos; pero el ahorro de tiempo y de azogue de su método eran más que suficientes para hacerlo atractivo en Centroeuropa y a la Corona española, preocupada por el abastecimiento de azogue para las minas de plata americanas. En cuanto el Ministro de Indias Gálvez supo de él envió a Fausto Elhuyar a Austria, a evaluar la posibilidad de introducirlo en Hispanoamérica.[47]

Desde las primeras décadas del siglo XVIII la Corona española había enviado españoles a otros países a estudiar y a hacer espionaje industrial. En 1778 la Corona envió a estudiar fuera de España a los hermanos Juan José y Fausto Elhuyar, pensionados por la Sociedad Patriótica de Vascongadas. Los hermanos estudiaron en la Escuela de Minas de Friburgo, visitaron Tirol, Carintia, Estiria y Carniola, y en el otoño de 1781 pasaron a Suecia, en cuya Universidad de Upsala escucharon las conferencias de los químicos Scheele y Bergmann. En junio de 1782 fueron examinados y alcanzaron la calificación suprema.[48] Los hermanos Elhuyar regresaron a España y en septiembre de 1782 la Sociedad Patriótica le encomendó a Fausto las cátedras de mineralogía y metalúrgica de su nueva Escuela de Minas de Vergara. Fue recién instalados en Vergara que los Elhuyar aislaron el tungsteno, y la memoria de sus experimentos fue publicada en los *Extractos de la Sociedad Vascongada de Amigos del País*.[49]

Según el mismo Barón Born, el método de beneficio que lleva su nombre no fue un "descubrimiento", sino una mejora del método combinando fundición con amalgamación descubierto en Alto Perú por el sacerdote español Alvaro Alonso Barba en el siglo XVII.[50] No solamente era honesto el Barón en darle crédito al Padre Barba, sino que quería compartir la tecnología que había desarrollado. En el otoño de 1786 tuvo demostraciones públicas de su método en Skleno, a las que asistieron observadores extranjeros y Fausto Elhuyar fue uno de ellos.[51] No hay evidencia de que ninguno de ellos recibió una invitación oficial, pero su presencia en Skleno le permitió al Barón Born proponer la creación de una Sociedad de Ciencias y Minería para la diseminación de los conocimientos útiles dividida en catorce secciones territoriales, incluyendo Nueva Granada y Nueva España. Desafortunadamente, este noble proyecto pereció con su originador, no oyéndose hablar de él después de la muerte del Barón Born en 1790.[52]

En una carta de septiembre de 1786 a Don Casimiro Gómez Ortega, primer Director del Jardín Botánico de Madrid, Fausto Elhuyar dice que estaba satisfecho con la nueva amalgamación, la cual era una perfección del método inventado por el Padre Barba en Potosí, en el siglo XVII, y expresa asombro de que los hispanoamericanos abandonasen la amalgamación "de cazo", tan superior a la "de patio" que estaban usando.[53] Poco después de su asistencia a las demostraciones en Skleno, el mineralogista español pasó a Friburgo, en donde se experimentaba también con el nuevo método, y más tarde a Viena, en donde contrató a un grupo de expertos, en su mayor parte alemanes, para que se trasladacen a América en una misión oficial a brindar ayuda técnica.[54]

El rey Don Carlos III envió a América tres expediciones para introducir e implementar el sistema del europeo Born: Juan José Elhuyar, enviado a Nueva Granada en 1786 para desarrollar allí el beneficio de los metales por el método de fundición, fue ordenado al año siguiente que lo introdujese allí; Fausto Elhuyar fue enviado a Nueva España; y el sueco Tadeo von Nordenflicht fue enviado al Perú con el mismo objeto en 1788. Juan José Elhuyar quedo teóricamente convencido de las ventajas de la amalgamación mecanizada, pero el que su cuñado Angel Díaz (miembro de su expedición) mencione los tres métodos de beneficio en su *Instrucción teoricopráctica que se forma para los mineros de veta del territorio y minas del gobierno de Popayán* de 1803 hace pensar que el método de Born no fue aceptado universalmente en Nueva Granada.[55] En Nueva España se hicieron experimentos costosísimos por los trenes de barriles giratorios y los hornos que el método centroeuropeo requería. A pesar de ser rápido, el sistema tampoco fue aceptable en Nueva España, allí específicamente porque requería cantidades enormes de combustible y porque no podía acomodar la gran cantidad de mineral producido. El problema presentado por la escacez de combustible en las zonas mineras de Nueva España lo imposibilitó. Este fue el caso también en Perú.

El Rey de España gastó 145,371 pesos en una misión que el virrey Revillagigedo describió como un fracaso, más tuvo el buen sentido de aceptar las recomendaciones de sus subordinados de desistir en su empeño modernizante.[56] Pero la misión de Fausto Elhuyar a Nueva España tenía también un aspecto académico: la fundación de un colegio de minería en Ciudad México. El Tribunal de Minería de México le había propuesta al Rey la formación de un colegio de minería en la capital de Nueva España desde los 1770s, poco después de su formación en 1776. Cuando el Rey envió la misión tecnológica para introducir el método de Born, también el encomendó a su director la organización de este colegio de minería. Elhuyar redactó el plan para la fundación del Real Seminario de Minería de México en 1791, siguiendo los patrones de las escuelas de minería en Friburgo y Vergara, y este abrió sus puertas en 1792.

Cuando el Barón von Humboldt visitó Ciudad México a principios del siglo XIX quedó impresionado favorablemente por sus instituciones, y seguramente se refería al Colegio de Minería cuando escribió que no había ciudad en el Nuevo Mundo (incluyendo los Estados Unidos en América) que tuviera establecimientos científicos como los México.[57] En verdad, el Colegio de Minería contó con excelentes profesores educados en instituciones prestigiosas, como Andrés del Río y el mismo Fausto Elhuyar, y produjo destacados alumnos, como Casimiro Chovell. Fue en un laboratorio del Colegio, en 1801, que el profesor del Río describió una sustancia roja desconocida la cual nombró eritronio, pero luego fue "redescubierta" por el sueco N. G. Sefstron, quien la llamó "vanadium".[58]

El Colegio (una tercera parte de cuyos costos era subvencionada por el Tribunal de Minería) debía asesorar a los mineros de Nueva España. En esto la misión de Elhuyar fue un éxito, porque tanto él como Sonneschmid y otros técnicos de la expedición adquirieron rápidamente el conocimiento de los procedimientos empleados por los mineros de Nueva España, y sus esfuerzos por entender científicamente lo que estos hacían empíricamente tuvieron resultados positivos. Por ejemplo, muchas minas se abrían siguiendo vetas falsas, y el conocimiento de la geología subterránea impartido por Andrés del Río desde 1794 le permitió a los mineros evitar tal error, habilitándoles a "leer las rocas".[59] Friedrich Sonneschmid, uno de los alemanes en la expedición, escribió un tratado en el que describe los procesos químicos en que el método "de patio" se basaba y llama a este "el primero y original método de amalgamación".[60]

Don Carlos IV expresó su confianza en el Colegio de Minería cuando por Real Orden de 19 de abril de 1798 autorizó la examinación de sus graduados más destacados para ser directores de minas e ingenieros en Perú, Buenos Aires, Guatemala, Quito y Chile.[61] Después de la independencia de México de la Corona española Elhuyar renunció la dirección del Colegio, pero Andrés del Río tomó su puesto, y este continuó sus operaciones bajo una serie de directores capacitados hasta el año 1867, cuando la ley estableciendo la Escuela Nacional Preparatoria le otorgó a esta la mayor parte de sus funciones.[62]

Hay dos obras ricas en datos sobre la expedición española que trajo la vacuna contra las viruelas a Hispanoamérica: *La vuelta al mundo de la expedición de la vacuna*, de Gonzalo Díaz de Yraola y *Los viajes de Don*

Francisco Xavier de Balmis, de Francisco Fernández del Castillo. De todas las expediciones científicas financiadas por la Corona española la expedición filantrópica de la vacuna fue la más humana, pero no la más desinteresada. Se conjetura que Don Carlos IV envió la expedición con la vacuna a sus reinos de Indias después de saber de la devastación causada por una epidemia de viruelas en Santa Fé de Bogotá en 1802. En su proclamación de la expedición filantrópica este rey menciona el dolor que le daba saber los daños que las viruelas causaban entre sus amados súbditos americanos, pero cuando le propuso a su Consejo que la Real Hacienda pagase todos los gastos de esta, le recordó que las epidemias decimaban a veces una tercera parte, y aún una media parte, de la población de regiones enteras en los reinos de Indias, causando bajas en la población, el comercio, la producción y los tributos.[63]

Las viruelas eran una cosa muy seria a principios del siglo XIX, porque no se conocía ninguna cura contra ellas. En aquella época en que se desconocían las bacterias no se tenía idea de como se producía el contagio. Lo más que se había llegado a hacer era aislar a los enfermos y quemar los efectos de las víctimas, como aconseja el Dr. Gil en una *Disertación físico-médica en la cual se prescribe un método seguro para preservar los pueblos de viruelas*, 150 copias de la cual el Ministro Gálvez hizo distribuir entre clérigos, médicos y principales, al virrey de Nueva España en 1785. Las viruelas eran muy democráticas, entrando aún en los palacios de los reyes de Europa y quizás fue el conocimiento personal de esa enfermedad lo que movió a Don Carlos IV a hacer alguno por erradicarla. Aunque también pudo haberlo hecho en reparación, porque antes de la llegada de los españoles los indígenas americanos vivían felizmente ignorantes de ellas. La primera epidemia de viruelas en América de la cual hay noticia tuvo lugar en la Isla Española (República Dominicana y Haití) en 1507. La debacle demográfica que siguió ya es conocida.[64]

Desde tiempos remotos existía en Asia y Africa la práctica de la variolización, la cual consistía en la inserción de pus o del polvo de postillas de un varioloso dentro de la piel de un sano, induciendo en este unas viruelas benignas. Esta práctica fue introducida en Europa por una dama inglesa en 1721, y de Inglaterra pasó a sus colonias en Norteamérica.[65] En Hispanoamérica fue introducida por el fraile chileno Matías del Carmen Verdugo en 1775.[66] El problema con la variolización era que el inoculado transmitía la enfermedad y por eso y por considerársela peligrosa fue prohibida en varios países. En España fue opuesta por la Academia Médica de Madrid hasta 1792.

Expedición de vacunación

La vacunación es otra historia y fue descubierta por el médico inglés Eduardo Jenner en 1796. La vacuna contra la viruela original consistía de la inoculación en una persona del líquido en las pústulas de las vacas afectadas de viruelas vacunas o del grano de un vacunado, y tenía la ventaja sobre la variolización de que un vacunado no transmite la enfermedad (aunque por otro lado, la inmunización producida por la vacuna es temporal). El Dr. Jenner publicó los resultados de sus experimentos en 1798, tras haberse negado a publicarlos en sus *Transactions* la Royal Society de Londres. En España las primeras referencias sobre su hallazgo aparecieron en 1800.[67] Una traducción al castellano de la obra de Jenner por Guillermo del Río, *Extracto acerca del origen y efectos de una enfermedad conocida con el nombre de viruela de las vacas*, fue publicada en Lima en 1802.[68]

Cuando el Dr. Francisco Javier Balmis se ofreció a dirigir una expedición llevando la vacuna a América y las Filipinas y le presentó a Don José Antonio Caballero, Ministro de Gracia y Justicia, un proyecto de reglamento y un itinerario, un proyecto había sido discutido y aprobado por el Consejo de Indias. La idea fue cosa del rey Don Carlos IV y el proyecto fue basado en recomendaciones del Dr. Juan Felipe Flores, Médico de Cámara del Rey, que este último presentó al Consejo de Indias el 28 de febrero de 1803 y el Consejo lo aprobó el 22 de marzo de ese año.[69] El 6 de junio el rey envió instrucciones a la Junta de Cirujanos de Cámara sobre el transporte de la vacuna y decretó una Real Orden a sus virreyes y gobernadores de Ultramar, haciéndoles saber su voluntad de financiar la expedición de la vacuna de su Real Hacienda, y de que la apoyasen y animasen a obispos y otros clérigos a apoyarla.[70]

El 23 de junio de 1803 la Junta de Cirujanos de Cámara recomendó al Dr. Balmis como director de la expedición y aunque sugirió cambios en su proyecto, asemejándole al que ellos habían aprobado en las recomendaciones del Dr. Flores, aceptó su idea de un director único. La Junta nombró a José Salvany Director Asistente y el Ministro de Marina recibió la orden de preparar un navío para la expedición.[71] El 28 de junio el Dr. Balmis recibió el nombramiento oficial como director de la Real expedición marítima de la vacuna y prosiguió a hacer imprimir 500 copias de su traducción del manual de vacunación de Moreau de Sarthe y ordenar 2000 ampollas para transportar el suero vacunal. Su proyecto incluía el transportar vacuna "en vivo" mediante la vacunación en serie de un grupo de niños durante la travesía y la Corona se comprometió a proteger a los niños que fueron con la expedición hasta que consiguieran un trabajo apropiado o al llegar a la mayoría de edad. En La Coruña se unieron a la expedición veintidós niños de la Casa de Expósitos de ese ciudad, junto con Isabel López Gandalla, la rectora de esa institución.[72]

La expedición salió de La Coruña en la corbeta "María Pita" el 30 de noviembre de 1803 y meses más tarde llegó a Puerto Rico. En Puerto Rico la vacuna había sido introducida por el cirujano Don Francisco Oller, quien la había conseguido en la isla (entonces danesa) de Santo Tomás, y como el gobernador les recibió con una acogida fría, los expedicionarios marcharon para Venezuela, en donde fueron recibidos con más entusiasmo. El Ayuntamiento de Caracas les dio un recibimiento apoteósico y el Capitán General dispuso la creación de una Junta Central de la Vacuna. En Puerto Cabello se dividió la expedición, quedando un grupo con dirección a Nueva España y Filipinas bajo el Dr. Balmis y otro con la misión de llevar la vacuna a Suramérica bajo el Dr. José Salvany.[73]

Balmis partió con la expedición a Nueva España pasando por Cuba, en donde la vacuna había sido introducida por Doña María de Bustamante, procedente de Puerto Rico, de quien el Dr. Romáy tomó el suero. Al llegar Balmis a Cuba procedió a la formación de una Junta de Vacunación, la cual se refundió con la Sociedad Patriótica de Amigos del País de La Habana.[74] En junio de 1804 la expedición llegó a Yucatán y Francisco Pastor y cuatro niños fueron a Guatemala, a donde llegaron un mes más tarde. La vacuna había llegado a Guatemala el 16 de mayo, remitida de Veracruz por Ignacio Pavón y Muñoz, y Don Narciso Esparragosa Gallardo estaba vacunando cuando Pastor llegó. Bajo la asesoría de Francisco Pastor se creó y aprobó un reglamento para la Junta Central de la Vacuna de Guatemala.

El recibimiento al Dr. Balmis en Veracruz al llegar la expedición a ese puerto el 24 de julio de 1804 fue menos acogedora. Allí recibió del virrey Iturrigaray una copia de *La Gaceta de México* "para que supiese que estaba introducida la vacuna."[75] Algunas autoridades dicen que la vacuna fue introducida en México de La Habana por el Dr. Juan de Arboleda a principios de 1804.[76] El Dr. Balmis le contestó al virrey desde Veracruz que emprendería su viaje para la capital a fin de establecer el modo de conservar el suero de la vacuna en ella y entregarle los veintidós niños que había sacado de La Coruña.

Al llegar a Ciudad México el 9 de agosto de 1804, el Dr. Balmis no tuvo recibimiento oficial, y no encontrando rastro alguno de la vacuna atribuyó la pérdida de la vacuna recibida antes de su llegada a que el virrey había confiado la vacunación a personas poco o nada instruidas. La expedición no recibió mucho apoyo en Ciudad México y durante su estadía en Nueva España fue ignorada por el virrey Iturrigaray, pero tuvo acogidas apoteósicas en Guadalajara y Antequera de Oaxaca (cuyo obispo exhortó a sus curas diciéndoles que no había ninguno "tan indolente que se crea desobligado y se atreva a decir groseramente que él es médico de las almas y no de los cuerpos, porque acreditaría así su ignorancia y falta de caridad, debiendo saber que quien pudiendo conservar la vida corporal de su prójimo la omite es un verdadero homicida").[77] El Comandante General de las Provincias Internas consiguió llevar la vacuna hasta Chihuahua, Sonora y Texas y en Acapulco Balmis vacunó 300 personas.[78]

Mientras tanto el Dr. Salvany se había dirigido con la otra parte de la expedición a Cartagena de Indias, a donde llegó el 24 de mayo de 1804, después de sufrir un naufragio cerca de Barranquilla. Desde Cartagena mandó vacunar en Portobelo y Panamá, estableció una Junta de la Vacuna y recogió diez niños de un orfanato para ir vacunándolos de dos en dos en el curso de la navegación Magdalena arriba que había de conducirlos a Santa Fé de Bogotá. En su recorrido de Cartagena a Santa Fé hizo varias paradas, vacunando un total de 56,327 personas. El virrey de Nueva Granada, Don Antonio de Amar y Borbón, protegió la labor de la expedición y creó la Junta de la Vacuna en Santa Fé. El 8 de marzo de 1805 la expedición salió de Santa Fé para Popayán, en donde fueron bien recibidos el 27 de mayo. Al saber que se había desatado una epidemia de viruelas en Quito, la expedición se dirigió allí inmediatamente, y en el trayecto los expedicionarios hicieron cientos de vacunaciones e instruyeron sobre la vacuna a los facultativos en los pueblos por donde pasaron.[79]

Al llegar la expedición a las cercanías de Quito el 16 de julio de 1804, salió a recibirla una muchedumbre encabezada por las autoridades, la cual tomó a los niños portadores de la vacuna en hombros, llevándoles en triunfo a la ciudad. El 12 de septiembre la expedición salió de Quito, pasando por Latacunda, Ambato, Riobamba y Cuenca, en donde hicieron vacunaciones y dejaron instrucciones para la preservación de la vacuna.

La vacuna fue introducida en Montevideo por un negrero portugués, Antonio Machado de Carvalho, en esclavos que llevaba del Brasil.[80] El gobernador Ruiz de Huidobro logró hacerla llegar "en vivo" a Buenos Aires, en negritos vacunados (como Balmis la había llevado a través del Atlántico en españolitos) y allí se propagó gracias al entusiasmo del virrey Marqués de Sobremonte, quien la envió al virrey del Perú y al gobernador de Chile. La vacuna llegó a Chile de Buenos Aires en 1805, siendo Fray Pedro de Manuel Chaparro el primero en administrarla en ese reino.[81] Cuando la expedición de la vacuna llegó a Lima esta ya estaba propagada, y fue mal recibida por los médicos limeños, quienes cobraban 4 pesos por administrarla.[82]

Después de establecer en Lima una Junta Central de la Vacuna el 20 de agosto de 1806, con el apoyo del nuevo virrey Don José Abascal, el Dr. Salvany llegó a vacunar hasta 22,726 personas en el Perú.[83] A principios de 1807 envió al Dr. Manuel Julián Grajales y al enfermero Boldaños con la vacuna a Chile y al asistente Rafael Lozano Pérez a Huancavelica, Huamanga y Cuzco. Los expedicionarios a Chile fueron bien recibidos por los chilenos, aunque estos ya conocían la vacuna, y vacunaron a miles de ellos.[84] El asistente Lozano también tuvo buen recibimiento en Huancavelica, Huamanga y Cuzco, donde vacunó a 24,041 personas. Camino a La Paz, el Dr. Salvany administró la vacuna en Chinca, Santiago de Almazor e Ica —en donde corrió el rumor de que la expedición se llevaba a todos los niños que se vacunaban y las madres huyeron al monte escondiendo sus hijos, a pesar de los esfuerzos del Ayuntamiento y los curas.[85] En Ica el Dr. Salvany enfermó y allí quedó del 28 de abril hasta el 28 de julio de 1807. Una vez con suficientes fuerzas para continuar su viaje pasó vacunando por Villa Nasca, Acarí, Carareli, Cumaná, Uchumayo, Arequipa, Tiabaya, Sabandía, Puno, Vilqui, Pomata y Cepita, hasta que llegó a La Paz, en donde murió del corazón.[86]

Después de tanta inversión en las ciencias, era de esperarse que España e Hispanoamérica jugaran un papel importante en la historia de su desarrollo en los dos últimos siglos. A principios del siglo XIX las ciencias estaban más avanzadas en España que en Rusia, y en México que en los Estados Unidos de América (si se puede creer al Barón Humboldt lo que dice en su *Ensayo político sobre el Reino de la Nueva España*). Se ha sugerido que las guerras de independencia (de Francia en el caso de España y de la Corona española en el caso de Hispanoamérica) destruyeron vidas e instituciones claves al desarrollo de las ciencias hispánicas. Yo añadiría las luchas entre Liberales y Conservadores que durante el siglo XIX (con la excepción de Cuba, Puerto Rico y Chile) mantuvieron a las naciones de habla castellana en una casi perpetua guerra civil.

En su ensayo "Science and Independence in Latin America", el historiador Thomas F. Glick concluye que irónicamente el movimiento independentista , que había sido animado en Nueva Granada (Colombia) por el estudio de las ciencias, tuvo el efecto de abortar este, ya que dependía de la munificencia de la Corona y del mantenimiento de comunicaciones abiertas entre los centros científicos de los varios reinos de Indias y la transmisión de la ciencia y la tecnología europeas a la sociedad hispánica de la América española que esta promovía por razones utilitarias.[87] Según Michael M. Smith en su ensayo "The 'Real Expedición Marítima de la Vacuna' in New Spain and Guatemala", los disturbios de las guerras de independencia destruyeron la cadena de centros de vacunación. La conservación de la vacuna se hizo esporádica y a veces era imposible conseguirla, aún en las ciudades importantes.[88]

Uno puede preguntarse si vale la pena sacar de la oscuridad las expediciones científicas financiadas por los reyes de la casa de Borbón en Hispanoamérica cuando sus efectos fueron tan pocos y fugaces. Reflexionando sobre los casos expuestos, no podemos más que creer que sí. Por el interés humano de los personajes fascinantes que en ellas participaron (aún los reyes, a quienes los gobernantes hispanoamericanos que les sucedieron han imitado en lo despótico —siguiendo, se dice, su tradición— pero la mayor parte de las veces olvidando imitarles en lo que tuvieron de ilustrados); por lo que su estudio nos puede enseñar sobre el intercambio de ideas y tecnologías entre Europa y América en el siglo XVIII; y por lo que podamos aprender de sus aciertos y sus errores. La inversión de la Corona española en las ciencias representada por las expediciones botánicas con miras a encontrar plantas útiles es un ejemplo de inversión a largo plazo comendable. Más que criticar a Don Carlos IV y sus consejeros por su percepción de que la inversión en una causa humanitaria como la expedición de la vacuna produce beneficios materiales comparables a su costo, bien podemos considerarles apologistas de políticas de salud pública. Finalmente, la flexibilidad mostrada por el Rey al aceptar que el sistema centroeuropeo para el beneficio de la plata que quería implantar no funcionaba clama ser imitada en algunas naciones de Nuestra América.

NOTAS

1. La primera misión botánica a Nueva España fue la de Francisco Hernández, Médico de Cámara de Felipe II, a quien este rey ordenó en enero de 1570 informarse de las plantas medicinales de Nueva España. Hernández consignó el resultado de sus desvelos en 38 volúmenes manuscritos. Desgraciadamente el rey decidió hacer publicar solamente un extracto de esta obra y le comisionó esa labor al napolitano Nardo Antonio Recchо. El compendio de este no vio la prensa hasta 1648. Una copia del manuscrito de Hernández fue descubierta en España en el siglo XVIII, la cual Don Casimiro Gómez Ortega hizo publicar.

2. Antonio Lafuente, "Las expediciones científicas del setecientos y la nueva relación del científico con el estado", *Revista de Indias* 47 (1987), 373.

3. Neftalí Zúñiga, *La expedición científica de Francia del siglo XVIII en la Presidencia de Quito* (Quito: IPGH, 1977), p. 13.

4. Robert Jones Shafer, *The Economic Societies in the Spanish World, 1763-1821* (Syracuse, NY: Syracuse University Press, 1958), pp. 7-8.

5. Ibid., p. 17.

6. Francisco Javier Puerto Sarmiento, "Las expectativas metropolitanas respecto a las expediciones botánicas", en *La ciencia española en Ultramar* (Actas de las I Jornadas sobre España y las expediciones científicas en América y Filipinas), coordinado por Alejandro R. Díaz Torre et al. (Madrid: Ediciones Doce-Calles, 1991), p. 130.

7. Shafer, *Economic Societies*, pp. 136-144.

8. Ibid., p. 337.

9. Ibid., p. 193.

10. Fermín del Pino Díaz y Angel Guirao de Vierna, "Las expediciones ilustradas y el estado español", *Revista de Indias* 47:180 (1987), 429.

11. Lafuente, "Expediciones científicas", p. 429.

12. Iris H. W. Engstrand, *Spanish Scientists in the New World: The 18th Century Expeditions* (Seattle: University of Washington Press, 1981), p. 45.

13. José Vericat, "A la búsqueda de la felicidad perdida: La expedición de Malaspina o la interrogación sociológica del Imperio", *Revista de Indias* 47:180 (1987), 612.

14. Del Pino Díaz y Guirao de Vierna, "Expediciones", p. 409.

15. Arthur Robert Steele, *Flowers for the King: The Expedition of Ruiz and Pavón and the Flora of Perú* (Durham: Duke University Press, 1964), p. 57.

16. Diego Mendoza, *La expedición botánica de José Celestino Mutis al Nuevo Reino de Granada y memorias inéditas de Francisco José de Caldas* (Madrid: Librería General de Victoriano Suárez, 1909), p. 93.

17. Juan Carlos Arias Divito, *Las expediciones científicas españolas durante el siglo XVIII: La expedición botánica de Nueva España* (Madrid: Ediciones Cultura Hispánica, 1968), p. 21.

18. Steele, *Flowers for the King*, pp. 47-52.

19. Puerto Sarmiento, "Expectativas metropolitanas", p. 133.

20. Steele, *Flowers for the King*, pp. 60-63.

21. Ibid., p. 64.

22. Ibid., p. 99.

23. Ibid., p. 131.

24. Ibid., p. 136.

25. Ibid., p. 153.

26. Ibid., p. 159.

27. A. González Bueno, "La expedición botánica a los reinos del Perú y Chile (1777-1831): Un análisis de sus resultados", en *La ciencia española en Ultramar* (Madrid: Ediciones Doce-Calles, 1991), p. 186.

28. Steele, *Flowers for the King*, pp. 44-45.

29. Mendoza, "Expedición botánica", p. 94.

30. Eduardo Mendoza Varela, *Regreso a la expedición botánica* (Bogotá: Litografía Arco, 1983), pp. 107-108.

31. Thomas F. Glick, "Science and Independence in Latin America (with Special Reference to New Granada)", *Hispanic American Historical Review* 71 (1991), 313.

32. Ibid., p. 314.

33. Mendoza Varela, *Regreso*, p. 116.

34. Arias Divito, *Expediciones científicas*, p. 22.

35. Este diario de viaje ha sido traducido al inglés y publicado por Lesley Byrd Simpson como *Journal of José Longinos Martínez, Notes and Observations . . .* (San Francisco, 1961).

36. Engstrand, *Spanish Scientists*, p. 10.

37. Este ensayo etnográfico ha sido traducido al inglés y publicado por Iris Higbie [Engstrand] Wilson como *Noticias de Nutka: An Account of Nootka Sound in 1792 by José Mariano Mocino* (Seattle, 1970).

38. Engstrand, *Spanish Scientists*, p. 154.

39. Ibid., p. 177.

40. Ibid., p. 183.

41. R. Rodríguez Noval et al., "La influencia de las expediciones botánicas ilustradas en las farmacopeas españolas", en *La ciencia española en Ultramar* (Madrid: Editorial Doce-Calles, 1991), pp. 238-239.

42. Marcel Roche, "Early History of Science in Spanish America", *Science* 194 (19 de noviembre de 1976), 807.

43. Mendoza, *Expedición botánica*, p. 133.

44. Ibid., p. 134.

45. A. P. Whitaker, "The Elhuyar Mining Mission and the Enlightenment", *Hispanic American Historical Review* 31:4 (1951), 576.

46. Mikulas Teich, "Born's Amalgamation Process and the International Metallurgic Gathering at Skleno in 1786", *Annals of Science* 32 (1975), 309.

47. Guillermo Mira, "Misiones mineras a América en la segunda mitad del siglo XVIII", en *La ciencia española en Ultramar* (Madrid: Ediciones Doce-Calles, 1991), p. 115.

48. Arturo Arnaiz de Freg, "D. Fausto de Elhuyar y de Zubcic", *Revista de Historia de América* 26 (1939), 76.

49. Ibid., pp. 76-79.

50. Teich, "Born's Amalgamation Process", p. 309.

51. Ibid., p. 330.

52. Ibid., pp. 331-333.

53. Francisco Pelayo, "Las actividades mineras de J. C. Mutis y Juan José Elhuyar en Nueva Granada", *Revista de Indias* 50:189 (1990), 465.

54. Mira, "Misiones mineras", p. 115.

55. Pelayo, "Actividades mineras", p. 470.

56. En 1791 el mexicano José Gil Barragán inventó una máquina de amalgamación que operaba con el mineral frío y en vez de barriles usaba una tina de molinetes, pero a pesar del apoyo inicial del virrey Revillagigedo y de haberse usado en algunos reales mineros con resultados positivos no fue aceptada universalmente y fue olvidada. Cuando México tuvo máquinas de amalgamación en el siglo XIX estas fueron importadas de Europa. El historiador Elías Trabulse ha escrito extensivamente sobre el invento de Gil Barragán en su artículo "Aspectos de la tecnología minera en la Nueva España a finales del siglo XVIII".

57. Clement G. Motten, *Mexican Silver and the Enlightenment* (Philadelphia: University of Pennsylvania Press, 1950), p. 63.

58. Roche, "Early History of Science", p. 808.

59. Motten, *Mexican Silver*, p. 17.

60. Ibid., p. 52.

61. Walter Howe, *The Mining Guild of New Spain and Its Tribunal General, 1770-1821* (Cambridge: Harvard University Press, 1949), p. 342.

62. Ibid., p. 360.

63. Michael M. Smith, "The 'Real Expedición Marítima de la Vacuna' in New Spain and Guatemala", *Transactions of the American Philosophical Society*, New Series, 64, pt. 1 (1974), p. 15.

64. Donald R. Hopkins, *Princes and Peasants: Smallpox in History* (Chicago: University of Chicago Press, 1983), pp. 204-213.

65. Ibid., p. 7.

66. John Tate Lanning, *Academic Culture in the Spanish Colonies* (Port Washington, NY: Kennika Press, 1971), p. 120.

67. Elvira Arqueola, "La expedición Balmis y la difusión de la vacuna", en *La ciencia española en Ultramar* (Madrid: Ediciones Doce-Calles, 1991), p. 251.

68. Lanning, *Academic Culture*, p. 123.

69. Smith, "The 'Real Expedición'", p. 12.

70. Ibid., pp. 14-15.

71. Ibid., pp. 16-17.

72. Gonzalo Díaz de Yraola, *La vuelta al mundo de la expedición de la vacuna* (Sevilla: Escuela de Estudios Hispanoamericanos de Sevilla, 1948), p. 34.

73. Ibid., p. 41.

74. Ibid., p. 42.

75. Ibid., p. 51.

76. Lanning, *Academic Culture*, p. 124.

77. Díaz de Yraola, *La vuelta al mundo*, p. 57.

78. Ibid., p. 70.

79. Ibid., pp. 72-74.

80. Ibid., pp. 75-78.

81. Enrique Alfonso, . . . *Y llegó la vida* (Buenos Aires: Espasa-Calpe, 1950), p. 208, nota 106.

82. Lanning, *Academic Culture*, p. 123.

83. Díaz de Yraola, *La vuelta al mundo*, p. 81.

84. Ibid., pp. 84-85.

85. Lanning, *Academic Culture*, p. 123.

86. Díaz de Yraola, *La vuelta al mundo*, p. 88.

87. Ibid., p. 92.

88. Glick, "Science and Independence", p. 334.

89. Smith, "The 'Real Expedición'", pp. 67-68.

BIBLIOGRAFIA SELECTA

Alfonso, Enrique. *Y llegó la vida: Estampas del descubrimiento y difusión de la vacuna antivariólica*. Madrid: Espasa-Calpe, 1950.

Archila, R. *La expedición de Balmis en Venezuela*. Caracas: Tipografía Vargas, 1969.

Arias Divito, Juan Carlos. *Las expediciones científicas españolas a América en el siglo XVIII: Indice documental*. Buenos Aires: Instituto Bibliográfico Antonio Zinng, 1983.

———. *Las expediciones científicas españolas durante el siglo XVIII: Expedición botánica a Nueva España*. Madrid: Ediciones Cultura Hispánica, 1968.

Arnaiz de Freg, Arturo. "D. Fausto de Elhuyar y de Zubcic". *Revista de Historia de América* 6 (1939), 75-96.

Barras de Aragón, Francisco de las. "Noticias y documentos de la expedición del Conde de Mopox a la Isla de Cuba". *Anuario de Estudios Americanos* 9 (1952), 513-548.

Beltrán, Enrique. "Las Reales Expediciones Científicas a Nueva España", en José Luis Peset, ed., *La ciencia moderna y el Nuevo Mundo*. Madrid: Consejo Superior de Investigaciones Científicas, 1985. Pp. 217-227.

Brading, D. A. *Miners and Merchants in Bourbon Mexico, 1763-1810*. Cambridge: Cambridge University Press, 1971.

La ciencia española en Ultramar. Actas de las I Jornadas sobre España y las expediciones científicas en América y Filipinas. Alejandro R. Díaz Torre, Tomás Mall, Daniel Pacheco F. y Angeles Alonso Flecha, coord. Madrid: Ediciones Doce-Calles, 1991.

Del Pino Díaz, Fermín y Angel. *Guirao de Vierna*. "Las expediciones ilustradas y el estado español". *Revista de Indias* 47:180 (1987), 379-429.

Díaz de Yraola, Gonzalo. *La vuelta al mundo de la expedición de la vacuna*. Sevilla: Escuela de Estudios Hispanoamericanos de Sevilla, 1948.

Engstrand, Iris H. Wilson. *Spanish Scientists in the New World: The 18th Century Expeditions*. Seattle: University of Washington Press, 1981.

Espinosa y Tello, José, ed. *Relación del viaje hecho por las goletas "Sutil" y "Mexicana" en el año 1792*. Madrid: Imprenta Real. 1802. (Reimpresa en Colección Chimalistac. Madrid: José Porrúa Turanzas, 1958.)

Fernández del Castillo, Francisco. *Los viajes de Don Francisco Xavier de Balmis: Notas para la historia de la expedición vacunal de España a América y Filipinas (1803-1806)*, 2ª edición. México: Sociedad Médica Hispano-Mexicana, 1985.

Glick, Thomas F. "Science and Independence in Latin America (with Special Reference to New Granada)". *Hispanic American Historical Review* 71 (1991), 307-334.

Herrera, F. L. "Botanistas de fines del siglo XVIII: primeros escritos de vulgarización científica en el Perú". *Revista del Museo Nacional* (Lima), v. 6, pp. 95-124.

Hopkins, Donald R. *Princes and Peasants: Smallpox in History*. Chicago: University of Chicago Press, 1983.

Humboldt, Baron Alexander von. *Ensayo político sobre el Reino de la Nueva España*. México: Editorial Porrúa, 1966.

———. *Viaje a las regiones equinocciales del Nuevo Continente*. 5 vols. Caracas: Monte Avila Editores, 1985.

Lafuente, Antonio. "Una ciencia para el estado: La expedición geodésica hispano-francesa al virreinato del Perú, 1734-1743". *Revista de Indias* 43:172 (1983), 549-629.

Langue, Frederique. "Bibliografía minera colonial". *Anuario de Estudios Americanos* 45, sup. 1 (1988), 137-162.

Lanning, John Tate. *Academic Culture in the Spanish Colonies*. Port Washington, NY: Kennikat Press, 1971.

Longinos Martínez, José, editado y traducido por Lesley Byrd Simpson. *Journal of José Longinos Martínez, Notes and Observations of the Naturalist of the Botanical Expedition in Old and New California and the South Coast*. San Francisco: John Howell, 1961.

Lozoya, Xavier. *Plantas y luces en México: La Real Expedición Científica a Nueva España (1787-1803)*. Barcelona: Ediciones del Serbal, 1984.

Mendoza, Diego. *La expedición botánica de José Celestino Mutis al Nuevo Reino de Granada y memorias inéditas de Francisco José de Caldas*. Madrid: Librería General de Victoriano Suárez, 1909.

Mendoza Varela, Eduardo. *Regreso a la expedición botánica*. Bogotá: Litografía Arco, 1983.

Mociño, José Mariano, traducido y editado por Iris Higbie [Engstrand] Wilson. *Noticias de Nutka: An Account of Nootka Sound in 1792, by José Mariano Mociño*. Seattle: University of Washington Press, 1970.

Motten, Clement G. *Mexican Silver and the Enlightenment*. Philadelphia: University of Pennsylvania Press, 1950.

Mutis, José Celestino, compilada por Guillermo Hernández de Alba. *Escritos científicos de Don José Celestino Mutis*. Bogotá: Editorial Kelly, 1983.

Novo y Colson, Pedro de. *Viaje político-científico alrededor del mundo por las corbetas "Descubierta" y "Atrevida" al mando de los Capitanes de Navío D. Alejandro Malaspina y D. José Bustamante y Guerra, desde 1789 a 1794*. Madrid: Imprenta de la viuda e Hijos de Abienzo, 1888.

Pelayo, Francisco. "Las actividades mineras de J. C. Mutis y Juan José Elhuyar en Nueva Granada". *Revista de Indias* 50:189 (1990), 455-471.

Roche, Marcel. "Early History of Science in Spanish America". *Science* 194 (19 de noviembre de 1976), 806-810.

Sessé y Lacasta, Martín de y José Mariano Mociño. *Flora mexicana*. México: Sociedad Mexicana de Historia Natural, 1885.

———. *Plantae novae hispanie*. México: Sociedad Mexicana de Historia Natural, 1889.

Shafer, Robert Jones. *The Economic Societies in the Spanish World, 1763-1821*. Syracuse, NY: Syracuse University Press, 1958.

Smith, Michael M. "The 'Real Expedición Marítima de la Vacuna' in New Spain and Guatemala". *Transactions of the American Philosophical Society*, n.s., 64, pt. 1 (1974).

Steele, Arthur Robert. *Flowers for the King: The Expedition of Ruiz and Pavón and the Flora of Peru*. Durham: Duke University Press, 1964.

Teich, Mikulas. "Born's Amalgamation Process and the International Metallurgic Gathering at Skleno in 1786". *Annals of Science* 32 (1975), 305-340.

Trabulse A., Elias. "Aspectos de la tecnología minera en la Nueva España a finales del siglo XVIII". *Historia Mexicana* 30:3 (1981), 311-357.

Ulloa, Antonio y Jorge Juan. *Relación histórica del viaje a la América meridional de orden se S. M. en el Reyno del Perú*. Madrid, 1748.

Vericat, José. "A la búsqueda de la felicidad perdida: La expedición de Malaspina o la interrogación sociológica del Imperio". *Revista de Indias* 47:180 (1987), 559-615.

Whitaker, Arthur P. "The Elhuyar Mining Mission and the Enlightenment". *Hispanic American Historical Review* 31:4 (1951), 557-585.

Zúñiga, Neftalí. *La expedición científica de Francia del siglo XVIII en la Presidencia de Quito*. Quito: IPGH, Sección Nacional del Ecuador, 1977.

4. Indigenous Visions of the Book

Barbara A. Miller

Why examine how the indigenous people of the Americas perceived Western literacy, books, and writing? All too often we see this topic through the filter of our own socio-cultural bias without realizing that we, especially we librarians, are reifying the goodness of books and literacy in our own personal lives. But communications media such as books and writing cannot and should not be separated from the message they carry nor the social context in which they function. We may laugh at the vocabulary used to describe non-Western cultures as savage or barbarian and at the arguments about the level of civilization achieved by these cultures because they lacked the technological sophistication of their conquerors. But arguments based on an evolutionary model of development which place the Western linear sense of history and alphabetical writing at the pinnacle of civilized achievement still underpin our judgment.

In this paper I will highlight the communications technologies utilized by the natives at the time of the Conquest, including the painted fold-screen books of the Nahua and the Maya and the *quipu* of the Inca. Then I will discuss briefly the society introduced by the Spanish with its monopoly on modes of expression and with its dependence on the written word. Finally, I will discuss two reactions to Spanish books, writing, and literacy as expressed in native texts both written and pictorial: first, the book as a symbol of conquest, communication failure, and forced acculturation; and, second, writing as a means to resist colonial domination.

Be forewarned that the quotations used have been filtered through European languages, both English and Spanish, for I cannot read nor write in any indigenous language. Like all who attempt to study this topic, I find myself at the mercy of those who collected and preserved or destroyed this material, be they conquistadors, priests, historians, anthropologists, publishers, librarians, or the indigenous peoples themselves. Thus a brief statement on sources is necessary.

Sources

The main sources for this paper include various sixteenth-century texts including Nahua pictorial codices, the works of Bernardino de Sahagún, and the Quiche Maya *Popol Vuh.*[1] Guamán Poma de Ayala wrote his monumental letter to King Philip III, *Nueva Cronica y Buen Gobierno,*[2] in the first decades of the seventeenth century, while the *Chilam Balam of Chuyamel Maya*[3] is one of many versions of Chilam Balam (or Jaguar Priest) written by anonymous Yucatec authors and dates from the eighteenth century.

I have used secondary sources to help me locate both written and pictorial examples in English and Spanish translations of these various published primary documents. This task was made harder by the lack of indexes in many versions and by the fact that even those with indexes often did not include this topic. I am especially in debt to the compilations of Miguel León-Portilla and his efforts to publish the other side of the conquest story, such as *El Reverso de la Conquista*[4] and *Broken Spears.*[5] The work of James Lockhart in his *The Nahuas After the Conquest,*[6] of Gordon Brotherston in his new book *Book of the Fourth World: Reading the Native Americans through their Literature,*[7] and of Rolena Adorno in her numerous studies of Guamán Poma de Ayala also helped enormously.[8]

Antecedents

The peoples of the Americas never perceived history in the linear fashion of Western Civilization, but as a repeating, cyclical pattern. This worldview focused on the maintenance of the orderly and repetitive cycle of the seasons: planting, rain, and harvest upon which society's survival depended. Their records documented patterns of events, not sequences. To debate whether these records are "true" writing is not within the scope of this study, but it must be noted that the indigenous peoples of the new world generated records which served many of the same purposes as the alphabetic records in Europe, and in some respects they were more efficient in accomplishing their tasks (e.g., the Inca *quipu* or knotted string is much easier to carry long distances than a book).

The Spanish would introduce their own constellation of communication modes. Superficially, some of the uses to which these were put did not differ markedly from indigenous modes. However, the social contexts within which communication modes functioned to transmit knowledge were radically dissimilar. Table 1 lists similarities and differences in the types of records and their use. Mesoamericans and Spaniards recorded administrative, historical, and religious information in writing, while the Inca utilized the knotted cords for this purpose. Europeans often point out that in the

Table 1: Communication Modes and Uses

Record Use Type	Spaniards	Mesoamericans	Andean
Administrative/ bureaucratic	Written	Pictorial/ written	Quipu (knotted cords)
Historical/ dynastic	Written	Pictorial/ written and oral	Quipu and oral, textile?
Religious/ educational	Written, oral, and pictorial	Pictorial/ written, oral	Quipu and oral, textile?
Recreational/ literature personal	Written and oral	Oral	Oral

Americas a special class of interpreters was needed to translate these records, but the same must also be said of Spanish records. Otherwise, there would be no reason to have priests, lawyers, or historians to explain written texts. Both Americans and Europeans used pictorial representations to explain religious concepts. However, while Europeans used pictures to illustrate texts or, as in the case of the stained glass windows of European cathedrals, to illustrate Catholic catechism to nonliterate worshipers,[9] Americans used pictures to convey major portions of the text's message.[10]

Precontact Communication Modes

None of the cultures of Mesoamerica found it surprising that the Spanish wrote with pen and ink, nor did they find books unusual. They did find those books to be "poorly painted," but they recognized the advantages of alphabetic writing. Those who were allowed to learn it adjusted rapidly, though for many years they would combine their pictorial writing with the new alphabetic writing. Lockhart notes that Nahua handwriting was uniformly better than the Spanish.[11]

Mesoamerican pictographic writing had been in use since the time of the Olmecs in the first millennium B.C. More than mnemonic devices, these writing systems placed a high value on visual imagery and the marking of time. Many show elements of a developing phoneticism. In the last twenty years it has been proved that the Classical Maya developed a phonetic script capable of expressing spoken language completely.[12]

The ability to write was limited to a small group of elite artisans and priests or wise men who would paint, carve, or write texts as well as interpret them for the rest of the populace. In most Mesoamerican cultures the word for writing also means painting, thus illustrating the close relationship between visual modes of expression. They and the texts they read served as mediators between the physical and spiritual world; they read the signs of space and time. But writing was also put to more mundane uses such as compiling tribute lists and histories of conquests.

"Uttered flower" and "Painted song" (Nahuatl)

In the *Cantares Mexicanos* manuscript we find many Nahua poems which underscore the esteem in which artists, singers, and scribes were held by the Nahua. They also illustrate how all the modes of communication worked together, enriching discourse with visual imagery. Here is one Nahua canto:[13]

As white and yellow maize I am born.
The many-colored flower of the living flesh rises up
and opens its glistening seeds before the face of our mother.
In the moisture of Tlalocan, the quetzal water-plants
open up their corollas.
I am the work of the only god, his creation.
Your heart lives in the painted page,
you sing the royal fibers of the book,
you make the princes dance,
there you command by the water's discourse.
He created you,
he uttered you like a flower,
he painted you like a song:
a Toltec artist.
The book has come to an end:
your heart is now complete.
Here through art I shall live forever.
Who will take me, who will go with me?
Here I stand, my friends.
A singer, from my heart I strew songs.
My fragrant songs before the face of others.
I have carved a great stone, I paint thick wood.
My song is in them.

Another example was recorded by Sahagún during a debate which took place in 1524 between the twelve original Franciscan friars to come to Mexico and the priests of Quetzalcoatl.[14] After the Spaniards spoke, the priests were introduced by a Mexican noble in this manner:

> There are those who guide us,
> Who govern us,
> Who look after us,
> Who make the offerings and burn the incense;
> And these priests of Quetzalcoatl, as they are called,
> Show us how to venerate our gods,
> Whom we serve, as wings and tails serve birds.
> They are the ones who must know the litanies ...
> It is they who see, who observe,
> The orderly progress of the skies,
> And how light is divided from darkness.
> It is they who are reading,
> They who are telling what they read,
> They who loudly turn the pages of the books.
> They who have in their grasp the red ink, the black ink,
> And the paintings;
> They lead us, they guide us,
> They show us the way.
> They ordain how the year is borne, and counted,
> How the count of days and destinies, the cycle of twenty,
> Follows its course.
> This is their vocation;
> It is they who speak of the gods.

"Original Book and Ancient Writing" (Maya)

Few Maya codices survived the ravages of time, the violence of Spanish conquest, and the Spanish monopoly on the forms of visible expression. We are left with stone carvings on Classic Maya buildings and stelae, painted vases, and the fragments of four codices which survived from the Post-classic period, but some texts survived in modified form by being converted into alphabetic script. The writers of *Popol Vuh* of the Quiche Maya and the various *Chilam Balam* of the Yucatan Maya continued a literary tradition which spanned thousands of years.[15] The continuity of Maya belief and writing can be seen in the sections of the *Popol Vuh* which relate the Quiche version of the Maya Hero-Twins creation story. Coe found specific references to the same story on Classic Maya vases and plates.[16]

The importance and reverence the Maya gave to their writers and books can be heard in the following passage from the *Popol Vuh*:[17]

They were great lords, they were people of great genius. Plumed Serpent and Cotuha were lords of genius, and Quicab and Cauizimah were lords of genius. They knew whether war would occur; everything they saw was clear to them. Whether there would be death, or whether there would be famine, or whether quarrels would occur, they knew it for certain, since there was a place to see it, there was a book. Council Book was their name for it.

These texts are deliberately obscure to confuse outsiders. It is hard to tell if the authors write of the past, present, or future. The distinction was unimportant, for they wrote of all three at the same time. For the Maya writing was the key to the cosmos. It opened the door to (communicated with) the Overworld.

"A Piece of String" (Andean)

The multicolored knotted strings known as *quipus* were used by the peoples of the Andes to record accounts and dynastic histories and to relate cosmology. Stored in rooms known as *Cápac marca huasi* (rich salons), the *quipu* were cared for by trained elite imperial bureaucrats called *Tucuy-rícuc* (All Seers). More than librarians, these *quipu-camayuc* (*quipu* experts) were the only segment of the population who knew how to interpret the complex system of knots. Guamán Poma mentions that an Inca ruler would keep a secretary to tend his archives, another to record commands, an accountant, as well as others necessary for good administration.[18]

In a world such as the Andes, the surrounding landscape held a place of equal importance in Andean cosmology to that of time. The same word *Pacha* is used for both "earth" and "time" in the Quechua language. With its radiating cords knotted at precise, but variable, intervals, the *quipu* had a unique ability to express geographic as well as numeric and time concepts.[19] While Westerners have, in general, been unable to accept the *quipu* as a writing technology, there is no reason that it could not have expressed language concepts. Between the colors, knots, and string lengths, it could have been possible to represent a vast amount of information. In the computer age, it should not surprise us that mathematics can be used to communicate.

As rulers of a vast empire, the Inca appreciated the need for rapid and accurate dissemination of information. To that end, they created a system of royal highways and *chasqui* (runners) who, with *quipu* tied around their waists, would relay messages across the empire in a matter of days. Evidence that this system was maintained and used on behalf of the Spanish conquistadores can be found in a letter written in 1547 by Don Martín, an Indian nobleman, to Gonzalo Pizarro, brother of Francisco Pizarro. Don

Martín wrote that he had sent an Indian, who spoke good Spanish, to Trujillo to find out what was happening there. "As soon as he finds out, your lordship can be certain that he will bring back a true account on his quipu of the men, ships and captains. When he comes, I will go with what news that he brings to give your lordship account of everything. . . ."[20]

Guamán Poma declared that secretaries who used the *quipu* had ". . . such skill that the knots in their cords had the clarity of written letters."[21] He identifies *quipu* records and their interpreters as his major source of information.[22] He even claimed that so much information was available that he was hard pressed to convert it into alphabetic writing.[23]

Spanish and European Literacy

The society Spain transferred to the Americas had its roots in the Middle Ages. It contained a blend of both literate and oral traditions, though the literate was dominant. During the centuries before the conquest and the colonization of the Americas, European literati had convinced themselves of the supremacy of alphabetic writing over both oral and nonalphabetic modes of discourse.[24]

Europeans placed governmental, judicial, and scholastic authority in written documents. Likewise, Christianity, along with Judaism and Islam, was and is known as a "religion of the book." Nowhere was this more true than in Spain. Even the authority and justification for the conquest came from a written document, the *requerimiento*. The Spainiards used this written act of possession to establish their right to rule by reading it to uncomprehending natives.[25] The so-called cult of the book or the belief that all knowledge was contained in books would also influence the European ability to evaluate native texts.[26]

A good illustration of the native reaction to the European "cult of the book" comes to us from late-seventeenth-century French Canada (outside Latin America, but the circumstances were similar): a Friar attempting to convince the natives, this time the Iroquois, of the superiority of Christianity. He fails miserably. "These Savages, who have a large share of common sense, often ask'd me, Did your *Spirits* know of our being here before you came hither? I answered them, No. You do not learn therefore all things by Scripture; it tells you not all things, reply'd they."[27] Many Spanish chroniclers, theologians, and scholars were at a loss to explain the presence of unknown peoples on an unknown continent. Some would insist that the natives had descended from the lost tribes of Israel. Even the name "Indian" perpetuates the "cult of the book," as the name refers to the people Columbus expected to find from his readings of known texts.

Mediators between Text and Community

The priestly orders maintained control of education of both Spaniard and native alike. They developed the policy which at first encouraged the development of native language grammars to aid in the task of converting the native population. They decided who would be educated and to what level.

Literacy among the Indians was restricted to a Hispanicized elite. These indigenous elites attempted to retain their former status without sacrificing their place in Indian society. They served as a bridge suspended between the Spanish and their peoples, but often they were not socially accepted by either group. Many became completely Hispanicized and merged with the colonial elite, exploiting their own people just as the Spanish did. Others continued to serve their local population as scribes or notaries. In fact, Bartolomé de las Casas, the first Christian bishop of Chiapas, remarked that no native town ever lacked a manuscript painter to serve its population.[28]

Other elite natives became skilled at manipulating the Spanish judicial system on behalf of themselves or their communities, attempting to defend their constituents against unfair tribute burdens. They earned a reputation as litigious people, flooding courts with petitions and suits. These actions required an understanding of the use of the written word, if not actual literacy.

Encounters with Literacy and Books

Text as Symbolic Object

From the first encounter with the *requerimiento* Native Americans experienced Western literacy and written documents as conquest. From the burning of native texts to the imposition of a new educational system, the introduction of Western writing brought change to indigenous society. It should be no surprise that to the indigenous peoples of the Americas Western books and literacy came to symbolize conquest, miscommunication, and forced acculturation.

A Symbol of Conquest

The book played a central role in the conquest of Peru and the destruction of indigenous notions of order and balance. From the beginning, the Andean world has had a traumatic and confused relationship with the written word. The story of the events which took place in Cajamarca, on November 16, 1532, is repeated in chronicles written by both Spaniards and Indians. Ansion points out that it is not the truth of the occurrence that is actually important, but rather the fact that it remains etched in the collective Andean conscience even today.[29]

When Pizarro met Atahualpa in the plaza at Cajamarca, the Friar Vicente de Valverde came armed with a book (see figure 1). He admonished the Inca to convert to the one true faith. Atahualpa replied, according to Guamán Poma, that he would not change his belief in his own gods. He asked Valverde on what authority were his beliefs based and the friar showed him the book he held.

"The Inca then said: 'Give me **the book** so that it can speak to me.' **The book** was handed to him and he began to eye it carefully and listen to it **page by page**. At last he asked: 'Why doesn't **the book** say anything to me?' Still sitting on his throne, he threw it on the ground with a haughty and petulant gesture."[30] Friar Valverde, shocked by this treatment of the Holy Bible, demanded punishment. Pizarro ordered his men to attack, and the slaughter began. Atahualpa failed the test of the "cult of the book."[31]

A Symbol of Communication Failure

Mutual incomprehension marked the first encounters between the Spanish and the Inca. The two worlds from which they came were completely alien to each other. Wachtel uses a Quechua play, which reenacts the conquest, to illustrate that, even today, the native view of the first encounters is one of communication failure. The actor who plays the Spaniard moves his lips, but never utters a sound. The interpreter, Felipillo, must translate everything for him.[32]

Titu Cusi Yupanqui's *Relación de la Conquista del Perú*, written around 1570, is the oldest surviving written document of native origin in Peru.[33] It provided the first behind-the-scenes details of the struggle against Spanish colonial rule. Titu Cusi begins by showing the Spaniards and Inca without means to common discourse as demonstrated by mutual refusal of reciprocity. Pizarro pours the *chicha* (corn beer) offered by Atahualpa on the ground, and Atahualpa retaliates by throwing the Bible down. One hundred pages later, Titu Cusi counterbalances the first scene, with another, more peaceful one between the author and Fray Marcos García. García accepts the Inca's hospitality, and the Inca accepts Christian writing in the form of the catechism. As Salomon states, "Reciprocity of speech is under way."[34]

A Symbol of Forced Acculturation

The indigenous peoples of America were not unfamiliar with the practice of burning the records of a defeated enemy and the rewriting of history according to the victor. The Codice Matritense records that after an Aztec victory over Azcapotzalco, Itzcoatl had Aztec history rewritten:[35]

Fig. 1. Friar Valverde comes armed with a book. (Guamán Poma, *Nueva Cronica*, p. 384 [386].)

They preserved an account of their history
but later it was burned,
during the reign of Itzcoatl.
The lords of Mexico decreed it,
the lords of Mexico declared:
'It is not fitting that our people
should know these pictures.
Our people, our subjects will be lost
and our land destroyed,
for these pictures are full of lies....'

The depth of their understanding shows in a drawing of Franciscan friars burning books depicted in the *Lienzo de Tlaxcala*.[36] It is the ideas contained in the books which are shown burning, not their physical containers (see figure 2).

Throughout the colonial period and into the present the native peoples of the Americas continued to express their distrust of European writing, though those cultures with a writing tradition do not reject the written word completely. The Great Dance of the Conquest performed in eighteenth-century New Spain contains a speech by Cuauhtemoc in which he admonishes Moctezuma for his actions or rather inaction during the conquest.[37]

. . . . They come to mock you. All those who come here are second rate or Spaniards who lost out, who come telling you that in their country there are great cities, talking of another king at the head of the empire of Castile by the name of Charles the Fifth, [and] of a Catholic religion.

These are only stories, lies. I do not believe in other books [that is other than indigenous codices]. I feel that their words are only like dreams. . . .

The encounter at Cajamarca became immortalized in a colonial legend known as the Incarrí which Andean storytellers repeat to this day. The following, excerpted and translated from Alencastre's *Historias fantásticas del Perú colonial*, was collected in the 1970s.[38] It illustrates Andean peoples' distrust of the written word and of Western education still felt today.[39]

God, all powerful, who is our father . . . had two sons: the Inca and Sucristus [Jesus Christ]. The Inca told us: "Speak!," and we learned to speak. Since then we teach our children so they can speak. The Inca asked Pacha Mama [mother earth or mother time] to feed us and teach us to farm. The llamas and the cows obeyed us. It was a time of abundance. . . .

Since Jesucristo was young and strong, he wanted to beat his older brother, the Inca. "How will I beat him?," he said. The moon felt sorry for him, and she told him: "I can help you," and she caused **a piece of paper with written words** to fall to him.

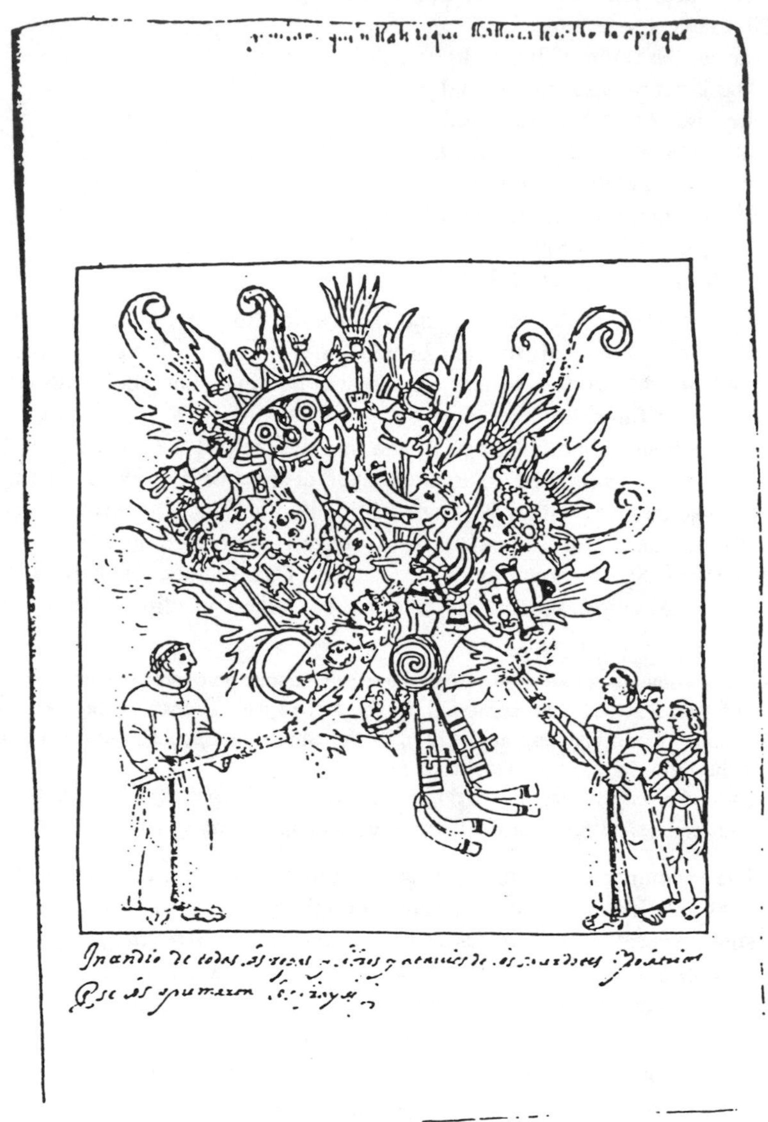

Fig. 2. Franciscans burning books. (From the *Lienzo de Tlazcala*; reprinted in León-Portilla, *Los Franciscanos*, between pp. 18-19.)

Jesus said: "With that the Inca is going to be frightened." In a dark field, he showed him **the paper** and the Inca was afraid when he could not understand **the writing**. "What things are those drawings? What does my brother want?," he said and he fled; he went far away. . . .

The Ñaupa Machu [literally old primitive] was happy to learn that the Inca had died. The Ñaupa Machu lived in a mountain named **"school."** She was joyful to learn that they had beaten Pacha Mama. During this, two sons of the Inca passed by. They were looking for their parents. Ñaupa Machu told them: "Come, come. I'm going to reveal to you where the Inca is, where Pacha Mama is!" The children contentedly went to the **"school."** The Ñaupa Machu wanted to eat them.

In the end, Pacha Mama didn't love the Inca anymore. The Inca made friends with Jesucristo and now they are together, as two brothers. . . .

The children were very afraid and they escaped. Since that time, all the children are supposed to go to **school**; and, like the sons of Pacha Mama, almost all children don't like to go to **school**, they escape. . . .

This tale confirms the indigenous population's perception that education is an acculturation process. By making friends with the outsiders, the Inca is no longer loved by mother earth. The Inca is no longer in balance with his world.

Writing as a symbol of alienation is also a strong theme among the Wakuenai, an Arawak-speaking tribe living along the upper reaches of the Rio Negro who regard whites as semihumans whose souls take the form of books and papers. To them writing is a symbol of social stratification. According to Hill and Wright, writing separates whites from nature and from their fellowmen by dividing them into occupations. The soul of the missionary is a bible; the trader has a financial log for a soul; and the anthropologist's soul is his field log.[40] This makes sense since Western society does tend to "pour its soul" into its work.

Writing as Resistance

Guamán Poma's *Nueva Cronica* and Titu Cusi Yupanqui's *Relación* are more than literary texts; they are also acts of resistance. They were intended to be weapons in the battle to expose Spanish abuses. They hoped to convince the Spanish monarch of the legality of their position. Chang-Rodríguez suggests that the *Nueva Cronica* and the *Relación* are the products of their authors' "faith in the power of the written word, appropriated from the Europeans. . . ."[41]

Like Guamán Poma and Tuti Cusi, the Maya wrote to save their cultures. Often writing in secret and in obscure language, they attempted to use writing to preserve their cultural heritage. The *Popol Vuh* opens in this manner:[42]

This is the beginning of the Ancient Word, here in this place called Quiche. Here we shall inscribe, we shall implant the Ancient Word, the potential and source for everything done in the citadel of Quiche, in the nation of the Quiche people.

And here we shall take up the demonstration, revelation, and account of how things were put in shadow and brought to light. . . .

They accounted for everything—and did it too—as enlightened beings, in enlightened words. We shall write about this now amid the preaching of God, in Christendom now. We shall bring it out because there is no longer a place to see it, a Council Book . . . as it is called. There is the original book and ancient writing, but he who reads and ponders it hides his face. . . .

Conclusion: The Violence of the Book a Legacy for Today

The *Chilam Balam of Chumayel* ends with the following prophesy:[43]

These words compiled here are said for the ears of those who have no father and for those who have no mother. These words should be hidden, as the precious jewels are hidden. . . . There is no truth to the words of strangers. The children of the deserted great houses, the children of the great men of the deserted, unpopulated houses, they will say what is certain about those who came here, Father. What prophet, what priest, will be the one to correctly interpret the words of these writings?

Today, in language that echoes this prophesy, Rigoberta Menchú, Nobel Peace Prize recipient, recognizes the distinction between technology and social context. In her memoirs, dictated in 1982 just three years after she learned to speak Spanish, she remembers what her father told her: "My children, don't aspire to go to school, because schools take our customs away from us."[44] She was glad that she had never been sent to school to learn lies taught as history. Hearing about these schools taught her ". . . that even though a person may learn to read and write, he should not accept the false education they give our people."[45]

Most important to her is that her people think for themselves. They, not the government nor any outsider, should decide for themselves what is truly relevant. As a community they have been able to survive by rejecting all outside aims. They kept their true selves secret. Enduring hatred, misunderstanding, and ridicule, they pretended not to think, and so they were thought to be stupid. But why waste the effort to communicate if no one will listen? She concludes:[46]

But we have hidden our identity because we needed to resist, we wanted to protect what governments have wanted to take away from us. They have tried to take our things away and impose others on us, be it through religion, through dividing up the land, through schools, through books, through radio, through all things modern. . . . We don't want to because we know that they are weapons they use to take away what is ours.

The continuity of negative indigenous views of Western literacy and books reminds us that communications technologies cannot be separated from the social context in which they are used. Technology alone will not improve the life of the indigenous peoples of this continent until the social context in which they are forced to function changes.

NOTES

1. Translation consulted: Dennis Tedlock, trans., *Popol Vuh: The Mayan Book of the Dawn of Life* (New York: A Touchstone Book, Simon & Schuster, 1985).

2. Version and translation consulted: Felipe Guamán Poma de Ayala, *Nueva Cronica y Buen Gobierno*, 3 vols., eds., John V. Murra, Rolena Adorno, and Jorge L. Urioste (Madrid: Historia 16, 1987); Felipe Huamán Poma de Ayala, *Letter to a King: A Peruvian Chief's Account of Life Under the Incas and Under Spanish Rule*, ed. Christopher Dilke (New York: Dutton, 1978).

3. Translation consulted: Miguel Rivera, ed., *Chilam Balam de Chumayel* (Madrid: Historia 16, 1986).

4. Miguel León-Portilla, *El Reverso de la Conquista* (Mexico: Editorial Joaquín Mortiz, 1980).

5. Miguel León-Portilla, ed., *Broken Spears: The Aztec Account of the Conquest of Mexico*, expanded and updated edition, translated from Nahuatl into Spanish by Angel María Garibay K., and into English by Lysander Kemp (Boston: Beacon Press, 1992).

6. James Lockhart, *The Nahuas After the Conquest: A Social and Cultural History of the Indians of Central Mexico, Sixteenth through Eighteenth Centuries* (Stanford, CA: Stanford University Press, 1992).

7. Gordon Brotherston, *Book of the Fourth World: Reading the Native Americans through Their Literature* (Cambridge: Cambridge University Press, 1992).

8. Such as Rolena Adorno, *Guamán Poma: Writing and Resistance in Colonial Peru* (Austin: University of Texas Press, 1991).

9. M. T. Clanchy, "Reading the Signs at Durham Cathedral," in Karen Schousboe and Mogen Trolle Larsen, eds., *Literacy and Society* (Copenhagen: Akademisk Forlag, 1989), pp. 171-182.

10. Lockhart, *The Nahuas*, p. 334.

11. Ibid., p. 342.

12. Michael D. Coe, *Breaking the Maya Code* (New York: Thames and Hudson, 1992).

13. *Cantares Mexicanos*, fol. 27r-27v, quoted in Brotherston, *Fourth World*, p. 160.

14. *Colloquios y Doctrina Christiana*, recopilados y dispuestos por fray Bernardino de Sahagún, 1564, fol. 34v.-36r. as quoted in Miguel León-Portilla, *Los Franciscanos Vistos por el Hombre Nahuatl: Testimonios Indígenas del Siglo XVI* (Mexico: Centro de Estudios Bernardino de Sahagún, A.C., 1985), pp. 29-30.; English translation: Ronald Wright, *Stolen Continents: The 'New World' through Indian Eyes* (Boston: Houghton Mifflin, 1992), pp. 146-147.

15. Gordon Brotherston, "Continuity in Maya Writing: New Readings of Two Passages in the Book of Chilam Balam of Chumayel," in Norman Hammond and Gordon R. Wiley, eds., *Maya Archaeology and Ethnohistory* (Austin: University of Texas Press, 1976), p. 243.

16. Coe, *Breaking the Maya Code*, pp. 220-222.

17. Tedlock, *Popol Vuh*, p. 219.

18. Huamán Poma, *Letter to a King*, pp. 18, 43.

19. Marcia Ascher and Robert Ascher, *Code of the Quipu: A Study in Media, Mathematics, and Culture* (Ann Arbor: University of Michigan Press, 1981), p. 158.

20. James Lockhart and Enrique Otte, trans. & eds., *Letters and People of the Spanish Indies: Sixteenth Century*, Cambridge Latin American Studies, no. 22 (Cambridge: Cambridge University Press, 1976), pp. 158-159.

21. Huamán Poma, *Letter to a King*, p. 101.

22. Guamán Poma, *Nueva Cronica*, p. 367 [369].

23. Ibid., p. 359 [361].

24. Anthony Grafton, *New Worlds, Ancient Texts: The Power of Tradition and the Shock of Discovery* (Cambridge, MA: Belknap Press of Harvard University Press, 1992), pp. 1-2.

25. Patricia Seed, "Taking Possession and Reading Texts: Establishing the Authority of Overseas Empires," *The William and Mary Quarterly*, 3rd Series, 49:2 (April 1992), 184-209.

26. For a discussion on the "cult of the book" see Luis Borges, "Del Culto de los Libros," in *Prosa Completa*, vol. 2 (Barcelona: Bruguera, 1980), pp. 229-233.

27. Louis Henepin, *A New Discovery of a Vast Country in America*, reprinted from the Second London Issue of 1698, ed. Reuben Gold Thwaites, vol. 2 (New York: Kraus Reprint, 1972), pp. 535-536.

28. As quoted in Thompson, "A Commentary on the Dresden Codex," *Memoirs of the American Philosophical Society* 93, 6-7.

29. Juan Ansion, "Una Visión Andina del Libro," in *Bibliotecas Populares: Identidad y Proceso* (Lima: CIDAP-TAREA, 1987), p. 169; the relationship between Andeans and the book has also become one of the more popular research topics of the last few years. See, for example, Constance Classen, "Literacy as Anticulture: The Andean Experience of the Written Word," *History of Religion* 30:4 (May 1991), 404-421; Sabine MacCormack, "Atahualpa y el Libro," *Revista de Indias* 49:184 (September-December 1988), 693-714.

30. Huamán Poma, *Letter to a King*, p. 109.

31. Rolena Adorno, "Selections from the Symposium on 'Literacy, Reading, and Power,' Whitney Humanities Center, November 14, 1987," *Yale Journal of Criticism* 2:1 (Fall 1988), 221.

32. Nathan Wachtel, *Vision of the Vanquished: The Spanish Conquest of Peru through Indian Eyes (1530-1570)*, trans. Ben Reynolds and Sian Reynolds (New York: Harper & Row, 1977), p. 39.

33. Diego de Castro Titu Cusi Yupanqui, *Relación de la Conquista del Perú* (Lima: Biblioteca Universitaria, 1973).

34. Frank Salomon, "Chronicles of the Impossible: Notes on Three Peruvian Historians," in Rolena Adorno, ed., *From Oral to Written Expression: Native Colonial Period*, Foreign and Comparative Studies/Latin American Series, no. 4 (Syracuse, NY: Maxwell School of Citizenship and Public Affairs, Syracuse University, 1982), p. 15.

35. León-Portilla, *Broken Spears*, p. xxxviii.

36. León-Portilla, *Los Franciscanos*, between pp. 18-19.

37. León-Portilla, *Broken Spears*, pp. 163-164.

38. Gustavo Alencastre Montufar, *Historias fantásticas del Perú colonial*, Lecturas Peruanas Escogidas, ser. 1, no. 1 (Cusco: Editorial Garcilaso, 1976), pp. 188-192.

39. These excerpts from Spanish to English by the author. The emphasis is entirely mine.

40. Jonathan D. Hill and Robin M. Wright, "Time, Narrative, and Ritual: Historical Interpretations from an Amazonian Society," in Jonathan D. Hill, ed., *Rethinking History and Myth: Indigenous South American Perspectives in the Past* (Urbana: University of Illinois Press, 1988), pp. 92-93.

41. Raquel Chang-Rodríguez, "Writing as Resistance: Peruvian History and the *Relación* of Titu Cusi Yupanqui," in Adorno, ed., *From Oral to Written Expression*, p. 56; see also Adorno, *Writing and Resistance*.

42. Tedlock, *Popol Vuh*, p. 71.

43. Rivera, *Chilam Balam*, pp. 159, 163-164; English translation by the author.

44. Rigoberta Menchú, *I, Rigoberta Menchú: An Indian Woman in Guatemala*, ed. Elizabeth Burgos, and trans. Ann Wright (London: Verso Editions, 1984), p. 169.

45. Ibid., p. 170.

46. Ibid., pp. 170-171.

The Environment and Society Today

5. La especie Araucaria y su relación con el pueblo pehuenche: El caso de la comunidad de Quinquen

Gabriel Sanhueza Suárez

Resumen

El Araucaria o Pehuén (*Araucaria araucana*) es una especie de pino que se desarrolla principalmente en la Cordillera de los Andes de Chile. Se caracteriza por gran longevidad superando incluso los 1,200 años de edad. Crece en ecosistemas poco diversificados que presentan condiciones de gran rigurosidad climática.

El Araucaria tiene un crecimiento muy lento, incrementando su tamaño en un promedio anual de 3,5 cm. y su diámetro en 1 mm. De esta forma alcanza diámetros explotables recién a los 500 años.

Debido a los incendios, a la explotación irracional y a la corta ilegal, esta especie se vio en los últimos decenios fuertemente amenazada. Es así, como el propio organismo estatal denominado Corporación Nacional Forestal (CONAF), la clasificó en 1985 de "especie vulnerable a la extinción."[1] Además el Araucaria está protegida por la Convención de Comercio Internacional de Especies Amenazadas de Extinción (CITES).[2]

Este árbol ha sido fundamental para la sobrevivencia del pueblo pehuenche —que significe la gente del Pehuén, un grupo reducido de indígenas Mapuches que habitan en restringidas comunidades en lo alto de la Cordillera de los Andes. Su nombre expresa su estrecho contacto con el Araucaria, que les sirve desde alimento básico tradicional hasta ser símbolo de su espiritualidad.

Parte de las comunidades pehuenches estuvieron hasta los inicios del año 1990 amenazadas por empresas madereras, que pretendieron explotar económicamente los bosques de araucarias, considerando el alto valor comercial de esa madera.

Estos intentos se habían visto favorecidos y respaldados ampliamente, desde fines del año 1987, debido al decreto 141 del Ministerio de Agricultura, que permitió la explotación de Araucaria, hasta entonces considerada Monumento Natural en todo el país.[3] Este decreto derogó el Decreto Supremo 29, publicado en abril de 1976, que prohibía en forma absoluta cualquier corta o destrucción de la especie dentro del territorio nacional con fines comerciales.

Este documento entrega antecedentes de la especie Araucaria y la situación de la comunidad de Quinquen, Departamento de Curacautín, Novena Región de Chile, una de las más amenazadas por empresas forestales que deseaban cortar sus bosques vírgenes milenarios. Al mismo tiempo alerta sobre la situación de peligro del Araucaria en el país. Por último, propone acciones concretas para la defensa de los bosques amenazados, base de sustentación de las comunidades pehuenches.

Se destaca como fundamental la realización de una exitosa campaña nacional e internacional de información y defensa activa de la especie Araucaria, que culminó el 19 de marzo de 1990, cuando el gobierno de transición democrática del Presidente Patricio Aylwin, a través del Ministerio de Agricultura, restituyó de nuevo el carácter de Monumento Natural a la especie.

Antecedentes de la comunidad de Quinquen

La comunidad de Quinquen, con una extensión de 6,680 hectáreas, considerando la montaña y el valle, se encuentra ubicada en el Departamento de Curacautín, Novena Región del país, alrededor de los 39 grados latitud sur y los 71 grados de longitud oeste, donde nace el río Bio-Bio. La comunidad está formada par 22 familias, involucrando un total de 130 personas. Tienen como vecinos a otras 4 comunidades, con menor número de familias.

Las montañas, que alcanzan una altura de 1,800 m. sobre el nivel del mar, poseen un bosque virgen de Araucaria, con ejemplares que superan los 1,400 años de antigüedad, en combinación con la especie Lenga (*Northofagus pumilio*). Este bosque tiene una extensión aproximada de 1,500 hectáreas y es considerado por los expertos forestales el mejor bosque de Araucarias del país.

Las condiciones geomorfológicas y climáticas de la zona son rigurosas. En el invierno la nieve puede alcanzar más de dos metros de altura, y la temperatura llega hasta 25 grados Celsius bajo cero.

Las familias de Quinquen han construido sus casas de madera en el valle, las que no cuentan con las condiciones necesarias para enfrentar la rigurosidad del clima andino. La madera es solamente labrada rústicamente con hacha.

En la comunidad no existe una escuela, a pesar que los niños que se encuentran en edad escolar son alrededor de 30. La no escolaridad es elevada, ya que sólo unos pocos visitan la escuela de Sierra Nevada, distante a 30 kilómetros. Tampoco existe una Posta de Primeros Auxilios. La salud de la población está visiblemente deteriorada.

La economía de la comunidad es absolutamente marginal, fundamentalmente porque el suelo es pobre, no se presta para un desarrollo agrícola.

La subsistencia se basa en la crianza reducida de animales, ovejas, chivos, caballos y cerdos. Las mujeres y los jóvenes durante el largo invierno hacen tejidos tradicionales, que venden durante el verano a los turistas que pasan por el sector. Todas las familias de Quinquen subsisten en condiciones extremadamente pobres, por una parte por el aislamiento geográfico y la dureza de las condiciones climáticas y por otra la incapacidad de una acumulación económica primaria.

El pino Araucaria (Pehuen) constituye un elemento fundamental en la subsistencia de la comunidad. Este árbol es para el pueblo pehuenche por una parte sagrado y expresión de la espiritualidad del pueblo, pero fundamentalmente es también la fuente de su alimento básico, a través de su fruto, el piñón.

La comunidad se traslada anualmente en los meses de febrero, marzo y abril hasta los bosques de Araucaria para cosechar los piñones, acompañados de sus animales, que viven bajo al sistema de "veranada".[4] Es la fase de recolección de piñones, durante la que cada familia recoge alrededor de 4.000 kilos. Esto será utilizado, por una parte, como alimento para los animales durante el largo invierno y primavera, y fundamentalmente para la venta o trueque, de manera de poder obtener los alimentos que necesitan para la larga temporada invernal.

La comunidad Quinquen conserva aun grandes rasgos culturales típicos. Entre ellos hablan aun el "mapudungún", idioma de los mapuches, en el cual se expresan mejor que en el castellano. Este último idioma es ignorado por una parte significativa de las mujeres de la comunidad.

Mantienen asimismo sus propias creencias, que se transmiten a través de la traducción oral. Llevan a cabo ceremonias tradicionales, como el "ngillatun",[5] cuando comienza la época de cosecha de los piñones. Conservan sus propias danzas, como el "loncomeo", y producen también una chiche tradicional, llamada "mundai", así como harina, ambas de piñones. La mayoría de los adultos, sin embargo, expresan que muchas de las costumbres y creencias se están perdiendo, fundamentalmente entre los jóvenes.

Destaca, sin embargo, el profundo conocimiento de su medio ambiente, de los bosques, las plantas, el clima, los cerros, los animales y las aves. Poseen una sabiduría y un gran entendimiento de la naturaleza, a través de generaciones. Impresiona, sobre todo, su decisión de impedir cueste lo que cueste que sus bosques de Araucarias sean destruidos, pues comprenden que de ocurrir eso, significará la muerte de identidad cultural, de su economía tradicional, de su relación social. Es decir, la disgregación de toda la comunidad.

Historia de la comunidad Quinquen

En el año 1880 llega Lonquimay hasta el valle de Quinquen la familia indígena Meliñir, probablemente arrancando de la "Guerra de Pacificación"[6] y en busca de alimento. En el valle forma una comunidad para permanecer y habitarla en forma permanente.

Veintiocho años más tarde se instala —a aproximadamente 30 kilómetros del valle de Quinquen— Guillermo Schweitzer, dueño del fundo "El Porvenir de Lolen" (propiedad agropecuaria de gran extensión). Este solicita permiso al cacique de nombre Manuel Meliñir para que sus reses pastoreen en época de verano en el valle, ofreciéndole pago a cabo de ello. El cacique acepta, y Schweitzer cancela el talaje durante 10 temporadas, negándose posteriormente, a seguir haciéndolo. Es entonces cuando señala que él es dueño del valle, por habérselo comprado al Estado. Agrega que la comunidad podrá seguir viviendo y ocupando el lugar sin problema, pues él lo ocupera sólo en primavera y verano.

En 1920, Guillermo Schweitzer hipoteca el valle de Quinquen, ante la Caja Agraria de la época a cambio de un préstamo en dinero. Como no cancela el préstamo oportunamente este organismo le confisca sus propiedades, incluso el valle de Quinquen, habitado por la comunidad Meliñir.

Posteriormente, en el año de 1936, la Caja Agraria procede a rematar las propiedades confiscadas, adjudicándose el valle de Quinquen, Agustín Lamoliatt, quien también promete a la comunidad indígena que habita el valle, que puede seguir haciéndolo sin preocupaciones.

Los problemas comienzan en el año 1946 cuando se instalan dos amerraderos de la Sociedad Lamoliatt y Lledo, los que comienzan a cortar las Araucarias del sector.

En el año 1964 la comunidad Quinquen sufre una fuerte represión encabezada por un maderero de apellido Fahrenkrog Buttendiek, quien con la ayuda de la fuerza policial pretende dar un escarmiento a los indígenas, y poder así posteriormente cortar las Araucarias. Muchos indígenas quedan heridos, uno de ellos paralítico para siempre. Los más ancianos cuentan hasta hoy verdaderas historias de horror de esa jornada, ya que muchos de ellos fueron introducidos por horas amarrados en el río, mientras otros permanecieron largamente atados a los pinos, como forma de castigo.

Después de esta represión, los indígenas del valle de Quinquen solicitan al Presidente Eduardo Frei, en el año 1964, que se les entreguen los títulos de dominio de las tierras que han ocupado por largo tiempo. Se inicia así un largo período de tramitaciones, sin que obtengan resultados positivos; y sin que siguiera haya sido considerado sus derechos como auténticos propietarios del valle.

La lucha de los últimos años

Por el contrario, tanto la llamada Sociedad Gallatue,[7] perteneciente a la familia Lamoliatt-Lledo como la empresa denominada Focura,[8] se disputan en los tribunales chilenos el valle de Quinquen habitado por los pehuenches desde el siglo pasado.

Este proceso se inicia en 1987 en el Juzgado de Curacautín, bajo la responsabilidad del Juez Oscar Vinuela, quien en noviembre de 1988 ordenó un peritaje a un topógrafo como antecedente para resolver el problema de deslindes que ambas firmas plantean. Este peritaje fue realizado a fines de noviembre de 1988 y resolución del juez favoreció en primera instancia a la comunidad de Quinquen.

La que está en juega para las dos empresas son los bosques de Araucarias vírgenes aun, gracias a la presencia de los pehuenches, que no han permitido que estos sean tocados. Las dos empresas se habían especializado en la corta de Araucarias y Focura nunca ocultó de que si el juicio le era favorable, de inmediato presentaría un Plan de Manejo para la corta del árbol ante el Director Regional de CONAF[9] en Temuco.

Los dirigentes máximos de la comunidad de Quinquen, preocupados por estas amenazas, viajaron a fines de noviembre de 1988 a Santiago para entregar una carta a las autoridades de gobierno, exponiendo su problema, que consiste fundamentalmente en obtención de los títulos de dominio sobre las tierras en que viven y que han solicitado hace 24 años e impedir que sean cortados sus Pehuenes (Araucarias).

Durante su permanencia en la capital, los dirigentes solicitaron ayuda al Comité Nacional Pro Defensa de la Fauna y Flora (CODEFF), fundamentalmente en torno a la segunda petición: evitar que la Araucaria sea explotada. CODEFF es un organización de conservación y protección ambiental con 25 años de existencia en Chile.

La situación en la que se encontraba el país estaba caracterizada, por una parte, por un total apoyo de la empresa privada por parte del gobierno; unida a la decisión de esta de utilizar al máximo la posibilidad de obtener ganancias rápidas, durante el año de 1989 antes de la vuelta de la democracia que entonces ya era de prever.

A esto se une desde hace ya muchos años la incapacidad de la Corporación Nacional Forestal (CONAF) —por la falta de personal y de implementación material— para controlar y hacer efectiva la protección del Araucaria. El organismo estatal está siendo permanentemente sobre pasado. Es así, como denuncias provenientes de las comunas de Curarrehue, Curacautín, Malipeuco, Villarica, Pucon, Pitrufquen, Longuimay y otras aseguran que madereros inescrupulosos recurren al engaño de hacer uso de la autorización que tiene un fundo para explotar otros lugares y otro predios, donde la especie debería estar protegida.

Por su parte la Sociedad Lamoliatt-Lledo solicitó la expulsión de la comunidad pehuenche del valle, arguyendo que se encontraban viviendo en su propiedad sin autorización. En una insólita resolución, tanto la Corte de Apelaciones de Temuco, como posteriormente la Corte Suprema, máxima instancia judicial del país aceptaron esa argumentación y ordenaron en enero de 1990 la expulsión por la fuerza policial de las tierras que ancestralmente el pueblo pehuenche había ocupado.

El gobierno dilató durante meses el cumplimiento de esa orden judicial, debiendo finalmente, sobre todo frente a la gran presión ciudadana, llegar a un arreglo con la Sociedad, adquiriendo las tierras de Quinquen.

La campaña de defensa del Araucaria

La lucha de las empresas madereras por los bosques de Quinquen fue un claro ejemplo de los efectos que provocó el Decreto 141 del Ministerio de Agricultura, bajo el Gobierno de Pinochet, al desproteger el Araucaria entregándolo a la explotación comercial de las grandes empresas.

CODEFF señaló públicamente cuando apareció el Decreto, "aquí está en peligro no solamente una especie vegetal única en el mundo sino comunidades humanas para las cuales constituye un elemento fundamental de identidad y subsistencia".

Es decir la corta del Araucaria destruye al mismo tiempo la historia, subsistencia y religiosidad de una comunidad que depende de ella.

Todo lo anterior movió al Comité Nacional Pro Defensa de la Fauna y Flora (CODEFF) a organizar un grupo especial multidisciplinario que enfocó este problema con creatividad y rapidez, teniendo como fin fundamental la defensa de los bosques y de los pehuenches que han asegurado por más de cien años su existencia.

El CODEFF se planteó, tomando como ejemplo el caso de la comunidad de Quinquen, realizar una campaña de acciones permanentes de información, denuncias e investigación de la situación del Araucaria tanto a nivel nacional e internacional.

La campaña tuvo una duración de 18 meses y logró en el plano nacional, concitar el apoyo de numerosas organizaciones de distintos ámbitos sociales, generándose una gran presión en contra del gobierno de la época, encabezado por Augusto Pinochet.

En el plano internacional se recibió la solidaridad de centenares de organizaciones conservacionistas de todo el mundo, las que a través de cartas, declaraciones públicas e interpelaciones a las autoridades solicitaban la protección de la especie y el respeto a la cultura pehuenche.

Un papel fundamental durante toda la campaña lo jugó la comunidad Pehuenche de Quinquen, quienes resistiendo mucha presión jamás vacilaron en la defensa de sus bosques. Como ejemplo, se reproduce en el Anexo 1 un llamado formulado el 5 de junio de 1989, Día Mundial del Medio Ambiente.

Más meritorio es la actitud de la comunidad, si se considera que durante muchos meses estuvieron, en virtud de la sentencia de la Corte Suprema, de ser expulsados de sus tierras. Esta situación se solucionó finalmente, sólo en 1992, cuando el gobierno democrático compró 30 mil hectáreas del valle de Quinquen en más de 6 millones de dólares para evitar el desalojo de 22 familias pehuenches que había ordenado la justicia chilena.

La acción finalizó sólo en marzo 1990 cuando el gobierno de la Concertación reestableció la protección que tenía la especie hasta antes de la publicación del Decreto 141. Es decir, cuando se le reconoció de nuevo su carácter de Monumento Nacional a lo largo de todo el país, prohibiéndose su corta o explotación en todo el territorio natural por constituir uno de los acervos naturales más valiosos del patrimonio nacional tanto en lo científico como en lo histórico y cultural y simbolizar además las más auténticas y nobles tradiciones del pueblo mapuche.

NOTAS

1. Esa clasificación la hizo CONAF en el "Simposio de Flora Amenazada de Extinción", realizado en Santiago en el año 1985.

2. La Convención de Comercio Internacional de Especies Amenazadas de Extinción (CITES) fue ratificada por Chile el 20 de enero de 1975.

3. El Decreto Supremo 141 del Ministerio de Agricultura, del 26 de diciembre de 1987, autoriza la explotación forestal del Pino Araucaria incluso dentro de las llamadas Reservas Nacionales, terrenos con pendientes superiores a 80% y otros sectores que a juicio de CONAF deben tener protección, pero en los lugares restantes se permite la explotación. El cuerpo legal está redactado de tal forma, que en apariencia ratifica la condición de Monumento Nacional del Araucaria, status del que ya gozaba en todo el país por el Decreto 29 del mismo Ministerio, publicado el 26 de abril de 1976, y establecía en forma absoluta cualquier tipo de corta o destrucción de la especie en Chile.

4. Veranada, lugar de pastoreo estival utilizado en el manejo trashumante del ganado. Las familias se dedican durante ese período a la recolección de piñones así como de hierbas medicinales.

5. Ngillatun: ceremonia religiosa comunitaria, realizada al aire libre, siempre en el mismo lugar y que cobra vigencia en determinadas épocas del ciclo agrario. Con ella se pide a Dios (Ngueyen) generalmente que haya una abundante cosecha. También puede existir un ruego especial, como el término de una catástrofe, etc. En la comunidad de Quinquen, se efectúa en el mes de enero, para dar inicio al tiempo de recolección de piñones, junto a otros vegetales utilizados como remedios.

6. "Guerra de Pacificación", a partir de fines de la década del sesenta del siglo pasado. Una de las páginas más negras de la historia de Chile, caracterizada por el ingreso del ejército en el territorio mapuche, haciendo una guerra de exterminio en contra de la población civil. El objetivo era destruir la economía ganadera de los mapuches. Gran parte de la población se ve obligada a huir a la montaña.

7. Sociedad Gallatue: ubicado en el Departamento de Curacautín en la Novena Región. Se considera que la dictación del Decreto Supremo 141 tiene una razón oculta: la obligación que pesaba sobre el fisco de pagar una indemnización de varios millones de dólares a los propietarios de la Hacienda Gallatue. Así lo dispuso una sentencia de la Corte Suprema de 1914. Los dueños de la Sociedad reclamaron esa elevada suma ante la prohibición de explotar las Araucarias existentes en sus terrenos, debido a que eran consideradas Monumento Natural. La defensa del Estado frente a la demanda de Gallatue fue asumida por Sergio Gaete, ex Ministro de Educación y luego Embajador de Buenos Aires en el gobierno de Pinochet y se caracterizó por su deficiencia y errores realmente inexplicables.

8. Focura: Sociedad Maderera de Curacautín, creada en el año 1938 bajo el nombre de Patricio Moser en Curacautín. Es en la actualidad la empresa industrial maderera más importante de la Novena Región. El rubro principal es la producción de madera contra-enchapada (terciada) y aglomerada, utilizando con materia primera principalmente la Araucaria y otras maderas nativas como Coigue, Tepa y Lenga. Sus exportaciones a Argentina alcanzaron en el año 1988 a 800 mil dólares.

9. CONAF: Corporación Nacional Forestal, organización de índole gubernamental dependiente del fomento y desarrollo de políticas para el sector forestal del país. Posee como función adicional la administración, control y vigilancia del Sistema Nacional de Areas Silvestres Protegidas del Estado (parques naturales, monumentos naturales y reservas nacionales).

ANEXO 1

Carta de la Comunidad Mapuche de Quinquen

Nosotros, las 140 personas que vivimos en el Valle de Quinquen, pedimos que nos ayudan a impedir que corten los pehuenos, que son muy importantes para nuestra subsistencia.

El piñón es nuestro alimento, y también lo vendemos para poder comprar todo lo que necesitamos.

Este verano hemos cosechado muy pocos piñones, además con la erupción del Volcán Longuimay, el precio de nuestros animales ha bajado mucho.

Nuestros padres y abuelos han vivido en el valle desde el 1880. Todos estos años hemos cuidado permanentemente los bosque de pehuén, sin cortarlos, cuidándolos de los incendios y cosechando el piñón para vivir.

Pedimos a todos ustedes —especialmente a las autoridades— que nos ayuden a conservar nuestros bosques. Que se elimine la ley que permite cortarlos, porque el pehuén es parte de nuestra vida, nuestra tradición y cultura.

Pedimos también que se nos reconozca como dueños de esta tierra y se nos entreguen los títulos correspondientes.

Mauricio Meliñir	José Meliñir
Presidente	Secretario

5 de junio de 1985, Día Mundial del Medio Ambiente

6. Investigación y conservación de la cotorra margariteña

Jon Paul Rodríguez

Venezuela, por su ubicación al norte de Suramérica, está bajo la influencia de numerosos factores geográficos y climáticos diferentes. Es un país caribeño, atlántico, amazónico, andino y llanero. El resultado es una gran variedad de ecosistemas que van desde las nieves perpetuas de las cumbres de las montañas por encima de los 4500 m de altitud, hasta las zonas de desiertos, dominadas por extensas zonas de médanos de arena prácticamente desprovistos de vegetación.

Una consecuencia de esta gran variedad de ecosistemas es una de las biodiversidades más altas de la tierra. Por ejemplo, si se considera el caso de las aves, en Venezuela se ha registrado el 14.25% de las especies de aves del mundo (1300 especies), en un área inferior al 1% de la superficie del planeta.

Al igual que en otras partes del mundo, las especies y ambientes de Venezuela se encuentran sometidos a fuertes presiones de uso por parte de las sociedades humanas, con consecuencias muy serias para su sobrevivencia:

— cientos de especies de plantas y animales se encuentran amenazadas de extinción;
— 30% de la superficie del país ha sido desforestado;
— cada año se liberan 30 millones de toneladas de gases que producen el efecto invernadero y 5 millones de toneladas de gases que degradan la capa de ozono;
— diez cuencas hidrográficas importantes sufren serios problemas de contaminación;
— numerosas playas han sido declaradas no aptas para su uso;
— desde 1960 hasta 1990, Venezuela presentó un crecimiento poblacional de 290.66%, el valor más alto en Latinoamérica y cinco veces el promedio a nivel mundial.

Toda esta situación ha dado origen a una gran cantidad de iniciativas a nivel gubernamental y no gubernamental, destinadas a reducir el impacto de la sociedad sobre el ambiente y buscar fórmulas de utilización de los recursos naturales manteniendo su capacidad de generar bienes y servicios indefinidamente (uso sostenible).

Entre las labores gubernamentales más destacadas, resalta el sistema de parques nacionales venezolano. Más de 15% del territorio del país está protegido en la forma de parques nacionales (el valor más alto del mundo), y más de 40% del territorio se encuentra en alguna figura bajo régimen de administración especial.

Por otra parte, alrededor de cien organizaciones no gubernamentales (ONGs) ambientalistas desarrollan innumerables proyectos en todas las regiones del país.

Entre estas ONGs, se encuentra PROVITA, una asociación civil sin fines de lucro fundada en 1987, con el objetivo de conservar las especies y ambientes amenazados de Venezuela, haciendo énfasis en aquellos cuya situación sea más grave. PROVITA desarrolla sus actividades principalmente en los campos de la investigación científica (en ciencias naturales y ciencias sociales) y la educación ambiental.

Es una organización formada en su mayoría por voluntarios, de una gran cantidad de disciplinas. Es la convicción de PROVITA que los problemas de conservación deben ser abordados desde una perspectiva transdisciplinaria, integrando conocimientos de profesionales de la mayor cantidad de especialidades posible. Entre los voluntarios, se cuenta con biólogos, sociólogos, economistas, abogados, educadores, diseñadores gráficos e ingenieros de computación, entre otros. Adicionalmente, PROVITA mantiene un conjunto de profesionales a dedicación exclusiva, responsables de la administración y organización general de los programas y proyectos.

Uno de los proyectos más exitosos de PROVITA es el Proyecto por la Conservación de la Cotorra Margariteña. La cotorra margariteña (*Amazona barbadensis*) es una especie de loro restringida a pocas zonas de la costa de Venezuela y algunas islas del Caribe. En la isla de Margarita (Estado Nueva Esparta, Venezuela) encontramos una población conformada por cerca de 800 individuos, concentrados en la península de Macanao, en el extremo oeste de la isla. Esta población se encuentra sometida a un conjunto de presiones que permiten afirmar que, de continuar operando con la misma magnitud, extinguirían a la población en un lapso menor de cincuenta años: prácticamente 100% de los pichones son extraídos de los nidos para ser utilizados como mascotas y para ser vendidos en actividades de comercio ilegal, y las principales áreas de reproducción de esta ave están siendo desforestadas a consecuencia de actividades de minería de arena a cielo abierto que se llevan a cabo para mantener una pujante industria de la construcción (principalmente hoteles y villas turísticas) en el extremo este de la isla.

En 1990, y a raíz de toda esta situación, PROVITA conjuntamente con el servicio de fauna del Ministerio del Ambiente y los Recursos Naturales (Profauna-MARN) y Wildlife Conservation International (WCI), una división de la Sociedad Zoológica de Nueva York, acordaron iniciar un programa de conservación de esta ave incluyendo actividades de investigación, educación y guardería, con la participación adicional de la Guardia Nacional, la Armada de Venezuela, la Gobernación de Estado Nueva Esparta y el Fondo San Francisco (un propietario privado de grandes extensiones de tierra dentro del área de distribución de la cotorra en Margarita).

La responsabilidad de PROVITA está concentrada principalmente en investigación de la biología reproductiva y alimentaria del ave, monitoreo del tamaño poblacional, y el mantenimiento de aves en cautiverio y su posterior liberación al medio natural.

Cada año, con la asistencia de estudiantes de secundaria de la isla, se llevan a cabo censos de la población silvestre, antes, durante y después de la estación reproductiva. Estos censos permiten evaluar el efecto del proyecto sobre variaciones en el tamaño poblacional y, por supuesto, evidenciar si la población se encuentra en recuperación (lo cual es, obviamente, el objeto de este programa).

Adicionalmente, cerca de 40 nidos activos de cotorra son protegidos de los saqueadores, a fin de estudiar el proceso de crecimiento de pichones, sus causas de mortalidad natural, y experimentar métodos que permitan obtener una mayor productividad de estas aves en cada estación reproductiva. Asimismo, pichones que se encuentren en nidos en zonas de alto riesgo de saqueo son transferidos a los nidos protegidos a fin de aumentar su probabilidad de sobrevivencia. Igualmente, se introducen en estos nidos aquellos pichones que hayan sido decomisados por la Guardia Nacional de manos de saqueadores y traficantes.

En el caso de que al transferir pichones a los nidos de otros parientes ocurra un rechazo o se tema por su sobrevivencia, éstos son removidos y criados en cautiverio para su posterior liberación.

Los resultados de este programa han sido muy alentadores. En los últimos tres años, se ha logrado la incorporación de más de 120 pichones a la población silvestre a partir de los nidos que se encuentran protegidos por nuestro programa. Esta cifra es considerable, si se toma en cuenta que en los 15 años previos a la puesta en práctica de este plan de conservación es posible que el número total de aves incorporadas a la población silvestre sea inferior a este valor.

Por otra parte, a finales de 1992, se liberaron las primeras ocho aves criadas en cautiverio, de las cuales, cuatro estaban provistas con radiotransmisores para monitorear el proceso de adaptación a la vida silvestre. A los tres meses de liberadas, dos de las cuatro aves marcadas ya formaron pareja, resultados sin precedentes en relación a proyectos de reintroducción de loros en cualquier otra parte del mundo.

Finalmente, es importante mencionar el papel de los pobladores locales en la conservación de esta ave. PROVITA ha hecho un esfuerzo notable en incorporar a los habitantes nativos al programa de conservación. Hoy en día, personas que en el pasado se dedicaban a la extracción y comercialización de pichones trabajan en el proyecto y se han convertido en los principales protectores del ave. Asimismo, incontables estudiantes de las escuelas de la zona desarrollan actividades de divulgación y concientización como la realización de murales conservacionistas y festivales de conservación de la cotorra margariteña cada año. Por último, el gobierno estatal declaró a la cotorra como Ave Regional del Estado Nueva Esparta.

Todos estos resultados, así como la gran cantidad de personas que han participado en el programa, nos hacen pensar que la sobrevivencia de una de las especies más amenazadas de Venezuela ahora es una realidad.

7. Organización social y ecología: Una misma historia, un nuevo principio

Leonardo Meza Aguilar

Para los propósitos de este ensayo entiendo como organismos no gubernamentales a aquellos grupos organizados de la sociedad civil que desarrollan una acción en defensa de la descentralización, de la cultura local, la organización democrática y autónoma, los derechos humanos, la justicia social, la defensa del medio ambiente, etc. Todas estas actividades como respuesta a la insuficiente o nula actividad gubernamental al respecto de cada uno de estos aspectos. Es evidente que existe un antagonismo de fondo entre las distintas formas de ver la participación de los ciudadanos y sus organizaciones en la vida política y social de su comunidad. En consecuencia la hostilidad y choques entre autoridades y grupos no gubernamentales es inevitable.

La realidad de las relaciones entre las ONG y el gobierno en sus diferentes niveles e instancias es muy compleja y rebasa con mucho el planteamiento (esquemático) inicial, de un "antagonismo irreconciliable". En palabras de Dieter Paas, no obstante, es uno de sus rasgos más característicos.

Durante muchos años hubo un divorcio entre la mayoría de los equipos de apoyo y los sectores dirigentes de los movimientos populares. Los primeros concentraron su actividad en pequeños grupos parroquiales con muy poco impacto social. Los segundos marcharon sostenidos en sus propias fuerzas pero con grandes carencias y limitaciones. Aisladas de las organizaciones sociales más dinámicas—que tenían problemas para trascender—la mayoría de las ONG nacionales mantuvieron muy poca presencia. Un número de sus integrantes prefirieron incorporarse a la militancia partidaria o hacer carrera como funcionarios públicos que mantenerse en estas instituciones. Asimismo, si en otros países de Latinoamérica las ONG eran un espacio de trabajo para sectores desatacados de la intelectualidad, en México, salvo excepciones, la mayoría de los intelectuales realizaban sus actividades desde las universidades o el estado. Sólo en fechas recientes, en buena parte como resultado de la pauperización del trabajo académico en los centros de educación superior y ante la necesidad de encontrar nuevas fuentes de ingresos, distintos intelectuales se han acercado a las ONG. El hecho tiene que ver tanto con la desconfianza de muchas organizaciones sociales para recibir recursos del exterior, como del carácter cerrado y hasta cierto punto exclusivo de las relaciones entre las financiadores y algunos interlocutores nacionales.

El panorama ha cambiado sustancialmente en los últimos años de manera acelerada. El divorcio entre el sector popular y las ONG ha terminado. Los equipos de apoyo han cualificado su trabajo y sus propuestas de acción son mucho menos doctrinarias y más adecuadas para transformar la realidad. Su existencia institucional está mucho más cuajada. Sectores significativos de intelectuales y activistas populares con experiencia, que quieren hacer otro tipo de trabajo con un compromiso popular, han encontrado en ellas espacio de acción. [1]

Los diferentes movimientos populares ambientales han surgido en este marco de relaciones multideterminadas y estos no son la excepción en cuanto a la relación estrecha en su interior de las ONG y base social.

Intentar una tipología de las ONG escapa a las características de este trabajo. No obstante, es necesario por lo menos hacer un planteamiento aún cuando este sea esquemático que ubique los principios y quehaceres del amplio y diversificado mundo de los organismos no gubernamentales, conformados en torno de la búsqueda de soluciones a diferentes aspectos de la problemática ambiental.

Los primeros regularmente mantienen una relación más o menos estrecha con algunos miembros de las instituciones académicas y las del gobierno, incluso llegan a establecer mecanismos de colaboración, sobre todo en cuanto a aspectos de conservación de flora y fauna silvestre con organismos gubernamentales, se reconoce en estos grupos un componente de académicos importante (fundamentalmente profesionales de las ciencias naturales). En estas iniciativas civiles la relación con grupos de base es muy pobre y cuando existe siempre está subordinada a los intereses de conservación de especies, hábitats o paisajes. Sus relaciones con otros organismos gubernamentales son pobres también, a menos que se trate de otros similares y aún en estos casos son restringidos. Los temas sociales en su relación con los ecológicos son tratados siempre en segundo término. En muy pocas ocasiones incorporan a su quehacer y demandas consideraciones políticas y cuando lo hacen estas están relacionadas con la obligación del gobierno de incrementar su participación financiera en procesos de investigación para la protección ambiental. Estos grupos regularmente están vinculados para su financiamiento con organismos internacionales de corte conservacionista como el Fondo Mundial para la Vida Silvestre (WWF [World Wildlife Fund], por sus siglas en inglés), Nature Conservancy, etc. Alrededor de estos grupos giran un gran número de organizaciones más pequeñas que en menor escala tratan de llevar a cabo este mismo tipo de tareas. Ejemplos de estos grupos en México son entre otros, el Instituto de Recursos Naturales Renovables (IMERNAR), BIOCENOSIS y PRONATURA. El papel que han jugado en el conocimiento propiamente ecológico es importante y no debe ser minimizado.

El otro extremo lo ocupan los grupos y organizaciones que enfocan la crisis actual desde una perspectiva que vincula estrechamente los componentes ambientales y sociales, realizando un cuestionamiento al modelo de desarrollo actual, un cuestionamiento que incluye por supuesto los aspectos ideológicos. Tienen un quehacer mucho más político, su práctica los lleva a vincularse con otros grupos similares. Las iniciativas en este extremo tienen como una de sus características distintivas el hecho de estar fuertemente vinculadas a grupos de base, constituyéndose en grupos de apoyo para los movimientos sociales de base, tanto en aspectos técnicos como políticos y de gestión. Su práctica apunta a cambios profundos en la sociedad. En este extremo se encuentran una gran cantidad de grupos con muchos años de vida (más de 15 años), cuyos orígenes se encuentran en la promoción del desarrollo y que más o menos recientemente (unos 5 años) han iniciado la incorporación de aspectos ambientales a su práctica. Estos son a mi juicio los dos extremos entre los cuales podemos ubicar a los ambientalistas; entre ellos podemos encontrar una gran cantidad de variaciones y grupos que cada día se van sumando. Gudynas (1993) señala que en el registro del Centro Latinoamericano de Ecología Social (CLAES) se cuenta con un registro de más de 1500 organizaciones en la región, que tienen una preocupación primaria, o al menos una secundaria por el ambiente, aunque las estimaciones están alrededor de 4000. En este registro México ocupa el tercer lugar después de Brasil y Argentina.

No existe (por lo menos que yo conozca) para México un registro del número de organismos no gubernamentales en cuyo trabajo y motivo de organización esté la preocupación ambiental. No obstante los diversos registros parciales que existen sitúan el número de ONG ambientalistas en México alrededor de 300. Aunque no se puede señalar este número como definitivo, dada la alta movilidad del ambientalismo. No existen datos sobre el número de miembros que conforman a cada grupo; existen grupos con registro legal de asociación civil con cuatro miembros y asociaciones que reunen hasta 30 elementos. En la elaboración de un directorio en 1988 dentro de la Fundación Friedrich Ebert, nos encontramos con membresías dobles de algunos personajes, presidencias compartidas para algunos grupos, en fin una ubicuidad que da lugar a muchas dudas sobre el verdadero número de grupos y personas incluidas en este quehacer. [2]

Más allá del problema de situar numéricamente la existencia de ambientalistas, es importante destacar que es un movimiento que está en constante crecimiento en cuanto a su número y definición de las diferentes corrientes que se expresan hacia su interior. Para el caso de México, existen una gran cantidad de luchas y disputas internas en el movimiento ambientalista que han hecho crisis en diversas ocasiones y que se expresó claramente con la toma de posición de los grupos más relevantes en la conformación del llamado Foro Mexicano de la Sociedad Civil Hacia Brasil '92 (conocido en México como FOROMEX), formándose dos corrientes con concepciones diametralmente diferentes en cuanto al papel que deben jugar las ONG ambientalistas en la búsqueda del desarrollo sustentable, las formas de acción, las relaciones internas y externas de un movimiento de este tipo, las relaciones con el gobierno y partidos políticos, que finalmente expresan la toma de posición en los extremos anteriormente señalados. Finalmente esta toma de posición llevó a la extinción del FOROMEX.

No obstante lo anterior en México se han logrado mantener diversas instancias de coordinación para las diferentes tendencias que están avanzando en su consolidación. Las discusiones sobre como lograr avances en la protección del medio ambiente nos llevan por fuerza a considerar las diferentes acciones que los grupos ambientalistas desarrollan de acuerdo con la posición en la que se ubican en esos extremos señalados. Los problemas ambientales no pueden verse aisladamente, como si no tuvieran relación con el contexto económico, social y político en que se presentan. Lo ambiental constituye un espacio de confluencia de nuevos y viejos actores sociales comprometidos en un cambio sustancial de las actuales formas de vida social.

NOTAS

1. Dieter Paas, *El sector informal en América Latina: Una selección de perspectivas analíticas* (México: Centro de Investigación y Docencia Económicas, 1991).

2. Para profundizar en este tópico, consultar E. Kurzinger, *Política ambiental en México: El papel de las organizaciones no gubernamentales* (México: Instituto Alemán de Desarrollo, 1991).

8. Ecology in Central and North Mexico

George F. Elmendorf

As far as I can tell, the ecology movement in Mexico is not well known in the United States and is not reported or is misreported in U.S. newspapers and magazines. In fact, the government of Mexico has accepted and integrated ecological thinking and planning. In every state of the republic there is a *ley de ecología.* There is also a state dependency which is mandated to enforce the law. Under such pressure from private ecological groups the inherent contradiction between development and ecology has been recognized, and as a result the old SEDUE, which combined urban development and ecology, has been broken up and replaced by SEDESOL (Secretaría de Desarrollo Social). This entity has the responsibility for ecology at the federal level. SEDESOL in turn has an office in every state of the republic. In addition, every state has its own dependency for ecology and, beginning with Querétaro, has passed and is implementing a state *ley de ecología.* Many municipios, especially those where the state capital is located, have their own ecological offices and their own municipal laws of ecology.

México Norte and México Sur are mandated by the Library of Congress and by an ephemera consortium, headed by Princeton University, to collect ecology material at all levels. Since between them the two companies cover all the states of Mexico and visit, for collecting purposes, each state at least once a year, the entire country has been covered during the year since the SALALM conference in Austin, Texas. This paper is a result of that year of work.

It must first be said that as a developing country Mexico has special ecological problems with respect to the amount of economic and human resources available. It also has a significant indigenous population whose primary source for cooking and heating is wood, which leads to deforestation problems. There is also the inherent conflict between development needs and ecological considerations. Mexico, however, is addressing ecological problems with astonishing vigor and all available resources. The Canadian government's confidence in Mexico's approach to ecological issues is, I believe, the correct position. Criticism of the North American Free Trade Agreement (NAFTA) is both ignorant and ill-advised.

Mexico has recently been lauded by several international organizations for its progress in family planning and population control. The population curve is definitely moving in the right direction in Mexico. The national organization DIF is very involved in family planning and contraception. Two other organizations involved in family planning, sex education, and contraception are IMIFAP, the Mexican Institute of Family Investigation and Population, and MEXFAM, the Foundation for Family Planning. A recent Gallup poll in Mexico showed that up to 90 percent of Mexican parents favor sex education in the schools. Support for such programs is weaker in the North and in rural areas and stronger in the Federal District. Compared to the United States there is relatively little opposition. Women's groups strongly support the government position and direct much of their efforts in this area. Pro-life organizations are relatively ineffective in part because the federal government frames the population issue as a choice between family planning and abortion. The Catholic Church's opposition to contraception is less than vigorous owing to a tradeoff with the government, who recently relaxed a number of laws proscribing church activities.

Another very serious problem is water. I am unaware of a single state capital where the tap water is potable. The bottled water business in Mexico is booming. Mexico city has exhausted its current water resources, and nearby states with water problems of their own like Querétaro fear that the Federal District will draw down their own limited water resources. According to recent data, per capita water consumption is 180 liters per day in Paris and 360 liters per day in Mexico City. The difference can be attributed to lack of appropriate charges and leaks in the city's water network. The water pressure is so low that often water does not reach the storage tank on the roof of a two-story house. Any adequate solution to the water pipe situation will be very expensive. In addition to potable water problems, a relatively low percentage of Mexico's territory is economically arable. Irrigation is urgently needed in many areas. In Nayarit the Aguamilpa dam is close to completion. When it is completed, it will have a production capacity of 2 billion kilowatt hours per year and form a lake holding 5.95 billion cubic feet of water, which will make possible the irrigation of 185,325 acres of farmland. The cost will total approximately $756 million with 44 percent coming from the Federal Electric Commission, 30 percent from the World Bank, and 26 percent from private investors.

Finally, I would like to say a few words about the auto pollution situation. Magna Sin, the unleaded gas, is widely available throughout Mexico. All gas prices have been raised and Nova or leaded gas is now priced quite close to Magna to discourage use of Nova in systems designed for unleaded gas. Most, if not all, state capitals now have annual mandatory emissions testing, and the Federal District has biannual inspections.

Currently Mexico cannot produce enough unleaded gas to meet demand. Pemex recently acquired 50 percent of Shell Oil's Deer Park refinery on the Houston Ship Channel. The new partnership will allow Pemex to sell an average of 100,000 barrels a day of heavy Maya crude to the U.S. market and permit Shell to ship 45,000 barrels a day of unleaded gasoline to the Mexican market. Mexico is making a major effort to reduce automobile pollution.

Publications on ecology in Mexico come from four principal sources: federal, state, and municipal governments; universities and technical institutes; private ecological groups; and international organizations working in Mexico. Tamaulipas, Querétaro, and Estado de México are helpful examples of state-level ecology publications. In 1984 Tamaulipas, a border state and not a particularly rich one, drew up an ecology plan based on a municipio-level study conducted by the Secretaría de Ecología. Although never published, the reports are available in photocopy form along with a variety of pamphlets and other ephemera. The Secretaría de Ecología recently hired thirty young biologists and chemists and gave them six months of technical training concerning factory pollution, a good indication that at the state level Mexico is aware of the need for trained people in the ecology field and is doing something about it.

Querétaro is a small, relatively rich, and well-developed state, 200 kilometers from Mexico City. While in Querétaro a few months ago, I interviewed Heidi Thiel, president of the state's Association of Ecologists. The Directorio Verde published by SEDESOL lists 33 nongovernmental ecological organizations in Querétaro. While most are in the state capital, others are in San Juan del Río, Tequisquiapan, Cadereyta, Jalpa, Colón, and Amealco. The publications issued by these organizations would be classified as ephemera, designed for educational purposes and distributed gratis. The surprising development is that the Secretaría de Ecología of the state is co-publishing material with these nongovernmental organizations. The ecology groups focus on issues such as reforestation. One of the organizations, in Jurica, a suburb of Querétaro, is recycling paper, glass, aluminum, and biodegradable garbage and is developing a program to encourage factories to recycle on a much wider scale. The composting of biodegradable garbage is also about to move to the next step of producing and marketing organic fertilizer on a commercial scale. It should also be noted that INEA of Querétaro, the institute for adult education, has recently published a book on ecology in Querétaro. Heretofore literacy texts have been simple histories and the like.

Both the Universidad Autónoma de Querétaro and the Tecnológico now offer degrees in ecology and issue scholarly publications. The Secretaría de Ecología has published some five or six titles worthy of collecting. Additional studies have been completed; funds are needed to finance their publication.

The surprising aspect of the ecology movement in Querétaro is its momentum. Conferences are taking place; there is a one hour a week radio show devoted to ecology; speakers make presentations and distribute literature in primary and secondary schools.

The last example of state efforts in ecology is Estado de México. This state surrounds the Federal District on three sides. Its capital, Toluca, however, is located about 60 kilometers away over a range of mountains. The pass between the two is some 3000 meters high.

As in other states, there is a fairly large delegation of SEDESOL, the national organization. Some overlap occurs between SEDESOL and the Secretaría de Ecología, the state organization. A 62-page pamphlet explaining the organization and goals of the state organization was published in June 1992. In addition, the Consejo Consultivo de Protección al Ambiente del Estado de México, an organization of 135 nongovernmental organizations and individuals, primarily idealists, acts as a pressure point on the state government and as a conduit of information for the populace. Their first Informe describes their organization and work.

According to one of its members, the Consejo enjoys very cordial relations with the state government which, until recently, provided the organization with office space and financial assistance with the publication of the Informe. The more cynical or more knowledgeable among us might think this is a case of co-option, but I don't believe so. I believe that the state and the Consejo both know that if they don't do a lot fairly fast in the ecological field their state will become unlivable or, at the very least, an unpleasant and dangerous place to live.

The other noteworthy organization in Estado de México is the Centro Panamericano de Ecología Humana y Salud, an international organization associated with the World Health Organization. Located in Métepec, about 15 minutes by taxi from Toluca, the Centro has a library collection of between 15,000 and 18,000 monographs and serials and about 150 periodicals on health and ecology in Mexico and Latin America. The holdings are completely computerized and accessible through various databases. The Centro has issued over 100 publications which are, for the most part, very technical. It should also be mentioned that universities and technological institutes in Estado de México offer degree programs in ecology which are well advertised in posters.

The ecological situation in Mexico is desperate, but not now fatal. The Mexican government and much of the population realize that it is vital to their health and survival that they work vigorously to correct mistakes of the past and diligently to avoid them in the future. There is considerable internal pressure on the federal and state governments to make ecology a priority in policy planning, and some degree of awareness and cooperation on the part of industry and other developers. There is recognition of the built-in corruption and the large amounts of money involved. The situation is not conceptually different in the United States.

U.S. criticism of Mexico's environmental record is not helpful and seems to embody its own non-ecological agenda. In any case, it is viewed as insensitive and not appreciated in Mexico. The United States would do well to engage in joint projects on the border and technical and economic cooperation.

Lest I leave the impression that I am overly optimistic about the ecological situation in Mexico, I quote from a recent article in a Mexico City newspaper:

"Less than 10 percent of the toxic waste produced in Mexico is adequately treated or safely eliminated," the president of the National Council of Ecological Industrialists (Conieco) said Thursday. "Toxic waste treatment and disposal plants are the hot potato in the environmental industry," said Carlos Sandoval Olivera during a press conference at the Camino Real Hotel. "Everybody wants there to be toxic waste plants, but nobody wants to have them in their own backyard," he said. The only toxic waste disposal plant in the entire country is located in the northern state of Nuevo León.

9. Los compromisos de la Universidad de Guadalajara ante el desarrollo sustentable

Arturo Curiel Ballesteros

La educación ambiental y los problemas actuales

Son múltiples los problemas ambientales que en la actualidad enfrentamos y de una complejidad cada vez mayor. Si bien, los problemas de contaminación y de presión a los recursos naturales consecuencia de un crecimiento poblacional y del modelo de desarrollo vigente siguen siendo prioritarios en la escena mundial. Nuevas manifestaciones de crisis ambiental aparecen, como el adelgazamiento de la capa de ozono en la estratosfera, el cambio climático, los sorpresivos accidentes tecnológicos, y el daño crónico a la salud de algunos contaminantes, entre otros. Para dar respuesta a esta problemática planetaria, se ha identificado al medio ambiente como una dimensión necesaria del desarrollo, y a la educación como una de las estrategias para una gestión ambiental.

En Estocolmo, durante la Conferencia de las Naciones Unidas sobre el Medio Humano en 1972, la educación ambiental fue definida como un proceso que consiste en reconocer valores y aclarar conceptos, para comprender las interrelaciones entre el hombre, su cultura y su medio, fomentando aptitudes y actitudes a favor del medio ambiente, el natural y el modificado, esenciales para el bienestar de la humanidad. La educación ambiental, en su visión de Estocolmo, hace un llamado a una solidaridad entre países, a fin de impedir que la contaminación atraviese las fronteras, que se produzcan deformaciones nefastas en los intercambios comerciales y que surjan nuevos desequilibrios económicos y socioculturales.

Veinte años después, se realiza en Rio de Janeiro, la Conferencia de las Naciones Unidas sobre Medio Ambiente y el Desarrollo, donde se plantearon las Bases de Acción en un Programa de Medio Ambiente para el Siglo XXI (Agenda 21). El Capítulo 36 de la Agenda, se refiere al Fomento de la Educación, la Capacidad y la Conciencia, considerando tres objetivos principales:

1. Reorientación de la educación hacia el desarrollo sustentable
2. Aumento de la conciencia del público
3. Fomento de la capacitación.

Se reconoce que la educación, incluidas la enseñanza escolar, la toma de conciencia del público y la capacitación, es un proceso que permite que los seres humanos y las sociedades desarrollen plenamente su capacidad latente. La educación es fundamental para favorecer la participación pública efectiva en el proceso de adopción de decisiones. Para ser eficaz, la educación en materia de medio ambiente y desarrollo debe ocuparse de la dinámica del medio físico/biológico y del medio socioeconómico y el desarrollo humano (que podría comprender el desarrollo espiritual).

Educación ambiental y universidad

Desde la Conferencia Intergubernamental de Educación Ambiental de Tbilisi en 1977, se consideró que la participación de la universidad dentro de las estrategias de desarrollo de la educación ambiental, resulta fundamental en base a las potencialidades de este nivel de educación. Se señaló asimismo, que el reto de esta educación es de no incorporarla a los programas como una disciplina separada o un tema de estudio particular, sino como una dimensión que debe ser integrada en dichos programas, permitiendo tener una percepción integrada del medio ambiente y emprender una acción más racional y propia para responder a las necesidades sociales.

En la reunión de Bogotá de 1985, sobre Universidad y Medio Ambiente en América Latina y el Caribe se generó una carta sobre universidad y medio ambiente, donde se señala, que las universidades constituyen organismos vivos y actuantes, generadores y catalizadores de procesos integrados al cuerpo social, desde la actividad tradicional de producción y transmisión de conocimiento, hasta la práctica sistemática de transformación continua de la realidad.

La experiencia de la Universidad de Guadalajara

La Universidad de Guadalajara ha pasado por diversas experiencias de educación ambiental, desde una visión naturalista en los años 50, donde la botánica y la geografía generaron los primeros conocimientos sistematizados de los recursos naturales de nuestra región; hasta los tiempos actuales, en donde las tres funciones sustantivas se encuentran involucradas en una idea de medio ambiente como eje de problematización en el quehacer universitario. Para hacer frente a este reto, la Universidad de Guadalajara creó el 2 de octubre de 1990 un Comité Universitario de Ecología y Educación Ambiental, con los objetivos de:

1. Promover acciones concretas para desarrollar una cultura ambiental a partir de las funciones sustantivas de la universidad
2. Definir y dar a conocer la política universitaria sobre el medio ambiente
3. Promover hacia el interior de nuestra casa de estudios el desarrollo y coordinación de trabajos relacionados con el medio ambiente.

Algunas de las experiencias en educación ambiental de la Universidad de Guadalajara, se pueden citar en cada una de sus funciones sustantivas.

Investigación

La investigación ambiental en la Universidad de Guadalajara ha dejado de ser estática y segmentaria, para pasar a una etapa participativa, holística y de aportación crítica y científica en relación a problemáticas regionales concretas, asociadas a los principales temas de importancia mundial, como la biodiversidad, la ordenación territorial, la rehabilitación y restauración de ecosistemas, el control de la contaminación y lo referente a los análisis de impacto y riesgo ambiental. Al respecto, vale la pena remarcar dentro del desarrollo actual de proyectos, la investigación sobre riesgos ambientales en la zona metropolitana de Guadalajara, que es un proyecto que involucra doce dependencias universitarias, favoreciendo el trabajo interdisciplinario y el trabajo en equipo, y que aborda dentro del marco de la ordenación del territorio, la evaluación de riesgos naturales, así como la delimitación de riesgos tecnológicos que afecten a la salud de la población de forma aguda o crónica. También de importancia, son los proyectos referidos a la conservación de ecosistemas representativos del estado de Jalisco donde se realiza investigación permanente como parte de los programas de manejo. Tal es el caso de la Reserva de la Biosfera Sierra de Manantlán, sitio de máxima biodiversidad en el país, donde habita el maíz perene *(Zea diploperennis)*, como una de las 2,000 especies vegetales de la reserva. Otras áreas de trabajo permanente son el Bosque La Primavera, regulador hídrico-ambiental de la ciudad de Guadalajara, y símbolo del interés de protección de sus habitantes, que durante más de 30 años han demandado su conservación; el Lago de Chapala, que es el más grande de Mesoamérica; y las áreas de anidación de la Tortuga Marina, a donde llegan 4 de las 11 especies de tortuga que existen en el mundo.

Las investigaciones en el campo ambiental incluyen enfoques interdisciplinarios donde se relacionan desde estudios de ecología pura, hasta propuestas de reglamentos jurídico-administrativo a nivel estatal y municipal sustentados en el conocimiento cabal de la capacidad de sustentación de la tierra y de los procesos que podrían menoscabar o acrecentar su capacidad para sustentar la vida.

Docencia

Actualmente en el 65% de las licenciaturas y el 100% de los bachilleratos, se ha incorporado lo ambiental a la currícula. Se espera que durante el actual proceso de reforma, se incorpore la dimensión ambiental en todas las formaciones, haciendo énfasis en el impacto de las profesiones en el medio ambiente.

A nivel de posgrado, se han establecido diplomados sobre impacto y riesgo ambiental, ordenamiento territorio, control de la contaminación, manejo de áreas silvestres y gestión ambiental industrial.

Vale la pena resaltar que la Universidad de Guadalajara ha sido la sede durante tres años, de los cursos y talleres de interpretación ambiental, que se han formado especialistas a nivel nacional, con apoyo del Servicio de Parques Nacionales de Estados Unidos y la Secretaría de Desarrollo Social (antes SEDUE). Actualmente se realizan convenios con cinco universidades de los Estados Unidos y Canadá, para desarrollar programas de capacitación conjunta en el área ambiental.

Extensión

La educación ambiental en la Universidad de Guadalajara no sólo se realiza dentro de su comunidad, sino hacia la sociedad en general, a través de comunicaciones permanentes en la prensa y radio, foros sobre problemáticas identificadas por la sociedad y publicaciones periódicas. Sobresale el boletín de educación ambiental "E", que circula en toda Latinoamérica con el apoyo de la World Wildlife Fund, y la revista mexicana de educación ambiental, que próximamente saldrá con el apoyo del Instituto Nacional de Ecología.

La educación ambiental informal y abierta, se realiza cotidianamente en senderos establecidos por la Universidad de Guadalajara en áreas silvestres como Manantlán y La Primavera, y campamentos educativos donde se generan experiencias directas de niños, jóvenes y adultos, en programas de 2 a 15 días. Como mención especial, señalaremos el programa internacional de intercambio de jóvenes para la conservación, entre México y los Estados Unidos, cuya sede es la Universidad de Guadalajara, en convenio con SCA (Student Conservation Association) de los Estados Unidos.

Vale la pena destacar la realización de eventos sobre educación ambiental, entre los que destacan dos seminarios nacionales, y el Congreso Iberoamericano de Educación Ambiental, celebrado en noviembre de 1992, con apoyo del Programa de Naciones Unidas para el Medio Ambiente (PNUMA) y la UNESCO. Este trascendental evento reunió 500 congresistas de 25 países. Como parte de las conclusiones del congreso, se realizan actualmente acuerdos para integrar redes de formación ambiental para manejo de áreas silvestres, entre Costa Rica, México y los Estados Unidos, y con la Agencia de Cooperación Internacional de España para conformar una maestría de educación ambiental. Es de reconocerse, igualmente, la inducción a la participación comunitaria que se ha tenido en la universidad, en programas como el reciclado de papel.

Reflexiones finales

Los rasgos de la educación del mañana será una educación: científica, flexible, vitalista, activa, formativa, democrática y permanente. La práctica de la educación ambiental no debe de limitarse a la información ni a una área de conocimiento, sino a una sistematización de un método de acción que considere el descubrimiento, el conocimiento, la expresión, la crítica y la transformación del medio.

El ambiente va adquiriendo complejidad, y su comprensión requiere de un enfoque holístico y de acercamientos metodológicos que permitan aprender la convergencia de los diversos procesos que lo constituyen. La universidad debe de afrontar el reto de mantener una postura crítica y propositiva y formar gente capaz, no sólo para desempeñar un trabajo, sino ir articulando una realidad que permita un desarrollo sin comprometer el futuro de las generaciones venideras.

Estamos así, inmersos en una propuesta de valores que a su vez supone una modificación de actitudes, entre las que aparecen la responsabilidad, la solidaridad, el uso racional de recursos y la creatividad, con la práctica de la participación, la toma de decisiones, y el ejercicio del espíritu crítico. La formulación de una nueva cultura ambiental, que integre y relacione a la cultura urbana con una cultura de prevención y una cultura de la vida, se constituye en un principio actual de nuestra universidad.

La Universidad de Guadalajara tiene como misión el estudio de los problemas que atañen a la convivencia nacional, y en estos momentos, no puede haber una de mayor relevancia, que los problemas ambientales. El derecho a un ambiente sano y la obligación de conservarlo y aprovecharlo racionalmente, como una prerrogativa irrenunciable e indispensable para el adecuado desarrollo de la sociedad y la coexistencia de las personas.

10. Grupos ecológicos de Chile: Estado del arte

Marta Domínguez D.

En Chile las actividades económicas más dinámicas y rentables durante los últimos diez años, se han centrado especialmente en las zonas agrícolas, forestales y pesqueras, las que junto a su crecimiento, han quedado expuestas a un alto riesgo de impacto ambiental: pobreza y empobrecimiento de su población, contaminación de los ambientes físicos (aire, suelo y agua) y depredación de importantes recursos naturales. Se alade a ésto, la desprotección jurídica del medio ambiente que existe en Chile, hecho que se traduce en estas transgresiones. Esta situación ha provocado una creciente conciencia ciudadana de preservación del medio ambiente como condición indispensable para su sobrevivencia y ha generado la formación espontánea de grupos ecológicos locales que reaccionan ante la amenaza de deterioro de su componente ambiental físico y socio-cultural.

Así, hoy la ecología ha dejado de ser solamente una cuestión de especialistas profesionales e investigadores que debaten el problema en foros, seminarios, simposios, para transformarse en una cuestión social y en la movilización de grupos de pobladores, campesinos, mujeres, etnias indígenas y juventudes.

La revista recientemente editada por el Instituto de Ecología Política, titulada *En Movimiento: Boletín para los Consejos Ecológicos Comunales y el Movimiento Social*, editorializa:

> Existen numerosas experiencias de comunidades locales que se organizan en torno a exigir el fin de la contaminación de su medio ambiente, el cual es agredido por empresas que lo contaminan y sobreexplotan sus recursos naturales, o por el Estado que instala basurales, modifica los planos reguladores en beneficio de empresas y grupos de interés económico. . . . Reciente es el caso de la comuna de Huasco en la que campesinos y pescadores artesanales, presentaron un recurso de protección y ganaron el juicio en contra de la empresa CMP (Planta Productora de Acero Refinado), porque los residuos que generaba contaminaban sus costas afectando la producción del ecosistema.

Hay varios ejemplos más en el país: Ventana, donde funcionan las empresas ENAP (Empresa Nacional de Petróleo) y ENERSIS (Filial de CHILECTRA, Compañía Chilena de Electricidad); Talcahuano (fábricas de harina de pescado); Calama (mineral de cobre de Chuquicamata); Peumo (pesticidas); Estación Central (vertedero de basuras Lo Errázuriz); Pirque (Compañía Manufacturera de Papeles y Cartones); Maipo (Cemento Melón). En todos ellos intervienen grupos ciudadanos llamados Consejos Ecológicos Comunales (CECs), que luchan por sus derechos estableciendo nuevas relaciones con el Estado y las empresas, exigiendo ser escuchados y valorados como actores sociales válidos que merecen ser considerados en la toma de decisiones.

Para realizar este trabajo, se envió una carta circular a todos los grupos afiliados a la Red Nacional de Acción Ecológica (RENACE), la que, como explicamos más adelante, sigue siendo, junto al CIPMA (Centro de Investigación y Planificación del Medio Ambiente) y el Instituto de Ecología Política, la instancia de mayor significación en el campo de la investigación ecológica. La respuesta fue muy débil, de lo que se puede concluir que la literatura producida por los grupos es casi nula. Su labor es más de acción que de información. La literatura adicional que se conoce está compuesta de boletines, cartillas, prospectos, ocasionalmente artículos o inserciones en los periódicos, y la acción se realiza a través de talleres, encuentros, campañas, debates y convocatorias. Podemos deducir fácilmente que la escasez de literatura e información se debe a razones de financiamiento, pues continúan siendo los centros de investigación con respaldo de agencias de apoyo extranjeras, las realizan la investigación propiamente tal, y de estas investigaciones se informan los grupos locales para su acción.

Señalo a continuación los grupos ecológicos que efectúan acciones de defensa de su entorno ecológico, que alcanzan conocimiento nacional, pues la mayoría de ellos actúa casi en el anonimato.

De la publicación de CIPMA, "Las organizaciones no gubernamentales y el medio ambiente en los años '80: Una muestra itinerante", 1991, hemos extraído información que coincide con nuestro objetivo de dar a conocer "Grupos Ecológicos" que emergen de asentamientos humanos ubicados en zonas de pobreza crítica. Todas estas experiencias comparten una visión global inspirada en la acción local, hecho que ha sido escasamente reconocido dentro de la economía formal y por la ciencia institucionalizada que incluye las disciplinas dedicadas al medio ambiente. Durante la década de los '80, mientras las ONGs (Organizaciones No Gubernamentales) realizaban acciones de mejoramiento ambiental local en una especie de anonimato, la actividad científico-profesional sobre el medio ambiente estaba restringida a los diagnósticos y a la denuncia, escribe el CIPMA en la introducción de su publicación.

Podemos definir los grupos ecológicos por interés en su defensa.

Defensa del agua

1. El Grupo Red de Mujeres por la Tierra se moviliza en defensa de los ríos. Del río Maipo por construcción de calichera que contamina la fuente del 10% de agua que consume Santiago, la capital.

2. GABB (Grupo de Acción por el Bio-Bío). Lo defienden con encono contra los proyectos de ENDESA (Empresa Nacional de Electricidad), de construir seis represas entre ellas, la gran represa Pangue, en la zona del Alto Bio-Bío, destruyendo con ello el ecosistema de la etnia pehuenche.

3. Centro Mapuche Pehuenche del Alto Bio-Bío. Destacamos una inserción que habla de esta lucha: "Detengamos la construcción de represas en el Bio-Bío. ¿Por qué precipitarnos a destruir el patrimonio natural y cultural de Chile antes de que el Parlamento apruebe la Ley Ambiental? (*El Mercurio*, 13 de diciembre, 1992), firmado por Instituto de Ecología Política, Centro Mapuche-Pehuenche de Alto Bio-Bío, Centro de Alternativas de Desarrollo (CEPAUR), Comité Nacional Pro Defensa de la Flora y Fauna (CODEFF), RENACE, Centro El Canelo de Nos, Casa de la Paz y GABB.

4. Agrupación Pro Defensa del Laja. Mesas redondas de estudio sobre las consecuencias ecológicas de posibles instalaciones hidroeléctricas.

5. Grupo de Defensa de Salto del Petrohué en Parque Nacional Vicente Pérez Rosales, ante la amenaza de instalaciones hidroeléctricas.

6. Oficina de Greenpeace en Santiago de Chile. Grupo ecologista que comienza en 1993 y cuya oficina en Santiago será Regional del Pacífico Sur/Andes (Chile, Perú y Ecuador). Sara Larraín, representante en Chile, asevera que el 60% del presupuesto se asignará a investigaciones científicas para detectar problemas, determinar las causas y buscar las soluciones, a través de campañas y propuestas a los gobiernos, movilizaciones de presión por tóxicos, defensa de la ecología marina, la Antártida y los recursos forestales. En Chile se preocupará preferentemente de la contaminación oceánica y atmosférica. Ello significa, fauna costera, pesca, caza de cetáceos, lo que le significará lucha con los empresarios pesqueros y búsqueda de alternativas energéticas limpias y renovables. Desde su funcionamiento en Santiago, en público acude espontáneamente a inscribirse. Ha realizado ya acciones conjuntas con grupos chilenos frente a la amenaza de que el barco Akatsuki Maru que transportaba dos toneladas de plutonio, surcara aguas chilenas.

Defensa del bosque nativo

1. CONAF (Corporación Nacional Forestal) es un organismo dependiente del Ministerio de Agricultura, creado en 1973. Su rol consiste

en conservar, proteger e incrementar los recursos naturales del país, elaborar un catastro sobre ellos y ejercer la función administrativa sobre el patrimonio forestal del estado. Sus publicaciones incluyen boletines, guías de reconocimiento de plagas y arqueológicas, directorios, boletines bibliográficos, manuales, cartillas y las revistas *Chile Forestal* y *Chilean Forestry News*, ambas sobre el sector forestal chileno.

2. CODEFF (Comité Nacional Pro Defensa de la Flora y Fauna, Amigos de la Tierra), organización independiente permanentemente preocupada por la problemática ambiental, nos plantea a través de su documento *El futuro del bosque nativo chileno: Un desafío de hoy* (octubre 1992), su preocupación de que continúa el proceso de concentración de la propiedad de grandes superficies de bosque nativo (5 empresas poseen 162.800 de las 364.647 hectáreas). Su línea de publicaciones incluye documentos, textos y publicaciones periódicas como *Eco Tribuna*.

3. Comunidad de Quinquén, por la defensa de la tala indiscriminada del bosque nativo y sobre todo de la Araucaria de Chile. Este grupo, con una persistente acción, logró que la Araucaria fuera declarada Monumento Nacional.

4. Amigos del Pehuén, por la defensa de la Araucaria o Pehuén, árbol de cuyo fruto, el piñón, se alimenta la etnia indígena y en cuyo entorno coexisten.

5. Movimiento Ecológico Araucaria, Universidad de Concepción, Facultad de Ciencias Biológicas y Recursos Naturales, realiza también acciones en torno a la defensa de la Araucaria. La situación que afecta a la *Araucaria araucana* o Pehuén, es de particular gravedad, tratándose de una especie catalogada en situación de vulnerabilidad, declarada Monumento Nacional y de gran significancia para la comunidad indígena mapuche pehuenche, en su alimentación, religión y cultura. Su tala desconoce el derecho ancestral que poseen los indígenas con respecto a esta especie arbórea.

6. La Comisión Relacionadora de ONGs de la Novena Región, grupo independiente, organizó un encuentro en Temuco, el 27 de septiembre de 1991, cuyas ponencias están incluidas en la publicación *Pueblo mapuche y medio ambiente y organizaciones no gubernamentales ONGs* (1991). En el encuentro se dio a conocer que uno de los problemas principales del debate público en esta región, es la penetración de los bosques de pino y su impacto en la situación mapuche muy ligado al problema ambiental provocado por la industria forestal, a consecuencia de lo cual, nacen los movimientos indígenas integrados a la Coordinadora Indianista (CONACIN), a la Comisión Especial de Pueblos Mapuches (CEPI), y a la Organización Lonko Kilapán de Temuco, Chile.

Defensa de la tierra

1. Consejo de Todas las Tierras, organización mapuche que lucha por la recuperación de las tierras usurpadas a las comunidades mapuches, junto al CEPI y a la Organización Lonko Kilapán.

Defensa de la naturaleza en general

1. Foro Chileno de Organizaciones No Gubernamentales. En marzo de 1991, realizó en Ciudad de México una reunión paralela a la Reunión Ministerial Regional Preparatoria de la Conferencia de Naciones Unidas sobre Medio Ambiente y Desarrollo (UNCED), convocada por la CEPAL (Comisión Económica de las Naciones Unidas para América Latina y el Caribe), a la que asistieron tres organizaciones no gubernamentales chilenas: la Comisión Chilena de Derechos Humanos, el Instituto de Ecología Política y el Comité Nacional Pro Defensa de la Flora y Fauna. En este encuentro surgió la iniciativa de estructurar una instancia coordinadora que permitiera reforzar el planteamiento de la sociedad civil y de las ONGs chilenas en el marco del proceso preparatorio de la UNCED. Así quedó estructurado en 1991 el Foro Chileno de Organizaciones No Gubernamentales, cuya secretaría ejecutiva quedó en CODEFF.

En la publicación *Informe Nacional del Foro Chileno de Organizaciones No Gubernamentales*, se expresa el punto de vista respecto a la realidad chilena de más de treinta organizaciones, que dentro del Foro, reflexionan, discuten y trabajan en forma conjunta sobre los temas del medio ambiente y su vinculación profunda con el desarrollo.

2. Foro Global, paralelo a la Cumbre Oficial de Río de Janeiro '92, propone: "Trabajar para la implementación de los Tratados Internacionales, Convenciones, Leyes Nacionales y Locales, Códigos de Conducta sobre Medio Ambiente que puedan asegurar la participación de las ONGs en la Comisión de N.U. para el desarrollo Sustentable y en los programas de orientación para obtener un equilibrio entre el Norte y el Sur" (Thijs de la Court, "El Desafío Ecológico de los '90").

3. Grupo Verde, grupo independiente, compuesto por cinco parlamentarios de la XI Región de Aysén empeñados en defender la naturaleza del territorio, en una coalición suprapartidaria de análisis o acción, como se dio en debate frente a la debilitación de la capa de ozono y el hacinamiento de las ciudades. Trabajaron también en la fiscalización para prohibir el paso de carga radioactiva como el plutonio, la restricción del empleo de hormonas en la ganadería y la fiscalización para mejorar y resolver los problemas ambientales de la zona. Están: Vladislav Kusmicic (Partido Socialista); Víctor Barrueto (Partido por la Democracia); Jaime Orpis (Unión Demócrata Independiente); Baldo Prokurica (Renovación Nacional); y Antonio Horvath (Independiente).

4. Casa de la Paz. Entidad que realiza la campaña "Santiago Como Vamos '93", para despertar conciencia sobre la contaminación del aire en Santiago, por emanaciones tóxicas.

5. Movimiento Juvenil de Acción Ecológica Generación Alternativa. Realizan acciones y campañas tales como "Jornada de Ayuda a los Pehuenches y Mensaje Medioambiental", campaña en bicicleta hacia el sur de Chile, junto a jóvenes de Estados Unidos, Bolivia, Uruguay e Islas Canarias, llamada "Ecocicletada Latinoamericana", demostrando que la bicicleta constituye un medio de transporte no contaminante; promueven la construcción de ciclovías en zonas urbanas y carreteras. En Ralco, pequeña ciudad sureña, punto de llegada de los ciclistas, construyeron una sede social para el pueblo pehuenche.

6. RENACE (Red Nacional de Acción Ecológica), que acoge a 61 grupos, es un organismo no-gubernamental creado en 1987 para vincular a grupos, personas y organizaciones que han decidido coordinarse para intercambiar información y experiencias; contribuir a su capacitación; promover la realización de acciones comunes que contribuyan a la solución de los problemas ambientales que aquejan a Chile; incentivar el desarrollo de una sociedad ecológica en Chile. En la Red participan comités ciudadanos, centros académicos, grupos poblacionales, centros culturales, organismos de la mujer y colectivos de arte y comunicación. RENACE edita la revista mensual *Ecoprensa*, que comenzó a circular en 1989, y cuya finalidad es informar sobre todo lo que ocurre en relación al medio ambiente en Chile y el mundo.

7. CIPMA (Centro de Investigación y Planificación del Medio Ambiente), corporación académica creada en 1979 por iniciativa de un grupo de investigadores. Su línea de acción consiste en la promoción de un concepto de desarrollo que compatibilice el crecimiento económico y la equidad social con la conservación ambiental. CIPMA ha organizado hasta la fecha cuatro encuentros científicos, de los que ya ha publicado el informe final con los resultados. Entre sus publicaciones recientes, se tiene *Gestión ambiental en Chile* (octubre 1992); *Aportes al 4º Encuentro Científico sobre el Medio Ambiente*, que CIPMA realizó en mayo en Valdivia; *Santiago, diálogo en torno a la descontaminación del aire* (noviembre 1992), que difunde los temas tratados en el seminario sobre descontaminación atmosférica de Santiago, realizado por CIPMA en agosto 1992; *Bases para una ley general del medio ambiente en Chile* (1993) aporte el proceso de elaboración de una ley general del medio ambiente auspiciada por el gobierno. Además, publica la revista *Ambiente y Desarrollo* trimestralmente y los boletines informativos *Ambiente Ahora* y *PrensAmbiental.* Se encuentra preparando Dirper 1993, *Directorio de personas vinculadas al medio ambiente*, incluyendo a los funcionarios del nuevo régimen. CIPMA

es el nodo central de la Red Regional de Información sobre Medio Ambiente (REDMA) al que ya se han incorporado un nodo de la VIII Región que tendrá sede en el Centro EULA-Chile, en la Universidad de Concepción; la Universidad Católica del Norte, sede Coquimbo que se ha integrado como Centro Cooperativo al nodo de la Universidad de La Serena; nodo de la Universidad de Tarapacá; nodo de la Universidad de Atacama; nodo de la Universidad de Los Lagos.

Defensa de la calidad de vida

1. CECs (Comités Ecológicos Comunales) realizan acciones en demanda por mejorar la calidad de vida en sus territorios de barrio y comunas, y ya llevan dos años intercambiando ideas y experiencias.

2. Centro "Común y Silvestre" y "El Alter de San Bernardo" se han unido para dar vida al "Centro Juvenil Alternativo", un organismo que pretende acoger las inquietudes de los diferentes grupos de jóvenes que ven en la ecología "algo más que plantar un arbolito", como dicen ellos "un modo de vida".

Los partidos políticos también asumen su compromiso con la defensa de la calidad de vida de los chilenos.

1. Comisión de Medio Ambiente del PC, publica continuamente artículos en el diario *El Siglo*, tales como "La ecología en la vida cotidiana", "Impacto del smog", "Contaminación de alimentos, aguas y suelos"; planteó una plataforma de 16 puntos englobados en *Hacer Santiago una ciudad respirable*, a través de: saneamiento básico para todos el año 2000 (desrratizar Santiago); garantizar la seguridad ciudadana (más luz); convertir basurales, en parques y jardines; por derecho al descanso del trabajador, eliminar los ruidos molestos; por la cultura popular en las comunas (teatro, cine, museo, biblioteca, multicancha); por un ambiente vecinal humanizado (sin alcoholismo, sin brutalidad, sin miseria); convoca a movilización de protesta por el vertedero de basura "Lo Errázuriz"; la represa de Pangue (Alto Bio-Bió, por ENDESA); la devastación de los bosques magallánicos para transformarlos en astillas; por las 60.000 hectáreas de la Región Metropolitana destinadas a la provisión de hortalizas al país de las cuales 50.000 son regadas con aguas servidas.

2. Comisión de Medio Ambiente y Ecología del P.P.D. publicó *Medio ambiente y municipio* (1992), una guía dirigida a los candidatos a concejales y alcaldes por el rol que les cabe como representantes de las comunas.

3. Partido Humanista Verde efectuó una protesta frente a la embajada de Japón en Santiago por tránsito del Akatsuki Maru en aguas chilenas y realiza campañas de plantación de árboles a lo largo del país.

Defensa de la educación ambiental

Distintas instituciones están incorporando la educación ambiental en el país. En el Ministerio de Educación hay un equipo trabajando en la incorporación del tema del medio ambiente en los programas curriculares de la enseñanza básica y media.

En el plano de la enseñanza superior, existen programas de pregrado de post-título y post-grado de algunas universidades como la Pontificia Universidad Católica de Chile con el Programa de Magister en Asentamientos Humanos y Medio Ambiente, del Instituto de Estudios Urbanos; estudio de temas ambientales en el Departamento de Ecología de la Facultad de Ciencias Biológicas; desarrollo de estudios ambientales en el Departamento de Ingeniería Hidráulica de la Facultad de Ingeniería. La Universidad de Santiago de Chile con el Programa de Post-Título en Gestión Ambiental. Además en esta universidad existe el Area Ambiente dentro del Departamento de Ingeniería Geográfica de la Facultad de Ingeniería. Importante es el Proyecto EULA/Universidad de Concepción con el Doctorado en Gestión Ambiental. La Universidad Central cuenta con una Escuela de Ecología y Paisajismo, dentro de la Facultad de Arquitectura y Bellas Artes. La Universidad de la Frontera constituyó recientemente un Comité de Ciencias Ambientales formado por varios departamentos y dirigido por la Facultad de Ingeniería. El Instituto Nacional de Capacitación (INACAP) tiene la carrera de Ingeniería de Ejecución en Ordenamiento Ambiental. La Universidad Bolivariana imparte carreras en cuyos programas se incorpora la temática ambiental.

Cabe señalar también que la mayor parte de las Federaciones de Estudiantes de la Enseñanza Superior y Media, organizan jornadas y semanas universitarias en las cuales el tema de convocación ha sido el medio ambiente. El Comité Ecológico del Liceo Oscar Castro de la ciudad de Rancagua efectúa una Campaña de Recuperación de la Basura y Limpieza de Basurales en las poblaciones, en el marco de su Programa de Recuperación de Desechos, con gran éxito.

Siempre en el ámbito de educación ecológica destaca CONCIENCIA 21, que es una institución al servicio de las personas para capacitarlas e informarlas en temas de desarrollo ciudadano y organizacional, colocando énfasis en sus relaciones con el medio ambiente e incentivando su participación tanto en la toma de decisiones como en la acción misma. CONCIENCIA 21 tiene un alcance territorial que cubre las ocho regiones de mayor densidad poblacional del país, con un equipo de educadores y profesionales de alto nivel. Sus objetivos principales son: investigar, educar, asesorar y difundir acerca de los siguientes aspectos: la realidad medioambiental a nivel local, nacional y global; la conservación y cuidado del medio ambiente: aire, agua y tierra; conductas que contribuyan a crear un estilo de vida, de respeto y protección del medio ambiente; iniciativas para lograr la participación de las personas en actividades que ayuden a la protección del entorno, creen hábitos y generen labores comunitarias, tales como reciclaje, arborización y limpieza; proyectos de educación y capacitación en materias medioambientales y capacitación de líderes en la toma de decisiones. Para lograr estos objetivos, ofrece charlas, talleres, cursos, seminarios, proyectos juveniles, campañas, encuestas, foros, eventos. Todo ello, con el ánimo de producir un cambio en la mentalidad de las personas en lo que se refiere a la protección de su medio.

Mención aparte cabe para el Instituto de Ecología Política (IEP), organización no-gubernamental creada en 1987 para contribuir a la elaboración de un proyecto de desarrollo de una sociedad ecológica. Es institución independiente no alineada, que realiza una amplia labor mediante sus programas e investigaciones. Para el área juvenil, los Programas Eco-Fondo y Parlamento Escolar; para la ciudadanía, el Programa 25 Comunas por el Medio Ambiente y el área Internacional Brasil '92. Entre sus recientes publicaciones destaca la revista *En Movimiento*, boletín para los Consejos Ecológicos Comunales y el Movimiento Social; el *Ecomanual del reciclaje comunitario: Reciclando nuestro presente* (1992); el documento *Por una iniciativa de los pueblos de América: Análisis y propuestas alternativas a la Iniciativa para las Américas, del gobierno estadounidense* (1992); y el libro *El desafío ecológico de los '90* (1991; 1ª ed. en español); y algunos posters ecológicos. Participa apoyando todos los movimientos de defensa del medio ambiente del país. Durante la segunda quincena de enero de 1993, realizó el Segundo Encuentro Nacional de los Consejos Ecológicos Comunales, convocado por el Programa de Ecología y Participación del IEP. El Encuentro se realizó en conjunto con la reunión anual de RENACE. Estos grupos están siendo los más activos a nivel local, actualmente.

CEAAL (Consejo de Educación de Adultos para América Latina), como organización latinoamericana, está adherida a la Red de Educación Popular Ambiental, cuyo nodo central funciona en México. La Red edita el boletín *Pachamama*, de educación ambiental. El CEAAL tiene la publicación periódica *La Carta* que en su edición de julio-agosto 1992 incluye el texto completo del "Tratado de Educación Ambiental para Sociedades Sustentables y Responsabilidad Global", postulado de la Cumbre de Río, 1992.

El CODEFF también ha inaugurado un programa de educación con grupos escolares, que se desarrolla a través de juegos y dibujos ecológicos.

Defensa del desarme

El Comité Chileno por el Desarme y la Desnuclearización junto con el IEP y varios grupos ecologistas elevaron su protesta por el transporte de plutonio en barco japonés Akatsuki Maru, con 1,7 toneladas reprocesadas que surcaría aguas chilenas.

Defensa de la geosfera biosfera

El Comité Nacional para el Programa Internacional de la Geosfera Biosfera: Cambio Global (IGBP) fue creado en 1988 dependiente del Consejo Nacional de Uniones Científicas y apoyado por la CONICYT y coordinado por Humberto Fuenzalida, Director del Departamento de Geofísica de la Universidad de Chile, quien elaboró el documento "Cambio global del clima y sus eventuales efectos en Chile", para trabajar en forma más coordinada en el problema del calentamiento del planeta y sus consecuencias.

Defensa de la seguridad nacional

Para otro tema que está hoy en el centro del debate en el país, que es la seguridad de las personas, citaremos palabras de manuel Baquedano, presidente del Instituto de Ecología Política, quien reconstruye el concepto "Seguridad Nacional" y afirma:

> La seguridad se logra buscando relaciones armoniosas con el medio ambiente. El desafío de construir sociedades justas, dignas y seguras pasa por el respeto y redefinición de la relación hombre-naturaleza es decir la reconstrucción o mantenimiento de los ecosistemas naturales en una situación no contradictoria con los sistemas artificiales que crea el hombre. . . . El modelo económico neo liberal atenta contra el equilibrio. En un mundo finito, con recursos finitos, con problemas ambientales que hacen más escasos los recursos, se sigue con la lógica del crecimiento ilimitado. Es una contradicción que puede llevar a grandes conflictos. . . . La tarea de los ecologistas es también revolucionaria, ayudando a preparar los cambios radicales necesarios de la sociedad para enfrentar la amenaza ambiental. . . . La conciencia ambiental chilena es una conciencia que podríamos llamar "ingenua", se asocia "ecología" con no botar basura a la calle y plantar árboles. . . . Sociedad que despilfarra recursos va destruyendo su medio ambiente.

Area de gobierno

Con la recuperación democrática en Chile, el gobierno tomó una seria postura frente a los problemas ambientales del país, implementando una estrategia de crecimiento con equidad en la que comprometió, tanto a la ciudadanía, como a las instancias gubernamentales. Ahora está intentando plasmar su programa de mejoramiento ambiental en políticas concretas. Se ha puesto en marcha un conjunto de iniciativas legislativas que buscan crear un marco jurídico e institucional moderno que permita enfrentar los problemas ambientales armonizando los requerimientos del desarrollo con los de la preservación ambiental. Cabe destacar la Ley de Pesca, promulgada en 1991, el Proyecto de Ley de Bosque Nativo, el Proyecto de

Ley de Bases del Medio Ambiente ya presentados al Parlamento, y las Declaraciones de Monumentos Nacionales de algunos recursos en vías de extinción. A la fecha, existen dos proyectos de ley sobre política nacional ambiental ya presentados al Congreso, que corresponden al del partido Renovación Nacional conocido como el "Proyecto Piñera" y el de la Democracia Cristiana, conocido como "Proyecto Frei".

En el ámbito del Parlamento se han formado las Comisiones de Medio Ambiente del Senado y de la Cámara de Diputados. El diputado Gutemberg Martínez Ocamica, Presidente de la Comisión de Recursos Naturales, Bienes Nacionales y Medio Ambiente de la Cámara de Diputados, ha publicado el libro *Contaminación de Santiago* (1993), como resultado de la investigación de la Comisión que preside. También existe la Comisión Especial de Descontaminación de la Región Metropolitana, cuyo rol es enfrentar los problemas de contaminación atmosférica, hídrica, por residuos sólidos y acústica, plano en el que se han establecido medidas y sanciones drásticas. Su reciente "Balance 1992 y Programa 1993" (enero de 1993) y "Cuestionario sobre Descontaminación" (1993) dan cuenta de su trabajo al respecto.

El Ministerio de Transporte ha efectuado un ordenamiento y regulación general del transporte metropolitana que puede apreciarse en la *Guía de licitaciones de recorridos en la Región Metropolitana*, publicada por una empresa particular en convenio con el Ministerio. A su vez la Comisión Nacional del Medio Ambiente (CONAMA), que se extiende a nivel nacional, dependiente del Ministerio Secretaría General de Gobierno y cuyo rol es dictar las políticas nacionales, la legislación y la institucionalidad en el plano del medio ambiente, presentó un *Informe nacional a la Conferencia de las Naciones Unidas sobre Medio Ambiente y Desarrollo*, la llamada "Cumbre de la Tierra" (junio de 1992 Río de Janeiro), desplegado en tres puntos: I. Las tendencias del desarrollo y sus repercusiones en el medio ambiente; II. Las respuestas aplicadas a los asuntos relativos al medio ambiente y al desarrollo; III. Hacia el fortalecimiento de la gestión ambiental en Chile como una nueva función del Estado. También en 1992 CONAMA publicó *Repertorio de la legislación e relevancia ambiental vigente en Chile*, que permite una expedita identificación de la normativa jurídica aplicable a las diversas cuestiones y problemas regulados por el derecho chileno.

También apoyan esta labor del gobierno, las unidades ambientales de los ministerios, enfrentando los problemas de sus respectivos sectores, como ya lo vimos en el caso del Ministerio de Educación, de Transporte y Secretaría General de Gobierno. El Ministerio de Planificación y Cooperación (MIDEPLAN) tiene el control de los estudios de impacto ambiental que se está exigiendo a los proyectos de inversión. Su publicación, a dos años del gobierno de Aylwin, *Avanzando en equidad, proceso de integración al desarrollo, 1990-1992*, representa el balance de los avances alcanzados a través de la estrategia de desarrollo basada en el crecimiento y en la equidad. Según ellos, el balance es alentador.

Ocurre eso sí que la labor de estas instancias es más de acción que de investigación, de modo que más que nada se traduce en campañas de concientización, recomendaciones y eventos.

Turismo ecológico

La Corporación Nacional Forestal (CONAF) de la IX Región de Chile, en coordinación con SNASPE (Sistema Nacional de Areas Silvestres Protegidas del Estado), dispone para licitar, de 15.000 hectáreas de áreas naturales para turismo ecológico, con volcanes, lagunas, bosques nativos, ríos, cascadas, flora y fauna protegida en los parques nacionales.

Area internacional

Programa de Desarrollo y Medio Ambiente de las Naciones Unidas (PNUMA) realiza proyectos conjuntos con CEPAL.

PAN (Chile, Pesticide Action Network) funciona en la Casa de la Paz, de Santiago de Chile y recientemente publicó su primera cartilla, "Mujeres . . . Ojo con los Pesticidas", advirtiendo del daño que ellos causan a la salud y a la natalidad, por deformaciones congénitas.

Otros grupos

1. Agrupación de Periodistas del Medio Ambiente (APMA)
2. Grupos cuyo trabajo pasa inadvertido por ahora, como el de la Iglesia chilena.

No quisiera terminar sin aludir a la campaña presidencial de un candidato ecologista, el Premio Nobel Alternativo de Economía, Manfred Max-Neef, a quien sus seguidores llaman "el vocero de los temas ausentes", refiriéndose, entre otros, al tema de la ecología y el medio ambiente.

A nivel empresarial se destaca el Programa del Departamento de Medio Ambiente de la Sociedad de Fomento Fabril para capacitación en gestión ambiental, que desarrolla desde hace dos años con el apoyo de la Fundación Carl Duisberg.

11. Bibliografía chilena sobre ecología, 1989-1993

Marta Domínguez D.

Aceituno, Patricio, et al. *Congreso Ibero-Americano del Medio Ambiente Atmosférico, I.* Congresso Ibero-Americano do Meio Ambiente Atmosférico, I. Ibero American Conference on the Atmospheric Environment, I. Enero/Janeiro/January 7-11, 1991, Santiago de Chile. Abstracts. Universidad de Santiago de Chile, 1991.

Alvaray, Rodrigo, y Gustavo Marín. *Pueblo mapuche, medio ambiente y organizaciones no gubernamentales (ONGs).* Encuentro organizado por la Comisión Relacionadora de ONGs de la Novena Región de Chile, en Temuco el 27 de Septiembre 1991. Temuco, Chile, 1992.

Beer, Wendoline de, y César Padilla. *Desechos tóxicos domésticos.* RENACE, Red Nacional de Acción Ecológica. Santiago, 1991.

Boutros, Boutros-Ghali. *Paz, desarrollo medio ambiente.* Santiago: NU, CEPAL, 1992.

Cerda C., Rodrigo, Andrea Leiva, y Pablo Escobar. *Ecomanual del reciclaje comunitario: Reciclando nuestro presente.* Santiago: Instituto de Ecología Política, 1992.

Centro de Investigaciones de la Realidad del Norte (CREAR). *Tecnología y Ecología.* Iquique, Chile, 1989.

Centro de Investigaciones del Medio Ambiente (CIPMA). *Directorio de personas vinculadas al tema del medio ambiente en Chile.* Santiago, 1991.

———. *Santiago: Diálogo en torno a la descontaminación del aire.* Santiago, 1993.

Cereceda Troncoso, Pilar, y Ana María Errázuriz Körner. *Ecogeografía: Nueva geografía de Chile.* Santiago: Zig Zag, 1991.

Comisión Nacional de Investigación Científica y Tecnológica (CONICYT). *Cambio global: Un desafío para Chile. Chile en las fronteras de la ciencia.* Santiago, 1992.

Court, Thijs de la. *El desafío ecológico de los '90.*

Domínguez Díaz, Marta, comp. *El medio ambiente en Chile hoy: Informe y bibliografía.* Santiago: SEREC, 1991.

Echeverría V., Cristián. *La contaminación atmosférica en la ciudad de Santiago*. Cuaderno de Economía, no. 88. Instituto de Economía, Pontificia Universidad Católica de Chile, 1992.

FAO. *Conferencia Internacional para América Latina y El Caribe, 21a: Santiago de Chile, 9 al 13 de julio, 1990. Desarrollo rural sostenible en ecosistemas frágiles en América Latina y el Caribe*. Santiago, 1990.

Favero, Gabriel del, y Miguel González Pino. *Aportes a la discusión del Proyecto de Ley de Bases del Medio Ambiente*. Santiago: Centro de Estudios Públicos, CEP, 1993.

Gómez-Lobo, Andrés. *La Iniciativa para las Américas: Acuerdos de libre comercio y el medio ambiente*. Santiago: FLACSO/CIEPLAN, 1992.

González, Tomás, Monseñor. *Proteger y conservar la naturaleza creada por Dios*. Santiago: Ediciones Paulinas, 1992.

ILADES/PET. *Encuentro "El Desarrollo Sustentable: Desafíos para la Equidad"*, 4 y 5 de abril 1991.

Instituto Nacional de Estadísticas (INE), Departamento de Energía y Medio Ambiente. *Estadísticas del medio ambiente 1986-1990*. Santiago, 1991.

Liendo P., Oscar. *Contaminación hídrica en la cuenca de Santiago*. Santiago, 1991.

López B., Jorge, et al. *Bases para una Ley General del Medio Ambiente en Chile*. Santiago: CIPMA, 1993.

Martínez O., Gutemberg. *Contaminación en Santiago*. Santiago: Editorial Atena, 1993.

Ministerio de Hacienda/Ministerio Secretaría General de Gobierno. *Crecimiento con equidad: Balance y proyección económico-social del gobierno del presidente Aylwin 1990-1992*. Santiago, 1992.

Ministerio de Planificación y Cooperación (MIDEPLAN). *Avanzando en equidad: Un proceso de integración al desarrollo 1990-1992*. Santiago, 1992.

Naciones Unidas/CEPAL. *Evoluciones del impacto ambiental en América Latina y el Caribe*. Santiago, 1991.

———. *Medio ambiente y desarrollo en América Latina: Bibliografía seleccionada*. Santiago, 1992.

Partido por la Democracia (PPD). *Medio ambiente y municipio: Guía dirigida a candidatos*. Santiago, 1992.

Phillips Chilena. *Calendario Phillips Chilena. Tema: Medio ambiente en la pintura chilena y occidental. (Paisajes)*. Santiago, 1993.

Red Nacional de Acción Ecológica (RENACE). *Desechos y medio ambiente*. Cartillas Ecológicas. Santiago, 1991.

———. *Medio ambiente marino*. Cartillas Ecológicas. Santiago, 1991.

Reidt-Gritclifield, Linda. *El uso de permisos de emisión transables en el control de la contaminación atmosférica*. Santiago: Centro de Estudios Públicos, CEP, 1992.

Rodríguez, Alfredo, coord. *Encuentro Científico sobre el Medio Ambiente 4to., "Gestión Ambiental; Desarrollo Hoy sin Arriesgar el Mañana.* Valdivia, Chile, 6-8 marzo de 1992. 2 tomos. Santiago: CIPMA, 1992.

Römpczyk, Elmar. *Política ambiental: Conferencia de Río: ¿Espectáculo apenas mediano?* Santiago: CESOC/Fundación Friedrich Ebert, 1992.

———. *Política ecológica: Institutionalización e instrumentos*. Santiago: Fundación Friedrich Ebert, 1992.

Rosetti, María Pía. *Plan de acción nacional para el decenio en el área de la conservación del medio ambiente en beneficio de la infancia.* Santiago, 1991.

Saavedra, Igor, et al. *Gestión ambiental en Chile: Aportes del 4to. Encuentro Científico Sobre Medio Ambiente.*

Schatan, Jacobo, et al. *Por una iniciativa de los pueblos de América: Análisis y propuestas alternativas a la iniciativa para las Américas del gobierno estadounidense: Una visión desde Chile*. Santiago: Instituto de Ecología Política (IEP), Taller PIRET, Sociedad Chilena de Economía Política, PRIES–CONOSUR, 1992.

Serrano, Miguel. *Defendamos nuestra Patagonia*. Santiago, 1992.

Serrano Rodríguez, Pedro. *Reciclaje de basuras domésticas*. Cartilla Técnica. Centro el Canelo Nos, Programa de Ecología y Desarrollo Sustentable. San Bernardo, Chile, 1992.

Taylor, John L. *Guía sobre simulación y juegos para la educación ambiental*. Educación Ambiental, 2. Santiago: UNESCO/PNUMA, 1991.

———. *Tendencias, necesidades y prioridades en la educación ambiental desde la Conferencia de Tbilisi*. Educación Ambiental, 1. Santiago, 1.

Uribe P., Juan C. *Investigación Marea Roja en las provincias de Magallanes y Ultima Esperanza, XII Región. Informe final*. Informe de Investigación, no. 62. Punta Arenas: Instituto de la Patagonia, Universidad de Magallanes, 1992.

Urrutia, Mónica, et al. *Ecología y calidad de vida*. Santiago: Quercum, Centro de Desarrollo y Estudios Jurídicos y Sociales, 1992.

Vial, Joaquín, comp. *Desarrollo y medio ambiente: Hacia un enfoque integrador*. Santiago: CIEPLAN, 1991.

Publicaciones Periódicas

Ambiente Ahora. Informativo mensual de CIPMA.

Ambiente y Desarrollo. CIPMA.

Chilean Forestry News. Corporación Nacional Forestal, Santiago de Chile.

Chile Forestal. Corporación Nacional Forestal, Santiago de Chile.

Documentos de Trabajo CIPMA.
No. 23, "Información ambiental para la gestión", 1992.
No. 24, "Manejo de cuencas", 1992.
No. 25. "La conservación ambiental para la conservación de suelos", 1992.

Eco Prensa. Red Nacional de Acción Ecológica (RENACE).

Eco Salud. Colectivo de Atención Primaria, Salud Medio Ambiente.

Ecotemas. Comisión Nacional del Medio Ambiente VI Región.

Eco Tribuna. Comité Nacional de Defensa de la Flora y Fauna (CODEFF), Santiago de Chile.

Eco XXI: Revista para el Medio Ambiente. Auspiciada por el Ministerio de Bienes Nacionales. Chile.

Un Océano: Boletín Red de Avistamiento de Cetáceos. Comité Nacional de Defensa de la Flora y Fauna (CODEFF), Santiago de Chile.

Pachamama: Boletín de Educación Popular Ambiental de la Red Nacional de Educación Popular y Ecología del CEAAL.

Red Verde. Area de Comunicaciones, Guias y Scouts de Chile.

La Semilla. Grupo de Huertos Caro-Valledor-La Florida. Poblaciones de la Región Metropolitana, Santiago de Chile.

Otra Bibliografía

Aleuy, Francisco, et al. *Informe Nacional del Foro Chileno de Organizaciones No Gubernamentales: Extracto*. Santiago, 1992.

Benoit C., Iván. *Red List of Chilean Terrestrial Flora. Libro Rojo de la Flora Terrestre Chilena*. 2ª ed. actualizada. Santiago, 1989.

Canto H., Joan, et al. *Historia de una sobre explotación: Las ballenas*. Santiago, 1991.

Comisión Especial de Descontaminación de la Región Metropolitana. *Balance 1992—Programa 1993*. Santiago, 1993.

———. *Cuestionario sobre descontaminación*. Santiago, 1993.

Comisión Nacional del Medio Ambiente (CONAMA). *Chile: Informe Nacional a la Conferencia de las Naciones Unidas sobre Medio Ambiente y Desarrollo*. Junio, 1992.

———. *Repertorio de la Legislación de Relevancia Ambiental Vigente en Chile*. Enero, 1992.

Ormeño Ortíz, Eugenio, et al. *Educación para los desarrollos locales: Macrocomunas y sustrato material en la IX Región de la Araucanía*. Temuco, Chile, 1991.

Papic V., Vilma. *El Planeta de los Limpios*. Ecología en historieta. Santiago, 1992.

Parraguez, Eledino. *Cultura chilena y medio ambiente*.

Zegers Domínguez, Carolina, et al. *El futuro del bosque nativo chileno: Un desafío de hoy*.

12. Environment in Brazil: A Checklist of Current Serials

Carmen M. Muricy

This compilation is a selective list of current serials on environmental issues published in Brazil, based on the publications acquired by the Library of Congress, Rio de Janeiro Office. Most of the titles listed will be included in the next edition of the Library of Congress microfilm collection titled "Brazil Popular Groups Collection, Supplement 1990-92." The titles marked with an asterisk are in the main collection of the Library of Congress. It covers titles published by nongovernmental organizations, government agencies, and commercial houses. Information on first issue published and frequency is given whenever possible. A few important serials that have ceased publication are also mentioned. This list updates that published in Deborah L. Jakubs, ed., *Latin American Studies into the Twenty-First Century: New Focus, New Formats, New Challenges*, Papers of SALALM XXXVI (Albuquerque, NM: SALALM, 1993).

ABES-DF
a. 1– n° 01– fev. 1990– Irregular
Associação Brasileira de Engenharia Sanitária e Ambiental—ABES
Seção Distrito Federal
SCS Q. 6 - Bloco A - n° 81 sala 408 - Ed. José Severo
70326-90 Brasília, Distrito Federal

ABES-RJ
Associação Brasileira de Engenharia Sanitária e Ambiental—ABES
Seção Rio de Janeiro
Av. Beira Mar, 216 - 13º andar
20021-060 Rio de Janeiro, Rio de Janeiro

Alerta Amazônia: ecologia
v. 1- nº 1- nov. 1987- Monthly
INFORMAN—Sistema de Informação Científica e Tecnológica da Amazônia Brasileira
Universidade Federal do Pará
Biblioteca Central
Campus Universitário do Guamá
66075-900 Belém, Pará

*Amazônia: informação e debate**
v. 1- nº 1- jan. 1988- Irregular
Campanha Nacional de Defesa e pelo Desenvolvimento da Amazônia—CNDDA
Rua Araújo Porto Alegre, 71 - 10º andar
20030-010 Rio de Janeiro, Rio de Janeiro

*Amazônia brasileira em foco**
nº 1- 1967- Irregular
Campanha Nacional de Defesa e pelo Desenvolvimento da Amazônia—CNDDA
Rua Araújo Porto Alegre, 71 - 10º andar
20030-010 Rio de Janeiro, Rio de Janeiro

*Ambiente: revista CETESB de tecnologia** ISSN 0102-8685
Companhia de Tecnologia de Saneamento—CETESB
Av. Prof. Frederico Hermann Jr., 345, prédio 1, 1º andar, s. 100
05459-900 São Paulo, São Paulo

Ambiente e desenvolvimento
Irregular
Centrais Elétricas do Norte do Brasil S.A.—ELETRONORTE
Departamento de Meio Ambiente e Comunicação Social
SCN - Q. 6 - Conj. A - sala 113 - Ed. Venâncio 3000
70718-900 Brasília, Distrito Federal

Ambiente hoje
a. 1- nov./dez. 1988- Irregular
Associação Mineira de Defesa do Ambiente—AMDA
Rua Viçosa, 542-A
30330-160 Belo Horizonte, Minas Gerais

Anna Iekaré: nossa notícia
a. 1- nº 1- abr. 1990- Monthly
Conselho Indígena de Roraima—CIR
Av. Sebastião Diniz, 1672 W - Bairro São Vicente
69303-120 Boa Vista, Roraima

Antes que seja tarde
Grupo Ecológico Queremos Gente
Av. Tiradentes, 1067
94850-000 Alvorada, Rio Grande do Sul

Arqueo Notícias
Irregular
Fundação Brasileira para Conservação da Natureza—FBCN
Centro Técnico de Arqueologia-CTA
Museu da Fauna - Quinta da Boa Vista
20940-040 Rio de Janeiro, Rio de Janeiro
Continues: O Calendário

Bahia de Todos
Monthly
Grupo de Recomposição Ambiental
Av. Sete de Setembro, 1370
40080-001 Salvador, Bahia

Bem-te-vi
nº 1- jun. 1988- Irregular
Comité de Defesa da Ilha de São Luís
Beco do Couto, 56
65010-110 São Luís, Maranhão

Bicho-do-Mato
Irregular
Grupo Ecológico Sentinela dos Pampas—GESP
Rua Morom, 2031 - Centro
99010-034 Passo Fundo, Rio Grande do Sul

*Bio** ISSN 0103-5134
a.1- nº 1- set./out. 1989- Quarterly
Associação Brasileira de Engenharia Sanitária e Ambiental—ABES
Av. Beira Mar, 216 - 13º andar
20021-060 Rio de Janeiro, Rio de Janeiro
Supersedes *Engenharia sanitária*

Biodiversidade em notícias
nº 0- dez. 1990- Irregular
Fundação Biodiversitas para Conservação da Diversidade Biológica
Rua Maria Vaz Melo, 71 - Dona Clara
Caixa Postal 2462
30260-110 Belo Horizonte, Minas Gerais

Boletim (Grupo Seiva de Ecologia)
Grupo Seiva de Ecologia
Caixa Postal 55.190
04799-970 São Paulo, São Paulo

Boletim ANAÍ-BA
Associação Nacional de Apoio ao Índio
Rua Borges dos Reis, 46 lj. 54
40223-000 Salvador, Bahia

Boletim CIMI Sul
nº 1- abr. 1986- Irregular
CIMI Regional Sul
Caixa Postal 65
89800-000 Xanxerê, Santa Catarina

Boletim do CEDOC
nº 1, jan. 1988 - nº 5/6, set. 1988 Irregular
Fundação Nacional do Índio-FUNAI
SEPS - Q. 702/902 - Ed. Lex
70390-025 Brasília, Distrito Federal

*Boletim do Museu Paraense Emílio Goeldi: ciências da terra**
Irregular
Museu Paraense Emílio Goeldi
Biblioteca
Caixa Postal 399 - Campus de Pesquisa
66017-970 Belém, Pará

Boletim do NEMA
Irregular
Núcleo de Educação e Monitoramento Ambiental—NEMA
Rua Maria Araújo, 450
90620-000 Cassino, Rio Grande do Sul

Boletim ecológico (AMPRA)
a. 1- nº 1- jan. 1991- Monthly
Associação dos Moradores da Praça Cte. Xavier de Brito e Adjacências—AMPRA
Departamento de Ecologia
Rua Uruguai, 134/504
20510-060 Rio de Janeiro, Rio de Janeiro

Boletim ecológico (Projeto Sabor Natureza/Opçao pela Vida)
Projeto Sabor Natureza/Opção pela Vida
Av. Rodovalho, 78
88700-000 Tubarão, Santa Catarina

*Boletim FBCN** ISSN 0101-249
v. 1- 1966- Irregular
Fundação Brasileira para a Conservação da Natureza—FBCN
Rua Miranda Valverde, 103 - Botafogo
22281-000 Rio de Janeiro, Rio de Janeiro

Boletim FUNATURA
a. 1- nº 1- 1986-
Fundação Pró-Natureza
SCLN 107 - Bloco B - salas 201/13
Edifício Gemini Center II
70743-520 Brasília, Distrito Federal

Boletim informativo (ACAPRENA)
Associação Catarinense de Preservação da Natureza—ACAPRENA
Rua Antônio da Veiga, 140 Bloco T - sala 315
Caixa Postal 1507
89012-900 Blumenau, Santa Catarina

Boletim informativo (COIAB)
nº 1- mar. 1990- Irregular
Coordenação das Organizações Indígenas da Amazônia Brasileira—COIAB
Av. Joaquim Nabuco, 1572 - Centro
69020-031 Manaus, Amazonas

Boletim informativo (Movimento Ecológico Mater Natura)
a. 1- nº 001- 1987-
Movimento Ecológico Mater Natura
Caixa Postal 81
80001-970 Curitiba, Paraná

Boletim informativo (Sociedade para Estudos de Defesa Ambiental)
Sociedade para Estudos de Defesa Ambiental—SEDA
Centro de Ciências Biológicas da Saúde
Universidade Federal de Mato Grosso do Sul—UFMS
Caixa Postal 306
79070-900 Campo Grande, Mato Grosso do Sul

Boletim MAB
Irregular
Movimento de Atingidos por Barragens—MAB
Rua Santa Cruz, 281
04121-000 São Paulo, São Paulo

Boletim S.O.S. Mata Atlântica
Fundação S.O.S. Mata Atlântica
Rua Manoel da Nóbrega, 456
04001-001 São Paulo, São Paulo

Brasil environment
a. 1- nº 1- jan. 1991- Monthly
Secretaria da Imprensa da Presidência da República
Palácio do Planalto - 2º andar - sala 37
Praça dos Três Poderes
70150-900 Brasília, Distrito Federal
Published also in Portuguese: *Brasil meio ambiente*

Brasil X fome: movimento em busca de soluções
nº 1- jan. 1990-
Escola Livre de Agricultura Ecológica—ELAE
Caixa Postal 2133
11900-000 Registro, São Paulo

*Brasil florestal** ISSN 0045-270X
1970- Quarterly
Instituto Brasileiro do Meio Ambiente e dos Recursos Naturais Renováveis—IBAMA
SAIN - Lote 4 - Ed. Sede IBAMA
70800-900 Brasília, Distrito Federal

Brasil meio ambiente
a.1- nº 1- jan. 1991- Monthly
Secretaria de Imprensa da Presidência da República
Palácio do Planalto, 2º andar - sala 37
Praça dos Três Poderes
70150-900 Brasília, Distrito Federal
Published also in English: *Brasil environment*

*Brasil: meio ambiente e desenvolvimento**
Bi-weekly
Provent Convenções e Eventos Ltda.
Rua Uruguaiana, 10/2º andar
20050-090 Rio de Janeiro, Rio de Janeiro

*Brasil verde: quem é quem na ecologia**
Annual
Apoio Marketing e Editora Ltda.
SAAN - Q. 3 - Lotes 70/80
71220-900 Brasília, Distrito Federal

Bulletin (Preparatory Forum of Brazilian NGOs for UNCED-92)
Preparatory Forum of Brazilian NGOs for UNCED-92
Executive Secretariat
CEDI—Centro Ecumênico de Documentação e Informação
Rua Santo Amaro, 129 - Glória
22211-230 Rio de Janeiro, Rio de Janeiro

*Cadastro nacional das instituições que atuam na área do meio ambiente**
Irregular
Instituto Brasileiro do Meio Ambiente e dos Recursos Naturais Renováveis—IBAMA
SAIN - Lote 4 - Ed. Sede IBAMA
70800-900 Brasília, Distrito Federal

*Cadernos CEDOPE: Série I: ecologia, população e família**
nº 1- fev. 1988- Irregular
Universidade do Vale do Rio dos Sinos—UNISINOS
Centro de Documentação e Pesquisa—CEDOPE
Av. Unisinos, 950
93022-000 São Leopoldo, Rio Grande do Sul

Cadernos do meio ambiente
Irregular
Instituto Ambiental de Estudos e Assessoria
Rua Deputado João Pontes, 766
60040-430 Fortaleza, Ceará

*Os caminhos da terra**
a. 1- nº 1- maio 1992- Monthly
Editora Abril S.A.
Rua Marechal Câmara, 160/15º andar - sala 1533/34
20020-080 Rio de Janeiro, Rio de Janeiro

Canto da terra
nº 1- 1985-
Associação Pernambucana de Defesa da Natureza—ASPAN
Caixa Postal 7862
50732-970 Recife, Pernambuco

Carta verde: boletim informativo do mandato Carlos Minc-PT
Gabinete Carlos Minc
Praça XV, Palácio 23 de Julho, s.207
20010-090 Rio de Janeiro, Rio de Janeiro

*Catálogo brasileiro de engenharia sanitária ambiental-CABES**
1st ed.- dec. 1975- Annual
Associação Brasileira de Engenharia Sanitária e Ambiental—ABES
Av. Beira Mar, 216 - 13º andar
20021-060 Rio de Janeiro, Rio de Janeiro

CEACON informativo
Monthly
Centro de Estudos e Atividades de Conservação da Natureza—CEACON
Caixa Postal 20684
01498 - São Paulo, São Paulo

O Charão
Twice a year
Clube de Observadores de Aves—COA
Rua Gilberto Cardoso, 200/904
22430-070 Rio de Janeiro, Rio de Janeiro

Circular (Fórum das ONGs Brasileiras Preparatório para a Conferência da Sociedade Civil sobre Meio Ambiente e Desenvolvimento)
Irregular
Fórum das ONGs Brasileiras Preparatório para a Conferência da Sociedade Civil sobre Meio Ambiente e Desenvolvimento
Rua do Catete, 153
a/c Museu da República - Anexo I
22220-000 Rio de Janeiro, Rio de Janeiro

Circular técnica (Projeto PNUD/FAO/BRA/87/007)*
Quarterly
Instituto Brasileiro do Meio Ambiente e dos Recursos Naturais Renováveis—Projeto PNUD/FAO/BRA/87/007: desenvolvimento integrado no nordeste do Brasil
Av. Alexandrino de Alencar, 1399 - Tirol
39015-350 Natal, Rio Grande do Norte

Clima Brasil: boletim informativo
a. 1- nº 1- maio 1992- Irregular
Rede de Ação Climática - Clima Brasil
Caixa Postal 20785
01498 São Paulo, São Paulo

Correio ecológico
a. 1- nº 1- abr. 1991-
Fundação Pró-Natureza
SCLN 107 - Bloco B, salas 201/13
70743-520 Brasília, Distrito Federal

*CPAA informa**
a. 1- nº 0- 1989-
Empresa Brasileira de Pesquisa Agropecuária—EMBRAPA
Centro de Pesquisa Agroflorestal da Amazônia—CPAA
Rodovia AM-010, km 28
Caixa Postal 319
69048-660 Manaus, Amazonas

Desafío
1989- Bi-monthly
Asociación Interamericana de Ingeniería Sanitaria y Ambiental—AIDIS
Rua Nicolau Cagliardi, 354
05429-010 São Paulo, São Paulo

Desenvolvimento urbano e meio ambiente
Bi-monthly
Universidade Livre do Meio Ambiente
Rua Victor Benato, 210 - Pilarzinho
82120-110 Curitiba, Paraná

Documentos florestais
Irregular
Escola Superior de Agricultura "Luiz de Queiróz"
Departamento de Ciências Florestais
Av. Pádua Dias, 11
13418-900 Piracicaba, São Paulo

Eco Sirkis
Irregular
Alfredo Sirkis
Rua Francisco Muratori, 45
20230-080 Rio de Janeiro, Rio de Janeiro

Ecobrasil
Irregular
ECOBRASIL—Empresa Jornalística SC Ltda.
Rua Álvaro Alvim, 48/610
20031-010 Rio de Janeiro, Rio de Janeiro

Ecologia
Weekly
Jornal do Brasil S.A.
Av. Brasil, 500
20949-900 Rio de Janeiro, Rio de Janeiro
Weekly supplement to *Jornal do Brasil*, published between June 24, 1991–June 15, 1992; from May 25, 1992–June 15, 1992 daily published under the title "Ecologia & Cidade"

Ecologia e ação
Grupo Ação Ecológica
Estrada do Capenha, 275/801 - Bl. 2
22743-041 Rio de Janeiro, Rio de Janeiro

*Ecologia e desenvolvimento**
a. 1- nº 1- mar. 1991- Monthly
Editora Terceiro Mundo
Rua da Glória, 122/105-106
20241-180 Rio de Janeiro, Rio de Janeiro

Ecologizando: boletim informativo
a. 1- nº 1- jan./mar.- 1989-
Federação de Entidades Ecologistas Catarinenses—FEEC
Caixa Postal D-33
89201-972 Joinville, Santa Catarina

Ecopaulista
nº 1- 1989- Irregular
Assembléia Permanente de Entidades em Defesa do Meio Ambiente do Estado de São Paulo—APEDEMA
Caixa Postal 6866
01064-970 São Paulo, São Paulo

Ecopress (International Edition)
nº 0- oct. 1989- Monthly
Ecopress News Agency
Rua Sampaio Viana, 72
04004-000 São Paulo, São Paulo

EcoRio
a. 1- nº 1- maio 1991- Monthly
Andina Cultural Ltda.
Av. Rio Branco, 156 - grupo 3103
20040-003 Rio de Janeiro, Rio de Janeiro

Ecos
a. 1- nº 1- set. 1992- Irregular
Sociedade Nordestina de Ecologia—SNE
Rua Pessoa de Melo, 355
50610-220 Recife, Pernambuco

ECOTECH Newsletter
nº 3- maio 1992- Irregular
International Symposium and Exhibition of Environmental Technologies
Rua México, 11 slj. 201
20031-144 Rio de Janeiro, Rio de Janeiro
International Symposium in Rio de Janeiro, from May 29 to June 6, 1992

Em nome do amor à natureza
Irregular
Associação Ecologista em Nome do Amor à Natureza
Rua Otávio Corrêa, 62
90050-120 Porto Alegre, Rio Grande do Sul

Espaço, ambiente e planejamento
v. 1- nº 1- jan. 1986- Irregular
Companhia Vale do Rio Doce—CVRD
Superintendência do Meio Ambiente
Av. Graça Aranha, 26 - 14º andar
20030-000 Rio de Janeiro, Rio de Janeiro

Espeleo notícias
Quarterly
Fundação Brasileira para Conservação da Natureza—FBCN
Grupo Técnico de Espeleologia
Rua Miranda Valverde, 103 - Botafogo
22281-000 Rio de Janeiro, Rio de Janeiro

*Estudos avançados: coleção documentos: série ciências ambientais**
Irregular
Universidade de São Paulo—USP
Instituto de Estudos Avançados—IEA
Av. Prof. Luciano Gualberto, Trav. J, nº 374 - Térreo
05508-900 São Paulo, São Paulo

Exetinati copenati: o índio em manchete
a. 1- nº 1- maio 1987- Irregular
Fundação Nacional do Índio—FUNAI
Administração Regional de Bauru
SEPS - Q. 702/902 - Ed. Lex
70390-025 Brasília, Distrito Federal

Floresser
Irregular
Associação Mineira de Defesa do Meio Ambiente—AMDA
Rua Viçosa, 542-A
30330-160 Belo Horizonte, Minas Gerais

Folha ambiental
Irregular
Grupo Ambientalista da Bahia—GAMBÁ
Rua Borges dos Reis, 46 s/j - Boulevard Rio Vermelho
40223-000 Salvador, Bahia

A Folha da Frente Verde
Sociedade Grupo Ecológico Frente Verde
Av. 13 de Maio, 13 gr. 1410/11
20031-000 Rio de Janeiro, Rio de Janeiro

Folha da Mata Virgem
Irregular
Fundação Mata Virgem (The Rain Forest Foundation)
SCS Q. 8 - Bloco B - nº 60 - Ed. Venâncio 2000
70333-900 Brasília, Distrito Federal

Folha da Natureza
Bi-monthly
Fundação Zoobotânica do Rio Grande do Sul
Núcleo de Comunicação Social
Rua Dr. Salvador Franca, 1427
90690-000 Porto Alegre, Rio Grande do Sul

Folha de gaia
Monthly
Gaia Produções
Rua Arimatéia Cirne, 234 - Apiadouro
65030-000 São Luís, Maranhão

Folha do meio ambiente
a. 1- nº 1- mar. 1990- Bi-monthly
Forest Cultura Viva Ltda.
SCS Q. 08 - Bl. B- nº 60 - s. 228 - Ed. Venâncio 2000
70333-900 Brasília, Distrito Federal

Folha ecológica
Monthly
Folha Ecológica
Rua Senador Dantas, 75/2013
20031-201 Rio de Janeiro, Rio de Janeiro

Folha verde
Secretaria de Estado para Assuntos do Meio Ambiente—SEAMA
Av. Princesa Isabel, 629 - 6º andar
29010-361 Vitória, Espírito Santo

Folhinha da UVA
a. 1- nº 1- fev. 1991- Monthly
União Valeparaibana de Ambientalistas
Rua Dr. Emílio Winther, 40
12030-000 Taubaté, São Paulo

Fórum
a. 1- nº 1- abr. 1991-
Fórum de ONGs Brasileiras Preparatório para 92
Secretaria Executiva
CEDI-Centro Ecumênico de Documentação e Informação
Rua Santo Amaro, 129 - Glória
22211-230 Rio de Janeiro, Rio de Janeiro

Gaia: informativo mensal de movimentos ecológicos
Monthly
Caixa Postal 68029
Cidade Universitária
21944-970 Rio de Janeiro, Rio de Janeiro

O Geca
Grupo de Estudo Ecológico e Controle Ambiental
Av. Tiradentes, 161
12030-180 Taubaté, São Paulo

*Globo ecologia**
Editora Globo
Rua Itapiru, 1209
20251-031 Rio de Janeiro, Rio de Janeiro

Greenpeace América Latina
a. 1- nº 1- maio 1992
Greenpeace
Rua México, 21 sala 1301 A/B
20031-144 Rio de Janeiro, Rio de Janeiro

GRUMIN
a. 1- nº 1- feb. 1989- Irregular
Grupo Mulher - Educação Indígena - GRUMIN
Rua da Quitanda, 185 - s. 509
20091-000 Rio de Janeiro, Rio de Janeiro

A Gruta
Irregular
Espeleo Grupo de Brasília
Caixa Postal 00468
70359-970 Brasília, Distrito Federal

Habitat
a. 1- nº 1- jan. 89- Monthly
Associação Brasileira de Caça e Conservação—ABC
Rua Mourato Coelho, 1372
05417-002 São Paulo, São Paulo

Information on the '92 Global Forum
Irregular
Forum Global
Hotel Glória - Prédio Anexo - sala 366
Rua do Russell, 632
22212-010 Rio de Janeiro, Rio de Janeiro

Informativo (ADFG)
Monthly
Ação Democrática Feminina Gaúcha Amigos da Terra—ADFG
Rua Miguel Tostes, 694
90430-060 Porto Alegre, Rio Grande do Sul

Informativo ABES
Associação Brasileira de Engenharia Sanitária e Ambiental—ABES
Seção São Paulo
Rua Costa Carvalho, 234
05429-000 São Paulo, São Paulo

Informativo Brasil PNUMA
Bi-monthly
Instituto Brasil PNUMA
Av. Nilo Peçanha, 50 sala 1313
20020-100 Rio de Janeiro, Rio de Janeiro

Informativo da FBCN
Irregular
Fundação Brasileira para a Conservação da Natureza
Rua Miranda Valverde, 103 - Botafogo
22281-000 Rio de Janeiro, Rio de Janeiro

Informativo da SPVS
Irregular
Sociedade de Pesquisa em Vida Selvagem e Educação Ambiental—SPVS
Rua Gutemberg, 345 - Batel
80420-030 Curitiba, Paraná

Informativo IEA
Irregular
Instituto de Estudos Amazônicos—IEA
Rua Monte Castelo, 380 - Tarumã
82530-200 Curitiba, Paraná

Informativo Pró-Natura
a. 1- nº 1- nov./dez. 1992 Bi-monthly
Instituto Brasileiro de Pesquisas e Estudos Ambientais Pró-Natura
Av. Beira-Mar, 406/708
20021-060 Rio de Janeiro, Rio de Janeiro

Informativo SBE
Sociedade Brasileira de Espeleologia—SBE
Av. Brigadeiro Luís Antônio, 4442
01402-000 São Paulo, São Paulo

Informativo SBTA
Quarterly
Sociedade Brasileira de Tecnologia Ambiental—SBTA
SCLN 216 Bloco D nº 74
Caixa Postal 7068
71619-970 Brasília, Distrito Federal

Informativo SEMAX
Sociedade Ecológica e Meio Ambiente de Xaxim—SEMAX
Rua do Comércio, 1619
89810-000 Xaxim, Santa Catarina

*Ingeniería sanitária**
1948- Quarterly
Asociación Interamericana de Ingeniería Sanitária y Ambiental—AIDIS
Rua Nicolau Cagliardi, 354
05429-010 São Paulo, São Paulo
Previously published by AIDIS in United States, Mexico and Argentina

O Ipê
Associação Anapolina de Proteção ao Meio Ambiente—AAPMA
Rua Calixto Abdala, 76
Caixa Postal 876
75020-140 Anápolis, Goiás

JC
Irregular
Companhia Estadual de Águas e Esgotos do Estado do Rio de Janeiro—CEDAE
Rua Sacadura Cabral, 103/9º andar
20081-260 Rio de Janeiro, Rio de Janeiro

Jornal ABES
jan. 1975- Monthly
Associação Brasileira de Engenharia Sanitária e Ambiental-ABES
Diretoria Nacional
Av. Beira Mar, 216 - 13º andar
20021-060 Rio de Janeiro, Rio de Janeiro

Jornal CEFLAM
Irregular
Centro de Estudos Florestais da Amazônia—CEFLAM
Av. Dionísio Bentes, 210
68680-000 Tomé-Açu, Pará

Jornal da CETREL
a. 1- nº 2- jan. 1992- Irregular
CETREL S.A. Empresa de Proteção Ambiental
Via Atlântica, km 9
Pólo Petroquímico de Camaçari
42810-000 Camaçari, Bahia

Jornal da ecologia
Jornal da Ecologia
Rua Prudente de Morais, 554 - apto. 144
14015-100 Ribeirão Preto, São Paulo

Jornal do Brasil
jun. 1-15, 1992 Daily
Jornal do Brasil S.A.
Av. Brasil, 500
20949-900 Rio de Janeiro, Rio de Janeiro
Special English edition of *Jornal do Brasil*, published during the Earth Summit, 1992

Jornal do MPST
Irregular
Movimento pela Sobrevivência na Transamazônica
Caixa Postal 6
68371-970 Altamira, Pará

Jornal do Pró-Natura
a. 1- nº 1- verão 1990- Irregular
Instituto Brasileiro de Pesquisas e Estudos Ambientais—Pró-Natura
Rua da Quitanda, 20 - 4º andar
20011-030 Rio de Janeiro, Rio de Janeiro

Jornal Ecoturismo
Irregular
HJ Publicidade e Promoções Ltda.
Rua 7, nº 390 - Nova Porto Velho
78900 Porto Velho, Rondônia

Jornal EcoVerde
Monthly
Artijuca, Jornalismo e Promoções - ME - Ltda.
Rua Carlos Vasconcelos, 155 gr. 402
20521-050 Rio de Janeiro, Rio de Janeiro

Jornal Pró-Rio
a. 1- nº 1- abr. 1991- Monthly
Pró-Rio
Rua Uruguaiana, 10 - 2º andar
20050-090 Rio de Janeiro, Rio de Janeiro

Jornal Riocentro
Irregular
Centro Internacional Riocentro - Riotur S.A.
Av. Salvador Allende, 6555
22780-160 Rio de Janeiro, Rio de Janeiro

Jornal SODEPAN
nº 01- 1991-
Sociedade de Defesa do Pantanal—SODEPAN
Av. Américo Carlos da Costa, 320 - Parque Laucídio Coelho
79080-170 Campo Grande, Mato Grosso do Sul

Jornal verde: a ecologia levada a sério
a. 1- nº 1- jan. 1988- Irregular
Jornal Verde Comunicação Ecológica Ltda.
Rua Manuel Maria Tourinho, 880
01236-000 São Paulo, São Paulo

JornalECO
a. 1- nº 1- nov. 1988- Monthly
Secretaria de Estado do Meio Ambiente
Rua Tabapuã, 81 - 13º andar
04533-010 São Paulo, São Paulo

Marcha verde
Monthly
Federação Paranaense de Cineclubes, Movimento Cultural Marcha Verde
Caixa Postal 15023
80531-970 Curitiba, Paraná

*Meio ambiente**
a. 1- 2ª série, nº 1- jun./jul. 1989-
Thesaurus Editora
SIG - Quadra 8, Lote 2356
70610-400 Brasília, Distrito Federal

Mensageiro
abr. 1979- Bi-monthly
Conselho Indigenista Missionário—CIMI
Caixa Postal 2080
66090-970 Belém, Pará

Mira mirá: homem e árvore
a. 1- nº 1- mar. 1992- Monthly
CIMI Regional Norte
Rua Tapajós, 54
69025-140 Manaus, Amazonas

Movimento ecológico
Associação Brasileira de Ecologia—ABE
Av. Nilo Peçanha, 12 - gr. 801/3
20020-100 Rio de Janeiro, Rio de Janeiro

Museu ao vivo
a. 1- nº 1- jan. 1991- Quarterly
Museu do Índio
Assessoria de Comunicação Social
Rua das Palmeiras, 55 - Botafogo
22270-070 Rio de Janeiro, Rio de Janeiro

Mutação
Irregular
Associação de Prevenção do Meio Ambiente do Alto Vale do Itajaí—APREMAVI
Ladeira Joaquim Nabuco, 322
Caixa Postal 628
89160-000 Rio do Sul, Santa Catarina

Natureza viva
Instituto Brasileiro do Meio Ambiente e dos Recursos Naturais Renováveis—IBAMA
Assessoria de Comunicação Social e Imprensa
SAIN - Lote 4 - Ed. Sede IBAMA
70800-900 Brasília, Distrito Federal

Newsletter da FMV
Irregular
Fundação Mata Virgem
SCS - Q. 8 - Bloco B - nº 60 - Sala 501B - Ed. Venâncio 2000
70333-900 Brasília, Distrito Federal
Title varies : 1990-jun. 1991 FMV newsletter

Nova terra
nº 12- Quarterly
Centro de Estudos e Preservação da Natureza Nova Terra—HIPPOKAMPUS
Cidade Universitária
Caixa Postal 11461
05422-970 São Paulo, São Paulo

Pedra escrita
Irregular
Fundação Serra das Andorinhas
Caixa Postal 172
68500-000 Marabá, Pará

Penaha
a.1- 1987- Irregular
Fundação Nacional do Índio—FUNAI
Aministração Regional de Governador Valadares
SEPS - Q. 702/902 - Ed. Lex
70390-025 Brasília, Distrito Federal

Pêndulo
Irregular
Trinca Comunicação e Marketing Ltda.
Rua Sales Cabral, 26 - Térreo 2
22240-070 Rio de Janeiro, Rio de Janeiro

Pólo agora
a. 1- nº 1- set. 1990- Monthly
PetroRio-Petroquímica do Rio de Janeiro
Av. Rio Branco, 80 - 6º/7º andar
20040-000 Rio de Janeiro, RJ

*População & desenvolvimento** ISSN 0102-8332
a. 1- nº 1- mar. 1967- Bi-monthly
Sociedade Civil Bem-Estar Familiar—BEMFAM
Av. República do Chile, 230 - 17º andar
20031-170 Rio de Janeiro, Rio de Janeiro
From nº 159, 1990 on co-edition with Fundação Brasileira para Conservação da Natureza

*Porantim: em defesa da causa indígena**
Monthly
Conselho Indigenista Missionário—CIMI
SDS Edifício Venâncio III - sala 311
70393-900 Brasília, Distrito Federal

Projeto fauna
Irregular
Prefeitura de Campinas
Projeto Fauna
Av. Anchieta, 200/3º andar
13015-100 Campinas, São Paulo

Quero-Quero
a. 1- nº 1- mar. 1990- Bi-monthly
Secretaria de Estado da Educação
Grupo de Trabalho em Educação Ambiental—GTEA
Rua Antônio Luz, 101 - s. 605
88010-401 Florianópolis, Santa Catarina

Relatório anual Fundação Mata Virgem
Annual
Fundação Mata Virgem
SCS Q. 8 - Bloco B - nº 60 - sala 501B - Ed. Venâncio 2000
70333-900 Brasília, Distrito Federal

*Relatório de balneabilidade das praias paulistas**
Annual
Companhia de Tecnologia de Saneamento Ambiental—CETESB
Divisão de Biblioteca
Av. Prof. Frederico Hermann Jr., 345 - Alto de Pinheiros
05489-010 São Paulo, São Paulo
Continues: *Balneabilidade das praias paulistas*

Resenha ambiental
Secretaria de Estado de Meio Ambiente—SEMAN
Av. 13 de Maio, 33 - 24º andar
20031-000 Rio de Janeiro, Rio de Janeiro

Resenha & debate
nº 1- jun. 1990- Irregular
Museu Nacional
Projeto Estudos sobre Temas Indígenas no Brasil—PETI
Quinta da Boa Vista, s/nº
20940-040 Rio de Janeiro, Rio de Janeiro

*Revista da FEEMA**
a. 1- nº 1- set. 1991- Bi-monthly
Fundação Estadual de Engenharia do Meio Ambiente—FEEMA
Assessoria de Comunicação—ASCOM
Rua Fonseca Teles, 121/15º andar - São Cristóvão
20940-200 Rio de Janeiro, Rio de Janeiro

*Revista do COPAM**
Conselho Estadual de Política Ambiental—COPAM
Assessoria de Comunicação
Av. Prudente de Morais, 1671
30380-000 Belo Horizonte, Minas Gerais

*Saneamento ambiental**
a. 1- nº 1- jan. 1990- Monthly
Signus Editora
Rua Eugênio de Medeiros, 499/507
05425-001 São Paulo, São Paulo

*Saúde e meio ambiente**
Secretaria da Saúde e do Meio Ambiente
Fundação Estadual de Proteção Ambiental
Av. A. J. Renner, 10
90245-000 Porto Alegre, Rio Grande do Sul

Sinal verde: Green Light for Latin American Rivers
Irregular
União Protetora do Ambiente Natural—UPAN
Caixa Postal 189
93001-970 São Leopoldo, Rio Grande do Sul

Sobrevivência
Irregular
Associação Gaúcha de Proteção ao Ambiente Natural—AGAPAN
Caixa Postal 1996
90001-970 Porto Alegre, Rio Grande do Sul

SobreViver: jornal de ecologia e meio ambiente da Ilha do Governador
Rua Crundiúba, 71/101 - Ilha do Governador
21931-500 Rio de Janeiro, Rio de Janeiro

Sociedade de Preservação dos Recursos Naturais e Culturais da Amazônia—SOPREN
Sociedade de Preservação dos Recursos Naturais e Culturais da Amazônia—SOPREN
Alameda Lúcio Amaral, 193 - Jardim Independência
66040-240 Belém, Pará

SOS Terra
a. 1- nº 1- jan. 1991- Monthly
Movimento Conservacionista Teresopolitano—MCT
Rua Tocantins, 1475 - Alto
25950 Teresópolis, Rio de Janeiro

Terra
Bi-monthly
Terra
Caixa Postal 62560
22257-970 Rio de Janeiro, Rio de Janeiro

*Terra indígena** ISSN 0103-2437
Quarterly
Centro de Estudos Indígenas
Faculdade de Ciências e Letras/UNESP
Rodovia Araraquara/Jaú, km 1
Caixa Postal 174
14800-900 Araraquara, São Paulo

Terra viva
[nº 1]-12, jun. 3-15, 1992 Daily
Inter Press Service
Rua do Russel, 450/602
22210-010 Rio de Janeiro, Rio de Janeiro
The independent daily of the Earth Summit

O Trabalhador
Irregular
Secretaria de Meio Ambiente
Av. Princesa Isabel, 629/6º andar
29010-361 Vitória - ES

Transformação
Visão Mundial
Rua Antônio de Albuquerque, 788 - Térreo
30112-010 Belo Horizonte, Minas Gerais

Tupari
Monthly
Grupo de Trabalho Missionário Evangélico—GTME
Av. João Gomes Monteiro Sobrinho, 3419
Caixa Postal 642
78050-700 Cuiabá, Mato Grosso
Continues: *Boletim do GTME*

Um mais
Ação Democrática Feminina Gaúcha Amigos da Terra—ADFG
Rua Miguel Tostes 694
90430-060 Porto Alegre, Rio Grande do Sul

UNCED 92
Instituto de Pré-História, Antropologia e Ecologia—IPHAE
Caixa Postal 585
78900 Porto Velho, Rondônia

Uniambiente
a. 1- nº 0- dez. 1990- Bi-monthly
Comissão Interinstitucional sobre Meio Ambiente e Educação Universitária—CIMAEU
Av. Prof. Frederico Herman Jr., 345
05459-010 São Paulo, São Paulo

Urihi
Irregular
Comissão pela Criação do Parque Yanomami—CCPY
Rua Manoel da Nóbrega, 11 - conjunto 32
04001-080 São Paulo, São Paulo
English edition

Urtiga
Associação Ituana de Proteção Ambiental—AIPA
Caixa Postal 83
13300-000 Itu, São Paulo

O Verde
Irregular
Associação Para Proteção Ambiental de São Carlos—APASC
Praça Coronel Paulino Carlos, s/n
Caixa Postal 596
13560-040 São Carlos, São Paulo

Vidativa
nº 1- 1990- Bi-weekly
Associação Brasileira de Engenharia Sanitária e Ambiental—ABES
Diretoria Nacional
Av. Beira Mar, 216 - 13º andar
20021-060 Rio de Janeiro, Rio de Janeiro

Viva alternativa: porta-voz das entidades ambientalistas autônomas
nº 0- maio 1989- Bi-monthly
Esquadrão da Vida Produções Culturais
Caixa Postal 08581
70312-970 Brasília, Distrito Federal

Yanomami urgente
nº 1- 20 de abr. 1988- Irregular
Comissão pela Criação do Parque Yanomami—CCPY
Rua Manoel da Nóbrega, 111 - conjunto 32
04001-080 São Paulo, São Paulo
English edition

Yuimaki
Comissão Pró-Índio do Acre
Rua Manoel Cesário, 182 - Capoeira
69910-020 Rio Branco, Acre

New Technology for Communication: Video

13. Collecting Latin American Independent Video: The Independent Media Resource Exchange

Karen Ranucci*

At the Downtown Community TV Center, a community video center in Chinatown, New York, where I worked for ten years, I saw the possibilities of community empowerment and people empowerment through video. During the time I worked there, we made documentaries for PBS and freelanced for NBC Nightly News and the Today Show. As a reporter/producer, I would find the story, develop it, shoot it, and get it on television, for millions of Americans to see. It was a very seductive position to be in: to be an independent video maker with adequate budget to do the work I wanted to do, that is, place alternative messages on broadcast TV.

In my travels for NBC, particularly in Latin America, I became aware of the fact North Americans were being sent down to cover events in Latin America for Latin Americans. We would arrive in a location, generally during a crisis situation, with little language ability and no background or information. From my background in community television I looked around and said, "Wait a second. Don't these people have anything to say about themselves? Are these people doing community video like that in the United States?"

I took a leave of absence from my work at NBC and DCTV and spent several months traveling in Latin America looking for the answer. I contacted video groups in every country I visited and was incredibly impressed by the quality and authenticity of the materials that I saw. Latin America has a long history of film production, which reflects their own images. With the new video technology, many more people were able to become involved in expressing themselves about their lives. I have now dedicated myself to finding this work and bringing it to the United States.

As a result of my travels in 1985, I organized "Democracy in Communication," a traveling exhibition of popular video from many different countries of Latin America. I collected it, packaged it, translated it, subtitled it and distributed it, particularly to universities, community groups, art galleries and museums. As I began to let people know that this material

---

*Transcribed by Angela Carreño. Edited for publication.

existed I saw that there was actually a tremendous interest on the part of U.S. audiences. They had just never known that this material existed. One of the problems that came up in trying to bring this material to the United States was that of language. This material was in Spanish and Portuguese. How do we make that available to North Americans? I say "we" because I was an initiator of this kind of work, but everywhere I turned I found other people who were likeminded and interested in doing this sort of thing, and instantly collaborated in many different aspects of the work.

I started working at a university, Ramapo College in Mawa, New Jersey. One thing that we did to try to solve this problem of the translation question was to create, within the university, a translation course in the Spanish Language Department. The students would work with these materials. We would have a Spanish language transcript, and the entire class would work to translate it into English. Then those language students would work with Communication students. Like many universities, Ramapo had video facilities where they could put subtitling on video. The language students and the communication students put subtitles on the tapes. We were providing a service to the Latin American producers by translating their tapes for free. At the same time, the students were being turned on to these materials, and learning valuable translation and subtitling skills.

We published a booklet which explains that project, and how it can be duplicated at other universities. When we were distributing the booklet and letting other universities know about this material and our translation exchanges for material, the same question kept coming back to us: "Yes, that is great! We are very interested in this material. What are they and where are they?" However, I just had this little collection that I put together in 1985. That bigger question of "what are they and where are they?" now loomed over me.

This was why I created an organization called the International Media Resource Exchange, which is specifically dedicated to bringing up material from Latin America and getting it out there. What we are working on now, as we proceed with support from the Rockefeller Foundation and the MacArthur Foundation, is to create a database and an archive of these kinds of Latin American materials. We have begun to research all of the materials, made by Latin American and U.S. Latinos, that are available in the United States. Not only collecting the information on what is available and where it is available, but we are actually physically getting copies of these materials and have begun a process of evaluating them.

That evaluation is being done by professors around the country. Right now we are working with 280 professors from various universities who are evaluating these tapes. Their evaluations are helping us to identify the materials that are most useful in U.S. education. At the same time their descriptions, which are given from a user's point of view, and provide information about how they could be used in various kinds of courses, will make up the copy for a directory that we will be publishing. In the directory, you will be able to find material by subject, by title and by country.

Lists of tapes currently in hand that need to be evaluated can be supplied to anyone who might be interested in participating in the evaluation process. These also give a wider sense of the material that we are talking about.

In addition to doing all this work, we are not just going to publish a book; our organization will also be able to provide a telephone service. You will be able to call up and say "I am teaching a course on this or that, and I am looking for material on a specific subject." We can then provide a print-out of what exists.

This is very much a cooperative project. I know that a number of universities have large film collections already, and a large number of Latin American films within those collections. Any information about the materials in the collections in libraries will be very valuable in creating a centralized information source.

Further information about the project can be obtained from:

The International Media Resource Exchange
124 Washington Place
New York, NY 10014
Telphone: (212) 463-0108

14. Latin American Independent Video: Distribution and Information Sources

Angela M. Carreño

Caribbean Film and Video Federation
77 Route de la Folie
97200 Fort de France
Martinique FWI
Fax (596) 51-0665; telephone (596) 60-2142

Best source for information on Caribbean video. Direct correspondence to Suzy Landau, the Secretary-General of the Federation. The aim of the Federation is to develop the production and distribution of film and video by and about Caribbean people and all the backup facilities which that requires. The Federation's members include television producers, film directors, actors and film archivists with a shared involvement in Caribbean film, meeting across all differences of language, culture, and ideology.

Cine Acción
346 Ninth St., 2nd Floor
San Francisco, CA 94103
(415) 553-8135

Founded in 1980 to encourage and promote the production, distribution, and understanding of contemporary independent Latino film and video. Distributes a printed guide titled *CineWorks*.

Cinema Guild
1697 Broadway
New York, NY 10019
Fax (212) 246-5525; telephone (212) 246-5522

Shorts, documentaries, and feature films.

Center for Cuban Studies
124 W. 23rd St.
New York, NY 10011
(212) 242-0559

Cuban feature, performance, shorts, and documentary video.

DEC Films
229 College St.
Toronto, Ontario, Canada M5T-1R4
(416) 597-0524; 597-2287

Strengths in Central American and Chilean documentary.

The Empowerment Project
1653 18th St., Suite 3
Santa Monica, CA 90404
Fax (310) 829-2305; telephone (310) 828-8807

Distributes several U.S.-made documentaries on Central America, including the Academy Award-winning "Panama Deception" for $99.95. For orders contact The Empowerment Project at 3403 Highway 54 West, Chapel Hill, NC 27516.

Evergreen Video
228 West Houston St.
New York, NY 10014
(800) 225-7783

Feature film.

Facets Multimedia
1517 West Fullerton Ave.
Chicago, IL 60614
(800) 331-6197

Feature film.

Filmmakers Library, Inc.
133 East 58th St.
New York, NY 10022
(212) 355-6545

First Run/Icarus Films
153 Waverly Pl., 6th Floor
New York, NY 10014
Fax (212) 989-7649; telephone (212) 727-1711

Food First
145 9th St.
San Francisco, CA 94103
Fax (415) 864-3909; telephone (415) 864-8555

Global Exchange
2940 16th St., Room 307
San Francisco, CA 94103
(415) 255-7296

Home Film Festival
P.O. Box 2032
Scranton, PA 18501
(800) 633-3456 in PA; (800) 258-3456 elsewhere

Feature film.

Ideara Films
2524 Cypress St.
Vancouver, British Columbia, Canada V6J-3N2
(604) 738-8815

Ingram International
10990 E. 55th Ave.
Denver, CO 80239
(800) 356-3577

Formerly Tamarelle's; distributes feature films.

International Film Circuit Inc.
20 Nassau St., Suite 244
Princeton, NJ 08542
(609) 683-4223

Feature film.

International Media Resource Exchange
124 Washington Pl.
New York, NY 10014
(212) 463-0108

Popular independent video from Latin America.

Kino International Corporation
333 W. 39 St., Suite 503
New York, NY 10018
Fax (212) 714-0871; telephone (212) 629-6880

Limited listing; distributes the Colombian film *Rodrigo D: No Future* directed by Victor Gaviria.

Madera Cinevideo Education Division
620 E. Yosemite
Madera, CA 93638
(800) 828-8118 in CA; (800) 624-2204 elsewhere

Strength in Mexican documentary and feature film; catalog is not comprehensive; distributes the García Márquez collection of short stories on film and the historical documentary *Memorias de un mexicano.*

Media Network
39 West 14th St., Suite 403
New York, NY 10011
(212) 929-2663

Information service for U.S. independent media.

Movies Unlimited, Inc.
6736 Castor Ave.
Philadelphia, PA 19149
(215) 722-8298 in PA; (800) 523-0823 elsewhere

Feature film.

National Film Board of Canada
1251 Avenue of the Americas, 16th Floor
New York, NY 10020
(212) 586-5131

New Yorker Films
16 W. 61st St.
New York, NY 10023
(212) 247-6110

Mostly feature films; some documentaries.

Public Broadcasting Service/Public TV Library
475 L'Enfant Plaza Software
Washington, DC 20024
(202) 488-5000

Publications Exchange
8306 Mills Dr., Suite 241
Miami, FL 33183
Fax (305) 252-1813; telephone (305) 256-0162

Cuban feature, performance, and documentary videos.

South American Resources
40 East 62nd St.
New York, NY 10021
(212) 838-1732

Third World Newsreel
335 West 38th St., 5th Floor
New York, NY 10018
(212) 947-9277

Strengths in (1) video related to the black experience in Latin America and the Latin American black diaspora; one of the few good sources for non-Cuban, Caribbean film; and (2) videos from Sistema Radio Venceremos and the Film Institute of El Salvador.

Videoteca del Sur
84 E. 3rd St., Suite 5A
New York, NY 10003
Fax (212) 925-5730; telephone (212) 334-5257

Dedicated to the collection, preservation, and dissemination of alternative video from Latin American producers. Currently working on a catalog of videos available for rent and/or sale. Affiliated with Videotecas in Latin America and Montreal. Publishes *Magicamérica*.

Women Make Movies
225 Lafayette St., 2nd Floor
New York, NY 10012
Fax (212) 925-2052; telephone (212) 925-0606

Work by Latin American women, including work by the Sistren Project in Jamaica.

Xchange TV Film and Tape Library
c/o Martha Wallner
(212) 260-6565 or (212) 463-0108

Distributes Nicaraguan tapes produced by the Ministry of Agrarian Reform (MIDINRA) and the Taller Popular de Video "Timoteo Velásquez."

LATINA/Jorge Sánchez,
Atletas No. 2 Pasillo A-301
Col. Country Club, C.P. 04220
México, D.F.
Fax (525) 549-1380; telephone (525) 689-3850

A U.S. distributor of features and documentaries from throughout Latin America; excellent general source.

Latino Collaborative
280 Broadway, Suite 412
New York, NY 10007

An information service for mostly U.S.-born Latino independent producers who distribute their own film/video. Catalog available. Publishes a newsletter, *LC News/Newsletter of the Latino Collaborative*.

SELECTED READINGS

Arbeláez Ramos, Ramiro. *El espacio audiovisual en Colombia: Infraestructura y marco jurídico*. (N.P.): Universidad del Valle, 1992.

Covers current cinema, television, and video trends and developments in Colombia. Octavio Getino is coordinating efforts to publish similar studies on eight other Latin American countries.

Aufderheide, Patricia, and Lois Fishman, eds. *Latin American Visions Catalogue*. Philadelphia, PA: Neighborhood Film/Video Project of International House, 1989.

The catalog of an exhibit of Latin American cinema and video organized by the Neighborhood Film/Video Project of the International House of Philadelphia in 1990. Includes translated essays by Latin American film and video critics.

Boyd, Douglas A., Joseph D. Straubhaar, and John A. Lent. *Videocassette Recorders in the Third World*. New York, NY: Longman, 1989.

Burton, Julianne, ed. *The Social Documentary in Latin America*. Pittsburgh, PA: University of Pittsburgh Press, 1990.

Includes essays on feminist media production, Karen Ranucci's video collecting experiences, media production efforts of El Salvador's Radio Venceremos, Chilean, and Brazilian documentary.

Cham, Mbye, ed. *Ex-Isles: Essays on Caribbean Cinema*. Trenton, NJ: Africa World Press, 1992.

Fills a void in our understanding of non-Hispanic Caribbean film and video developments.

CineWorks: The Guide to Films and Videos by Cine Acción Members. San Francisco, CA: Cine Acción, 1993.

The members include U.S. and Latin American media artists, such as Lourdes Portillo, Gustavo Vázquez, and Carlos Avila. The guide provides titles and descriptions; running time and available formats; prices; and distribution/contact information.

Dinamarca, Hernán. *El video en América Latina: Actor innovador del espacio audiovisual*. Montevideo: Fundación de Cultura Universitaria, 1990.

Background information on the introduction and use of video in Latin America, including country summaries, Latin American distribution efforts, and major Latin American video festivals.

Ecrans d'Afrique: Revue Internationale de Cinéma, Télévision et Vidéo.

Began publication in 1992 in Burkina Faso, Africa. Covers the African diaspora. Excellent coverage of Caribbean video developments.

Fusco, Coco, ed. *Internal Exile: New Films and Videos from Chile.* New York, NY: Third World Newsreel, 1990.

Publication designed to accompany a touring film and video exhibition of media art produced by directors living and working inside Pinochet's Chile.

Fusco, Coco. *Young, British and Black.* Buffalo, NY: Hallwalls/ Contemporary Arts Center, 1988.

Monograph on Sankofa Film/Video Collective and Black Audio Film Collective, two highly productive Caribbean exile groups in the U.K.

Gutiérrez, Mario, ed. *Video, tecnología y comunicación.* Lima: Instituto para América Latina, 1989.

Luna, Lola G. "El video aplicado a la memoria de las mujeres latinoamericanas." *Boletín Americanista* 30:38 (1988), 141-150.

Magicamérica. New York, NY: Videoteca del Sur, 1991–.

Newsletter published by Videoteca del Sur on the popular video movement in Latin America.

Monte-Mór, Patrícia. "A produção de vídeo independente no Brasil: Dados para a su história." In Ann Hartness, ed., *Continuity and Change in Brazil and the Southern Cone: Research Trends and Library Collections for the Year 2000.* Papers of SALALM XXXV, Rio de Janeiro, Brazil, June 3-8, 1990. Albuquerque, NM: SALALM, 1990. Pp. 263-269.

Pick, Zuzana M. *The New Latin American Cinema: A Continental Project.* Austin: University of Texas Press, 1993.

Several of the essays incorporate a discussion of the video movement in Latin America.

Ranucci, Karen. *Directory of Film and Video Production Resources in Latin America.* New York, NY: AIVF, 1990.

Lists works, producers, and noteworthy organizations in Latin America. The International Media Resource Exchange is currently producing a database and directory that will identify, describe, and locate Latin American-made video materials.

Review: Latin American Literature and Arts 46 (Fall 1992).

The whole issue is devoted to contemporary Latin American film. Includes articles on Latin American women directors, film in the southern cone today, video in Latin America, and Latin American film and video festivals.

Suro, Federico. "Take Two on Video." *Américas* 44:2 (1992), 40-49.

Straubhaar, Joseph D. "The Impact of VCRs on Broadcasting in Brazil, Colombia, the Dominican Republic, and Venezuela." *Studies in Latin American Popular Culture* 8 (1989), 183-199.

———. "Television and Video in the Transition from Military to Civilian Rule in Brazil." *Latin American Research Review* 24:1 (1989), 140-154.

Velleggia, Susana, et al. *Experiencias en el espacio audiovisual: Argentina, Brasil, Chile, Uruguay*. Montevideo: Fundación de Cultura Universitaria, 1990.

Papers presented at a seminar held in Montevideo, November 10-11, 1989, sponsored by the Centro de Medios Audiovisuales and the Instituto de Comunicación y Desarrollo.

15. Independent Video in Brazil

Carmen M. Muricy

Brazil today is the world's eighth largest economy; it has the fourth largest television network, with the fifth largest circulation weekly magazine, and one of the worst income distributions on the planet. With 146 million people, Brazil has more homes equipped with televisions (73.8%) than refrigerators (71.1%). A slum dweller in São Paulo declared very plainly: "What do I need a refrigerator for? I have nothing to keep in it."

The profound relationship between social inequalities and the monopoly of information and mass media has often been noted. In Brazil, the executive branch of government still controls broadcasting station licenses, using them as tools of political manipulation.

There is great hope for the democratization of communication in the country later this year when Congress will vote on the Democratic Information Bill. Among other important features, the bill ends the monopoly and oligopoly in radio and television in all regions of Brazil and establishes rules for community television stations. It has the support of the Forum Nacional da Democratizacão da Comunicação, consisting of about 40 state and regional committees, which, in turn, unite more than 1,000 organizations. The Associação Brasileira de Vídeo Popular—ABVP (Brazilian Association for Popular Video) has assumed leadership of the popular movements in the Forum. This proposed legislation was widely discussed at the II Seminário Nacional de Vídeo Popular/VIII Encontro Nacional da ABVP (National Seminar of Popular Video/ABVP National Meeting), held in late 1992 in Belo Horizonte, Minas Gerais, and at the I Encontro de Vídeo Popular de Rio Grande do Sul (First Rio Grande do Sul Meeting on Popular Video), in Porto Alegre, also organized by the ABVP.

Within this context independent video has a marked presence in communication and in social movements in Brazil. This paper outlines the development of independent video in Brazil, emphasizing popular video, where there is creative pioneer work in progress.

History

Brazilian television was established in 1950. Six years later, with the development of videotape, live shows on television were replaced by recordings on tape. The first fifteen years, dominated by TV Tupi, were characterized by improvisation and creativity. After 1965, with political and technological changes, Rede Globo de Televisão assumed superiority, and its dominion continues to the present day. Other networks appeared, such as Rede Manchete and Sistema Brasileiro de Televisão (SBT), but they did not threaten the power of Rede Globo. The first videocassette recorders (VCRs) arrived in Brazil in the mid-1970s, legally imported by the television networks, followed by a great number of smuggled VCRs and underground cassettes. Brazilian home video appeared in 1982, leading to a major change in television viewing habits.

The 1980s were the years of redemocratization and development of new technologies in communication and information, when independent video production started. Its origins were in a universe uncompromised by the traditional television environment, led by artists, university graduates, and television professionals. Short-subjects, documentaries, and art-videos proliferated, produced by alternative and experimental groups. They exhibited their work in shows, festivals, and on television. In 1982 the First National Video Show (I Mostra Nacional de Vídeo) took place in São Paulo, followed in 1983 by I Vídeo Rio in Rio de Janeiro. The most prestigious event, Vídeo-Brasil International Festival (Festival Internacional de Vídeo Brasil), formerly known as Vídeo Fotóptica Festival (Festival Fotóptica de Vídeo) and held annually in São Paulo, is in its ninth year of presentation.

It is important to note the influence of independent producers on TV aesthetics in their use of language. This was the case of the São Paulo group called Olhar Eletrônico which received various national prizes. It became famous for its programs "23ª Hora" (23rd Hour) and "Olho Mágico" (Magic Eye) broadcast by TV Gazeta in São Paulo. Popular video, trying to break away from the governmental monopoly of information aimed at the masses, set up TVs in public squares and disseminated the works produced by popular movements and nongovernmental organizations (NGOs). Lacking funds, they minimized technical concerns and concentrated on the content of their products.

São Paulo and Rio de Janeiro, where most of the independent video producers work, maintain their leadership. Minas Gerais, Rio Grande do Sul, and Pernambuco are important centers as well.

Video has become a part of many aspects of Brazilian society, in cultural and educational projects. A variety of production and distribution networks related to specific groups such as schools, universities, government agencies, and cultural centers has developed.

In 1990 a pioneer catalog in the area, *Filmes e vídeos em ciência e tecnologia*, was published by IBICT (Instituto Brasileiro de Informação em Ciência e Tecnologia). It listed 1,811 titles produced by government and private institutions, including some produced abroad. This material was part of the database FILMES, created in 1989 and available to the public for research via the national network RENPAC (Rede Nacional de Pacotes), by accessing the database SEMEAR (Sistema de Linha Especializada em Armazenamento e Recuperação de Informação, On Line Specialized Information Storage and Retrieval System).

The Fundação Oswaldo Cruz (Rio de Janeiro) has a video unit, designed to promote the dissemination of health information. In 1992 it sponsored I Vídeosaúde: Mostra Nacional de Vídeo Sobre Saúde (I Health Video: National Exhibition of Health Videos), showing about 70 videos produced by 41 public agencies, nongovernamental organizations, and commercial companies.

In spite of the economic crisis of recent years, there is growth in videoclubs and in video rental establishments in the bigger cities. Cultural centers, such as the Instituto Cultural Itaú in São Paulo and the Centro Cultural Banco do Brasil in Rio de Janeiro, promote video showings.

Popular Video

Popular video, as noted above, started in the 1980s as a means of communication among the various social groups that fought for their rights, particularly in the areas of politics, labor, education, and religion.

In September 1984 about 40 groups met during the I National Meeting of Groups of Video Producers in Popular Movements in São Bernardo do Campo, São Paulo, to discuss a proposal to create an association of people who worked with popular videos. In November of the same year, the Associaçao de Vídeo no Movimento Popular was founded. It is known today as the Associação Brasileira de Vídeo Popular (ABVP). The activities of the ABVP increased, and after 1986 popular video expanded, with an ever growing number of groups and programs. In the labor movement area, the most important are TV dos Trabalhadores—TVT (Workers' Television), from São Bernardo and Diadema, São Paulo, TV dos Bancarios de São Paulo (Bank Clerks), and the Union of Workers in Telecommunications in Minas Gerais and in Rio Grande do Sul. Nongovernmental organizations (NGOs) are very active in the production of videos: among them are FASE—Federação de Órgãos para a Assistência Social (Federation of Social Assistance Agencies), ISER—Instituto de Estudos da Religião (Institute for Religious Studies), IBASE—Instituto Brasileiro de Análises Sociais e

Econômicas (Brazilian Institute for Social and Economical Analysis), and CECIP—Centro de Imagem de Criação Popular (Center for the Creation of Popular Images), all located in Rio de Janeiro.

Two noteworthy Catholic Church projects are the Produtora dos Salesianos in Minas Gerais and Verbo Filmes in São Paulo. The Centro de Trabalho Indigenista—CTI (Indian Work Center) located in São Paulo developed a project with a series of documentaries on Brazilian Indians. It showed the Indians' emotions when they saw their own images and documented the exchange of information and experiences among the various tribes. Projeto Vídeo nas Aldeias (Video in Villages Project) produced some nine videos, and O Espíritu da TV (Spirit of TV) received various national and international prizes (1990).

The nine-year-old ABVP, with 200 members, has been developing several projects that will promote the exchange of information among videomakers and producers in Brazil and throughout Latin America. Its activities focus on training, distributing videos and information, and promoting regional and national meetings. The association plans to organize a video library, establish new communication centers, and initiate a national network to facilitate regional and international communication through electronic mail. Its publications include a bimonthly bulletin *Vídeo Popular*, with 17 issues to date, and *Catálogo de vídeos*, issued in June 1992. The catalog lists 300 videos available at the ABVP collection. These are primarily documentaries on the Brazilian reality made by social movement groups and independent producers. The catalog is indexed by subject and includes credits and a synopsis for each title. The first edition was published by Cinema Distribuição Independente (CDI) in 1989.

CDI was established in 1979 by independent moviemakers, having collected more than 400 motion pictures in 16mm and 35mm, videos on social issues, highly creative fiction, animated cartoons, and experimental works. Today, besides its role as distributor of alternative films, it is an educational and informational center and a think-tank on cinema and video. CDI is a member of FEDALC—Federación de Distribuidoras Alternativas de América Latina y Caribe (Federation of Alternative Distributors of Latin America and the Caribbean).

Ethnic communities in Brazil have also been active in video production. The Jewish, Japanese, Portuguese, Arab, and other groups produce their own commercial television programs, usually broadcast on smaller television stations. The Jewish communities in Rio de Janeiro and São Paulo have produced two programs for many years: "Comunidade na TV" (Community at the TV), sponsored by the Jewish Federation of Rio de Janeiro since 1985, and "Mosaico," produced in São Paulo.

Various important experiments in the area of popular video are in progress. New groups and projects constantly emerge while others disappear, reflecting the shifting Brazilian political, economic, and social scenes.

Community Television

The four community television projects discussed below take place in poor communities, using modern video technology, and encourage people to reflect on their own problems in public.

TV Viva (Olinda, Pernambuco)

Initiated in 1984, TV Viva is a project of the Centro Cultural Luiz Freire (Luiz Freire Cultural Center), which produces and shows programs in Greater Recife and Olinda. The videos are informal, recorded in the streets with wit and art. They reflect the daily lives of the people, with all their joys and their difficulties. The public showings are on big screens, attracting hundreds of viewers. In 1987 TV Viva won first prize at the Festival do Novo Cinema Latino-Americano de Havana (Havana Festival of the New Latin-American Cinema) for its work in video communication.

TV Maré (Rio de Janeiro)

TV Maré started in 1989 as a result of a proposal by Caritas of the Archdiocese do Rio de Janeiro, which recommended using video for educational and entertainment purposes, with the direct participation of residents of poor areas. The Maré complex, a slum located in Bonsucesso (adjacent to Avenida Brasil, the Cidade Universitária, and the road known as Linha Vermelha), has some 150,000 inhabitants, living in ten communities. They began filming with a VHS camera, borrowed from Caritas. Caritas also offered vocational courses on videomaking. A video team was eventually formed which recorded daily events in the neighborhood and showed the videos on monitors placed in streets and other open areas.

TV Maxambomba (Nova Iguaçu, Rio de Janeiro)

TV Maxambomba (the name comes from a local expression) began in 1986 as the Popular Video Project, an initiative of CECIP—Centro de Criação de Imagem Popular (Center for the Creation of Popular Images), a nongovernmental organization dedicated to the production of audiovisual and graphic materials. In the working class suburb of Nova Iguaçu (population 2 million) a community television service which produces a monthly video magazine for exhibition in public squares was created. TV Maxambomba uses a giant screen mounted on top of a van to inform the community about issues ignored by commercial television. Local groups help create the video dramatizations. Concerns ranging from public health, to women's cooperatives, to taxes are discussed with widespread public participation.

TV Mocoronga (Santarém, Pará)

The Saúde e Alegria (Health and Joy) Project, active in Amazônia since 1987, promotes integrated development in health, environment, rural production, arts, and communication. It reaches 19 rural communities, contacting some 18,000 inhabitants. One of its programs, TV Mocoronga (Mocoronga refers to a native of Santarém), was created in July 1991. A crew records local events and covers community affairs and social movements of the area. In addition to television programs of local interest, it produces documentaries and educational and research videos.

16. Independent Video in Brazil: Useful Sources

Carmen M. Muricy

Catalogs

Exhibitions, Festivals, and Events

10 anos Vídeo Independente, 80/90. São Paulo: Elétrico Cineclube, n.d. 54 p.

O Cinema Cultural Paulista (6th: 1992: São Paulo, Brazil). *O Cinema Cultural Paulista, 8 a 13 de dezembro de 1992.* São Paulo: Museu da Imagem e do Som, 1992. 56 p.

Curtas dos anos 80 (1989: São Paulo, Brazil). *80 curtas dos anos 80.* São Paulo: Secretaria de Estado de Cultura; Museu da Imagem e do Som, 1989. 4 p.

Festival Internacional Vídeobrasil (9th: 1992: São Paulo, Brazil). *9º Festival Internacional Vídeobrasil, de 21 a 27 de setembro de 1992.* São Paulo: Associação Cultural Vídeobrasil; SESC, 1992. 100 p.

Festival Fotóptica Vídeobrasil (8th: 1989: São Paulo, Brazil). *VIII Festival Fotóptica Vídeobrasil, 28 de setembro a 1º de outubro.* São Paulo: Secretaria de Estado da Cultura; Fotóptica; Museu da Imagem e do Som, 1989. 32 p.

Festival Vídeo Educativo (1st: 1989: São Paulo, Brazil). *1ª Festival Vídeo Educativo.* São Paulo: Universidade de São Paulo, Escola de Comunicações e Artes—ECA, Curso de Rádio e Televisão—CTR; Associação Brasileira de Tecnologia Educacional—ABT/SP, 1989. 13 p.

Festival Vídeo Educativo (2nd: 1990: São Paulo, Brazil). *2º Festival Vídeo Educativo, 15 a 18 de maio/90.* São Paulo: Universidade de São Paulo, Escola de Comunicações e Artes—ECA, Curso de Rádio e Televisão—CTR; Associação Brasileira de Tecnologia Educacional—ABT/SP, 1990. 21 p.

FORUMBHZVIDEO (1991: Belo Horizonte, Brazil). *Festival de Vídeo de Belo Horizonte.* Belo Horizonte: Secretaria Municipal de Cultura, 1991. 96 p.

Fotoptica International Video Festival (8th: 1990: São Paulo, Brazil). *8th Fotoptica International Video Festival, 09 a 15 de novembro de 1990.* São Paulo: Museu da Imagem e do Som, 1990. 98 p.

Mostra de Filmes e Vídeos Ecológicos Franceses e Brasileiros (1992: Rio de Janeiro, Brazil). *Filmes e vídeos brasileiros.* Paris: Ministère de l'Environment; Ministère des Affaires Etrangères; Rio de Janeiro: Fundação Museu da Imagem e do Som, 1992. 24 p.

Mostra de Vídeos sobre Ecologia e Meio-Ambiente (1992: Rio de Janeiro, Brazil). *Terra à vista.* Rio de Janeiro: Centro Cultural Banco do Brasil, 1992. "Evento do calendário oficial da Rio Eco 92". 1 leaflet.

Retrospectiva Atlantic do Vídeo Independente (1992: Rio de Janeiro, Brazil). *Retrospectiva Atlantic do Vídeo Independente: a trajetória da produção brasileira, exibido na TVE de 05 a 09 de outubro de 1992.* Rio de Janeiro: Fundaçao Roquete Pinto, Rede Brasil de TVs Educativas; Centro Cultural Cândido Mendes, 1992. 1 leaflet.

São Paulo International Short Film Festival (3rd: 1992: São Paulo). *III São Paulo International Short Film Festival, 20th–30th August 1992.* São Paulo: Museu da Imagem e do Som, 1992. 80 p. "III Festival Internacional de Curtas Metragens de São Paulo".

Vídeosaúde. Mostra Nacional de Vídeo sobre Saúde (l: 1992: Rio de Janeiro, Brazil). *Catálogo geral.* Rio de Janeiro: Fundação Oswaldo Cruz, Superintendencia de Informação Científica e Tecnológica—SICT, Núcleo de Vídeo—NVT, 1992. 30 p.

Producers/Distributors

Associação Brasileira de Vídeo Popular. *Catálogo de vídeos,* junho/1992. São Paulo: ABVP, 1992.

Catálogo Cinevídeo 1989. São Paulo: Associação Brasileira de Vídeo Popular—ABVP; Cinema Distribuição Independente—CDI, 1989.

Catálogo de recursos pedagógicos: vídeos. São Paulo: Secretaria Nacional de Formação, CUT [1990]. 60 p.

Catálogo de vídeos: mulher e trabalho. Rio de Janeiro: Conselho Estadual dos Direitos da Mulher—CEDIM, 1992. 47 p.

Catálogo Videoteca de Economia. Rio de Janeiro: Conselho Regional de Economia—CORECON, 1ª Região, RJ, Núcleo de Valorização Profissional, n.d. 35 p.

Centro de Criação de Imagem Popular. *Lista de produções.* Rio de Janeiro: CECIP [1992].

Centro de Documentação e Pesquisa Vergueiro. *Agenda de recursos audiovisuais.* São Paulo: CPV [1990]. 3 v.

———. *Relação das entidades que trabalham com recursos audiovisuais.* São Paulo: CPV [1990]. 12 p.

Cinema Rio de Janeiro 1990 a 1992. Rio de Janeiro: Centro Cultural Banco do Brasil [1993]. 64 p.

FASE. *Catálogo de Vídeo.* Rio de Janeiro: Federação de Órgãos para Assistência Social e Educacional [1992]. 40 p.

Filmes e vídeos em ciência e tecnologia. Brasília: Instituto Brasileiro de Informação em Ciência e Tecnologia—IBICT, 1990. 615 p.

IBASE Vídeo. *Catálogo 93.* Rio de Janeiro: Instituto Brasileiro de Análises Sociais c Econômicas, IBASE Vídeo, 1993. 34 p.

ISER Vídeo. *Catálogo.* Rio de Janeiro: Instituto de Estudos de Religião, ISER-Vídeo [1992]. 6 l.

SOS Corpo. *Catálogo 92.* Recife: SOS Corpo, 1992. 22 p. "Vídeos": pp. 17-22.

TV Viva. *Vídeos realizados.* Olinda: Centro de Cultura Luiz Freire, TV Viva, 1992? 28 l.

Universidade de Brasília. *UnB verde vida.* Brasília: Universidade de Brasília, 1992. 72 p. "Videotapes": pp. 31-38.

———. Centro de Produção Cultural Educativa. *Catálogo dos vídeos produzidos pelo CPCE até 07/01/93.* Brasília: CPCE, 1993. 40 p.

Verbo Filmes. *Catálogo.* [São Paulo]: Verbo Filmes, n.d. 39 p.

Vídeo 89. São Paulo: Editora Nova Cultural Ltda., 1988. 800 p. (Guias Práticos Nova Cultural). "90 anos de cinema brasileiro: a memória resgatada pelo videocassete": pp. 692-698.

Vídeo 1993. São Paulo: Editora Nova Cultural Ltda., 1992. 896 p. (Guias Práticos Nova Cultural).

Vídeo verde: imagens ambientais registradas em 476 vídeos e filmes. Brasília: Fôlha Ecológica Comunicação Ltda., 1992. 121 p.

The Academia Brasileira de Vídeo. Videoteca Cultural Brasileira. *Catálogo 87-88.* São Paulo: 1987. 188 p.

Addresses of Producers, Distributors, and Institutions

Abril Vídeo
Av. Ermano Marchetti, 1272 - Agua Branca
05038-001 São Paulo, São Paulo
Telephone: (011) 832-1555

Associação Brasileira de Vídeo Popular—ABVP
Rua Treze de Maio, 489
01327-000 São Paulo, São Paulo
Telephone: (011) 284-7862 Fax: (011) 287-2259

Associação Brasileira de Vídeo Popular/ABVP-Centro-Oeste
SDS Edifício Venâncio III - cobertura
70393-900 Brasília, Distrito Federal
Telephone: (061) 223-8476/322-5404 Fax: (061) 223-8476

Associação Brasileira de Vídeo Popular/ABVP-Nordeste
Rua Vinte e Quatro de Janeiro, 150 Sul
64001-230 Teresina, Piauí
Telephone: (086) 222-8121 Fax: (086) 222-8122

Associação Brasileira de Vídeo Popular/ABVP-Norte
Av. Borges de Leal, 2284
68040-080 Santarém, Pará
Telephone: (091) 522-5090/523-1083 Fax: (091) 522-5748

Associação Brasileira de Vídeo Popular/ABVP-Sudeste
FASE-Setor de Audiovisual
Rua Bento Lisboa, 58 - Catete
22221-011 Rio de Janeiro, Rio de Janeiro
Telephone: (021) 285-2998 Fax: (011) 205-3099

Associação Brasileira de Vídeo Popular/ABVP-Sul
Rua José Pedro Gil, 31 - Agronômica
88025-030 Florianópolis, Santa Catarina
Telephone: (048) 222-8895 Fax: (048) 222-8895

Associação Cultural Vídeobrasil
Rua Cônego Eugênio Leite, 920
05414-001 São Paulo, São Paulo
Telephone: (011) 280-6031 Fax: (011) 64-5564

Centro Cultural do Banco do Brasil—CCBB
Setor de Cinema e Vídeo
Rua Primeiro de Março, 66 - 4° andar - sala 7
20010-000 Rio de Janeiro, Rio de Janeiro
Telephone: (021) 216-0290

Centro de Assessoría Multiprofissional—CAMP
Rua Vilamil, 98 - Santa Teresa
90840-190 Porto Alegre, Rio Grande do Sul
Telephone: (051) 233-4101/233-0901

Centro de Criação de Imagem Popular—CECIP
Rua Senador Dantas, 80 sala 201
20031-201 Rio de Janeiro, Rio de Janeiro
Telephone: (021) 533-0772/220-8316 Fax: (021) 533-0772

Centro de Defesa dos Direitos Humanos/CMBB Norte I
Projeto CDDN-Vídeo
Rua Ramos Ferreira, 260
69010-120 Manaus, Amazonas
Telephone: (092) 233-8072 Fax: (092) 233-8636

Centro de Estudos Avançados de Promoção Social—CEAPS
Projeto Saúde e Alegria
Caixa Postal 243
68100-970 Santarém, Pará
Telephone: (091) 522-5090 Fax: (091) 523-1083

Centro de Estudos e Práticas de Educação Popular—CEPEPO
Rua 25 de Junho, 2154
C.P. 1288
66035-790 Belém, Pará
Telephone: (091) 229-7323 Fax: (091) 229-7323

Centro de Trabalho Indigenista—CTI
Rua Fidalga, 548 - sala 13
05432-000 São Paulo, São Paulo
Telephone: (011) 813-3450 Fax: (011) 813-0747

Centro Ecumênico de Documentação e Informação—CEDI
Rua Santa Amaro, 129 - Glória
22211-230 Rio de Janeiro, Rio de Janeiro
Telephone: (021) 224-6713

Ciência Produções
Av. das Américas, 1917 - s. 229 - Barra de Tijuca
22631-000 Rio de Janeiro, Rio de Janeiro
Telephone: (021) 325-1712

Cinema Distribuição Independente—CDI
Rua Treze de Maio, 489
01327-000 São Paulo, São Paulo
Telephone: (011) 288-4694 Fax: (011) 284-0586

Cinemateca Brasileira
Rua Volkswagen, s/nº - Parque Conceição
04344-020 São Paulo, São Paulo
Telephone: (011) 577-4666 ext. 13

Companhia de Tecnologia de Saneamento Ambiental—CETESB
Av. Prof. Hermann Junior, 345
05489-90 São Paulo, São Paulo
Telephone: (011) 210-1100 ext. 380

Comunicação Edições Paulinas—COMEP
Rua Botucatu, 171
04023-061 São Paulo, São Paulo
Telephone: (011) 549-6799

Comunicação Mulher—COMULHER
Rua Rocha, 119/504 - Bela Vista
01330-000 São Paulo, São Paulo
Telephone: (011) 251-5626

Em Vídeo
Rua Sertões, 147 - Prado
30410-020 Belo Horizonte, Minas Gerais
Fax: (031) 335-7555

Ema Vídeo Ltda.
SCRN 708/9 Bl. E - loja 10
70740-780 Brasília, Distrito Federal
Telephone: (061) 274-6683/274-6432 Fax: (061) 347-3352

Estudos e Comunicação em Sexualidade e Reprodução Humana—ECOS
Rua dos Tupinambás, 239
04104-080 São Paulo, São Paulo
Telephone: (011) 275-7338 Fax: (011) 573-8340

Federação de Orgãos para Assistência Social e Educacional—FASE
Rua Bento Lisboa, 58 - Catete
22221-011 Rio de Janeiro, Rio de Janeiro
Telephone: (021) 285-2998

Federação de Orgãos para Assistência Social e Educacional—FASE
Rua São Paulo, 404
69033-180 Manaus, Amazonas
Telephone: (092) 671-6121

Fundação Oswaldo Cruz—FIOCRUZ
Núcleo de Vídeo
Av. Brasil, 4036 sala 514 - Manguinhos
21040-361 Rio de Janeiro, Rio de Janeiro
Telephone: (021) 280-9441/590-9122 ext. 257, 335, 311

Fundação para o Desenvolvimento de Educação
Rua Rodolfo Miranda, 636
01121-010 São Paulo, São Paulo
Telephone: (011) 228-1922 ext. 239

Fundação Roberto Marinho
Coordenação de Programas de Televisão
Av. Paulo de Frontin, 568 - Rio Comprido
20261-243 Rio de Janeiro, Rio de Janeiro
Telephone: (021) 273-3377 Fax: (021) 293-8912

Fundição Arte e Progresso
Vídeo Fundição
Rua dos Arcos, 24-50
20230-060 Rio de Janeiro, Rio de Janeiro
Telephone: (021) 532-4308

Instituto Brasileiro de Análises Sociais e Econômicas—IBASE
IBASE Vídeo
Rua Vicente de Souza, 29 - Botofogo
22251-070 Rio de Janeiro, Rio de Janeiro
Telephone: (021) 226-5412

Instituto Brasileiro de Arte e Cultura—IBAC
Coordenadoria de Cinema
Av. Brasil, 2482 - Benfica
20930-040 Rio de Janeiro, Rio de Janeiro
Telephone: (021) 580-9848/580-9292

Instituto Cultural Itaú—ICI
Centro de Informática e Cultura
Av. Paulista, 2424
01310-300 São Paulo, São Paulo
Telephone: (011) 257-8031/258-8920

Instituto de Estudos da Religião
ISER Vídeo
Ladeira da Glória, 98 - Glória
22211-120 Rio de Janeiro, Rio de Janeiro
Telephone: (021) 265-5747/205-7085 Fax: (021) 205-4796

Interior Produções Ltda.
Rua Barão de Jaguaripe, 243 - casa
22421-000 Rio de Janeiro, Rio de Janeiro
Telephone: (021) 521-5700/274-9868 Fax: (021) 205-4796

Interlab Som e Imagem Ltda.
Rua Turiassu, 376
05005-000 São Paulo, São Paulo
Telephone: (011) 62-9373/65-6651

Link Produções Audiovisuales Ltda.
Rua da Glória, 190/601 - Glória
20241-180 Rio de Janeiro, Rio de Janeiro
Telephone: (021) 232-7610 Fax: (021) 222-0927

M.W.L. Comunicação
Rua Paraíba, 737
15500-000 Votuporanga, São Paulo
Telephone: (017) 421-7311

Magnetoscópio Vídeo & Comunicação
Rua Siqueira Campos, 143 gr. 154
22031-070 Rio de Janeiro, Rio de Janeiro
Telephone: (021) 235-5069 Fax: (021) 257-5571

Manduri Produções
Av. Marte, 451 - Centro de Apoio I - Alphaville
06500-000 Santana de Parnaíba, São Paulo
Telephone: (011) 723-3599

Museu da Imagem e do Som—MIS
Av. Europa, 158
01449-000 São Paulo, São Paulo
Telephone: (011) 282-8074

Orion Cinema e Vídeo Ltda.
Rua Mourato Coelho, 972
05417-001 São Paulo, São Paulo
Telephone: (011) 212-3554 Fax: (011) 211-7059

Pulsar Artes e Promoções Ltda.
Rua Lopes Trovão, 89/401
24220-070 Niterói, Rio de Janeiro
Telephone: (021) 710-0465

Quinze Minutos Vídeo
Rua Maria Quitéria, 96/502
22410-040 Rio de Janeiro, Rio de Janeiro
Telephone: (021) 287-2691/247-0796 Fax: (021) 294-7691

Savaget Produções
Rua Santa Alexandrina, 343 casa 3 - Rio Comprido
20260-020 Rio de Janeiro, Rio de Janeiro
Telephone: (021) 502-5451 Fax: (021) 273-9087

Secretaria de Estado do Meio Ambiente
Coordenadoria de Educação Ambiental/Videoteca Videoambiente
Av. Nove de Julho, 4877 - 11° andar
01407-902 São Paulo, São Paulo
Telephone: (011) 852-1896 Fax: (011) 881-4618

SOS Corpo
Núcleo de Documentação e Produção de Materiais Educativos—NUDOC
Rua do Hospício, 859/ap. 14
50060-080 Recife, Pernambuco
Telephone: (081) 221-3018 Fax: (081) 221-3947

The Academia Brasileira de Vídeo
Praça Benedito Calixto, 113
05406-040 São Paulo, São Paulo
Telephone: (011) 883-0633 Fax: (011) 573-8340

TV dos Trabalhadores—TVT
Sindicato dos Metalúrgicos de São Bernardo do Campo e Diadema
Rua João Basso, 121
Caixa Postal 294
09721-100 São Bernardo do Campo, São Paulo
Telephone: (011) 452-3922/458-7102

TV dos Trabalhadores—TVT
Rua Ouvidor Peleja, 112
04128-000 São Paulo, São Paulo
Telephone: (011) 275-5913/579-2208 Fax: (011) 275-6318

TV Maré
Rua Capivari, 57 casa 1 - Bonsucesso
21042-090 Rio de Janeiro, Rio de Janeiro
Telephone: (021) 260-5468

TV Viva
Rua São Bento, 344 - Carmo
53020-080 Olinda, Pernambuco
Telephone: (081) 429-4109 Fax: (081) 429-4881

TVB—Sindicato dos Bancários de São Paulo
Rua do Comércio, 22/4° andar
01013-010 São Paulo, São Paulo
Telephone: (011) 37-7461

Universidade de Brasília—UnB
Centro de Produção Cultural Educativa—CPCE
ICC Norte - Módulo 5 - Campus Universitário
70910-900 Brasília, Distrito Federal
Telephone: (061) 274-6783

Universidade de São Paulo—USP
Escola de Comunicação e Artes—ECA
Av. Prof. Lúcio M. Rodrigues, 443
Cidade Universitária
05508-900 São Paulo, São Paulo
Telephone: (011) 813-3222 r. 2086 Fax: (011) 815-4272

Universidade Federal Fluminense—UFF
Núcleo Audiovisual
Rua Prof. Lara Vilela, 126
24210-590 Niterói, Rio de Janeiro
Telephone: (021) 719-3458

Usina do Gasômetro
Núcleo de Vídeo
Av. Presidente João Goulart, 551
90010-120 Porto Alegre, Rio Grande do Sul
Telephone: (051) 227-1383 Fax: (051) 221-6078

Ver e Ouvir
Rua Pascal, 791 - Campo Belo
04616-002 São Paulo, São Paulo
Telephone: (011) 533-2125/530-6509

Verbo Filmes
Rua Verbo Divino, 671
Caixa Postal 12.605
04719-001 São Paulo, São Paulo
Telephone: (011) 548-5744 Fax: (011) 521-6135

VTV Vídeo Ltda.
Rua Itapeva, 187
01332-000 São Paulo, São Paulo
Telephone: (011) 251-1313/284-4487 Fax: (011) 251-3740

Bibliography

Almeida, Cândido José Mendes de. *O que é vídeo*. 2d ed. Coleção Primeiros Passos, 137. São Paulo: Brasiliense, 1986. 96 p.

Ceccon, Claudius. "Brazilian Centre Shows That Video Is an Agent of Change." *Media Development* 36:4 (1989), 30-32.

Monte-Mór, Patrícia. "A produção de vídeo independente no Brasil: dados para a sua história." In Ann Hartness, ed., *Continuity and Change in Brazil and the Southern Cone: Research Trends and Library Collections for the Year 2000.* Papers of SALALM XXXV, Rio de Janeiro, Brazil, June 3-8, 1990. Albuquerque, NM: SALALM, 1992. Pp. 263-269.

Santoro, Luiz Fernando. *A imagem nas mãos: o vídeo popular no Brasil.* Novas Buscas em Comunicação, 33. São Paulo: Summus Editorial, 1989.

———. "O vídeo no Brasil—1986." *Cinejornal* 1 (1986), 3-54.

Vídeo popular, no. 1– August 1984– . São Paulo: Associação Brasileira de Vídeo Popular (ABVP). Bimonthly. Numbers examined: no. 13 (May/ June 1992) – no. 17 (January/February 1993).

"Vídeo popular: as outras cores da imagem." *Proposta* 14:43 (November 1989), 1-68.

New Technology for Information Management

17. Groping for Our Piece of the Elephant: Latin American Information on the Internet

Molly Molloy

What Is the Internet: Past, Present, Future?

The Internet has been described in a variety of ways:

- a network of networks based on the TCP/IP protocols (a common language that allows all the different computers on the net to communicate with each other)
- a community of people who use and develop the networks
- a collection of resources that are accessible via these networks.[1]

The Internet as it exists today is a global resource connecting millions of users which began over twenty years ago as an experiment by the U.S. Department of Defense. This global network encompasses over 10,000 connected networks, 1.3 million computers, and more than 12 million users (the number of individual users grows daily). The Internet servers (or nodes) communicate with each other using standard TCP/IP protocols, but the Internet also provides gateways to other networks and services that may use different protocols, such as Bitnet, Peacenet, or Fidonet. In addition, many commercial services such as CompuServe and Dialog can be accessed via the Internet.

The Internet has no real governing body. Krol describes it as something like a church with a "council of elders" (a volunteer group known as the Internet Architecture Board or IAB) which makes policies and sets standards for how the Internet should function. As in a church, Internet "members" may express their opinions, agreement, or disagreement with the Internet Architecture Board through meetings of another volunteer organization, the Internet Engineering Task Force (IETF), but to remain a "member" of the Internet, participant networks must agree to conform to the standards set by the IAB. If a network chooses not to conform (and all are free to do as they wish), then it will no longer be a part of the Internet. The Internet has no president, CEO, or Pope. Individual networks may have such authorities, but there is no single authority for the Internet as a whole. Each constituent network supports itself, and individual subscribers (such as universities) pay for their connections to the Internet.[2]

Within the United States and globally, constituent networks may be owned by government agencies, private enterprises, non-profit organizations, universities, and/or various combinations of such entities. Networks may differ considerably in resources, goals, size, and services offered. In spite of these disparities and what seems at times to be a chaotic lack of structure or governance, the Internet has been incredibly successful in terms of growth—the number of constituent networks has doubled each year since 1990. Weis points to two major reasons for this success: (1) the Internet satisfies user needs; (2) network technologies have developed as solutions to real operational problems.[3]

There are currently Internet connections in over seventy countries and access is spreading rapidly. While the great majority of network users live in North America and Europe, many developing countries are promoting network access as a way to raise education and technology levels. Networks such as Peacenet (run by the Association for Progressive Communications) provide relatively inexpensive gateways to the Internet in many developing countries.[4]

Speaking from the Latin American perspective, Daniel Pimienta, director of the REDALC (Red para América Latina y el Caribe) project, cites several other reasons why network communication can benefit developing countries:

- as an aid to distance education, computer communication may help to alleviate the economic crisis in education;
- network access facilitates communication among scholars who leave to study in the United States and Europe and their colleagues at home;
- the use of networks can raise awareness of both the costs and the value of information;
- communication via computer networks may help to reduce the effects of the brain drain from south to north as information begins to flow more freely in both directions.[5]

The future of the Internet (at least in the United States) promises more commercial use as private enterprises realize the value of network access. More commercial use will lead to more privatization. Individuals not affiliated with universities or government research entities can now purchase Internet access from a growing number of commercial providers. Government funding of the Internet in the United States via the NREN (National Research and Education network) or the NII (National Information Infrastructure) is now being considered by both the U.S. Congress and the White House. The U.S. interstate highway system provides a useful analogy in discussions of government participation in the development of a truly national network in the United States.

The trend toward commercialization and privatization will expand as more individuals come to view network access as a necessity.[6] Weis points out that widespread commercial use (and financing) of the Internet will depend upon the consideration of several key policy issues. These include:

- revision of current "acceptable use" policies that restrict the use of the Internet for commercial purposes;
- establishment of federal statutory protection for network service providers who might be found liable for libel, false advertising, obscenity, copyright violations, and so on because of the content of information that travels over the networks. Network service providers do not function as publishers (which are able to screen material and have the responsibility to protect themselves from liability). Telecommunications carriers cannot screen the information they transmit and are accorded statutory protection against liability. Most Internet service providers cannot screen messages, yet they currently have no statutory protection against liability for the content of those messages.
- integration of "development" networks employing experimental, leading-edge technologies, and heavily used "production" networks based on standard, proven technologies;
- planning to ensure that the Internet becomes an interconnected global resource, rather than clusters of isolated networks.[7]

The NSF (National Science Foundation) and various U.S. corporate entities, most notably AT&T, are collaborating to create network information centers, collectively known as InterNICs to provide directory information to the vast resources of the Internet, theoretically free of charge. These online directories of FTP sites, library catalogs, data archives, as well as e-mail addresses for individual net users could greatly enhance the ability of novice users to find information.[8]

Rationale for Librarians to Use Internet Resources and Services

Electronic communication is already well established in academic and research communities. At present, scientific and technical fields are ahead of the humanities and social sciences, but network use is growing among students and faculty in all areas. On many campuses, students are the heaviest users of e-mail, IRC (Internet Relay Chat), and Usenet News.

Respondents to an Internet use survey conducted by Rohm and Haas Company, a major chemical products manufacturer in Philadelphia, stated that they used electronic mail more than any other Internet service. In addition to personal communications, many respondents stated that they used Usenet newsgroups, electronic mail lists, and bulletin boards as tools for continuing education, current awareness, and to gather information to solve specific problems. Nearly a third of the respondents indicated that they used the Internet to facilitate collaborative research. Others used the Internet to connect to commercial services such as Dialog and found Internet access to be faster and more reliable than modem connections. Respondents expressed concerns relating to security and internal management issues. The Internet was seen as open and unregulated, thus outside the control of traditional management information systems. In addition, once the Internet had been accepted in the organization, its use required a great deal of training and support. The survey was sent to selected industrial, academic, and government organizations and to several Internet newsgroups and lists.[9]

Sharyn Ladner and Hope Tillman surveyed special librarians on their use of the Internet for reference and also found that electronic mail was the most heavily used and most popular Internet service. Many respondents indicated that by using electronic mail, both personal and lists, they were able to take advantage of the specialized expertise of hundreds of colleagues and to respond more quickly to difficult questions from their patrons.[10]

Librarians need to know what sources are available via the networks and how students, researchers, and faculty are using the nets to get information. At present, many students use the nets primarily for interactive games and other entertainment. However, as resource discovery tools improve, more students will look to the nets for research information.[11] Academic librarians need to learn about electronic mail lists, Usenet newsgroups, computer archives, and other sources of information on the Internet in order to be able to recommend the best of these information sources to the students and faculty they serve.

Reference librarians may be the best at evaluating the resources currently available on the Internet. When, for instance, is an Internet source the best thing to use to answer a query? For example, the *CIA World Factbook* and the *U.S. State Department Travel Advisories* are available on many gopher and WAIS servers. Depending on what server is selected, however, the user may or may not get the most up-to-date information. There is no regime in place right now for administering or regulating the information that is posted on the Internet. Each individual site can decide what newsgroups, databases, full-text sources, directories, library catalogs, and so on it will make available. Only at the site level is there any control over the accuracy or currency of the information posted.

Reference librarians and subject specialists, in cooperation with the Internet systems experts, are well qualified to administer and to critically evaluate Internet sources. Librarians can and should make the critical decisions concerning what information to place on the nets. What characteristics of the information should be considered?

- Is it already in the public domain, such as government documents, classics, or the Bible?
- Is it copyright protected? If the Internet carries proprietary information paid for by an institution, for example, a commercial product such as the University of New Mexico's Latin America Database, how will access by net-users from outside the institution be controlled?
- Is the information up-to-date and accurate? Who or what will maintain the information once it is posted onto the network?

The critical evaluation of information that librarians can provide will be even more important in the relatively uncontrolled and "peer-review-less" world of electronic publications. While there are a growing number of peer-reviewed electronic journals,[12] there have been few systematic efforts to evaluate information on the networks using traditional reviewing methods or criteria. One notable exception is a "list review service." Volunteers monitor new electronic mail lists for a period of time and then post reviews of the lists to various interest groups such as LIBREF-L-Discussion of Library Reference Issues.

In a technical discussion of the present and future of Internet resource discovery tools, Schwartz, Emtage, Kahle, and Neuman state that:

> In libraries, highly trained staff are responsible for organizing the available data. Library science has developed methods over hundreds of years to construct a model in which the user, with some experience, can navigate through, locate, retrieve and use the desired information. In contrast, in the Internet every user is also a potential "publisher" and "librarian." No one expects the average user to be able to organize his or her information with such skill. Moreover, because of the decentralized control of Internet information and the difficulty of providing coherent organization in such an environment, most Internet information is only minimally organized. The challenge for the designers of information systems is to help the user find the information that is of interest.[13]

Helping the user find the information that is of interest is precisely what reference librarians do. In addition, librarians generally try to provide more than "minimal organization" of information sources. A recent OCLC research report investigated the nature of electronic textual information on the Internet and addressed the practical and theoretical problems of creating MARC records for text files and other electronic objects available via networks as a first step in providing some sort of cataloging for this huge store of information.[14] Systems specialists, catalogers, and reference librarians working together can develop the access tools needed to enable users to find information on the Internet. We can become the "access engineers" and "knowledge cartographers" that Campbell refers to when he describes an essentially new role for reference librarians. Knowledge cartographers engage in continuous reconnaissance of existing and emerging sources of information and then provide knowledge maps to guide users to the information.[15]

Looking a bit further into the development of automated resource discovery tools, Schwartz et al. describe an automated process that sounds a lot like the traditional "reference interview":

> Searching in a distributed environment is challenging. Brute force methods such as broadcast can pose a tremendous burden on network resources if the information being sought resides on many machines. In this case, one needs a means by which to limit the scope of searches. One means is to request "advice" from the user about promising places to search. This technique is often helpful, because users may know more about a resource being sought than they initially specify . . ..[16]

Librarians use the reference interview to learn as much as possible about the user's information need so that the answers provided will satisfy the user. The give-and-take of the reference interview requires interpersonal communication skills that will probably never be matched by automated tools. However, their sheer numbers dictate that millions of network users will never have the opportunity to personally seek a librarian's guidance to navigate the Internet. Thus, librarians should take the lead in assisting the developers of the resource discovery tools that will continue to improve access to the current information anarchy on the Internet.

How to?

I hope I have mentioned a few compelling reasons why reference librarians should take an active role in using the Internet. In order to include network sources as an integral part of the accessible universe of information, however, librarians must become familiar with some of the sources available and the tools used to discover these sources. Some libraries, computer centers, academic departments, and commercial enterprises have begun to offer workshops and courses on Internet navigation, but many more individuals are "feeling their way" onto the networks and learning by experience.

One of the primary reasons that reference librarians and other information seekers will be inspired to get on the Internet is the possibility for raising current awareness. Fulfilling this need requires the willingness to explore. The adventurer soon discovers that every piece of information found, or contact made, or inquiry floated can open the way to a myriad of other resources. One of the best ways to do this is to subscribe to electronic mail lists (also called bulletin boards, listservs, discussion groups). These lists expand personal electronic mail networks to include hundreds of subscribers from all over the world with similar interests. Many library-oriented lists on the net cover almost any specialty in the field. After spending some time in one subject-oriented "region" of the Internet, the user begins to get to know the cultural landscape, the style of communication, and some of the personalities in the region. Then, the process of "knowledge cartography"—the reconnaisance and mapping of network information sources—can begin.

The best way for the novice user to start is to subscribe to one list that seems to have something to do with an area of interest. Soon, the announcements for new lists, related lists, new files available via FTP, new commercial databases, and more will start to flow to the user's open mailbox. Also, by getting onto a list, the new user will learn many techniques for navigating the Internet, such as how to send commands to subscribe or unsubscribe, how to find out who else is on a list, how to search the list archives (if they exist), how to retrieve files via anonymous FTP, and so on. As with any new technology, the best way to learn is to start doing it.

Lists such as HELP-NET (Chapter 19, "List of Lists for Latin America," below) were set up to help new users find things out. This and other lists maintain FAQ (frequently asked questions) files which are posted periodically to the list to broadcast basic information to new subscribers. In addition, it is part of "netiquette" or the "internet culture" for experienced users to answer new users' questions and to keep the information flow open and courteous. If a new user posts a very basic question, he/she will usually get private mail in response with suggestions for solving the problem. But to really learn, the new user has to take the time to follow suggested procedures and learn by doing.

One does not have to be an expert in all of the Internet resource discovery tools and how they work, but it is necessary for reference librarians and subject specialists to know what the different systems are and how they can be used to find information.

Internet Basics

Kinds of Information Available

Internet users may find the following kinds of information (this list is not meant to be all inclusive):

- the full text of papers, research reports, documents, etc.
- library catalogs
- computer software (special sites and interest groups for all hardware platforms)
- graphics, photographs, and video images
- maps
- music lyrics
- books

- discussion lists and their archives
- specialized databases
- news from wire services and published sources

Internet Services

The following paragraphs briefly describe some of the most popular Internet services.

ELECTRONIC MAIL (e-mail)—This communication tool includes personal mail and list mail. E-mail facilitates communication among colleagues and researchers and is used as a tool for personal and professional communication. Librarians have found it especially useful to solicit help with difficult reference questions. E-mail enables the user to take advantage of another library's collection vicariously. Through an electronic mail interest group, the user can pose one question to hundreds of people with similar knowledge and interests and often elicit dozens of replies. E-mail increases exponentially the chances of finding the right answer.

TELNET—Telnet is the standard protocol used to establish direct connections to computers on the Internet. It is used as a noun and adjective: telnet, the telnet protocol, the telnet address for, etc. Telnet can also be a verb: "Telnet to xyz.uvw.rst.edu." Or often: "I telnetted to Melvyl the other day and couldn't find my way home."

FTP (File transfer protocol)—This tool allows the user to connect to various Internet sites (remote computers) and to transfer files to and from these sites. Many sites maintain archives of files that may include text documents, computer programs, graphics, and so on that are available free to the user who asks for them via FTP.

USENET News—These newsgroups differ from electronic mail lists in that the individual user does not actually receive mail from a group. Rather, the user has access to a computer that subscribes to some or all of the Usenet newsgroups. The individual accesses the news via a connection to one of the connected computers and dips into the newsgroups of interest. The user can post messages to newsgroups, send mail, reply to and save messages, through an account on the computer where he/she reads news. These groups (some are parallel versions of electronic mail groups) cover virtually any subject. Some may seem totally silly (hamsters . . . the Simpsons . . . Star Trek, etc.), while others are quite serious. In a way, these groups are more resource efficient than electronic mail groups because the messages are not duplicated so many times. Thousands of users can read news on one computer and the message is only duplicated once. But the user must have an account on a computer that receives Usenet news or access to one via telnet.

IRC (Internet Relay Chat)—IRC allows people to talk to each other online in real time. The user can signal to another user online and invoke the IRC protocol which produces a split screen where each person's words will be displayed in different window. Depending on network traffic at the time of the online conversation, communication is instant or with only a few seconds delay.

Resource Discovery Tools

The resource discovery tools that might someday make keyword or subject access to the Internet possible are now being developed, but most remain in the developmental or experimental stage. Information sources on the Internet change constantly. Systematic monitoring or reconnaisance via targetted browsing in certain "regions" of the Internet is currently one of the best ways to find out what sources are available at any given time.[17]

ARCHIE—Archie is an Internet discovery tool that searches computer archives on the Internet by looking for keywords in the filenames of the millions of files stored on computers connected via the Internet. This works especially well for locating computer programs or known documents. Archie does not work nearly as well for locating materials on a subject. To use Archie, the user telnets to an archie site, logs in as "archie," and then sends search commands using keywords or filenames (if known). Archie sends a message back with the Internet addresses for the computer, the directory names, and filenames that enable the user to retrieve the entire file via FTP.

GOPHER—A software program developed at the University of Minnesota, Gopher allows the user to "burrow" through the Internet using a set of menus to point the way. Gopher employs the client-server model of computing in which the end-user uses a client program (residing on one computer) to access information by communicating with a server (running on a different machine). Rather than entering Internet addresses for the places where the information resides, the user simply points to an item on the gopher menu and the software actually makes the telnet connection to the remote site. Gopher provides a relatively uniform interface via the menu system so that the user can navigate without having to understand exactly what connections are being made or where the information is actually stored.[18]

VERONICA—As Archie is to FTP, so Veronica is to gopher. Veronica is a program that searches through all levels of gopher menus in "all the gophers in the world" and tells the user where to go to find particular information. Consistent with the current state of Internet discovery tools, results are only as good as the filenames are descriptive and informative. There is no controlled vocabulary on the Internet. A search of the Veronica server accessible via CNIDR (Clearinghouse for Networked Information Discovery & Retrieval), located at Research Triangle in North Carolina, using the terms "Latin America" yielded over 100 items. These included conference papers electronically published on the Internet, course syllabi, entries from directories of campus organizations, among others. Other items are from other gophers and choosing them puts the user in the other gopher system, making the telnet connection automatically.

WAIS (Wide Area Information Server)—While Archie searches through indexes of filenames of the files stored in computer archives on the net, WAIS searches the full text of documents for keywords. A WAIS search involves first choosing a file or set of files to search. WAIS servers provide a list to scan. Then the user enters keywords and retrieves relevant portions of the documents. WAIS was developed by a commercial enterprise, Thinking Machines, Inc., a company that builds connection machines (gigantic computer hardware for parallel processing). The main developer, Brewster Kahle, released a version of WAIS to the public via the Internet in 1991 in order to learn what kinds of uses would be developed to take advantage of its capabilities. Kahle has since left Thinking Machines to establish WAIS, Inc. to market and service the commercial version of the WAIS software. The public domain WAIS continues to be available on the Internet.

Using Internet for Reference: Practical Considerations for Latin Americanists

Many individual librarians and reference departments are experimenting with using Internet resources to answer questions and assist researchers, and there have been numerous calls for librarians to get involved in the process of "mapping" the Internet to make its resources more accessible.[19] The rest of this paper describes some of the practical ways reference librarians and scholars can use the networks to facilitate access to research information and scholarly communication.

Library Catalogs

Hundreds of library catalogs in the United States, Canada, Europe, Australia, and Latin America are now accessible via the Internet, and the numbers are constantly growing. Reference librarians and bibliographers can use Internet access to identify materials available in the best Latin American collections, to verify bibliographic information before sending an interlibrary loan request, and to alert users to the existence of research materials not held by the local institution. Researchers planning a trip can search the catalogs of possible destinations in advance and verify that the material exists ahead of time. In addition, reference librarians can search a variety of online systems and take advantage of special features of certain systems such as keyword searching, expanded subject headings, government document access, and so on. Some catalogs include local databases and access to specialized collections that may not be available through the major bibliographic utilities such as OCLC and RLIN.

Electronic Mail and E-mail Discussion Lists

There are many electronic mail discussion lists for Latin American countries and related topics. (For details, see Chapter 19, "List of Lists.") Reading these lists can be productive and/or time-consuming, and their value depends on the needs of the individual user or researcher. Many lists consist of conversations between students and others from a particular region or country, often studying or working in North America or Europe. The list may be used primarily to keep up with news and gossip from home. Other lists, however, regularly post "hard news" from wire services and newspapers, thus providing much more detailed and timely information from Latin America than can be obtained in the mainstream U.S. media. Some lists, such as ACTIV-L, have a clearly stated political agenda. As long as the user is aware of the bias and evaluates the information accordingly, these lists can be an excellent source of information from popular organizations in Latin America and from a variety of international organizations and interest groups. The Association for Progressive Communications (APC) networks (Peacenet, Econet, etc.) distribute information from grassroots human rights and environmental organizations in Latin America that is not available through mainstream sources. The APC has member networks in Uruguay, Brazil, Ecuador, and Nicaragua. These networks may provide the only gateway to the global Internet in certain countries.[20]

Electronic mail groups can also spark collaborative projects and lead to productive research relationships between scholars widely separated by geography and politics. For example, I received the following message from Professor Ivan Schulman of the Department of Spanish, Italian, and Portuguese at the University of Illinois (quoted with permission):

> For more than three years now, I have been exchanging scholarly material via e-mail with scholars at the Centro de Estudios Martianos (Havana) in connection with two projects: (1) the research connected to a Task Force for Scholarly Relations with Cuba (LASA) project on Marti and the United States. Four U.S. and four Cuban scholars have been involved . . .; (2) research and sharing of materials

for the volumes on the U.S. of the new critical edition of Marti's works being prepared at the Centro de Estudios Martianos. [This work is an example of] how scholars in the humanities and social sciences cooperate across national boundaries and in the face of the difficulties imposed by the embargo.[21]

As more scholars, librarians, and other researchers in Latin America obtain access to the Internet, opportunities for collaboration will increase. Monitoring electronic mail lists from and about Latin America is a good way to establish e-mail contacts in many Latin American countries. There may be only one Internet node in a country, thus it becomes relatively easy to find e-mail addresses once the node address is known. Librarians may be able to alert faculty and student researchers to opportunities for collaborative research and assist them in establishing electronic mail contacts with colleagues in Latin America.

Some electronic mail lists maintain archives of postings which can be searched. Searching e-mail list archives can be a very good way to retrieve relevant messages on a subject. Searching can be done interactively using listserv database commands which can be obtained by sending a request to any listserv. The user sends a "search database" command to the listserv where the list archives are stored. The listserv sends back an "index" of the hits produced by the search which contains the accession numbers, the dates, and the subject lines of the messages that match the search strategy. The user sends a "print" command to the listserv that includes the accession numbers of the relevant messages. The listserv then sends all of the requested postings back to the user's mailbox in one e-mail message. (I was able to use this method to search the ACTIV-L archives for a year of human rights reports and other news items on Peru for a professor researching how popular organizations in Peru are currently affected by repression from both right and left.)

The problem with relying on list archives to search this information is that not all lists maintain remotely searchable archives. Most are selectively archived by the moderator who chooses what is worth keeping. Others are automatically archived by the listserver, which may be programmed to archive all postings for a certain period of time. Networked reference librarians and subject specialists could take an active role in evaluating materials from lists for the purpose of setting up archives. One possible SALALM project would be to monitor the various Latin America-related lists. Find out which are archived, where, by whom, how often archives are purged, and so on. This would be a big and constantly changing job, but subject specialists would be best able to evaluate archived material to determine what should be saved. Latin Americanist librarians could communicate via our own networks (LALA-L) about the various list archives available for searching on the Internet.

As a caveat to the above, anyone who has subscribed to electronic mail lists for any time knows that most of the lists are unmoderated and contain a lot of personal communications, gossip, verbiage, and general silliness that is probably of no lasting value. As a caveat to this caveat, however, I would say that the Internet provides its users with a new means of communication which is still evolving and which has the potential to revolutionize scholarly communication. Those who participate in this evolving process will have a greater understanding of both the problems and the possibilities of this new communication paradigm.

Projects

Libraries are experimenting with ways to integrate Internet sources into the reference process. Many individual reference librarians are using the networks to seek answers to difficult reference questions. It is also important for reference librarians to work with systems experts to introduce network access tools to facilitate Internet navigation. HYTELNET Internet access software, created by Peter Scott, gives the IBM PC user instant access to Internet-accessible library catalogs, freenets, gophers, WAIS, and other Internet utilities.[22] The LIBS software, created by Mark Resmer and others at California State University, Sonoma, actually makes the telnet connections to library catalogs, gophers, WAIS, Veronica, and other Internet resource discovery tools such as Netfind (a way of locating directory information on individual users). The end user does not need to type in the telnet addresses, but can use all of these utilities via a menu system.[23]

At New Mexico State University Library, we are currently using the LIBS program—called LIBINFO on our local system. We are promoting it to faculty and students on a limited basis and have introduced the system to students in advanced bibliographic instruction sessions. Access is available not only in the Library, but also at the campus computing center and to all dial-up users of the NMSU campus network. We are also beginning a program to monitor network resources. Using the LIBINFO network access program, a group of volunteer librarians and other interested library staff will monitor library catalogs to find out what databases are available through each Internet-accessible catalog. We will record the information into a standard form and the data will be entered in an easy-to-query database program. The long-term goal is to continuously monitor all of the online catalogs and then move on into the gopher and WAIS services. At this stage we are especially interested in identifying periodical indexes and other databases accessible via the Internet that we can use to help answer basic reference questions.

Cyberlibrary, developed by Suzy Shaw of the Library Systems Office at University of Florida, provides online access to Internet reference sources such as the Art St. George list of telnet-accessible library catalogs, the Kovacs list of electronic conferences, the Strangelove list of electronic journals, and more. It also contains a "Latin American Information" menu item that provides access to several electronic mail lists on Latin America. The user can also search the State Department Travel Advisories via Cyberlibrary and several other electronic reference sources. Reference librarians worked with the systems experts to identify sources of Latin American information to incorporate into Cyberlibrary.[24]

The University of Texas at Austin Latin American Network Information Center (UT-LANIC) is a gopher server announced in April 1993. The UT-LANIC gopher offers a menu that will provide access to Latin American databases, library catalogs, special FTP-accessible file archives, and other services.[25]

The Chile Information Project (CHIP News) illustrates a creative use of technology to provide access to an electronic journal published by Princeton University and available by subscription via the Internet. Created by Harry Kriz at Virginia Polytechnic Institute using the SPIRES database development system distributed by Stanford University, CHIP News provides the user with a menu of databases, then an input screen to enter keywords, and then displays articles from the database that satisfy the query. The CHIP News database resides on an IBM mainframe at Virginia Tech and access is restricted to users with accounts on that computer.[26]

As more Latin American information becomes accessible in full-text electronic form via networks, reference and systems librarians will need to work together to make this information user-friendly to students and faculty.

Conclusion

I like to think of the Internet in terms of the parable of "The Blind Men and the Elephant." Everyone who ventures out onto the net finds something different and may form a unique perception of what the Internet is like and what kind of information access it can provide. The parable also implies that no one will get a completely accurate view of what the Internet is and all of the information accessible via the Internet. As the story concludes:

> Each (of the blind men) had felt one part out of many. Each had perceived it wrongly. No mind knew all . . . All imagined something, something incorrect.[27]

Perhaps it would be better to say that each individual's knowledge is incomplete. Considering the vast and mercurial nature of the Internet, it is impossible (and thankfully unnecessary) to know everything. Users would not really want the whole elephant on their desktops anyway. What is necessary is for each scholar/librarian to use the resource discovery tools now available to explore the network to find the resources most relevant to their research and clientele.

As librarians, we should lead the way in resource discovery by working with the technical experts to develop better ways to search the Internet. We should actively communicate with our constituents (networked and otherwise) about net resources by producing "network cartographies," in addition to bibliographies on student and faculty research interests. Every subject specialist can claim a region of the Internet to explore in depth, and then by working collaboratively we can become the "knowledge cartographers" and "access engineers"[28] that are needed in the electronic library environment.

NOTES

1. E. Krol and E. Hoffman, *Internet Draft: What Is the Internet?* (Internet Engineering Task Force FTP document, March 1993), 1. See also John Markoff, "The Staggering Scope of the Internet," *Digital Media* (April 20, 1992), 19-24.

2. Krol and Hoffman, *Internet Draft: What Is the Internet*, 5-6.

3. Allan H. Weis, "Commercialization of the Internet," *Electronic Networking: Research, Applications, and Policy* 2:3 (September 1992), 7.

4. Association for Progressive Communications, *Global Communications for Environment, Human Rights, Development and Peace* (GNET Archive, 1993). [FTP document, see bibliography for FTP address and instructions.] See also Graham Lane, *Communications for Progress: A Guide to International E-Mail* (London: Catholic Institute for International Relations, 1990).

5. Daniel Pimienta, *La comunicación mediante computadora: Una esperanza para el sector académico y de investigación del Tercer Mundo* (GNET Archive, May 1993), 3.

6. Susan M. Eldred, "Commercialization of the Internet/NREN: Introduction," *Electronic Networking: Research, Applications, and Policy* 2:3 (September 1992), 2-4; see also Jean Armour Polly, "NREN for All: Insurmountable Opportunity," *Library Journal* 118 (February 1, 1993), 38-41.

7. Weis, "Commercialization of the Internet," 10-11, 15.

8. InterNIC Directory and Database Services, electronic mail message, April 8, 1993, details the various services provided by InterNIC including Database Services, Directory of Directories, and Server Access. For more information, send an electronic mail query to <admin@ds.internic.net>.

9. Thomas J. Cozzolino and Thomas H. Pierce, Internet Summary Results, electronic mail message posted to LIBREF-L-Discussion of Library Reference Issues, April 20, 1993.

10. Sharyn J. Ladner and Hope N. Tillman, "Using the Internet for Reference," *Online* 17:1 (January 1993), 45-51.

11. Thomas Kinney points out that librarians should consider the importance of entertainment technologies in bringing networked information to the general public. See Thomas Kinney, "Memex Meets Madonna: Multimedia at the Intersection of Information and Entertainment," *Electronic Library* 10:3 (June 1992), 133-138.

12. Michael Strangelove, *Directory of Electronic Journals and Newsletters* (Ottawa: University of Ottawa, 1993). Available as an electronic mail file from <listserv@uottawa.bitnet> or an FTP document from <137.122.6.16> in the /pub/religion directory. For more information on retreiving the file contact Michael Strangelove at <441495@acadvm1.uottawa.ca>.

13. Michael F. Schwartz, Alan Emtage, Brewster Kahle, and B. Clifford Neuman, "A Comparison of Internet Resource Discovery Approaches," *Computing Systems* 5:4 (Fall 1992), 463-464.

14. Martin Dillon et al., *Assessing Information on the Internet: Toward Providing Library Services for Computer-Mediated Communication* (Dublin, OH: OCLC Office of Research, 1993).

15. Jerry Campbell, "Shaking the Conceptual Foundations of Reference," *Reference Services Review* 20:4 (Winter 1992), 32-33.

16. Schwartz, Emtage, Kahle, and Neuman, "A Comparison of Internet Resource Discovery Approaches," 464.

17. For more information on resource discovery tools and their development see the following: Peter Deutsch, "Resource Discovery in an Internet Environment—the Archie Approach," *Electronic Networking: Research, Applications, and Policy* 2:1 (March 1992), 45-50; Brendan Kehoe, *Zen and the Art of the Internet: A Beginners Guide* (2d ed. Englewood Cliffs, NJ: Prentice Hall, 1993) (the first edition is available from several FTP sites, including: nic.merit.edu in the directory: introducing.the.internet. Filename: zen.txt); B. Clifford Neuman, "Prospero: A Tool for Organizing Internet Resources," *Electronic Networking: Research, Applications, and Policy* 2:1 (March 1992), 30-37; Jean Armour Polly, "Surfing the Internet: An Introduction" (New York: Nysernet, December 1992) [FTP document; to retrieve FTP to <nysernet.org>. CD to /pub/resources/guides. Name of file <surfing.the.internet.2.0.txt>]; Schwartz, Emtage, Kahle and Neuman, "A Comparison of Internet Resource Discovery Approaches"; Curtis Simmonds, "Searching Internet Archive Sites with Archie: Why, What, Where, & How," *Online* 17:2 (March 1993), 50-55; Jane Smith, "CNIDR: Coordinating Internet User Tools," *Internet World* 4:2 (March 1993), 8-10.

18. Nathan Torkington, "Gopher: The Internet Resource Discoverer," electronic mail message posted to Usenet newsgroup <comp.infosystems.gopher>, October 11, 1992. Gopher descriptions are also found in many of the sources listed in note 17.

19. See, for example, G. H. Brett, "Accessing Information on the Internet," *Electronic Networking: Research, Applications, and Policy* 2:1 (March 1992), 10-12; Campbell, "Shaking the Conceptual Foundations of Reference"; Mary E. Engle, "Electronic Paths to Resource Sharing: Widening Opportunities through the Internet," *Reference Services Review* 19:4 (December 1991), 7-12; Erik Jul, "Of Internauts and Internots," *Computers in Libraries* 12:8 (September 1992), 52; Ladner and Tillman, "Using the Internet for Reference"; J. Still and J. Alexander, "Integrating Internet into Reference: Policy Issues," *College and Research Libraries News* 54:3 (March 1993), 139-140.

20. Association for Progressive Communications, *Global Computer Communications for Environment, Human Rights, Development and Peace* (GNET Archive, Brochure of the Association for Progressive Communications, 1993). [FTP document available from <dhvx20.csudh.edu> Directory <global_net> Filename <apc_brochure.txt>.]

21. Ivan Schulman, personal electronic mail communication, May 5, 1993.

22. Peter Scott, HYTELNET: Internet Access Software. [Available via FTP: <access.usask.ca> in the directory <pub/ hytelnet/pc> Filename: <HYTELN63.ZIP>. Also available in a UNIX version, created by Earl Fogel <fogel@skyfox.usask.ca>.]

23. Mark Resmer et al., LIBS: Internet access software. [To obtain LIBS software free of charge: FTP <sonoma.edu> in the directory /pub. Available in DOS or UNIX format. DOS has .com extension; UNIX has .tar.z extension.]

24. CYBERLIBRARY. Gainesville: University of Florida Library Systems Office. [To access via telnet: <telnet nervm.nerdc.ufl.edu> Login: <lib>. Also available via any gopher server that provides menu access to other gophers. Contact: Suzy Shaw <suzshaw@nervm.nerdc.ufl.edu>.]

25. UT-LANIC: Latin American Network Information Center. Austin: University of Texas, Institute of Latin American Studies. [Access via telnet <telnet lanic.utexas.edu> Login <lanic>. Also available via any gopher server with a menu system that allows access to "all gophers in the world." Choose North America, Texas, etc. For more information contact: Ning Lin, LANIC Technical Director <nlin@bongo.cc.utexas.edu> or Carolyn Poage <carolyn@emx.utexas.edu>.]

26. Harry Kriz, personal electronic mail communication, April 27, 1993.

27. Idries Shah, *World Tales: The Extraordinary Coincidence of Stories Told in All Times, in All Places* (New York: Harcourt Brace Jovanovich, 1979), p. 84.

28. Campbell, "Shaking the Conceptual Foundations of Reference," 32-33.

18. Internet Resources for Latin Americanists: A Working Bibliography

Molly Molloy

This bibliography contains references to articles, books, electronic files, and computer programs for learning about the Internet and for making the net's vast resources more accessible. It is in no way comprehensive, but simply a good beginning. I have tried to include items that might be especially useful to Latin Americanists.

Alley, B. "Gridlock on the Internet, or Too Much of a Good Thing." *Technicalities* 12:12 (December 1992), 1.

Editorial comment on Internet information overload. Raises issue of how (when? if?) librarians will catalog electronic lists, journals, newsletters.

———. "Internet, Learning Curves and Angst." *Technicalities* 12:9 (September 1992), 1.

Editorial on the need for Internet training for librarians and library users.

Association for Progressive Communications. Global Computer Communications for Environment, Human Rights, Development and Peace. GNET Archive, 1993.
Brochure of the Association for Progressive Communications. FTP <dhvx20.csudh.edu> Directory <global_net> Filename <apc_brochure.txt>.

Details of the APC organization; addresses of the APC member networks all over the world, including Uruguay, Brazil, Ecuador, Nicaragua.

Brett, G. H. "Accessing Information on the Internet." *Electronic Networking: Research, Applications, and Policy* 2:1 (March 1992), 10-12.

Editorial article in special issue on Internet resources. Using the kudzu metaphor for out-of-control growth and chaos on the Internet, Brett discusses the Networked Information Retrieval concept as the meeting ground between the two major cultures of information technologies: library/information sciences and the computing/networking technologies. Brett believes that these two groups working together can begin to create order from potential chaos.

———. "Navigating the Internet: A Beginning." *North Carolina Libraries* 50 (September 1992), 143-146.

Advice for new net users on learning to make sense of the resources available on the net. Recommends starting with paper-based sources, e-mail, and progressing toward the use of interactive services.

Campbell, J. D. "Shaking the Conceptual Foundations of Reference: A Perspective." *Reference Services Review* 20:4 (December 1992), 29-35.

Discusses a new role for reference librarians as "knowledge cartographers" and "access engineers" who will create "maps" and other tools for accessing the information available on electronic networks.

Churbuck, D. C. "Good-bye, Dewey Decimals." *Forbes* 151:4 (15 February 1993), 204.

Describes WAIS and Project Gutenberg as pioneers in creating a completely electronic library.

Cogan, S. "The Internet for Scholars in the Humanities." *Michigan Academician* 25:2 (December 1993), 179-187.

Provides a good brief overview of Internet resources of special interest to scholars in the humanities, such as the ARTFL database from the University of Chicago, Dartmouth's Dante Project, Project Gutenberg, the Brown University Humanist listserv, etc.

"Communications, Computers and Networks: How to Work, Play and Thrive in Cyberspace." *Scientific American* (special issue) 265:3 (September 1991).

A very good introduction to the technical, as well as the social/political, issues of computers and networks. Numerous articles by different authors.

CYBERLIBRARY. Gainesville: University of Florida Library Systems Office.
To access via telnet: <telnet nervm.nerdc.ufl.edu> Login: <lib>. Also available via any gopher server that provides menu access to other gophers. Contact: Suzy Shaw <suzshaw@nervm.nerdc.ufl.edu>.

Cyberlibrary provides online access to Internet reference sources such as the Art St. George list of telnet-accessible library catalogs, the Kovacs list of electronic conferences, the Strangelove list of electronic journals and more. It also contains a "Latin American Information" menu item that provides access to several electronic mail lists on Latin America. The user can also search the State Department Travel Advisories via Cyberlibrary and several other electronic reference sources.

Deutsch, P. "Resource Discovery in an Internet Environment—The Archie Approach." *Electronic Networking: Research, Applications, and Policy* 2:1 (March 1992), 45-50.

Description of Archie, an electronic tool for locating information by keywords in file archives accessible via Internet.

Dillon, M., et al. *Assessing Information on the Internet: Toward Providing Library Services for Computer-Mediated Communication.* Dublin, OH: OCLC Online Computer Library Center, Office of Research, 1993.
This document is available on the Internet via FTP as of April 1993. To retrieve, FTP to <ftp.rsch.oclc.org> Login as anonymous, send your userid as password. CD to /pub/ internet_resources_project_/report. The complete report exists in several files in this directory. The basic text is <internet.ps>. The <README> file describes the contents of the various appendices; <appende.ps> is a working bibliography on libraries and the Internet. The file is currently in postscript format. An ASCII version will be posted when available and announced on PACS-L and OCLCNEWS. A printed, bound version can be ordered from OCLC for $20.

Report of the OCLC Internet Resource Project which investigated the nature of electronic textual information on the Internet and the practical and theoretical problems of creating MARC records for text files and other electronic objects available via computer networks. The report contains a wealth of information—good technical descriptions of various Internet resources and access tools. Also reports on an experiment in cataloging electronic texts using USMARC format. The bibliography is extensive and provides excellent access to the (mostly nontechnical) literature on the Internet up to late 1992.

ECUANET: Corporación Ecuatoriana de Información. Corporación Ecuatoriana de Información.
Access via any gopher menu which provides access to gopher servers worldwide. Contact for ECUANET: Xavier Baquero, Director <xbaquero@ecnet.ec> or <ecuanet@cscns.com> or <info@ecnet.ec>.

ECUANET provides Internet access and services to more than 500 users in Ecuador as of May 1993. Via the ECUANET gopher, users can access library catalogs, other gophers, Archie and a variety of (standard) Internet services. Also provides a news service, "Diario Hoy," which is also sent to the ECUADOR e-mail list subscribers.

Eldred, S. M., and M. J. McGill. "Commercialization of the Internet/NREN: Introduction." *Electronic Networking: Research, Applications, and Policy* 2:3 (September 1992), 2-4.

Editorial in special issue of the journal *Electronic Networking* devoted to various aspects of commercialization of the Internet.

Engle, M. E. "Electronic Paths to Resource Sharing: Widening Opportunities through the Internet." *Reference Services Review* 19:4 (December 1991), 7-12.

Discussion of reference use of remote online catalogs via the Internet.

Gerich, E. "Expanding the Internet to a Global Environment but . . . How to Get Connected?" *Computer Networks and ISDN Systems* 23:1 (November 1991), 43-46.

Policy paper that discusses the growth of the Internet and relations between the US NSFNET and international networks connected to the Internet.

Jacobson, T. L., and S. Zimpfer. Non-Commercial Computer Networks and National Development. GNET Archive, 1993.
FTP from <dhvx20.csudh.edu> Directory <global_net> Filename <networks_and_dev.txt>. Article to be published in *Telematics and Informatics*.

Discusses the growing role of computer networks in developing countries in the context of other communications media.

Jul, E. "Of Internauts and Internots." *Computers in Libraries* 12:8 (September 1992), 52.

Discusses the need for librarians to play an active role in developing more access tools for navigating the Internet.

Kehoe, B. *Zen and the Art of the Internet: A Beginners Guide.* 2d ed. Englewood Cliffs, NJ: Prentice Hall, 1993.
The first edition is available from several FTP sites, including: nic.merit.edu in the directory: introducing.the.internet. Filename: zen.txt. The new version is published as a book and contains new information and some corrections.

Maybe the best self-help guide to Internet resources including explanation of Internet addressing, how to use Archie and WAIS, how to connect to freenets, and much more.

Kinney, T. "Memex Meets Madonna: Multimedia at the Intersection of Information and Entertainment." *Electronic Library* 10:3 (June 1992), 133-138.

Article proposes that current multimedia and networking technologies will lead to the development of personal information storage and retrieval systems similar to the Memex described in 1945 by Vannevar Bush. Librarians should consider the importance of entertainment technologies in bringing networked information to the general public and the effect this could have on the future of libraries.

Kovacs, D., et al. *Directory of Scholarly Electronic Conferences.* 6th revision. Kent, OH: Kent State University Libraries, 1993.
Exists as a set of electronic files. Files can be retrieved via e-mail or FTP. Send e-mail messages to <listserv@kentvm.kent.edu> with the message line: get filename.filetype. To retrieve via FTP, ftp ksuvxa.kent.educate. Look in the library directory for a list of the files. Also available in this directory as keyword-searchable hypercard stacks. For more information contact Diane Kovacs <dkovacs@kentvm.kent.edu>

Provides good subject access to hundreds of electronic discussion lists. Subject divisions in this revision include: anthropology, education, geography and area studies, library science, linguistics, political science, business, biological sciences, computer science, etc. <ACADLIST.FILE2> contains the area studies lists, including many on Latin America. FILE2 also includes the library science lists. The

<ACADLIST.README> contains detailed information about retrieving the files and about subscribing to the lists. The entries note whether or not the list is moderated and/or archived.

Krol, E., and E. Hoffman. "Internet Draft: What Is the Internet?" *Internet Engineering Task Force (IETF)* (1993).
Available via FTP from the Internet-drafts directory at several sites. To obtain, ftp to ftp.nisc.sri.com or ds.internic.net. Login as 'anonymous' and use 'guest' or your address as password. CD to Internet-drafts. Send command: get draft-ietf-uswg-fyi- 00.txt. According to the document, these "Internet drafts" are valid for six months. For questions send via e-mail to [internet-drafts@cnri.reston.va.us].

An example of many documents available over the network via FTP. This document answers the question: What is the Internet? It is a modified version of a chapter in Ed Krol's 1992 book *The Whole Internet User's Guide*. Contains a lot of information on current issues of privatization and commercialization of the Internet.

Krol, E. *The Whole Internet User's Guide and Catalog*. Sebastopol, CA: O'Reilly & Assoc., 1992.

Comprehensive guide to the network, how it works, acceptable use, security, and other issues.

Ladner, S., and H. Tillman. "Using the Internet for Reference." *Online* 17:1 (January 1993), 45-51.

Results of a survey of 54 special librarians indicated that most reference librarians use the Internet primarily to facilitate communication via personal e-mail and though the use of e-mail discussion lists. Internet was also used for searching remote databases including remote libary catalogs, and for file transfer and other data exchange.

Lane, G. *Communications for Progress: A Guide to International E-Mail*. London: Catholic Institute for International Relations, 1990.

Excellent overview of electronic communications intended as a manual for nonprofit organizations. Good technical background with details on networks accessible in developing countries.

LaQuey, T., and J. C. Ryer. *The Internet Companion: A Beginner's Guide to Global Networking*. Reading, MA: Addison-Wesley, 1993.

Foreword by Vice President Al Gore. Explains Internet origins, netiquette, and other basics. Includes chapter on network legends.

Markoff, J. "The Staggering Scope of the Internet: A Thicket of Networks Wound 'Round the Globe." *Digital Media* 1:11 (20 April 1992), 19-24.

Brief history of the Internet, with an overview of Internet resources: mail, conference, FTP files, databases, WAIS, and other experimental access tools.

Martin, J. "There's Gold in Them Thar Networks! or Searching for Treasure in All the Wrong Places." Columbus: Network Working Group, Ohio State University, January 1993.
Document available via FTP from: nic.merit.edu in the directory: introducing.the.internet. Check this directory for other good introductory documents, including the 1st edition of "Zen & the Art of the Internet."

A good introductory article containing much information about specific FTP sites and what they offer. Also how to use the "whois" feature to locate e-mail addresses, a bibliography, etc.

McGee, A. R. African, African American, African-Caribbean, African Latin Internet/Bitnet Mailing Lists.
Retrieve latest version of this list-of-lists via FTP from: <ftp.netcom.com> in the directory: <pub/amcgee>. Also available via e-mail to: <mcgee@epsilon.eecs.nwu.edu>.

Art McGee regularly posts updates of this list to many of the Latin American interest groups and other e-mail discussions. The list includes many of interest to Latin Americanists.

Michelson, A., and J. Rothenberg. "Scholarly Communication and Information Technology: Exploring the Impact of Changes in the Research Process on Archives." *American Archivist* 55 (Spring 1992), 236-315.

Main article in special issue devoted to electronic information and archives. Detailed discussion of many technology issues important to librarians, archivists, and researchers. Most important trends in scholarly communication affecting archives are end-user computing and connectivity.

NAFTA: North American Free Trade Agreement.

The full text of the NAFTA document is available from several ftp archives: <ariel.unm.edu> <csf.colorado.edu> <athena.law.columbia.edu> and probably more. An Archie search yielded only the ariel site, but the other addresses were given as answers to various inquiries.

The NAFTA document is quite long and unless you have a lot of disk space available and facility for electronically storing and searching the document, you may not want to retrieve it. You can, however, search the text via WAIS (Wide Area Information Server) at <sparc-1.law.columbia>. See WAIS entry below.

Neuman, C. B. "Prospero: A Tool for Organizing Internet Resources." *Electronic Networking: Research, Applications, and Policy* 2:1 (March 1992), 30-37.

For information contact the author/creator B. Clifford Neuman [bcn@isi.edu]. For information on the Prospero prototype contact [info-prospero@isi.edu].

An example of an Internet discovery tool under development, Prospero is a distributed file system based on the Virtual System Model which provides tools to help users organize Internet resources by using existing directories and indexes and incorporating more informal sources (such as asking a colleague for information) into a file system that the user can navigate through to find the desired information.

Nickerson, G. "Connecting to the Internet." *Computers in Libraries* 13:3 (March 1993), 21-24.

Describes e-mail, Archie, FTP, discussion groups, telnet, etc.

———. "LIBSOFT: The Library Software Archive." *Computers in Libraries* 12:10 (November 1992), 56-57.

To access the archive ftp to <hydra.uwo.ca>.

Describes the LIBSOFT archive, an FTP site at the University of Western Ontario that contains library software and information to help librarians use the Internet. The article provides a lot of good detail on FTP commands for retrieving both text and binary files.

Notess, G. "The Internet Meets Online." *Online* 17:2 (March 1993), 84-86.

Online searching of commercial databases such as Dialog over the Internet. Also gives examples of how Archie can be used to discover text files on the Internet.

O'Brien, R. The APC Computer Networks: Global Networking for Change. GNET Archive, 1993.
Retrieve via FTP from the GNET Archive. FTP <dhvx20.csudh.edu> Directory <global_net> Filename <apc_net.txt>. Paper also published in the July 1992 edition of the *Canadian Journal of Information Science*.

Analysis of how social activists all over the world are using computer communications to enhance networking, focusing specifically on the Association for Progressive Communications.

Page, M. "A Personal View of the Internet." *College and Research Libraries News* 54:3 (March 1993), 127-132.

Overview of the Internet, glossary of Internet terminology, brief discussion of NREN and other policy issues.

Pimienta, D. La comunicación mediante computadora: Una esperanza para el sector académico y de investigación del Tercer Mundo. La experiencia de REDALC en América Latina y el Caribe. GNET Archive, May 1993.
Paper available from the GNET Archive via FTP <dhvx20.csudh.edu> in the directory <global_net> Filename <cmc_acad_investig.txt>.

First paper of the GNET archive published in Spanish. Pimienta gives various reasons why network communication aids development. Description of the REDALC project.

Polly, J. A. "NREN for All: Insurmountable Opportunity." *Library Journal* 118 (1 February 1993), 38-41.

Policy discussion on NREN geared toward access for public libraries and schools. Includes "A Guide to Internet/NREN" bibliography of the most popular reading on NREN and Internet.

———. *Surfing the Internet: An Introduction.* New York: Nysernet, December 1992.
To retrieve this electronic document FTP to <nysernet.org>. CD to /pub/resources/guides. Name of file <surfing.the.internet.2.0.txt>.

This is a longer version of Polly's article in the June 1992 issue of *Wilson Library Bulletin.* It describes many ways that a librarian might use the Internet to communicate via e-mail, locate information, etc. Contains detailed information on how to search for files using Archie, gopher, WAIS. Bibliographic information on many basic Internet access sources.

Resmer, M., et al. LIBS: Internet access software.
To obtain LIBS software free of charge: FTP <sonoma.edu> in the directory /pub. Available in DOS or UNIX format. DOS has .com extension; UNIX has .tar.z extension.

Software for Internet access. Provides telnet connections to Internet-accessible libraries, gophers, WAIS servers, and other Internet access tools. Installation requires DOS or UNIX expert.

Robbin, A. "Social Scientists at Work on Electronic Research Networks." *Electronic Networking: Research, Applications, and Policy* 2:2 (June 1992), 6-30.

Report of research on how a group of social scientists used CMC (computer mediated communication) to obtain access to online data.

Saizar, P. A Guide to the Latin-American Mailing Lists, 1992.
This list appears at intervals on various e-mail lists. Contact compiler: <saizar@osu.edu>.

This list was used by Kovacs in the Latin American section of the "Directory of Scholarly Electronic Conferences." The latest update I have seen is January 1992. The document includes basic instructions for subscribing to the lists and some information on membership and subject matter of the lists.

Saunders, L. M. "The Virtual Library Revisited." *Computers in Libraries* 12:10 (November 1992), 51-54.

Deals with human/management issues involved with creating the virtual (electronic) library.

Schwartz, M. F., et al. "A Comparison of Internet Resource Discovery Approaches." *Computing Systems* 5:4 (September 1992), 461-493.

Taxonomy and analysis of Internet resource discovery tools, such as WHOIS, Archie, WAIS, Netfind, Gopher, etc.

Scott, P. HYTELNET: Internet Access Software.
Available via FTP: <access.usask.ca> in the directory <pub/hytelnet/pc> Filename: <HYTELN63.ZIP>. Also available in a UNIX version, created by Earl Fogel <fogel@skyfox.usask.ca>.

This program gives the IBM PC user instant access to Internet-accessible library catalogs, freenets, gophers, WAIS, etc. Requires some expertise in DOS and/or UNIX systems, file transfer, and dealing with compressed files.

Simmonds, C. "Searching Internet Archive Sites with Archie: Why, What, Where, & How." *Online* 17:2 (March 1993), 50-55.

Good description of how Archie works for searching computer archives. Texts of interactive Archie searches.

Smith, J. "CNIDR: Coordinating Internet User Tools." *Internet World* 4:2 (March 1993), 8-10.

Located at Research Triangle Park in North Carolina, CNIDR, the Clearinghouse for Networked Information Discovery and Retrieval, provides some structure and organization for both the creators and users of Internet navigation software tools. For more information on CNIDR and on current versions of available tools contact: <info@cnidr.org>.

St. George, A., and R. Larsen. *Internet Accessible Library Catalogs and Databases* [ftp document]. University of Maryland, University of New Mexico, 1993.
Available as an FTP file from <ariel.unm.edu> in the <library> directory with the filename <internet.library>.

This file provides telnet addresses and user information for library catalogs in the U.S., Canada, U.K., Mexico, and several other countries. New catalogs are always becoming available, and the directory is updated frequently. Many libraries are also installing software (such as gopher, libs, etc.) that make the telnet connection automatically.

Still, J., and J. Alexander. "Integrating Internet into Reference: Policy Issues." *College and Research Libraries News* 54:3 (March 1993), 139-140.

Brief discussion of one reference department's efforts to use Internet.

Strangelove, M. Directory of Electronic Journals & Newsletters, Edition 2.1. Ottawa: University of Ottawa, July 1992.
Available in two large files via electronic mail. Send an e-mail message to: <listserv@uottawa.bitnet>. In the body of the message type: <get ejournl1 directry> <get ejournl2 directry>. You may also be able to retrieve via interactive listserv commands. Also available via FTP <137.122.6.16> CD <pub/religion>. File is <electronic-serials-directory.txt>. According to the author, a new version of the list will be coming out in June/July 1993.

One of the first attempts to maintain a listing of electronic journals and newsletters. Useful for identifying potential information sources on the net. Entries usually contain details for subscribing.

Tennant, R., et al. *Crossing the Internet Threshold: An Instructional Handbook*. Berkeley: Library Solutions Press, 1992.

Guide for training users on the Internet.

United Nations Development Programme. UNDP Gopher.
Telnet address [nywork1.undp.org, port 70]. For information contact Lorraine Waitman, Dag Hammarskjold Library [lwaitman@nygate.undp.org].

This gopher server contains a directory of the U.N. system, UNCED documentation with WAIS search facility, UNDP field office telecommunications catalog, press highlights, etc. New information is added daily.

UT-LANIC: Latin American Network Information Center. Austin: University of Texas, Institute of Latin American Studies.
Access via telnet <telnet lanic.utexas.edu> Login <lanic>. You can also access via any gopher server with a menu system that allows access to "all gophers in the world" or something else like that. Just choose North America, Texas, etc. For more information contact: Ning Lin, LANIC Technical Director <nlin@bongo.cc.utexas.edu> or Carolyn Poage <carolyn@emx.utexas.edu>.

Announced in April 1993, the UT-LANIC gopher offers a menu that will provide access to Latin American databases, access to library catalogs and other services. Experimental.

WAIS Searchable Information of Interest to Latin Americanists.

To connect to WAIS: <telnet 192.31.181.1 or quake.think.com> Login: 'wais'. The LIBS software described above provides seamless access to WAIS.

WAIS allows keyword access to various archived electronic files. Browse the list to see what is available. This does change often and there are other WAIS sites out there. Some e-mail list archives are searchable via WAIS. The following files and sites currently available may be of interest to Latin Americanists: <nafta at sparc-1.law.columbia> <us-budget-1993 at sunsite.unc.edu> <columbia-spanish-law-catalog at pegun.law.columbia.edu> <clinton-speeches at sunsite.unc.edu> <us-state-department-travel-advis at gopher.stolaf.edu> <world- factbook at cmns-moon.think.com>. You can also search the Kovacs list of Academic E-mail Conferences via WAIS <acdemic_email_conf at munin.ub2.lu.se>. This makes more sense once you get into the WAIS server at quake.think.com. You can browse through the list, select files to search, enter keywords, and retrieve relevant texts from the files.

Weis, A. "Commercialization of the Internet." *Electronic Networking: Research, Applications, and Policy* 2:3 (September 1992), 7-16.

Describes Internet history and growth and the current trend toward commercial use of the Internet. Emphasizes the need to revise acceptable-use policies to account for private use and investment, the need for statutory treatment of liability issues for network providers, the need to integrate development networks based on leading edge technologies with heavily used production networks based on proven technologies, and the need for more global planning.

Wyman, W. J. "Internet and Foreign Language Instruction: A Report from Behind the Front Lines." *IALL: Journal of Language Learning Technologies* 26:1 (December 1993), 26-33.

Humorous review of Internet resources from the perspective of a language teacher.

Yanoff, S. Internet Services List. Milwaukee: Computer Services Division, University of Wisconsin-Milwaukee.

Updated about every 2 weeks. Obtain via FTP <csd4.csd.uwm.edu> Directory <pub> filename <inet.services.txt>. Also available via <gopher csd4.csd.uwm.edu> or subscribe to the USENET list alt.internet.services.

An eclectic list of special Internet files and services. Arranged in alphabetical order; browse list to become aware of new things on the net.

19. List of Lists for Latin America

Molly Molloy

This "list of lists" was compiled from several sources. I used Kovacs' List of Scholarly Electronic Conferences as a starter. I also found Art McGee's list of lists very useful since it is updated and posted to many lists quite often. Keep in mind that electronic interest groups come and go frequently. Some, like PACS-L or LASNET, are very well established. PACS-L and many of the other library-related lists are archived for a certain time period and the archives can be searched. Others may be quite ephemeral. I have tried to include the personal e-mail address of someone associated with the list when possible. To find out more, just send a query to that person.

This list does not aim to be complete, but it is a good place for Latin Americanists to begin establishing network connections. Please contact me with additions and/or subtractions from the list so I can keep the database current.

Note: The instruction "To subscribe" used below means to send an e-mail message to that address. "To post" means to send a message to the entire list.

ACTIV-L: Peace, Democracy, Freedom, Justice [electronic mail list].
To subscribe: <listserv@mizzou1.missouri.edu>. To post: <activ-l@mizzou1.missouri.edu>.

This is a very busy list covering all kinds of progressive/radical political issues. Of interest to Latin Americanists because many activist/human rights groups post news and bulletins from numerous Latin American countries. Excellent source for news from El Salvador, Guatemala, Haiti, Peru, and other countries. Also postings from environmental, trade, and development organizations.

ARENAL: Lista de discusión para hispanos/as que desean acabar con la homofobia . . . [electronic mail list] 1993.
To subscribe: <listserv@lut.fi>. For questions send e-mail to <mayorga@cis.udel.edu> or <dsoto@ucs.indiana.edu>.

New list announced in April 1993 for gay/lesbian latinos and discussion of gay issues. No other information at present.

ARGENTINA [electronic mail list].
To subscribe: <argentina- request@asterix.eng.buffalo.edu>. To post: <argentina@asterix.eng.buffalo.edu>. A separate address is used for news <argentina-noticias@ois.db.toronto.edu>.

Argentina discussion and news group.

ARQUITECTURA-L: Discussion of Latin American Architecture [electronic mail list].
To subscribe: <listserv@conicit.ve>. To post: <arquitectura-l@conicit.ve>. List administrator: Gonzalo Velez, <gvelez@conicit.ve>.

New list announced April 1993.

AVIFAUNA: Neotropical Birds and Conservation [electronic mail list].
To subscribe: <listasrc@rcp.pe>. To post: <avifauna@rcp.pe>.

A new list announced April 1993 from the International Council for Bird Preservation and the Red Científica Peruana. For information e-mail questions to <phillips@cipa.ec> or to Jose Soriano <js@rcp.pe>.

BORIKEN: Puerto Rico Culture and Society [electronic mail list].
To subscribe: <listserv@enlace.bitnet>. To post: <boriken@enlace.bitnet>. For other list and subscription information contact: Rafael Pirazzi <r_pirazzi@upr1.upr1.clu.edu>.

General discussion of Puerto Rican society and culture. The ENLACE listserv, located at the Universidad de Puerto Rico, also administers several other discussion groups on other issues.

BRAS-NET: Brazilian Discussion Group/Network [electronic mail list].
To subscribe: Non-European users: <bras-net- request@cs.ucla.edu>. European users: <bras-net-request@uk.ac.man.cs>.

Several other Brazilian interest groups exist. To get more general information on these other lists, try sending an e-mail message to: <gomide@brfapesp.bitnet> or to: <listserv@fapq.fapesp.br>.

CARECON: Caribbean Economy [electronic mail list].
To subscribe: <listserv@vm1.yorku.ca>. To post: <carecon@vm1.yorku.ca>.

Discussion of issues related to the Caribbean economy.

CENTAM-L: Central America Discussion Group [electronic mail list]. To subscribe: <listserv@ubvm.cc.buffalo.edu>. To post: <centam-l@ubvm.cc.buffalo.edu>.

Very active discussion group for people from Central America and others interested in the region. Many members are students in the United States from Central American countries. News, human rights reports, and other information posted regularly from the region.

CHILE-L: Chile Discussion Group [electronic mail list]. To subscribe: <listserv@usachvm1.bitnet>. To post: <chile-l@usachvm1.bitnet>.

General discussion on Chile.

CLACSO-INST-L: Red Electrónica de Ciencias Sociales en América Latina—Institutional Information and CLACSO-ACCESO-L: Regional Social Science News [electronic mail lists]. To subscribe: <listserv@ax.ibase.br>. To post: <clacso-inst-l@ax.ibase.br> or <clacso-acceso-l@ax.ibase.br>. Questions to: Gustavo Navarro <rtgus@arcriba.bitnet> or <rtgus@criba.edu.ar> or <clacso@ax.apc.org> .

New lists announced in April 1993. CLACSO-INST-L will include an electronic newsletter, "Carta de CLACSO."

COMEDIA: Hispanic Classic Theatre [electronic mail list]. To subscribe: <listserv@arizvm1.ccit.arizona.edu>. To post: <comedia@arizvm1.ccit.arizona.edu>.

Discussion of Hispanic classic theatre.

DEVEL-L: Technology Transfer in International Development [electronic mail list]: Volunteers in Technical Assistance. To subscribe: <listserv@auvm.american.edu>. To post: <devel-l@auvm.american.edu>. Administered by Volunteers in Technical Assistance. For more information contact: <vita@gmuvax.gmu.edu>.

Exchange of information on technology and development. Good source for finding out about publications (electronic and otherwise). Maintains archive of ftp files.

ECUADOR: Ecuadorean Network [electronic mail list].
To subscribe: <rone@skat.usc.edu> and ask to subscribe to the list. To post: <ecuador@skat.usc.edu>.

Excellent source for news from Ecuador. Daily news bulletins from "Diario Hoy" are posted to the list.

ESPORA-L: Spanish-Portuguese History [electronic mail list].
To subscribe: <listserv@ukanvm.cc.ukans.edu>. To post: <espora-l@ukanvm.cc.ukans.edu>.

Discussion and exchange of information on the history of the Iberian peninsula. Multilingual—Portuguese, Spanish, English, Catalan, etc.

FOLLAC: Folklore Latino, Latinoamericano y Caribeño [electronic mail list].
Mailing list for discussion of Latin American folklore. To join list send a message to Emily Socolov at: <owner-follac@ccwf.cc.texas.edu>. To post: <follac@ccwf.cc.utexas.edu>. Moderator's address: University of Texas—Austin, Folklore Studies.

List began in Spring 1993. Multilingual. Described as a mailing list for "all people interested in the folklore and traditional, expressive culture of the hemisphere."

GNET: Global Networking [electronic mail list].
To subscribe: <gnet- request@dhvx20.csudh.edu>.

This lists posts announcements of research papers and other documents available from the GNET Archives, an ftp site <dhvx20.csudh.edu>. The archive contains many papers on global networking, use of networks in less developed countries, communication in international development, and other related topics.

HELP-NET: Internet and Bitnet User Help [electronic mail list].
To subscribe: <listserv@templevm.bitnet>. To post: <help-net@templevm.bitnet>.

Good list for new network users. Get answers to many technical questions. Contains a list of FAQ (frequently asked questions) files to help new users.

HILAT-L: Higher Education in Latin America [electronic mail list].
To subscribe: <listserv@bruspvm.bitnet>. To post: <hilat-l@bruspvm.bitnet>. For information contact Simon Schwartzman, Universidade de São Paulo, Research Group on Higher Education <sschwart@bruspvm.bitnet>.

Intended as a means of information interchange about research on higher education in Latin America by disseminating information about research projects, publications, meetings, etc.

IBASE-TEXTS-L@ibase.br [electronic mail list]: Brazilian Institute of Social and Economic Analyses.
To subscribe: <listserv@ibase.br>. To post: <ibase-texts-l@ibase.br>. For more information send e-mail to <ibase@ax.ibase.br> or <ibase@ax.apc.origin>.

This list contains texts prepared by the Brazilian Institute of Social and Economic Analyses, IBASE, a nongovernmental research, service, and consultancy organization based in Rio de Janeiro. IBASE prepares information packages in several formats including text, video, radio, etc. on Brazilian social, economic, political, and cultural issues. IBASE's main goal is democratization of information. (This information obtained from the new list announcement posted to ACTIV-L on May 11, 1993.)

LALA-L: Latin Americanist Librarians' Announcements List [electronic mail list].
To subscribe: <listserv@uga.cc.uga.edu>. To post: <lala-l@uga.cc.uga.edu>. Moderator: Gayle Williams <gwilliam@uga.cc.uga.edu>.

Announcements and discussion for Latin American Studies librarians and others.

LASNET: Latin American Studies Network [electronic mail list].
To subscribe: <lasnet- request@emx.utexas.edu>. To post: <lasnet@emx.utexas.edu>. Moderator: Ning Lin <ilasut@emx.utexas.edu>.

Purpose of LASNET is to facilitate communication among Latin Americanists internationally. LASNET includes a directory of over 300 subscribers. Contains mostly "official" announcements like upcoming conferences, new publications, new lists, etc.

LATAM-INFO: Latin America Academic Information [electronic mail list]. To subscribe: <latam-info- request@mailbase.ac.uk>. To post: <latam-info@mailbase.ac.uk>.

Similar to LASNET, but based in U.K. Dissemination of information and discussion of matters of common concern to subject specialists, librarians, students, and others in Latin American studies.

LATCO: Business and Trade with Latin America [electronic mail list]. Portland, OR: Latin American Trade Council of Oregon, February 1993.
To subscribe: <lserv@psg.com>. To post: <latco@psg.com>. Produced by the Latin American Trade Council of Oregon. Moderators: Tom Miles <tmiles@well.sf.ca.us> and Walter Morales <walter@psg.com>.

Discussion list for trade and economic data, analysis, opinions and experience, sources of information about Latin American business and industry, conference announcements, etc. Multilingual.

LATINO-L: Latino E-Mail List [electronic mail list]. Amherst: University of Massachusetts, 1993.
To subscribe: <latino-l- request@amherst.edu>. To post: <latino-l @amherst.edu>.

List for communication among Latino students in the U.S. This list was announced in February 1993. Not a lot of traffic since that time.

MCLR: Midwest Consortium for Latino Research [electronic mail list].
To subscribe: <listserv@ibm.cl.msu.edu>. To post: <mclr@ibm.cl. msu.edu>.

Dialogue among Latinos living in the United States.

MEXICO-L: Knowing Mexico: People, Places, and Culture [electronic mail list]. Monterrey, Nuevo León, MX: ITESM.
To subscribe: <listserv@tecmtyvm.mty.itesm.mx>. To post: <mexico-l @tecmtyvm.mty.itesm.mx>.

An active list with members from many countries, all with an interest in Mexico. Good source for getting network information on Mexico. Mostly in Spanish.

NATIVE-L: Indigenous Peoples Information; NAT-LANG: Languages of Indigenous Peoples; NATCHAT: Indigenous Peoples Discussion [electronic mail lists].
Three separate lists available for subscription via: <listserv@tamvm1.tamu.edu>. To post: <native- l@tamvm1.tamu.edu> <natchat-@tamvm1.tamu.edu> <nat- lang@tamvm1.tamu.edu>.

These lists deal with various issues related to indigenous peoples worldwide. Politics, culture, and information sources are all discussed. Participants include academics, activists, students, etc. Good news source for information on environment, human rights, politics, etc. in Latin America, especially for Guatemala, Brazil, Ecuador, Peru, and other countries with large indigenous populations.

PACS-L: Public Access Computer Systems Forum [electronic mail list]. Houston, TX: University of Houston Libraries.
To subscribe: <listserv@uhupvm1.bitnet>. To post: <pacs-l@uhupvm1>.

Major list for information on library computer systems, including network information, OPACS, CD-ROM databases, etc.

PERU: Discussion Group [electronic mail list].
To subscribe: <owner-peru@cs.sfsu.edu>. To post: <peru@cs.sfsu.edu>. List administrator: Herbert Koller <herb@busybe.sf.ca.us>.

General discussion on Peru. Probably 5-10 news postings daily from various wire services and international newspapers. Mostly in Spanish.

REDALC: Reseau Amérique Latine et Caraibes/Latin American and Caribbean Networks [electronic mail list].
To subscribe: <listserv@frmop11.cnusc.fr>. To post: <redalc@frmop11.cnusc.fr>.

Discussion of the creation and status of Latin American and Caribbean computer networks.

SIRIAC-L: Latin American Networks [electronic mail list]. Puerto Rico: Sistema Integrado de Recursos Informáticos y Científicos.
To subscribe: <listserv@enlace.bitnet>. To post: <siriac-l@enlace.bitnet>. For more information on other lists or subscriptions contact: Roberto Loran <r_loran@racin.clu.net>.

An interest group for discussion of the present and future of Latin American networks.

USENET NEWS on Latin America: <soc.culture.latin-america> <soc.culture.mexican> <soc.culture.caribbean> <alt.culture.argentina> <soc.culture.portuguese> <soc.culture.spain> [Usenet newsgroups].
To read USENET news you must have access via a news reader on your local system or through access to another system. Find out about local access by contacting your computer center.

These newsgroups discuss almost anything relating to society, politics, travel, culture, etc. for the regions described. Various languages, mostly Spanish and English. Much information is cross-posted to other lists. At least one of these <soc.culture.mexican> contains a FAQ (frequently asked questions) file that provides a lot of good information.

20. The Latin American Information Base

Kinloch Walpole

Latin America is the world's single greatest challenge to electronic information specialists. The region is an electronic information void. Attempts to penetrate this void are unnecessarily expensive, excessively time consuming, and often unproductive.

This characterization does not mean that there are no databanks or that primary research is not computerized. The void is not the consequence of a conspiracy or monopoly, but rather the natural product of the absence of any single unifying force to make existing information known and available.

This lack of information distorts perceptions, retards development, and promotes speculative chaos. Three notable attempts to penetrate this void have resulted in limited success. The most noteworthy success has been the effort of the Universidad de Colima to search out and produce CD-ROMs containing databases produced throughout Latin America. The Universidad Nacional Autónoma de México Facultad de Filosofía y Letras has published a listing of about 700 local databases within Latin America. Another notable project is the Red de Redes (Network of Networks), coordinated by ALIDE with the active participation of BIREME, CLADES (CEPAL), IBASE, and REDUC. Although nascent, these efforts do demonstrate potential for making information available from Latin America.

At present, there is more information available on Latin America in the archives of various international organizations, commercial databases, and national governments than there is from databases originating in Latin America itself. As a consequence, history, science, economics, and development are being controlled from the exterior rather than from the interior in individual countries.

Compounding the problem is the fact that existing information is not neatly categorized by region, country, and subject, but rather is contained within more general subject areas collected on a global basis. For example, the single best source of generalized economic data on a particular country is usually the databanks of the United Nations, World Bank, Dialog, InfoQuest, or the U.S. government. These data are international in character and all too often ignore national and regional fluctuations or disparities. However, there is no source within any Latin American country that makes such regional information readily available to a global, national, or regional audience.

Readily available information is easily accessible to organizations, institutions, and individuals from inside or outside any given country at a reasonable cost. Many existing CD-ROMs or databases appear to be attempting to recoup the entire start-up cost on the first sale. In all fairness, though, CD-ROMs hold large amounts of information and information gathering and data entry can be very expensive. Often this information is not classified and could be made available. However, first one must know that it exists, where it is located, and who controls it. It is not unusual for officials of a government, department, university, or institution to be unaware of the existence of the information or who the gatekeeper might be. Thus, access to information can depend on personal contacts cultivated over a long period of time, sometimes known as the "old boy networks."

Vast amounts of computerized primary research data remain virtually hidden from both Latin America and the rest of the world. This material is essential to the development of new knowledge and to the well-being of Latin American populations.

What Is Being Done Now

This paper describes the origin of a hemispheric resource which was initiated to fill the void encountered by hemispheric information specialists. The objective of this resource is twofold: (1) to increase the overall knowledge base of the hemisphere, and (2) to facilitate interaction among people and organizations in the hemisphere. Both objectives support the goal of making existing information more readily available to all. The development of an up-to-date database that not only lists the available information resources but also catalogs communication networks with their institutional subscribers will further the development and exchange of new knowledge from primary sources.

Major information gateways are well known and accessible to organizations and individuals with sufficient financial assets. What is lacking, however, is a listing of databases and networks associated with primary research and specialized information.

Such alternate sources of information are not only overshadowed by the giant information gateways but also lack the ability to make their presence known. The Latin American Information Base (LAIB) is intended to provide a forum where this second tier of information producers can communicate and exchange information. There are several very tangible and immediate benefits associated with increased communication among these primary information producers. Avoiding duplication of primary research is probably the most important one. In addition, the efficacy of further primary research on similar subjects is invariably improved by an initial analysis of existing research. Quality primary research is the basic building block of new knowledge, knowledge that can dramatically improve the economics and life styles within the hemisphere.

Latin American Database Interest Group

The Latin American Database Interest Group (LADIG) is an informal organization of computer information professionals from the academic, commercial, and governmental arenas. The co-chairs are Lourdes Feria from the Universidad de Colima in Mexico and Roberto Guerra from the Universidad Nacional Autónoma de México. The immediate past chair was Sue Mundell from the U.S. Library of Congress. An important point to bear in mind about LADIG is that it is a group of information professionals who are acting on their own behalf.

The objectives of LADIG should not be confused with those of the Seminar on the Acquisition of Latin American Library Materials (SALALM). The two organizations share a relatively large number of members in common and have a mutual interest in electronic storage and retrieval of information within the hemisphere. The development and movement of information within the hemisphere is an important part of SALALM's agenda, but it is LADIG's sole focus. Despite this difference in emphasis, the two organizations interact on a regular basis.

Although LADIG's membership consists of individuals, several institutions and organizations have supported LADIG's activities in a significant way. These include the Universidad de Colima, University of Texas, Coordinadora Regional de Investigaciones Económicas y Social (CRIES), Red Científica Peruana, and the National Information Service Corporation (NISC). Their support extends to the distribution of the Latin American Information Base (LAIB) through electronic means. However, it is important to remember that LAIB has not and does not receive any financial support from any source. Thus, LAIB is not biased in the direction of any particular institution, organization, or political subdivision. The result is freer exchange of information.

The Latin American Information Base Project

The Latin American Information Base project collects information on databases, CD-ROMs, and networks by and of interest to the Latin American community. We do not actually collect these databases, CD-ROMs, or networks per se, but rather describe their contents in the originator's own words and provide a contact address so that interested parties can get in touch with the owners. To this end, we have developed a database that we distribute free to anyone interested in the subject.

The current version of LAIB, a DOS database written in the Clipper programming language, contains English, Spanish, and Portuguese modules and over 800 records. Currently, we are beta testing a Windows version in English, the Latin American Information Base for Windows (LAIBWIN). When the beta test is complete, in March 1994, a Spanish module will be added, with a Portuguese module to follow in June 1994. A DOS version (LAIBDOS), identical to the Windows version, will be distributed within 60 days of the completion of beta testing. This LAIBDOS will supersede the current LAIB.

Both LAIBWIN and LAIBDOS are updated and reissued when 50 records have been added to the contents or quarterly at a minimum. The program is updated by distribution to the networks that carry it free of charge. In the United States, the University of Texas makes LAIB available to any interested party on its Internet server LANIC and the Latin American Trade Council's Internet bulletin board LATCO. Similar arrangements have been made with universities or individuals in Mexico, Peru, and Guatemala, and with organizations in Nicaragua and Costa Rica. The program is also contained on CD-ROMs produced in both Mexico (Universidad de Colima) and the United States (National Information Service Corp.).

Several aspects of the development of LAIB make it a unique and incredibly successful project. First, it had to be developed and produced at minimal cost. All expenses had to be absorbed by the individuals who worked on its development. Second, it was necessary to devise a distribution system that would be available to everyone in the hemisphere at minimal cost. Third, the information contained in LAIB is not filtered in any manner. Whatever information LADIG received on any network, database, or CD-ROM was copied verbatim into the database with no editing or translation. Last, the program was written with English, Spanish, and Portuguese access modules so that the information would be available to any person in the hemisphere.

Mechanics of Presentation

The development of the actual program has been more revolutionary then evolutionary. LADIG had no institutional knowledge upon which to base a project of this type or magnitude. Nor did LADIG ever envision the quantitative expansion the program experienced. At the outset, in 1992, the project was intended for use by computer professionals. Consequently, it was written as a DOS application in Clipper. However, a much larger user group developed, and extensive help screens were required. Also, responding to popular demand, an electronic network database was added to the program. In addition, some of the original features which were useful to computer professionals caused confusion among the larger body of users. The program and its four databases has grown to about five megabytes, with no end in sight.

To solve many of the problems associated with the first edition, a second version of LAIB—LAIB for Windows (LAIBWIN)—has been developed. The Windows platform was chosen for several reasons. A more friendly user interface was required, and the mechanical proficiency of the program had to be improved. The Windows platform addresses both issues. It allows maximum effort to be applied to the design of the actual program while Windows itself takes care of secondary features such as memory handling, printing, mouse movements, and so on which would otherwise be excessively time consuming.

Visual Basic was chosen as the programming language for several reasons. Because Visual Basic was developed by the same company that developed Windows, it seemed that this company would provide the best interface with Windows. Also, the existing databases in LAIB could be integrated into the new program with very minor modifications and little labor. As to mechanical efficiency, Visual Basic incorporates Structured Query Language as a part of its search techniques. This makes searches very efficient and also eliminates the requirement for the 30 +/- indexes that the preceding DOS version required. Because Visual Basic 3.0 for Windows contains the Windows Access database engine, the database functions are easier to program and operate more efficiently. Of interest to programmers is the fact that Visual Basic comes with its own total compiler. Therefore, unlike most Windows database languages, Visual Basic can stand alone as a completely separate entity. What this means of course is that it can be distributed freely without copyright infringement.

Language

The language aspect of the program continues to be the greatest obstacle, partly because uniform, agreed-upon standards for technical and computer terms in English, Spanish, and Portuguese are lacking. Perhaps more important, however, is the scarcity of competent translators. The first LAIB program underwent the full circle of Spanish and Portuguese word changes. It is hoped that most of the terms can be carried over to the new database. The help screens, however, need total revision and, consequently, some new translations.

Solving the mechanical aspects of presenting the information is only the first of three core issues. The remaining two are distribution and collection.

Distribution

For several reasons, the Internet and electronic bulletin boards were chosen as a primary means of distribution. In general, they represent the fastest, cheapest, and most efficient mechanisms available. Unfortunately, this is not the case in all countries. Often, inadequate electronic hardware precludes the rapid transfer of data or the costs are prohibitive. Where any type of monopoly exists, not only do costs tend to be high but also equipment tends to be antiquated, reducing the speed of information transfer. As a rule of thumb, a 2400-baud modem can generally transmit five megabytes of data in about 45 minutes. LADIG is able to transmit at 14,400 baud to those who want to go directly to the source. However, in some countries antiquated telephone equipment limits transfer rates to 300 or 1200 baud. Unfortunately, some of these same systems charge as much as 5 cents for a byte of information, making the cost of large-scale database transmission prohibitive. About the only way around this problem is to mail 3.5 inch disks to primary distribution points for local reproduction and distribution.

Collection

The collection of information is also a continuing obstacle for LAIBDOS and LAIBWIN. This is related, in part, to the relative newness of the program. The first version of the program was released for beta testing at La VI Feria Internacional del Libro de Guadalajara in 1992; the final program was released in May at SALALM 93. In essence, the program has been available for about six months. In its present version, it has just under 1,600 records. Some 800 of these are listings of databases, gateways, networks, and CD-ROMs. Another 800 or so are Internet e-mail addresses of universities, colleges, organizations, and individuals in Central America, Bolivia, and Argentina. All e-mail listings from any country within the hemisphere are welcome and will be entered and distributed as fast as resources permit. In addition to e-mail addresses, there are approximately 100 listings for commercial networks, which include their telephone numbers and contact persons in each country in the hemisphere.

Future Development

The core problem remains: what about the secondary level of information sources within the hemisphere? Currently, we make use of two approaches. The first is the "old boy network," spreading the word in the circles within which the membership of LADIG operates. The second and most productive approach is to participate in international conferences where LADIG is able to reach out to other information professionals. We constantly search both for new information and for electronic platforms such as electronic bulletin boards which have national prominence in order to distribute the program.

At present, the program suffers from a deficiency that we hope will be temporary. Most of the source references are listings of information platforms from commercial distributors because these have been the easiest to locate and their information is easily accessible. However, other, more basic sources are needed. Sometimes a database is shown as available from various distributors. We decided to list each information source, whatever its form, because we have no idea what platforms are actually available to the end user.

It is beyond the scope and resources of the project to list pricing information. The variables of licensing, currency changes, editions, and so on fluctuate too much.

The last major problem concerns the accuracy of information contained within the LAIB databases. The information provided represents a best effort. Sometimes the information is secondhand but it is listed anyway. The goal is to provide a thread, at a minimum, to the sources of the databases, networks, and CD-ROMs. Compounding the problem of information quality is the transient nature of some of the organizations that collect the information. For example, in the case of academic research, the students who did the research graduate and move on to other pursuits. Professional information companies are merged, bought, and sold. Universities and governmental offices suffer from institutional amnesia because of the turnover of key personnel. Our solution to this problem is to correct any error when it is pointed out to us.

To a certain extent, the program is self-cleansing and self-correcting. After the addition of 50 records, the updated database is sent to each distribution point. Each update includes the most recent corrections. We believe this will be a satisfactory correction procedure.

Summary

The Latin American Information Base is a continuing attempt to forge links between and among organizations and institutions throughout the hemisphere. A more responsive and freer flow of information should enhance the well-being of individuals and organizations in Latin America.

21. Computadoras, comunicaciones y bases de datos en Guatemala: Nuevas oportunidades y una propuesta

Grete Pasch

En este trabajo se describe brevemente el desarrollo y la situación actual de la computación y las comunicaciones en Guatemala, presentando algunos ejemplos de bases de datos locales y exponiendo los problemas que hay para accesarlas. Finalmente, se propone la creación de directorios de bases de datos en línea que ayuden a localizar y utilizar mejor estos recursos.

Dos tipos de información: Interna y externa

Toda organización tiene que manejar su información interna, tanto a nivel operacional, como a nivel estratégico. Esta información interna incluye presupuestos de gastos, planificación y control de producción, estadísticas de ventas o de prestación de servicios, facturación y cobros, control de personal, etcétera.

En el caso de organizaciones de investigación y de servicios de información, la información generada también incluye, por ejemplo, reportes de resultados de investigación, estadísticas, bibliografías, y en el caso específico de las bibliotecas, el mismo catálogo de la colección. Este segundo tipo de información, que aquí llamaré "externa", es en el que casi todos pensamos al escuchar el término "bases de datos". En Guatemala no nos hemos dedicado hasta ahora, a desarrollar bases de datos de este tipo. Sin embargo, esto no significa que no exista experiencia en el uso de la computación y en el mantenimiento de bases de datos de tipo administrativo, de uso interno, como se ve a continuación.

Usos de la computación en Guatemala

Las primeras computadoras en Guatemala fueron instaladas en la década de los 40 por IBM. Entre sus primeros clientes estuvieron el IRCA (International Railway Company of America, que luego se volvió FEGUA, Ferrocarriles de Guatemala), la United Fruit Company, el Banco de Guatemala, el Crédito Hipotecario Nacional y, de manera muy importante, la Universidad de San Carlos de Guatemala (Arias 1992; Estévez 1981). El gobierno pronto se convirtió en el mayor cliente de IBM, y esta compañía fue tan importante que, aún hoy en día, el término Centro IBM se usa para referirse a algunos centros de cómputo, aunque ya no tengan máquinas

IBM. NCR (National Cash Register) llegó en los años 50, Hewlett Packard en los 60, y luego Basic Four, Data General, Wang, y otros durante los 70.

El uso de la computadora se expandió rápidamente durante la década de los 80, cuando aparecieron las computadoras personales. En Guatemala aparecieron docenas de compañías dedicadas a la venta de 'clones' y al desarrollo de sistemas comerciales. La competencia fue y continúa siendo tan dura, que con tal de vender una máquina, muchas de estas compañías regalan a sus clientes cualquier paquete de software que deseen —por supuesto, en copias ilegales, o "pirateadas", como se dice comúnmente.

El mercado de computación en Guatemala es relativamente pequeño, pero muy moderno. Se dice que cualquier paquete que sale al mercado hoy en los Estados Unidos estará mañana mismo en Guatemala. Aunque muchos clientes comerciales son conservadores y prefieren las soluciones probadas (e.g., IBM AS400), otras compañías están migrando hacia ambientes UNIX sobre 386, 486 y arquitecturas RISC (sobre todo de SUN Microsystems e IBM), comunicándose con TCP/IP, instalando aplicaciones cliente/servidor, y utilizando bases de datos distribuidas (Informix, Oracle). Esto ha sido posible gracias a los avances en la educación de la computación, como se ve en la siguiente sección.

Educación en "Informática"

Las computadoras personales también introdujeron cambios en la educación secundaria. En Guatemala es posible obtener certificados especializados de educación media, tradicionalmente en estudios de magisterio, contabilidad, ó secretariado. En 1980 el Ministerio de Educación aprobó el primer "Bachillerato de Computación". Este fue tan exitoso, que pronto se fundaron al menos 20 colegios similares. Además de los cursos generales de bachillerato, los alumnos toman cursos de computación, incluyendo nociones de análisis de sistemas y el uso de paquetes comerciales de aplicación como procesadores de palabras, hojas electrónicas, y programación de bases de datos que corren en computadoras personales (e.g., dbase IV, FoxPro).

Las cinco universidades del país ofrecen diversas carreras en computación: desde cursos de dos años para programadores, a carreras de ciencias de computación, electrónica, e ingeniería de sistemas (que toma cinco años completar), hasta maestrías en bases de datos y en investigación de operaciones. Estas carreras abrieron a finales de los años 70. Desde entonces se han graduado unos 350 profesionales a nivel de licenciatura o ingeniería. Actualmente hay alrededor de 2,000 estudiantes en estas carreras en las cinco universidades. Entre los catedráticos, muchos han obtenido grados académicos en los Estados Unidos, México y/o Europa.

Hace diez años quizás habría media docena de profesionales con postgrados en computación; hoy en día hay unos 60.

Todos estos datos son aproximados, debido a que no existen estadísticas publicadas al respecto. Esto cambiará cuando la Asociación de Informática de Guatemala (ADIG) logre patrocinar un esperado estudio de "diagnóstico del sector informático" del país. ADIG ha ido complementando las oportunidades educativas en informática, mediante publicaciones y la organización de seminarios y otros eventos, entre los cuales destaca la Convención Anual de Informática. Esta actividad se realiza desde 1982, en conjunto con la Asociación de Gerentes de Guatemala (AGG). Atrae unos 35,000 visitantes a las exhibiciones de equipos y servicios de computación que exponen unas 70 empresas de la región. La parte académica de la Convención consta de conferencias, seminarios y talleres prácticos, a los que asisten unas 550 personas.

Pero qué hay del manejo de la información "externa"?

Como decíamos al principio, toda organización debe manejar su información interna. Hoy en día existen sistemas para agilizar ese manejo, cuyo desarrollo e implementación es bien conocido y utilizado por muchas organizaciones en Guatemala.

Pero qué sucede con la información externa? Sobre todo para la toma de decisiones estratégicas, un administrador necesita conocer su entorno: estar al tanto de cambios en los mercados mundiales, conocer lo nuevo en tecnología, mantener contactos con profesionales que se dedican a la investigación en su área, etc. Mientras que en otros países se reconoce la utilidad de mantener bibliotecas corporativas, en Guatemala pareciera que muchos profesionales no vuelven a poner un pie en la biblioteca una vez salen de la universidad. Mientras en otros países se desarrollan redes y sistemas de consulta a bases de datos de referencia, en Guatemala resulta difícil justificar su adquisición y utilización. Cómo consiguen los profesionales guatemaltecos la información necesaria para mantenerse actualizados y para la toma de decisiones?

A continuación presento las tres razones que veo para esta falta de demanda de servicios de información.

Hay pocas bases de datos disponibles

Las bibliotecas y archivos que forman la base tradicional de fuentes de información nunca han recibido la prioridad necesaria para desarrollar buenas colecciones ni buenos servicios. Por lo tanto, los usuarios se han acostumbrado y/o decepcionado de lo que está disponible. El sistema educativo en general no propicia la investigación por parte de los estudiantes, limitándolos a comprar y estudiar en "el" libro de texto del curso. Ni siquiera los profesores acuden a las bibliotecas. En resumen el sistema no crea "buscadores de información".

Afortunadamente, existen algunos centros de investigación donde la situación es diferente, donde se mantienen centros de información e incluso se están creando bases de datos de uso público. Algunos ejemplos son:

> El CIEN (Centro de Investigaciones Económicas Nacionales), una institución privada, mantiene una base de datos de indicadores sociales sobre educación, población y salud. Esta se encuentra en Lotus y es muy usada para producir y publicar estadísticas.
>
> El INE (Instituto Nacional de Estadística) se ha ido modernizando y mantiene gran parte de su información en computadoras personales. Durante 1993 se espera llevar a cabo el Censo de Vivienda y Población. Todos los datos que se recopilen serán ingresados en una base de datos y agregados a nivel de sectores y municipios.
>
> El Banco de Guatemala, por ser el guardián de las divisas del país, mantiene una base de datos actualizada sobre estadísticas cambiarias, inflación, importaciones y exportaciones, que son publicadas regularmente.
>
> La Bolsa de Valores Global cuenta con un sistema en línea de información de valores, que puede ser accesada remotamente por cualquier persona interesada.
>
> ASIES (la Asociación de Investigaciones Económicas y Sociales) también de carácter privado, está creando una base de datos cartográfica, digitalizando los mapas detallados de todo el país con el propósito de relacionarlos con una base de datos de las características de suelos y vegetación.
>
> El CCEBU (Comité de Cooperación entre Bibliotecas Universitarias) ha estado trabajando desde 1988 en la creación de un "Catálogo Unido de Referencia" y un "Catálogo Unido de Tesis Universitarias". Cada universidad ingresa su parte a una base de datos, y luego se intercambian diskettes.

Esto, en cuanto a bases de datos locales. El uso de bases de datos disponibles a nivel internacional es muy limitado, por las razones que se detallan en las siguientes secciones. Sin embargo, deseo mencionar que existen autores que tienen la objeción de que estas bases de datos internacionales (Dialog, BRS, STN, etc.) no son relevantes para el usuario latinoamericano porque no contienen información sobre América Latina. Al contrario, estas bases de datos podrían sernos de mucha utilidad para aprender y mantenernos al día de los avances políticos, sociales, económicos y tecnológicos a nivel mundial —si tuviéramos acceso a ellas.

El acceso a bases de datos es difícil y costoso

En primer lugar, las instituciones que crean bases de datos no lo hacen en CD-ROMs ó en línea, pues no se tienen los recursos para imprimir discos ni para mantener un sistema funcionando y que dé servicios remotos al público. El Banco de Guatemala tiene mucha información en cintas magnéticas, el INE piensa distribuir los resultados del censo en diskettes, y para utilizar la base de datos geográfica de ASIES el interesado probablemente tendría que contar con los paquetes de software adecuados, ó consultarla in situ.

En segundo lugar, en Guatemala aún no tenemos conexión a Internet, y contamos con un sistema de telecomunicaciones anticuado que hace muy costoso el acceso remoto. Por ejemplo, el ICAITI (Instituto Centroamericano de Investigación y Tecnología Industrial) es la única institución que cuenta con una computadora, un modem, línea telefónica y personal entrenado para realizar búsquedas en Dialog. Parte considerable del costo de cada búsqueda lo constituye el costo de las llamadas telefónicas necesarias para conectar con Dialog en California ya que GUATEL, la Empresa Guatemalteca de Telecomunicaciones, tiene una tarifa de un dólar por minuto de conexión a los Estados Unidos.

Todo esto cambiará en cuanto se logre la conexión con Internet. La Comisión Nacional de Informática, de la cual formo parte, ha propuesto un proyecto de interconexión que está ahora en discusión para su aprobación por el Consejo Nacional de Ciencia y Tecnología. En cuanto sea aprobado y se liberen los fondos (que ya están disponibles), el nodo podrá ser instalado. Sin duda, GUATEL jugará un papel decisivo en ayudar a hacer posible este proyecto. Dado el papel tan importante que juega GUATEL, y como el acceso a bases de datos depende en gran parte de las telecomunicaciones, voy a expandirme un poco en el caso de GUATEL.

La Ley Orgánica de GUATEL le confiere "la exclusividad de prestar el servicio público de telecomunicaciones", tanto de servicios existentes, como de "*todos aquellos de la misma naturaleza que en el futuro se desarrollen.*" Por lo tanto, hoy en día esa ley da potestad a GUATEL para regular e interferir en el desarrollo de cualquier modalidad de telecomunicación (teléfonos, telégrafo, radio, televisión), incluyendo las que aún no se hayan inventado (Ibargüen 1992).

Este monopolio estatal ha creado varios problemas. Además de que el costo del servicio es elevado, la calidad del mismo deja mucho que desear, pues las comunicacione se interrumpen abruptamente, hay que hacer diez intentos antes de lograr hacer una llamada, las líneas son tan viejas y tienen tanto ruido que es imposible transmitir datos, etc.

El problema más grave es que GUATEL no logra satisfacer la demanda existente. "Sabemos del caso de numerosos . . . empresarios y personas particulares que, interesados en obtener una línea telefónica, se ven obligados a visitar frecuentemente GUATEL, rogando que les asignen una línea".[1] En 1990 había 2,000 teléfonos públicos para una población de más de 9,000,000 de personas, y un total de 200,000 líneas, ó sea, menos de 2 teléfonos por cada 100 habitantes, y 0.4 teléfonos por cada 100 habitantes en las áreas rurales. Esto, comparado con el promedio latinoamericano de 6 líneas por 100, ó con el 95 por 100 de los Estados Unidos y la mayor parte de Europa, nos indica que GUATEL tiene mucho trabajo que hacer. Se ha iniciado un proyecto para instalar 250,000 líneas adicionales con la colaboración de AT&T, MCI, Italtel, Intelsat, Siemens, Alcaltel, Mitsui, Ericcson y COMSAT. A pesar de esto, la demanda esperada para el año 2000 sólo llegará a ser cubierta en un 30% (GUATEL 1993).

Como dicen que mal de muchos, consuelo de tontos, a muchos les basta con saber que la situación es similar en todos los países centroamericanos —excepto en Costa Rica. Allí se goza de un mejor servicio; hay 9 teléfonos por 100 habitantes, y se está instalando una red de fibra óptica que enlaza 4 ciudades.

Costa Rica también tuvo el primer nodo regular tipo uucp desde agosto de 1990, gracias al apoyo del Programa de las Naciones Unidas para el Desarrollo y la Agencia Canadiense Internacional para el Desarrollo, que pagó parte considerable de los costos de comunicaciones. Es más, desde noviembre de 1990 la Universidad de Costa Rica, gracias al apoyo de IBM, OEA, BID y otros, cuenta con un link satelital vía Pan Am Sat, dedicado a la transmisión de datos, específicamente, a la interconexión con Bitnet —y desde febrero de 1993, al primer nodo Internet de Centroamérica (de Teramond 1993).

Mientras, en Guatemala, la transmisión de datos internacionalmente puede hacerse sólo a través de GUATEL. En 1990, durante el gobierno del presidente Vinicio Cerezo, se autorizó la creación de la empresa Telepuerto, que instaló una antena y empezó a ofrecer servicios de transmisión y recepción de datos vía satélite. Pese a las protestas de esta compañía (Prensa Libre, 1/5/93) y de los guatemaltecos que ven la importancia de contar con estos servicios, sus operaciones fueron canceladas por el nuevo gobierno. Luego, GUATEL inauguró su propio servicio de transmisión de datos, operando exclusivamente a través de COMSAT (Intelsat).

Como GUATEL es signatario de COMSAT, podrían dificultarse los trámites de la Comisión Nacional de Informática para lograr una conexión con Internet. Hasta ahora, la Comisión estaba considerando la posibilidad de enlazarse de manera similar a como lo hizo Costa Rica, o sea, usando la conexión de bajo costo que está ofreciendo la National Science Foundation en cooperación con Pan Am Sat y Sprint. Los datos bajarían en Homestead (Florida) y serían enrutados sin ningún costo al "FIX East", o sea, el punto principal de entrada a Internet de la costa este de los Estados Unidos. Esperamos que GUATEL y los miembros de COMSAT permitan esta conexión, ya que sería en beneficio de la educación y la investigación en Guatemala.

El usuario desconoce las bases de datos

Como hemos visto, hay problemas en la creación y uso de las bases de datos ya que éstas no son muy numerosas, ni son fácilmente accesibles. Además, como se ha mencionado repetidamente en la literatura sobre el tema, existe el problema de no saber qué bases de datos hay ni dónde están, ya que no contamos con directorios completos ni actualizados.

Harold Colson y otros miembros de SALALM y de otras organizaciones han publicado listas de bases de datos que son un buen punto de partida. DIBALC, el Directorio de Bases de Datos de América Latina y el Caribe de la UNAM, y LAIB del Latin American Database Interest Group de SALALM, son dos esfuerzos descritos en otros capítulos en volumen. Cierta ayuda en línea puede también encontrarse en el LANIC, el Latin American Network Information Center de la Universidad de Texas, Austin.

Las desventajas de los directorios impresos, es que pierden su actualidad tan pronto como se van a la imprenta. Además, todo directorio tiene que ser constantemente actualizado, lo cual implica un gran esfuerzo de investigación por parte de los editores. WAIS, los "knowbots" y otros agentes de búsqueda de información en las redes sólo toman en cuenta la información en línea, mientras que sería ideal que se incluyeran todos los formatos: en línea, en diskettes, en cintas, en CD-ROM, y cualquier otro que se haga disponible en el futuro. El acceso también debe poderse hacer "off-line", e incluso, usuarios que no tienen acceso a Internet deberían poder solicitar y recibir información sobre bases de datos.

Como veo que los directorios disponibles actualmente no responden a todas estas necesidades, presenté una propuesta a OEA para la creación de un modelo de "Directorio Automatizado de Bases de Datos Latinoamericanas" (Pasch 1992). La idea realmente es sencilla: mantener un directorio en línea, que sea accesible en forma interactiva, o vía mensajes de correo electrónico, ó vía fax o correo normal. La actualización de esta "base de datos de bases de datos" la harían los mismos creadores de bases de datos que quieran ser incluidos. Ellos también se encargarían de enviar cambios y adiciones cuando estos sucedan, ya sea "entrando" interactivamente al sistema central e ingresando los detalles en un archivo temporal, ó enviando un mensaje de correo electrónico en un formato standard, ó por medio de un fax que sería ingresado por el encargado del sistema.

La información para cada base de datos podría hacerse en formato MARC e incluir los campos típicos de una descripción bibliográfica. Cada registro tendría además del nombre de la base de datos, su productor, lugar de origen, etc., una descripción completa de lo que incluye, cómo accesarla, cuánto cuesta, etc. El directorio aportaría los siguientes beneficios:

Crear un directorio de fácil acceso que siempre contenga información actualizada.

Motivar a los creadores de bases de datos para dar a conocer sus esfuerzos, y que puedan encontrar a otros interesados en la labor que realizan, es decir, fomentar la comunicación entre investigadores.

Motivar a estudiantes y catedráticos para que vayan conociendo las nuevas fuentes de información disponibles, y que vayan contribuyendo a la recopilación de bases de datos.

Tener una sóla dirección donde los interesados puedan dirigirse para obtener información sobre la información que buscan —o sea, fungir como un servicio de referencia en modo electrónico. Cualquiera podría también enviar un mensaje con una sóla palabra ("HELP" o "AYUDA") y obtener mayor información sobre el servicio.

En Guatemala contamos con los conocimientos técnicos para implementar y probar esta idea a nivel centroamericano —pero haría falta la ayuda económica de alguna institución para llevarla a cabo.

NOTA

1. "Hasta cuándo, señores de GUATEL?" *ENLACE* 181 (7 de diciembre de 1992), 1.

REFERENCIAS

Arias de Blois, Jorge. 1992. Entrevista personal. Guatemala, marzo de 1992.

Comisión Nacional de Informática e Información Científico-Tecnológica. 1993. *Proyecto de interconexión con Internet*. Guatemala: Consejo Nacional de Ciencia y Tecnología, abril, 1993.

Estévez, Jorge A. 1981. "Desarrollo de la computación en la empresa guatemalteca." *Online* 1, no. 1 (marzo-abril).

GUATEL. 1993. *GUATEL XXII Aniversario*. Guatemala: Prensa Libre (Suplemento Especial), 14 de abril.

Hurtarte Gordillo, Francisco Javier. 1993. "Se inicia privatización de activos estatales." *Prensa Libre* (Guatemala), 4 de mayo.

Ibargüen S., Giancarlo. 1992. "Privatizar las ondas de radio", en *La Privatización: Una oportunidad!*, editado por Juan F. Bendfeldt y Hugo Maúl. Guatemala: CEES.

Nettleton, Greta. 1991. *The Role of Telecommunications in Guatemala's Development*. Arlington, VA: Institute for International Research.

Organización de Estados Americanos, Departamento de Asuntos Científicos y Tecnológicos. 1992. *RedHUCyT: Red Hemisférica Inter-Universitaria de Información Científica y Tecnológica.* Washington, DC, 12 de noviembre.

Pasch, Grete. 1992. *Directorio automatizado de bases de datos latinoamericanas.* Propuesta de Proyecto para SIBOLTI. Guatemala.

de Teramond, Guy F. 1993. *Description of the Research Network Initiative in Costa Rica.* Costa Rica: Universidad de Costa Rica.

22. Bibliografía nacional salvadoreña

Emmanuelle Bervas-Rodríguez

Historia del proyecto

Antecedentes

En las últimas décadas la región centroamericana se convirtió en un escenario crítico de importantes transformaciones y sucesos que atrajeron la atención internacional, evidenciado importantes dificultades y carencias para la investigación tanto en materia de fuentes confiables de información y documentación, como en la accesibilidad de las mismas. Esta situación se ha visto agravada en el caso salvadoreño por el deterioro o la destrucción de importantes fondos documentales como el de la Biblioteca Nacional y el de la Universidad Nacional.

El proyecto "Conclusión de la Bibliografía Nacional Salvadoreña y reclasificación y recatalogación de la Biblioteca Gallardo" nació del encuentro entre Rachel Barreto, en ese entonces Bibliotecaria Regional de USIS para Centroamérica, y M. A. Gallardo, actual director de la Biblioteca, en el curso de 1991, como producto de la preocupación común por llenar el vacío y superar las dificultades antes señaladas en materia de fuentes documentales.

Entre los elementos que explican la importancia, la viabilidad y la pertinencia del proyecto, figuran el creciente interés internacional por los asuntos centroamericanos, la ausencia de una bibliografía nacional salvadoreña, la riqueza documental ya reconocida de la Biblioteca Gallardo y el avance logrado por el proyecto original inconcluso de la Bibliografía iniciado a principios de los 80 por George Elmendorf y Bernardo Melero. La existencia en la Biblioteca Gallardo de los 18,000 registros de ese primer inventario, sin duda fue un factor que facilitó la obtención en 1992 de los primeros apoyos para el actual esfuerzo (Rachel Barreto, Oficina Regional para Bibliotecas en México/USIS, Plumsock Fund, Programa Fulbright).

En este mismo orden, debe recordarse que la Bibliografía tiene como fechas límites 1800-1990, utiliza el formato LCMARC, toma como modelo la Bibliografía Nacional Nicaragüense y sería editada en dos presentaciones, impresa y en disco compacto.

Montaje técnico del proyecto

1. Primera fase de montaje desde julio 1991 hasta abril 1992: la biblioteca comenzó por separar y colocar sala por sala, los distintos materiales publicados en El Salvador, por salvadoreños, o sobre El Salvador. Luego, inició su proceso de informatización con la adquisición de una computadora y un lector CDROM. A su vez adquirió las herramientas necesarias para el trabajo de catalogación y clasificación: *Reglas de Catalogación Angloamericanas*, 2a ed. (RCAA2), *Lista de Encabezamientos de Materia para Bibliotecas* (LEMB), 2a ed., *Bilindex*, última edición en español del Sistema de Clasificación Decimal de Dewey. Se consiguió el Banco de Datos Bibliográficos de la Biblioteca del Congreso conocido como CDMARC, y se compró el programa LOGICAT para la catalogación.

En esta etapa, la catalogación descriptiva se realizaba en español y se atribuían a los registros epígrafes en español.

En cuanto a los 18,000 registros del inventario Elmendorf, mecanografiados en hojas amarillas, con el formato MARC incompleto y codificados según las RCAA2, se decidió organizarlo por autores, cambiando su orden original por títulos. Error que nos hizo consumir mucho tiempo, que facilitó la búsqueda por autores, pero la complicó por todas las publicaciones emanadas de entidades.

A nivel del personal, se contaba con dos bibliotecarias, una a tiempo completo, encargada de la atención del público y de la gestión corriente de la biblioteca, otra a medio tiempo que se ocupaba de la reclasificación de las publicaciones periódicas y con una digitadora a medio tiempo.

Se catalogaron unos 600 registros salvadoreños. Las conclusiones que sacamos de este período fueron que el programa LOGICAT que permite solamente el nivel 1 de descripción, era insuficiente para las necesidades de una bibliografía nacional, que la formación del personal no era lo suficientemente sólida y que la metodología de trabajo no estaba aún bien definida.

2. Una segunda fase del montaje y verdadero comienzo de la Bibliografía Nacional, inició con la llegada del becario Fulbright Iván Calimano, en mayo de 1992, por un período de cuatro meses. Se sumó al equipo Lucy Romero quien había participado en el inventario Elmendorf.

Se consiguieron una computadora ACL y un módulo para la impresión de fichas. Después de una detenida evaluación de los programas disponibles, Calimano introdujo el programa "BibBase" para ingresar los registros en la computadora, con el nivel 2 de descripción. Este nos permite además importar registros de CDMARC, así como duplicar registros fácilmente. Se tomó la decisión de redactar la catalogación descriptiva en inglés y de atribuir a los registros epígrafes en inglés y español.

Con este fin se adquirió *Anglo-American Cataloging Rules*, 2d ed., revisión 1988, *Library of Congress Subject Headings*, 15th ed., 1992, con su *Subject Cataloging Manual: Subject Headings*, 4th ed., 1991.

Además de CDMARC, se cuenta también con un folder de PREMARC, con una lista de 1,800 registros seleccionados por su origen geográfico nacional.

Iván Calimano formó a todo el personal al formato LCMARC y a los AACR2.

Se decidió crear dos bases: la Base BNS conteniendo todos los registros de la Bibliografía Nacional Salvadoreña, con las menciones BMG o NON-BMG, correspondientes a si los libros se encuentran o no en la biblioteca, y la Base BMG de la biblioteca propiamente dicha, en la cual se incluirá, luego de completar la bibliografía, el resto de la biblioteca.

El método de trabajo es el siguiente: parear los libros con los formularios del inventario Elmendorf; buscar en CDMARC y luego en el folder PREMARC. A este nivel, se califica el registro según el origen de la catalogación: Original, CDMARC o PREMARC; se le atribuye un número único de identificación que comienza por BNS y se completa la información de los formularios, o, en el caso de no encontrarles —sea que la obra solo exista en la Gallardo o que sea posterior al inventario Elmendorf— se redacta la catalogación completa en un formulario nuevo. Al mismo tiempo se completa el Fichero Manual de Autoridades que nosotros creamos y que comprende a todas las personas, todas las entidades, y los epígrafes que no existen en el LCSH, ni en LEMB, ni en Bilindex.

Los formularios se entregan a la digitadora, quien les ingresa y les imprime para su revisión, luego se archivan en orden numérico de BNS.

Una de las bibliotecarias se encarga de trasladar a la base BMG los registros BMG, convertir al español la catalogación en inglés, suprimir los epígrafes en inglés y añadir el número de clasificación Dewey. La digitadora, al final, imprime las etiquetas y las fichas.

Desarrollo del proyecto

Primer balance, septiembre 1992

Fines de agosto, después de cuatro meses de trabajo, se tenía un poco más de 1,800 registros, lo que, teniendo en cuenta todas las dificultades de tipo técnico y laboral, equivale al trabajo realizado a tiempo completo, durante ocho meses, por una persona, el cual es un buen resultado. Los registros se repartían en 50% de catalogación original, 21% provenientes de PREMARC y 29% de CDMARC.

En septiembre, por limitaciones de personal, la gestión de la base BMG y la clasificación, ya no estaban aseguradas. Por otra parte, se constató que sobre los 1,800 libros catalogados, apenas unos 150 estaban clasificados. Era una situación insostenible para la biblioteca. Se tomó entonces la decisión de detener la catalogación y de dedicar los esfuerzos casi exclusivamente a la clasificación, refiriéndose sistemáticamente a la base, libro en mano.

Esta pausa fue al mismo tiempo beneficiosa porque permitió identificar errores, imprecisiones y omisiones, de tipo organizacional: ciertas obras no estaban catalogadas, otras, calificadas de NON-BMG, eran BMG; otras, con la mención Original, se encontraban en el folder PREMARC; otras tenían una localización solo BMG, porque los formularios Elmendorf no habían sido encontrados, faltaban en el Fichero de Autoridades fichas o referencias; de tipo intelectual: algunas obras no deberían haber aparecido en la base porque los autores no eran salvadoreños y no habían sido editados en El Salvador; otras no tenían fecha y ameritaban ubicación por lo menos a nivel de década; algunos epígrafes eran erróneos o imprecisos; de tipo mecánico: subsistían errores tipográficos, que podían alterar hasta la transcripción de títulos y de autores.

Todos estos errores pueden explicarse por varias causas: la extrema falta de espacio, tanto en el área de trabajo, como en los estantes —lo que explica la facilidad con que los libros se mezclan—, el ritmo intenso de trabajo sostenido, productor de un porcentaje normal de errores, un conocimiento insuficiente de los autores, y faltas de atención en la revisión de los registros.

La conclusión que se impuso fue la de un mayor rigor en la organización del trabajo y, sobre todo, de poner el acento sobre la investigación bibliográfica propiamente dicha.

Análisis de problemas bibliográficos

Dado que la elaboración de una bibliografía no se evalúa tan solo en términos estadísticos: hay un aspecto cualitativo fundamental, toda una parte de investigaciones que consumen mucho tiempo, pero que son necesarias para lograr una bibliografía que sea una fuente segura y un instrumento confiable.

Se han podido localizar algunos errores en la bibliografía de Grieb y en la *Bibliografía nacional nicaragüense*, como por ejemplo el hecho de que Manuel Castro Ramírez aparezca en la primera como un solo autor cuando en realidad son dos, ambos juristas, el padre internacionalista y el hijo penalista; en la segunda, vemos la atribución del epígrafe Nicaragua—Historia—Hasta 1838, al libro de Salvador Calderón Ramírez, *"Arriba El Salvador!"*, cuando en realidad se trata de la participación de tropas salvadoreñas al mando del General Ramón Belloso, en la Batalla de Masaya contra William Walker, en 1856.

Si bien es cierto que un pequeño porcentaje de errores puede ser considerado como normal, debe hacerse todo lo posible por reducirlo al mínimo, para lo cual es necesario profundizar la investigación siempre que lo permitan las fuentes y los documentos. El Fichero de Autoridades —Personas, Entidades, Materias— constituye el instrumento fundamental para sistematizar las investigaciones y por lo tanto es también condición sine qua non para una buena bibliografía.

Un Fichero de Autoridades Personas, exhaustivo y exacto, conteniendo, además de las formas elegidas de los nombres, notas biográficas, la mención de fuentes y, si posible, la lista completa de las obras publicadas por los autores, será ante todo la condición esencial para una recolección eficaz y completa del material bibliográfico salvadoreño, en el país mismo y en el extranjero durante la última fase del proceso.

En cuanto a su elaboración, pensamos que, en lo concerniente al establecimiento de los asientos —por supuesto en la estricta observancia de los AACR2— la decisión está en nuestras manos, por el hecho que poseemos mayores fuentes de información. Es decir, nosotros no podemos seguir siempre las formas establecidas por la Biblioteca del Congreso.

En lo que concierne las personas, los problemas a los que nos vemos confrontados son los siguientes: primero, la tradicional resolución de seudónimos, anagramas, heterónimos, homónimos, iniciales, con el propósito de establecer las referencias necesarias. Por ejemplo, es interesante ver como Ricardo Arenales, que colaboró con el Diario del Salvador a principios del siglo y escribió un libro sobre el terremoto Corpus Christi de San Salvador de 1917, y que tiene por verdadero nombre Miguel Angel Osorio, no es otro que el gran poeta colombiano Porfirio Barba Jacob.

Lamentablemente, no se cuenta con la Lista de Autoridades Personas de la Biblioteca del Congreso, pues ella es la verdadera llave para el manejo de la base. Bastan dos ejemplos para constatar lo anterior: Darlee, Irina aparece como Rukavishnikova-Darlee, Irina, y Jesualdo, como Sosa, Jesualdo.

La precisión de las fechas de nacimiento y muerte, que deseamos sistemática, es algunas veces un verdadero rompe-cabezas: éstas varían seguido de un repertorio al otro. Por ejemplo, la variación la más espectacular es la de la fecha de nacimiento de Francisco Gavidia, para la cual existen cinco fechas en tres años diferentes. José Mata Gavidia en su libro *Magnificencia espiritual de Francisco Gavidia* las recoge y las analiza. Y a pesar que una fecha hipotética sea más probable que la otra, ninguna es segura. CDMARC ha escogido el año 1864, lo mismo que la *Bibliografía Nacional Nicaragüense*. La biblioteca de la UCA ha escogido 1863. Y otros toman 1865. Nosotros propondremos 1863-1865, lo que refleja el estado de nuestro conocimiento y no una opción arbitraria.

La determinación de la nacionalidad, algunas veces difícil a establecer, es otro problema: no solamente al nivel de inclusión de los autores en la bibliografía, sino también por el hecho que nosotros optamos por calificar la literatura en los epígrafes, por lo que la bibliografía debe aparecer en un orden alfabético de autores y títulos y no bajo una forma sistemática.

Hay que destacar un fenómeno bastante frecuente en Centroamérica, el hecho que algunos escritores nacen en un país, se forman, publican, se casan en otro. El guatemalteco Ramón Uriarte es el padre del salvadoreño Juan Ramón Uriarte; el salvadoreño José Mata Gavidia fue rector de la Universidad de San Carlos en Guatemala; el nicaragüense Toruño desarrolla toda su actividad literaria y se casa en El Salvador; Alberto Guerra Trigueros es a la vez nicaragüense y salvadoreño.

Este fenómeno migratorio por razones políticas, económicas o de conveniencia personal, sobrepasa el ámbito centroamericano. Algunos autores se establecen y a veces se integran completamente en su país adoptivo, publicando allí en parte o totalmente sus obras. Este es el caso de los salvadoreños Gilberto González y Contreras en México y Cuba, Alice Lardé de Venturino en Chile, y en España, Carlo Antonio Castro en Mexico, e, inversamente, del chileno Luis Lagos y Lagos y del colombiano Isaías Gamboa en El Salvador.

En algunos casos, no se permite la duda, y en otros ella subsiste: debemos o no incluir estos autores? Como debemos calificar, en el caso de la literatura, sus poesías, sus novelas, sus ensayos? Y quien va tomar la decisión?

En lo que concierne a las entidades, se trata de determinar sus asientos, sus fechas de fundación y disolución, sus cambios de nombre, etc. Constituido de esta forma, el fichero puede servir en el futuro como un instrumento de trabajo para la historia de las instituciones.

En lo que concierne las materias, por una parte, tenemos la adaptación necesaria al español de los epígrafes que existen solamente en el LCSH, mucho más voluminoso que LEMB y que no tienen equivalencia en el BILINDEX; por la otra, la creación de epígrafes queda restringida a los casos que nos parecen valer la pena. A titulo de ejemplos, Putative marriage y Matrimonio putativo —noción que no existe en el derecho anglosajon— o Bombas, Salvadoran y Bombas salvadoreñas, que corresponde a una forma de poesía popular, nosotros la hemos conservado en inglés bajo la forma española, sobre el modelo de Coplas o Décimas, porque es un término intraducible.

La creación de epígrafes se impone también en el dominio de la historia, particularmente en la de El Salvador y, más generalmente, de la

América Central. Las listas de cuales disponemos son insuficientes, desde el punto de vista de la periodización —con divisiones muy vastas—, como de los hechos históricos precisos, demasiado poco numerosos. Pero, no tenemos la competencia histórica para hacerlo.

Frente a estos problemas, disponemos de dos tipos de ayuda, las fuentes bibliográficas y los recursos humanos.

Las fuentes bibliográficas son numerosas: bibliografías, biografías, diccionarios, antologías, libros de historia local, memorias, recortes de periódicos, etc. Contienen muchísima información que nos puede servir. Su explotación sistemática nos parece indispensable, pero es una tarea larga y ardua, porque la mayoría de ellas no contiene un índice, o porque no son igualmente fiables. Por lo tanto, convendría hacer una evaluación de su grado de fiabilidad. Por ejemplo, en *El desarrollo literario de El Salvador* de Toruño, las fechas para un mismo autor cambian de una página a la otra. Una obra de Gilberto González y Contreras, publicada a La Habana en 1934, aparece en Toruño y Hugo Lindo con el título *Rojo en azul*, y con el título *Bajo el azul* en el *Panorama de la literatura salvadoreña* de Gallegos Valdés y en el *Historical Dictionary of El Salvador*.

Paralelamente a las fuentes bibliográficas, nos parecen muy importantes los recursos humanos. Existen en El Salvador numerosas personas que podrían ayudarnos, porque han vivido como testigos o protagonistas los hechos históricos de una gran parte de este siglo, porque han participado en la historia cultural o porque tienen una competencia particular en un dominio dado. Convendría construir una red de informadores con el propósito de alcanzar —eso sería lo deseable— la conformación de una comisión encargada de revisar regularmente lo que hemos elaborado, para responder a nuestras preguntas, despejar nuestras dudas y tomar decisiones, por ejemplo en el dominio de la nacionalidad de los autores.

Por una feliz coincidencia, un grupo de historiadores, dirigidos por el Dr. Knut Walter, que ha sido comisionado por el Ministerio de Educación, con el apoyo financiero de México, para redactar un nuevo texto escolar de historia de El Salvador, solicitó la colaboración de la Biblioteca Gallardo. Después de varias semanas de búsqueda bibliográfica, estos investigadores se reunieron en nuestras instalaciones a principio de abril y al término de dicha reunión nos proporcionaron una lista de epígrafes más completa, más al día, la cual será de una gran utilidad.

Para finalizar con esta parte, quisiera citar el caso de un folleto muy interesante que se encuentra en la Gallardo, porque ilustra todos los procesos de búsqueda, con ayuda de fuentes bibliográficas y de personas, y el tiempo que a veces se debe de consagrar a la redacción de un solo registro. Se trata de una publicación anónima, sin fecha, impresa en

Guatemala, que tiene por título *Juan Pueblo en exilio*. Son versos satíricos con connotación política, ilustrados por caricaturas firmadas. El primer paso fue de saber si entraba en la bibliografía, quien era este Juan Pueblo, a que período histórico hacía referencia y a que personajes políticos se hacía alusión. Una primera persona contactada sugirió el nombre como autor de los versos a Pedro Geoffroy Rivas y la fecha de 1945. Con estos dos elementos, revisando ciertas obras, se pudo constatar que Geoffroy Rivas había creado el personaje de Juan Pueblo —figura alegórica del pueblo salvadoreño— en el periódico *La Tribuna* del cual fue director en 1944. Sin embargo, no fue el único en utilizar el personaje. Alfonso Morales, Manuel Aguilar Chávez y Manuel José Arce y Valladares también se sirvieron de esta alegoría. Por lo tanto, había que probar si Geoffroy Rivas había estado en el exilio en Guatemala en 1945 y encontrar otra pista que permitiera atribuirle de forma segura la paternidad de esta obra. Uno de los historiadores que se reunieron en la Gallardo hacía justamente una investigación sobre Juan Pueblo, pero ignoraba la existencia de este folleto, otro señala, a su vez, que el caricaturista, A. Pineda Coto, vive aún y reside en Costa Rica. Nuestro próximo paso es el de contactarlo. En resumen, es necesario realizar a veces todo un trabajo de detective, pero vale la pena y entra bien en el marco de una bibliografía nacional.

Segundo balance, abril 1993

De septiembre del 1992 a abril del 1993, aumentamos a casi 2,600 el número de registros, lo que evidencia un ritmo más lento, a pesar del refuerzo durante dos meses de Iván Calimano, tal como ya se ha explicado.

Las estadísticas son las siguientes: catalogación original 54% (con leve alza), CDMARC 24% (con leve baja), PREMARC 22% (equivalente). Este último deberá de ser el objeto de una reevaluación (pudo observarse gracias a Grieb), por el hecho que el Folder PREMARC no contiene las obras publicadas por salvadoreños en el extranjero o sobre El Salvador. De los registros, 13.5% son NON-BMG y 86.5% BMG; hay que destacar que 20.9% son registros únicos, es decir que se encuentran solo en la Gallardo.

Perspectivas y problemas

Evaluación del trabajo a completar

Primeramente en la Biblioteca Gallardo: se evaluó el fondo salvadoreño en aproximadamente 5,000 obras. Falta por lo tanto catalogar la mitad. Asimismo, será necesaria una revisión de los estantes, ya que un cierto número de libros seguramente escaparon a la primera selección.

También será necesario definir rigurosamente los criterios de integración de las obras que correspondan a Centroamérica.

La integración de los formularios Elmendorf será la siguiente etapa. Se puede suponer que faltarían unos 14,000. El trabajo que dicha etapa representa dependerá de la política que se adopte, si integramos tal cuales los formularios, con las modificaciones necesarias (epígrafes, descripción conforme a la última edición de AACR2), o bien si decidimos verificar los libros uno por uno en las bibliotecas mencionadas, para recoger los datos que hayan podido escapar y confirmar o anular la localización, en razón de la destrucción parcial de ciertos fondos.

De todas maneras, habrá que visitar las bibliotecas del país para inventariar y localizar las obras posteriores al inventario Elmendorf, aparecidas entre 1983 y 1990, e inventoriar algunos fondos olvidados o recientes, como la Biblioteca Judicial Dr. Ricardo Gallardo.

En lo que toca a la fase de recolección del material salvadoreño en las bibliotecas extranjeras, me limitaré al caso de Francia, en razón de un sondeo que realicé en julio de 1992. Al respecto, parece oportuno señalar y recordar el trabajo similar que Arturo Taracena hizo para la *Bibliografía nacional nicaragüense*, recuperando 180 registros únicos. Debido a la relativamente reciente informatización de los fondos de las bibliotecas, una investigación rápida sobre las bases disponibles cubriría un período aproximado de 20 años, permitiendo recolectar documentos poco difundidos, tésis, memorias, publicaciones de Comités de Solidaridad con El Salvador, etc. Antes de 1970, la investigación sería larga y difícil. Sin embargo, la Biblioteca Nacional ha emprendido la conversión retrospectiva de sus fondos sobre la base BN-Opale, que debería estar terminada en 1996. Algunos fondos que no han sido integrados al fichero general, Fonds Angrand, Société de Géographie, merecen ser explorados. En todo caso, habrá que disponer de listas selectivas de autores susceptibles de haber publicado en Francia, médicos, juristas, economistas, cónsules, etc. El interés de investigar en las bibliotecas francesas, y más generalmente en las bibliotecas europeas, será, no tanto la cantidad de los títulos recuperados —sin duda mucho menor que el de las grandes bibliotecas norteamericanas ricas en fondos latinoamericanos—, como el porcentaje significativo de registros únicos.

En fin, la última fase de la bibliografía será el esfuerzo de recuperación en las bibliotecas privadas de las obras "desaparecidas", es decir aquellas obras que no se encuentran ni en la Gallardo, ni en los formularios Elmendorf, ni en las bibliotecas extranjeras, y las cuales, de acuerdo con sondeos realizados regularmente, constituyen un número importante.

Problema de los recursos humanos y financieros

El proyecto Barreto, presentado a la National Endowment for the Humanities en el curso del año 92, a pesar de su calidad, pertinencia y costo relativamente modesto, no fue aprobado.

El equipo reducido que nosotros formamos —la desproporción con el equipo que trabajó sobre la *Bibliografía nacional nicaragüense* es enorme, aún teniendo en cuenta la economía que representa el inventario Elmendorf— no podrá, en un plazo razonable, llevar a cabo las numerosas tareas que le corresponden: catalogación, investigaciones bibliográficas, comunicaciones.

La Fundación Dr. Manuel Gallardo, que financia el funcionamiento de la biblioteca gracias a los ingresos parciales provenientes de una finca de café, no puede, en la coyuntura actual de baja de los precios del café, reclutar más personal, menos aún si se tiene en cuenta que se debe hacer frente a obras de preservación urgentes, que necesitarían también de una ayuda externa, lucha contra la polilla, microfilmación de ejemplares únicos, en mal estado, etc.

La cooperación inter-bibliotecas en El Salvador, que habría podido aportar el refuerzo de una catalogación compartida, todavía se encuentra en un estado embrionario. La formación del personal de biblioteca es aún insuficiente, a pesar del progreso logrado recientemente, especialmente gracias a los seminarios y cursos impartidos por Iván Calimano y otros profesionales nacionales y extranjeros.

En fin, la recolección de material salvadoreño en el extranjero es una tarea que, a nivel técnico y financiero, sobrepasa nuestros recursos actuales.

De parte de la Fundación Gallardo existe la determinación de realizar todos los esfuerzos posibles para continuar nuestro trabajo, y no dejar en el olvido del tiempo un proyecto que ha logrado superar las críticas etapas iniciales, estableciendo las bases para la consecución de una Bibliografía Nacional Salvadoreña que representa para el país la recuperación de parte importante de su patrimonio cultural y, a nivel internacional, la obtención de un valioso instrumento de investigación.

BIBLIOGRAFIA

Barreto, Rachel C. 1991. "The National Bibliography of El Salvador: 1800-1990: Final Proposal." S.l., s.n., 115 p. Sin publicar.

Gallardo, Miguel A. 1992. "Conclusión de la Bibliografía Nacional de El Salvador y reclasificación de la Biblioteca Gallardo: Perfil del proyecto." *SALALM Newsletter* 20(3), 87-91.

Calimano, Iván E. 1992. "La Biblioteca Gallardo y la Bibliografía Nacional." *Boletín de la Asociación de Bibliotecarios de El Salvador* 2(3/4), 71-75.

Nicaraguan National Bibliography, 1800-1978 = Bibliografía nacional nicaragüense, 1800-1978. 1986-1987. Redlands, CA: Latin American Bibliographic Foundation. Managua, Nicaragua: Biblioteca Nacional Rubén Darío. 3 vols.

23. La recuperación de información en línea por medio de la Red UNAM: El caso del Centro de Información Científica y Humanística

Saúl Armendáriz Sánchez y
Enrique Barreto Pastrana

Introducción

La recuperación de información bibliográfica en línea es un fenómeno que se inicia en los años 60 con la base de datos MEDLARS de la Biblioteca Nacional de Medicina de los Estados Unidos. Es a partir de esa década que comienza un cambio radical en el manejo, recuperación y almacenamiento de información biblio/hemerográfica a través de medios electrónicos y modernas telecomunicaciones. El valor de la información en línea es sin duda relevante, debido a que un gran número de investigadores, estudiantes, docentes, etc., pueden accesar a ella por medios modernos de comunicación en una forma casi inmediata y a un costo bajo.

El proceso en la selección y adquisición de información que puede alimentar a las bases en línea es laborioso y no es sino hasta los 70 que la metodología se mejora y surgen formatos internacionales de intercambio de información para este tipo de herramientas. En esta misma década, se intensifica la consulta de bases de datos en línea por medio de telecomunicaciones y redes de cómputo amplias y locales, que permiten enriquecer el contenido de las mismas, como el caso de OCLC (Online Computer Library Center), donde la alimentación de la base se da a través de los miembros participantes de la red. Esto es en relación a bases de los Estados Unidos, pero en el caso de América Latina se desarrollan en otro contexto, debido a que en estos países no se cuenta en esos momentos con los avances tecnológicos en materia de computación y telecomunicaciones de los países de primera línea.

Un ejemplo representativo de ello son las bases de datos del Centro de Información Científica y Humanística (CICH) de la Universidad Nacional Autónoma de México, que inicia su proyecto en el año de 1972, primeramente de consulta local y posteriormente de consulta en línea y en red por medio de la Red UNAM, que une a un gran número de investigadores, docentes y alumnos de México por medio de contactos electrónicos, principalmente por correo electrónico y redes académicas como Bitnet e Internet.

Sírvanse estas notas para enmarcar el contenido del trabajo, que desarrollaremos a continuación.

Las bases de datos a nivel internacional

Los avances tecnológicos han permitido a la humanidad, en esta década de los 90, accesar en forma inmediata a grandes volúmenes de información bibliográfica a nivel nacional e internacional. La aparición de las bases de datos en línea, primeramente, y en CD-ROM, como una segunda etapa, permiten sin lugar a duda almacenar una sorprendente cantidad de referencias de material documental para ser consultadas en forma local o a través de redes de cómputo.

Por lo que respecta a las bases de datos que pueden ser consultadas en línea a nivel internacional, tenemos un total de 4,447[1] hasta junio de 1992, pero consideramos que este número es mucho mayor debido a que no todas las bases de datos en línea de los países en vías de desarrollo son incluidas en este directorio. Por tal motivo, es obvio que casi la mayoría de bases en línea pueden ser consultadas vía telecomunicaciones en redes locales y amplias de información.

En lo relacionado a los CD-ROM (Compact Disc-Read Only Memory) a nivel internacional, tenemos un total de 2,914 títulos, de los cuales sólo el 24.91% (726 títulos) cuentan con formato para ser consultados en red.[2] El uso de redes tanto locales como amplias para la consulta de bases de datos en línea y CD-ROM es fundamental, por el hecho de que gracias a estas tecnologías la información bibliográfica viaja a una velocidad casi instantánea y llega a un buen número de usuarios cercanos o lejanos a la base de datos que estan consultando, con la posibilidad de recuperar el documento primario posteriormente.

Redes universitarias de información en México

Las redes de cómputo han representado desde sus inicios una alternativa viable para el manejo y recuperación de grandes volúmenes de información a nivel local y extramuros de cualquier institución. En el caso de México, su desarrollo se ha dado principalmente en instituciones de carácter académico y en otros organismos como bancos, casas de bolsa, etc., pero son en las redes de información universitarias donde se manejan el mayor índice de base de datos en línea de tipo bibliográfico. Cuatro ejemplos claves en el país son la Red de la Universidad Autónoma Metropolitana (RUAM), la Red del Instituto Politécnico Nacional (Red IPN), la Red Universitaria de Teleinformática y Comunicaciones (RUTIC) y la Red de Cómputo de la Universidad Nacional Autónoma de México (Red UNAM),[3] todas ellas de universidades estatales de México.

La primera de ellas, RUAM, es la desarrollada en la Universidad Autónoma Metropolitana, cuyo objetivo es unir a los tres campus (Xochimilco, Iztapalapa y Azcapotzalco) y la rectoría de este organismo. El proyecto inicia en 1988 y su topología es en forma de estrella, cuyo nodo central será el edificio de Rectoría General, enlazándose vía telefónicas las tres unidades, por medio de líneas privadas instaladas por TELMEX (Teléfonos Mexicanos). En la Unidad Iztapalapa se localiza el nodo principal de salida a Bitnet e Internet, mientras tanto en la Unidad Xochimilco se ubica el nodo de Telepac.

En esta red es importante resaltar que la consulta a bases de datos bibliográficos en línea se lleva a cabo principalmente a las bases del material documental que se encuentra procesado dentro de las unidades participantes. Esto es importante, debido a que es una forma de accesar vía telecomunicaciones a bases de datos locales creadas con recursos propios. Independientemente de la red amplia, cada unidad cuenta con su propia red local de cómputo, con la que se enlazan todos sus edificios.

La Red del Instituto Politécnico Nacional (Red IPN) es otra red universitaria mexicana que en estos momentos se encuentra en desarrollo y pretende unir a todas las unidades académicas del país pertenecientes a ese instituto, a través del canal once de televisión y sus repetidoras en el territorio nacional. Gracias a esta red, la consulta a bases de datos bibliográficas nacionales e internacionales será de gran apoyo a los académicos, alumnos e investigadores de esta importante universidad del país.

La RUTIC es el proyecto más ambicioso de este tipo, debido a que pretende ser "una red de comunicaciones vía satélite, entre las instituciones de educación superior para la transmisión de voz y datos, para complementar las redes de comunicación e información de los subsistemas universitarios y tecnológicos, bases de datos y redes de información internacionales".[4] En estos momentos se está llevando a cabo la segunda etapa del proyecto que consiste en la unión, por medio de la red, de 35 universidades del país, con una topología tipo estrella, conectándose gracias al sistema de satélites Morelos y Solidaridad.

Por lo que respecta a la Red UNAM, esta es una de las redes que cuentan con el mayor grado de avance, funcionando con altas tecnologías de información como son enlaces satélites, fibra óptica y contactos a través de la red local de cómputo, encabezándola la super computadora CRAY, que se encuentra en la Dirección General de Servicios de Cómputo Académico (DGSCA). Esta red permite accesar a la comunidad universitaria a un gran número de bases de datos de carácter bibliográfico, tanto a nivel campus universitario como de otros organismos del país.

Las bases de datos en la UNAM

Dentro de la UNAM existen un gran número de bases de datos bibliográficos que pueden ser consultados de tres formas: en CD-ROM, en sitio, y en línea.

Las bases en CD-ROM

Algunas de las bases de datos en CD-ROM producidas con información bibliográfica de la UNAM son:

(a) LIBRUNAM
(b) BIBLAT (Bibliografía Latinoamericana)
(c) IRESIE
(d) ARIES
(e) Algunas bases incluidas en el CD-ROM del proyecto Colima 1 y 2
(f) ARTEMISA
(g) SINF

De estas siete sólo las bases BIBLAT y LIBRUNAM pueden ser consultadas en red local o amplia por medio de la Red UNAM, conectándose vía fibra óptica al servicio del CICH y la Dirección General de Bibliotecas (DGB), o vía satélite o teléfono si están fuera del campus universitario.

Independientemente de las bases producidas con información bibliográfica y referencial de la UNAM, existen dentro de la Universidad un número aproximado a los 153 títulos de CD-ROM que adquiere la UNAM, y que se incrementan año con año. Muchos de ellos con excelentes posibilidades de ser trabajados en red.[5] De este total (153), solamente dos títulos son los que el CICH está explotando en red local en su Laboratorio de Aprendizaje DIALOG-CICH, las cuales son MEDLINE y ERIC.

Es gracias a esta tecnología óptica que más del 90% de las 164 bibliotecas existentes en la UNAM, ofrecen el servicio de consulta a bancos nacionales e internacionales de información, por el hecho de que la Red UNAM no ha conectado en su totalidad a los organismos inmersos dentro y fuera del campus universitario, por diversos factores técnicos. Así mismo, no todos los organismos participantes en la Red UNAM cuentan con la infraestructura que les permita salir en línea a la consulta de bases de datos.

Las bases locales

Las bases de datos de carácter bibliográfico que únicamente pueden ser consultadas en el lugar de su producción son varias, entre las que se encuentran las comprendidas en la obra *Bancos de información en ciencias sociales y humanidades: Directorio*,[6] que hasta septiembre de 1992 comprendía 27 bancos de este tipo dentro de las instituciones que conforman el campus universitario y otros organismos que mantienen estrecha relación con la UNAM.

Dentro del CICH existen diversas bases con estas características, entre las que se encuentran: HELA (Hemeroteca Latinoamericana), CIIN (Ciencia de la Información) y FRONTERA. Aparte de estas bases de datos que se encuentran dentro de la UNAM, también se presentan otras que se ubican en diversas instituciones a lo largo del territorio nacional y que solamente pueden ser consultadas en el sitio de su producción.

Tomando como elemento principal el *Directorio de bases de datos de América Latina y el Caribe*,[7] se detectó que existen en México 66 bases de datos de consulta local, independientemente de las que posee la UNAM. Ello demuestra que en el país se están llevando a cabo una proliferación de "bases de datos locales" y que se puede considerar como una línea a seguir en los últimos cinco años, con un excelente enfoque, debido a que en su totalidad el material documental de los registros recuperados en cualquier búsqueda se localizan en forma inmediata dentro del organismo productor de la base.

Otro fenómeno que ha provocado la evolución de estas bases en México, se debe principalmente a las no muy buenas telecomunicaciones que permitan unir a las bases en red o ser consultadas en línea, fenómeno que se da principalmente en algunos estados de la República Mexicana. La consulta de la información de las bases de datos en línea por medio de redes en el país, se presenta a partir de la segunda mitad de la década de los 70. Su presencia se da principalmente en las instituciones de investigación y educación superior y es en ellas mismas, como se vio anteriormente, donde se inician grandes proyectos de redes de cómputo.

Las bases en línea

La UNAM se ha distinguido a nivel latinoamericano, por la gran producción de bases de datos, tanto locales, en CD-ROM y en línea, y la ha llevado a ocupar un lugar importante dentro del país, como una de las primeras en este aspecto. Las bases en línea juegan un papel importante en el desarrollo científico, cultural, educativo y económico de la universidad y es gracias a la Red UNAM que pueden ser consultadas por casi todas las instituciones de este organismo, así como por otros usuarios físicos y morales que lo requieran.

Entre las bases de datos en línea que en un futuro inmediato pueden ser consultadas por medio de la Red UNAM, tenemos:

(a) BIVE (Banco de Información en Medicina Veterinaria y Zootecnia): Coordinado por la Facultad de Medicina Veterinaria y Zootecnia. Se conforma de 25,000 registros, tomados de revistas, tesis, monografías y literatura no convencional de los países de Hispanoamérica, Portugal y Mozambique.[8]

(b) ARIES (Acervo de Recursos de Instituciones de Educación Superior): Base que comprende información de investigaciones de más de 21 universidades estatales del país.

(c) MECS (México Ciencias Sociales): Base producida por la Facultad de Ciencias Políticas y Sociales, con aproximadamente 12,000 registros, obtenidos de diversos títulos de publicaciones periódicas.

(d) SINF (Banco de Información Hemerográfico en Ciencias Sociales): Número de registros 70,000. Base desarrollada por el Instituto de Investigaciones Bibliográficas.[9]

Por lo que respecta a las bases que en la actualidad sí pueden ser consultadas en línea, tenemos:

(a) BIBLAT (Bases del CICH): Comprende las bases de datos CLASE (Citas Latinoamericanas en Ciencias Sociales y Economía) con 84,111 registros; ASFA-México (Aquatic Science Fisher Abstracts) con 38,250 registros; PERIODICA (Indice de Revistas Latinoamericanas en Ciencias) con 82,146 registros; BIBLAT (Bibliografía Latinoamericana) con 63,313 registros; y MEXINV (Investigación Científica y Humanística Mexicana) con 59,221 registros.

(b) Las de la Dirección General de Bibliotecas (DGB), que son: LIBRUNAM: con aproximadamente 400,000 registros de libros de las 164 bibliotecas de la UNAM; SERIUNAM: con el registro de 15,153 títulos y 379,418 acervos de publicaciones periódicas; TESIUNAM: información de las tesis de grado de las diferentes dependencias de la UNAM, con un total de 182,036 registros.[10]

Es sin duda que estas bases son la puerta que permitirá, en un futuro inmediato, a un buen número de ellas poner al servicio de la comunidad universitaria su información, para ser consultadas por medios electrónicos y modernas telecomunicaciones.

Estas últimas bases de consulta en línea pueden ser accesadas por Telepac, Red UNAM, Internet y Bitnet, dependiendo el lugar de donde se esté accesando y las características de equipo con que se cuenta. Como se ve, son más el número de bases de tipo local que las que se existen en línea, debido a que muchas de estas bases locales cuentan con un número menor a los tres mil registros.

Para accesar a las bases antes mencionadas se requiere de equipo como:

(a) Línea telefónica
(b) Modem
(c) Conexión a Telepac
(d) Equipo de cómputo
(e) Clave de acceso
(f) Conexión Red UNAM, entre otros.

El acceso a las bases en línea del CICH

La UNAM cuenta con una infraestructura de telecomunicaciones denominada por Red UNAM. Esta red está creciendo continuamente, pero a finales del año pasado se tenían las siguientes características en su infraestructura: 600 km. de fibra óptica, 65 redes locales conectadas a la red, 64 centros locales enlazados vía fibra óptica, red tipo Ethernet, enlace satelital, red de microondas privada para conectar los diversos campus de la UNAM y conexión a Internet y a la Red Mexicana de Telecomunicaciones (Telepac) que usa X.25.

Por otro lado cabe hacer mención que faltan unos 100 centros de conectarse a la Red UNAM. Internet permite contar con servicios de correo electrónico, enlaces a otros hosts vía Telnet y transferencia de archivos vía FTP.

El CICH es uno de los centros conectados a la Red UNAM vía fibra óptica. Cuenta con un nodo directo y dos nodos indirectos de acceso Internet. El nodo directo Internet es un equipo Digital MicroVAX 3400 con sistema operativo ULTRIX que permite desarrollar todas las capacidades de TCP/IP como son correo electrónico, Telnet y FTP.

Respecto a los otros dos nodos, se tratan de dos mini computadoras Hewlett Packard 3000 con sistema operativo MPE V. Una de estas dos máquinas es una micro HP 3000 que es el host de las bases de datos de las suscripciones a publicaciones periódicas de la UNAM. La segunda máquina es una HP 3000-48 que es el host de las bases de datos producidas por el CICH: CLASE, PERIODICA y BIBLAT.

Las dos máquinas HP han estado conectadas desde 1986 a la Red Mexicana de Telecomunicaciones que usa el protocolo X.25 también soportado por la Red UNAM, aunque no a través de fibra óptica, con una confiabilidad no muy buena.

Las dos máquinas HP se conectan a Internet por medio del nodo MicroVAX a través de una interfase física que las conecta a la fibra óptica. El enlace lógico de estas dos máquinas a la MicroVAX se hace gracias al software llamado Win/TCP, instalado en las HP, que permite la transferencia entre X.25 y TCP.

Los usuarios externos con acceso a Internet primero entran con un Telnet usando la dirección IP de la MicroVAX cuyo nombre es selene.cichcu.unam.mx y cuya dirección es 132.248.9.1. Deben proporcionar un usuario y un password autorizado. Una vez en selene, el usuario a través de otro Telnet entra a la micro HP 3000 y de ahí pasa con otro comando a la HP 3000-48 donde debe proporcionar otro nombre de usuario y su password. En esta última máquina se localizan las bases de datos del CICH. Los usuarios interesados en tener claves para accesar las bases de datos del CICH pueden mandar un correo electrónico a la clave: enrique@ selene.cichcu.unam.mx.

Las bases de datos en línea del CICH usan el software llamado MINISIS, que es la versión de ISIS para mini computadoras producido por el International Development Research Centre (IDRC) de Canadá. En MINISIS se tiene dos maneras para que los usuarios externos consulten las bases de datos del Centro. La primera está pensada para las personas que conocen los comandos del procesador de búsqueda de MINISIS. Estos comandos se digitan en español aunque también se puede habilitar usuarios con comandos en inglés y aún en Francés.

Aparte de conocer el manejo de los comandos de búsqueda, los usuarios que usan este método deben proporcionar el nombre de la base de datos que van a utilizar y que puede ser CLASE, PERIODICA, ASFA, o BIBLAT. Cabe mencionar que existen ayudas en línea para el uso de estos comandos pero están pensadas para apoyar a usuarios con conocimientos del procesador de búsqueda. Cuando un usuario está habilitado para usar este método, inmediatamente entra al procesador de búsqueda y no puede usar otros procesadores de MINISIS.

En el segundo caso, se habilitan usuarios que usen una interfase llamada MENUDIS que a través de menús permite que dichos usuarios lleven a cabo consultas a las bases de datos. Esto facilita la labor del usuario porque no debe conocer comandos especiales como en el primer caso aunque el proceso de búsqueda es más lento.

Dado lo anterior, se recomienda a los usuarios externas que usan MENUDIS que se conecten al host cuando no hay mucho tráfico en las telecomunicaciones, como puede ser temprano (entre las 7:00 y las 10:00 horas) o tarde (después de las 17:00 horas) de cualquier día laboral. En este sentido, cabe señalar que se está considerando la posibilidad de cambiar las bases de datos a otro host que sea más veloz en su respuesta para que los accesos tanto internos como externos y todos los procesos de mantenimiento a estas bases de datos sean más eficientes.

Generalmente los fines de semana las HP 3000 permanecen apagadas, pero esta política se espera que cambie de tal manera que permanezcan encendidas las 24 horas. El CICH ha recibido diversas sugerencias en relación a que ponga el acceso a las bases de datos bibliográficas sin restricciones, es decir, de manera anónima como es el caso en algunas universidades en los Estados Unidos. Estas sugerencias se están ponderando y tal vez en un futuro cercano se brinde este servicio. Para los usuarios de otros países esto sería una gran ventaja, debido a que Internet usa uno de los satélites mexicanos de comunicaciones.

El acceso a través de Internet a las bases de datos del CICH es relativamente nuevo, debido a que se inició en mayo de 1992. La mayoría de los usuarios que usan este medio se encuentran en la Ciudad de México. Los usuarios de dependencias de la UNAM usan directamente la Red UNAM y los que no pertenecen a la UNAM generalmente accesan al host del CICH por medio de modems que se enlazan a un servidor de comunicaciones ubicado en la Dirección General de Servicios de Cómputo Académico (DGSCA), que es la dependencia universitaria que administra la Red UNAM. También accesan usuarios que cuentan con nodos Internet en sus instalaciones, como es el caso de la Universidad de Guadalajara y la Universidad Iberoamericana. Fuera de México, se han otorgado claves a usuarios de la Louisiana State University y la University of Wisconsin en los Estados Unidos y al IDRC en Canadá.

Para saber quienes accesan a las bases de datos se llevan a cabo estadísticas por cada usuario que permiten producir reportes mensuales de estos accesos por usuario por base de datos. Por el momento el cobro por estos accesos no tiene costo alguno, pero se han iniciado pláticas al respecto en el CICH para determinar en un futuro si es o no necesario modificar esta política.

NOTAS

1. *Directory of Online Databases*, K. Young Marcaccio, ed. (Detroit, MI: Gale Research, 1992), vol. 13, no. 1.

2. *CD-ROM Directory on Disc*, 8a ed. (London: TFPL, 1992).

3. Saúl Armendáriz Sánchez et al., "Redes universitarias de información en México", ponencia presentada en el V Coloquio sobre Automatización de Bibliotecas, Colima, Colima, 1991.

4. "Red Universitaria de Comunicaciones Vía Satélite: Memoria técnica primera etapa", Documento interno, 1991, p. 3.

5. Saúl Armendáriz Sánchez, "La prospectiva en la adquisición de CD-ROM en la UNAM: Un estudio a cinco años", ponencia presentada en el Primer Congreso Norte-Sur de Información ONLINE '93 (México, D.F., 1993).

6. *Bancos de información en ciencias sociales y humanidades: Directorio* (México, D.F.: UNAM, 1992), pp. 1-36.

7. *Directorio de bases de datos de América Latina y el Caribe* (DIBALC), coord. E. Barberena (México, D.F.: UNAM, Facultad de Filosofía y Letras, 1992), pp. 97-118.

8. A. M. Román de Carlos, J. Maldonado M. y M. Martínez Z., "El banco de información BIVE y su impacto en la investigación en medicina veterinaria", ponencia presentada en el Primer Congreso Norte-Sur de Información ONLINE '93 (México, D.F., 1993), p. 1.

9. *Bancos de información en ciencias sociales*, pp. 22, 25; DIBALC, pp. 97, 100, 116.

10. DIBALC, pp. 113, 115, 118.

OBRAS CONSULTADAS

Armendáriz Sánchez, Saúl. "La prospectiva en la adquisición de CD-ROM en la UNAM: Un estudio a cinco años". Ponencia presentada en el Primer Congreso Norte-Sur de Información ONLINE '93. México, D.F., 1993.

Armendáriz Sánchez, Saúl, et al. "Redes universitarias de información en México". Ponencia presentada en el V Coloquio sobre Automatización de Bibliotecas, Colima, Colima, 1991.

Bancos de información en ciencias sociales y humanidades: Directorio. México, D.F.: UNAM, 1992.

Castillo, A., S. H. Hernández R. y R. Rojas G. "Redes computacionales para la comunidad académica". *Ciencia y Desarrollo* 16:9 (1990), 107-118.

CD-ROM Directory on Disc. 8a ed. London: TFPL, 1992.

Directorio de bases de datos de América Latina y el Caribe: DIBALC. Coord. E. Barberena. México, D.F.: UNAM, Facultad de Filosofía y Letras, 1992.

Directory of Online Databases. K. Young Marcaccio, ed. Vol. 13, no. 1. Detroit, MI: Gale Research, 1992.

Kuhlmann R., R., y A. Buzo. "Redes de comunicación: Estado actual y perspectivas". En *Congreso Nacional Bases de Datos y Redes de Comunicación: Memoria.* México, D.F.: UNAM, 1987.

"Red Universitaria de Comunicaciones Vía Satélite: Memoria técnica primera etapa". (Documento interno.) 1991.

Román de Carlos, A. M., J. Maldonado M. y M. Martínez Z. "El banco de información BIVE y su impacto en la investigación en medicina veterinaria". Ponencia presentada en el Primer Congreso Norte-Sur de Información ONLINE '93. México, D.F., 1993.

Situación actual y perspectivas de las telecomunicaciones en México. México, D.F.: PNUD-UIT, 1991.

24. Red nacional de colaboración en información y documentación en salud

Gladys Faba Beaumont

El Centro Nacional de Información y Documentación en Salud (CENIDS) perteneciente a la Secretaría de Salud, propuso el desarrollo de un proyecto de Red Nacional de Información y Documentación en Salud en México, con el interés de fortalecer el desarrollo de los servicios de información que se prestan actualmente en el país.

La RENCIS tiene dos años de trabajo activo a partir de la fecha de establecimiento de la misma. Originalmente comenzó a funcionar con sólo seis nodos (CENIDS, UNAM-CICH, Facultad de Medicina de la Universidad de Nuevo León, Universidad de Tabasco, IMSS y Universidad de Colima) durante el primer año de vida y en el segundo se han incorporado dos nodos más, los de la Universidad de San Luis Potosí y la Universidad de Baja, California.

Durante el mes de junio de 1992 abrió sus servicios a los usuarios de la RENCIS de manera formal proporcionando principalmente el servicio de obtención del documento fuente.

Antecedentes

El crecimiento exponencial de la información científica generada en el área de la salud, y los sorprendentes avances ocurridos en la aplicación de la informática y telemática en los sistemas de información, transforman a ésta en un insumo cada vez más accesible y necesario para el desempeño de las tareas profesionales, técnicas y administrativas. Actualmente, un profesional o trabajador de la salud que no está bien informado, difícilmente puede desempeñarse dentro de un nivel de competencia y calidad.

En México el desarrollo explosivo de los sistemas de información se ha introducido con características especiales y podríamos decir, con ciertas dificultades tales como:

(a) Existe una distribución desigual de los recursos en las instituciones y en las diferentes regiones del país. Los servicios de información están prácticamente concentrados en el Distrito Federal (alrededor del 90%), quedando la gran mayoría de los estados con dificultades para el acceso a fuentes de información científica actualizada.

(b) Las instituciones que cuentan con fuentes de información automatizadas no siempre disponen de los documentos originales. En otras palabras, ofrecen al usuario un servicio incompleto ya que la parte importante de las fuentes de información, es el artículo original, el cual no está disponible en las bibliotecas cercanas.

(c) En el área de la salud, México cuenta con alrededor de 300 bibliotecas, de las cuales cerca del 15% de ellas cuenta con acervos relativamente completos y adecuados a las necesidades de la comunidad científica.

(d) Existe escasez de personal capacitado que pueda operar eficientemente los recursos disponibles, para establecer programas de intercambio, préstamos o adquisición de acervos de otras bibliotecas, para proporcionar servicios de búsqueda bibliográfica.

(e) En los centros de información y documentación en salud se han visto restricciones en sus programas de diseminación de información y distribución de servicios de información. La utilización de las fuentes de información, se originan por iniciativa o necesidad del usuario, más que por una estrategia de oferta de servicios, por parte de los centros de documentación. En este enlace entre los cursos bibliográficos y el usuario comúnmente no se sabe localizar las fuentes de información.

Estas condiciones han fundamentado la necesidad de utilizar las bondades de los avances tecnológicos y establecer una infraestructura tecnológica que abra la posibilidad de compartir los recursos y los servicios de información disponibles en los centros de información y los acervos bibliográficos. En la medida en que se facilite el acceso a las fuentes secundarias y primarias de información será posible ofrecer a los profesionales y trabajadores de la salud la oportunidad de mantenerlos actualizados sobre los avances y hallazgos de la ciencia y de la tecnología. Esto indudablemente revertirá en un mejoramiento de la calidad de la atención médica y del buen desarrollo de los programas nacionales de salud.

Debido al acelerado desarrollo de los sistemas automatizados de información, es posible establecer sistemas interactivos de intercambio de información bibliográfica y contar con una gran diversidad de fuentes en información por costos cada vez más accesibles y en un mínimo de tiempo.

El Centro Nacional de Información y Documentación en Salud, al estar integrado en la estructura de la Secretaría de Salud (SSA), presenta una ventaja estratégica, para convocar al establecimiento de una Red Nacional de Información y Documentación en Salud y hacer realidad la coordinación de servicios de información en el campo de la salud. Más de 60% de la investigación en salud se realiza en instituciones del Sistema Nacional de

Salud; alrededor de 3,000 residentes al año participan en los programas de posgrados en hospitales de la Secretaría de Salud; alrededor de 2,500 internos de pregrado anualmente se distribuyen en diversos hospitales. Se incorporan y realizan sus trámites cada inicio de año en la Secretaría de Salud para desarrollar su servicio social en los programas de atención médica de control y fomento, así como en el de vigilancia sanitaria.

De acuerdo al informe preliminar elaborado por CENIDS sobre el proyecto "Esfuerzos de Investigación en Universidades Públicas y Privadas en México", en el área de Ciencias Biológicas y de la Salud tenemos la siguiente distribución de universidades con programas en esta área: 47.6% se localizan en instituciones públicas y el 52.3% en privadas de un total de 86 instituciones que incluyen facultades y universidades ubicadas en diferentes lugares del país quienes generan un universo potencial de usuarios que requerirán más y mejores servicios de información.

Estos grupos junto con la comunidad de médicos, profesores e investigadores representan un campo de atención especial, en el cual deben desarrollarse programas de promoción y difusión del uso de la información disponible en las fuentes existentes en el país.

Los administradores de las instituciones de la salud representan también un universo potencial de atención por parte de los servicios de la Red.

Los servicios que proporciona la RENCIS cubren el universo potencial de acuerdo a las instituciones que conforman los nodos de la siguiente forma: IMSS, 5 hospitales de especialidad; CENIDS, 46 hospitales generales; Tijuana, 50 hospitales, lo que da un total de 120 hospitales ubicados en los diferentes estados en los que se encuentran los nodos, según datos proporcionados por cada nodo.

El funcionamiento de la Red permite establecer estrategias de difusión y distribución de información, y con ellas, poner al alcance de los profesionales, estudiantes y trabajadores de la salud, las diversas fuentes de información nacionales, latinoamericanas o internacionales, al menor costo y en el menor tiempo. El trabajo sistemático de difusión y promoción de la información científica y técnica favorecerá un mayor acercamiento entre el usuario y los recursos de información.

Objetivos de la Red

1. Constituir la Red como instrumento de apoyo básico para ofrecer información tanto a la comunidad científica como a los profesionales incorporados en los servicios de atención a la salud con el propósito de ayudar en su buen desempeño profesional y en elevar la calidad de atención médica.
2. Ofrecer el documento fuente en el menor tiempo posible.

3. Facilitar el acceso a la información científico y técnica en salud a instituciones de las distintas entidades federativas del país.
4. Difundir información científica relevante y relacionada con los problemas prioritarios de salud.
5. Apoyar la capacitación técnica de los profesionales y técnicos que ofrecen servicios de información, así como apoyar los cursos de información docente y la atención en las comisiones de la salud.

Concepción de la Red

La RENCIS surge como un proyecto viable y real, posible de aplicarse a la estructura de los recursos de información existentes a nivel nacional. Anteriormente se habían realizado algunos intentos para integrar redes de información las cuales fueron fracasando por falta de operacionalidad.

Se habían realizado ya varios intentos de red, sin poder concretarse alguna. Es en este ámbito en el cual surge la RENCIS, como un proyecto viable y objetivo en México del cual hemos visto concretizadas varias de las metas fijadas como: la elaboración de un Catálogo Colectivo de Publicaciones Periódicas, la creación de una Base de Datos en Texto Completo de Revistas Mexicanas, funcionamiento del correo electrónico, disminución de los tiempos de recuperación de los documentos, entre otros.

Organización de la Red

Para el cumplimiento de los objetivos planteados, la RENCIS se encuentra organizada a través de un Consejo Ejecutivo y tres Comités de Trabajo: Comité Técnico, Comité de Servicios y Comité de Desarrollo Tecnológico.

El Comité Ejecutivo coordina las actividades realizadas en los Comités de Trabajo. Algunas de las funciones que llevan a cabo son: apoyar técnicamente al Consejo Ejecutivo para la toma de decisiones en cuanto a infraestructura computacional se refiere, instalación de equipos de cómputo en cada una de las estaciones de trabajo de los nodos, definir los servicios a otorgar por los diferentes nodos de la red, definir horarios de servicios entre los nodos así como la tarifa a aplicarse por la prestación de servicios entre los nodos, diseñar e implementar nuevas metodologías y normalización de registros para transferencia y generación de productos RENCIS, entre otros.

Características de los nodos que integran la Red

Con el objetivo de crear una red dinámica e integral se consideraron los siguientes criterios de incorporación:

(a) Ubicación geográfica

Los nodos que integran la Red están distribuidos estratégicamente de tal manera que facilitan la diseminación de los servicios de información al mayor número de estados en el país. Para ello se consideró la incorporación de nodos que aseguren la oferta de servicios de información en las zonas norte, centro, sur y este del país.

(b) Infraestructura tecnológica
Se seleccionaron los nodos que cuentan con equipos de cómputo y medios de comunicación que agilicen el intercambio y abaraten costos del intercambio de recursos y servicios bibliográficos.

(c) Tradición de servicio de información
Se consideró importante que los nodos integrantes de la RENCIS tuvieran experiencia y tradición en el desarrollo de los servicios de información.

(d) Disponibilidad de acervos bibliográficos
La continuidad y permanencia de la adquisición de acervos bibliográficos por parte de los centros de documentación y bibliotecas que formarán parte de la Red, es de gran importancia ya que refleja la solidez y disposición de desarrollo de las instituciones que los sostienen. Esto asegura que los nodos estarán en condiciones de ofrecer un servicio permanente.

Acervo documental

De los datos preliminares obtenidos de la primera edición del CD-ROM ARTEMISA, la RENCIS a través de sus nodos tiene disponibles más de 11,000 colecciones distribuidas en 103 bibliotecas en diferentes entidades federativas, además de contar con bases de datos en CD-ROM como MEDLARS, LILACS, ONCODISC, DIALOG, ERIC, y en línea DIALOG, MEDLINE.

Estrategias

Conocer la demanda de información

Elaborar estudios de mercado

Establecer convenios de cooperación entre los hospitales y nodos

Utilizar la comunicación por correo electrónico

Fortalecer la red, proporcionando apoyo que permita conocer las necesidades que se van generando con el propósito de apoyar con nuevos servicios

Desarrollar un programa de suscripciones que permita dar mayor diversidad en cuanto a la adquisición de nuevos títulos de revistas, proporcionando los criterios para realizar un mejor aprovechamiento de los recursos presupuestales

Crecer gradualmente propiciando el desarrollo de una infraestructura que permita tener una cobertura en todos los estados del país los cuales deberán contar con un nodo de la RENCIS en un período de nueve años.

Cobertura a nivel nacional de servicios

En el entendido de que los servicios de información que ofrece la Red deberán alcanzar a la mayor parte de los profesionales y trabajadores de la salud, en particular a aquellos que se desempeñan en hospitales y centros de salud, los nodos de la RENCIS iniciaron un inventario de instituciones de atención a la salud y educativas a las cuales la Red ofrecerá sus servicios y apoyará a sus profesionales para contribuir en un proceso de atención médica con mayores rangos de actualización y calidad.

Los principales resultados de este estudio señalan que los nodos de la Red estarán en posibilidad de cubrir alrededor de 20 instituciones con servicios de información en los diferentes estados del país, sobresaliendo cerca de 120 hospitales generales ubicados en los cinco estados del país y en el Distrito Federal que serán las instituciones a las que los diferentes nodos de la Red, otorgarán servicios de información a través de un programa de diseminación selectiva de información, lo que a su vez permitirá actualizar a cerca de 1,000 médicos residentes y potencialmente alrededor de 2,000 médicos adscritos a estas instituciones.

Un elemento importante en este proyecto es la coordinación con las instituciones hospitalarias, con las que se está preparando el desarrollo de un programa de orientación a usuarios, el cual tendrá como objetivo central facilitar el acceso al manejo de información científica y tecnológica en salud dirigido a quienes atienden los procesos de atención a la salud, el desarrollo de la investigación científica, la administración de recursos y la formación de recursos humanos.

Servicios que proporciona

Recuperación de documentos

Por medio de la interacción en Red y el préstamo interbibliotecario se recupera el documento fuente, facilitando y agilizando la transferencia de información de un nodo a otro ayudando a que esta llegue al usuario en el más corto tiempo y al más bajo costo posible.

El número de artículos solicitados a través de la RENCIS durante el semestre comprendido entre los meses de julio y septiembre de 1992 fue de 3,113 documentos.

Acceso a bases de datos nacionales e internacionales

Utilizando las bases de datos en CD-ROM y en línea se atienden las solicitudes de los usuarios que requieren la elaboración de alguna estrategia, accesando a bases de datos como POPLINE, CANCERLINE, MEDLINE, LILACS, ADONIS, entre otros.

Durante este período, los nodos de la Red realizaron un total de 1,957 investigaciones bibliográficas, en línea y en disco compacto.

Diseminación selectiva de información

En este sentido se elaboran boletines de diseminación selectiva de información con el objetivo de generar una mayor demanda de información y con ello ofrecer las alternativas de conocimientos a los usuarios del área de la salud.

Se está trabajando con la evaluación de diversos softwares, con el propósito de poner a funcionar boletines por correo electrónico, etc.

Capacitación técnica en el manejo de servicios de información automatizada

Este es un programa de capacitación al personal de los nodos en el manejo de sistemas automatizados, en procesos técnicos, acceso a redes amplias, manejo de correos electrónicos, técnicas de indizado de literatura científica, entre otros.

Los cursos impartidos durante el año pasado por la RENCIS fueron sobre los siguientes temas: La Recuperación de Documentos, El Uso de las Bases de Datos, El Registro de las Publicaciones Periódicas, entre otros.

Orientación a usuarios

La orientación de usuarios constituye un área de atención importante de esta Red porque frente a la densidad de información se requiere una selección y localización de la información oportuna y necesaria para el buen desempeño profesional. En este sentido se están elaborando varios proyectos para brindar mayor apoyo a la formación de usuarios de información.

Funcionamiento de la Red en la prestación de servicios

Al principio el correo electrónico comenzó a operar con ciertas dificultades, ya que por una parte existía desconocimiento de como funcionaba y temor al usar nuevas tecnologías. En la primera etapa los mensajes que se enviaron eran prácticamente de carácter informal, y en poco tiempo se adoptó como un medio de comunicación ágil y oportuno. Actualmente se envían un promedio de 100 mensajes al mes, la mayoría de ellos se refiere a la solicitud de información.

Avances de la Red

1. Un programa de suscripciones que permita ampliar la disponibilidad de revistas científicas para asegurar la localización de artículos originales dentro del país.
2. Un sistema de localización ágil de artículos en bibliotecas localizadas en las ciudades fronterizas con Tijuana y con Nuevo León, lo cual disminuirá costos y reducirá tiempos de localización y entrega de los documentos al usuario.
3. Edición de un disco compacto con literatura científica mexicana en salud en texto completo y con el catálogo colectivo de publicaciones periódicas en biomedicina y salud.
4. Operación de la base de datos con información sobre problemas prioritarios en salud.
5. Establecimiento de un sistema ágil de interacción entre los nodos con hospitales y unidades de primer nivel de atención.

Algunas debilidades de la Red

Uno de los principales problemas es la carencia de recursos humanos en el área informática y esta situación ha creado dificultades para operar en el área de la teleinformática. Se ha tenido que trabajar arduamente y con mucho empeño con el personal especialista en sistemas para transformar el lenguaje informático en lenguaje de servicios.

25. La automatización de las bibliotecas de la UNAM: Su influencia en las bibliotecas mexicanas y en la conducta del usuario

Adolfo Rodríguez Gallardo y
Felipe Martínez Arellano

Este trabajo pretende cubrir dos aspectos: En primer lugar ofrecer un panorama sobre la automatización del Sistema Bibliotecario de la UNAM, el cual está integrado por 164 bibliotecas, así como señalar la influencia que este hecho ha tenido en otras bibliotecas mexicanas, a través de la utilización en diversas actividades bibliotecarias de tres grandes bancos de datos creados por la UNAM: LIBRUNAM, SERIUNAM y TESIUNAM, los cuales registran las colecciones de libros, series y tesis respectivamente. Por otro lado, describir cómo estos bancos de datos, junto con los catálogos en línea de acceso público, han influido en los servicios que presta la Biblioteca Central de la UNAM, así como el cambio que ha generado en la conducta de los usuarios, mencionando algunas acciones que serán necesarias para enfrentar dicho cambio.

A lo largo de la historia, los avances tecnológicos han sido bien recibidos y empleados por las bibliotecas: hace casi un siglo, los bibliotecarios fueron de los primeros en adoptar la luz incandecente; otro medio siglo después, empezaron a utilizar el aire acondicionado en los edificios para bibliotecas; y cuando la fotocopiadora empezó a utilizarse en otros lugares, además de la oficinas, las bibliotecas fueron uno de estos primeros sitios.[1]

Por otro lado, nuestra época se caracteriza por el empleo de una tecnología, donde predomina la utilización de las computadoras y nuevos sistemas de comunicación, lo cual ha venido a cambiar de una manera substancial las actividades que se llevan a cabo en nuestras bibliotecas, pues muchas de ellas han incorporado estos avances tecnológicos en la realización de sus actividades.

En muchas de las bibliotecas mexicanas, al igual que en las de otros países, el uso de las computadoras para la realización de las actividades diarias ha sido incorporado de una manera gradual y sistemática, cambiando la forma en que estas actividades son organizadas y modificando los servicios que se prestan a nuestros usuarios.

Durante el decenio 1970-1980 empezaron a tener lugar dentro de las bibliotecas mexicanas varios proyectos de automatización, dentro de los cuales destaca el emprendido por la Dirección General de Bibliotecas de la Universidad Nacional Autónoma de México (UNAM), la cual coordina el sistema bibliotecario de esta institución, formado por 164 bibliotecas para el apoyo de la docencia e investigación.

A partir de la implementación de este proyecto, las bibliotecas de la UNAM empezaron a utilizar sistemas automatizados para la producción y mantenimiento de catálogos, así como en las actividades de adquisiciones, continuando con circulación, servicios de referencia, control de publicaciones seriadas y actualmente catálogos en línea de acceso público.

Es importante señalar que la Dirección General de Bibliotecas a través de su Departamento de Adquisiciones Bibliográficas tiene centralizado el ejercicio de la partida presupuestal destinada a la compra de libros. De esta forma que se tiene automatizado el control de 193 códigos programáticos, mismos que corresponden a 149 bibliotecas presupuestadas, permitiendo tener al día el registro contable en forma global y de cada biblioteca; generar estados de cuenta mensual; elaborar formatos para trámite de pago a proveedores, entre otros, así como poder consultar los estados de cuenta para saber las cantidades ejercidas y disponibles.

Asimismo, como producto de este proyecto de automatización, la UNAM ha creado tres grandes bases de datos: LIBRUNAM, SERIUNAM y TESIUNAM, las cuales contienen los acervos de los libros, publicaciones periódicas, y tesis existentes en esta institución y que además han tenido un gran impacto en la forma en que se realizan las actividades y en los servicios ofrecidos, tanto en las bibliotecas de la UNAM, como en las pertenecientes a otras instituciones.

El banco de datos LIBRUNAM

Una de las actividades que mayor cantidad de tiempo y recursos consume es el proceso técnico de libros, por lo que LIBRUNAM surgió como una herramienta para poder efectuar de una forma rápida las actividades de catalogación y clasificación de los materiales pertenecientes a este sistema de bibliotecas, las cuales se llevan de una manera centralizada y de esta forma poder generar los juegos de tarjetas necesarios para la conformación de los catálogos en cada una de las diversas bibliotecas. LIBRUNAM contiene la información correspondiente a la ubicación de todos y cada uno de los libros existentes en las 164 bibliotecas del sistema bibliotecario de la UNAM, por lo que también podemos afirmar que su función es ser un catálogo colectivo de los acervos de las bibliotecas de esta institución.

Actualmente el banco de datos LIBRUNAM está conformado por cerca de 500,000 registros de títulos de libros que corresponden a 3,500,000 volúmenes y la información puede ser recuperada por: autor, título, tema, ISBN, editorial, clasificación, o bien por una búsqueda libre, es decir, es factible buscar un término en todas y cada una de las áreas de la ficha catalográfica. Asimismo, es posible efectuar combinaciones de los puntos de acceso anteriores: autor/título, autor/tema, autor/editorial, etc. Además se pueden hacer búsquedas por cualquier combinación de puntos de acceso, o realizar búsquedas libres que permiten localizar la información por una palabra sin importar su ubicación. También se pueden hacer búsquedas en los que se cometan errores ortográficos y la máquina los corrige.

La Dirección General de Bibliotecas con el propósito de agilizar las actividades de procesos técnicos utiliza diferentes fuentes de información automatizada como son Bibliofile, CDMARC-Bibliographic, entre otras.

En el caso de Bibliofile, es una de las primeras fuentes de información utilizada para realizar la búsqueda y recuperación en forma impresa de los registros ya catalogados por la Biblioteca del Congreso.

En lo que se refiere a CDMARC-Bibliographic, podemos decir que se realiza la transferencia de la información, ya que después de realizar la búsqueda, ésta es salvada y bajada a un disco flexible. Después con un programa diseñado por el Departamento de Informática de la Dirección General de Bibliotecas, son modificadas las etiquetas MARC-LC a MARC-DGB y posteriormente los registros son dados de alta en LIBRUNAM. Lo anterior permite optimizar tiempos y recursos en el proceso técnico, principalmente en la codificación y captura de la información.

Con la finalidad de verificar los términos que se emplean como encabezamientos de materia en los registros, actualmente se está llevando a cabo un proyecto que tiene como finalidad la construcción de un catálogo de autoridad. Como producto de este proyecto se tiene construido y en operación una base da datos conteniendo aproximadamente 30,000 registros de autoridad con sus correspondientes referencias de *Véase* y *Véase también* y el equivalente de los términos en inglés.

Se han generado tres versiones de LIBRUNAM en disco compacto, la primera de ellas en el mes de noviembre de 1988, la segunda en agosto de 1989 y la tercera en el mes de octubre de 1992.

Aunque LIBRUNAM tuvo su origen como una herramienta para apoyar los procesos técnicos, dadas sus características y la información que contiene, está siendo también empleado como una fuente de referencia que permite a los usuarios de las diversas bibliotecas de la UNAM y de otras instituciones, conocer en que lugar se encuentran los materiales que son de utilidad a determinado usuario y de esa forma puede acudir a la biblioteca correspondiente para consultarlos, o bien hacer uso del servicio de préstamo interbibliotecario.

El banco de datos SERIUNAM

SERIUNAM surge como un banco de datos, cuya finalidad principal era registrar y dar a conocer a la comunidad de la Universidad Nacional Autónoma de México, la ubicación de los títulos y acervos de las publicaciones periódicas adquiridas por compra, canje y donación en las diversas bibliotecas de su sistema bibliotecario. Sin embargo, a partir de 1992 se convierte en un banco de datos que cuenta con información de otras bibliotecas pertenecientes a universidades e instituciones de educación superior del país, centros de investigación, así como organismos gubernamentales y paraestatales, entre otros. Acualmente contiene información de aproximadamente 33,506 títulos existentes en 163 bibliotecas pertenecientes a la UNAM y en otras 62 bibliotecas de 18 instituciones de diversos puntos del país.

El incluir acervos de otras instituciones marcó un cambio substancial en el contenido y utilidad de SERIUNAM. De un banco de datos que contenía los títulos de las publicaciones seriadas localizadas en las bibliotecas de la UNAM, se convirtió en un banco de datos que incluye los acervos de las publicaciones periódicas de diversas bibliotecas mexicanas. Por otro lado, las características del programa de recuperación de información permiten básicamente tres opciones:

1. Conocer las bibliotecas donde se encuentra determinada revista.
2. Conocer qué números o fascículos de una revista o publicación seriada tiene una biblioteca en particular, o bien todas aquellas donde se encuentra.
3. Conocer qué biblioteca tiene determinado número de una revista que al usuario le interesa en particular.

Es importante señalar que en la actualidad el banco de datos SERIUNAM puede ser consultado en línea o en disco compacto y que el número de bibliotecas participantes crece continuamente.

El banco de datos TESIUNAM

Dentro del sistema bibliotecario de la UNAM, la Biblioteca Central es una de las más grandes debido a la magnitud y naturaleza de sus colecciones, dentro de las cuales se encuentran las tesis presentadas por los egresados de esta institución. Uno de los requisitos indispensables para que los alumnos de la UNAM puedan efectuar los trámites necesarios para su titulación es entregar una copia de su tesis en la Biblioteca Central, lo que ha permitido tener la información necesaria para la creación y actualización del banco de datos TESIUNAM.

Como se ha mencionado anteriormente, TESIUNAM proporciona información acerca de las tesis presentadas por los egresados de la UNAM, pero también se incluyen algunas presentadas en diversas universidades de los estados. La mayoría están o estuvieron incorporadas a la UNAM, pero hay unas pocas que simplemente enviaron su información con el objeto de enriquecer el banco.

La información en este banco de datos puede ser recuperada por el autor, el título o el asesor, entre otras opciones. Una vez que el usuario recupera la información sobre las tesis que le son de utilidad, puede consultarlas en el Departamento de Tesis de la Biblioteca Central o bien en la biblioteca de la escuela o facultad donde fueron presentadas.

Formas de acceso a los bancos

Con la finalidad de que las diversas bibliotecas de este sistema puedan consultar los tres bancos de datos mencionados anteriormente, la Dirección General de Bibliotecas ha dotado a cada una de ellas de una microcomputadora XT provista de un modem de respuesta automática, con lo cual pueden efectuar búsquedas y recuperación en línea desde sus respectivas instalaciones. La conexión es efectuada a través de vía telefónica, existiendo diez canales disponibles para que las bibliotecas puedan accesar a estos bancos de datos.

Adicionalmente del equipo mencionado anteriormente, también se ha dotado a las bibliotecas de un lector de discos compactos, ya que estos bancos de datos también han sido producidos empleando esta tecnología. En este sentido podemos decir que TESIUNAM ha sido producido en disco compacto el pasado mes de marzo y SERIUNAM será producido a finales de mayo.

Otra de las posibilidades de acceso a estos bancos de datos es a través de la red de telecomunicaciones Telepac o por medio de Internet, lo cual hace posible que cualquier biblioteca localizada en algún punto de México o del mundo pueda tener acceso a esta información.

Impacto en las actividades y servicios bibliotecarios

La utilización de sistemas automatizados afecta invariablemente la forma en la cual son organizadas o llevadas a cabo las actividades de la biblioteca. En el caso del sistema bibliotecario de la UNAM, el proyecto de automatización ha tenido un impacto básicamente en tres tipos de actividades: préstamo, procesos técnicos y servicios de referencia.

El tener registrados en el banco de datos LIBRUNAM los materiales existentes en todas y cada una de las bibliotecas del sistema, ha permitido la creación de archivos individuales para cada una de ellas que han sido la base para la implementación de un sistema de préstamo automatizado denominado CIRULA, el cual es utilizado en un considerable número de las bibliotecas de la UNAM.

Este sistema permite las siguientes funciones: dar de alta usuarios a través de la captura de sus datos personales; modificación de los datos de los lectores; generación, actualización y cancelación de credenciales en las cuales es utilizado un código de barras para identificar a cada usuario; registro de préstamos, refrendos y devoluciones de libros; consulta sobre cantidades adeudadas por concepto de retraso en la devolución de los libros y cancelación de éstas cuando es presentado el recibo correspondiente; consulta sobre los libros que tiene prestados un usuario; generación de cartas y etiquetas para los usuarios morosos.

El empleo de este sistema automatizado de circulación, conjuntamente con la utilización de códigos de barras en los libros y en las credenciales de los usuarios, han permitido un mejoramiento y agilización en los servicios y una optimización de los recursos destinados a éstos. De este sistema se han hecho tres versiones, la última de ellas para equipos multiusuarios.

En relación a los procesos técnicos, obviamente, estas actividades han sido una de las que mayor impacto han recibido, manifestándose lo anterior en un abatimiento en el rezago de los materiales por catalogar y en una disminución en los tiempos en que los materiales son procesados técnicamente.

De todos es conocido que uno de los principales problemas a que se enfrentan las bibliotecas es al rezago en el proceso técnico de los materiales, al cual la Dirección General de Bibliotecas de la UNAM no podía ser ajena. Previamente a la implementación del banco de datos LIBRUNAM, los volúmenes de material sin catalogar alcanzaban proporciones gigantescas. Sin embargo, en nuestros días no existen esas grandes líneas de espera y el tiempo promedio que tarda un libro en ser catalogado es de dos a cuatro semanas.

Este impacto en los procesos técnicos, no únicamente es perceptible en las bibliotecas de la UNAM, sino también en las bibliotecas de otras instituciones, donde el banco de datos LIBRUNAM es utilizado como una fuente para realizar sus procesos técnicos, tomando los registros existentes en éste y haciéndole las modificaciones pertinentes en base a sus propias necesidades.

La existencia de estos bancos de datos, indudablemente también ha tenido un efecto en los servicios de referencia, tanto en las bibliotecas de la UNAM, como en las de otras instituciones, a través de su consulta en línea o por medio del disco compacto.

Estos bancos de datos les permite a los estudiantes, investigadores y maestros, contar con una amplia bibliografía sobre determinado autor o tema en apoyo a sus actividades académicas.

Por otro lado, a los administradores de bibliotecas les ayuda en la selección del material, los procesos técnicos, así como en la elaboración y generación de catálogos.

En el caso específico de SERIUNAM, el que las bibliotecas mexicanas cuenten con un banco de datos con tal riqueza de información les permite hacia futuro:

Conocer y compartir sus recursos a través de un instrumento confiable, accesible y económico, y de esta forma evitar duplicar esfuerzos y recursos.

Utilizar en una forma más adecuada los recursos destinados a la adquisición de publicaciones seriadas pudiendo emprender programas cooperativos de adquisición de este tipo de materiales.

Completar las colecciones existentes en diversas instituciones, constituyendo un acervo de singular importancia para el apoyo de las actividades académicas y de investigación que se llevan a cabo en diferentes instituciones del país.

Elaborar bancos de datos especializados en diversas áreas del conocimiento humano.

El catálogo en línea de acceso público CD-UNAM

Como parte del programa de automatización del sistema bibliotecario de la UNAM, el año pasado fue puesto a disposición de los usuarios de la Biblioteca Central y de otras 32 bibliotecas el catálogo CD-UNAM, el cual ha venido a substituir los catálogos de tarjetas existentes en estas bibliotecas.

CD-UNAM es una serie de programas de cómputo desarrollados en la Dirección General de Servicios de Cómputo para la Administración de la Universidad Nacional Autónoma de México, diseñados especialmente para el manejo de todo tipo de información de bibliotecas, a través de CD-ROMs. Contiene rutinas para el manejo de información tipo texto, prácticamente de toda forma. Puede manejar bancos de datos en general, fichas y textos de gran longitud, entre otros. "Fue concebido como un sistema multimedia, por lo que puede manejar imágenes en múltiples formatos, así como sonido".[2]

La utilización de este catálogo en línea de acceso público en las bibliotecas de la UNAM, en substitución de los tradicionales catálogos de tarjetas, ha traído consigo una serie de ventajas entre las cuales podemos citar las siguientes:

1. Mediante esta forma de consulta, el usuario tiene acceso al catálogo automatizado de su biblioteca, ya que el mantenimiento se llevará a cabo semanalmente, o si es necesario, con menor frecuencia, dependiendo del volumen de

adquisición que se presente. De ello resulta un cambio radical con relación a los tradicionales catálogos en fichas, cuya actualización requiere de mayor tiempo, arrastrando un retraso permanente de varias semanas o meses.

2. El usuario tiene posibilidad de búsqueda de información con mucha mayor precisión ya que existe una enorme flexibilidad en la forma como puede recuperarla. Por otro lado no tiene que afrontar el riesgo de encontrar errores en la alfabetización, como puede suceder en el caso de catálogos en forma de tarjetas de cartón, en los cuales la inserción y por consiguiente la alfabetización de las tarjetas, se realiza de manera manual, con la consiguiente posibilidad de error.

3. El usuario dispone de varias opciones para establecer sus estrategias de búsqueda de la información. Básicamente, utilizando el sistema que ahora la Universidad pone a su disposición, puede acceder a la información por alguna de las siguientes formas, o bien la combinación de algunas de ellas: autor, título, tema, clasificación editorial, pie de imprenta, International Standard Book Number (ISBN) y serie.

4. El tiempo que el usuario dedica a la consulta de los catálogos se reduce en forma notable, ya que indudablemente el proceso automatizado es mucho más rápido que el manual. Esto finalmente redunda en menor tiempo de espera para la consulta, mayor rapidez también para el acceso físico al libro deseado y una agilización general del servicio de préstamo en la biblioteca.

5. Por otro lado, para la Universidad esto significa una reducción en los costos de mantenimiento de los catálogos. Se tiene calculado que el 25% del esfuerzo que se realiza anualmente para la impresión de tarjetas de catálogo, está destinado solamente a la reposición de aquéllas que se encuentran muy gastadas por el uso o bien han sido sustraídas de las gavetas.[3]

Consideraciones finales

Como podemos darnos cuenta a través de todo lo anteriormente expuesto, la automatización dentro de las bibliotecas de la UNAM y la existencia de estos tres grandes bancos de datos, han tenido un fuerte impacto en las actividades y servicios que se ofrecen en las bibliotecas pertenecientes a la institución, como en otras de diversos organismos.

En relación al empleo de la tecnología, las bibliotecas mexicanas, al igual que las de otros países, han adoptado dos posturas: en algunas bibliotecas existe una actitud positiva hacia el empleo de la nueva tecnología, y en otras se nota una actitud más pasiva, pues continúan trabajando de una manera tradicional, evitando todo el tiempo que les sea posible su utilización, no obstante lo anterior, tarde o temprano la utilización de las computadoras en las bibliotecas se volverá común, afectando la forma en que hemos organizado nuestras actividades, la manera en que las realizamos, los servicios que ofrecemos y la conducta de nuestros usuarios.

Respecto a éste último, la existencia de catálogos en línea de acceso público en las bibliotecas de la UNAM ha tenido una serie de cambios en la forma en que los usuarios se comportan puesto que:

Se ha incrementado el número de usuarios que asisten a la biblioteca.

La opinión de los usuarios por los servicios que la biblioteca presta ha mejorado.

El usuario tiene mayor éxito al buscar información en un catálogo en línea, en comparación con un catálogo de tarjetas.

Esta serie de efectos que el uso de la tecnología trae consigo, hace que los bibliotecarios nos enfrentemos a un cambio dentro de nuestras bibliotecas, pues nuestro papel como intermediarios entre las necesidades del usuario y los recursos de la biblioteca, se enfatiza, por lo que tenemos que estar conscientes de que nuestro papel en el futuro no deberá ser circunscrito a enseñar a nuestros usuarios como usar un catálogo en línea, sino más bien, a utilizar los recursos y servicios de la biblioteca dentro de una concepción global, es decir, enseñarlos a utilizar la biblioteca como un recurso que apoya sus actividades académicas.

NOTAS

1. H. Kenner, "Computers, Libraries, Scholars", *Ex Libris* 9:1 (1986), 1-3.

2. Universidad Nacional Autónoma de México, Dirección General de Bibliotecas, *Catálogo de libros de las bibliotecas de la UNAM, 1992* (México, D.F.: UNAM, Dirección General de Servicios de Cómputo para la Administración, 1992), disco compacto.

3. Universidad Nacional Autónoma de México, Dirección General de Bibliotecas, *Los catálogos automatizados en las bibliotecas de la UNAM* (documento mecanografiado), pp. 1-3.

26. The Impact of Electronic Resources on Bibliographic Instruction at the University of New Mexico General Library

Mina Jane Grothey

Introduction

Over the last twenty years there has been a proliferation of electronic resources available in academic libraries. Over the last ten years, many of these resources plus a whole array of new ones have become available to the public. What are librarians doing to teach library users about these resources, both about their existence and about how to get the most from them? Have these resources made library instruction easier or harder? This paper does not have the answers to these questions, but will look at how one institution is attempting to answer them.

Electronic resources include online public catalogs most commonly referred to as OPACs, CD-ROMs, end user online systems, mediated online searching, and the Internet. Another resource more frequently handled by the computer center is data tapes or files which are often run on a mainframe computer.

Anita Lowry in her article "Beyond BI: Information Literacy in the Electronic Age" states

> The information environment has become more complex because users have more choices of information sources—print, microform, CD-ROM, online—and because these sources vary greatly in structure, mechanics, and purpose. New skills knowledge and modes of conceptualization are needed in the search process if users are to fully exploit computer-based information sources.[1]

How do we teach these "new skills knowledge and modes of conceptualization"? This paper looks at a variety of ways to answer this question, with specific reference to electronic resources in the field of Latin American studies.

Although Latin American studies does not account for a large portion of the available electronic resources, some major resources are available electronically. The *Hispanic American Periodicals Index* (*HAPI*), published by the UCLA Latin American Center, comes in both an online version and recently on CD-ROM, as well as in print. The *Latin America Data Base* (*LADB*), produced by the University of New Mexico Latin American Institute, also comes in both forms. The North-South Center of the

University of Miami produces *Info-South*, available in a direct online version, via Dialog, on CD-ROM, and published quarterly as *Info-South Abstracts*. The University of Texas Benson Latin American Collection is now available on CD-ROM along with the *Handbook of Latin American Studies* (*HLAS*) from v. 50: Humanities (1990) to date. The two-volume CD-ROM version of these titles is called *Latin American Studies* and is produced by National Information Services Corporation. Volume 1: Multidisciplinary includes the Benson Collection, *HAPI*, and *HLAS*, and Volume 2: Current Affairs and Law contains *Info-South*, *LADB*, and *Hispanic Law Index*.

Another resource being developed at the University of Texas at Austin is UT-LANIC (University of Texas—Latin American Network Information Center), which will be a gopher system to provide Latin American users with access to academic databases and information services worldwide.

It has been possible to access UTCAT, the online public catalog for the University of Texas at Austin, via the Internet and thereby gain access to information on the holdings for the Benson Collection. Catalogs for other libraries with large Latin American collections are also available on the Internet.

For more information on electronic resources in Latin American studies, see other chapters in this volume and the article by Peter Stern written for historians in *Colonial Latin American Review*.[2]

The University of New Mexico (UNM) General Library is a medium-sized research library currently ranked 53rd by the Association of Research Libraries. The Latin American/Iberian collections are one of the strengths of the library, and public services are provided specifically for students in all areas of Latin American studies. I serve as a reference librarian and a Latin American specialist in the Zimmerman Library, the general, education, humanities, and social sciences library. Additional support for public service is provided by the Curator for Latin American and Iberian Collections and personnel on the Ibero-American cataloging team. In addition to Zimmerman Library, the Parish Memorial Library, covering business, economics, and management, provides special Latin American reference service. Parish has a public access terminal for *HAPI*, *LADB*, and *Info-South*.

Electronic Resources

We talk about electronic resources as if the term refers to a single entity when in reality the variety of types of resources demands a variety of instructional approaches. The first electronic resource most library users encounter is the online public access catalog (OPAC). Too often we now assume familiarity with searching OPACs and overlook teaching this resource to our users. The needs of the users range from the most basic to the very complex. The University of New Mexico's student body is composed of people with a wide variety of library experience. Also the UNM General Library actively serves the local community. So the user's experience with computers can range from nonexistent to expert. One day I helped a woman totally unfamiliar with using a keyboard. Even for the inexperienced computer user, I had always assumed a familiarity with a typewriter keyboard. This experience made me more alert to the experience level of the user and illustrates the need to recognize different levels of experience when conducting group instruction sessions.

The UNM General Library online public catalog, LIBROS (LIBRary Online System), is a version of Innopac. It is a menu driven system, which is supposed to make it user friendly. One problem is that not everyone takes the time to read the screens. Even reading the screens doesn't help, however, if one doesn't know what to look for or what possibilities exist. Instruction sessions on the OPAC can help in this area by alerting users to the potentialities of the system.

Recently, I spoke to a graduate Spanish literature class and offered hints for getting the most from LIBROS. For example, LIBROS has some name authority information. A search for "subject Lorca," for instance, will produce a cross reference to the form of the name as entered in the catalog. I also distinguished between searching by subject heading and by keyword, pointing out the benefits of both types of searching. Our system allows keyword searching by subject, title, corporate author, and contents notes, but not personal authors. The term "subject" refers to searching by Library of Congress subject headings, which can provide a cleaner search. If the student doesn't know the subject heading or can't find an appropriate heading, then keyword searching is best. I also talked about how to limit a search and how to read a serials record. These are examples of topics that can be covered in a presentation on using the OPAC.

Users can find some of what they want without instruction, but to get the most from the OPAC, instruction is necessary. For many users, searching the OPAC will be their first experience with Boolean operators. Learning to use Boolean operators is a skill transferable to many other electronic resources. Depending on the OPAC software, Boolean search techniques may be implicit rather than explicit, which makes it more difficult for users to understand their usage.

Innovative Interfaces, Inc. is working on making searches of catalogs from other vendors appear the same as Innopac. Currently this feature is being tested at the University of Arizona. Will such a feature be a true help? Or will it only mask differences among systems? Seeing a different menu or access instructions is a clue to the user that the techniques for searching this OPAC may differ from techniques used elsewhere. Another complication in searching the OPAC is that it can serve as a gateway to bibliographic databases or other electronic resources.

Sometimes the OPAC may contain records from more than one library system. For example, LIBROS includes records from New Mexico Institute of Mining and Technology, located 75 miles south of Albuquerque. Having records from other libraries can cause confusion unless the patron can elect to include or exclude locations other than the local library. Patrons become upset when they do not have immediate access to the materials from other libraries.

Since OPACs are often available by remote access, a whole new user group has opened up for instruction. Some institutions have placed instructions and/or tutorials on the local computer information system to meet this need.

Another aspect of instruction for LIBROS is teaching this resource in Spanish. The University of New Mexico has several programs for students from Latin America. The two principal programs are LAPE (Latin American Programs in Education), which offers a Master's degree in Educational Administration and MAPAS (Master's in Public Administration in Spanish). While participating students do not need to know English since the courses are taught in Spanish, other university services are not as readily available in Spanish. The library provides limited services in Spanish, such as bibliographic instruction and reference services. Release 8 of Innopac will have the ability to provide Spanish language screens. I look forward to having these screens available for this special group of users. In the meantime, brief Spanish language instructions have been written, but to fully use the system the Spanish language users need to understand the English language menu options and how to use subject headings in English. Keyword searching using Spanish words does help overcome some of the reliance on English.

The second most frequently used electronic resource is the compact disc with read only memory referred to as the CD-ROM or optical disc technology. Zimmerman Library Reference has five CD-ROM stations, including *ERIC* (two stations); *Psyclit*; one station with *Readers' Guide Abstracts*, *Social Sciences Index*, *Chicano Database*, *Ethnic NewsWatch*, and *Religious and Theological Abstracts*; and one station with the *Modern Language Association (MLA) Bibliography*, *Dissertation Abstracts International*, U.N. documents, *Philosopher's Index*, *The Movie Database*, and the *Bible*. The reference area also has a terminal which provides public access to CARL (Colorado Alliance of Research Libraries) including *UnCover* and *ERIC*. We do not yet have the *Latin American Studies* CD-ROMs.

Deanna Nipp in her article "Back to Basics" points out some of the unique aspects of instruction for CD-ROM use.

> Although CD-ROM should be taught in the context of the entire array of collections and services a library offers, there are some goals that may be seen as specific to CD-ROM instruction:
>
> First librarians must deal with the mechanics of CD-ROM systems. . . . Users must first understand the database—the disciplines and subdisciplines it includes. . . . Users must also understand the unique function of this tool, its role among other similar tools and its relationship to them. . . . Users must understand the format of a record in the database. . . . They must understand Boolean logic. . . . They must be able to evaluate results and consider altering their strategies if results are not satisfactory. . . .
>
> Existing programs and the environment in which they are developed and implemented affect CD-ROM instruction. Many of the basics the CD-ROM user needs to understand are covered in instructional programs that already exist. The user must be able to formulate an appropriate research question, identify the most appropriate access tool, and recognize the elements of a citation. . . .
>
> Librarians can set up conditions for transference of learning from the basics to the new CD-ROM format.[3]

One problem in teaching CD-ROM versions of an index is that time discussing the print version is reduced in order to cover everything in a one hour session. Students are so interested in computerized tools that they do not pay attention to the print sources. How do you structure a session to attract and retain their interest? If you start with the print source, the students are impatient for you to move on to the computerized version. If you discuss the computerized version first, they lose interest thereafter. The importance of understanding the structure of the index, whether in print or on computer, is difficult to convey.

Sometimes different indexes use the same software for the computerized versions. For example, Zimmerman Reference has the Silverplatter versions of *ERIC* and *Psyclit*. The function keys and other search features are the same. Students are often confused about why they don't find the same types of materials on both computers.

A question being asked by bibliographic instruction librarians is how much time should be spent on teaching equipment and computer skills as well as software and quirks of the database. Because of the variety of computer experience of the users, striking a balance can be difficult. Users need to know that the formal session is not their only opportunity to learn these skills. It should be stressed that when users actually do searches on CD-ROM indexes, they should feel comfortable in asking reference personnel for assistance.

An important aspect of teaching CD-ROMS is the opportunity for students to practice during the session. It is particularly helpful if examples and exercises relate to the topic of the class. Without adequate facilities for hands-on practice, instruction works better on an informal basis.[4]

Electronic resources have produced an interesting phenomenon exemplified in the following quotes.

> As CD-ROM usage continued to increase, the reference staff confirmed Craig Gibson's statement that, because students often consider CD-ROM indexes and online catalogs as magical devices, the need for teaching research concepts is now greater than ever before. Reference faculty found it imperative that these technologies be taught, as he suggested, "within a larger information-gathering or search strategy process."[5]

> There is some concern that staff and patrons alike are too enamored of the new tools, at the expense of traditional (and sometimes better) reference works. . . . Some librarians are concerned that users are not critical enough when it comes to electronic resources. . . . Most would rather wait than use printed sources, even if the print may be more appropriate.[6]

Zimmerman Reference department staff have experienced referrals to *ERIC* as if it was a broad subject index. Some students, even after hearing about more appropriate indexes, insist on using *ERIC* because it is on computer. Having access to *UnCover* has helped provide the broad subject access not available on our other sources. But still students seem unwilling to use the best resource for their topic, if that resource is not available on computer.

Along the same lines, recently there was a discussion on LIBREF-L, the listserve for reference librarians, called "electronic resources addictive" or "right database?". The following comments are excerpted from this discussion.

> I have encountered students at the desk who will only use CD-ROMs or any other electronic resource and when told their topic does not lend itself to the scope of what we have . . . change their topic rather than use a paper index despite the existence of appropriate paper indexes. . . . The rallying cry should be "Paper isn't obsolete. Everything isn't on the screen!"[7]

> What does surprise and concern me is the apparent collusion on the part of some librarians—and professors—who simply go along with this rather than urge students to evaluate their sources. It seems to me also to be a factor in the tendency of some who feel that periodicals (articles) are intrinsically more important to students than books. . . . We would, . . . be following—not leading—the students down the path of least resistance.[8]

> The problem doesn't seem to be a BI problem, but a BIBLIOGRAPHIC problem: how can we make material in the paper sources more accessible and usable? Paper indexing is often INAPPROPRIATE for a topic. . . . Trying to find [the] material in standard indexes is more time-consuming and frustrating than it could conceivably be worth! . . . Users don't WANT to use non-computerized indexes because print indexes are mostly inferior! . . . We've given our users

CD-ROM glimpses of the Ultimate Encyclopedia. Why are we surprised when they are upset and frustrated with less? How can we reconcile them to the clumsiness of extant systems? . . . Aside from warning users that the Final Source doesn't exist, and trying to make them accept the necessity of pale copies, what CAN BI do about this?[9]

This phenomenon has serious consequences for bibliographic instruction. Have we become so concerned about teaching electronic resources that we are shortchanging the importance of print sources? How do we stress to students the importance of using the best source for their research no matter what the format happens to be? On the other hand, if a student needs just a few sources for a short freshmen level essay, does it matter if the student changes the topic in order to use an electronic resource?

At a recent meeting of the SALALM Bibliographic Instruction Subcommittee, a participant wondered whether having the *Handbook of Latin American Studies* available on CD-ROM would encourage people to use the older volumes in print.

The two resources discussed above were designed from the beginning to be used by the public and without charge. For this reason the role of the librarian has been to help the patron learn how to use these resources to obtain the best results. Other resources, databases provided by a vendor such as Dialog, were first the province of the librarian who did mediated searches for the user. In most libraries these searches were offered on a fee basis, often at a subsidized rate to members of the university community. Over the last few years these services have been marketed to the general public. First Dialog, the system with which I am most familiar, offered Knowledge Index to the general public. Next came Classmate, a program designed for use by students. Classmate allows students, once they have completed a formal training course, to search a limited number of databases at a special rate. The formal training sessions include instruction in Boolean logic as well as the commands needed to search the system. Information to be used in the sessions is provided by Dialog. Training sessions are offered on a regular basis to any student. Librarians still help users decide which databases are best for their topic and help develop search strategies.

A professor in the University of New Mexico sociology department requires his students in an upper level class to learn and to use Classmate to access *Sociological Abstracts*.

I do not recommended Classmate to students in Latin American studies because many of the databases these students need are available on CD-ROM or free. Since the University of New Mexico is part of the Latin American Database Consortium, we have free access to *HAPI OnLine*, *LADB*, and *Info-South*. A public terminal is available at the Parish Memorial Library and a terminal will soon be available in Zimmerman Reference.

Instruction in the use of these systems has been mostly one-on-one. Printed guides are also available at the terminal.

In an article in *Online*, the authors describe this as a growing area since "end-user options fit right into the new generation's expectations and experiences."[10] These expectations have been referred to pejoratively as fast-food expectations because of user demand for immediate information and instant gratification.

As end-user searching has increased, the demand for mediated online searching has decreased. We try to find a free or cheaper source first, but some databases are still only available through commercial services. So we do mention this option during instruction sessions. Some users prefer to pay us to do a search because they think it saves time.

Another new feature is the full text database, which originated primarily with newspapers. One full text database available for Latin Americanists is the *Latin America Data Base* (*LADB*), produced by the Latin American Institute at the University of New Mexico. It is a group of three, previously four, electronic newsletters. The three titles are SourceMex, economic news and analysis on Mexico; Chronicle of Latin American Economic Affairs; and NotiSur, Latin American political affairs. These newsletters are written by staff members based on newspaper and wire service reports from Latin America and Europe. The newsletters can be read as such or searched by subject to find articles on particular topics. Because this database is produced locally, our students have a unique opportunity to acquire training directly from the database producer. Access to the system is available to students free through TECHNET, the New Mexico statewide computer network. This database is also accessible at the Parish Memorial Library. Carolyn Mountain, the Ibero-American specialist at Parish, says she needs to help users with particular problems that occur during a search rather than give instruction on basic use of the *LADB*.

Another area of great potential is the Internet. I participated in a session to demonstrate Latin American resources available on the Internet. With two librarians and a staff member from CIRT, our computer center, we were able to do individual hands-on instruction. The session included information on access to the local system UNMINFO which is provided by CIRT (Computer and Information Resources Technology). UNMINFO provides remote access to LIBROS and to catalogs of other libraries via the Internet, and provides a connection to TECHNET for access to *LADB*.

Introducing the Internet to library users raises the question of the role of the campus computer center. Some institutions have computer centers which teach basic computer skills and may even teach about the Internet. Elsewhere, the library has primary responsibility for instruction about the Internet.

At UNM, a task force of people from both the General Library and from CIRT has been established to address this issue. One mission of the task force is to help people from each area understand what is currently being done and to coordinate future activities.

Teaching Technology

A number of recent articles have addressed the issue of teaching emerging technologies. Also, *Teaching Technologies in Libraries: A Practical Guide*, by Linda Brew MacDonald, Mara R. Saule, Margaret W. Gordon, and Craig A. Robertson (G. K. Hall, 1990), covers the different types of resources and the use of computers and other methods to teach these resources.

The following comments from the first chapter, which provides an overview, introduce some of the problems encountered in teaching technologies.

> Because of the inherent differences between computerized and printed reference sources and between the ways users react to these sources, teaching electronic information sources becomes a new and different instructional challenge.
>
> While we may recognize the need for teaching users how a particular information technology works there are compelling reasons not to do much special training for library technologies. Since there is no charge on a CD-ROM system, users can learn as they search. Spontaneous searchers will in most cases discover what they need in order to do a successful basic search. . . . They generally want as little instruction as possible in order to get an answer to their research questions. . . .
>
> Library staff time in designing and executing instructional materials and sessions, as well as ongoing administrative costs, can make special training programs for computerized information systems too costly. . . . Even though the costs of teaching technologies may be high and, on the surface, the benefits of training may be questionable, designing pedagogically sound instructional programs for library technology is nonetheless extremely important for both the library and the library user.[11]

As this passage illustrates, part of the debate is about whether it is necessary to teach electronic resources. Are the time and effort needed worthwhile? If users are satisfied with the results they get, should we librarians worry that they haven't used the resources to get the best results? If systems are truly user friendly, is there a need for instruction?

Most of us would say that although systems are called user friendly, in fact, just about everyone needs help in learning how to do an effective search. The electronic search process is composed of two parts: (1) the database being searched and (2) the software being used to search the database. In the past, information about how a database or index is constructed, what information is covered, and how that information can be accessed was the core of an instructional session. With the same information in computerized form, the instructor must also get users comfortable with the computer equipment and the software.

To further complicate matters, few subjects can be covered by using just one resource. This means one must know how to search different resources often with different software. How do we ease the user's transition from one software application to another or from one type of electronic resource to another?

Too often students just want to retrieve specific information and are not interested in learning about database structure and how one index fits into a total picture of resources available in a subject area.

Concepts that carry over from one electronic resource to another include Boolean searching and controlled vocabulary. If the user understands Boolean operators and search sets, these concepts work in searching a CD-ROM product, in end-user searching, and to some extent in searching an OPAC. "Constructing an effective search strategy, using the concepts of question analysis, sets, and Boolean logic, is the single most important searching skill that an end user can master."[12]

> Searching for information via microcomputer offers faster retrieval of a greater range of materials using more dynamic and varied search modes. The searcher can go "deeper" into the bibliographic record to find what she needs, free from the constraints of linear, controlled vocabulary searching in printed indexes and abstracts. She can combine terms, limit which fields she chooses to search, search a range of years at once. Not the least of the advantages to computerized searching is the ability to print off results once a search has been completed; patrons can work effectively in the library without paper and pencil.[13]

Librarians are familiar with teaching the Library of Congress subject headings (LCSH) which can lead to teaching how to use a thesaurus, especially since the more recent editions of the LCSH are presented in a thesaurus format. Both of these tools introduce students to the concept of a controlled vocabulary. Understanding the difference between seraching with a controlled vocabulary and searching with keywords or free text is essential to conducting an effective search.

Another important aspect is understanding the entire research process and not just what a certain electronic resource can do. For example, in Latin American studies, researchers rely not only on the Latin American specific resources, but must also consult the general resources for the same subject area. In literature, for example, a researcher working on a Latin American author would need to search the *MLA International Bibliography* as well as *HAPI*.

Just because information comes from a computer makes it no more reliable than information found in print sources. Learning how to evaluate the results of a search is an important part of the research process, as the following quote from Saule points out.

The list of citations itself, however, does not provide indications of how trustworthy, complete, or valuable the information in the cited documents will be for the searcher. It is important to teach patrons how to evaluate the citations that they have retrieved. For example, searchers should be able to distinguish between journals and magazines and to understand the differences in content, audience, and focus between the two types of periodicals. The number of pages that an article comprises is an important indication of its usefulness for certain purposes. Finally, the language used in article titles also provides clues to the potential value of the article itself; the searcher should examine whether the language is technical, nontechnical, or colloquial in order to see whether the level of articles is appropriate for the information need.[14]

As mentioned earlier, one of the common problems in dealing with the user's reliance on computer sources is a reluctance to use resources available only in print.

The searcher needs to know the range of sources available, their relative strengths in terms of particular questions, and the benefits and limitation of their format (for example print, online, or optical disc). . . . Providing guidelines for determining which technology for which information need is an important part of the overall search strategy process.

The differences between print sources and computerized information sources highlight the need for approaching these with a different instructional manner.[15]

Many library users remain unfamiliar with using computers, a point to remember when doing library instruction, especially to a group that includes older students. Part of the instruction session should offer the opportunity for people to get comfortable with the computer itself. Librarians must be sensitive to the possibility that a user is wary of using a computer. Telling the patron that it is easy doesn't really help. At the reference desk, it is possible to go with the user to a terminal to illustrate some of the basics. During an instructional session, if equipment is not available for hands-on practice, handouts or transparencies can be used to show special features such as function keys. I have had the experience of telling a user to press F4, meaning the function key on a separate part of the keyboard, and the user types in the letter F and the number 4 and wonders why nothing happens.

In an article about the gender gap in using computers and its possible effect on bibliographic instruction, Elizabeth Cardman takes the position that women are less likely to be familiar with computers than are men and offers several suggestions for overcoming this gap.[16] In fact, in the Zimmerman Reference Department we find more of an age gap than a gender gap. When older library users learn that the majority of our catalog is now only available on computer, they are hesitant about using LIBROS without some assistance.

Those familiar with computers often assume that all computer terminals access the same information. Although signs are posted above the computer terminals which operate the various CD-ROMs available in the Reference Department, users frequently assume they can search any database on any terminal.

In the UNM General Library we kept our Wyse terminals for our online catalog when the library switched from Carlyle to Innopac. To make matters even more confusing, the name of the catalog, LIBROS, remained the same. Not only did the software for searching change, but the amount of material in the online catalog greatly increased.

This section explored some of the issues involved in teaching electronic resources: teaching concepts versus skills, teaching the research process as a total package, and the need to help patrons familiarize themselves with the equipment used to access electronic resources. The next section discusses methods for teaching electronic resources.

There is a wide variety of ways to give instruction about these resources, ranging from informal instruction while on the reference desk (often called one-on-one) to full length credit courses. For most libraries it is not a case of using only one method, but of taking advantage of as many as possible.

> Traditional methods have always worked best when faculty corroborated by understanding library resources and incorporating them into coursework and assignments. This corroboration has been somewhat lacking with respect to new technologies simply because faculty have been unaware of the new resources or have used them only for special purposes.[17]

> It is useful to target faculty first because of their strong liaison to students. . . . For many of the faculty, new vistas opened up regarding ease of research, thoroughness of searching and creative interrelating of subject areas through using Boolean operators.[18]

For the reasons mentioned in the above quotes many libraries have designed and presented special workshops on electronic resources just for faculty members. Unfortunately we have not yet done this at the University of New Mexico.

Workshops, not only for faculty but also for other library users, are a popular form to teach electronic resources. Loretta Caren describes a series of workshops put on by the Rochester Institute of Technology library in her article titled "New Bibliographic Instruction for New Technology."[19]

> The theme of [the] R[ochester] I[nstitute of] T[echnology]'s program is "connections" including: (1) a historical review, (2) local connections, (3) bibliographic connections, and (4) document delivery connection and future connections.

The seminars are planned for one and one-half to two hours each. . . . These seminars are designed to be multimedia presentations. . . . [The] introduction sets the stage for the seminar as a lively and exciting journey and puts the forthcoming "connections" into perspective.

Perhaps the most valuable aspect of the seminar is the opportunity to build channels of communication between the library and the faculty and to provide a mechanism for input from patrons for current and future library services. It is more than an instructional vehicle in that it promotes liaison and communication.[20]

Workshops are one example of a formal method of teaching. The credit course is another. "Some libraries are trying to add a one- or two-credit course to the required undergraduate curriculum in order to cover adequately the many dimensions of research, both print and computer-based."[21] The University of New Mexico General Library offers a two-credit course called "Information Research Strategies" which covers electronic as well as print resources.

Through my literature search, I found two articles that present very different examples of credit courses. A course at a community college in Florida is described in "Delivering Hi-Tech Library Instruction" by Rudy Widman and Jimmie Anne Nourse.[22] The second article looks at the course called "Research in the Humanities: A Practicum on Resources and Methods" being taught in the Graduate School of Arts and Sciences of Columbia University.[23]

When CD-ROMs first appeared in reference departments, many began offering demonstrations of these new resources. The Zimmerman Reference Department offers CD-ROM demonstrations on a walk-in basis for Silverplatter (*ERIC* and *Psyclit*) two days a week and for Wilson (*Readers' Guide Abstracts*, *Social Sciences Index*, and *MLA*) one day a week. It is also possible to request a demonstration by appointment for these CD-ROMs and for those not part of the regular schedule. "Voluntary separate workshops in database searching are sparsely attended and do not address the importance of learning over time."[24] Others have found that to increase attendance it helps to ask users to sign up in advance.

Now . . . most of the classes also include a block of time for demonstrating and discussing compact disc technology. . . . In beginning level classes . . . students should be informed about the availability of the CD-ROM resources and encouraged to attend the CD-ROM drop-in sessions. . . . It is anticipated that, as time goes on, more upper division and graduate-level classes will request BI for certain databases. . . . The classes are likely to include more than just the demonstration and discussion of compact discs. For fullest use of a database, users need to understand Boolean logic, appropriate use of connectors, the importance of thesauri for accessing information, the value of truncation symbols, and crystallizing a topic into the most concise statement possible for identifying the main concepts to search. With this knowledge, users can search in depth rather than superficially. Also, students who recognize the importance of learning skills to access both traditional and new sources become very serious about learning and desirous of help.[25]

A method of bibliographic instruction with long standing has been course-related sessions in which the materials presented are tailored to the needs of a particular class.

> The heart of most BI programs, at least in academic libraries, has been the one-hour instructional session; in this one class period, the librarian generally distributes a bibliography of sources pertinent to the course or to a class project, offers a search strategy, and discusses the scope of uses of individual reference sources. Most instruction librarians, however, have found one hour inadequate for teaching both print and computerized sources. . . .
>
> It is particularly difficult to address the varying levels of knowledge, experience, and attitudes of different students in the one-hour session. Furthermore, course-integrated instruction reaches only a very small percentage of automated reference systems users.[26]

The Zimmerman Reference Department still relies on this method of instruction. For some graduate classes we have been able to schedule two hours which allows us one hour to present the traditional print resources and the second hour to discuss and demonstrate the appropriate electronic resources. Sometimes the two sessions are back to back while at other times we can convince professors to come to the library twice. Part of the problem is that faculty are often unwilling to devote more than one class period to learning about the library and its resources.

One professor in sociology brings his class to the library for one hour a week for four weeks. This allows us to divide the presentation into sessions on (1) books, (2) print indexes, (3) electronic indexes, and (4) government publications.

Renovation and construction projects at the UNM General Library have hampered my working with public access to Latin America-related electronic resources; however, a benefit resulting from the construction has been a library instruction classroom. The room has been equipped with 15 dual floppy terminals which can access LIBROS and UNMINFO and one hard disk terminal which in addition to communications software is set up with Wilson and Silverplatter software for CD-ROM demonstrations. By using an overhead projector and an LCD panel, we are able to demonstrate how to search LIBROS and the CD-ROMs. It is in this room that I gave the aforementioned demonstration on using the Internet. I tried one large group which had all the terminals working and found it difficult to help all those who had questions or problems. Because of the equipment limitations, students can not do hands-on CD-ROM work, but can practice with LIBROS.

Using computers to teach electronic resources is an idea that intrigues me. I have had no experience in this area, but I can offer the following quotes from others who have.

> Computer-assisted instruction (CAI) has been used in libraries to train both patrons and employees, to cover both particular subject resources and general library orientation. Good CAI can provide consistent high-quality, interactive instruction at any time of the day, night, or weekend. . . . [Using CAI for basic instruction] allows librarians to focus their efforts on assisting advanced undergraduate and graduate students in specific disciplines and on developing enhanced CAI modules.[27]

> Using teaching technologies, such as help screens, online tutorials, videotapes, CAI, expert systems, and artificial intelligence, to instruct library users in computerized literature searching can overcome some of the problems presented by traditional instruction methods. If it is well done, instructional technology provides the searcher with many of the same attractions as the searching technology itself; it is available at all times; it is fast; its pace is user-controlled; it is interactive; it can give immediate positive reinforcement for correct responses; it can address the needs of a variety of users; it can be turned off or left if the learner has had enough.
>
> For the librarian, using technology as a teaching aid can save time and money. Once the initial costs of designing and implementing the teaching modules have been borne, instruction technology can free the reference librarian from giving lengthy, repetitive searching instructions. In most cases, computer-based instruction packages can be easily updated to reflect changes in software or systems. Technological media can also be used to teach concepts in a way that printed instructional sheets or workbooks cannot; it is interactive and, depending on the software or medium being used, can build conceptual frameworks and create mental models slowly. . . . Technology-aided instruction . . . is simply one component in an overall instructional program. The most important aspect of the library instruction curriculum is the content of the instructional sessions.[28]

Probably the most well known example of the OPAC as a total reference package is the Gateway system used at Ohio State University. Information accessible as part of the online catalog allows users to search the catalog, indexes, encyclopedias, and even see where items are located in the reference area. At the 1991 meeting of SALALM, Ted Riedinger spoke about this system and what it has for Latin American studies. For additional information on the Gateway and its use in freshmen survey classes, see the article by Fred Roecker and Thomas Minnick in *Working with Faculty in the New Electronic Library*.[29]

One advantage of a gateway system mounted on the public catalog is its availability at all times. Users do not have to sign up for instruction or come to the library only when reference staff is available. In the past printed workbooks were used to provide self-paced instruction. "While workbooks can be valuable for the motivated learner, they cannot accurately reflect the interactive nature of database searching."[30]

Another way to help people as they actually use resources is the point-of-use guide which is available right at the computer. There is debate over the effectiveness of these guides. How long should they be? How comprehensive? For the CD-ROMs in the reference department we provide both lengthy guides on how to use the different products and also a single page "quick guide." Observation has shown that instead of consulting the guides before beginning a search, users resort to them when they get into trouble.

Signs are also posted on the terminals explaining the major function key operations such as how to print. But when there is more than one software application on a terminal, it becomes very confusing because users don't know which package they are using.

The physical facilities and financial position of a library will dictate which of the different methods of instruction can and will be employed. The variety and possibilites are as unlimited as the resources being taught.

Conclusion

It is clear that electronic resources will continue to have an impact on how libraries offer bibliographic instruction. But rather than just complicating matters, computers may also be able to bring us new instruction methods so we can reach more users.

"The feeling of confidence in the library and its services is particularly important in face of the rapidly changing technological mix in libraries. The library that the patron enters today may look entirely different tomorrow."[31] One of the greatest challenges for librarians is how to keep up with all the new electronic resources so we can teach them to our users. Change is occurring so quickly that it is difficult to keep up. Each new resource can require learning another technology.

In their article "The Impact of Electronic Reference on Reference Librarians," Tenopir and Neufang feel that

> Users are making more demands on librarians, providing more challenges to reference work and often leading to enhanced services. . . . One change is in the attitude library users have about the library and about the research process. They are coming more often to the library and going away more satisfied. . . . [Librarians] are trying out new instructional techniques . . . with CD-ROM [making] library instruction more effective for a wide range of students. . . . Most agreed that their instruction has improved and has gotten more interesting.[32]

The librarian who does bibliographic instruction can play a very important role in humanizing technology for the library user. This point is made by Elizabeth Frick:

> the instruction librarian is a prime actor in creating a humane environment even in a highly technical setting. The best instruction creates a sense of the significance of

the project within the overall world of information and fosters in the patron confident pride in an efficient, effective search. The bibliographic instruction librarian teaches control of the information environment, and while the instruction librarian can take no responsibility for the self-esteem of the patron in other areas of life, the context in which information access is addressed, is ours to create.[33]

As librarians who do bibliographic instruction in the area of Latin American studies, we need to work together to keep abreast of the electronic resources in the field and of the methods to teach these resources to our users.

NOTES

1. Anita Kay Lowry, "Beyond BI: Information Literacy in the Electronic Age," *Research Strategies* 8 (Winter 1990), 22.

2. Peter Stern, "Coaxing the Historian into the New Information Age," *Colonial Latin American Review* 1 (1992), 201-221.

3. Deanna Nipp, "Back to Basics: Integrating CD-ROM Instruction with Standard User Education," *Research Strategies* 9 (Winter 1991), 43-44.

4. Carol Tenopir and Ralf Neufang, "The Impact of Electronic Reference on Reference Librarians," *Online* 16 (May 1992), 58.

5. Caroline Blumenthal, Mary Jo Howard, and William R. Kinyon, "The Impact of CD-ROM Technology on a Bibliographic Instruction Program," *College & Research Libraries* 54 (January 1993), 12-13.

6. Tenopir and Neufang, "The Impact of Electronic Reference on Reference Librarians," 59.

7. Richard Heinzkill, "Electronic Resources Addictive," in LIBREF-L [listserve], [Kent, OH: Reference Office, Kent State University Libraries; libref-l@kentvm.bitnet; 10 Apr 1993, 11:40:51] message id: <O1GWUFC673ZOA4M21X>; [lines 1-6].

8. A. Gerald Anderson, "RE: Electronic Resources Addictive," in LIBREF-L [listserve], [Kent, OH: Reference Office, Kent State University Libraries; libref-l@kentvm.bitnet; 10 Apr 1993, 18:30:36] message id: <O1GWVT7R7RE4A4M21X>; [lines 6-16].

9. Jennifer Heise, "RE: Electronic Resources Addictive," in LIBREF-L [listserve], [Kent, OH: Reference Office, Kent State University Libraries; libref-l@kentvm.bitnet; 13 Apr 1993, 18:08:17] message id: <O1GWYZQCKB88A4M21X>; [lines 1-33].

10. Tenopir and Neufang, "The Impact of Electronic Reference on Reference Librarians," 58.

11. Mara R. Saule, "Teaching for Library Technologies," in Linda Brew MacDonald, Mara R. Saule, Margaret W. Gordon, and Craig A. Robertson, eds., *Teaching Technologies in Libraries: A Practical Guide* (Boston, MA: G. K. Hall, 1990), pp. 23, 12-13.

12. Ibid., p. 19.

13. Ibid., p. 2.

14. Ibid., p. 20.

15. Ibid., pp. 19, 5.

16. Elizabeth R. Cardman, "Gender Gap in Computer Use: Implications for Bibliographic Instruction," *Research Strategies* 8 (Summer 1990), 116-128.

17. Loretta Caren, "New Bibliographic Instruction for New Technology: Library Connections' Seminar at the Rochester Institute of Technology," *Library Trends* 37 (Winter 1989), 367.

18. Blumenthal, Howard, and Kinyon, "The Impact of CD-ROM Technology on a Bibliographic Instruction Program," p. 13.

19. Caren, "New Bibliographic Instruction for New Technology," pp. 366-373.

20. Ibid., pp. 368-369, 371.

21. Saule, "Teaching for Library Technologies," pp. 23-24.

22. Rudy Widman and Jimmie Anne Nourse, "Delivering Hi-Tech Library Instruction: A Hands-On Approach," *Laserdisk Professional* 2 (November 1989), 50-54.

23. Lowry, "Beyond BI," pp. 22-27.

24. Saule, "Teaching for Library Technologies," p. 24.

25. Blumenthal, Howard, and Kinyon, "The Impact of CD-ROM Technology on a Bibliographic Instruction Program," pp. 13-14.

26. Saule, "Teaching for Library Technologies," p. 23.

27. Harold B. Shill, "Bibliographic Instruction: Planning for the Electronic Information Environment," *College & Research Libraries* 48 (September 1987), 436.

28. Saule, "Teaching for Library Technologies," pp. 24-25.

29. Fred Roecker and Thomas Minnick, "The Portal and The Gateway: Library Technology in the Freshman Survey Class at the Ohio State University," in Linda Shirato, ed., *Working with Faculty in the New Electronic Library: Papers and Session Materials Presented at the Nineteenth National LOEX Library Instruction Conference held at Eastern Michigan University 10 to 11 May 1991, and related resource materials gathered by the LOEX Clearinghouse* (Ann Arbor, MI: Published for Learning Resources and Technologies, Eastern Michigan University by Pierian Press, 1992), pp. 41-69.

30. Saule, "Teaching for Library Technologies," p. 24.

31. Ibid., p. 21.

32. Tenopir and Neufang, "The Impact of Electronic Reference on Reference Librarians," pp. 58-59.

33. Elizabeth Frick, "Humanizing Technology Through Instruction," *Canadian Library Journal* 41 (October 1984), 266.

BIBLIOGRAPHY

Anderson, A. Gerald. "RE: Electronic Resources Addictive." In LIBREF-L [listserve]. [Kent, OH: Reference Office, Kent State University Libraries; libref-l@kentvm.bitnet; 10 Apr 1993, 18:30:36] message id: <01GWVT7R7RE4A4M21X>; [16 lines].

Blumenthal, Caroline, Mary Jo Howard, and William R. Kinyon. "The Impact of CD-ROM Technology on a Bibliographic Instruction Program." *College & Research Libraries* 54 (January 1993), 11-16.

Cardman, Elizabeth R. "Gender Gap in Computer Use: Implications for Bibliographic Instruction." *Research Strategies* 8 (Summer 1990), 116-128.

Caren, Loretta. "New Bibliographic Instruction for New Technology: Library Connections' Seminar at the Rochester Institute of Technology." *Library Trends* 37 (Winter 1989), 366-373.

Frick, Elizabeth. "Humanizing Technology Through Instruction." *Canadian Library Journal* 41 (October 1984), 263-267.

Hallman, Clark N. "Technology: Trigger for Change in Reference Librarianship." *Journal of Academic Librarianship* 16 (September 1990), 204-208.

Heinzkill, Richard. "Electronic Resources Addictive." In LIBREF-L [listserve]. [Kent, OH: Reference Office, Kent State University Libraries; libref-l@kentvm.bitnet; 10 Apr 1993, 11:40:51] message id: <01GWUFC673ZOA4M21X>; [22 lines].

Heise, Jennifer. "RE: Electronic Resources Addictive." IN LIBREF-L [listserve]. [Kent, OH: Reference Office, Kent State University Libraries; libref-l@kentvm.bitnet; 13 Apr 1993, 18:08:17] message id: <01GWYZQCKB88A4M21X>; [33 lines]

Lowry, Anita Kay. "Beyond BI: Information Literacy in the Electronic Age." *Research Strategies* 8 (Winter 1990), 22-27.

MacDonald, Linda Brew. "Instruction for and with CD-ROM." In Linda Brew MacDonald, Mara R. Saule, Margaret W. Gordon, and Craig A. Robertson, eds., *Teaching Technologies in Libraries: A Practical Guide*. Boston, MA: G. K. Hall, 1990. Pp. 1-27.

MacDonald, Linda Brew, Mara R. Saule, Margaret W. Gordon, and Craig A. Robertson, eds. *Teaching Technologies in Libraries: A Practical Guide*. Boston, MA: G. K. Hall, 1990.

Moscoso, Purificación, and Ching-chih Chen. "Optical Technologies on Library Reference Work." *Microcomputers for Information Management* 7 (June 1990), 85-114.

Nipp, Deanna. "Back to Basics: Integrating CD-ROM Instruction with Standard User Education." *Research Strategies* 9 (Winter 1991), 41-47.

Roecker, Fred, and Thomas Minnick. "The Portal and The Gateway: Library Technology in the Freshman Survey Class at the Ohio State University." In Linda Shirato, ed., *Working with Faculty in the New Electronic Library: Papers and Session Materials Presented at the Nineteenth National LOEX Library Instruction Conference held at Eastern Michigan University 10 to 11 May 1991, and related resource materials gathered by the LOEX Clearinghouse*. Ann

Arbor, MI: Published for Learning Resources and Technologies, Eastern Michigan University by Pierian Press, 1992. Pp. 41-69.

Saule, Mara R. "Teaching for Library Technologies." In Linda Brew MacDonald, Mara R. Saule, Margaret W. Gordon, and Craig A. Robertson, eds., *Teaching Technologies in Libraries: A Practical Guide*. Boston, MA: G. K. Hall, 1990. Pp. 1-27.

Shill, Harold B. "Bibliographic Instruction: Planning for the Electronic Information Environment." *College & Research Libraries* 48 (September 1987), 433-453.

Shirato, Linda, ed. *Working with Faculty in the New Electronic Library: Papers and Session Materials Presented at the Nineteenth National LOEX Library Instruction Conference held at Eastern Michigan University 10 to 11 May 1991, and related resource materials gathered by the LOEX Clearinghouse*. Ann Arbor, MI: Published for Learning Resources and Technologies, Eastern Michigan University by Pierian Press, 1992.

Stern, Peter. "Coaxing the Historian into the New Information Age." *Colonial Latin American Review* 1 (1992), 201-221.

Tenopir, Carol, and Ralf Neufang. "The Impact of Electronic Reference on Reference Librarians." *Online* 16 (May 1992), 54-60.

Widman, Rudy, and Jimmie Anne Nourse. "Delivering Hi-Tech Library Instruction: A Hands-On Approach." *Laserdisk Professional* 2 (November 1989), 50-54.

Chinese Immigrant Communities in Central America and the Caribbean

27. Connecting East and West: The Chinese in Panama, 1850-1914

Nelly S. González

Panama . . . Pablo Neruda looked at his map and saw the slender waist of America. Anthropologists see it as a land bridge between the cultural groups of Mexico and South America. For Balboa in 1513, it was the path to personal glory and discovery of the Pacific Ocean.

Throughout history, Panama's geography has been its destiny. And this geography has also been the destiny of the many peoples—from North and South and from East and West—who have come to Panama. This paper concerns the destiny of one such people—the Chinese—who emigrated to Panama between the years 1850 and 1914.

The discussion covers the size, characteristics, and consequences of this migration, referring to academic studies on this subject. This essay aims, first, to evoke greater appreciation of human diversity in Latin America in general, and in Panama in particular. In the words of the Mexican philosopher José Vasconcelos, Latin America is the place where "a new race will come into being, made of the treasury of all the previous races, the final race, the cosmic race."[1] Second, the study attempts to provide a better understanding of the Chinese laborers' contribution to the building of the Interoceanic Railroad and the Panama Canal which connected the Pacific and Atlantic oceans. Third, the paper endeavors to share a sense of the lasting cultural contributions of the Chinese to Panamanian society.

During the mid-seventeenth century, Chinese started emigrating to the Western Hemisphere. The Manchus had overthrown the Ming dynasty and established the Ch'ing dynasty in 1644. The turmoil caused a great deal of suffering and desperation among the Chinese people. Hence, they began seeking a place where they could find work and better living conditions. Overseas Chinese emigration to Latin America comprises four important periods: (1) 1550-1850; (2) 1850-1900; (3) 1900-1950; and (4) 1950 to date.[2]

The abolition of the slave trade in the New World and the opening of China by Great Britain in the infamous Opium War created and shaped the Coolie Agency System.[3] Through the Agency, all Europeans in need of workers for their enterprises (plantations, mines, railroads, etc.) took advantage of the Treaty ports and created a system to supply needed laborers upon request. Thus, a successful new industry involving "coolie brokers" and "coolie trade centers" began. Between 1856 and 1872, thousands of "coolies" were shipped to the New World.[4]

The high demand for coolie laborers increased the high price paid for each of them—$3.00 per coolie, an amount that, according to a communication sent by Dr. Bowring to the Earl of Malmesbury on January 5, 1853, was "more than a month's pay for honest labor."[5] Abuses in labor contracts were the norm, and mistreatment of Chinese immigrants was common during their recruitment and transportation. There were many cases of decoy and kidnapping. To add to the already deplorable situation, "gambling and traps" were used in the process. For example, the laborers were deceived into thinking that they would be well paid and well treated.[6] The "coolies," a term given to Chinese emigrants,[7] were transported in dedicated ships which were generally overcrowded. The prospective laborers, both men and women, were allocated a small space to live and sleep.

The first recorded migration of Chinese workers to Panama took place in the period 1850-1855. Approximately 800 Chinese from Hong Kong arrived to work on the construction of the Panama Railroad. The railroad was built by an American company called Compañía del Ferrocarril de Panamá (Panama Railroad Company).[8]

The need for railroad construction was created by the extraordinary movement of people in search of a new life. In 1849 gold was discovered in California and Oregon and the news in Europe brought gold-seekers to the new goldfields. In moving from the East to the West coast of the Americas, people had to pass through Panama. The building of the railroad was intended to facilitate transportation.

The Panama Railroad Company, according to Newton, "constructed villages of stilted shacks in which workmen were grouped according to their nationality. The rationale for this separation was to avoid conflict since some groups displayed considerable hostility towards others."[9]

Moreover, Lancelot S. Lewis writes that "racial restrictions were placed on the workers by the railroad officials in compliance with requests from the Panamanian government."[10] With these restrictions, "the workers were not allowed to leave their work camps and if seen outside the camp they would be immediately sent back, or taken back by the police." One could conclude that "this isolation could easily have been the cause or one of the causes for the mass frustration among the Chinese who apparently loved their freedom of movement."[11]

The tales of horror of Chinese employment with the railroad company are represented by the deaths of so many of them. Perhaps as many as one-half of the workers died of malaria, yellow fever, or suicide.[12] According to Fessenden N. Otis, a place named Matachin "gave rise to the myth that the place was so named because of the many Chinese who lost their lives at this location, since the word 'mata' means to kill, and 'chino' means Chinese. But, besides the myth, the coincidence is that indeed the Matachin region had been a Spanish settlement as early as 1678."[13]

Initiated in 1850, the railroad was completed by 1855. Its construction had considerable economic significance. The railroad connected the Pacific and Atlantic oceans, and about 65 steamboats, 7 of them war boats, arrived into Panama Bay, generating rent of $26,000 with expenditures of only $16,000. This was a success for the new republic.[14]

The human price paid to build the railroad was great. C. Reginald Enock writes that "the sufferings and death of the greater number of 800 Chinese who were imported by the railway company as laborers on construction work, who embarked from their own country for the new land without any knowledge of the conditions which awaited them, are among the most terrible and pathetic in the history of Panama. Many committed suicide. . . . There is a tradition that every tie on the railway represented one human life lost. . . ."[15]

Upon completion of the railroad in 1855, several laborers became stranded in the isthmus of Panama.[16] It is estimated that during the first three months, 4,225 passengers arrived in 24 steamboats and 22 "veleros." From these, 1,721 passengers proceeded to the north in a span of only 24 hours.[17] The survivors scattered around the region, some staying in Panama and others going to Jamaica.[18] "Some settled and prospered in the larger cities of Colon and Panama City . . . others resumed their rural way of life in the interior towns of the country," according to C. Reginald Enock.[19] "Their descendants today are shown in the extraordinarily mixed population of the isthmus."

The construction of the Panama Canal followed the successful completion of the railroad. The first plan of the Canal was conceived by the French company the Société Civile Internationale du Canal Interocéanique, after the construction of the Suez Canal. They concentrated on making explorations and surveys, but bankruptcy halted their efforts. This was followed by the Panama Canal Company, which also failed and closed in 1887.[20] The French Campagnie Universelle then attempted to carry on the project and continued recruiting and importing Chinese laborers. Like many enormous enterprises, it was plagued with problems of organization and in the actual construction of the canal. Hence, this company's efforts were also a failure.

This paper addresses only the Chinese laborers' contribution to this engineering marvel. It does not describe the historical evolution of Panama as an independent nation nor the treaties and political maneuverings that culminated in Panama's secession from Colombia and the transfer of the administration of the Canal Zone to the United States "in perpetuity of the use and control of any other lands and waters outside the zone, which may be necessary and convenient for the construction, maintenance, operation, sanitation, and protection of the Canal."[21]

The building of the Canal began in earnest with the active participation of the United States under President Theodore Roosevelt. The failure of the previous enterprise owing to corruption, mismanagement, and poor work production provided strong support for a different managerial approach in the construction of the Canal. "A few days after the ratification of the treaty with Panama, a commission was appointed by President Theodore Roosevelt to undertake the organizational management of the work."[22]

This commission turned out to be unsatisfactory because of a lack of cooperation and understanding among its authorities. To remedy the situation, President Roosevelt, by exercise of executive authority, decided that administration and construction would be implemented by military engineers, and Colonel Goethals was appointed in full control as absolute administrator.[23]

The labor force during the first period of the Canal construction did not include Chinese laborers. At the beginning the intent was to import thousands of Chinese laborers, but there were enough workers from the West Indies and Europe. It was only after 1906 that "steps were taken to secure a supply of Chinese labour."[24] The completion of the Canal paralleled the railroad construction in the difficulties and miseries it brought to the Chinese workers. Many were stricken with yellow fever, malaria, and pneumonia especially during the rainy season.[25]

Further recruitment of Chinese into the labor force was hindered by American trade unions[26] and some Panamanians who regarded the Chinese as an economic threat.[27] Beginning with selling cheap food in restaurants for Canal employees,[28] the Chinese had ventured into the retail grocery business and were so successful that by 1940 "'going to the Chino's' was synonymous with 'going to the grocery store.'"[29] President Arnulfo Arias Madrid attempted to control Chinese retail activity through the nationalization of commerce which barred all foreigners from retail trade. Panamanians, however, were not attracted to this industry so there was no option but to let the Chinese, Jews, and Indians once again manage their small stores.[30]

Not only have the Chinese participated substantially in the construction of the two major Panamanian infrastructure projects (the railroad and the Canal), but they also have had a great influence in the daily life and social customs of Panama which has prevailed through the years. The legacy of Chinese culture is embedded in Panamanian lifestyle from its cuisine to its festivities, including the use of fireworks, parasols, and lanterns. Children play with beautiful kites inspired by Chinese designs which fly to the heavens, as if with a prayer for universal integration. It has "become evident that the world can not remain regionalized, as it has been before."[31]

In conclusion, it is clear that Chinese immigrants have played an important role in the economic and cultural development of Panama. The Interoceanic Railroad and the Panama Canal, major economic assets in Panamanian society, were constructed at the cost of extreme suffering and death of many Chinese. Moreover, the rich Chinese influence in the culture of Panama in particular, and of Latin America in general, is evident to this day. Such blending of two races and cultures represents vividly what José Vasconcelos refers to as the "final race, the cosmic race."[32]

NOTES

1. José Vasconcelos, *La raza cósmica* (Barcelona: Agencia Mundial de Liberación, 1942), p. 130.

2. Ainslie T. Embree, ed., *Encyclopedia of Asian History*, vol. 3 (New York, NY: Charles Scribner's Sons for the Asian Society, 1988), pp. 164-167.

3. Yen Ching-Hwang, *Coolies and Mandarins: China's Protection of Overseas Chinese During the Late Ch'ing Period (1851-1911)* (Singapore: Singapore University Press, 1985), p. 36.

4. Sing-wu Wang, *The Organization of Chinese Emigration, 1848-1888* (San Francisco, CA: Chinese Materials Center, 1978), p. 138.

5. *British Parliamentary Papers: Command Papers (1852-1853)*, no. 16, p. 433.

6. *The Organization of Chinese Emigration, 1848-1888*, pp. 59-60.

7. Samuel Wells Williams, *Chinese Emigration* (New York, NY: C. Scribner's Sons, 1879), p. 9.

8. Enrique José Arce and Ernesto J. Castillero, *Guía histórica de Panamá* (Panama: Editora Nacional, 1942), p. 94.

9. Velma Newton, *The Silver Men: West Indian Labour Migration to Panama 1850-1914* (Kingston: Institute of Social and Economic Research, University of the West Indies, 1984), p. 119.

10. Lancelot S. Lewis, *The West Indian in Panama: Black Labor in Panama, 1850-1914* (Washington, DC: University Press of America, 1980), p. 18.

11. *Star and Herald* (Panama: Star and Herald Press, September 4, 1854).

12. Ramón Arturo Mon Pinzón, "A Century of Chinese Immigration to Panama," in Luz M. Martínez Montiel, ed., *Asiatic Migrations in Latin America* (Mexico: El Colegio de México, 1981), pp. 22.

13. Fessenden N. Otis, *Isthmus of Panama: History of the Panama Railroad* (New York, NY: Harper Brothers Publishing Co., 1867), p. 133.

14. *Guía Histórica de Panamá*, p. 99.

15. C. Reginald Enock, *The Panama Canal (Its Past, Present, and Future)* (London and Glasgow: Collins' Clear-type Press, 1914), pp. 43-44.

16. *The West Indian in Panama: Black Labor in Panama, 1850-1914*, p. 20.

17. *Guía Histórica de Panamá*, p. 99.

18. Robert Tomes, *Panama in 1850* (New York, NY: Harper and Brothers, 1855), p. 121.

19. *The Panama Canal (Its Past, Present, and Future)*, p. 44.

20. Ibid., p. 69.

21. Ibid., p. 100.

22. Ibid., p. 105.

23. Ibid., p. 171.

24. Ibid., p. 185.

25. Jean Dorsenne, *La vie sentimentale de Paul Gauguin* (Paris: L'Artisan du Livre, 1927), pp. 51-52.

26. *The Panama Canal (Its Past, Present, and Future)*, p. 178.

27. *The Silver Men: West Indian Labour Migration to Panama 1850-1914*, p. 133.

28. Ibid., p. 133.

29. John Biesanz and Mavis Biesanz, *The People of Panama* (New York, NY: Columbia University Press, 1955), p. 102.

30. Jean G. Niemeier, *The Panama Story* (Portland, OR: Metropolitan Press, 1968), p. 196.

31. Manuel Gonzáles Galván, "Asian Influences in the Colonial Art of the Americas," in Ernesto de la Torre, ed., *Asia and Colonial Latin America* (Mexico: El Colegio de México, 1981), pp. 141-144.

32. *La raza cósmica*, p. 130.

SELECTIVE BIBLIOGRAPHY

Bibliographies

Bailey, Juan, and Freya Headlam. *Intercontinental Migration to Latin America: A Select Bibliography*. London: Institute of Latin American Studies, University of London, 1980.

Bibliografía especializada: Relaciones de Panamá con los Estados Unidos, Canal de Panamá. PanamA: Biblioteca Nacional de Panamá, Ministerio de Educación, 1977.

Bishop, Joseph Bucklin. *Goethels, Genius of the Panama Canal: A Bibliography*. New York; London: Harper & Brothers, 1930.

Bradley, Anita. *Trans-Pacific Relations of Latin America: An Introductory Essay and Selected Bibliography*. New York, NY: International Secretariat, Institute of Pacific Relations, 1942. Bibliography: pp. 83-108.

Bray, Wayne D. *The Controversy Over a New Canal Treaty Between the United States and Panama: A Selective Annotated Bibliography of United States, Panamanian, Colombian, French, and International Organization Sources*. Washington, DC: Library of Congress,

Superintendent of Documents, U.S. Government Printing Office, 1976.

Library of Congress. Division of Bibliography. *List of References on the Panama Canal and the Panama Canal Zone*. Washington, DC: n.p., 1919.

Handbooks, Dictionaries, and Encyclopedias

Encyclopedia of Asian History. Ainslie T. Embree, editor in chief. New York, NY: The Asia Society; Charles Scribner's Sons, 1988. V. 3, pp. 164-167.

Handbook of Latin American Studies. Gainesville: University of Florida Press.

Isthmian Canal Commission (U.S.). *Panama Canal, Official Handbook.* 3rd ed., rev. and enl. Ancon: 1913.

Indexes

Hispanic American Periodicals Index. Los Angeles: Latin American Center, University of California, Los Angeles, 1975–.

Historical Abstracts. Santa Barbara, CA: ABC-Clio, 1955–.

Monographs

Arce, Enrique José, and Ernesto J. Castillero. *Guía histórica de Panamá.* Panama: Editora Nacional, 1942.

Bakenhaus, Reuben Edwin. *The Panama Canal, Comprising Its History and Construction, and Its Relation to the Navy, International Law and Commerce*. New York, NY: n.p., 1915.

Barker, Samuel H. *The Panama Canal and Restoration of the American Merchant Marine*. Washington, DC: n.p., 1912.

Barrett, John. *Panama Canal, What It Is, What It Means . . .*. Washington, DC: Pan American Union, 1913. Brief bibliography, pp. 118-120.

Biesanz, John B., and Mavis Biesanz. *The People of Panama*. New York, NY: Columbia University Press, 1955.

Billot, Feliz. *L'ouverture du canal de Panamá et les interets des colonies françaises des antilles et d'oceanie*. Paris: n.p., 1913.

Bishop, Farnham. *Panama: Past and Present*. New York, NY: The Century Co., 1913.

Bishop, Joseph B. *Uncle Sam's Panama Canal and World History.* New York, NY: World Syndicate Co., 1913.

British Parliamentary Papers: Command Papers (1852-1853), no. 16.

Bullard, Arthur (Albert Edwards, pseud.). *Panama: The Canal, the Country, and the People*. New York, NY: The Macmillan Company, 1911.

Carlos, Rubén D. *Reminiscencias de los primeros años de la República de Panamá (1903-1912)*. Panama: La Estrella de Panamá, 1968.

Castillero Reyes, Ernesto de J. *Historia de la comunicación interoceánica y de su influencia en la formación en el desarrollo de la identidad nacional panameña*. Panama City: Imprenta Nacional, 1939.

Chidsey, Donald Barr. *The Panama Canal: An Informal History*. New York, NY: Crown Publishers, 1970.

Ching-Hwang, Yen. *Coolies and Mandarins: China's Protection of Overseas Chinese During the Late Ch'ing Period (1851-1911)*. Kent Ridge, Singapore: Singapore University Press, 1985.

Core, Susie Pearl. *Trails of Progress*, or, *The Story of Panama and Its Canal*. New York, NY: The Knickerbocker Press, 1925.

Dorsenne, Jean. *La vie sentimentale de Paul Gauguin*. Paris: L'Artisan du Livre, 1927.

Du Val, Miles Percy. *And the Mountains Will Move: The Story of the Building of the Panama Canal*. Stanford, CA: Stanford University Press; London: G. Cumberledge, Oxford University Press, 1947.

Enock, C. Reginald. *The Panama Canal (Its Past, Present, and Future)*. London and Glasgow: Collins' Clear-type Press, 1914.

Forbes-Lindsay, Charles H. *Panama, the Isthmus and the Canal*.

Fried, Morton H. *Colloquium on Overseas Chinese*. New York, NY: International Secretariat, Institute of Pacific Relations, 1958.

García, Rubén. *El Canal de Panamá y el ferrocarril de Tehuantepec*. Mexico: n.p., 1934.

Goethals, George Washington. *The Panama Canal*. N.p., n.d.

Gonzáles Galván, Manuel. "Asian Influences in the Colonial Art of the Americas." In Ernesto de la Torre, ed., *Asia and Colonial Latin America*. Mexico: El Colegio de México, 1981. Pp. 141-144.

Haskin, Frederic Jennings. *The Panama Canal*. Garden City: Doubleday Page, 1913.

Hopkins, Albert Allis. *Our Country and Its Resources*. New York, NY: Munn & Co., Inc., 1918.

Howarth, David. *Panama: Four Hundred Years of Dreams and Cruelty*. New York, NY: McGraw-Hill Book Company, 1966.

Lewis, Lancelot S. *The West Indian in Panama: Black Labor in Panama, 1850-1914*. Washington, DC: University Press of America, 1980. Pp. 17-20.

Lifton, Robert Jay. "On Psychohistory." In Herbert Bass, ed., *The State of American History*. Chicago: Quadrangle Books, 1970.

Marshall, Logan. *The Story of the Panama Canal*. Philadelphia: n.p., 1913.

McCullough, David G. *The Path Between the Seas: The Creation of the Panama Canal, 1870-1914*. New York, NY: Simon & Schuster, 1977.

Ministry of Foreign Affairs. *Annual Reports*. Panama City: Imprenta Nacional, 1904, 1906, 1910, 1912, 1914, 1916, 1918, 1922, 1942, and 1960.

Mon Pinzón, Ramón Arturo. "A Century of Chinese Immigration to Panama." In Luz M. Martínez Montiel, ed., *Asiatic Migrations in Latin America*. Mexico: El Colegio de México, 1981. Pp. 21-35.

Morner, Magnus. *Race Mixture in the History of Latin America*. Boston: Little, Brown and Company, 1967.

Newton, Velma. *The Silver Men: West Indian Labour Migration to Panama (1850-1914)*. Kingston: Institute of Social and Economic Research, University of the West Indies, 1984. Pp. 116-149.

Niemeier, Jean Gilbreath. *The Panama Story*. 1st ed. Portland, OR: Metropolitan Press, 1968.

Núñez, Enrique Bernardo. *La galera de Tiberio: Crónica del canal de Panamá*. Caracas: Dirección de Cultura, Universidad Central de Venezuela, 1967.

Otis, Frederic N. *A History of the Panama Railroad and of the Pacific Mail Steamship Company*. New York, NY: n.p., 1867.

The Panama Canal: Fiftieth Anniversary: The Story of a Great Conquest. Balboa Heights: Panama Canal Information Office, 1964.

Panama. Secretaría de Relaciones Exteriores. *Memoria*. Panama: n.p., 1907–?

Panama. Laws, Statutes, etc. The civil code of the Republic of Panama and Amendatory Laws continued in force in the Canal zone, Isthmus of Panama, by executive order of May 8, 1904. Washington, DC, 1905.

Panama-Pacific International Exposition Company. *Universal Exposition, 1915, Celebrating the Opening of the Panama Canal*. San Francisco, CA: n.p., 1915.

Papers relating to the construction of the Panama Canal. Washington, DC: n.p., 1909.

Payne, Fanny Ursula. *The Parted Sisters, an Allegorical Play in One Act*. New York, NY: n.p., 1914.

Pennell, Joseph. *Joseph Pennell's Pictures of the Panama Canal*. Philadelphia, PA: Lippincott, 1912.

Pepperman, Walter Leon. *Who Built the Panama Canal?* New York, NY: n.p., 1915.

Porras, Hernán. *Panamá, 50 años de República: El papel histórico de los grupos humanos en Panamá*. Panama City: n.p., 1953.

Reclus, Armand. *Exploraciones a los istmos de Panamá y Darian en 1876, 1877 y 1878*. San José: Editorial Universitaria Centroamericana, 1972.

Richard, Henry Earle. *The Panama Canal Controversy: A LectureDelivered Before the University of Oxford*. London: n.p., 1913.

Root, Elihu. *Panama Canal Tolls: Speech in Reply in the Senate of the United States*. Washington, DC: n.p., 1914.

Siber, William Luther. *The Construction of the Panama Canal*. New York, NY: n.p., 1915.

Smith, Darrell Hevenor. *The Panama Canal: Its History, Activities and Organization*. Baltimore, MD: John Hopkins Press, 1927.

Smith, William Alden. *Panama Canal Tolls: Speech in the Senate of the United States*. Washington, DC: n.p., 1914.

Special Publications and Documents. *Federal Compendia of Population*. Panama City: Statistics and Census Department.

Tomes, Robert. *Panama in 1855*. New York, NY: Harper and Brothers, 1855.

Tracy, Edith Hastings. *The Panama Canal During Construction*. New York, NY: n.p., 1914.

United States. Isthmian Canal Commission. *Letter from the Isthmian Canal Commission to the Advisory Board of Engineers Upon Plans for the Panama Canal*. Washington, DC: n.p., 1905.

United States. President (1901-1909: Roosevelt). *Message of the President on the Panama Canal Communicated to the Two Houses of Congress*. December 17, 1906; Milwaukee, 1907.

United States Congress. Senate Committee on Interoceanic Canals. *The Panama Canal*. Washington, DC: n.p., 1912.

United States Congress. House Committee on Interstate and Foreign Commerce. *The Panama Canal*. Washington, DC: n.p., 1912.

Vasconcelos, José. *La raza cósmica*. Barcelona: Agencia Mundial de Liberación, 1942.

Wang, Sing-wu. *The Organization of Chinese Emigration, 1848-1888*. San Francisco, CA: Chinese Materials Center, 1978.

Williams, Samuel Wells. *Chinese Emigration*. New York, NY: C. Scribner's Sons, 1879.

Theses and Dissertations

Agrioyanis, José. "El movimiento migratorio de Panamá y su aporte económico." Ph.D. dissertation, University of Panama, 1954-1955.

Cobamanos, Mireya, and Edda Dutury. "El istmo de Panamá: Historia del ferrocarril nacional by F.N. Otis (N.Y., 1867)." Ph.D. dissertation, University of Panama, 1968.

Delgado, Nicolás. "Inmigración, estudio socio jurídico." Ph.D. dissertation, University of Panama, 1970-1971.

García Aponte, Isaías. "Autenticidad e inautenticidad en lo Panameño." Master's thesis, University of Panama, 1953-1954.

Hoffman, Irlanda de. "Algunas características de la autopercepción del Panameño." Master's thesis, University of Santa María la Antigua, 1975.

Jímenez, Javier O. "La inmigración en Panamá desde 1904." Master's thesis, University of Panama, 1975.

Meagher, Arnold Joseph. "The Introduction of Chinese Laborers to Latin America: The 'Coolie Trade': 1847-1874." Ph.D. dissertation, University of California, Davis.

Solís, Didia, and Bolívar Pinto. "La colonia China de Panamá: Un estudio histórico y social." Ph.D. dissertation, University of Panama, n.d.

Vásquez, Dora Alicia de. "Un estudio transcultural en tres grupos de niños Panameños (Caribbean, Chinese and Farmers' Ancestors)." Master's thesis, University of Santa María la Antigua, 1975.

28. Chinese Immigration to Mexico from the Nineteenth Century to 1911

Karen T. Wei

Migration of the Chinese to foreign lands has had a long-standing history. Continuous overseas migration and settlement in significant numbers, however, did not occur until the sixteenth century. While the majority of the Chinese migrants settled in Southeast Asia, a small number found their way to the West and Mexico via the Manila galleon before the mid-nineteenth century.[1] During the second half of the nineteenth century demands for labor in newly discovered gold mines, railroad construction, and plantation interests attracted large numbers of Chinese to the United States and Latin America, and some of these later migrated to Mexico. The number of Chinese settled in Mexico only became significant, however, after the Mexican and Chinese governments signed the Treaty of Amity and Commerce in 1899, permitting free immigration between the two countries.[2]

This paper traces the history of Chinese immigration to Mexico from the nineteenth century to 1911, the end of the Porfirio Díaz regime; surveys the distribution of the Chinese in the country; and explores the social and economic status of the Chinese in Mexican society. I also discuss the anti-Chinese campaign in Mexico and its impact on Chinese immigrants.

History of Chinese Immigration to Mexico

During the course of Chinese history, the Imperial government of China never encouraged emigration of her subjects to foreign countries. On the contrary, Imperial decrees prohibited such movement, and penalties were imposed on those who sought to leave. China, however, consistently maintained foreign contacts throughout her long history. In 1870, restrictions on settling abroad were removed and the migration of Chinese became active.[3] The large migration of the Chinese in the nineteenth century can be attributed to population pressures on resources, scarcity of tillable land, and disruption of the economy. A series of historical events leading toward the poor living conditions in China included the Opium War, the T'ai-ping Rebellion, the Yunnan Rebellion, the Sinkiang Revolt, and various natural disasters. As a result, the Chinese people, particularly those residing along the coastal provinces who had had contact with foreigners since the late

Ming dynasty in the mid-seventeenth century, sought to leave their unstable homeland and seek better economic opportunities in foreign countries.

Trans-Pacific contacts with the New World were opened when Miguel López de Legaspi, an explorer supported by the court of the Spanish King Philip I, was sent to establish contact with China. Legaspi sailed from New Spain to the Philippines in 1564, and, although not entirely successful in his expedition, discovered that Chinese ships sailed frequently to the Philippines.[4] It was obvious that the Philippines would be important in trans-Pacific relations since the Philippine city of Manila was used as a base for merchants and missionary expeditions to the Asiatic continents. Ever since then one of the most important routes between the western world and the Far East passed from Mexico to Manila.[5]

Nao de la China and Galéon de Manila, Spanish ships which carried commercial goods, military supplies, and missionaries, sailed between Acapulco and Manila on a regular basis and from there to China and other regions of the Far East.[6] The galleons carried valuable goods—mainly silk, brocades, linen, tea, porcelains, perfumes, and spices—to the West and on return trips carried silver bullion exported from Peru and Mexico. Many Chinese sailors who served with the crew of the Manila galleons became the first Chinese to reach Mexico, and a few of them actually remained settled in the New World during the Spanish Colonial period,[7] that is, the seventeenth century, when Mexico was still a colony of Spain.

The galleon trade between Acapulco and Manila which dominated the trans-Pacific routes during the sixteenth, seventeenth, and eighteenth centuries came to an end around 1815 when Spain lost control of her colonies.[8] Other European vessels continued serving the Orient and America. The movement of luxury items from the Far East to Latin America became less important, however, and was gradually replaced by the movement of Asian laborers and coolies. The supply of Negro slaves from Africa had been cut off, and the demands of Latin American mines and plantation interests were high. It was estimated that in the mid-nineteenth century between a quarter to a half a million Chinese laborers were sent to Peru, Cuba, Chile, and the Hawaiian Islands.[9]

Following the wars for independence from Spain, Mexico was in constant turmoil for fifty years until Porfirio Díaz took control in 1877. President Díaz strongly promoted economic development by welcoming foreigners and foreign capital. He firmly believed that foreign investment, technology, and labor were essential to the rapid economic development of Mexico. Díaz therefore encouraged immigration in order to provide the necessary capital and labor for mining, railroad construction, and agriculture.[10] The Chinese began arriving on Mexican soil in considerable numbers during this time, coinciding with the regime of Porfirio Díaz (1877-1911).

The growth of the Chinese immigrant population in Mexico accelerated when the United States government passed the Chinese Exclusion Act of 1882. Although during the same period Chinese immigration to other Latin American countries such as Cuba, Peru, and Colombia was quite large, the Chinese population in Mexico was never significant until 1899, when the governments of Mexico and China signed the Sino-Mexican Treaty of Amity and Commerce, allowing free immigration and travel between the two countries. Mexico and China also agreed to allow immigrants to work as laborers or to engage in commerce without restrictions. As a result, the Chinese immigrants became more noticeable and their numbers expanded rapidly.

Survey of the Distribution of Chinese in Mexico

The majority of the Chinese arriving in Mexico settled in the northern states and were concentrated in bigger cities. There were also varying numbers of Chinese in other parts of the country. The following section is a brief survey of the distribution of the Chinese in Mexico.

The first Chinese to arrive in Mexico were tradesmen and crewmen in service on ships of the Manila galleon during the Spanish colonial period. Entering from the port of Acapulco, the number of people who actually settled there was insignificant. In the seventeenth century, a small number of Chinese arrived in Mexico and opened businesses such as barber shops in Mexico City before 1635.[11] Again, the number was too small to be noticeable. In the last quarter of the nineteenth century, however, Chinese immigrants, in response to the demands for laborers in mining, railroads, and plantation interests, and escaping the turmoil and poor living conditions in China, began to arrive on the coast of Mexico, entering through the Pacific coasts ports of Mazatlán and Guaymas.[12] The number of Chinese immigrants began to increase in 1882 when the United States issued the Chinese Exclusion Act, terminating Chinese immigration to the United States. Because of the proximity of northern Mexico to the United States, many Chinese migrated south of the U.S. border to enter into northern Mexico for settlement. In 1899, the governments of Mexico and China signed the Treaty of Amity and Commerce, allowing Chinese complete freedom to live and work in Mexico. There was a great demand at the time for industrious Chinese workers in mining, plantations, and railroad construction. The Chinese immigrants to Mexico thus became more significant and more widely spread throughout the country.

In 1890, Sonora recorded 229 Chinese in the total population of 56,000. In 1893, there were Chinese reported in Baja California, Sinaloa,

Chihuahua, Tamaulipas, Coahuila, and Sonora.[13] It was estimated that there were around 900 Chinese residing in Mexico in 1895. The census of 1900 indicated about 2,700 Chinese; by 1910, the number had increased to more than 13,000 (some estimated between 20,000 to 40,000); and by 1930, nearly 19,000 were recorded, and Chinese formed the second largest foreign group in Mexico, next to the Americans.[14] The distribution of the Chinese was uneven, concentrated mainly in northern states with Sonora consistently ranked first among all the states reported owing to its close proximity to the United States. Through the years the states with the most Chinese population included Sonora, Chihuahua, Sinaloa, Coahuila, and Baja California. Chinese also resided in the southern states of Yucatán and Oaxaca. The Chinese population in other areas was very sparse.

One very distinct feature of the Chinese population in Mexico was that the majority were young males, while female immigrants from China were very few. Over the years, female immigrants comprised only between 6 and 14 percent of the total Chinese immigrant population. As a result, intermarriages between Chinese male immigrants and Mexican females occurred during the early years before a prohibition on such unions was established in the twentieth century.[15]

Social and Economic Status of the Chinese in Mexico

When the Chinese came to Mexico in the latter part of the nineteenth century, they were expected to replace the Negro slaves as coolies or contract laborers in mines, railroad construction, and plantations. Unlike their counterparts in the American West and in other Latin American countries, however, many of the Chinese in Mexico did not take the laboring jobs. Instead, with small amounts of capital, they engaged in trade and commerce as independent entrepreneurs. Those who came and sought work on the railroads, mines, and plantations also progressed gradually into the sale of vegetables and fruit and invested in the wholesale and retail grocery trade.[16]

In 1890, by taking advantage of the frontier development needs, Chinese were very prominent in many shoe and rough clothing businesses, laundries, and gardening services. By 1900, they had moved into wholesale and retail grocery and drygoods businesses, controlling essential necessities via grocery trade. They also participated actively in local economies by contributing substantially to local tax revenues.[17] Nonetheless, Chinese entrepreneurs, though hard working and law abiding, were not particularly welcome by local Mexicans. Instead, when the Chinese began to prosper, although modestly, many Mexicans considered them a threat for the following reasons: (1) while the other immigrants from North America and Europe and some wealthy Mexicans were in control of the big businesses such as the mines, the Chinese controlled many small businesses which the Mexicans regarded as within their reach; (2) while Mexican businessmen operated independently, Chinese businessmen formed a large international network that connected them to sources of credit and merchandise; (3) Chinese businesses were generally well stocked with large quantities and more varieties of merchandise and could therefore undersell their Mexican counterparts; (4) the Chinese who controlled laundries and gardening were viewed as taking away work from Mexican women; (5) the Chinese did not employ enough Mexicans in their businesses; and (6) the prominence and prosperity of the Chinese in the local economy, particularly in northern Mexico, was an embarrassment in the wake of increased Mexican nationalism.

As in the case of Chinese immigrants in other parts of the world, the close correlation between the economic situation of the Chinese and the anti-Chinese agitation in Mexico was no surprise. The resentment culminated in the anti-Chinese movement during the Mexican Revolution. When the Díaz regime was unseated in 1911, protection of foreigners also diminished. The forces of the Revolutionary leader Francisco Madero attacked northern Mexico in the hope of eliminating Díaz's power; the mob that accompanied the forces slaughtered more than 300 Chinese in Torreón, Coahuila, on May 13, 1911.[18] The massacre discouraged Chinese immigration into the area and the effect of the attack lingered on.

During the two decades following the tragic event, anti-foreign demonstrations became more heated. In 1931, the hostility toward the Chinese, compounded by the Great Depression, led to the expulsion of the Chinese from Sonora, the largest Chinese colony in Mexico. The Chinese immigrants in Mexico never recovered from these devastating incidents.

Like other immigrants, the Chinese suffered the impact of the revolution. There were losses of life and property and the Chinese presence in Mexico diminished. After a prosperous beginning, Chinese immigrants in Mexico were quickly expelled during hard times, as they became targets of aggression during the Mexican Revolution and the Depression.

NOTES

1. Edgar Wickberg, "Overseas Chinese," in Ainslie T. Embree, ed., *Encyclopedia of Asian History*, vol. 3 (New York, NY: The Asia Society; Charles Scribner's Sons, 1988), pp. 164-167.

2. Chien-ch'eng Yang, ed., *Chung-hua Min Tsu Chih Hai Wai Fa Chan* (Taipei: Chung-hua hsüeh Shu Yüan Nan-yang Yen Chiu So, 1983), pp. 217-218.

3. Anita Bradley, *Trans-Pacific Relations of Latin America* (New York, NY: Institute of Pacific Relations, 1942), pp. 65-66.

4. Eugenio Chang-Rodríguez, "Chinese Labor Immigration into Latin America in the Nineteenth Century," *Revista de Historia de América* 46 (December 1958), 375-397.

5. Lino Gómez Canedo, "Mexican Sources for the History of the Far East Missions," in Ernesto de la Torre, ed., *Asia and Colonial Latin America*, XXX International Congress of Human Sciences in Asia and North America, Mexico City, Mexico, August 3-8, 1976 (Mexico City: El Colegio de México, 1981), pp. 7-19.

6. Gómez Canedo, pp. 7-19.

7. Chang-Rodríguez, p. 377.

8. Bradley, p. 10.

9. Magnus Mörner, *Race Mixture in the History of Latin America* (Boston, MA: Brown & Co., 1967), pp. 131-132.

10. Leo M. Jacques, "Have Quick More Money Than Mandarins: The Chinese in Sonora," *Journal of Arizona History* 17:2 (Summer 1976), 201-218.

11. Homer H. Dubs and Robert S. Smith, "Chinese in Mexico City in 1635," *Far Eastern Quarterly* 1:4 (August 1942), 387-389.

12. Evelyn Hu-DeHart, "Coolies, Shopkeepers, Pioneers: The Chinese of Mexico and Peru (1849-1930)," *Amerasia Journal* 15:2 (1989), 91-116.

13. Evelyn Hu-DeHart, "Immigrants to a Developing Society: The Chinese in Northern Mexico, 1875-1932," *Journal of Arizona History* 21:3 (Autumn 1980), 275-312.

14. Bradley, p. 62.

15. Hu-DeHart, "Immigrants," p. 302.

16. Hu-Dehart, "Coolies," p. 97.

17. Leo M. Jacques, "Chinese Merchants in Sonora, 1900-1931," in Luz M. Martínez Montiel, ed., *Asiatic Migrations in Latin America*, XXX International Congress of Human Sciences in Asia and North America, Mexico City, Mexico, August 3-8, 1976 (Mexico City: El Colegio de México, 1981), pp. 13-20.

18. Leo M. Dambourges Jacques, "The Chinese Massacre in Torreón (Coahuila) in 1911," *Arizona and the West* 16:3 (Autumn 1974), 233-246.

BIBLIOGRAPHY

Bradley, Anita. *Trans-Pacific Relations of Latin America*. New York, NY: Institute of Pacific Relations, 1942.

Chang-Rodríguez, Eugenio. "Chinese Labor Migration into Latin America in the Nineteenth Century." *Revista de Historia de América* 46 (December 1958), 375-397.

Cumberland, Charles C. "The Sonora Chinese and the Mexican Revolution." *Hispanic American Historical Review* 40:2 (May 1960), 191-211.

Dubs, Homer H., and Robert S. Smith. "Chinese in Mexico City in 1635." *Far Eastern Quarterly* 1:4 (August 1942), 387-389.

Embree, Ainslie T., ed. *Encyclopedia of Asian History*. Vol. 3. New York, NY: The Asia Society; Charles Scribner's Sons, 1988.

Gómez Canedo, Lino. "Mexican Sources for the History of the Far East Missions." In Ernesto de la Torre, ed., *Asia and Colonial*

Latin America. XXX International Congress of Human Sciences in Asia and North America, Mexico City, Mexico, August 3-8, 1976. Mexico City: El Colegio de México, 1981. Pp. 7-19.

Hu-DeHart, Evelyn. "Coolies, Shopkeepers, Pioneers: The Chinese of Mexico and Peru (1849-1930)." *Amerasian Journal* 15:2 (1989), 91-116.

———. "Immigrants to a Developing Society: The Chinese in Northern Mexico, 1875-1932." *Journal of Arizona History* 21:3 (Autumn 1980), 275-312.

———. "Racism and Anti-Chinese Persecution in Sonora, Mexico, 1876-1932." *Amerasia Journal* 9:2 (Fall/Winter 1982), 1-28.

Jacques, Leo M. "The Anti-Chinese Campaign in Sonora, Mexico, 1900-1931." Ph.D. dissertation, University of Arizona, 1974.

———. "The Chinese Massacre in Torreón (Coahuila) in 1911." *Arizona and the West* 16:3 (Autumn 1974), 233-246.

———. "Chinese Merchants in Sonora, 1900-1931." In Luz M. Martínez Montiel, ed., *Asiatic Migrations in Latin America*. XXX International Congress of Human Sciences in Asia and North America, Mexico City, Mexico, August 3-8, 1976. Mexico City: El Colegio de México, 1981. Pp. 13-20.

———. "Have Quick More Money Than Mandarins: The Chinese in Sonora." *Journal of Arizona History* 17:2 (Summer 1976), 201-218.

Jamieson, Tulitas. *Tulitas of Torreón: Reminiscences of Life in Mexico*. El Paso: Texas Western Press, 1969.

Lo, Jung-pang. *K'ang Yu-wei: A Biography and a Symposium*. Tucson: University of Arizona Press for the AAS, 1967.

Martínez Montiel, Luz María. *Asiatic Migrations in Latin America*. XXX International Congress of Human Sciences in Asia and North America, Mexico City, Mexico, August 3-8, 1976. Mexico City: El Colegio de México, 1981.

Meagher, Arnold J. "The Introduction of Chinese Laborers to Latin America: The 'Coolie Trade,' 1847-1874." Ph.D. dissertation, University of California, Davis, 1975.

Mörner, Magnus. *Race Mixture in the History of Latin America*. Boston, MA: Little, Brown & Co., 1967.

Sanderson, Susan, Phil Sidel, and Harold Sims. "East Asians and Arabs in Mexico: A Study of Naturalized Citizens (1886-1931)." In Luz M. Martínez Montiel, ed., *Asiatic Migrations in Latin America*. XXX International Congress of Human Sciences in Asia and North

America, Mexico City, Mexico, August 3-8, 1976. Mexico City: El Colegio de México, 1981. Pp. 173-186.

Torre, Ernesto de la, ed. *Asia and Colonial Latin America.* XXX International Congress of Human Sciences in Asia and North America, Mexico City, Mexico, August 3-8, 1976. Mexico City: El Colegio de México, 1981.

Turner, John Kenneth. *Barbarous Mexico.* Austin: University of Texas Press, 1969.

Wallace, Mildred Young. "I Remember Chung." *Journal of Arizona History* 20:1 (Spring 1979), 35-46.

Wickberg, Edgar. "Overseas Chinese." In Ainslie T. Embree, ed., *Encyclopedia of Asian History.* Vol. 3. New York, NY: The Asia Society; Charles Scribner's Sons, 1988. Pp. 164-167.

Yang, Chien-ch'eng, ed. *Chung-hua Min Tsu Chih Hai Wai Fa Chan.* Taipei: Chung-hua Hsüeh Shu Yüan Nan-Yang Yen Chiu So, 1983.

29. Chinese Immigration to the Caribbean

Joyce C. Wright

The Chinese in the Caribbean

Nowhere in the world has the mixing of races been as widespread as in the Caribbean since 1492. One may ask, Why the interest in Chinese immigrants? Having recently celebrated the five hundredth anniversary of the Encounter with the Americas, it is fitting to explore the impact of the Chinese in Caribbean society.

This paper presents an overview of Chinese immigration to the region. According to Knight and Palmer (1989), the Caribbean is a diverse region. Since that fateful event in 1492, the region has oscillated between the center and the periphery of international affairs, sometimes the victim of "benign neglect," other times the venue for the flexing of American military muscle to subdue legitimate local aspirations or score points in an extra-regional geopolitical rivalry between the superpowers. International interest in the Caribbean has intensified and waned with predictable regularity. Its historical trajectory permanently impressed by the twin experiences of colonialism and slavery, the Caribbean has produced an unusual collection of societies with a population mélange that differs from that in any other region in the world. There, Europeans, Native Americans, Africans, and Asians came together to create a new society, a new economy, and a new culture, an eclectic blend of all its components. Chinese immigration to the Caribbean flourished during the mid-seventeenth century, partly as a consequence of the political upheaval in China, when the Manchus overthrew the Ming dynasty and established the Ch'ing dynasty in 1644. Because the turmoil caused a great deal of suffering and desperation, the Chinese people began to emigrate from their homeland in search of work that would enable them to make a small fortune and then return to China. Today the Chinese heritage is deeply imbedded in Caribbean culture and its legacy is evident in both the daily life and social customs of the region.

Several studies have addressed the subject of Chinese immigration to the Caribbean. Apparently, an influx of Chinese shopkeepers settled in Jamaica (see Johnson 1983). Bonaich (1973) provides a useful overview of Asian immigrant entrepreneurs in the United States, in which she focuses on the important economic role of Asian immigrants. In contrast to most ethnic minorities, they occupy an intermediate rather than low-status position. They tend to hold positions in trade and commerce, and as other "middlemen" such as agent, labor contractor, rent collector, money lender, and broker. They play the role of middleman between producer and consumer, employer and employee, owner and renter, elite and masses.

Evelyn Hu-DeHart's research reveals that

> Chinese immigrants in parts of Jamaica were instrumental in developing agriculture in frontier areas and virgin land. Most importantly, in creating modern commercial infrastructure where none, or only very rudimentary forms had existed. This particular role that the Chinese carved for themselves throughout the Caribbean cast them the role of "middleman minorities," whereby they occupy a middle stratum between an elite (local or foreign) and the native masses (Hu-DeHart, n.d.).

The Chinese in Jamaica illustrate business competition with a subordinate group. According to Lind (1958:156), "The establishment of Chinese grocery shops had extended throughout the island prior to 1911 and had thus brought vividly to the attention of the entire population that these once humble laborers were displacing the native Jamaicans as the shopkeepers of the country."

Like any foreigner who arrives to new soil, the Chinese were quick to recognize and exploit new economic opportunities created by land and natural resource development, the transformation of peasants into wage laborers, and the subsequent expansion of the local consumer market. For example, in Mexico and Peru, they were ambitious shopkeepers and were given the name "Chino" which has become synonymous with the corner grocer. This term is also prevalent in the United States, especially in large cities such as New York, Boston, Chicago, San Francisco, and Los Angeles.

Hurwitz and Hurwitz (1971) reported that a majority of Chinese immigrated to Jamaica between 1911 and 1921, and they came in far fewer numbers. In 1921, Chinese numbered 3,696 as compared to 18,600 East Indians. The East Indians, by and large, remained in agriculture, but the Chinese almost immediately sought commercial occupations. They dominated the grocery trade for many decades in North Kingston and the rural parts of the island. In 1943, more than 75 percent of the Chinese population of 12,394 were engaged in trade, white-collar, manufacturing, and service occupations, with more than half in trade alone. Today the ethnic Chinese population is over 25,000 in Jamaica, 20,000 in Trinidad, and 10,000 in Guyana.

Brereton (1989) calls the Chinese the "Newer Immigrant." Like the Indians, Chinese laborers were imported to work on the plantations. They brought their own language and culture. Some adopted Christianity and mixed freely with Creoles, while others held on to traditional cultural patterns into the mid-twentieth century. Throughout the Caribbean the "Chinese shopman" is a common figure.

Overseas Chinese Nationals and People of Chinese Origin

There are approximately twenty million Chinese nationals and people of Chinese origin residing outside of China. It is generally agreed that most of them, 17-18 million, are in Southeast Asia. Nearly 300,000 are in other parts of Asia. There are about 3 million in North and South America, less than 300,000 in Europe, and some 170,000 in Oceania. Africa and the Caribbean have the smallest Chinese community (Brereton 1989:96).

Overseas Chinese Contributions to Their Countries of Residence

The peaceful nature of Chinese immigration was clearly demonstrated by their pursuits in the countries of residence. The early immigrants sailed southward and brought goods and skills. They cultivated cash crops such as tea, sugarcane, and mulberry; employed techniques for processing tea and sugar, and for silk-reeling, silk-weaving, and farming; and manufactured farm tools (James 1989:1369).

Wherever they went overseas, the Chinese opened up the wilderness, flattened hills and filled gullies, dug ditches, paved roads, reclaimed land, and opened mines, turning wastelands and thick forests into thriving farms and towns, with blood and sweat. They joined local workers of different ethnic groups in developing the tea plantations in Java, tobacco and and pepper plantations in Sumatra, tin mines in Gbanga and Belitung, rubber plantations in Malaya, farmlands in Sorwak and South Vietnam, sugar plantations in Hawaii, vegetable gardens in Brazil, plantations in Guyana and Chile, cotton fields in Mexico, the Amur gold mine in Russia, the port of Vladivostok, the Siberian railway, and gold mines in South Africa, Australia, and New Zealand. In the United States and Canada, one still sees dwelling houses of overseas Chinese workers who engaged in mining or gold-panning. Railways in the United States and Canada bear historical witness to the contributions made by overseas Chinese workers to the countries of residence (James 1989:1370).

Many Chinese immigrants became petty traders who helped stimulate the urban and rural economies. They went into remote mountain areas to purchase local products and transported them to towns for processing or export. In turn, they brought daily necessities to underdeveloped, barely accessible peasant villages. They were quite popular among the local people. During a visit to Jamaica in 1991, a tour guide commented that "the Chinese are highly visible and an indispensable part of the working person's daily struggle for survival."

Over the years, the Chinese have been respected for their industriousness, dedication, and skills. The question for Caribbean and Asian scholars is, Why were Chinese immigrants brought to the Caribbean region? Some historians believe that, like the Indians and Portuguese laborers, they were brought in to further divide the society. As Brereton states, the Chinese, Indians, and Portuguese would always "stand by the whites" (1989:96).

Conclusion

The presence of Chinese in the Caribbean region today is not the result of any expansionist design on their part. On the contrary, the vast majority left China because foreign invasions, civil war, political disorder, and intractable economic problems made living in, or returning to, China unattractive if not impossible. Both Chinese and foreign historians agree that as far back as ancient times, Chinese left China to work or to settle abroad.

BIBLIOGRAPHY

Bonaich, Edna. 1973. "A Theory of Middleman Minorities." *American Sociological Review* 38:583-594.

Brereton, Bridget. 1989. "Society and Culture in the Caribbean." In Franklin W. Knight and Colin A. Palmer, eds., *The Modern Caribbean.* Chapel Hill: University of North Carolina Press.

Hu-Dehart, Evelyn. N.d. "From Area Studies to Ethnic Studies: The Study of the Chinese Diaspora in Latin America.

Hurwitz, Samuel, and Edith F. Hurwitz. 1971. *Jamaica: A Historical Portrait.* New York, NY: Praeger Publishers.

James, C. V. 1989. *Information China: The Comprehensive and Authoritative Reference Source of New China.* Compiled and translated by The Chinese Academy of Social Sciences. New York, NY: Pergamon Press.

Johnson, Howard. 1983. "The Anti-Chinese Riots of 1918 in Jamaica." *Immigrants and Minorities* 2:50-63.

Knight, Franklin B., and Colin A. Palmer. 1989. "The Caribbean: A Regional Overview." In *The Modern Caribbean.* Chapel Hill: University of North Carolina Press.

Lind, Andrew. 1958. "Adjustment Patterns Among Jamaican Chinese." *Social and Economic Studies* (University College of the West Indies) 7 (June), 144-164.

30. Los chinos en Cuba, 1847-1959

Rosa Q. Mesa

El movimiento de chinos en el Hemisferio Occidental ha sido tratado en términos de la experiencia de California, pero muy poco se ha estudiado con respecto a la inmigración china a otras partes de América como Cuba, Perú y las Indias Occidentales Británicas. Este movimiento incluyó un cuarto de millón de personas. Aproximadamente 125,000, o sea el 48%, fueron a Cuba. Cerca de 100,000, o sea el 38%, fueron a Perú, y 18,000 (18%) fueron a las Indias Occidentales Británicas. El resto fue a las Indias Occidentales Holandesas y Francesas, a Brasil y a Chile.

Al iniciarse la década de 1840, la falta de esclavos había hecho crisis en la industria azucarera cubana. Muchos esclavos habían alcanzado su libertad al expirar los doce años fijados por la Real Cédula de 1838. Su importación clandestina era en extremo difícil y el precio del esclavo se había elevado a cantidades incosteables.

Para algunos historiadores fue Francisco Diago, dueño del ingenio "Tinguaro", con la cooperación de Francisco Pairós Herrera, el que puso en práctica el proyecto de Manuel B. Pereda de introducir trabajadores chinos. Otros historiadores mencionan a Julián de Zulueta, un comerciante español, el que realizó la gestión decisiva y quien abrió el camino a la introducción de emigrantes asiáticos. Hubiere sido uno o el otro el autor de la idea, lo cierto fue que en junio de 1847 llegó al puerto de La Habana el primer cargamento de 574 chinos procedentes del puerto de Amoy. En este lejano lugar del continente asiático se había producido un levantamiento popular contra los señores feudales de la zona, la rebelión había fracasado y las cárceles políticas estaban llenas de rebeldes.

Julián de Zulueta entró en contacto con altos funcionarios de la Dinastía de Fukien y pagó un buen precio por cada prisionero de guerra que le vendieran bajo contrato firmado y con un salario de cuatro pesos mensuales. Los primeros chinos llegaron al Puerto de La Habana en los bergantines españoles "El Oquendo" y "El Delfín". Estos primeros chinos llegados a Cuba era una pequeña parte de los complotados en una conspiración contra los señores feudales de Fukien e iniciaron la adición de otro elemento étnico a la población de la Isla, ya racialmente dividida.

La presencia de los chinos, conducidos en condiciones de lamentable servidumbre a pesar de su origen de hombres libres, es fácil de explicar. En primer lugar, aunque la inmigración china era radicalmente ilegítima, pues las leyes de su país la prohibían, la venalidad de los funcionarios de China y el deseo de emigrar de una gran parte de la población empobrecida y numerosa, hizo fácil contratar a los chinos del sur del país, particularmente en las áreas de Cantón y de Amoy. En segundo lugar, a pesar de ser una inmigración de asiáticos, fue auspiciada por la Comisión de Población Blanca de la Junta de Fomento de España. En tercer lugar, debido a la persecución de la trata africana por Gran Bretaña, se había agravado la crisis de brazos en la Isla. Gran Bretaña contribuyó a la trata de chinos indirectamente al abrir a cañonazos el comercio con China (1841-1844) y directamente aportando barcos e intermediarios comerciales para la contratación de los colonos y su conducción a Cuba hasta 1860.

El origen de la expresión "Coolie" (o culí en castellano) es oscuro, pero algunos historiadores están de acuerdo en que es de origen indio y viene del bengali "Kuli" o del hindú "quilí", ambas palabras con significado de "trabajador a sueldo". Se piensa que los ingleses, después de la ocupación de Hong Kong, trajeron la expresión desde la India. De Hong Kong el uso del término se extendió rápidamente.

Dos años después del arribo de los primeros culíes, ya se confrontaban dificultades y fugas de chinos dada la dureza de los trabajos. En abril de 1849, Federico Roncalli, gobernador de Cuba, promulgó un Reglamento mediante el cual se establecían y aplicaban sanciones y castigos corporales a los asiáticos que se rebelaban contra los trabajos impuestos. El Reglamento de Roncalli provocó una confrontación con la Audiencia de Puerto Príncipe, la que determinó que el gobernador carecía de facultades para establecer castigos corporales. La audiencia alegaba que los asiáticos no eran esclavos sino trabajadores libres, aunque en la práctica se equiparaba al colono con el esclavo.

En la *Revista Económica* que se publicaba en La Habana, se estimaba que entre 1853 y 1874 habían llegado a Cuba 124,835 chinos, de los cuales 95, 631 procedían de Macao y el resto de Swatow, Amoy, Cantón, Whampoa, Hong Kong, Saigón y Manila. El ministro inglés en Madrid, Lord Lowden, se dirigió al Ministro de Relaciones Externas de España el 6 de junio de 1854 señalando que en el Real Decreto del 22 de marzo de 1854 referente a la importación de chinos a Cuba, no se consignaba el término del contrato, lo cual significaba una forma encubierta de esclavitud. Hacia 1856 traer un culí a Cuba ascendía a cien pesos, y el precio de venta variaba entre 150 y 250 pesos, pero algunos se vendieron hasta en 400 pesos.

Agentes de las compañías de tráfico recorrían China, contratando a los infelices culíes por un término de ocho años, asegurándoles el pasaje a Cuba, la alimentación, ropa y vivienda y cuatro pesos mensuales de jornal. La trata se había desplazado de Africa a China.

El viaje de los chinos no difería en horror del de los esclavos. Todo se hacía de la misma forma, pero en mayor escala y a la luz del día. Los barcos "clipper" que conducián a los culíes tenían que navegar a través de tres océanos. Navegaban por el Pacífico hacia el sur hasta el estrecho de la Sonda donde tomaban rumbo suroeste, cruzando el Océano Indico por el extremo sur de Africa. Una vez en el Atlántico tomaban rumbo noroeste, haciendo escala en la Isla de Santa Elena, hasta el Caribe, cruzando entre Trinidad y Barbados. Frente a las costas de Cuba navegaban hacia el oeste a través de la costa sur de la Isla, rumbo al Cabo de San Antonio, el que rodeaban en dirección al puerto de La Habana, único puerto autorizado para el desembarco de culíes.

La navegación duraba de acuerdo con el barco empleado y fluctuaba entre 80 y 230 días. Como es de suponer, la mortandad era muy elevada. Para evitar la larga travesía por los cabos de Buena Esperanza y Hornos, comenzó a emplearse la ruta de Panamá, atravesando el istmo en ferrocarril desde el Pacífico hasta el Atlántico, desde donde se transportaban los chinos a Cuba en barcos de vapor.

La mortandad en la travesía, según la Oficina del Censo de 1899, se elevaba al 13%, y el trato con los infelices chinos era más inhumano que con los africanos. El maltrato, el engaño y la explotación de los agentes de las compañías extranjeras en China eran de tal dureza que el 27 de enero de 1857 el Cónsul de España en Amoy se dirigió a Madrid denunciado:

> De cada 100 chinos que ultimamente se han embarcado para La Habana puedo asegurar a V.E. que 90 son cazados como bestias feroces y llevados violentamente a bordo de los buques para ser conducidos a aquellas apartadas regiones o bien seducidos con engañosas promesas, ocultándoseles el país a donde los transportaban y la clase de trabajo al cual se obligaban. Esta conducta criminal introdujo bien pronto la alarma por estas dilatadas costas. . . . [Los tripulantes de los barcos] tenían el cargo de dedicarse a la persecución de los miserables pescadores a quienes arrebataban de sus pequeñas embarcaciones, dejando en la mayor orfandad numerosas familias. . . .

El 10 de octubre de 1864, España firmó con China el Tratado de Tientsin mediante el cual se eliminaban los agentes y se autorizaba a los hombres a embarcarse solos o en unión de sus familiares.

La vida infra-humana del colono chino, tanto durante la travesía como la dureza del trabajo a que se sometió, fue la causa de la alta mortandad. Entre 1853 y 1861, la tasa de defunciones alcanzó el 29.6% y en igual número de años, entre 1861 y 1869, se elevó al 62%. En 1861 el número de chinos residentes en Cuba ascendía a 34,834, de los cuales solamente 57 eran mujeres. De los miles de chinos traídos a Cuba, si acaso mil fueron mujeres. La razón por la casi total ausencia de mujeres chinas en Cuba era primeramente económica: con lo que ganaban los hombres no se podía mantener una familia. En segundo lugar, ninguna mujer china decente podía convencerse a emigrar.

En el caso de los negros, la constumbre fue de importar 35% de mujeres y 65% de hombres. La vida de éstos era mejor que la de los chinos, que no tenían mujer. Los problemas que confrontaron los chinos incluyeron la falta de una vida sexual normal, especialmente para los chinos que se encontraban en los ingenios y haciendas, lo cual resultó en la sodomía y el homosexualismo entre los chinos. En las ciudades, la cohabitación entre chinos y mulatas era frecuente.

¿Cuántos culíes chinos vinieron a Cuba? Existe buena información estadística sobre la inmigración, mucho mayor que sobre la europea y antillana del siglo XX y más aún que sobre la africana del XIX, de la cual solo existen conjeturas. La existencia de esta buena información se debió a que la inmigración fue un tráfico legal y que a los promotores les interesaba divulgar sus resultados financieros para obtener clientes y nuevos aportes de capital.

El más intenso tráfico a Cuba y al Perú comenzó en 1847 y terminó en 1874. Durante esos 28 años, 343 barcos trajeron 125,000 chinos emigrantes a Cuba, cerca de diez veces el número de chinos que desembarcaron en el Caribe Británico. Otros 276 barcos hicieron el viaje de China al Perú.

Había tres modos de emigrar de china a mediados del pasado: (1) el emigrante podía pagar su propio pasaje, (2) el emigrante recibía el pasaje como préstamo pagadero con interés después de éste llegar al país (este era el sistema de crédito), y (3) el emigrante firmaba un contrato con un patrono por un número fijo de años a un salario fijo (este era el sistema de contrato). En otra forma de contrato, el trabajador adquiría una deuda con su patrono por el importe de su pasaje, cuya deuda se iba amortizando con parte de su salario.

El contrato cubano era generalmente por un período de ocho años a cuatro pesos al mes más la alimentación. El número de horas de trabajo diario dependía del tipo de labor a realizar. Un contrato típico no tenía escape de cumplir los ocho años ni de modificar el salario. Los colonos recibían dos comidas al día, con abundancia de almidones, carne y pescado salado. La ropa era la misma que se le daba a los esclavos negros —dos mudas al año. La vivienda en los ingenios eran bohíos aparte del área de los negros, o una sección del "barracón". El contrato inglés era mucho más benigno. El tratamiento arbitrario y abusivo a los emigrantes chinos en Cuba y en Perú hizo historia en el sistema de contratos de trabajo y fue aceptado libremente por las autoridades y la sociedad.

En 1849 la legislación cubana que regulaba el tratamiento de los colonos asiáticos e indios incluía el número de azotes que podían aplicacarse a los colonos si desobedecían o se negaban a trabajar. Los colonos que trataban de fugarse se condenaban a llevar grilletas durante dos meses por el primer atentado de fuga, cuatro meses por el segundo y seis meses por el tercero. Además tenían que dormir en el cepo, atados de pies y manos. En las 36 plantaciones que existían en la isla, trabajaron 2,916 chinos, cuyas edades oscilaban entre 18 y 54 años.

Un resultado del inhumano tratamiento a que eran sometidos los esclavos y los colonos a mediados del siglo XIX fue la alta proporción de suicidos registrados oficialmente en ambos grupos. La esclavitud doméstica ha sido descrita hasta los primeros años del 1880 como paternalista y suave. Pero el crecimiento de la industria azucarera hizo más dura para siempre la ya dura vida de los esclavos rurales. La demanda de excesivas horas de trabajo (de 16 a 18 horas diarias), durante la zafra de diciembre a junio, hizo a esclavos y chinos, incapaces de resistir el esfuerzo físico y los castigos corporales, se quitaron la vida. Un análisis del suicidio en Cuba demuestra que en 1886 la isla tenía la tasa más alta de suicidios en el mundo, y que los chinos se suicidaban quince veces más frecuentemente que aun los esclavos negros.

En 1861, comenzaron las grandes industrias tabacaleras y cigarreras en La Habana y los chinos comenzaron a trabajar en fábricas de tabacos y cigarros. También había carpinteros, albañiles, mecánicos, herreros, estibadores, etc. A partir de 1855, miembros de los primeros grupos de colonos comenzaron a cumplir sus contratos con los patronos azucareros y los hacendados. Al liberarse, muchos se iban para la capital. Otros fueron liberados debido a serios accidentes que sufrieron que no les permitían continuar el rudo trabajo físico. En esta época comenzaron a aparecer en la isla un grupo de vendedores ambulantes chinos que vendían frutas, vegetales, verduras y carnes. También habían vendedores de joyería, quincalla y loza. En 1858 se estableció un pequeño restaurante chino en La Habana cuyo dueño era Luis Pérez. Su verdadero nombre era Chung Ling.

Cuando los chinos se bautizaban en la iglesia católica, se les daba nombre de bautismo español. Con respecto al apellido, a veces los chinos escogían uno español o continuaban usando su verdadero apellido.

En 1858 un mercado de frutas y verduras se estableció en la calle Zanja. El dueño era Abrahan Scull, cuyo nombre chino era Lan Si Ye. En la Calzada del Monte una tienda de víveres fue establecida por Pedro Plá Tan (Chi Pan). En los años inmediatamente anteriores a la guerra de 1868, los chinos descontratados ya se habían establecido en toda la isla.

Al llamamiento de Carlos Manuel de Céspedes en el ingenio "La Demajagua" el 10 de octubre de 1868, acudieron los criollos de todos las clases sociales. Los que tenían esclavos o colonos los libertaron y ambos patronos y trabajadores se unieron en la lucha por la independencia. En número crecido engrosaron los chinos las filas mambisas, incluso dotaciones o cuadrillas completas. Por su valentía arrojo y determinación alcanzaron los chinos grados en el ejército libertador. Entre otros, podemos mencionar al capitán Liborio Wong, ayudante del general Modesto Díaz; al comandante Sebastián Siang, con 400 otros chinos a las órdenes del General Tomás Jordán de la expedición del "Perritt". En el ejército de Las Villas era donde abundaban más chinos mambises y donde se distinguieron extraordinariamente. Son dignos de mencionarse el capitán Juan Díaz, el teniente Tancredo, Antonio Moreno y otros que habían sido bautizados y adoptado los apellidos de sus antiguos amos.

El año 1871 fue un año crítico en la revolución debido a la escasez de armas y municiones y la presión del enemigo. Los alzados de Las Villas tuvieron que pasar a Oriente acosados por el hambre, las enfermedades y el ejército español. Entre ellos estaba el chino Juan Anelay quien, a pesar de lo parco de su conocimiento del español, dio un discurso elocuentísimo ante los orientales y así obtuvo las provisiones y armas necesarias para continuar la lucha. Capturado por los españoles, Anelay demostró su patriotismo y coraje cuando, amarrado, resistía como una fiera. Solo las palabras "Viva Cuba Libre" cruzaron sus labios mientras que lo mataban a palos.

Otro ejemplo del heroísmo de los chinos tuvo lugar en las batallas que se sucedieron en la provincia de Camagüey —la Sacra, Palo Seco, Naranjo, la famosa batalla de las Guásimas donde 1,300 mambises derrotaron a 3,000 españoles. Unos 500 chinos pelearon con tezón cubriendo la retirada, destacándose los nombres del capitán Juan Sanches (Lam Fu King) quien había sido soldado en China, el teniente José Pedroso, los sargentos Andrés Cao, José Fong y José Tolón, quien alcanzó el grado de capitán.

En 1864 el general español Jovellar decretó la organización del cuerpo de guerrilleros. No hubo ningún chino que aceptara semejante deshonra. Todos los combatientes chinos estaban en el ejército mambí.

El comandante José Bu, amigo y hombre de confianza de Máximo Gómez, y el capitán José Tolón fueron los únicos chinos que junto a los generales extranjeros Máximo Gómez y Carlos Roloff, calificaban como cubanos nativos y podían ser electos presidentes de la República de acuerdo con la constitución de 1901, por haber servido con las armas en las manos en ambas guerras por más de 10 años.

Al firmarse la Paz del Zanjón, el reconocimiento de sus luchas y aceptación de la realidad de la composición de las filas mambisas, en uno de sus artículos se concedió "la libertad a los esclavos o colonos asiáticos que se hallen hoy en las flas insurrectas".

No es posible hacer relación de los numerosos chinos, antiguos combatitentes de la Guerra de los Diez Años o nuevos participantes, que brindaron sus vidas y esfuerzos a la Guerra del 95. Concluida ésta, se dedicaron a sus negocios y ocupaciones habituales, sin reclamar sus pagas de veteranos, pero todos ostentando orgullosos la medalla de veterano mambí.

La características de la raza china —lealtad, espíritu de sacrificio, devoción al deber— les hacían inmunes a las tentativas de soborno o intentos de traición. Fueron leales hasta la muerte, ascendieron paulatinamente y venciendo inumerables obstáculos los grados de la carrera militar. Hubo chinos en la guardia personal del general Antonio Maceo, hecho que por si solo constituía un reconocimiento al valor. Otros llegaron a ganarse la confianza y amistad del "viejo zorro", general en jefe de los ejércitos libertadores, Máximo Gómez. Por eso Gonzalo de Quesada, discípulo de Martí, afirma una frase que quedó grabada en piedra en el monumento que la república dedicó a la memoria de los mambises chinos. En el obelisco de la calle Línea en el Vedado, está el siguiente epitafio: "NO HUBO CHINO CUBANO TRAIDOR; NO HUBO CHINO CUBANO DESERTADOR".

La inmigración colectiva bajo contrato de colonos chinos se había suspendido en 1877. La población china disminuyó en los censos por dos razones básicas: (1) solo venían hombres y muy pocas mujeres, y (2) los hijos de chinos con mujeres de color no eran clasificados como chinos sino como mulatos o pardos. Hasta el principio de la Primera Guerra Mundial (1914-1918), a solo unos pocos chinos se les permitió emigrar a Cuba como estudiantes. Ante la gran demanda de azúcar y la escasez de brazos se importaron obreros haitianos y jamaicanos, y no fue hasta dos años después de la terminación de la primera guerra que se autorizó la inmigración de obreros chinos.

Hacia los años veinte Cuba tenía una población china de 24,000 personas, en su mayoría varones. La mayor o menor necesidad de brazos baratos y los altibajos del mercado azucarero eran los factores determinantes en las sucesivas prohibiciones o autorizaciones para la inmigración china. Desde el primer envío de chinos a Cuba en 1847 hasta la Segunda Guerra Mundial, aproximadamente 300,000 chinos emigraron a la Isla. Solamente Perú proporciona un paralelo a esta migración en los países hispanos. Por consiguiente, fue Cuba la que tomó la iniciativa en hacer desaparecer la discriminación racial de los occidentales hacia los chinos.

En 1939 la legislatura cubana revalidó una orden dada por el gobierno militar americano en 1902 por la cual se aplicaban a Cuba las mismas leyes de inmigración de los Estados Unidos en esa época. La entrada de chinos se restringía entonces a diplomáticos, familias, mercaderos y turistas. Un nuevo tratado firmado en noviembre de 1942 adoptó una política completamente distinta. Este tratado contenía la base para una perpetua amistad y la promesa de cooperación mutúa para la paz universal bajo principios de justicia entre China y Cuba.

De toda suerte, el chino, como el negro, ha dejado su sello o huella indeleble en la nacionalidad cubana, no solo en lo étnico, sino también en lo cultural y costumbrista. Como todo pueblo emigrado, el chino trajo sus costumbres y algunos malos hábitos de difícil erradicación: el juego de la charada china, el mah jong (dominó chino), el fan tan (botones). Y sobre todo entre ellos el vicio de fumar opio que había sido introducido a su país desde la India.

La charada china se introdujo en Cuba entre 1876 y 1878. Se extendió y popularizó con una velocidad extraordinaria entre la población cubana hasta convertirse en parte integral de la cultura popular. La charada es una especie de lotería que consiste de un dibujo de un chino mandarín vestido con traje típico a cuyo alrededor están colgados 36 "bichos" (animales u otros objetos) específicamente distribuidos. Las personas apuestan a los números basándose en sueños, premoniciones o el "verso" que el "banquero" da como adivinanza. El banquero por lo regular escoge el número menos "cargado."

El pueblo chino, amante de sus tradiciones, costumbres y ritos, conmemoraba en Cuba el Año Nuevo Chino, el Día de los Difuntos, el Festival de los Faroles, y otras fiestas de calendario lunar que se conservaron durante un largo período. En el Año Nuevo las sociedades chinas organizaban la Danza del Dragón. Los bailarines se vestían de rojo, color que es para ellos símbolo de la felicidad y el bienestar, y manipulaban el dragón, animal sagrado de su mitología, que ejecutaba pasos de danza. El Día de los Difuntos los chinos iban en caravana al cementerio donde adornaban las tumbas de sus seres queridos con lámparas y papeles rojos y encendían velas con palitos de sándalo.

La música ritual de las ceremonias religiosas chinas no recibió en Cuba tanto favor como la música popular que se empleaba en el teatro de la ópera y la folklórica que cantaban los cortadores de caña y los vendedores ambulantes. Estos anunciaban a las amas de casa los productos que llevaban con pregones que iban acompañados de melodías rítmicas y simples. La proximidad de un chino vendedor de dulces se anunciaba por el repique peculiarísimo e inconfundible de un palillo contra el costado del tablero que el asiático llevaba en la cabeza. La famosa danza "Ahí viene el chino" de Lecuona imita la melodía seguida por los chinos vianderos. La escala pentatónica china aparece con frecuencia en las canciones y danzones cubanos.

La trompeta china de cinco notas fue muy usada en los mítines políticos por su estridencia. La flauta china, según Severo Sarduy, es el centro de la música cubana. El considera que la orquesta cubana es quizás el caso único de síntesis total de las tres culturas —la española, la africana y la china. La corneta china se hizo parte de los carnavales de Santiago de Cuba. La conocida conga "Al carnaval de Oriente me voy" se tocaba con el acompañamiento de estas cornetas, sopladas por músicos chinos, blancos o negros con igual maestría.

La comida china gustaba por su sabor, variedad, fina presentación y la abundancia de productos frescos que utilizaba. Amantes del clima tropical, los chinos supieron aprovechar la riqueza de las viandas, verduras, mariscos y pescados que les brindaba la Isla. Con las frutas cubanas como el anón, el mamey, el caimito y la guanábana, preparaban helados que se distinguieron siempre como los mejores. En las fondas chinas surgió el cubanismo "comerse una completa" que significaba saborear una comida abundante con muchas viandas —y barata.

El típico chino ha pasado a formar parte de la literatura y el folklore cubanos. Muchos autores cubanos describieron en sus obras unas veces las características físicas y morales del chino, otras sus tradiciones, costumbres, juegos, su manera peculiar de hablar español, etc.

Entre las voces chinas que pasaron al lenguaje cubano popular se encuentran "chaucha" que significa "comida." Otras palabras, como nombres de animales y comidas, términos de juegos y relacionadas con el fumar opio también pasaron al habla cubana, pero con menos frecuencia.

Los chinos, considerados colonos blancos libres bajo contrato dentro de la semántica esclavista cubana, constituyeron el último aporte significativo a la población de la Isla. A partir de la llegada de los primeros colonos asiáticos hasta 1959, el chino cubano pasó de su sugesión a un estatus ambivalente y trágico durante el período colonial hasta ser parte integrante del pueblo cubano, a cuyas luchas de independencia contribuyó como combatiente para distinguirse como ciudadano útil y digno de la república.

BIBLIOGRAFIA

Chang, Ching Chiek. "The Chinese in Latin America: A Preliminary Geographical Survey with Special Reference to Cuba and Jamaica". Tesis para doctorado, University of Maryland.

Ching-Hwang, Yen. *Coolies and Mandarins: China's Protection of Overseas Chinese during the Late Ch'ing Period, 1851-1911*. Singapore: University Press, National University of Singapore, 1985.

"La colonia china de Cuba es ya centenaria." *Carteles* 29:6 (February 8, 1948), 14-17.

Corbitt, Duvon C. "Chinese Immigration in Cuba." *Far Eastern Survey* 133 (julio 1944), 130-133.

"Cuba. Dirección de Estadística." *Anuario estadístico de Cuba 1952*. La Habana: Comité Estatal de Estadística, 1952.

"Cuba. Dirección General de Estadística." *Compendio del Anuario estadístico de Cuba 1952*. La Habana: Comité Estatal de Estadística, 1952.

Jiménez Pastrana, Juan. *Los Chinos en las luchas por la liberación cubana, 1847-1930*. La Habana: Instituto de Historia, 1963.

Tejeiro, Guillermo. *Historia ilustrada de la colonia china en Cuba*. La Habana, 1947.

Uhuesada, Gonzalo de. "The Chinese Question: Los Chinos y la Revolución Cubana." Prólogo del Dr. Ti-Tsun Li, Enviado Extraordinario y Ministro Plenipotenciario de la República de China en Cuba. *North American Review* (La Habana) XV (1946), 144.

Varela, Beatriz. *Lo Chino en el habla cubano*. Miami, FL: Ediciones Universal, 1980.

Cuban Bibliography

31. La bibliografía cubana: Inventario de nuestra cultura

Araceli García-Carranza

La bibliografía cubana no sólo describe y controla el inventario editorial del país sino que es obra de obligada consulta para el estudio de la historia y la cultura cubanas: documento vivo y memoria que atesora nuestras experiencias como pueblo. Veamos como desde los albores del siglo XVIII podemos seguir el paso a la creación intelectual descrita en los repertorios de carácter nacional.

Siglo XVIII

Cuba colonial careció totalmente de atención cultural hasta este siglo. No teníamos imprenta, ni universidades, ni bibliotecas. La Metrópoli ejercía férrea censura y abogaba todo intento que superase ese estado de ignorancia. Cuba era colonia pobre carente de metales preciosos y por ello sólo interesaba como Llave del Golfo y centro estratégico y operacional de las flotas: el puerto de La Habana era tránsito obligado de los navegantes que iban y venían de Europa. Sin embargo, ya desde el siglo XVII existía un movimiento editorial relacionado con Cuba que demuestra la monumental obra de Carlos Manuel Trelles y Govín, *Bibliografía cubana de los siglos XVII y XVIII.* Trelles menciona 850 títulos de libros, folletos y manuscritos desconocidos en su mayoría, con noticias bibliográficas de los cubanos que aparecen en estos documentos. Esta biblioteca cubana describe la documentación correspondiente en cuatro secciones: en la primera, folletos escritos por cubanos en Cuba o fuera de Cuba (130 autores y 270 títulos); en la segunda enumera más de 200 folletos impresos en La Habana durante el siglo XVIII y 83 impresos en Santiago de Cuba; en la tercera describe 130 manuscritos; y en la cuarta, 290 títulos impresos en México, España y otros países europeos, en los cuales hay referencias a Cuba. Trelles da a conocer en este inventario precioso los orígenes de nuestra literatura aunque un número muy escaso de estos documentos integran hoy nuestro acervo bibliográfico nacional. (La mitad de los autores cubanos a que se refiere Trelles no aparecen en el *Diccionario bibliográfico* de Francisco Calcagno por lo que ambas obras se complementan en el estudio de los autores de los siglos XVII y XVIII cubanos.)

De manera que la cultura cubana no empieza como se ha repetido durante años con el gobierno de Don Luis de las Casas, época de la publicación del *Papel Periódico de la Havana*, y cuando se crea la Real Sociedad Patriótica de Amigos del País. Recuérdese que la primera publicación periódica conocida que circuló en nuestro país fue la *Gazeta de la Havana*. Según algunos historiadores este periódico apareció el 17 de mayo de 1764, pero sólo conocemos los ejemplares que posee la Biblioteca Nacional de Cuba: un número de 22 de noviembre de 1782 y un suplemento publicado el 15 de noviembre de este año. Muchos años antes nuestra cultura ya se hacía sentir cuando abre sus puertas la Real y Pontificia Universidad de la Habana en 1728 y prueba de ello es la obra redactada a mediados del siglo XVIII por el fraile habanero José Fonseca o José González Alfonseca titulada *Noticias de los escritores de la Isla de Cuba* la cual estuvo en poder del erudito mexicano Juan José de Eguiara y Eguren, autor de un *Diccionario histórico y bibliográfico de todos los autores nacidos en Nueva España (México)* del cual sólo publicó el primer volumen que abarca las tres primeras letras. (El manuscrito llegaba hasta la letra J.) No obstante haberse perdido esta obra de Fonseca, con el sólo dato de su existencia es posible refutar a Aurelio Mitjans quien en su notable *Estudio sobre el movimiento científico y literario de Cuba*, se refiere a un siglo XVIII cubano pobre con algunos ensayos poéticos, varios predicadores, tres cronistas y un zoólogo. Trelles con su *Bibliografía cubana de los siglos XVII y XVIII* da la razón a Fonseca, y no a Mitjans al mencionar 30 oradores sagrados, 17 poetas, 5 autores dramáticos, 12 jurisconsultas, 12 teólogos, 5 cronistas y otros escritores más autores de libros y folletos de diversos asuntos. Porque no olvidemos que aunque mucho se ha discutido en torno a la fecha de introducción de la imprenta en Cuba el famoso bibliógrafo mexicano José María de Beristaín y Souza afirma que fue en 1707, fecha que impugnó Bachiller y Morales, pero que Trelles acepta, por ello describe como el primer libro cubano el folleto de Francisco González del Alamo *Disertación sobre que las carnes de cerdo son saludables en las islas de Barlovento* publicado en la Habana en 1707. (González del Alamo fue el primer fisiólogo que hubo en Cuba y uno de los primeros médicos cubanos que enseñó medicina en el Convento de San Juan de Letrán.) José Toribio Medina, el más notable bibliógrafo y bibliófilo hispanoamericano, también acepta esta obra como el primer libro cubano. Por lo que sólo estos datos dan fe de la existencia de la obra de González del Alamo, la cual no conocemos y por tanto no ha llegado a integrar el acervo cultural de nuestros días.

La primera obra conocida data de 1723 y se trata de la *Tarifa general de precios de medicina* impresa por el flamenco Carlos Habré. A pesar de su valor histórico y bibliográfico presenta una composición tipográfica desigual y burda muy lejana de la tradición que existía en Gante, Francia, país de donde procedía Habré.

Ya más avanzado el siglo el portugués Antonio Parra estudia nuestra flora y fauna, muy especialmente los peces, y publica en 1787 el primer libro de ciencia cubano, *Descripción de diferentes piezas de historia natural, la más del ramo marítimo*, representadas en setenta y cinco láminas grabadas en metal. Esta obra resulta un clásico en nuestra bibliografía por su contenido y belleza gráfica.

En la última década del siglo XVIII a pesar de la censura se publican entre libros y folletos tanto como lo que se publicó desde el primer impreso hasta 1790. El movimiento editorial cubano se acentúa a partir de 1791, de manera que de 1790 a 1799 se imprimen en Cuba 100 folletos, casi tanto como lo que se publicara desde el primer impreso hasta 1790.

Es innegable que a pesar del atraso colonial en el siglo XVIII la cultura cubana sobresalió inclusive por encima de la cultura de otras colonias de España ya que Cuba fue uno de los primeros países, exactamente el quinto, que tuvo imprenta.

Siglo XIX

Pero si mayor parte de la bibliografía cubana del siglo XVIII correspondió a obras publicadas fuera de Cuba, aunque relacionadas con nuestro país, a la bibliografía cubana del siglo XIX le corresponde un movimiento editorial considerable publicado en Cuba, desde principios de esta centuria. Los talleres tipográficos de: Boloña, Mora, Palmer, y Seguí abiertos desde fines del siglo XVIII ya imprimían diversos tipos de obra, como las del médico y literato cubano Tomás Romay quien publica en 1805 su *Memoria sobre la introducción de la vacuna en la isla de Cuba*. Conferencia de 14 páginas en la cual da a conocer el modo de vacunar, los caracteres del grano vacuno, el tiempo oportuno de tomar el benéfico pus, las dificultades que se le presentaban a los facultativos y la verdadera y falsa vacuna. A partir de esta obra Romay publica valiosos aportes científicos que rompen con la rigidez y cerrazón del pensamiento escolástico.

En este siglo se suceden tres libertades de imprenta, hechos que promueven en 1812, 1820 y 1869 el movimiento editorial cubano. En 1812 se promulga en Cuba por la Constitución de Cádiz la primera libertad de imprenta la cual no aportó gran cosa a la cultura cubana, ya que se publicaron en esta ocasión libelos políticos muy soeces. Sin embargo, paradójicamente, esta etapa cuenta con la sobresaliente figura del Padre Varela quien por primera vez publica en español sus textos de *Moral* (1812) y sus *Lecciones de filosofía* (1818) haciendo accesibles las verdades científicas de la época con sus libros impresos en nuestro idioma, y no en latín, tal como se hacía hasta entonces. Varela es el primer conformador de nuestro pensamiento político. En El Habanero, primera expresión cubana del periodismo puesto en función de la independencia, plantea valientemente la separación definitiva de Cuba de la metrópoli.

En año 1820 es la fecha de la segunda libertad de imprenta surgida por la toma del poder de los liberales en España. En esta etapa se publicaron periódicos que defendían la causa separatista y propagaban las ideas revolucionarias americanas. Emigrados revolucionarios radicados en Cuba publican periódicos que ejercen notable influencia en la cultura de la época y en las ideas de los jóvenes. La prensa criolla como *El Americano Libre* (1822) y *El Revisor Político y Literario* (1823) entre otros, hacen patente la asimilación de la ideología de la Revolución Francesa en Cuba. Pero cuando se restablece el régimen absolutista en España, la libertad de imprenta desaparece por el justificado temor de la metrópoli a que las ideas revolucionarias y el sentimiento separatista del continente americano tuvieron eco en nuestra Isla. Por esta razón en 1825 se implantan las facultades omnímodas para los capitanes generales. La censura férrea provocaría un año después que la Sociedad Económica de Amigos del País dejara de publicar la *Revista Bimestre Cubana* y no pudiera crear la Academia Cubana de Literatura cuya defensa costó a Saco su destierro. Sólo quedaba a los intelectuales las tertulias literarias y las revistas, publicaciones periódicas por separatas "amables", "amenas", "para las damas" que tenían formato de libro.

Ya en 1839 con el establecimiento de los talleres litográficos en La Habana aumenta la calidad y cantidad de libros ilustrados y a mediados del siglo XIX, y también debido al auge de la industria azucarera, la Imprenta en la Litografía de Luis Marquier publica el más hermoso libro de la época, *Los ingenios* (1857), de Justo Germán Cantero, ilustrado con las litografías del francés Eduardo Laplante.

Período colonial

Es por estos años que Antonio Bachiller y Morales publica en La Habana sus *Apuntes para la historia de las letras y de la instrucción pública en la Isla de Cuba* (1859-1861) donde incluye: Publicaciones periódicas —Catálogo razonado y cronológico hasta 1840 inclusive, que apareció en la sección segunda de la tercera parte del volumen dos y el Catálogo de libros y folletos publicado en Cuba desde la introducción de la imprenta hasta 1840, inserto en la sección segunda de la cuarta parte del tercer tomo. Esta primera bibliografía no sólo marca el inicio del primer período bibliográfico de nuestra historia, el llamado Período Colonial, sino que es fuente imprescindible para el estudio de la cultura cubana

. . . los Apuntes para las Letras Cubanas —según expresara nuestro José Martí— en que no hay nada que poner, salvo un poco de órden, porque ya en sus relatos, ya en sus biografías de hombres ilustres, de Arangos y Peñalveres, de Heredia y Varela, de los Castillos y de la Luz, está, desde sus albores hasta la mitad de este siglo, cuanto recuerda de sus maestros e institutos Cuba reconocida. . . . [O.C. t. 5, p. 149]

Unos años después de publicada esta obra, en octubre de 1868 estalla la Revolución de Yara y en 1869 Domingo Dulce establece la tercera libertad de imprenta para calmar un tanto la exaltación de la guerra pero, por el contrario, desató violentas pasiones políticas en la prensa por lo que fue prohibida al mes y días. En esta época, precisamente el 22 de enero de 1869, ocurren los sucesos del Teatro Villanueva, los Caricatos Habaneros provocaron el ataque armado por parte de los voluntarios. En realidad el programa de la representación era toda una provocación revolucionaria. De esta etapa es notable sin embargo la labor de la prensa clandestina que edita proclamas y leyes en los territorios libres; y en la manigua *El cubano libre*, fuente imprescindible para el estudio de múltiples facetas de la Guerra Grande. (Es importante destacar en años posteriores títulos que recogen las experiencias de los diez años de guerra: *Cuba heroica* y *Desde Yara hasta el Zanjón*, de Enrique Collazo; *La Revolución de Yara*, de Fernando Figueredo Socarrás; y *La República de Cuba*, de Antonio Zambrana.)

No obstante este conflicto bélico la obra de Bachiller influye en sus contemporáneos, eruditos que aprovecharon la tregua fecunda para publicar en la *Revista de Cuba* y en *El Curioso Americano*, aportes bibliográficos que completaron su catálogo primero. Así aparecen en la *Revista de Cuba* las listas de Eusebio Valdés Domínguez, Francisco Jimeno y Domingo del Monte; y en *El Curioso Americano* la lista de Manuel Pérez Beato. Un año después de terminada la Guerra de los Diez Años, en 1879 aparece en la *Revista de Cuba* el primer aporte para hacer más completo el catálogo de Bachiller. Se trata de la *Bibliografía cubana*, de Eusebio Valdés Domínguez; y en esa misma revista se insertan después otras listas bibliográficas que forman Francisco Jimeno, Domingo del Monte y el propio Bachiller; completa esta lista de adiciones la que publicar Manuel Pérez Beato en *El Curioso Americano* de 1892 a 1893, donde agrega un segundo apéndice de Bachiller y Morales.

La lista de Domingo del Monte titulada *Biblioteca cubana* que incluyó 170 libros inéditos e impresos sobre Cuba, fue compilada en Paris en 1846. A pesar de la fecha (que aparentemente lo sitúa aportes de Bachiller) es un indiscutible suplemento a los *Apuntes para la historia de las letras y de la instrucción pública en la isla de Cuba*, pues no es posible pensar que Bachiller comenzara su obra después de 1846 teniendo en cuenta lo monumental de la misma, que es labor de un solo hombre, y las dificultades de la época. Domingo del Monte, inequívocamente nuestro segundo bibliógrafo, publicó este listado en el tomo 11 de la *Revista de Cuba*, en 1882.

Período del aporte extranjero

Al Período Colonial encabezado por la obra de Antonio Bachiller y Morales le sigue el Período del Aporte Extranjero. Durante este período la Biblioteca del Congreso de Washington publica, en 1898, la obra del bibliógrafo Appleton P. Griffin *List of Books Relating to Cuba* cuya segunda parte contiene una cartografía compilada por P. Lee Phillips (de esta obra se hizo una segunda edición). También en este mismo año se publican en Nueva York las obras *Finding List of Books Relating to Spain and Her Colonies* y *Reading List of the Books on Cuba and the Present War with Spain*, esta última compilada por Anne S. Woodcock para la Grosvener Library de Buffalo.

Europa no se mantuvo ajena a este interés bibliográfico. Un francés, Charles Chadenat, publica en Paris, también en 1898, para la serie *Le bibliophile américaine*, un estudio titulado *Cuba y Puerto Rico*.

Mención aparte merece la labor erudita de José Toribio Medina; el más notable bibliógrafo y bibliófilo hispanoamericano, autor de decenas de obras sobre la imprenta en América. Su obra más importante la publica precisamente en estos años finiseculares. Se trata de la *Bibliografía hispano americana (1493-1810)*, editada en seis volúmenes en Santiago de Chile (1898-1902). También por estos años este erudito polígrafo chileno publica en Santiago de Chile, en 1904, su obra *La imprenta en la Habana*, la cual contiene notas bibliográficas de interés y abarca un período amplio de nuestra historia editorial, desde 1707 hasta 1870. Medina descubre 169 títulos de folletos habaneros del siglo XVIII, y 96 de 1801 a 1870. (Otra de sus obras abarcadoras del período 1754-1823, y titulada *Notas referentes a las primeras producciones de la imprenta en algunas ciudades de la América Española*, no es ajena a Cuba pues en ella aparecen descritos siete folletos impresos en nuestro país.)

Paralelamente a estas obras extranjeras sobre Cuba existen aportes nacionales que cierran el siglo XIX de la bibliografía cubana. Resultan el trabajo de Leandro González Alcorta titulado *Datos para la historia de Vuelta Abajo: exploraciones bibliográficas* (Pinar del Rio, 1902) y la obra de Luis Marino Pérez, *Apuntes de libros y folletos impresos en España*, que trata expresamente de Cuba (La Habana, 1907).

Siglo XX

La bibliografía cubana en el siglo XX abarca cuatro períodos fundamentales: Período de predominio de Carlos Manuel Trelles (1907-1916), Los años huecos o laguna bibliográfica (1917-1936), Período de predominio de Fermín Peraza (1937-1959) y el Período de predominio de la Biblioteca Nacional de Cuba, institución que desde 1959 es autor corporativo del más importante trabajo bibliográfico realizado en el país. Sin olvidar el trabajo de otras instituciones como la Casa de las Américas y la Academia de Ciencias de Cuba, instituciones que han colaborado, en esta etapa, al desarrollo de la bibliografía en Cuba.

Predominio de Carlos Manuel Trelles y Govín

El período de predominio de Carlos Manuel Trelles abarca los primeros años de la República cuando la producción bibliográfica cubana destaca lo heroico nacional, los escritores de la época relatan los hechos históricos vividos: José Miró Argenter, jefe de Estado Mayor, en su obra *Cuba, crónicas de la guerra* (1899), verdadero diario de las campañas de Antonio Maceo, narra en detalles las grandes acciones de armas de la Revolución y relata y comenta sus experiencias personales para dar a conocer la guerra de independencia; Enrique Collazo publica sus obras *Cuba independiente* (1900), *Cuba intervenida* (1910) y *Cuba heroica* (1912), testimonios inapreciables de quien fue autor y testigo de gran parte de los hechos que narra desde los años en que se incubó la Revolución del '95 hasta la segunda intervención norteamericana; Vidal Morales y Morales se sitúa entre los historiadores más ilustres de la América de habla hispana con su *Iniciadores y primeros mártires* (1901); y Julio César Gandarilla protesta contra la Enmienda Platt en su obra *Contra el yanqui* (1913).

La vibrante oratoria de Manuel Sanguily, el periodismo militante de Juan Gualberto Gómez y el pensamiento de Enrique José Varona hacen valer ante la intervención el sentimiento patriótico nacional. Y en estos mismos años de la República de la Enmienda Platt la gigantesca obra de Carlos Manuel Trelles y Govín opaca los esfuerzos de bibliógrafos cubanos y extranjeros porque ella compendía todos los intentos criollos y foráneos precedentes para llenar una necesidad cultural. Trelles acomete en el campo de la bibliografía general la tarea de recomenzar en el siglo XVII con todas las obras hechas por cubanos fuera de Cuba, para continuar describiendo hasta sus días todo título que sobre Cuba interesara a la cultura cubana.

Su obra fundamental, inventario precioso de la cultura cubana desde el siglo XVII hasta 1916, resulta la *Bibliografía cubana de los siglos XVII y XVIII* (Matanzas, 1907), la *Bibliografía cubana del siglo XIX*, en ocho volúmenes (Matanzas, 1911-1915) y la *Bibliografía cubana del siglo XX*, en dos volúmenes (Matanzas, 1916-1917). A ésto debemos añadir sus bibliografías especiales, entre ellas: *Biblioteca científica cubana* (Matanzas, 1918-1919), *Biblioteca geográfica cubana* (Matanzas, 1920), *Biblioteca histórica cubana* (Matanzas, 1922-1926) y su *Bibliografía de la Universidad de La Habana* (La Habana, 1938).

Es curioso señalar lo que Trelles expresara, en 1914, al analizar el movimiento editorial cubano en el siglo anterior y en los años que corrían del 20:

No creo que el patriotismo me ofusque al afirmar que es sorprendente la labor intelectual de Cuba, teniendo en cuenta su escasa población, y que estuvo sujeta hasta hace poco a una dominación asaz, dura y recelosa, preocupada apenas de la difusión de las luces, como lo demuestra el hecho de que a los 400 años de estar gobernada por España, el 75% de los cubanos no supiesen leer ni escribir, . . . Y si a esto se agrega el despotismo que . . . ahogaba, con su previa censura, la mayor parte de las manifestaciones realizada por los hijos de este país por medio de la imprenta, se comprendiera entonces que la labor de los cubanos ha sido extraordinario, luchando en condiciones tan desventajosas, y que, no obstante circunstancias tan adversas, podemos figurar y figuramos hoy, entre las naciones más adelantadas de la América Latina, o sea la Argentina, Chile, México y el Brasil.[1]

Los años huecos o laguna bibliográfica

Al interrumpir Trelles la compilación de la bibliografía general después de 1916, se dedica a las bibliografías especiales y a trabajos de investigación histórica. Deja suelta entonces la guía que vertebraba el panorama cultural de Cuba. El resultado: 20 años vacíos de bibliografía nacional. Esta bibliografía nacional retrospectiva ya ha sido compilada y publicada por la Biblioteca Nacional José Martí, en cinco volúmenes, de cuatro años cada uno, correspondiente al período 1917-1936: los llamados años huecos o laguna bibliográfica, desde la monumental obra de Carlos Manuel Trelles hasta la primera de Fermín Peraza. También para el estudio de la cultura cubana en esta etapa resultan repertorios de valor e interés la *Revista Bimestre Cubana*, los catálogos de la Librería Cervantes y las *Crónicas* de León Primelles que aunque no son propiamente bibliográficas recogen casi todo lo acontecido y lo publicado en Cuba desde 1915 hasta 1922. Otras fuentes de indiscutible consulta para el estudio de esta etapa lo son las secciones de crítica de libros de la *Revista Bimestre Cubana* y de *Cuba Contemporánea.*

En estos años la deuda del continente ascendía a más de 100 millones en 1927 y los verdaderos intereses del pueblo eran abandonados en medio de una situación convulsa debida fundamentalmente a las ambiciones del patio. Se promueve entonces la más desenfrenada politiquería.

En 1919 Emilio Roig de Leuchsenring publica su obra *La ocupación de la República Dominicana por los Estados Unidos y el derecho de las pequeñas nacionalidades de América* en la cual denuncia la situación creada por la intervención al no poder esa República satisfacer los intereses y demás términos del Convenio Financiero con los Estados Unidos.

Este período gris de la nación se rompe en 1923 con la Protesta de los Trece, lidereada por Rubén Martínez Villena, antecedente valedero del

Grupo Minorista que en 1927 firmaría un manifiesto premonitorio por la revisión de los valores falsos, por el arte nuevo, por la reforma de la enseñanza pública, por la independencia económica de Cuba, contra el imperialismo yanqui y contra las dictaduras políticas unipersonales en el mundo, en América y en Cuba.

El año 1927 es el año de la *Revista de Avance*, órgano que sirvió de expresión a creadores y críticos de avanzada. En este año Ramiro Guerra publica *Azúcar y población en las Antillas*, primera historia de Cuba con fundamentación económica, obra fundamental de la bibliografía cubana, libro básico de nuestra cultura, que denuncia la pérdida de nuestra soberanía, la entrega del suelo cubano al extranjero y el coloniaje que provocó el latifundismo.

En los predios literarios de la antigua laguna bibliográfica escritores como Miguel de Carrión, José Antonio Ramos, Carlos Loveira y Luis Felipe Rodríguez expresan en sus obras la corrupción republicana y su frustración social. Miguel de Carrión en sus novelas *Las honradas* (1917) y *Las impuras* (1919) da la imagen moral de la mujer de la época y denuncia las más infames lacras sociales, sin descuidar la penetración extranjera de que fue víctima Cuba después de las intervenciones norteamericanas; José Antonio Ramos con su drama *Tembladera* (1918) disecciona las deformaciones de la clase burguesa, y con su novela *Caniquí* (1936) busca en el pasado las raíces de nuestra identidad nacional; Carlos Loveira relata el acontecer de la vida cubana durante la guerra de independencia y se extiende hasta las primeras décadas de la república en sus novelas *Generales y doctores* (1920) y *Juan Criollo* (1927); y Luis Felipe Rodríguez vuelca su talento y su amor en el campo cubano para convertirse en el cuentista mayor de su tiempo con sus *Relatos de Marcos Antilla* (1932).

La década de los 30 se abre paso con la poesía de Nicolás Guillén quien publica sus *Motivos de son*, obra que asombró a la crítica y con la cual nuestro poeta nacional llevó el molde rítmico del son a la poesía cubana; de 1931 son sus versos mulatos *Songoro Cosongo* y de 1934 *West Indies Ltd.* Comienza entonces a gestarse una poesía revolucionaria y vigorosa que se identifica con la historia del país. Tres años después Guillén publica *Cantos para soldados y sones para turistas* (1937), versos con los que apela, en insuperable lenguaje poético, a la conciencia de los trabajadores para que estos sean soldados de sus pueblos.

Por otra parte la obra de Don Fernando Ortiz, hombre de fecunda existencia e inmensa erudición, luchador incansable contra el delito del recismo y fundador por estos años de la Sociedad Hispano Cubana de Cultura y de la revista *Ultra*, también se abre paso desde 1923, año de sus discursos cubanos *En la tribuna*. En esta obra su prologuista Rubén

Martínez Villena previó lo que Don Fernando significaría para la cultura cubana.

Período de predominio de Fermín Peraza

En 1938 apareció el primer tomo del *Anuario bibliográfico de 1937*, de Fermín Peraza quien reinicia la tarea bibliográfica y la continúa hasta el momento que decide salir de Cuba en 1960; deja publicada inclusive la bibliografía correspondiente a 1959. (El Anuario como tal se publica hasta 1952, ya que a partir de 1953 aparece y continúa como *Bibliografía cubana.*) En 1962 Peraza comienza a publicar en Gainesville, Florida, la *Bibliografía cubana*, a partir de 1960, con lo cual a pesar de sus deficiencias, debidas principalmente a su confección fuera del país, complementa la nuestra que sufre el bloqueo impuesto por el gobierno americano, bloqueo que nos afecta principalmente, por el no acceso a fuentes extranjeras de cubanos o sobre Cuba.

Esta segunda etapa de nuestra bibliografía en el siglo XX tuvo su antecedente en la VII Conferencia Internacional de las Repúblicas Americanas, reunida en Montevideo en 1933 donde se planteó el gran auge de estos estudios en el mundo y especialmente en América. En esta Conferencia se aprobó un acuerdo referente a la bibliografía americana, en el que se resolvía proponer a cada uno de los países de América la compilación de sus respectivas bibliografías nacionales tanto corrientes como retrospectivas y se recomendaba para su organización, el modelo norteamericano.

La bibliografía de fines de la década de los 30 y primeros años de los 40 cuenta con las primeras obras poéticas de Eugenio Florit, José Lezama Lima, Mirta Aguirre y Eliseo Diego; y con obras fundamentales para el estudio de nuestra historia como el *Manual de historia de Cuba: económica, social y política* (1938), de Roig de Leuchsenring, y el *Contrapunteo cubano del tabaco y el azúcar*, de Don Fernando Ortiz. Ramón Guirao y Rómulo Lachatañeré publican por estos años *Orbita de la poesía afrocubana* (1938), y *'Oh, mio Yemayá'*, respectivamente, obras clásicas para el estudio de la cultura negra en Cuba. Luis Felipe Rodríguez y Enrique Serpa denuncian con sus novelas *Ciénaga* (1937) y *Contrabando* violentos conflictos sociales. Y en el ámbito internacional antiimperialista el escritor y combatiente Pablo de la Torriente Brau, testigo excepcional de los hechos que narra sobre su participación en la guerra civil española, lega para la historia testimonios de lucha tales como *Peleando con los milicianos* (1938) y *Aventuras del soldado desconocido cubano* (1940).

Un poco más avanzada la década de los 40 y principios de los años 50 el entusiasmo que el pueblo había depositado en los regímenes auténticos se resquebraja totalmente. La literatura sigue siendo un oficio raro del cual nadie podía vivir, y los creadores siguen pagando por las ediciones de sus libros. A pesar de esta situación crítica en 1944 comienza a publicarse nada menos que la revista *Orígenes*, cristalización final de una serie de revistas que comenzaron a publicarse a mediados de la década de los 30. Esta revista define una generación literaria que se aferra a la tradición criolla, en proceso de demolición por la presencia del capital norteamericano. Y a pesar de su empeño en la actividad literaria al margen de lo político, la revista y el grupo representan una etapa de "entrerrevoluciones" —así la define Graziella Pogolotti— entre la frustración del movimiento del 30 y la curva ascendente del proceso revolucionario que se produce a partir de los años 50.

En esta etapa de "entrerrevoluciones" correspondiente a los años 40 y 50 figuras tales como Alejo Carpentier, José Lezama Lima, Cintio Vitier, Eliseo Diego, Samuel Feijoó y Onelio Jorge Cardoso producen una obra literaria; y en el campo de la investigación histórica Raúl Cepero Bonilla publica *Azúcar y abolición* (1948), el más brillante ensayo histórico escrito en Cuba hasta su tiempo y punto de partida de la también brillante historiografía que surgiera posteriormente.

Por estos años la obra de Don Fernando Ortiz alcanza lugar cimero dentro de la bibliografía cubana por su monumentalidad (*La africanía de la música folklórica de Cuba*, 1950; *Los bailes y el teatro de los negros en el Folklore de Cuba*, 1951; *Los instrumentos de la música afrocubana*, 1952); y por último la significativa obra de Emilio Roig de Leuchsenring, *Cuba no debe su independencia a los Estados Unidos* (1950), vibrante denuncia contra la ingerencia norteamericana; *La guerra libertadora cubana de los treinta años* (1952), valioso aporte esclarecedor de todas las cuestiones fundamentales de la lucha de Cuba por su independencia; y su *Martí, antiimperialista* (1953), obra fundamental de la historiografía cubana.

Este ciclo de frustración nacional culminaría con un período de terror y sangre: la dictadura. Frente a la situación imperante Fidel Castro encabeza la lucha armada ya a fines de 1956. Y en los últimos años de este período (1952-1958) prolifera la prensa clandestina contra la tiranía de Batista. Esta colección ofrece inestimables datos sobre los acontecimientos en la sierra y en el llano, y se caracteriza por un depurado sentimiento patriótico. Gran parte de esta colección resulta antecedente editorial al triunfo de la Revolución y es atesorada por la Biblioteca Nacional: institución que publicó el catálogo correspondiente a este fondo, en 1965.

Período de predominio de la Biblioteca Nacional José Martí

A fines de 1959 la Biblioteca Nacional, una vez departamentalizada y sin abandonar la tarea inmediata de organización, acomete la compilación del movimiento editorial del país, actual y retrospectivo, y en 1961 logra publicar un primer intento bibliográfico de carácter nacional, un catálogo titulado *Movimiento editorial en Cuba 1959-1960*, con motivo de una exposición de libros, folletos y revistas, que mostraba la producción de las editoras cubanas, y por tanto mostraba uno de los más importantes logros de la Revolución.

La sociedad cubana desde entonces sufre profundos cambios en toda su estructura. La cultura en manos del pueblo responde en 1961 con la exitosa y trascendental campaña de alfabetización sobre casi un millón de analfabetos, y la creación de la Imprenta Nacional. Posteriormente, el 8 de marzo de 1962, se crea la Editora Nacional, pero la necesidad de un desarrollo acelerado promueve en 1967 la creación del Instituto del Libro, convertido en 1970 en Instituto Cubano del Libro e incorporado como Dirección de Editoriales al Ministerio de Cultura en 1976. El desarrollo alcanzado en el mundo editorial cubano exigió posteriormente la recreación del Instituto del Libro como órgano rector del libro en Cuba.

En cuanto a la edición de la *Bibliografía Nacional* posterior a 1959, no es hasta 1968 que aparece publicado el período 1959-1962, el cual contiene las descripciones de más de 2700 títulos. Entre otros, la segunda edición (1959) de la *Historia de la literatura cubana* de Salvador Bueno sería punto de partida del gigantesco movimiento editorial que con fines didácticos se haría realidad unos años después. Esta obra, de gran utilidad al estudiantado, realiza los valores patrióticos de los grandes de nuestra literatura.

Otras obras representativas de la creación literaria y artística se publican en 1960: *Los pasos perdidos*, de Alejo Carpentier; *Dador*, de José Lezama Lima; *Bertillón 166*, de José Soler Puig; y, *Análisis funcional de la cultura*, de Ezequiel Martínez Estrada. Estas dos últimas obras, premios de novela y ensayo del Primer Concurso Literario Hispanoamericano de la Casa de las Américas, que devendría el más importante y prestigioso concurso de esta especialidad en la América de habla hispana. En este mismo año, la Imprenta Nacional da sus primeros frutos; se inicia con la publicación de la obra de los grandes maestros de la literatura universal partiendo de la tirada masiva de *El ingenioso Hidalgo Don Quijote de la Mancha*, primera edición cubana de este título, en cuatro tomos, con viñetas e ilustraciones de Gustavo Doré y un dibujo de Pablo Picasso.

En cuanto a publicaciones periódicas, a mediados de 1959, exactamente el 10 de abril, aparece la revista *Verde Olivo*, vehículo de formación, información, orientación y educación de los miembros de las Fuerzas Armadas Revolucionarias. Por su parte, el Instituto Cubano del Arte y la Industria Cinematográfica, inicia la publicación de la revista *Cine Cubano*, la cual recogería desde sus primeros pasos el desarrollo de nuestra producción cinematográfica, expresión artística, del perfil cultural de la nueva Cuba. En el campo de la literatura, la poesía revolucionaria se abre paso con el *Himno a las milicias* y el *Libro de Rolando* de Alvarez Baragaño y Rolando Escardó respectivamente; la novela *Tierra inerme*, de Dora Alonso, resulta premio en el Segundo Concurso Literario Hispanoamericano de la Casa de las Américas. Ya a fines de este año, aparece la revista *Cuba Socialista*, encaminada fundamentalmente al desarrollo político-ideológico de cuadros y militantes revolucionarios.

En 1962 la Dirección de Publicaciones de la Universidad Central de Las Villas edita *Prosa de Prisa*, una compilación de crónicas que Nicolás Guillén publicara en Cuba y en el extranjero el los años 1938 y 1961; y la Unión de Escritores y Artistas de Cuba publica en sus Ediciones Unión *Con las mismas manos*, selección de poesías de Roberto Fernández Retamar; por su parte, la Casa de las Américas en su Tercer Concurso Literario Hispanoamericano otorga premio de cuento a Raúl González de Cascorro con su obra *Gente de Playa Girón*; y la Editora del Ministerio de Educación publica la imprescindible obra del doctor José Antonio Portuondo *Bosquejo histórico de las letras cubanas*.

Con el año 1962 se cierra el período (1959-1962) que dio lugar a la primera compilación bibliográfica de carácter nacional después del triunfo de la Revolución.

En 1967, un año antes de la publicación de la *Bibliografía cubana* (1959-1962), por razones editoriales, se publica el período 1963-1964, y en otro volumen aparte el movimiento editorial 1965.

En el período 1963-1964 también se desglosa la información de la *Bibliografía* en un índice analítico. Más de 1200 citas bibliográficas ponen de manifiesto el esfuerzo editorial e intelectual del país. Ya a fines de 1963, nuestro novelista Alejo Carpentier declara a la periodista mexicana Elena Poniatowska que el Gobierno Revolucionario había editado dieciséis millones quinientos mil volúmenes. En este mismo año, Carpentier publica en Ediciones *R* su novela *El siglo de las luces* (editada posteriormente, catorce veces en español y traducida a más de veinte idiomas); y en Ediciones Unión, *Guerra del tiempo, tres relatos y una novela*. Un año después, en 1964, la Unión de Escritores y Artistas de Cuba publica, por primera vez en Cuba, *El reino de este mundo*.

Por otra parte, el también pujante movimiento editorial de la Universidad Central de Las Villas edita, entre otros títulos, el testimonio poético de Nicolás Guillén, quien refleja, en su obra *Tengo*, la realidad de la Revolución Cubana y la epopeya de la Sierra Maestra; Samuel Feijoó desentraña, una vez más, las realidades y la cubanía de nuestro campesinado con su novela *Juan Quinquin en Pueblo Mocho*, obra que es llevada al cine en 1967; y Renée Méndez Capote recuerda para la historia los quehaceres de la república "enmendada", en sus *Memorias de una cubanita que nació con el siglo*.

En el campo de la investigación, Julio Le Riverend Brusone, en 1963, publica *Historia económica de Cuba*, documento básico que respondió a una necesidad inminente del proceso revolucionario: la escasez de libros para el estudio de esta materia.

Un año después, en 1964, aparece *El ingenio: complejo económico social cubano del azúcar*, de Manuel Moreno Fraginals, donde se analiza el desarrollo histórico de la industria azucarera cubana como elemento fundamental de nuestra estructura económica. Por estos años el empeño de la política editorial por editar auténticas obras científicas logra la publicación, entre otros títulos, de la tercera edición ampliada y corregida del *Diccionario botánico de nombres vulgares cubanos* de Juan Tomás Roig, que edita el Instituto Nacional de Reforma Agraria.

Nuevas secciones presentan la *Bibliografía cubana 1965*: un índice de títulos correspondiente a libros y folletos; las publicaciones seriadas aparecidas o cerradas durante el año, relación de gran utilidad con vistas a futuros repertorios especializados; biobibliografías de autores fallecidos durante el año, contribución básica para un diccionario biográfico; y el Suplemento, que, a partir de este año 1965, recoge aquellos títulos que por causas diversas no figuraron en sus años correspondientes.

La sección de biobibliografías, aunque en ningún modo resultó una innovación de las compilaciones nacionales cubanas, sin embargo, ha ofrecido un verdadero servicio de presente y futuro a la cultura cubana. Hasta 1988, esta sección había publicado 96 biobibliografías, esquemas de la vida y la obra de los más relevantes cubanos, y guías imprescindibles para el estudio de nuestra cultura.

El ámbito literario cubano de 1965 registra en la colección Contemporáneos de la Unión de Escritores y Artistas de Cuba (UNEAC), los ensayos de Graziella Pogolotti en su primer libro, *Examen de conciencia*, y la novela de Edmundo Desnoes *Memorias del subdesarrollo*, llevada al cine en 1968; en el ámbito científico, el Museo Histórico de Ciencias Médicas Carlos J. Finlay de la Academia de Ciencias de la República de Cuba publica las obras completas de Tomás Romay y de Carlos J. Finlay, ambos títulos compilados y prologados por el doctor José López Sánchez.

Las compilaciones nacionales de los años 1966-1970, aparecidas en el período 1968-1972, no presentan variantes formales, sino la misma organización que la compilación 1965. No obstante, el auge editorial de estos años pone de manifiesto las posibilidades de creación que promueve el ascenso del proceso revolucionario.

Dos obras de interés histórico se publican en 1967: *Historia de Cuba* del Ministerio de las Fuerzas Armadas Revolucionarias e *Ideología Mambisa*, ambas del historiador Jorge Ibarra, obras que se complementan al ofrecernos con criterio marxista la descripción de los acontecimientos históricos y la ideología que forjó nuestra nacionalidad respectivamente.

Otro empeño bibliográfico importante en este período resultó la edición del *Atlas Nacional de Cuba* (1970), publicado por la Academia de Ciencias de Cuba y la Academia de Ciencias de la URSS, obra elaborada durante cinco años por especialistas y científicos cubanos y soviéticos conjuntamente.

Títulos representativos de la creación literaria en este período resultan *Biografía de un cimarrón* (1966), de Miguel Barnet, el testimonio de un esclavo publicado por el Instituto de Etnología y Folklore de la Academia de Ciencias de la República de Cuba; *Ensayo de otro mundo* (1967), obra de Roberto Fernández Retamar que incluye su importante interpretación marxista "Martí en su tercer mundo"; *Muestrario del mundo o Libro de las maravillas de Boloña* (1968), poesías de Eliseo Diego; y *El acoso*, de Alejo Carpentier, publicado por primera vez en Cuba en 1969, estos tres últimos títulos editados por el Instituto del Libro.

Por su parte, en la colección Contemporáneos, la UNEAC publica *Tientos y diferencias* (1966), de Alejo Carpentier; *Paradiso* (1966), de José Lezama Lima; *El Gran Zoo* (1967), de Nicolás Guillén; *Testimonios* (1968), de Cintio Vitier; y *Visitaciones* (1970), de Fina García Marruz. La Biblioteca Nacional José Martí resulta autor corporativo de los tres tomos de *La crítica literaria y estética en el siglo XIX cubano* (1969-1974), de Cintio Vitier.

En esta segunda mitad de la década de los 60 aparecen importantes revistas políticas y culturales que aún se publican por resultar serios instrumentos de información de nuestra vida nacional: *Revolución y Cultura* (1967), *Signos* (1969), *Cuba en el Ballet* y *Santiago* (1970). Prensa Latina continuaría la publicación de la revista *Cuba* (1962) como *Cuba Internacional* (1969); y el periódico *Granma* inicia en 1966 su *Resumen Semanal* en español, inglés, francés y portugués.

Nuevos horizontes enfrenta la *Bibliografía cubana 1971*, la cual marcó un hito en nuestro desarrollo bibliográfico, al hacer patente que cambio y permanencia cultural resultan conceptos que se complementan. Más abarcadora que las anteriores compilaciones, esta obra comenzó a reflejar la realidad cultural revolucionaria con sus variadas y pujantes manifestaciones. En efecto, en el III Encuentro de Bibliotecas Públicas, celebrado en La Habana en octubre de 1971, se acuerdan nuevas secciones que a partir de ese año describirían en nuestro repertorio bibliográfico nacional carteles o afiches, catálogos de exposiciones, las producciones cinematográfica y discográfica y las emisiones postales del país.

En la producción editorial 1971, resultan fuertes editores el Instituto Cubano del Libro (ICL) y su Editorial Ciencias Sociales, la Casa de las

Américas y la Unión de Escritores y Artistas de Cuba. El ICL y la Casa de las Américas editan las novelas revolucionarias *Los negros ciegos*, de Raúl Valdés Vivó, y *La última mujer y el próximo combate*, de Manuel Cofiño, entre otras obras de creación literaria. (Esta última novela fue premio Casa de las Américas 1971.)

La Editorial Ciencias Sociales se hace eco del centenario del fusilamiento de los estudiantes en 1871, con la publicación de la más completa investigación sobre este hecho, realizada por el doctor Luis Felipe LeRoy y Gálvez. La UNEAC publica en su colección Contemporáneos *Crítica sucesiva*, conjunto de profundas valoraciones de Cintio Vitier; y en Ediciones Unión, el ensayo de Pedro Deschamps Chapeaux *El negro en la economía cubana del siglo XIX*. Capítulos de este ensayo (Premio UNEAC 1970) habían aparecido, desde 1968, en la sección "Historia de las gentes sin historia" de la *Revista de la Biblioteca Nacional José Martí*.

Posteriormente, los repertorios bibliográficos de carácter nacional, de los años 1972-1976, siguieron ofreciendo la misma información que la *Bibliografía Cubana 1971* aunque introduciendo dos variantes formales desde 1974: la *Bibliografía Cubana 1974* presenta al final de la compilación de libros y folletos, los asientos bibliográficos de autores cubanos en el extranjero (obras de cubanos publicadas en otros países o traducidas a otros idiomas), y modifica el contenido del índice analítico, ya que aparecen las *Colecciones y Series* y las *Editoriales Extranjeras y Nacionales* al final del mismo.

En esta etapa (1972-1976) se consolida y perfecciona el sistema editorial del país, el cual se integra totalmente, en 1975, en editoriales. Miles de títulos son editados ante las crecientes necesidades educacionales e intelectuales del país.

Con respecto a la producción bibliográfica destinada a la educación, el Instituto Cubano del Libro enfrenta las necesidades de la mayor explosión demográfica estudiantil registrada en la historia de nuestro país; y, solamente en 1974, destina a la educación 23.2 millones de ejemplares. *La educación en revolución*, obra publicada en este mismo año, resulta un precioso documento que enriquece sobremanera la bibliografía cubana de la educación al ofrecer una síntesis de la política educacional y cultural de la Revolución, así como una panorámica de los logros obtenidos en este sector.

La Editorial Ciencias Sociales publica importantes títulos de mensaje patriótico inspirados en realidades pasadas y en la lucha por la independencia nacional y la justicia social: en 1973, *Antonio Maceo, apuntes para una historia de su vida*, de José Luciano Franco, obra cuya primera edición data de 1951, y que constituye uno de los esfuerzos más serios que se hayan realizado para explicar en toda su complejidad el tiempo y la obra de

Antonio Maceo, como asegura su prologuista el doctor José Antonio Portuondo; en 1974, *Carlos Manuel de Céspedes*, escritos del prócer independentista, recopilados por los profesores Fernando Portuondo y Hortensia Pichardo; y *El Ala Izquierda Estudiantil y su época*, de Ladislao González Carbajal; en 1975, *El barracón y otros ensayos*, importante obra de interés demográfico y económico, resultado de muchos años dedicados a la investigación por el sabio profesor Juan Pérez de la Riva. Otros éxitos editoriales de Ciencias Sociales, en 1975, resultan la segunda edición de las *Obras completas* de José Martí, el más grande hombre del siglo XIX cubano, y las primeras ediciones del Instituto de Historia del Movimiento Comunista y la Revolución Socialista de Cuba, con motivo de la celebración del Primer Congreso del Partido Comunista de Cuba. El Instituto de Historia publica el primer tomo de *El movimiento obrero cubano, documentos y artículos*, que abarca desde el origen de las primeras organizaciones obreras, a mediados del siglo XIX, hasta la fundación de la primera central sindical y el primer partido marxista-leninista de la clase obrera cubana en 1925; y *Mella, documentos y artículos*, la más completa recopilación de la acción y del pensamiento del lider revolucionario. En 1972, el escritor Enrique Cirules gana el Premio Testimonio en el Concurso 26 de Julio del MINFAR con la obra *Conversación con el último norteamericano*. La Casa de las Américas otorga premio, en 1975, al testimonio de Raúl González de Cascorro titulado *Aquí se habla de combatientes y bandidos*, sobre la lucha frente a los bandidos en el Escambray.

Pero no solamente se describen en la bibliografía nacional de este período obras de interés histórico. También la creación literaria continuaba su ascenso: en 1972 la UNEAC publica *La rueda dentada* y *El Diario que a diario*, del poeta nacional Nicolás Guillén; en 1973, la colección Biblioteca Básica de Autores Cubanos edita *Poesía mayor* de José Martí, el poeta mayor de nuestra lengua en su tiempo, con la selección y prólogo del inolvidable doctor Juan Marinello; en 1974, la Editorial Arte y Literatura lanza *El recurso del método* y *Concierto Barroco*, de nuestro primer narrador Alejo Carpentier; y, en 1975, la Casa de las Américas publica en su colección Cuadernos Casa, *Del incausto a la sangre: Sor Juana Inés de la Cruz*, de la doctora Mirta Aguirre. También nuevas novelas se inscriben en la narrativa policial: entre otras *No es tiempo de ceremonias*, de Rodolfo Pérez Valero (Premio MININT 1974). Finalmente, en este período bibliográfico, la Editorial Gente Nueva pone en manos de niños y jóvenes la mejor lectura; a su esfuerzo editorial se debe el bellísimo libro *Juegos y otros poemas*, de Mirta Aguirre. Otro editor de obras infantiles y juveniles lo es la Casa de las Américas, institución que premia en 1976 a Nersys Felipe por sus *Cuentos de Guane*.

En 1977, la *Bibliografía cubana*, como instrumento práctico de información y como registro de nuestra producción editorial, incluye una nueva sección que describe gran parte de la edición de mapas publicados en Cuba desde 1959. Este importante portador presenta las descripciones cartográficas en orden cronológico. La información específica es ofrecida mediante un índice analítico y, al final, en orden alfabético, aparecen las instituciones editoriales responsables de la edición de atlas, mapas y planos en nuestro país. Por las características propias de estos materiales no ha sido posible una frecuencia estable en esta sección, aunque en ningún modo ésta podría ser ni siquiera anual. Recientemente la sección de mapoteca en coordinación con el Departamento de Bibliografía Cubana ha logrado incluir de nuevo esta sección en la Bibliografía Nacional 1990. Esta masa informativa actualiza la sección anterior y sigue el paso a los materiales cartográficos publicados en Cuba desde 1977 hasta esa fecha.

Los títulos más significativos de este año fueron editados por las editoriales de Ciencias Sociales, Arte y Literatura y Letras Cubanas, así como por la UNEAC, la Casa de las Américas y el Centro de Estudios Martianos. La Editorial Ciencias Sociales publica la colección de documentos *Política cultural de la Revolución Cubana*; el valioso trabajo de documentación y análisis *La Revolución del 33*, de Leonel Soto, en tres tomos, el cual constituye un aporte esencial al conocimiento de ese fenómeno histórico y del período en cuestión; *Etiopía, la revolución desconocida*, de Raúl Valdés Vivó; y el testimonio de Ricardo Martínez Víctores *7 RR—La historia de Radio Rebelde*, entre otros títulos que, por su contenido, resultan verdaderas contribuciones de interés histórico, político y social. La Editorial Arte y Literatura logra cuidadosas ediciones en distintos géneros de la literatura cubana: en poesía, la edición facsimilar del *Ismaelillo*, de José Martí, a cargo de Angel Augier; *Poesía*, de Juan Marinello; y *Fragmentos a su imán*, de José Lezama Lima; en novela *Oppiano Licario*, también de Lezama, obra prologada por Manuel Moreno Fraginals, y *Tres novelas de humor (Pancho Ruta y Jil Jocuma, La jira descomunal, y Tumbaga*) de Samuel Feijóo; en historia y crítica, las investigaciones elaboradas en la Biblioteca Nacional José Martí: *Flor oculta de poesía cubana*, de Fina García Marruz y Cintio Vitier; *Suite para Juan Francisco Manzano*, de Roberto Friol, y *Para una vida de Santiago Pita*, de Octavio Smith. La UNEAC en su colección Contemporáneos publica las *Elegías*, de Nicolás Guillén, y su poesía para niños *Por el mar de las Antillas anda un barco de papel* publicada en primera edición, de 144 ejemplares mimeografiados y numerados, bellísima iniciativa de nuestro Poeta Nacional para recaudar fondos para el XI Festival de la Juventud y los Estudiantes; posteriormente fue publicada en edición de lujo por la Editorial Letra Cubanas. La Casa de las Américas, por su parte, selecciona para su Premio 1978, *Contra viento y marea*, del Grupo Areíto. Este último, Premio La Juventud en Nuestra América, concedido a jóvenes cubanos que emigraron siendo niños a los Estados Unidos. También la UNEAC otorga su premio de testimonio a la obra de Jesús Díaz, *De la patria al exilio*, basada en esta misma experiencia de jóvenes cubanos en busca de su identidad nacional. Por último, el Centro de Estudios Martianos publica en su colección Estudios Martianos *Siete enfoques marxistas sobre José Martí* y el número uno de su Anuario. A partir de estos títulos el Centro de Estudios Martianos publicaría títulos decisivos para el estudio de la vida y la obra del Apóstol.

La *Bibliografía Cubana* de los años 1979-1981 fue publicada cada año, en dos tomos de tamaño menor con vistas a facilitar el uso y manejo de una considerable información, descrita en forma casi exhaustiva. Algunas modificaciones técnicas rectifican las descripciones bibliográficas de revistas, de catálogos de exposiciones y de la producción cinematográfica a partir de 1979. En este mismo año se inicia la descripción de programas, documentos de primera mano para la historia de nuestra cultura, y en 1980 se incorporan las obras musicales impresas, relación alfabética que requirió una considerable labor de búsqueda al extenderse su descripción bibliográfica, en forma retrospectiva, hasta 1972. Otra innovación abre nuevas perspectivas a la bibliografía nacional al ampliar su información biobibliográfica, la cual estuvo limitada hasta 1979 a la vida y obra de literatos y científicos cubanos fallecidos cada año. A partir de 1980 esta sección incluye además datos de la vida y la obra de artistas cubanos insignes.

La consulta de este repertorio arroja un saldo favorable a la Editorial Letras Cubanas la cual publica selecciones, compilaciones y antologías de grandes figuras de la cultura cubana. En 1979: *Teatro*, de Carlos Felipe; *Poesía y prosa*, de José Zacarías Tallet; y *Crítica literaria*, de Enrique José Varona. En 1980: *Letras*, de Dora Alonso; *Poesía y prosa*, de Manuel Navarro Luna; y *Prosa*, de José Manuel Poveda. Y en 1981: *Estudios literarios*, de Mirta Aguirre; *Para el perfil definitivo del hombre*, de Roberto Fernández Retamar; *Obra poética*, de Nicolás Guillén; *La pedrada: selección poética*, de Fayad Jamis; *Cuentos escogidos*, de Onelio Jorge Cardoso; *Imagen y posibilidad*, de José Lezama Lima; *Cartas cruzadas*, de Pablo de la Torriente Brau; y *Antología poética*, de Cintio Vitier. Apreciable rescate de distintos géneros literarios: teatro, poesía, prosa, ensayo y cartas, representativos dentro de la cultura cubana.

Si analizamos la creación poética de este período podríamos destacar los poemarios *Pasajes de una época*, de Nancy Morejón; *Ciudad, ciudad*, de Francisco de Oraá; *La extraña fiesta*, de Emilio de Armas; *Palabras juntan revolución*, de Lourdes Casal; *A través de mi espejo*, de Eliseo Diego;

Imitación de la vida, de Luis Rogelio Nogueras; y *La fecha al pié*, de Cintio Vitier. Por otra parte la más alta creación novelística se debió a Alejo Carpentier y a Miguel Barnet quienes publican en 1979 y 1981, respectivamente, sus novelas *El arpa y la sombra* y *Gallego*. También se publican libros de conferencias tales como: *Razón de ser* y *La novela latinoamericana en vísperas de un nuevo siglo*; ideario estético y literario de nuestro primer narrador Alejo Carpentier. Por último investigaciones históricas como: *Comercio clandestino de esclavos*, de José Luciano Franco y *Nación y cultura nacional*, de Jorge Ibarra, son obras que descansan sobre una sólida base documental, y enriquecen sobremanera la historiografía contemporánea cubana.

En 1982 la Bibliografía Nacional sufre nuevas modificaciones en beneficio de un mayor perfeccionamiento técnico: su periodicidad bimestral pretendió acelerar al flujo de la información; y para la descripción de libros y folletos se utilizó la norma basada fundamentalmente en la ISBD(M) International Standard Bibliography for Monographic Publications preparada por la Oficina de la FIAB para el Control Bibliográfico Universal (CBU).

Y para inventariar este último período que parte de 1982 el Premio de la Crítica, instituido por el Ministerio de Cultura y otorgado por primera vez a las obras editadas durante este año, es guía inapreciable para determinar una selección bibliográfica representativa de lo mejor de nuestra literatura de estos años. En esta década de los 80 hace historia de la obra histórica la Dra. Carmen Almodóvar con su antología crítica de la historia cubana en las épocas colonial y neocolonial (1986 y 1989); la obra activa y pasiva del Generalísimo Máximo Gómez es publicada en apreciables títulos y ediciones con motivo del CL aniversario de su natalicio; y José Luciano Franco, historiador entre historiadores, hace historia de la legislación y administración colonial en Cuba.

La compilación bibliográfica nacional correspondiente a 1989 que debió publicarse en 1990 sufre también modificaciones dada la situación actual del país con respecto a las medidas necesarias tomadas con las publicaciones periódicas. A duras penas el Departamento de Publicaciones de la Biblioteca Nacional José Martí ha logrado la publicación de los dos primeros bimestres de este año, y con el apoyo del Instituto del Libro otro volumen que abarca la información correspondiente a los bimestres 3-6 con una indización auxiliar y con las biobibliografías de las figuras fallecidas en 1989. De manera que esta experiencia renueva la bibliografía cubana anual a partir de la compilación de 1990.

En resumen, la bibliografía nacional cubana, a pesar de su carácter general, es inventario de nuestra cultura y valga aclarar que en este caso las bibliografías temáticas o especializadas no sólo complementan las bibliografías nacionales sino que también resultan inventario de la cultura en todas las ramas del saber. Inventarios imprescindibles al estudioso porque la bibliografía es depositaria de esa cultura heredada que ha oprimido y oprime el cerebro de los vivos.

Este recorrido a través de la bibliografía cubana que tiene su mejor expresión en la Bibliografía Mínima Cubana, obra de más de 1000 títulos y de carácter selectivo que en la actualidad conforma lo mejor de una biblioteca cubana (esta obra ha sido compilada por mi hermana Josefina García-Carranza y por mi y aún está pendiente su publicación), ha pretendido ser inventario de lo mejor de nuestra cultura, inventario de la historia, la literatura y la cultura de un pueblo, que es fundamento y razón de su reafirmación como nación.

NOTA

1. Carlos Manuel Trelles, *Los 150 libros más notables que los cubanos han escrito* (Habana: Impr. El Siglo XX, 1914).

32. Caracterización de la historiografía cubana en el período colonial

Carmen Almodóvar Muñoz

En cultura podemos afirmar que existe una correspondencia entre el lento proceso de desarrollo económico-social y la tardía aparición de nuestra historiografía particular. Se observa un incremento de la población en la primera mitad del siglo XVIII, el cultivo del tabaco alcanza en estos años su mayor producción, aumenta el número de ingenios y la ganadería ocupaba un lugar prominente en la riqueza de la Isla; tomando en cuenta lo anteriormente expuesto puede considerarse que Cuba había alcanzado en aquellos tiempos una economía relativamente equilibrada.

La cultura también mejora durante las décadas a las que hacemos referencia. El clero, que controlaba la enseñanza, muestra interés en algunos casos, por la preparación literaria de los alumnos; la enseñanza superior cobra vida con la fundación del Seminario de San Basilio el Magno (1722) y de la Universidad de La Habana (1728). Si a esto unimos la aparición de la imprenta en la Isla (1723), la labor desplegada por el Obispo Jerónimo Valdés como promotor cultural y el contacto con marinos y militares franceses que visitaban asiduamente el país, consideramos lógico que surgieran los primeros exponentes de la historiografía cubana en el alborear de los grandes cambios institucionales de la colonia.

Los "pioneros" de este aludido quehacer —el Obispo Morell de Santa Cruz, el regidor Arrate, el abogado Urrutia y Nicolás J. de Ribera— elaboran sus obras alrededor de 1760, cuando la influencia de los cronistas aún está muy presente en el ámbito latinoamericano que abre sus puertas a la historia de sus pueblos. Por supuesto, cada uno de ellos impone a los trabajos que escriben su propia tónica, su "visión" del pasado sobre el cual indagan. Morell —de hecho— nos brinda una historia de la iglesia de Cuba. Es la expresión vernácula de la historiografía eclesiástica contrareformista no sólo por el tema sino por las apreciaciones que el autor expone en la obra. El controvertido Obispo que escribe la *Historia de la Isla y Catedral de Cuba* (1754-1761) sitúa en el mismo nivel de importancia la historia secular y la eclesiástica de la colonia; su "celo católico" constituye un freno para generar un sentimiento de nacionalidad. No obstante lo anterior, se advierten en su historia algunas tímidas manifestaciones que denotan diferencias entre el clero peninsular y el criollo.

Félix de Arrate sí nos brinda la primera expresión historiográfica de un sentimiento de la nacionalidad cubana. Su "Patria" es La Habana, una parte del imperio español, con características específicas, que ama y exalta. En su *Llave del Nuevo Mundo Antemural de las Indias Occidentales* (1761) defiende los intereses de la oligarquía habanera, a la cual pertenece y además se rebela contra la "desigualdad" entre españoles y americanos, destacando con "pasión" los "méritos" de la sociedad que representa y de cuyos valores está convencido. Pero a nuestro juicio lo más interesante del trabajo de Arrate se evidencia en sus reflexiones acerca de la esclavitud, institución sobre la cual no discute su legitimidad. Advierte, con agudeza, que la calidad del trabajo de los negros esclavos es inferior al de los indios y además considera que estos últimos podían resultar más baratos, en tanto un trabajador "libre" se despedía cuando su rendimiento no era el esperado.

Arrate, a diferencia de Morell, es un hombre de su tiempo; el regidor habanero quiere dar a su "Patria" la historia de que carece; en esto coincide con Ignacio de Urrutia, quien aspira como él a ser útil y legar a la posteridad esa historia "particular" necesaria. Ahora bien, el concepto de "amada patria" de uno y otro es diverso. Para Arrate su concepto es eminentemente local; para el "leguleyo" Urrutia los límites patrios se amplían, alcanzando la totalidad del país.

El autor del *Teatro histórico, jurídico, político militar de la Isla Fernandina de Cuba* (1789) tiene un concepto pragmático de la historia cuya finalidad es utilitaria. De todos los "pioneros" a los que estamos aludiendo es Urrutia el que se propone un objetivo más amplio; su *Teatro* tiene pretensiones de una historia general de Cuba que respalde el ideario del "despotismo ilustrado". La obra de Urrutia no cumple sus propósitos habida cuenta que no contaba para ello con los medios materiales y culturales necesarios; sin embargo, el solo hecho de plantearse acometer tamaña empresa en aquella época merece un reconocimiento especial. Urrutia es duramente criticado por el presbítero José Agustín Caballero, suscrito a las ideas racionalistas, tan debatidas entre nuestros intelectuales en los primeros años del siglo XIX; el Padre Caballero lo tilda de "pedante" e influido por la más "rancia escolástica", que él abomina.

N. Joseph de Ribera, cuya *Descripción de la Isla de Cuba* (1757) prácticamente era desconocida hasta hace pocos años para los historiadores cubanos, cierra este grupo de "iniciadores" en el terreno historiográfico. Ribera, como Urrutia, toma en cuenta toda Cuba como provincia de España cuando se refiere al desarrollo de la Isla; las reformas que propende tienen sus orígenes en el despotismo ilustrado, en las ideas de los fisiócratas y han de hermanarse —salvando las lógicas distancias— con los planteamientos de Francisco de Arango y Parreño en su antológico *Discurso sobre la agricultura de La Habana y medios de fomentarla* (1792) donde se "imponen": su condición de "habanero" y que la ocupación inglesa había marcado el "despegue" en el desarrollo de la Colonia.

Ninguno de los ya mencionados historiadores de la segunda mitad del siglo XVIII sometan a crítica las fuentes que utilizan; unos como Arrate y Urrutia confieren importancia a las citas y se detienen a consignar la bibliografía consultada. Otros, como Morell, pasan por alto este "detalle". El estilo tampoco es similar, mientras en Arrate se impone la influencia neoclásica, en Urrutia se advierten dos tipos de discurso: uno barroco, plagado de citas eruditas y otro mucho más sobrio y alejado de la historiografía escolástica.

El siglo XIX supone un cambio que no puede obviarse en el proceso historiográfico cubano. Se abre con la obra de Antonio J. Valdés, *Historia de la Isla y en especial de La Habana* (1813), que denota la influencia del Iluminismo, de los postulados racionalistas defendidos por Caballero en su controversia con los abanderados del escolasticismo decadente. Valdés también "quiere ser útil a la patria", que es Cuba, aunque inscrita dentro de los límites del imperio español. Influido probablemente por Juan J. Rousseau y su *Contrato Social*, así como de otras figuras de la Ilustración, en el libro de Valdés se observan algunas críticas acertadas referidas en algunos casos a la contemporaneidad, que constituye el centro de atención de dicho historiador.

El autor somete a crítica las fuentes consultadas, que si bien son insuficientes en cuanto al tratamiento de los primeros siglos. No podemos decir lo mismo en relación a los años correspondientes al gobierno del Marqués de Someruelos, ya que la información acopiada al respecto es numerosa. Valdés se anota un tanto a su favor cuando incluye en su *Historia* la toma de La Habana por los ingleses; en las páginas dedicadas al importante hecho de armas, se hace patente la ineptitud demostrada por las autoridades españoles que dirigen la defensa de la "plaza", así como el apoyo prestado por muchos vecinos de la capital para impedir el desembarco inglés en tierra cubana: protegen "el suelo que les vio nacer".

Es un español, Jacobo de la Pezuela, el que contando con el apoyo documental requerido logra lo que tanto habían intentado sin éxito los cubanos: la tan acariciada *Historia de la Isla* con el apoyo de fuentes documentales. El resultado alcanzado por Pezuela no es impensado sino fruto de muchos años de investigación, donde le sirven de antecedente el *Ensayo histórico de la isla de cultura* (1848) y el *Diccionario geográfico, estadístico, histórico de la Isla de Cuba* (1863-1866). La "imparcialidad" documental constituye el sello acreditativo del historiador gaditano, quien bajo esta aparente "objetividad" mantiene en toda su obra un ideario colonialista, sin dar ni el más mínimo margen a reformas que tendiesen a disminuir las "tensiones" existentes entre la colonia y su metrópoli. La *historia de la Isla de Cuba* (1868-1878) de Pezuela es sin duda alguna uno de los aportes más significativos que en aquel momento se hace a nuestra historiografía particular, independientemente de los intereses que represente el autor. Por supuesto, nadie niega el cúmulo informativo de la obra ni la calidad de las fuentes, de ahí que todos los que escriben con posterioridad —díganlo o no— revisan y se "sirven" de este arsenal de datos. Pero los cubanos que alimentaban reformas para el país no podían suscribir las tesis defendidas por el historiador al que hemos hecho mención. Era preciso contraponer a su documentada *Historia* otra que respondiese a la óptica cubana y naturalmente a los intereses de la opción reformista, que a la sazón había ganado bastantes adeptos en el seno de nuestra oligarquía desde finales del siglo XIX.

Pedro J. Guiteras es el encargado de dar respuesta a la obra del investigador gaditano; lo hace serenamente, sin tratar de exacerbar los ánimos, imponiéndose la "objetividad" en el tratamiento de los hechos, incluyendo en estos el odiado gobierno del General Tacón, que aborda desapasionadamente. Aunque partidario de la abolición gradual y con indemnización para los propietarios, no comparte la idea de la igualdad socio-política del negro; las concepciones anti-esclavistas de Guiteras están íntimamente ligadas a su ideología de clase, lo que representa una seria limitación en lo concerniente a nacionalidad. Si bien nunca expresa explícitamente este concepto, se infiere que es coincidente con el de José A. Saco, quien influye en las ideas políticas del historiador matancero, al calor de una fraterna amistad que les une durante años y en la que prima la franca admiración del autor de *Cuba y su gobierno* (1853) por su contemporáneo.

Cuando Guiteras escribe su obra cumbre, *Historia de la Isla de Cuba* (1865-1866), tiene presente su experiencia pedagógica, de ahí en el campo de la historia tiene una concepción pragmática y didáctica de la misma; aunque en la época en que redacta este trabajo están en alza las ideas románticas —tanto en Europa como en los Estados Unidos— sus concepciones historiográficas mantienen una estrecha "comunión" con el racionalismo dieciochesco, sin desconocer algunos elementos incorporados por el referido romanticismo a la historiografía general. A pesar de que no pudo consultar fuentes de primera mano como Pezuela, su *Historia*, como afirma Juan Marinello en *Revista de Avance* (1927), "fue en su día un libro de vanguardia".

Si la elaboración de una historia general y sistemática de Cuba constituye para los "naturales del país" una meta de compromiso ineludible, el tema relacionado con la esclavitud y su posible abolición no "atrae" tanto su interés, en tanto que resulta muy controvertido. Fundamentalmente son los extranjeros los que toman la palabra para expresar sus criterios en cuanto a la trata y la esclavitud, para manifestar sus puntos de vista acerca de las ventajas de la abolición para el futuro desarrollo de la Isla: Humboldt, Turnbull, Madden y La Sagra son ejemplos de ello.

Humboldt, en su *Ensayo político de la Isla de Cuba*, que circula a partir de 1807, hace patente su condena al tráfico clandestino de esclavos; influido por el ideario liberal burgués de la época se adhiere a los partidarios del abolicionismo. En este "clásico" que todos hemos utilizado en alguna ocasión, el científico alemán hace certeras consideraciones, en cuanto a las medidas que debían tomarse en cuenta para enfrentar una abolición gradual de la esclavitud en nuestro territorio. Humboldt no sólo advierte el problema sino que brinda soluciones al mismo, y lo hace sin perder de vista los intereses de los productores cubanos, preservando el predominio económico-social de estos. Aunque sus "reformas" no son atendidas ni "entendidas" en aquel momento por quienes debían hacer tenido oídos receptivos, cabe subrayar que sus opiniones trascienden a la postre y su *Ensayo* es uno de los títulos más consultados por los que estudian la temática en los años siguientes.

Turnbull y Madden, cada uno con su estilo personal, dejan bien sentados los intereses del abolicionismo inglés, cuyas ideas sustentan y defienden respectivamente en *Travels in the West, Cuba; with Notices of Porto Rico, and the Slave Trade* (1840) y *The Island of Cuba* (1849). En sus "esencias" ambas obras tienen mucho en común, pero mientras Turnbull somete a crítica las fuentes seleccionadas, se apoya en datos estadísticos para fundamentar sus criterios y argumenta con relativa "objetividad" cómo se desenvuelve la vida de los esclavos en la Isla, entre otras cosas; Madden se motiva más por exponer al lector los "horrores" de la esclavitud y el funcionamiento "sui géneris" de la legislación colonial, con respecto a los tratados firmados entre España e Inglaterra para dar término al tráfico negrero. No se preocupa por criticar las fuentes que consulta y como el mismo afirma en su libro, "no pretende analizar los hechos" a los que se refiere sino simplemente "citarlos". Consideramos que el trabajo de Turnbull es más profesional que el de Madden y su información más completa; la frontera del idioma, pues no se traduce al español, es a nuestro juicio la causa de que *Travels in the West* no fuese citada por los historiadores cubanos y Richard Madden "aparentemente" merece la preferencia de estos. El español Ramón de la Sagra consagra parte de su importante quehacer a la historia económica de Cuba, al estudio de su población; necesariamente se pronuncia sobre el tema de la esclavitud y comparte el abolicionismo inglés. En tanto entiende que la esclavitud frena el desarrollo tecnológico de la agricultura en la Isla y los nuevos cánones colonialistas que La Sagra defiende no pueden llevarse a efecto manteniendo viva una institución ya caduca. Sin "historias", que han dado lugar a contrapuestas opiniones acerca de su calidad y objetivos propuestos, dejan un saldo informativo que nadie puede ignorar —ni siquiera sus detractores— y sus reflexiones en torno al desarrollo alcanzado en la Isla a mediados del pasado siglo, así como sobre los problemas fundamentales de la Colonia en aquellos momentos, son tenidos en cuenta por muchos de sus contemporáneos, sus obras constituyen durante décadas fuentes de obligatoria referencia.

El examen de la supresión del tráfico de esclavos africanos y su interrelación con el adelanto o atraso de la agricultura cubana, entre otros aspectos relacionados con el tema de la esclavitud, tienen en el bayamés José Antonio Saco un perspicaz analista. Entre los múltiples asuntos que aborda en su vasta "papelería" la polémica esclavista ocupa el sitio preferente; esto sin desconocer su erudita *Historia de la esclavitud* (1875) donde Saco afirma que la esclavitud siempre había existido y sobre estas "bases" justifica la permanencia de dicha institución en la Colonia.

Independientemente de que el concepto de nacionalidad del historiador bayamés tiene limitaciones que no se pueden obviar, llamamos la atención en cuanto al contexto en el que Saco se desenvuelve, que necesariamente hace mella en su forma de pensar y actuar; a pesar de excluir al negro, negarle un lugar preferente entre los fundadores de la nacionalidad cubana al autor de la *Memoria sobre la vagancia en la isla de Cuba* (1831), supone asumir una actitud extremista al enjuiciar el pensamiento de este ilustre patricio. Partidario de la abolición del tráfico africano, su ideario no rebasa los límites del reformismo, encontrando la expresión óptima de su cubanía en el análisis donde se proyecta abiertamente contra la anexión a los Estados Unidos, y "alerta" de sus peligrosas consecuencias para quienes aman la Isla. Sus "Papeles" constituyen un monumento intelectual de gran valor para la historiografía y cultura cubanas; revisarlos es tarea inicial, obligatoria, para todos los que indagan sobre la problemática esclavista en nuestro país.

El también erudito Antonio Bachiller y Morales, aunque con óptica diferente a la de Saco —habida cuenta que sus presupuestos investigativos son de otra índole— cobra interés por la historia de la esclavitud en Cuba, en especial durante el siglo XIX, relacionándola con el movimiento abolicionista mundial en su libro *Los Negros* (1887). El "Padre de la Bibliografía Cubana" canta "loas" a Inglaterra por su actitud abolicionista. Aprecia diferentes opiniones entre los "grupos de poder" que se mueven en redor de la esclavitud y los problemas que la misma entrañaba al país: sus consideraciones referentes al abolicionismo y su repercusión en la Isla son interesantes en el momento en que ve la luz el trabajo, máxime que representaba la primera aproximación sistemática al referido tema en Cuba, aunque en apretada síntesis.

Bachiller y Morales, sin embargo, no sobresale en nuestra historiografía particular por lo anteriormente expuesto acerca de la temática esclavista, sino por su aporte a la historia de la cultura cubana, de lo que es una muestra representativa su trabajo *Apuntes para la historia de las letras y de la instrucción pública en la Isla de Cuba* (1859-1861), donde se insertan dos de sus principales contribuciones a la bibliografía de asuntos cubanos: el "Catálogo razonado y cronológico de publicaciones periódicas". Su amplia producción, caracterizada por una preocupación erudita, brinda el mayor caudal informativo posible, nutriéndose de las mejores fuentes "asequibles", pero no adecuándose en cuanto a métodos de exposición a la historiografía erudita; tampoco maneja los elementos de la crítica externa de las fuentes, en tanto demuestra pericia y agudeza al aplicar la crítica interna a las mismas. Bachiller, al igual que Saco, ocupa por sobrados valores un destacado lugar en el siglo XIX y por ende su labor realza nuestra historiografía.

Nos enfrentamos a una síntesis y por tanto sólo traemos a colación aquellos elementos que no pueden pasar inadvertidos al analizar, a grandes rasgos, la historiografía cubana enmarcada en la sociedad colonial. De ahí que pasemos finalmente a desarrollar algunas ideas relacionadas con la temática independentista, que cubre las últimas décadas del pasado siglo como centro de interés por parte de los historiadores nativos.

De manera general, quienes abordan las guerras que se libran en el país a partir de 1868 han sido testigos o protagonistas de los hechos, de ahí que son sus "vivencias", las fuentes testimoniales las que nutren preferentemente a estos cubanos que circunstancialmente se convierten en historiadores o como muchos prefieren llamarles, "cronistas de la guerra".

Los que se inspiran en la Guerra Grande —Fernando Figueredo, Enrique Collazo, Antonio Zambrana, etc.— tienen que girar de una u otra forma en torno a Carlos Manuel de Céspedes. En tanto hasta la muerte del "Padre de la Patria" no se puede hacer historia de los años 1868-1873 sin tenerlo muy presente: el alzamiento, la toma de Bayamo, la Asamblea de Guáimaro, por mencionar algunos hechos significativos, tienen que enjuiciarse investigando la actitud asumida por el "Iniciador" en cada una de los casos. Y es más, aún después de muerto su "presencia" no puede desconocerse, de ahí que sea este prócer el que acapare más que ninguna otra personalidad de la época, el interés de quienes al escribir se valen —en primer lugar— de los recuerdos, de las "fuentes orales".

Las raíces del Pacto del Zanjón, las verdaderas causas y gestores de esta "paz sin independencia", también constituyen un centro de miras para los estudiosos de la Guerra de los Diez Años. En aquellos momentos la mayor parte de los que nos legan una obra justifican el Pacto, aduciendo múltiples razones, particularmente esta "defensa" es en esencia una autodefensa. Sin entrar en modo alguno a enjuiciar los hechos, sí queremos subrayar que hoy entendemos sus razones, dado que no resultaba fácil para hombres como Máximo Gómez, admitir sin inmutarse el epíteto de "traidor" a la causa revolucionaria, cuando se habían dedicado diez años de la vida a luchar por la independencia de Cuba.

Tanto en el caso de Céspedes como en el del Pacto, los testimoniantes sientan las bases de criterios que luego serán "interiorizados" durante décadas por los que se refieren a la temática con posterioridad, es decir durante la república neocolonial. Pocos indagarán más allá de lo afirmado por Collazo, Figueredo, Gómez o Sanguily; esta influencia excesiva, este repetir una y otra vez lo expuesto por los "cronistas", sin poner en "entredicho" sus afirmaciones, sin contrastar sus "vivencias" con la documentación existente en los archivos, ha retrasado durante largo tiempo una interpretación justa de hechos y personalidades históricos. No culpamos a Collazo ni a Sanguily por no haberse "distanciado" suficientemente de los sucesos que analizan, porque resulta muy difícil ser "juez y parte" a la vez; consideramos que gracias a la información que nos brindan y a pesar de sus limitaciones, se sientan las bases para el estudio de nuestras guerras de liberación nacional con títulos tan conocidos como: *Desde Yara hasta el Zanjón* (1893) de Collazo, *La República de Cuba* (1873) de Zambrana, *La Revolución de Yara* (1902) de Fernando Figueredo, *Convenio del Zanjón* (1878) de Ramón Roa, etc. Si de "culpables" se trata demos paso a la verdad, los que les suceden en el tiempo y ahí nos incluimos también nosotros, nos "acomodamos" a lo dicho y sólo fragmentariamente se hacen aportes, que han permitido paso a paso llenar vacíos historiográficos y acercarnos mucho más a la verdad histórica, justa meta de todo investigador.

El período inter-guerras, que irradia luz ante la presencia martiana, no cuenta con muchos exponentes que expliquen cuanto acontece en los tiempos del llamado "reposo turbulento"; los autonomistas, grandes oradores, poco nos legan en el terreno que analizamos; aún del propio Martí, cuyo ingente quehacer constituye el centro motor de cuanto acontece con vistas a la preparación de la "guerra necesaria" desde la década del 80, tampoco nos han llegado completas sus consideraciones acerca de la Guerra iniciada en Demajagua el 10 de octubre de 1868. Contamos con los trabajos de Enrique Trujillo, en particular el titulado *Apuntes históricos* (1896), en el que trata de "empañar" a toda costa la labor revolucionaria de José Martí y critica inmisericordemente al Partido que dirige, buscando la división de las fuerzas proclives a la independencia, agrupadas en el exilio. Fuentes periodísticas y las vivencias personales de Trujillo constituyen la "materia prima" del aludido libro; a pesar de la carga "subjetiva" contenida en sus páginas, entendemos que no debe desecharse la información de las mismas, ya que se incluyen elementos de interés relacionados con algunos problemas surgidos en el seno de la emigración, poco abordados a posteriori. También debemos anotar el aporte de Luis Estévez y Romero a la historiografía de esta etapa, *Desde el Zanjón hasta Baire* (1899), escrito con el apoyo de fuentes bibliográficas, publicísticas y documentales, con el objetivo de exaltar el importante papel desempeñado por el Partido Autonomista para "salvar a la Patria" de la errada política metropolitana e impedir que una nueva guerra tocase a nuestras puertas. A pesar de la relativa "imparcialidad" del autor y de las características del texto —que básicamente es una suma de documentos— hay que reconocer que el libro ha mantenido su vigencia hasta la actualidad; la ausencia de otros títulos relativos a la temática que superase la labor precedente, impone esta situación. La Guerra del 95, aunque recogida en excelentes "impresiones" en muchos de los "Diarios de Campaña" que escriben los testigos de aquella campaña militar, editados en plena "República", tiene en José Miró Argenter respuesta inmediata con sus *Crónicas de la Guerra* que parcialmente publica al año de terminada la contienda y luego, de manera completa en 1909. Miró se basa ante todo en el Diario de operaciones que había redactado en el escenario de los hechos, a partir de aquí construye sus *Crónicas* con la aspiración de que estas se conviertan en una "fuente legítima" para las generaciones que no habían presenciado las heroicidades de Maceo, Gómez y demás combatientes del Ejército Libertador. La realidad ha superado los "pronósticos" a pesar de todos los detractores del "panegirista" de la Invasión; si bien esta fuente sólo constituye un punto de partida para el conocimiento de la gesta del 95, esta contribución imbuida de sentimiento patriótico, similar al de Collazo y Figueredo, coadyuva a la forja de conciencias nacionalistas, tan necesarias durante los años que suceden al fin del status colonial en Cuba: a mi entender es su mayor mérito.

La historiografía cubana colonial abre caminos que son retomados ulteriormente en las décadas del siglo XX; los cambios que se operan en esta ciencia en nuestro ámbito suponen un salto cualitativo a partir de la década del 20. Si bien los tiempos cambian y la historiografía se renueva, al volver los ojos a ese siglo y medio que queda atrás nos sentimos satisfechos con este legado "colonial" que es el firme cimiento sobre cual descansa nuestra historiografía hasta la actualidad.

33. Notas para el estudio de la historiografía del movimiento obrero cubano

Luis Hipólito Serrano Pérez

El nacimiento del proletariado y de la historia del movimiento obrero cubano están íntimamente ligados al surgimiento y desarrollo de la economía capitalista que se abre paso en nuestro país en el siglo XIX. En este proceso influyen también importantes acontecimientos sociales y culturales que tienen lugar en la arena internacional, como son los movimientos migratorios, la difusión de nuevas ideologías y la formación de organizaciones de trabajadores.

Para que se tenga una idea de como acontecen en Cuba estas transformaciones, pudiera señalarse que si en 1827 los ingenios movidos por máquinas de vapor, expresión elocuente del modo de producción capitalista, ascendían sólo al 2.5% del total de las fábricas de azúcar existentes en el país, ya en 1861 alcanzaban la cifra del 70.7%.[1]

Posteriormente tiene lugar en este importante sector de la economía cubana el clásico proceso de concentración de la producción. Así tenemos, que en 1894, con una cantidad de ingenios 3.4 veces menor que en 1861, se alcanza una producción 2.3 veces mayor de azúcar.

A lo anteriormente expresado se suma el hecho de que en Cuba surge en 1837, antes inclusive que en España y otros países de América, la primera línea de ferrocarril que logra alcanzar 27 km y en 1898, al terminar la dominación colonial española, se extiende a 1,717 km. También en 1854 se establece como vía de comunicación el telégrafo Morse.

Si en 1841 la mano de obra esclava constituía el 43.3% de la población, ya en 1861 bajó a 26.5% y al lograrse en 1886 la abolición definitiva de la esclavitud, aunque se carece de un estudio confiable al respecto, se estima que la mayoría de los 200,000 esclavos liberados pasaron a engrosar las filas del proletariado agrícola, sector más importante de la clase obrera en aquella época, mientras que otros se convirtieron en campesinos, obreros asalariados en las ciudades, artesanos y muchas mujeres se dedicaron a las labores domésticas.[2]

Para paliar el grave problema de la creciente demanda de mano de obra más calificada, que había provocado este desarrollo y modernización en la sociedad cubana, se tomó el camino de la importación de trabajadores bajo el disfraz de contratados. Por esta vía entraron al país obreros procedentes de Islas Canarias, Galicia, Cataluña, China y otras regiones. Se calcula que entre 1853 y 1873 arribaron a nuestro país 132,435 chinos.[3]

La industria tabacalera alcanzó también un gran desarrollo al suprimirse el estanco del tabaco en 1817, y quedar libre el cultivo, venta y exportación de este producto. Así tenemos que en 1861 en La Habana y sus alrededores laboraban 516 tabaquerías con 15,128 trabajadores y en el resto del país 701 con 4,480. Un proceso similar tendrá lugar en las cigarrerías, que en 1836 eran 21 y agrupaban 46 obreros y en 1861 habían 38 talleres con un total de 2,300 cigarreros.

Por ello la historiografía del movimiento obrero abarca en su desarrollo diversas y variadas temáticas, que incluyen no sólo problemas organizativos sino también cuestiones ideológicas, políticas, culturales y migratorias.

Nacida originalmente de las mismas filas de la clase trabajadora, donde algunos militantes asumieron la tarea de registrar las luchas proletarias con fines diversos, llámense políticos, educativos y culturales o sociales, la historiografía del movimiento obrero fue estructurándose en estrecha vinculación con las tendencias ideológicas prevalecientes en el mundo laboral.

En un primer intento, sin que constituya una definición acabada, sino más bien una aproximación a una periodización de la historiografía del movimiento obrero cubano, sobre la cual tendremos que retornar, tras el breve paréntesis que hacemos para redactar estas notas para la 38ª reunión de SALALM, el autor de este trabajo advierte una primera etapa que abarca desde 1865 hasta 1887, caracterizada por las ideas reformistas, iluministas, cooperativistas, sectarias, raciales, religiosas, sociatorias y opuestas en el orden político a la lucha por la independencia nacional. Estas ideas en su conjunto eran esencialmente utópicas. La ilusión, de que con apelaciones a los sentimientos humanitarios de los patronos y mediante la elevación del nivel cultural de los obreros era posible cambiar la mentalidad y la actitud de los capitalistas, se debía al hecho de que no tenían una comprensión precisa del carácter de las contradicciones de clases entre los capitalistas y los obreros.

Un segundo momento se extiende desde 1887 a 1925 en que surgen y se desarrollan vigorosamente las ideas anarcosindicalistas, cuya doctrina predicaba un socialismo que daría lugar al establecimiento de industrias autónomas, poseídas y dirigidas por los trabajadores sin la presencia de la propiedad del estado y, por otra parte, reducía el papel de los sindicatos a meras agencias de lucha por reivindicaciones económicas.

Una tercera etapa que abarca desde 1925 hasta 1959 en que están presentes con gran fuerza e influencia las ideas comunistas, las que se enfrentan resueltamente a las tendencias reformistas anarcosindicalistas y al desdén de los historiadores burgueses que soslayaron, por regla general, cuando no ignoraron el papel de los trabajadores en las luchas de nuestro pueblo. En su primer congreso en agosto de 1925, el Partido Comunista acordó como tarea política estratégica la de que todos sus militantes trabajaran en los sindicatos, y organizaran a los campesinos, las mujeres y los jóvenes.

Una cuarta etapa se inicia con el triunfo de la Revolución Cubana el primero de enero de 1959, en que se abre un amplio cauce para que discurran las investigaciones y divulgación de obras sobre la clase trabajadora y sus organizaciones, desde su surgimiento hasta nuestros días, y el rescate de los materiales escritos por obreros e intelectuales que legaron trabajos de incuestionable valor sobre aspectos del accionar proletario.

Un repaso sobre la producción bibliográfica acerca del tema que nos ocupa, evidencia que exiten, por lo menos, dos tipos de escritores: aquéllos que fueron protagonistas de la historia que narran e interpretan, y los que desde una óptica académica o científica se interesan en recoger las experiencias de la clase trabajadora.

En el primero de ellos estamos en presencia de obras que constituyen testimonios imprescindibles para la reconstrucción de la dinámica social y las motivaciones espirituales que incidieron en las luchas, los éxitos y los fracasos de los trabajadores. Generalmente estos materiales carecen de una bibliografía que allane el camino para la localización de las fuentes.

A éstos se suma el hecho de que una buena cantidad de materiales responde más a objetivos divulgativos que científicos. Esto lo señalamos no porque consideremos incompatibles los mundos de la política y la academia, sino porque constituye en fenómeno que nos puede ayudar a explicar el particular desarrollo de los estudios en el campo del movimiento obrero. Tal situación resulta comprensible, si tenemos en cuenta que en nuestra región han tenido lugar importantes convulsiones sociales.

Los trabajos realizados desde el ámbito de la ciencia histórica, suponen la búsqueda sistemática de información, aunque en ocasiones ésta resulta insuficiente para la comprobación de las hipótesis. Recordemos que los historiadores conceden especial significación a la documentación primaria, pues buscan en ésta los testimonios que permitan esclarecer los hechos, situarse en la época, conocerla y sentirla.

Un rasgo característico presente como tendencia en la literatura que aborda el movimiento obrero, con alguna que otra excepción que no falta, es que privilegia el análisis de las instancias de mediación creadas por los trabajadores.

Ello evidencia lamentablemente una ausencia de estudios de la clase obrera como un todo, que tome en cuenta su proceso de constitución, su vida cotidiana, su conformación cultural, su papel y aporte a la economía de la sociedad, el contexto de las relaciones de clases y de las relaciones de poder.

Debemos subrayar el hecho de que la mayoría de los proyectos de investigación en el campo histórico apunta principalmente hacia los orígenes de la clase trabajadora, sus esfuerzos organizativos y de reivindicación laboral y política en el transcurso del siglo pasado y hasta mediado del presente.

La historia de la actualidad, como expresa el Dr. Julio Le Riverend, aun cuando se enriquece con muchos hechos económicos, políticos y sociales del momento, no está suficientemente tratada. En ello incide el criterio de que lo actual no es apto para historiarlo, y requiere tiempo; pero el problema de la posibilidad de una historia al día no depende del puro transcurso del tiempo sino de lo que pueda decir el historiador.

El análisis de la historiografía del movimiento obrero revela que ha habido no pocos trabajos, y por consiguiente muchos escritores, estrechamente vinculados a lo actual de cada momento. La historia en este sentido adquiere carácter militante y los resultados de las indagaciones aportadas por estos investigadores en ocasiones están invariablemente teñidas con diversas posiciones políticas.

Por otro lado, una gran parte de la historiografía se expresa en forma de ensayos, artículos y folletos. En las etapas más tempranas adquiere un valor particular la prensa, pues la dinámica de los acontecimientos favorece el tramiento urgente de los más acuciantes problemas; pero al margen de ello las publicaciones periódicas permiten reconstruir los hechos históricos con gran certeza y precisión y llegan a ser fuentes de obligada consulta.

La prensa obrera deviene desde sus inicios en institución clave del movimiento obrero, defensora de la organización sindical y política de la clase trabajadora y vehículo de sus manifestaciones culturales. A pesar de la elevada tasa de analfabetismo entre los proletarios, la prensa obrera es leída diariamente en alta voz por los lectores de los talleres de tabaco y llevada por militantes y organizadores a las plantaciones azucareras donde solía ser analizada y discutida.

Aunque las investigaciones sobre el movimiento obrero han tenido un enorme avance en los años posteriores a 1959, aún no se ha logrado consolidar una tradición historiográfica en las organizaciones sindicales. Ello ha provocado un débil desarrollo de una cultura favorable a la preservación de su legado, a lo que se suma un criterio equivocado respecto a lo que valora y se considera histórico.

Es común escuchar que lo verdaderamente importante, y por ello debe resguardarse con las actas de constitución, las fotografías y los periódicos antiguos, pero no así los documentos de los congresos, las declaraciones, las cartas, proclamas y otros. Con este criterio se corre el peligro de que muchos documentos importantes y valiosos pueden perderse.

Por otro lado, se mantiene en algunos trabajos el predominio de una historia bastante ideológica, por decirlo así, sobre el movimiento obrero, a partir obviamente de las alineaciones políticas de los analistas en donde, casi siempre se considera el movimiento como la vanguardia revolucionaria absoluta y se le atribuye a priori ciertos méritos, ciertas perspectivas, ciertos deberes ignorando su desarrollo, madurez política y experiencia.

Para el estudio del movimiento obrero cubano existen no pocas obras de gran valor, de aquí que las consideraciones que haremos en las páginas siguientes son el resultado de la lectura de algunas monografías, ensayos, folletos y otros materiales que considero indispensables para el estudio y conocimiento de la clase trabajadora cubana.

Vale significar que estas reflexiones no agotan de manera alguna la copiosa bibliografía que aborda este tema. Nos anima el propósito de ofrecer una pequeña muestra representativa del quehacer investigativo histórico del movimiento obrero.

Una de estas importantes obras es *La Aurora y los comienzos de la prensa y de la organización obrera en Cuba*, y su autor es el destacado intelectual J. Antonio Portuondo. En esta monografía se presenta un cuadro completo de las luchas y vicisitudes de los organismos obreros y de sus legítimas pretensiones para obtener un justo mejoramiento para su clase.

Tomando como eje la historia del semanario *La Aurora*, Portuondo nos lleva con prosa elegante, precisa y eficaz al mundo de los artesanos y a sus primeros esfuerzos serios en el orden de la Ilustración y de sus formas de lucha por la obtención de sus derechos, en una sociedad aquejada por todos los inconvenientes de una absoluta miseria social e intelectual.

Una muestra como reflejo de las ideas sociales de la burguesía liberal, en la mentalidad de los obras y propagandistas en el seno de éstos, fue Saturnino Martínez, fundador de *La Aurora*, inspirador también de las lecturas de tabaquerías y el primer líder de los trabajadores tabacaleros.

Español, de origen asturiano, Saturnino vino a Cuba muy joven y trabajó en distintos oficios hasta que se hizo tabaquero. Más tarde logró que se le designara bibliotecario en la Sociedad Económica de Amigos del País, labor que realizaba de noche después de terminada la jornada laboral. El trabajo en la biblioteca le permitía conocer las publicaciones de carácter liberal llegadas de España.

La Aurora, editado entre los años 1865 y 1868, sirvió para denunciar las condiciones infrahumanas de los obreros, los salarios de hambre que percibían, la insalubridad y el hacinamiento en los talleres, los precios prohibitivos de los alquileres y de los artículos de primera necesidad. En las luchas contra esos males apelaba a los sentimientos cristianos de que hacían ostentación los patronos y los exhortaba a que trataran a los obreros de acuerdo con la prédica del evangelio. De otra parte, *La Aurora*, partidaria de las ideas de la Ilustración, trataba de persuadir a los obreros de que los malos tratos y abusos que sufrían se debían esencialmente a su retraso cultural.

En el primer número de *La Aurora* se anunciaba ya el propósito de ésta de ilustrar en todo lo posible a los artesanos y en él figuraba también la siguiente:

Cuando en el seno de los pueblos empieza a sentirse el desarrollo de las ideas de civilización y progreso, no hay fuerza posible a detener el espíritu de impulsión que lo anima. Las ciencias y las artes, el comercio y la industria, los ricos y los pobres, todos en armónicas y legítimas aspiraciones se empeñan en disipar el fantasma del error que cierne sus alas sobre la multitud que empieza a despertar de su letargo. Por eso los pueblos han efectuado con éxito admirable tan grandes evoluciones en su rápida jornada. Por eso en los fastos de la inteligencia humana se cuentan siglos de actitud asombrosa, y siglos de letargo profundo. Por eso a través de sombra de unos siglos se vislumbra todavía la luz espléndida de otros. Afortunadamente nosotros pertenecemos a un siglo que no queda envuelto en el sudario del olvido, antes por el contrario su actividad general será memorable en las épocas venideras. Pertenecemos a un tiempo en que las ideas de unificación, se van haciendo extensivas a todas las clases; en que los trabajadores materiales van adquiriendo el rango que injustamente se les negara y en que todo se va hermanando por medio de la ley ingénita del programa.[4]

Resulta en esta "Profesión de Fe" una conciencia incipiente de los trabajadores que no se presenta en posición enérgica e intransigente, sino más bien muestra tímidas señales de una clase que empieza a nacer y sus ideas son diluidas en un fraternalismo de características definidamente colaboracionista con las demás clases sociales.

La divulgación de las doctrinas económicas fueron refrendadas en este semanario con la presencia de José de Jesús Márquez y sus gestiones en cuanto a la fundación de sociedades cooperativas, y dado su desconocimiento de las leyes que rigen el modo de producción capitalista, atribuía a las cooperativas de producción y consumo un papel que jamás tuvieron.

El interés de lograr la igualdad por la instrucción y la fe en el impulso nivelador del progreso, se reafirma en casi todos los números de este semanario, idealista y reformista, que cumplió una importante función a pesar de que sus animadores no llegaron a comprender el carácter de las contradicciones de clases entre los capitalistas y los obreros.

Otra obra importante, dirigida al estudio y significación de la prensa obrera en la etapa más temprana del surgimiento del movimiento proletario, es la compilación de la Dra. Aleida Plasencia dedicada a Enrique Roig de San Martín y *El Productor*.

En este libro apreciamos altamente el estudio que se hace del papel desempeñado por el semanario *El Productor* (1887-1890), consagrado a la defensa de los intereses económico-sociales de la clase obrera y órgano oficial de la Junta Central de Artesanos de La Habana a partir de #39 (29-3-1888).

En el artículo editorial del primer número, el 12 de julio de 1887, aparecieron claramente expresadas las razones de la publicación.

Nuestra misión, al parecer en el estadio de la prensa, es de muy distinta índole. Tratar de reunir a los obreros todos en una aspiración común y confundirlos en la santa causa de su regeneración social, es nuestro principal papel. Para ello habremos de poner en juego, ora los recursos que la ciencia habrá de prestarnos, ora la enérgica protesta en contra de toda opresión, ya parte de los llamados burgueses o ya los pequeños caciques que, entre nosotros, como entre todas las clases sociales han llegado por desgracia, a entronizarse.

De esta manera, le hacían un llamamiento a la unidad clasista del proletariado no sólo para enfrentarse a sus explotadores: la burguesía, sino también a los dirigentes reformistas, que desviaban a la clase obrera del verdadero camino. Para ello, se utilizarían tanto los conocimientos teóricos como la enérgica protesta contra la opresión.

Desde sus inicios, *El Productor* laboró por la creación de una federación de trabajadores cubanos, semejante a la organización que existía en España, por lo que sus planteamientos se vinculaban a las orientaciones internacionalistas del "socialismo revolucionario" (anarquismo), los que junto con una serie de confusiones ideológicas constituirían la guía fundamental de un pensamiento más radical.

La etapa más brillante de este semanario discurrió bajo la dirección de Enrique Roig San Martín, nacido en La Habana el 5 de noviembre de 1843, quien se convirtió en un gran líder obrero. Fue el primero en señalarle a los trabajadores cubanos el camino de la lucha de clases y el que logró unificar a un gran número de trabajadores a fines del siglo XIX. Sin embargo, pese a sus extraordinarias condiciones de dirigente, no escapó a ciertas confusiones ideológicas a causa de la propaganda que llegaba de España de filiación anarcosindicalista.

Desde las páginas de *El Productor* se libraron incontables batallas por la unidad y la organización de los trabajadores, por el mejoramiento de las condiciones de vida y trabajo, por su derecho a la huelga y a la lucha contra la opresión y la explotación de las clases dominantes, y por la formación de una conciencia internacionalista en el proletariado.

La primera campaña librada por *El Productor*, encabezada por Roig, fue a favor de la creación de una nueva organización proletaria cubana que culminaría con un congreso obrero.

Más tarde bajo el título "Realidad y Utopía", se publica una serie de editoriales en los que se plantea de forma concreta como avanzan las ideas socialistas en Cuba. Roig demuestra como éstas son aceptadas por los obreros porque no se presentan redentoras hipócritas ofreciéndoles grandes bienes a cambio de una candidatura. El socialismo, en cambio, ofrece fórmulas que ponen la redención de los obreros en sus manos.

El último artículo, el sexto, reitera que la abolición de las clases, antes que la del Estado, será también hija de dicha apropiación. "Cuando la apropiación de la producción por la sociedad sea un hecho, y cuando por consiguiente, la humanidad esté en aptitud de dominar las condiciones que hoy la rodean, entonces el hombre someterá a su inspección el conjunto de aquellas condiciones y será verdaderamente dueño de la naturaleza.[5]

Tales conceptos no se habían expuesto nunca en Cuba y ciertamente tenían que preocupar al gobierno y a la burguesía, de los cuales debería esperarse una reacción violenta, y por ello en el artículo "Vanos empeños" expresa: "Es necio empeño, inútil batallar, la pretensión de oponer diques a la corriente de las ideas grandes y generosas".[6] En el artículo "Nuevas arterias", Enrique Roig señala:

> Desde la aparición de *El Productor* en el estadio de la prensa hasta la fecha, hemos venido abogando en sus columnas por la formación de un partido obrero en la Isla de Cuba, que venga á engrosar el ya formado en los países más cultos del mundo con el fin de contribuir con nuestras escasas fuerzas á la realización del gran acontecimiento que se prepara; acontecimiento que, á nuestro juicio, habrá de poner a los obreros en la plena posesión de sus derechos conculcados.[7]

No cabría dentro de estas apretadas páginas una visión ni siquiera coherente del papel trascendental que desempeñaron *La Aurora* y Enrique Roig, sin expresar que mostraron a los obreros cubanos el camino de las luchas de clases, y defendieron al proletariado frente al capital.

En cuanto a sus ideas, como bien apunta la Dra. Aleida Plasencia, Roig no estaba por la independencia nacional de Cuba. Su criterio del internacionalismo proletario cae en la estrecha limitación de negar el movimiento de liberación nacional. A pesar de sus ideas utópicas y equivocadas y de su evidente influencia anarquista es sin lugar a dudas la figura más vigorosa del movimiento obrero en su época.

El tercer momento dentro de la historiografía del movimiento obrero cubano, se caracteriza por la lucha de los comunistas contra las tendencias reformistas y anarquistas que tratan de obtener ventajas materiales y el reconocimiento de sus derechos dentro de la sociedad capitalista basados en sus fuerzas sindicalistas, sin vincularse con las actividades políticas del país.

El poderoso movimiento huelguístico que se origina y desarrolla en los primeros años de la década del 30, evidencia la significación y el papel activo de la clase obrera cubana y a la vez pone de manifiesto errores en la dirección de este movimiento. Aquellos épicos y gloriosos acontecimientos históricos son recogidos en importantes obras entre las que se destacan *La Revolución del 33* de Leonel Soto, *La Revolución del 30: sus dos últimos años* de José A. Tabares del Real y otras, que describen las fuerzas dinámicas que intervienen en esta coyuntura revolucionaria, valoran los aciertos políticos, señalan los errores y destacan la lucha de los obreros fundamentalmente en los centrales azucareros donde logran establecer los soviets.

En 1938 comienza a editarse *Noticias de Hoy*, diario de filiación comunista que realizó un intenso trabajo orientado a fomentar y fortalecer la unidad dentro del movimiento obrero y la conciencia antiimperialista del pueblo cubano y en favor de las ideas socialistas. En sus luchas en aras del cumplimiento de su deber sufrió persecuciones, asaltos, clausuras e inclusive fueron destruidos sus talleres. Ello no impidió que en sus páginas continuaran saliendo escritos en favor de la clase obrera salidos de la pluma de destacados intelectuales que habían asumido la causa del proletariado.

Otra obra importante de este período la constituye *Los Fundamentos del Socialismo en Cuba*, escrita por Blas Roca, redactada con precisión científica y poesía revolucionaria en un lenguaje proletario y que hace un recuento histórico y un profundo análisis de la sociedad cubana, de los males que la aquejan y señala el camino para cambiar la situación. Por eso esta pequeña gran obra sirvió para educar y formar a la vanguardia de los trabajadores cubanos, por ello no es de extrañar que fue editada siete veces.

La publicación de este libro en 1945, devino punto de partida en el terreno de la lucha revolucionaria, al mostrar a la clase obrera y al pueblo que los diferentes movimientos reivindicativos dirigidos a lograr un poco más de pan, democracia y libertad para las masas populares tenían que proponerse metas superiores, es decir, alcanzar el socialismo.

La cuarta etapa comienza en el 1959, período en que se abren todas las posibilidades para que historiadores de oficio o aficionados, saquen sus notas y escriban sus testimonios y vivencias sobre los trabajadores, sus luchas, sus anhelos y esperanzas.

Los importantes y profundos cambios que tienen lugar en la vida de la sociedad cubana, a partir de ese momento, posibilitaron la apertura de nuevos caminos para la historiografía del movimiento obrero cubano.

Así tenemos que el Gobierno Revolucionario dicta la Ley No. 714 de 1960, mediante la cual en uno de sus artículos establece que: *Nadie está facultado para destruir sin autorización del Archivo Nacional documento alguno*. A partir de ese momento comienza un vigoroso movimiento dirigido a dejar constituido en cada provincia del país un archivo, que permitiera la recuperación y conservación de las fuentes documentales. Igual impulso recibirían las bibliotecas públicas en el país, las que tras un sostenido crecimiento y perfeccionamiento lograron alcanzar todo un sistema nacional armónicamente estructurado.

Simultáneamente empiezan a publicarse obras inéditas que narraban las luchas de los trabajadores y que en el pasado reciente resultaban imposible de ser editadas, porque no eran del interés de las clases que detentaban el poder, pues estos recuentos históricos se enfilaban a desenmascarar la situación de miseria y vicisitudes por las que había discurrido la vida del proletariado cubano.

A este impulso inicial, le seguiría un esfuerzo sostenido de investigadores, obreros, dirigentes, estudiantes y otros, que apoyados por las organizaciones políticas y de masas del país, formando parte de un gran movimiento, dejarían en letras impresas decenas y centenares de trabajos.

En 1966, como resultado de los acuerdos adoptados en el XII Congreso Obrero de la Central de Trabajadores de Cuba, la Comisión Nacional de Divulgación creó el Museo Histórico del Movimiento Obrero con el propósito de mostrar a las futuras generaciones las luchas de los trabajadores y del movimiento sindical. Para ello se dio a la tarea de recuperar los materiales que atesoraban los sindicatos y luchadores obreros y logró obtener más de 30,000 fuentes que incluyen documentos, folletos, publicaciones periódicas, fotografías y otros.

En mayo de 1973 se crea el Instituto de Historia del Movimiento Comunista y de la Revolución Socialista de Cuba, el cual fue dotado de los recursos humanos y técnico-materiales indispensables. Esta institución asume como tarea principal la de trabajar en las investigaciones históricas y en el estudio, la preparación científica y publicación de obras sobre la historia de la revolución cubana, el movimiento obrero, sindical y comunista.

Después de transcurridos varios años de intenso trabajo de investigación, y de enfrentar no pocas diferenciadas, la primera de ellas fue los insuficientes estudios sobre el movimiento obrero con rigor científico, a lo que se sumaba la pérdida y dispersión de una buena parte de la documentación y la carencia de investigadores históricos de experiencia en este tema que fueran capaces de redactar una historia rigurosamente científica.

No obstante, en esas condiciones, el Instituto publicó en 1977 una compilación de documentos y artículos sobre el Movimiento Obrero Cubano y más tarde, cubriendo una de las grandes lagunas de la historiografía cubana, sacó a la luz pública en 1988 la *Historia del movimiento obrero cubano 1865-1958* en dos tomos.

Esta obra representa un aporte significativo, lúcido y documentado de la historia del proletariado cubano desde sus orígenes hasta el año 1958. El libro es de obligada lectura para quien pretenda adentrarse en el heroico mundo de las luchas proletarias en Cuba, pero ello no excluye que en el mismo afloren lagunas y otras insuficiencias que devienen estímulo para nuevos y mayores empeños en los que se enfrascan nuestros historiadores de hoy.

NOTAS

1. Raúl Cepero Bonilla, *Azúcar y abolición* (La Habana: Editorial de Ciencias Sociales, 1971), p. 33.

2. Oscar Pinos Santos, *Historia de Cuba: Aspectos fundamentales* (La Habana: Editorial Nacional de Cuba, 1964), p. 99.

3. Juan Jiménez Pastrana, *Los chinos en la historia de Cuba 1847-1930* (La Habana: Editorial Ciencias Sociales, 1983), p. 38.

4. *La Aurora*, 22 de octubre de 1866.

5. *El Productor*, 12 de abril de 1888.

6. *El Productor*, 10 de mayo de 1888.

7. *El Productor*, 7 de junio de 1888.

34. Desarrollando una colección cubana en el exterior

Lesbia Orta Varona

Cuba siempre ha ocupado un lugar prominente como parte de las colecciones de distintos organismos de los Estados Unidos ya que "la geografía estableció y reforzó un vínculo natural entre Cuba y los Estados Unidos", según Howard F. Kline, que fuera director de la Fundación Hispánica de la Biblioteca del Congreso. Estos vínculos dieron como resultado la creación de importantes colecciones cubanas a todo lo ancho del país. Bástenos citar el trabajo de Appleton Prentiss Clark Griffin cuando era bibliotecario asistente de la Biblioteca del Congreso, que compiló una obra titulada *Lista de libros relacionados con Cuba* y que fue publicada como el Documento Oficial del Senado de los Estados Unidos no. 161, de la Segunda Sesión, y que fue editado en 1898. Este documento constituye uno de los primeros proyectos de bibliografía cubana en la Biblioteca del Congreso y refleja el interés mostrado hacia Cuba desde el siglo pasado.

El término colección de acuerdo con Domingo Buonocore en su *Diccionario de Bibliotecología* "presupone una idea selectiva y ordenadora, esto es, un conjunto bibliográfico armonioso y homogéneo que responde a un criterio dado". Y sigue diciendo "ese sentido auténtico de colección, ha sido desnaturalizado por el abuso, aplicándose el término a cualquier grupo heteróclito de libros". Esta definición de colección ha sufrido algún cambio y vemos que la American Library Association en su *Glosario de Bibliotecología y Ciencias de la Información* define a ésta como "un grupo de material bibliográfico que tiene una característica común".

¿A qué nos referimos al hablar del desarrollo de una colección cubana en el extranjero? Ciertamente se trata de una colección homogénea, pues el tema es Cuba, comprendiendo literatura, arte, educación, ciencia, tecnología, política, etc., escritas por cubanos dentro de Cuba y en nuestros tiempos también los que viven fuera de ésta, así como de los especialistas en el tema. De aquí se deriva la problemática en el desarrollo de tal colección.

En las últimas tres décadas lo que se publica dentro de Cuba ha sido de difícil adquisición, ya que nunca ha existido un sistema que permita la adquisición y la actualización del material con la necesaria continuidad que facilite una operación con un fácil engranaje. En otras palabras, la comunicación con Cuba no se ha facilitado: la telefónica es casi inexistente, el correo se pierde o no llega a la persona indicada por el constante cambio de personal en los organismos encargados de viabilizar las órdenes o pedidos, o simplemente aclarar dudas o reclamos.

Los bibliotecarios fuera de Cuba hemos tenido que acudir a todas las fuentes imaginarias para poder obtener el material cubano, muchas veces comprando publicaciones a través de América del Sur, México, España o Canadá, cuando hubiera sido tan fácil obtenerlas directamente desde los Estados Unidos. Hay bibliotecas que pueden utilizar el canje para el material que solo se puede adquirir por este medio. Bibliotecas como la nuestra (Universidad de Miami), donde el sistema de canje no existe, se encuentra impotente para soslayar este vacío. En algunos casos se ha conseguido contacto con alguna que otra persona, la cual nos ha hecho saber qué publicaciones necesitan sus organismos, las cuales hemos comprado y enviado a cambio de las publicaciones ofrecidas en canje. Estas operaciones duran poco tiempo, por el cambio de personal responsable antes mencionado.

Algunas bibliotecas ofrecen a sus bibliotecarios la opción de viajes de adquisición a otros países. Cuando esto sucede, muchos bibliotecarios norteamericanos han podido visitar Cuba, después de un largo proceso para obtener visas de visitantes o de investigadores. En estos casos, las personas que visitan Cuba pueden obtener mucho material y establecer contactos directos, que les facilitan el envío de material por algún tiempo. Los que por otra parte no tenemos la ventaja de visitar para comprar, nos quedamos sin esta oportunidad de adquirir material de primera mano. A grosso modo he mencionado algunas de las dificultades existentes para el bibliógrafo encargado de obtener material proveniente de Cuba.

Partiendo de la base de que la cultura cubana es una, aunque exista la dicotomía: Cuba-dentro, Cuba-fuera, de que la Florida se encuentra en una zona precisa donde la posición geográfica, la demografía y la etnografía la une a Cuba; y siguiendo la trayectoria de vínculos con Cuba establecida por la Universidad de Miami desde su fundación, la administración de la Biblioteca de la Universidad de Miami, aconsejada por las bibliotecarias cubanas que desde el principio de la década de los sesenta se incorporaron a la institución, estableció la política de adquirir todo el material que de Cuba y sobre Cuba se encontrara, incluyendo aquel producido por cubanos fuera de Cuba, para lograr una colección cubana total.

A tales efectos nos dimos a la tarea de no sólo adquirir lo publicado, sino también tratar de adquirir todo material sin condición de formato que sirviera en el futuro como fuentes primarias para el estudio de la diáspora cubana. Esta tarea ha sido muy difícil debido a que la atomización de los cubanos ha hecho que estos se encuentren diseminados por todo el mundo. Una característica del cubano es que no importa donde resida, siempre para él es necesario manifestarse y escribe y publica, haciendo difícil la tarea de localizar y obtener lo por él producido. Esto, unido al hecho de que existe una nueva generación de cubanos cuyos nombres son en la mayoría de los casos desconocidos y de que escriben en otros idiomas que no es el castellano, hace la labor de recolección mucho más compleja.

Como existe una similitud de hechos históricos, bástenos un recorrido por la bibliografía de Lilia Castro de Morales, *Impresos relativos a Cuba, editados en los Estados Unidos de Norteamérica*, para reconocer la importancia de poder ordenar y agrupar todo lo que fuera de Cuba se había publicado desde 1762 hasta 1955. Esta tarea en nuestro presente la comenzó el Dr. Fermín Peraza, cuando continuó publicando el *Anuario Bibliográfico Cubano* en el extranjero. Esta publicación duró de 1937 hasta 1966, cuando cambió el título a *Revolutionary Cuba* y se publicó hasta la muerte del autor. El Dr. Peraza incorpora a su bibliografía cubana lo poco que al principio de los años sesenta se publicaba por los cubanos fuera de Cuba. Esto se ha continuado hasta cierto punto con la publicación anual *Cuban Studies* que la Universidad de Pittsburgh encabeza, y que incluye en su bibliografía libros y artículos sobre Cuba, publicados dentro y fuera de la misma. Otros esfuerzos se realizan para dar a conocer esta producción cubana en el exterior con estudios como el de Esperanza Bravo de Varona, *Cuba Exile Periodicals at the University of Miami Library*, publicado por SALALM en 1987, y que reune los títulos de las publicaciones periódicas aparecidas fuera de Cuba desde 1962 hasta 1986 y que según ella representan "una crónica de las esperanzas y aspiraciones del pueblo cubano en el exilio, de la lucha para mantener la unidad de propósito, y de la necesidad de preservar, añadir y transmitir nuestro ancestro cultural".

Esta dedicación exige algo más que el mecanismo de adquirir material para enriquecer una colección cubana fuera de Cuba. Estos esfuerzos de poner a la mano este tesoro de fuentes primarias solo es el comienzo de una meta: adquirir, organizar y viabilizar la producción cubana como un total indivisible.

No hemos olvidado que para que esta colección llegue a generaciones venideras de cubanos y estudiosos de Cuba, es necesario su preservación. Varios proyectos a este fin se están llevando a cabo en distintas bibliotecas de los Estados Unidos. Mucho material cubano está siendo microfilmado en la actualidad, sobre todo las publicaciones periódicas, por el Intensive Cuban Collecting Group, un grupo formado por bibliotecas con colecciones cubanas de gran magnitud como son la Biblioteca del Congreso, Yale, Princeton, y otras.

En lo que a nosotros se refiere, nuestra biblioteca actualmente forma parte de un proyecto subvencionado por un fondo especial del gobierno de los Estados Unidos, organizado por SOLINET (Southeastern Library

Network), en el cual toman parte un grupo de bibliotecas académicas, públicas y estatales para preservar el material que cada organismo considere único o de gran importancia. Nuestro aporte es la preservación de gran parte de nuestra colección cubana. Hasta el momento 2,850 libros y folletos se han microfilmado. Este es un proyecto de tres años de duración que terminará en agosto del año en curso.

Hemos expuesto a grandes rasgos las dificultades, pero también en mi caso, las satisfacciones, que conllevan el coleccionar y facilitar el material cubano a los que estudian a Cuba. Creemos que al coleccionar este material, estamos salvaguardando una cultura que ha producido a través de los siglos, grandes figuras reconocidas mundialmente, en todas las ramas del saber. La historia de Cuba ha demostrado que no hay lugar para una escisión sino para una continuación.

The Hispanic Division of the Library of Congress

35. La Division Hispánica y el desarrollo de las colecciones de la Biblioteca del Congreso

Georgette Magassy Dorn

En esta breve exposición trataré de esbozar el papel que desempeña la División Hispánica en el desarrollo de las colecciones luso-hispánicas de la Biblioteca del Congreso, un fondo bibliográfico extraordinario para estudios latinoamericanos, ibéricos y del Caribe. Calculamos que en 1993 las colecciones luso-hispánicas y del Caribe cuentan aproximadamente con 2,200,00 libros y revistas y 9.5 millones de "piezas", es decir, un diez por ciento del acervo de libros y revistas de la Biblioteca.

Creada en 1800 y ubicada en el edificio del Capitolio (aún a medio construir), la pequeña colección que integraba la Biblioteca del Congreso fue destruida en 1814 cuando las tropas británicas ocuparon e incendiaron parte de la ciudad de Washington. Al año siguiente, el ex-presidente Thomas Jefferson vendió su biblioteca privada de 6,700 tomos —la tercera que había reunido— al Congreso de los Estados Unidos. La biblioteca de Jefferson representaba el panorama intelectual de la época desde la antigüedad clásica hasta el siglo de las luces.[1] Con los libros de Jefferson ingresaron 190 obras referentes a temas hispánicos, la mayoría de ellas sobre la exploración y conquista de Iberoamérica y las Antillas como, por ejemplo, tres libros de Bartolomé de las Casas, *Del imperio soberano sobre las Indias*, *Istoria della destruzzione dell Indie occidentale* y su *La découverte des Indes occidentales*. Jefferson poseía además libros de Garcilaso de la Vega, Agustín de Zárate, López de Gómara, Juan de Torquemada, Francisco Javier Clavigero y muchos más. En su colección se hallaban también obras literarias —varios libros de Cervantes, *La Araucana* de Alonso Ercilla y Zúñiga y un interesante juego de nueve tomos de poesía titulado *Parnaso español*. El interés de Jefferson hacia todo el hemisferio pudo verse en uno de sus escritos en 1809 en que decía que "México es uno de los países más interesantes de nuestro hemisferio que bien merece nuestra atención."[2]

Durante gran parte del siglo XIX se añadieron pocas obras hispánicas, siendo la mayoría de índole legal, comercial y algunos mapas, especialmente a partir de 1848. En 1865 la Smithsonian Institution cedió sus fondos sobre las humanidades y ciencias sociales (unos 44,000 volúmenes) a la Biblioteca del Congreso. El enfoque de la Smithsonian se concentró desde aquel tiempo en las ciencias naturales. Dentro de los materiales cedidos por dicha institución se econtraban muchos libros hispánicos como *Recuerdos de provincia* de Domingo F. Sarmiento, seguido con la traducción inglesa de *Facundo*, donada por la traductora Mary Peabody Mann. En 1866 la Biblioteca del Congreso estableció relaciones de canje de publicaciones con gobiernos extranjeros y academias científicas y de letras. El director de la Biblioteca del Congreso Ainswoth Spofford consiguió en 1870 que la institución fuera designada como depositaria de obras registradas con derecho de autor, con lo cual el aumento anual del acervo empezó a crecer con regularidad.[3]

Debido al sostenido crecimiento del acervo, la Biblioteca se instaló en su edificio propio en el año 1897. Las colecciones hispánicas, por su parte, aumentaron considerablemente después de la guerra hispano-norteamericana, pues llegaron materiales de toda índole sobre Cuba, Puerto Rico, y las Islas Filipinas. Fue entonces que ingresó la colección de Henry Harisse de libros raros y mapas sobre la primera etapa de la conquista de América la cual incluía, entre varios tesoros, una carta original de Pedro Mártir d'Anghiera.[4] En los albores del siglo XX y bajo la dirección de Herbert Putnam, la Biblioteca del Congreso ya era de hecho la "biblioteca nacional" de los Estados Unidos.

El filántropo norteamericano Archer M. Huntington efectuó su primera donación de fondos a la Biblioteca en 1927 para la compra de libros "relacionados con el arte, la literatura y la historia de España, Portugal, e Hispanoamérica".[5] Gracias a la continua generosidad de Huntington, la Biblioteca pudo crear la posición de especialista en cultura hispánica y el embajador de España en Washington, Juan Riaño y Gayangos, fue el primero en desempeñar esa posición por unos meses. En 1931 el fraile agustiniano español, David Rubio, fue nombrado consultor, cargo que desempeñó con gran distinción hasta 1941. Rubio adquirió más de 200,000 libros hispánicos para la Biblioteca, además de manuscritos, mapas, partituras de música e incluso material folklórico de Puerto Rico y Venezuela, y obras hispánicas oriundas de Texas y Nuevo México, así como también cintas grabadas por el folclorista John Lomax. Otros tesoros acumulados a lo largo de los años incluyen el Código de Colón, el llamado Código Sneyd que formaba parte de la colección John Boyd Thatcher, el primer informe veneciano sobre los descubrimientos de Colón, tratados mexicanos sobre lenguas indígenas, la colección de miles de páginas copiadas en el Archivo de Indias, como por ejemplo la colección *Papeles Cubanos*, y manuscritos cartográficos de la Real Escuela de Navegación de Cádiz.[6]

Huntington donó fondos en 1936 para establecer la Fundación Hispánica, hoy llamada División Hispánica, dotándola de una Sala

Hispánica de lectura y de espacio para especialistas. La dependencia abrió sus puertas al público el día 12 de octubre de 1939. En esa solemne ocasión el director de la Biblioteca, Archibald MacLeish, dijo que en esta "sección de la Biblioteca del Congreso . . . se preservarán, estudiarán y honrarán la literatura y la ciencia de aquellas otras repúblicas que comparten con la nuestra el nombre Americano; y que a la vez comparten con la nuestra las memorias de esperanza humana y de valor humano que este vocablo evoca —que evoca más que nunca en la historia del hemisferio en que vivimos".[7] La Sala Hispánica se convirtió enseguida en un centro de estudios ibéricos y latinoamericanos.[8]

El primer director de la División Hispánica, Lewis Hanke, trajo consigo de la Universidad de Harvard, dónde enseñaba, la edición de la bibliografía anual titulada *The Handbook of Latin American Studies*, la cual continúa siendo la bibliografía anotada más importante para Latinoamérica y el Caribe. El equipo del *Handbook* y los 120 colaboradores han contribuido de una manera muy especial, a través de los años, a la formación de lo que es la colección luso-hispana. Lewis Hanke y Marietta Daniels Shepard fueron pioneros en impulsar la cooperación entre bibliotecarios del hemisferio del norte y del sur.

En 1942, por sugerencia del director de la Biblioteca del Congreso, el poeta Archibald MacLeish, y bajo la dirección de Francisco Aguilera, quien siguió en calidad de especialista en cultura hispánica al P. Rubio, se comenzó la recopilación de grabaciones en el Archivo de Literatura Hispánica en Cinta Magnética. El primer escritor que grabó selecciones ante el micrófono fue el poeta uruguayo Emilio Oribe. En 1993 el archivo cuenta con 591 grabaciones. Las grabaciones se llevan a cabo por los mismos autores. Algunas también comprenden entrevistas y más recientemente, hasta videocintas. Entre las luminarias representadas en el archivo, se encuentran Gabriela Mistral, Pedro Salinas, Juan Ramón Jiménez, Miguel Angel Asturias, Gabriel García Márquez, Ana María Matute, Vicente Aleixandre, Camilo José Cela, Octavio Paz, Mario Vargas Llosa, José Donoso, Julio Cortázar, Nélida Piñón, Juan Rulfo, Agustín Yáñez, Carlos Fuentes, Elena Poniatowska, Eunice Odio, Claribel Alegría, entre muchos otros.[9]

Mientras que durante la época de Hanke, de 1939 a 1951, el énfasis de la División Hispánica enfocaba las humanidades, con la publicación de bibliografías como *The Art of Latin America* (1942) y la formación de una colección iconográfica titulada *The Archive of Hispanic Culture*, el siguiente director, Howard F. Cline, bajo cuya dirección funcionó esa dependencia de 1952 a 1971, concentró más en las ciencias sociales y la organización del campo de los estudios latinoamericanos. Fue durante la época de Cline que la División Hispánica colaboró en la fundación de SALALM (Seminario para la Adquisición de Materiales Latinoamericanos de Biblioteca), en la reorganización de la Conference on Latin American History, en la creación en 1966 de la asociación interdisciplinaria internacional Latin American Studies Association (LASA) y la Society for the Study of Spanish and Portuguese History (1970). Además, Cline dio ímpetu a la publicación de dos ediciones del *National Directory of Latin Americanists* (1967 y 1971), tres ediciones de *Latin America, Spain and Portugal: An Annotated Bibliography of Paperback Books (1967, 1971, 1976)*, una pequeña bibliografía titulada *Ladino Books in the Library of Congress* (1963), la monumental obra *The Handbook of Middle American Indians* (University of Texas, 1964-1976, 16 vols.) con lo que se pudo sistematizar para el mundo de la investigación el nuevo campo de etnohistoria, y la publicación de una serie de artículos sobre códices y *Relaciones Geográficas*. Cline organizó una serie de artículos en revistas sobre fondos archivísticos sobre Latinoamérica en Europa, comenzó la preparación de un proyecto extenso de listar manuscritos luso-hispánicos en la División de Manuscritos y asimismo la preparación de guías a los manuscritos de la Biblioteca como, por ejemplo, los manuscritos en las colecciones de Edward Harkness y Hans P. Kraus.[10] Cline propuso la creación de la Oficina de la Biblioteca del Congreso en Rio de Janeiro que es ahora tan importante para desarrollar las colecciones brasileñas como las grandes bibliotecas de investigación de Norteamérica.

Durante la época de la directora Mary Ellis Kahler (1973-1978) —que después ocuparía el puesto de directora en Rio— la labor editora de la División Hispánica continuó concentrándose en bibliografías y la preparación de guías como la de la colección de manuscritos portugueses y una porción del acervo de la colección Kraus, titulada *Las Casas as a Bishop* (1980). Durante el período 1975-1984 más de 300 autores fueron grabados en cinta magnética, como asimismo la primera sesión en videocinta en que Borges habló a los empleados de la Biblioteca del Congreso (1976).

El siguiente director, William E. Carter (1978-1983), distinguido antropólogo, impulsó la compilación de la tercera edición del *National Directory of Latin Americanists* (1965) y una bibliografía titulada *Human Rights in Latin America*. Carter prestó atención a la sistematización de la adquisición de materiales y fomentó la creación de la Sección Hispánica para Adquisiciones en la Exchange and Gift Division.

El último director, Cole Blasier (1988-1993), uno de los fundadores de LASA, que vino a dirigir la División después de una distinguida carrera en la Universidad de Pittsburgh, consiguió que se nombrara una especialista luso-brasileña (la Dra. Iêda Siqueira Wiarda) y una especialista en México (la Dra. Barbara Tenenbaum, además de un especialista en adquisiciones (Edmundo Flores). Estos nombramientos fueron los primeros aumentos de personal en treinta años. Puede decirse que durante la época de Blasier, por primera vez, la División Hispánica tiene en cuenta el cuadro total de las colecciones cuando recomienda materiales nuevos. La División ha colaborado no solo en la adquisición de libros, sino también de materiales iconográficos, películas, mapas, manuscritos, grabaciones y partituras.

Las colecciones de la Biblioteca proporcionan tal vez el centro más importante para estudiar derecho luso-hispánico empezando con ediciones del código fundamental español las *Siete Partidas*. La División de Derecho Hispánico de la Biblioteca ha editado una larga serie de guías a la legislación de todos los países luso-hispanos y desde hace unos veinte años mantiene una base de datos en computadora de legislación latinoamericana.

De sumo interés, también, es el acervo de publicaciones oficiales impresas, como por ejemplo memorias de ministerios de los países luso-hispanos. De hecho, un proyecto de colaboración con SALALM y la Asociación de Bibliotecas de Investigación ha sido el de copiar en microfilme una serie de memorias, un proyecto que estuvo a cargo de Donald Wisdom y que ahora lo está completando mi colega Edmundo Flores.

Y finalmente, la División Hispánica, con la asidua cooperación de muchas entidades dentro de la misma Biblioteca, ha recopilado varias series de folletos y materiales efímeros. Con la estupenda ayuda del historiador Brian Belanger —que es catedrático en Saint Anselm College en Manchester, New Hampshire, quien catalogó la colección en 1991— la Biblioteca acaba de microfilmar *Mexican and Central American Ephemera 1980-1991* en 44 rollos.

En conclusión, esta vasta colección es el legado intelectual y obra de un gran número de personas que a través de casi dos siglos han contribuido al desarrollo de las colecciones luso-hispánicas. Quisiera destacar aquí las contribuciones de Thomas Jefferson, Herbert Putnam, Archer M. Huntington, David Rubio, Lewis Hanke, Francisco Aguilera y Howard F. Cline en el desarrollo de las colecciones. Este acervo presenta fuentes muy importantes para el investigador y el bibliotecario. Teniendo el apoyo activo de profesionales en los Estados Unidos y en todo el mundo hispánico, contando con la simpatía y con la participación de muchos en el trabajo compartido, la División Hispánica se complace y, por lo menos, trata de ser una de las instituciones principales dedicadas al estudio de la cultura ibero-hispánica.

NOTAS

1. John Y. Cole, *For Congress and the Nation: A Chronological History of the Library of Congress* (Washington, DC: Library of Congress, 1979), pp. 3-7; Frederick R. Goff, "Jefferson, The Book Collector", *Library of Congress Quarterly Journal* 29:1 (1972), 33-39;

Thomas Jefferson Library: A Catalog with the Entries in His Own Order (Washington, DC: Library of Congress, 1989).

2. La cita de Thomas Jefferson aparece en *The Hispanic Room in the Library of Congress* (Washington, DC: Library of Congress, 1981), p. 1; *Catalogue of the Library of Thomas Jefferson*, Millicent Sowerby, comp. (Washington, DC: Library of Congress, 1952), vol. 5, pp. 94-97; *Thomas Jefferson's Library: A Catalog with the Entries in His Own Order*, James Gilreath y Douglas L. Wilson, eds. (Washington, DC: Library of Congress, 1989), pp. 102-105; Georgette Magassy Dorn, "Hispanic Books in the Library of Congress", en *Philosophy and Literature in Latin America*, Jorge J. E. Gracía y Mireya Camurati, eds. (Albany: State University of New York Press, 1989), pp. 173-175.

3. David C. Mearns, *The Story Up to Now: The Library of Congress, 1800-1946* (Washington, DC: Library of Congress, 1947), pp. 12-13.

4. Frederick R. Goff, "Henry Harisse, Americanist", *Inter-American Review of Bibliography* 3 (enero-abril 1953), 3-10.

5. *Annual Report of the Librarian of Congress for the Fiscal Year Ending 1927* (Washington, DC: Government Printing Office, 1927), p. 10.

6. Dorn, *Inter-American Review*, vol. 29, pp. 339-341; *Fundación Hispánica*, p. 19.

7. Palabras pronunciadas en la inauguración de la Sala Hispánica, en *La Fundación Hispánica en la Biblioteca del Congreso* (Washington, DC: Imprenta Panamericana, 1940), p. 4.

8. *Las actividades hispánicas de la Biblioteca del Congreso, con un discurso de Archibald MacLeish* (Washington, DC: Government Printing Office, 1945), pp. 2-3.

9. Francisco Aguilera y Georgette Magassy Dorn, *The Archive of Hispanic Literature on Tape: A Descriptive Guide* (Washington, DC: Library of Congress, 1974), y Georgette Magassy Dorn, "El Archivo de Literatura Hispánica de la Biblioteca del Congreso", *Revista Interamericana de Bibliografía* 39:1 (1989), 50-62.

10. *The Harkness Collection in the Library of Congress: Manuscripts Concerning Mexico, A Guide*, con traducciones por J. Benedict Warren (Washington, DC: Government Printing Office, 1974), y J. Benedict Warren, *Hans P. Kraus Collection of Hispanic American Manuscripts: A Guide* (Washington, DC: Library of Congress, 1974).

36. The *Handbook of Latin American Studies:* Fifty Years in the Development of a Field and a Publication

Dolores Moyano Martin

The creation and development of the *Handbook of Latin American Studies* are inseparable from the development of the field itself and from its founding father, first editor of the *Handbook*, the historian Lewis Hanke. It is a testimony to Hanke's foresight and insight that a series launched in the 1930s should have lasted into the 1990s. In his Editor's Note to the first volume, published in 1936, Hanke already anticipated the singularity of Latin American studies, the uniqueness of our field, a recalcitrant terrain more resistant than most to the narrow approach: "The field of Latin American culture is a particularly fertile region for that integrated investigation which ignores conventional academic divisions and considers the problem as a whole." Hanke insisted that the *Handbook* be designed "to forward such broadly conceived study and to emphasize the unity of the field." Such an interdisciplinary approach, Hanke noted, would make "it easier for the specialists to keep abreast of current literature in their own corners of the field," while giving "them the opportunity to peer over the fences which set them apart from their fellows and to observe each other's movements." In a 1988 interview, Hanke observed that "the 47 volumes of the *Handbook of Latin American Studies*, largely developed by historians, have been a spectacular demonstration of the interdisciplinary approach and how impossible it is to study Latin America without taking into account sources and interpretations written in many languages." The significance of the internationalization of history was precisely the subject of the 1988 presidential address to the American Historical Association by Japanese historian Akira Iriye, who praised Hanke specifically for his pioneering role in establishing closer ties with foreign historical communities, initiatives that "have left a valuable legacy to build on for the further internationalization of the profession."[1]

The *Handbook* was the original product of a conference of Latin Americanists held in 1935 in the offices of the Social Science Research Council in New York City. The fields of anthropology, economics, geography, government, history, and literature were represented by 15 scholars from nine universities: Harvard, Yale, Chicago, Michigan, Wisconsin, North Carolina, Ohio, Clark, and Catholic University of America in addition to the Library of Congress and the American Geographical Society. The historians were Clarence H. Haring, Lewis Hanke, and A.S. Aiton; the anthropologists John M. Cooper, Carl E. Guthe, and Clark Wissler; the economists Max S. Handman and Chester L. Jones; the geographers Preston E. James, Robert S. Platt, and Raye R. Platt; the political scientist Herman G. James; the literary critic Sturgis E. Leavitt; and the librarian C. K. Jones. Hanke's policy of recruiting scholars who would work for the *Handbook* without remuneration while upholding very high standards began with these individuals, several of them the original *Handbook* contributors. In the 1930s, only a handful of academics labored in the study of Latin America, a lonely and unrecognized pursuit in the United States at the time. Later, however, these early contributors became the founding fathers of many fields of study in this country. Their work is exemplified by Samuel Putnam's splendid essays on Brazilian literature; Irving Leonard's pioneering work on the Spanish American colonial period; George Kubler's essays on Latin American art; Gilbert Chase's chapters on the music of the region; and in the social sciences, the contributions of Robert Redfield, Alfred Métraux, and T. Dale Stewart on anthropology. When these scholars retired, they usually passed on the responsibility to a best student or respected colleague. In this manner, a relay race of excellence was established that makes the roster of past and present contributors to the *Handbook* a veritable *Who's Who* of scholars in every field we cover.

Lewis Hanke, the *Handbook*'s first editor, was also one of the first scholars to emphasize that Latin American studies did not and should not mean Spanish American studies "with Brazil ignored or neglected,"[2] because "a true Latin Americanist must have some real acquaintance with Brazil."[3] In fact, one of the earliest volumes, *HLAS 3,* published in 1937, was dedicated to the Instituto Histórico e Geográfico Brasileiro on its 100th birthday and already included separate chapters on Brazilian art, economics, education, geography, history, and literature. The *Handbook*'s special interest in Brazil continues to this day and is exemplified by the depth and breadth of the coverage of the country's literature in *HLAS 52:* seven chapters by as many scholars covering the Brazilian novel, short story, crônica, drama, poetry, criticism, and translations from the Portuguese into English.

The first two *Handbook* volumes were produced with the financial support of the American Council of Learned Societies, the next seven volumes were underwritten by grants from the Rockefeller Foundation, and volume 10 was made possible by a transfer of funds to the Library of Congress from the State Department's Committee on Scientific and Cultural

Relations. In 1944, the Library assumed full responsibility, and volume 11 (1948) was the first entirely financed by the Library of Congress.[4]

An odd coincidence in the history of our field in the United States is that Latin American studies, and as a consequence, the *Handbook*, prospered in wartime. For example, the most important historical journal in the field, the *Hispanic American Historical Review (HAHR)*, was created during World War I, with the first issue appearing in 1918.[5] Of World War II, Hanke writes that the years 1939-1945 witnessed an extraordinary mingling of scholars of the Americas in all fields. The war confined most of their activities to the American continent, and the result was beneficial for the growth of Latin American studies in the United States. For the first time there were numerous Latin American professors and intellectuals teaching and working at American institutions and universities. Among the more notable figures were the Brazilians Erico Veríssimo at California and Gilberto Freyre at Indiana; the Colombian Germán Arciniegas at Chicago; the Paraguayan Pablo Max Ynsfrán at Texas; the Dominican Pedro Henríquez Ureña at Harvard; and the Peruvian Luis Alberto Sánchez at the Library of Congress. Moreover, the United States Army's Specialized Training Program gave enlisted Americans the opportunity to study foreign languages "under circumstances in which the students were actually expected and enabled to speak Spanish or Portuguese fluently."[6]

Not only would the *Handbook* prosper during the war years, but additional publications and relevant programs launched in the late 1930s and throughout the 1940s would have a long-term impact on the direction and development of Latin American studies in the United States. Among them were the *Revista de Historia de América*, created in 1938 by the Pan American Institute of Geography and History under the editorship of Silvio A. Zavala; the *Revista Iberoamericana*, sponsored in 1939 by the Instituto Internacional de Literatura Iberoamericana; the prescient journal *Afroamérica*, created in 1940 by the International Institute of Afro-American Studies; and the historical quarterly *The Americas*, established in 1944 by the Academy of American Franciscan History. Other developments included the establishment of the Institute of Social Anthropology at the Smithsonian Institution and its production of the outstanding multivolume *Handbook of South American Indians*. Among its authors were three contributors to the *Handbook*, the anthropologists John Murra, Alfred Métraux, and Betty J. Meggers. Additional important events were the first Inter-American Conference on Philosophy held at Yale University in 1943, and the first Conference on Latin American Art, sponsored by the Council of Learned Societies and held in New York in 1945; and in the same year, the establishment of an office devoted to the promotion of Latin American music in Washington, D.C.: the Pan American Union's Music Division.[7]

The next notable expansion of Latin American studies in the United States would take place in the 1960s, the decade of the Cuban Revolution and the Vietnam War. This expansion was most visible in the social sciences, particularly economics and political science, fields in which there was a dramatic rise in the quality and quantity of the literature published. The launching of the Alliance for Progress in the early 1960s encouraged Latin American nations to compile and publish economic and social statistics which provided the necessary data for more scholarly and sophisticated analysis as well as for long-term projections. The explosion of publications in the social sciences in the 1960s resulted in the *Handbook* splitting into two components in 1964: humanities and social sciences, each represented by a separate volume to be published in alternate years.[8]

The role of our three academic publishers in the development and promotion of the *Handbook* should be emphasized. Harvard University, which published the volume from 1936 through 1947, took a gamble by launching a series in a neglected field; the University of Florida Press, which published the *Handbook* from 1948 through 1978, encouraged the first major expansion of the field throughout the 1960s and 1970s, decades of extraordinary growth and interest in Latin American studies; and our present publisher, the University of Texas Press, which has been issuing the *Handbook* since 1979, supported us not only through additional growth in the 1980s but encouraged us throughout the difficult conversion to automated publishing that culminated in *HLAS 50.*

The great boom in Latin American fiction of the 1960s and 1970s is also reflected in the extraordinary growth of the *Handbook*'s literature section. In *HLAS 1,* the entire literature section consisted of 40 pages prepared by three contributors. In *HLAS 50,* literature commands 202 pages and reflects the labors of 31 contributors.

Another field which the *Handbook* pioneered and nurtured from its very beginning in the 1960s is ethnohistory. And the 1980s, according to one well-known ethnohistorian, have witnessed "an explosion in the writing of indigenous history."[9] In the early 1960s, there were only a few stalwart scholars working in this field, practically all of them having served as contributors to the *Handbook.* These pioneers were the then Chief of the Hispanic Division of the Library of Congress, Howard Cline, in addition to Charles Gibson, H. B. Nicholson, and Donald Robertson, all of them Mesoamericanists. John Murra was the only one who in the 1960s was studying the history of Andean populations. In contrast, we note that in *HLAS 52,* published in 1993, some of the best and most prolific recent research is devoted to the Central Andes, a field now dominated by Peruvian scholars. And among them a consensus has developed that Peru's indigenous history "profoundly activates the nation's present," and that her true past is that of her native Americans.[10]

From its inception, ethnohistory has exemplified the direction and praxis of Latin American studies today. Those who wanted to study the past record of indigenous populations soon realized that attainment of such knowledge was impossible without acquiring additional expertise in unfamiliar and, what were then, arcane fields. Today, such cross-disciplinary incursions are not only taken for granted but required of scholars with "historians venturing into the realm of the pictorial; art historians examining the alphabetic text in colonial codices; and anthropologists and archaeologists studying the colonial period."[11] In fact, observes one historian of the Dutch Caribbean, "it is remarkable that anthropologists have written most of the historical works" on slavery and about Maroon societies in Suriname, Curaçao, Aruba, and other formerly Dutch territories in the Americas.[12]

Throughout the half century of its existence, the *Handbook* has also taken the lead in supporting research and publishing the first annotated bibliographies in emerging fields of study that were not included among the traditional disciplines covered by the *Handbook*. Past examples are "Latin American Law," "Latin American Statistics," and "Latin American Labor and Social Welfare." Emerging fields whose development the *Handbook* encouraged in the 1960s and 1970s were "Latin American Folklore" and "Latin American Film." In *HLAS 54* there will be a chapter titled "Electronic Resources on Latin America: An Overview of the Last Ten Years," by Harold Colson, University of California, San Diego. In ensuing volumes, Colson will alternate his chapter on electronic resources in the social sciences with Peter Stern, Rutgers University, who will contribute the chapter on these resources in the humanities.

The print edition of the *Handbook* is an annual annotated bibliography of about 5,000 items, alternating yearly between the social sciences and the humanities. Roughly 60 percent of *Handbook* entries cover monographs; about 40 percent consist of chapters from books as well as journal articles selected from more than 1,600 serial titles published worldwide in more than 10 languages. Disciplines covered are, for the Humanities volume: art, ethnohistory, history, literature, music, and philosophy; for the Social Sciences volume: anthropology (i.e., archaeology and ethnology), economics, geography, government and politics, international relations, and sociology. Offprints of selected disciplines are available for purchase through the Latin American Studies Association.[13]

To produce each *Handbook* volume we depend on three constellations that must be coordinated to work in tandem: (1) the editorial staff at the Library of Congress; and beyond the Library, (2) the scholars at their universities or other institutions; and (3) University of Texas Press which publishes and markets the volume.

At present approximately 130 willing scholars contribute their chapters without pay. One of the reasons we have such an extraordinary collection of Latin American materials at the Library of Congress is due, in no small measure, to the policing role these scholars have played for more than 50 years as to the quality and quantity of our acquisitions in their fields. Whenever we mail them the books received for a particular biennium, they let the *Handbook* staff know of any gaps, which regions, countries, or topics are being neglected, and what new serials titles we should acquire or discontinue. The *Handbook* Advisory Board of eight recognized scholars which oversees and reviews the contributors' performance at their regular meetings has also played an invaluable role in the development and pursuit of scholarship in Latin American studies.

With the publication of *HLAS 50* in 1991, the *Handbook*'s editorial process is completely automated, with data entered in MARC format into one of the MUMS files at the Library of Congress. At present (August 1993), the *Handbook* has an editorial staff of five permanent employees who perform most of their tasks on computer terminals connected to the Library's mainframe. The *Handbook* is merely one of numerous applications that make use of the Library's computer facility, one which encompasses more than 3,200 terminals, 160 disk drives, 75 million bytes of stored information, and which processes more than 20,000 online transactions per day. As of *HLAS 50*, the *Handbook*'s output program generates yearly proofs and a computer tape that contains the data for that year's print volume, including computer-generated document markup codes. Bibliographic information for each item sent to *HLAS* contributors for possible annotation in the print volume is initially input into the database. In the case of monographs, *HLAS* staff copies the Library of Congress's computer catalog information drawn from the BOOKS file to the Generalized Bibliographies (or GenBib) database, a shared file designed especially for bibliographers at the Library of Congress. The "cloned" book records are then edited by *HLAS* staff for bibliographic clarity and *Handbook* style. For analytic entries, including individually annotated journal articles and chapters taken from books, bibliographic records are created from scratch by *HLAS* staff. These *HLAS*-created records combine traditional cataloging rules with *Handbook* style guidelines. For all annotated records, the staff adds *Handbook* subject index terms, and the author index is verified and amplified. In brief, the *Handbook*'s database combines the best aspects of both bibliographies and online catalogs. For example, online catalog records include evaluative annotations prepared by scholars who specialize in that particular field; and catalog information usually excluded from print bibliographies because of space limitations is still available in the online record for use by researchers and librarians. Moreover, bibliographic information for unannotated items remains in the database available for searching. At present (August 1993), the *Handbook* database contains more than 44,000 bibliographic records. This figure is growing by an additional 8,000 entries annually, of which about 5,000 are annotated by scholars and appear in the printed volume.[14]

A future project and major goal of the *Handbook* is to provide machine-readable access to past volumes *(HLAS 1* through *HLAS 49).* Sue Mundell, Senior Assistant to the Editor of *HLAS*, is studying ways to facilitate access to this wealth of information by examining existing technologies as well as private-sector funding possibilities, given shrinking government budgets. A textual database could be created for the more recent volumes (i.e., *HLAS 41* through *HLAS 49)* by drawing data from existing typesetting tapes; for volumes published prior to automated typesetting, the *Handbook* staff plans to use optical scanning. Finally, with the advent of full-text databases, the *HLAS* staff looks forward to a time when it will be technically and legally feasible to scan the full text of articles, chapters, and perhaps books into our database for full-text use by scholars and librarians. We hope that this future and ideal database will, if created, be compatible with either the retrospective or the present *Handbook* MARC database.[15]

Throughout its more than a half a century of existence, the *Handbook* has served as a mirror reflecting developments in the humanities and social sciences. As such, it is the principal gauge which allows us to trace the evolution of major fields, including the rise and fall of fashions, ideologies, and conceits as well as the recurrence of certain constants.[16] In this sense, the *Handbook* has served as the world's historical record for Latin American studies in this century. We hope that the automated version will play a similar role in the next century.

NOTES

1. Lewis Hanke, "Editor's Note," *HLAS 1* (Cambridge, MA: Harvard University Press, 1936), p. xiii; David Bushnell and Lyle N. McAllister, "An Interview with Lewis Hanke," *Hispanic American Historial Review* 68:4 (November 1988), 673; Akira Iriye, "The Internationalization of History," *The American Historical Review* 94:1 (February 1988), 2; Dolores Moyano Martin, "Editor's Note," *HLAS 50* (Austin: University of Texas Press, 1990), p. xxi.

2. Lewis Hanke, "The Development of Latin American Studies in the United States: 1939-1945," *The Americas* (Academy of American Franciscan History, Washington, DC) 4 (July 1947/April 1948), 40.

3. Lewis Hanke, "The Early Development of Latin American Studies in the U.S.," in David J. Robinson, ed., *Studying Latin America: Essays in Honor of Preston E. James* (Syracuse, NY: Syracuse University, Department of Geography, 1980), p.113.

4. Hanke, "The Development of Latin American Studies," p. 35.

5. J. Franklin Jameson, "A New American Historical Journal," *Hispanic American Historical Review* 1:1 (February 1918), 10.

6. Hanke, "The Development of Latin American Studies," pp. 37, 58-59.

7. Ibid., pp. 36-37, 51-53, 60-61.

8. Earl J. Pariseau, "Editor's Note," *Handbook of Latin American Studies*, Vol. 26 (Gainesville: University of Florida Press, 1964), pp. ix-x; Earl J. Pariseau, "Editor's Note," *Handbook of Latin American Studies*, Vol. 27 (Gainesville: University of Florida Press, 1965), pp. ix-x.

9. S.L. Cline, "Ethnohistory: Mesoamerica," *HLAS 52* (Austin: University of Texas Press, 1993), p. 78.

10. Noble David Cook, "Ethnohistory: South America," *HLAS 52* (Austin: University of Texas Press, 1993), p. 87.

11. Cline, "Ethnohistory," p. 78.

12. Rosemarijn Hoefte, "History: The Caribbean, the Guianas, and the Spanish Borderlands," *HLAS 52* (Austin: University of Texas Press, 1993), p. 208.

13. For further information on the offprints, contact LASA Secretariat, 946 William Pitt Union, University of Pittsburgh, Pittsburgh, PA 15260. Telephone: (412) 648-7929; FAX: (412) 624-7145.

14. P. Sue Mundell, "Electronic Dissemination of the *Handbook of Latin American Studies*: Present and Future," in *Proceedings of the North South ONLINE 93 Information Meeting* (Mexico City, 1993), forthcoming.

15. Ibid.

16. The latest instance of the *Handbook*'s serving as the historical record and principal reference for a particular field is exemplified by a major work edited by David W. Dent, *Handbook of Political Science Research on Latin America: Trends from the 1960s to the 1980s* (New York, NY: Greenwood Press, 1990). This work draws its conclusions almost exclusively from *Handbook* data.

37. The Library of Congress Office, Rio de Janeiro

James C. Armstrong

The Library of Congress (LC) office in Rio de Janeiro, one of six such offices worldwide, acquires monographs, serials, and a variety of nonprint media for the Library from Brazil and Uruguay. It also acquires Brazilian serials, in a growing cooperative acquisitions program, for 44 U.S. research libraries, including the National Library of Medicine. This program began in 1990. The office, with a Brazilian staff of 20, is headed by James C. Armstrong, field director. There is also a part-time representative in São Paulo.

The Rio office opened in 1966 as a National Program for Acquisitions and Cataloging office serving the Library of Congress, for acquiring Brazilian publications. Uruguay was added in FY86. Consideration is being given to covering Guyana, Suriname, and French Guiana on a continuing basis.

The Rio office acquisitions staff uses a variety of techniques to ensure that as many publications as possible are examined and obtained. A key resource is a newspaper clipping service, which yields a daily harvest of items about new publications, reviews, news of publishers, and so on. Visits to Rio bookstores and acquisitions trips (8 to 10 per year) to major publishing cities, as well as letter-writing campaigns, are all useful and productive. A major factor in the success of the Rio office's acquisitions is the staff itself: seven acquisitions librarians, with a cumulative total of 57 years of experience, on a state-by-state basis, are supported by four clerical staff. The Rio-92 environment conference was the occasion for a major collecting effort. Occasionally, special efforts are made to identify new sources, such as independent video producers.

Brazil's chronic inflation creates many problems for the Rio LC office, ranging from frequent salary adjustments to rapidly escalating serial subscription costs. Moreover, inflation acts as a brake on the development of Brazil's publishing industry. Although the number of commercially published books remains relatively stable, printing production, in terms of numbers of copies printed, declined sharply from 1986 to 1990, with a noticeable recovery in 1991. Some publishers have reported very successful first quarters in 1993.

While there are many commercial publications, a major part of Brazil's publishing output is noncommercial in nature and derives from governmental and nongovernmental organizations.

Typically, about two-thirds of the Brazilian publications acquired by the Rio office are received on an exchange and gift basis, from approximately 5,500 exchange partners. In FY92 this amounted to more than 20,000 out of a total of over 33,000 pieces acquired for LC. (See tables 1-3.)

The office's cataloging section has been using the Minaret computer cataloging system since 1990. Cataloging output increasingly consists of full-level cataloging records, with a declining number of preliminary records. Close contact is maintained with LC's cataloging divisions for review purposes. Special emphasis is given to cataloging materials selected for the *Handbook of Latin American Studies*. The section is online with the MARC database for searching purposes. Cataloging input is done via diskette mailed to Washington.

Both acquisitions and cataloging sections use the CD-ROM version of the MARC database for searching. An "Overseas Acquisitions Subset" of this is also used; it is far more efficient to search, being on a single disk rather than seven. There are currently some 58,772 entries for Brazilian imprint on this, and 5,991 for Uruguay.

A special project undertaken by the Rio office has been the collection and organization of materials for "Brazil's Popular Groups: A Microfilm Collection of Materials Issued by Socio-Political, Religious, Labor and Minority Grassroots Organizations, 1966-1986" (32 reels), which is available from the Library's Photoduplication Service. A "Supplement 1987-1989" (43 reels) is available, and a "Supplement 1990-1992" will be filmed in 1994.

Over 500 copies of the *Accessions List: Brazil and Uruguay* are distributed. In the future, if it survives financial constraints, this will be a more legible product, generated from Minaret-based cataloging.

Table 1. Library of Congress Office,
Rio de Janeiro: Acquisitions–Brazil[a]

(Pieces FY88—FY92)

	FY 88	FY 89	FY 90	FY 91	FY 92
Purchase					
Monographs	1,374	1,297	1,031	1,182	1,594
Serials	7,760	7,149	7,053	10,327	11,000
Other forms	269	176	150	145	67
Total	9,403	8,622	8,234	11,654	12,661
Exchange and Gift					
Monographs	3,476	2,815	1,954	2,804	3,061
Serials	12,475	13,276	13,630	9,897	13,909
Other forms	3,302	2,384	1,812	1,891	3,494
Total	19,253	18,475	17,396	14,592	20,464
Summary					
Monographs	4,850	4,112	2,985	3,986	4,655
Serials	20,235	20,425	20,683	20,224	24,909
Other forms	3,571	2,560	1,962	2,036	3,561
Total	28,656	27,097	25,630	26,246	33,125

[a] The office subscribes to 537 serial titles and receives approximately 2,288 serial titles under exchange and gift arrangements.

Table 2. Library of Congress Office, Rio de Janeiro: Acquisitions–Uruguay[a]

(Pieces FY88—FY92)

	FY 88	FY 89	FY 90	FY 91	FY 92
Purchase					
Monographs	485	321	169	424	263
Serials	1,032	799	977	934	998
Other forms	14	48	6	2	18
Total	1,531	1,168	1,152	1,360	1,279
Exchange and Gift					
Monographs	197	199	173	103	93
Serials	788	929	931	1,368	653
Other forms	123	201	66	82	63
Total	1,108	1,329	1,170	1,553	809
Summary					
Monographs	682	520	342	527	356
Serials	1,820	1,728	1,908	2,302	1,651
Other forms	137	249	72	84	81
Total	2,639	2,497	2,322	2,913	2,088

[a] The office subscribes to 124 serial titles through Montevideo bookdealers and receives approximately 226 serial titles under exchange and gift arrangements.

Table 3. Library of Congress Office, Rio de Janeiro:
Combined Receipts for Library of Congress and Participants

(FY92)

	Source			Form of Material			
	Purchase	Gift	Exchange	Monographs	Serials	Miscellaneous	Total FY
Library of Congress	13,940	7,908	13,365	5,011	26,560	3,642	35,213
Participants	20,448	294	0	395	20,347	0	20,742
Total	34,388	8,202	13,365	5,406	46,907	3,642	55,955

38. The Hispanic Division and the Reduction of Luso-Hispanic Arrearages since 1989

Edmundo Flores

The efforts of the Hispanic Division of the Library of Congress (LC) to reduce arrearages have been ongoing for a number of years. This report documents the progress made since September 1989, when the Librarian of Congress, James Billington, established the goal of reducing the Library of Congress's overall arrearage, which then stood at 39,682,153 items. The timetable calls for the elimination of 11.3 million items from the arrearage by December 31, 1993. As of mid-May 1993, the arrearage had been brought down to 30,656,490 items, a reduction of 9,025,663 items or 22.7 percent. All available staff are working hard to ensure that the Library will reach its arrearage reduction goal for 1993 by processing 2.3 million items between now and December. Arrearage reduction continues to have a high priority in the Library of Congress; the ultimate goal in this effort will be to accomplish an 80 percent arrearage reduction by the end of 1999.

Division Arrearages

During 1990-1991, the Hispanic Division's Pamphlets I Collection was organized and processed. Of the 12,379 pamphlets that made up this collection, 7,979 received collection-level cataloging and were microfilmed, and 261 records were created in LC's MUMS online file. The remaining 4,400 pieces, many of them duplicates, were discarded. Items in this collection, all published before 1950, have been made accessible through broad subject categories, such as economics and education, for each of 22 countries.

A special collection titled Mexican and Central American Political and Social Ephemera 1980-1991, which was cataloged and prepared for microfilming in fiscal year 1991, is now available on 45 reels of microfilm. This collection consists of 3,100 items, organized by country and divided into the following ten subjects: human rights, refugee groups, women/feminist groups, environmental organizations, urban groups, labor groups, political parties, youth groups, ecumenical movements, and homosexual groups. Other libraries have shown an interest in this collection and have purchased the microfilm from LC.

Over the years, the Hispanic Division's Pamphlets II Collection had expanded to include 13,250 items. During 1992-1993, this entire collection was processed—5,500 items were discarded, and the remaining 7,750 were organized by subject and country. A total of 341 MUMS online records have been created. This collection will be on microfilm before the end of the year.

A collection of Spanish Drama Plays, consisting of 194 items, will also be prepared for microfilming in calendar year 1993.

During 1992-1993, the Luis Dobles Segreda (Costa Rican) Memorial Collection, consisting of about 700 volumes, received the attention of Reynaldo Aguirre, one of the Division's senior bibliographers, who created an author index. Arrangements are under way to complete the organizational work on this collection in preparation for microfilming this calendar year.

The microfilming preparatory work on the Puerto Rican Memoria Collection has been nearly completed in the Hispanic Division. This collection, which consists of about 500 pamphlets divided into six subjects—economic conditions, education, literature, religion, science, and medicine—will be microfilmed in 1994.

Library-Wide Luso-Hispanic Arrearages

The Hispanic Division also is assisting in efforts to reduce the Library's overall Luso-Hispanic arrearages.

Beginning in early 1991, the Hispanic Division began cooperating with the Hispanic Cataloging Team to help reduce the Luso-Hispanic arrearage of the former Whole Book Cataloging Section by reviewing materials that may not be suitable for full-level cataloging. No predetermined goal (in numbers) has been set for this arrearage reduction effort, but the project is expected to be ongoing as long as the need exists. So far, 751 pieces have been reviewed by Division specialists Everette Larson, Edmundo Flores, Barbara Tenenbaum, and Iêda Wiarda. The pieces were evaluated and earmarked for full-level cataloging, minimal-level cataloging, collection-level cataloging, discard, or the Division's own pamphlet files. This project is saving catalogers months of work.

In cooperation with the Preliminary Cataloging Section, Division staff in 1991 began an analysis of unsearched Spanish and Portuguese language materials in the former Shared and Descriptive Cataloging Division's arrearage—most of which has been housed in the Adams Building for 20 years or more. The goal of this project is to identify material for deselection and for less than full-level cataloging. At the beginning of the Division's involvement, there were between 15,000 and 20,000 books and pamphlets in this unsearched and recordless arrearage. With the assistance of Division staff, this arrearage has been reduced to about 5,000 pieces.

For many years, the Panama Canal Zone Library's materials were kept in LC's warehouse in Landover, Maryland. This material is of national historical importance and contains such items as photographs of the construction of the Canal and of Panama City, Colón, and Panamá la Vieja. Dr. Juan Manuel Pérez, another of the Division's senior bibliographers, examined and evaluated all these materials, consisting of about 60 boxes, and selected a variety of maps and manuscripts for LC's collections. Among the books and pamphlets in this collection were numerous political magazines from the 1940s and 1950s as well as many on the French Canal. Pérez also assisted curators in the Prints and Photographs Division in evaluating their portion of the collection, some 3,000 items, assuring the retention of valuable historical material.

Finally, in January 1993 Pérez and Tenenbaum began a project to eliminate 170 cartons of material in the Library's long-standing Serial Division's Hispanic arrearage. In March of this year, Tenenbaum and Pérez completed the evaluation of the Mexican portion of this arrearage, a total of 18 cartons (3,133 pieces), and discarded 89 percent (2,775 pieces) of the material. They then evaluated 6,849 pieces in the 25-carton Pan American Union Collection; this work was completed in June after discarding 6,485 pieces (95 percent). Some 127 cartons remain to be processed in this arrearage reduction effort.

The Hispanic arrearage as of July 1993 can be summarized as follows:

Spanish-language Materials	3,902 items
Portuguese-language Materials	962 items
Hispanic Pamphlets II	7,750 items
Doble Segreda Collection	700 volumes
Spanish Plays	194 items
Serial Division	127 boxes

Gift and Exchange

39. Acquisition of Latin American Serials: Three Methods

Paula Sullenger

Foreign serials are vital for most academic libraries. How to obtain these titles, however, is a matter of debate in the library community. Many are acquired as gifts and exchanges, methods which have fallen out of favor in recent years. For those involved in collection development, these can be valuable tools for obtaining material which might not otherwise be acquired. For budget-conscious administrators they can be exotic, expensive-looking programs that need to be cut back. For those involved in acquisitions, they can be frustrating procedures which seem to be more trouble than they are worth. Staff time has always been important, but it is considered a crucial element in these times of decreasing budgets. Many librarians feel that gifts and exchanges take up too much valuable time to be worthwhile.[1]

Nature of Study

According to management personnel in the Serials Department at the University of North Carolina at Chapel Hill, materials received as gifts and exchanges require more staff time and effort than those received through more common channels such as vendors. This study was conducted in the hope of providing data on whether or not there is a basis for this perception. Titles studied were limited to those received from Latin American countries (except French-speaking countries), Spain, and Portugal, hereafter referred to inclusively as Latin American titles. The purpose of the study was to determine the amount of staff time spent on Latin American serial titles, and to compare the workload of items received as exchanges or gifts to those titles received through purchase. The study involved only aspects of the processing workflow associated with the Serials Department. Excluded are the tasks carried out by the Collection Development staff, such as the initial contact with partners, establishing exchanges and gifts, and resolving the occasional problems turned over to them.

Assumptions

The researcher's hypothesis was that there would be little or no difference in the amount of staff time spent on Latin American serial titles received as gift or exchange compared to purchases. The investigator hoped to prove the following three assumptions:

1. There is little difference in amount of staff time spent on exchanges and gifts compared to time spent on material received as paid subscriptions.
2. There is little difference in amount of claiming that is performed.
3. There is little difference in response rates to claims.

Literature Review

Gift and exchange programs have been discussed in the library literature sporadically over the past few decades. The 1980s saw an increased amount of attention focused on the issue, owing to a large extent to Kovacic's 1978 survey of gift and exchange programs. His study outlined general principles and staffing patterns of programs at that time. He mentioned cost studies performed by various institutions which seemed to prove that gifts and exchanges were cost-effective measures of obtaining materials.[2]

Since that study, only Carl Deal has approached the topic so broadly. Deal surveyed thirteen Association of Research Libraries (ARL) administrators in order to assess the standing of foreign exchange programs and how they are perceived. His findings indicate that personnel in these programs are decreasing, compared to Kovacic's findings.[3] There is also a greater emphasis on the exchange of serials than monographs.[4] Most of the libraries reported that they give more than they receive and will have difficulties maintaining their programs at their present levels. They are hesitant to begin new exchanges.[5] These types of surveys deal with librarians' perceptions and feelings. Only a few quantitative studies have been undertaken.

Most articles dealing with exchanges focus on cost studies. A majority of these give positive results; that is, the studies show that the value or amount of material received by the library is greater than the value or amount that the library sends out. Galejs reported a benefit of over $5,000 in his survey.[6] Earlier, Lane reported a profit of $34,000 for Columbia's exchange program in 1952.[7] The University of California, Berkeley conducted a study and found that "the cost of acquisition by exchange compared favorably with the cost of purchase."[8]

However, a 1982 study at Duke University found that the "balance" of their Soviet serial exchanges was not in their favor and that they had a "deficit" of about $2,000.[9] The costs of such programs have risen and the procedures have changed. One of the major changes is that, in the past, many university presses donated copies of their journals to libraries to be used in the exchange programs. This practice has ceased in many instances and now the libraries must pay for the journals they send on exchange. This practice is known as "bartered" exchange and is clearly less favorable to the library.

These cost benefit analyses primarily involve the prices of the material involved from both partners and other factors such as personnel costs, shipping and distribution, and office supplies.[10] Items usually not considered in such analyses, because of the difficulty in quantifying them, include office space, equipment and storage, and overhead. Duke University considers these types of costs to be insignificant and that quantifying such items would not be very productive.[11]

In 1978, Kovacic pointed out that there had been no studies comparing the costs of acquiring materials through gifts and exchanges with the costs of ordering them through regular means.[12] A search of the literature reveals that only Berkeley has conducted such a study since then.[13]

Most of these studies conclude that more quantitative analyses need to be done. According to Kovacic:

> It would be extremely helpful if a number of reliable cost-effective studies would be done at those libraries where such studies have not previously been conducted. Several comparative studies between the cost of acquiring gift and exchange material and the cost of acquiring ordered material would also be very useful. It would be of particular interest to have cost-effective studies for those libraries where gift and exchange functions are not centralized but rather integrated into various work units.[14]

Deal points out that most such studies have focused on Soviet exchanges and that more studies are needed for other regions of the world.[15]

Most articles on gifts and exchanges contain statements such as this remark by UCLA's Margaret McKinley:

> Our basic concern is that a lot of work is required to maintain exchange agreements. Exchanges always demand more staff time. This staff time is needlessly expended if the publications in question are available for purchase. Serials acquired on exchange cannot, for us, ever be cost-effective.[16]

While perceptions such as this are common, no data are ever presented to back them up.

A study that attempts to look at this question objectively is Fairbanks's comparison of claim rates for exchange titles and claim rates for titles received as paid subscriptions. Her findings show that:

> the claim rate [was] lowest for domestic exchanges and highest for foreign exchanges with little difference between the claim rates for domestic and foreign subscriptions. Thus, claim rates appear to be determined not by the method of acquisition, but by the ease of communication between the library and publisher.[17]

Fairbanks points out that librarians' perceptions of exchanges may be a self-fulfilling prophecy. Since many libraries only use exchanges when no other means are available, titles received on exchanges are those that agents, for whatever reason, cannot or will not handle. The titles by their very nature are less reliable, often published sporadically and arriving late. Because these titles are usually foreign, a language barrier can frequently affect communication between the library and the supplier.[18] It is hoped that this study will validate Fairbanks's findings and help give more credibility to gift and exchange as a valid means of acquisition.

Chapel Hill Serials Department

At the time of this study, the Serials Department at the University of North Carolina at Chapel Hill was still a manual operation. When an issue was received, it was checked in on the manual record and then routed to its proper location. An automated serials system had just been acquired and staff were inputting the manual records into it in order to bring the system online during the course of this study. By the end of the study period, the check-in procedure for many records was automated, but Latin American and some other titles were still entered manually.

Invoice records were manually recorded at the beginning of the study, but were switched online during its course, so that some invoices were authorized manually and some were authorized online. The change in procedure did not affect the focus of this study. Invoice authorization in both automated and manual systems consists of verifying the title and order number, and that the invoice is received from the correct vendor. The order number is written on the invoice, as is the fund which pays for that title. For the manual record, the invoice number, amount paid, and date of authorization are entered on the manual record. Sometimes it is necessary to make additional copies of the invoice.

Claims are generally handled through form letters. A postcard-size "claim card" is used for the first claim for all serials. There are various form letters, some specifically for gifts and exchanges. The form letter most commonly used for Latin American titles has text written in English, Spanish, and Portuguese. The claimer specifies whether the title is received as a gift, subscription, or exchange. Occasionally, there are situations which cannot be handled through form letters and an original letter must be composed. Thus, as far as claiming is concerned, there is no difference in procedure for claiming based on the method of acquisition.

Methodology

Because no automated system was in place at the beginning of the study, the records were manually searched to find titles received from the study areas, that is, Latin American countries except French-speaking countries, Spain, and Portugal. The record specifies whether a title is an exchange, gift, or subscription. In the case of subscriptions, the agent's name is on the card. In the case of exchanges, the exchange partner and title sent in exchange are on the records. This exchange information is maintained by the subject bibliographers in the Collection Development Department and therefore the Serials staff's information might not necessarily be up-to-date.

These titles were then divided into lists of gifts, exchanges, and subscriptions. After the lists of titles were made up, a note (indicating that the title was involved in the study) was placed with those titles on the manual record. When these titles were received, the Serials staff placed them in a separate area. Because of the amount of staff time that would have been involved in taking the appropriate statistics, the Serials staff did not directly participate in the study. The investigator was trained in the procedures and processed all the Latin American serial titles received, keeping a log of the action performed and time spent on each title.

The activities monitored were:

Generating claim notices
Retrieving records from outstanding order files
Updating records in outstanding order files
Resolving complex problems discovered while updating
Mailing claim notices
Verifying invoices for the Accounting Department
Photocopying invoices
Refiling the records in outstanding or in-process files
Purging files of outdated records
Recording claim responses received from supplier[19]

The data were collected over a five-month period (October 1991-February 1992). They were kept on a form with space to record the title in question, action performed, and amount of time spent doing so (rounded off to the nearest half-minute). Simple checking in of titles was not part of the study because it was felt that there would be no difference in checking in for a title whether it was a gift, exchange, or subscription. If a title was checked in during the study period that fact was noted, but no other data were kept on it.

Results

The search of the Kardex revealed 595 serial titles received from Spain, Portugal, and Latin American countries (except French-speaking countries). Of those titles, 301 are paid subscriptions (50 percent of total titles), 219 (37 percent) are exchanges, and the remaining 75 titles (13 percent) are gifts. Of these 595 titles, only 157 titles (26 percent) were received (checked in) during the study period. Of these checked-in titles, 85 titles (54 percent) were paid subscriptions, 50 (32 percent) were exchanges, and 22 (14 percent) were gifts.

Since the information was easy to obtain, it was decided to duplicate Fairbanks's study somewhat and see how many of each type of title were being claimed before the study actually began. In September 1991, 178 titles had been claimed and were awaiting a response. Eighty-six paid subscription titles had been claimed (29 percent of the total number of paid titles), with 72 exchange titles (or 33 percent of the total number of exchange titles) and 20 gift titles (28 percent of total gift titles) being claimed.

While the exchange titles had slightly higher claim rates, there was not a significant difference. This result differs from Fairbanks's examination, which found a sharply higher claim rate for foreign exchanges than for foreign subscriptions.[20] However, her data were based on a sample from the total collection, while this study was limited to titles from a particular region.

The titles actually used in the study differed somewhat from the checked-in titles. The criterion for inclusion in this study was that the title needed some form of complex action taken. The most common examples of such an action are claiming and invoice authorization. As mentioned above, simple check-in was not such a factor.

There were 170 titles used for this study, or 29 percent of the total number of titles. One hundred paid subscription titles accounted for 59 percent of the titles used in the study. Fifty-one exchange titles needed some action taken and accounted for 30 percent of the titles used in the study. Only 19 gift titles, or 11 percent of titles used for the study, needed some action during the five-month time period. These numbers are in almost the same proportion as the number of total titles received. Therefore, a reliable sample seems to have been obtained.

The 170 titles in the study were received from the following countries: Mexico, 37; Spain, 35; Argentina, 24; Brazil, 18; Venezuela, 13; Chile, 10; Colombia, 10; Portugal, 15; Ecuador, 3; Costa Rica, 3; Uruguay, 3, Cuba, 2; Paraguay, 2; Puerto Rico, 2; Dominican Republic, 1; Peru, 1; and Nicaragua, 1.

Claims

Not surprisingly, claiming and its associated research (for example, verifying addresses for titles not received through a subscription agent) accounted for the largest category of actions taken (49 percent). Eighty-seven claim notices were generated during this time period. (This number does not refer to *titles* as a few titles had more than one claim notice sent out during the course of the study.) Forty-eight of these notices (or

55 percent) were generated by paid subscriptions, 27 notices (31 percent) came from exchange titles, and the 12 remaining (14 percent) were generated by gift titles.

Looked at another way, 48 percent of the actions performed on paid titles were claim related. For exchange titles, 52 percent of the actions were claim related, and 63 percent of the actions for gift titles were claim related.

While these data were being compiled, the investigator had occasion to wonder if, in the paid subscription category, there were more claims on titles received direct from the publisher (whether a university, private society, governmental organization, etc.) than on titles received through an agent. After checking the data, it was found that this was not the case. Of the 48 claim notices sent for paid subscriptions, only 17 were generated by titles received "Direct" from the publisher. The remaining 31 titles were received through an agent.

The investigator also looked at the types of claiming necessary. In other words, were the titles claimed during the study period being claimed for the first time, or were second or third claim notices being sent? A look at the paid titles showed that, of the 48 claims generated, 27 (56 percent) were being claimed for the first time. The remaining 44 percent had the following distributions: 15 second notices, 4 third notices, 1 fourth notice, and 1 fifth notice.

For the 27 exchange title claims: 11 (40 percent) needed a first claim. The remaining 60 percent had the following distribution: 9 second claims, 4 third claims, 2 fourth claims, and 1 fifth claim. For the 12 gift claims, only 2 (17 percent) were being claimed for the first time. The remaining 10 titles (83 percent) were being claimed for the second time.

Invoices

The second major category identified in the study is invoicing. Fifty-six items were invoiced during this time period. (Again, this number does not refer to titles because one title could receive more than one invoice notice during the study.) All of the titles invoiced of course were paid subscriptions. It was interesting to note, however, that on more than one occasion an invoice was received asking for payment for a title which was received as a gift or exchange from another source.

Claim Responses

Thirty-three claim responses were noted during the course of the study. A claim response can take various forms. For example, if the item claimed is later received, a claim response statistic is noted by the Serials staff. A message from the supplier is also counted, whether this message states that the item is being sent, has not yet been published, or that the supplier has no record of the item in question.

Receipt Coupons

Some suppliers send a "receipt coupon" with the item. This coupon takes the form of a postcard or letter asking the receiver to note the title, date, volume, issue number, and so on of the item received and to return the coupon so that the supplier knows that it was received. In the case of exchange titles, the supplier may also want to know the same information about the title sent in exchange. Most of these coupons say that future receipt of the title depends on the return of the coupon. Fifteen titles received had a receipt coupon attached, 11 exchanges and 4 gifts. There were no paid titles with coupons received during the course of the study.

Address Changes

Several years ago (in 1984) the library collection, including the Serials Department, moved from the Wilson Library to the new Davis Library. At that time, letters were sent to all suppliers of serials notifying them of the Serial Department's new address. The Department still occasionally receives items bearing the old address and when they come in, a new change of address notice is sent to the supplier, asking them to change their records and use the new address. Sixteen items needed this treatment during the course of the study: 11 exchanges, 4 gifts, and 1 subscription title, which was received "Direct" and not through an agent. Two exchange titles accounted for four of the address changes, as notices were sent twice during the investigation. It is unknown why these institutions have not been able to change the Serials Department's address after so many years have elapsed.

Ceased Titles

Eight titles, 7 exchanges and 1 gift, "ceased" during the course of the study. The majority of these titles were canceled by the Serials Department owing to non-receipt of the items and lack of response on the part of the supplier. Only one was canceled because it had ceased publication.

Transfers

Two subscription titles were transferred from one agent to another. One title had been claimed and the supplier responded that it had no record of such an order, so a new agent was found. For the second title, the decision to change agents had been made prior to this study, but the actual transfer occurred during the study period.

Other

Seven of the actions fell into a miscellaneous category. One exchange title had undergone a title change sometime in the past which was not noticed until the title changed once again during the study period. A second exchange required a note to the Latin American bibliographer to resolve some difficulties. The third exchange title required consultation with a departmental library when two exchange partners wanted to send the same title. The Latin American bibliographer also was notified of this situation.

Four subscription titles required special attention. One title required correspondence with the publisher. A second subscription title was claimed but the supplier had no record of a subscription with the Davis Library and another supplier had to be found. A third required extensive correspondence because the supplier continued sending an invoice notice for the same material although it had already been paid. The fourth situation involved sending a reply regarding a title that had been canceled two years before.

Time

The paid subscription titles required 370.5 minutes of labor, or 57 percent of the study time. The exchange titles required 204 minutes of labor, or 34 percent of the study time. The gift titles required 78.5 minutes, or 12 percent of the study time. The proportion of time spent on each type of title is almost exactly equal to the proportion of each type of title in the study.

Conclusion

As can be seen from the above results, there is no real difference in the amount of work involved per title for Latin American serials based on the method of acquisition.

Assumption #1, that there is little difference in the amount of staff time spent on exchanges compared with time spent on paid titles, was found to be valid. This analysis shows that the staff time spent on the titles and the number of tasks to be performed in each category (paid, exchange, and gift) are proportional to the total number of titles in each category. There is a small difference in the type of task performed on them (paid subscriptions require invoicing while exchanges and gifts often use return cards), but this has little effect on the overall picture. One cannot say that gifts and exchanges are more problematic than paid subscriptions.

Assumption #2, that there is little difference in the amount of claiming between the three means of acquisition, was not upheld conclusively. While there is little difference in the amount or type of claiming between paid and exchange titles, gift titles show a greater proportion of claims needed, and, at least during the study period, require a greater proportion of repeated claims.

Assumption #3, that there is little difference in claim response rates, was not addressed owing to the short time span of the study.

The data show that gifts and exchanges are not more problematic than paid subscriptions. It would probably be safe to assume this conclusion would be applicable to other gift and exchange programs for serials. The data would probably be transferable to other Third World countries.

It is precisely the foreign exchanges that constitute the majority of exchanges in academic libraries. This was true in Kovacic's 1978 study[21] and Deal found it to be true ten years later.[22] Even McKinley admits that exchanges are essential for supporting area studies.[23] Given that foreign publications are essential for many large academic libraries, perhaps librarians should not be so quick to dismiss an exchange opportunity.

The balance of exchange could not be determined at Chapel Hill from this study, mostly because of the manner in which exchange records are kept. If, however, a library can determine that its balance of exchange is reasonable, then exchanges could very well be a cost-effective method of acquisitions. Major expansion of such programs is not expected as a result of this analysis, nor is it greatly desired. Barker, an advocate of exchanges, is quick to point out that exchanges have "a critical point beyond which equilibrium is lost and stability and control become difficult or impossible."[24]

Limitations

While every effort was made to include all Latin American serial titles received as a part of the study, inevitably some slipped by. The Kardex staff on occasion brought such a title to the attention of the investigator to be included, but still there were a few which were not caught. However, since the data show such a clear proportional orientation, it is doubtful that these few titles would alter the results in any significant manner.

This study does not address some of the areas of research which past investigators have called for. Staff time and effort were measured, but not costs per se. One of the major concerns of librarians is the cost of setting up the gift or exchange, which is the area where they feel that much of the staff time is spent. This aspect was not covered in this study because no new titles were set up. (One new paid subscription title was received, unfortunately, right after the study period was over.)

Some factors that could not be analyzed include postage costs and costs associated with other library or university departments. Postage at the University of North Carolina at Chapel Hill is added at another location by the University Mail Service; it would be difficult to determine the actual postage costs for the Latin American serials titles. The majority of exchange records for Latin American serials are maintained by the Latin American-Iberian Resources department. Data on costs and staff time of this department could not be gathered for this study.

This study and the others mentioned give only an overview of some aspects of the total operations. To obtain the kind of data necessary for a complete and accurate comparison of the methods of acquisition, a long-range comprehensive examination is necessary. At least two years should be given to such an undertaking. Logs would need to be kept by staff members, noting time spent on a title, action taken, supplies used, and so on. Such a log would need to be kept by every staff member involved with exchange and gift titles and not limited to one department as this study was. All supplies and times would need to be given a dollar amount in order to have a real cost study.

A major drawback to this study is the short time period covered. At least two years, and probably more accurately five years, would be necessary for a comprehensive analysis. It can easily be seen that this type of study would be prohibitively time-consuming and expensive for most libraries. Until such a study is done, however, librarians must rely on the smaller existing studies which address the issues most important to their organization. If staff time is an area of concern for libraries, then this study and Fairbanks's research suggest that librarians should rethink their assumption that gifts and exchanges are more labor-intensive than traditional means of acquisition.

NOTES

1. Carl Deal, "The Administration of International Exchanges in Academic Libraries: A Survey," *Library Acquisitions: Practice and Theory* 13 (1989), 202; Margaret McKinley, "The Exchange Program at UCLA: 1932-1986," *Serials Review* 12 (September 1986), 74.

2. Mark Kovacic, *The Organization and Function of Gift and Exchange Programs in Eighteen Selected U.S. Academic Libraries* (Washington, DC: Council on Library Resources, 1978), p. 60.

3. Deal, "Administration of International Exchanges," p. 201.

4. Ibid., p. 203.

5. Ibid., p. 205.

6. John E. Galejs, "Economics of Serials Exchanges," *Library Resources and Technical Services* 16 (Fall 1972), 516-517.

7. Alfred H. Lane, "Economics of Exchange," *Serials Slants* 3 (July 1952), 22.

8. Joseph W. Barker, "A Case for Exchange: The Experience of the University of California, Berkeley," *Serials Review* 12 (Spring 1986), 69.

9. Jana K. Stevens, Jade G. Kelley, and Richard G. Irons, "Cost-Effectiveness of Soviet Serials Exchanges," *Library Resources and Technical Services* 28 (1982), 153.

10. Galejs, "Economics of Serials Exchanges," pp. 514-15; Stevens, Kelley, and Irons, "Cost-Effectiveness of Soviet Serials Exchanges," p. 154.

11. Stevens, Kelley, and Irons, "Cost-Effectiveness of Soviet Serials Exchanges," p. 154.

12. Kovacic, *The Organization and Function of Gift and Exchange Programs*, p. 71.

13. Barker, "A Case for Exchange," p. 69.

14. Kovacic, *The Organization and Function of Gift and Exchange Programs*, p. 74.

15. Deal, "Administration of International Exchanges," p. 205.

16. McKinley, "The Exchange Program at UCLA," p. 74.

17. Deborah Fairbanks, "Claim Rates for Exchanges and Subscriptions," *Serials Review* 16 (Fall 1990), 56.

18. Ibid.

19. ALCTS Technical Services Costs Committee, "Guide to Cost Analysis of Acquisitions and Cataloging in Libraries," *ALCTS Newsletter* 2 (1991), 50-51.

20. Fairbanks, "Claim Rates for Exchanges," p. 58.

21. Kovacic, *The Organization and Function of Gift and Exchange Programs*, p. 50.

22. Deal, "Administration of International Exchanges," p. 201.

23. McKinley, "The Exchange Program at UCLA," p. 76.

24. Barker, "A Case for Exchange," p. 71.

BIBLIOGRAPHY

ALCTS Technical Services Costs Committee. "Guide to Cost Analysis of Acquisitions and Cataloging in Libraries." *ALCTS Newsletter* 2 (1991), 49-52.

Barker, Joseph W. "A Case for Exchange: The Experience of the University of California, Berkeley." *Serials Review* 12 (Spring 1986), 63-73.

Deal, Carl. "The Administration of International Exchanges in Academic Libraries: A Survey." *Library Acquisitions: Practice and Theory* 13 (1989), 199-207.

Fairbanks, Deborah. "Claim Rates for Exchanges and Subscriptions." *Serials Review* 16 (Fall 1990), 55-59.

Galejs, John E. "Economics of Serials Exchanges." *Library Resources and Technical Services* 16 (Fall 1972), 511-520.

Kovacic, Mark. *The Organization and Function of Gift and Exchange Programs in Eighteen Selected U.S. Academic Libraries.* Washington, DC: Council on Library Resources, 1978.

Lane, Alfred H. "Economics of Exchange." *Serials Slants* 3 (July 1952), 19-22.

McKinley, Margaret. "The Exchange Program at UCLA: 1932-1986." *Serials Review* 12 (September 1986), 75-80.

Stevens, Jana K., Jade G. Kelley, and Richard G. Irons. "Cost-Effectiveness of Soviet Serials Exchange." *Library Resources and Technical Services* 26 (1982), 151-155.

40. El canje de material bibliográfico en la Biblioteca Daniel Cosío Villegas de El Colegio de México

Micaela Chávez Villa

El Colegio de México fue fundado en 1940 como una Asociación Civil. Es una institución de carácter universitario dedicada a la investigación y a la formación académica, principalmente a nivel de posgrado, en algunas ramas de las ciencias sociales y las humanidades.

Para cumplir con sus funciones está organizado en siete centros de estudios: Históricos, Lingüísticos y Literarios, Internacionales, Económicos, Demográficos y Urbano, Asia y Africa y Sociológicos.

Además de las investigaciones que se realizan en estos Centros, existen algunos programas surgidos de necesidades nacionales que requieren estudios específicos. Entre estos programas podemos mencionar: Estudios Interdisciplinarios de la Mujer, Ciencia y Tecnología, Diccionario del Español de México, Medio Ambiente y Formación de Traductores.

Bases

Para el canje de material bibliográfico, la Biblioteca ha establecido las siguientes bases:

Los convenios de canje y donativo se formalizan normalmente a través del Departamento de Desarrollo de Colecciones de la Biblioteca. Este Departamento ofrece el canje de:

1. Publicaciones impresas por El Colegio de México, por las publicaciones impresas por las instituciones con las que se establece el canje (originales por originales)
2. Duplicados de la Biblioteca, por duplicados de las bibliotecas con las que se establece el canje
3. Monografía por monografía o revista por revista
4. Título por título (sin tomar en cuenta el número de volúmenes que tenga cada uno de ellos), volumen por volumen, o precio de lista.

Selección

El costo de adquisición, de cada obra, es solamente una parte del que paga El Colegio por ponerla a disposición de los lectores. Al costo inicial de adquisición debe añadirse normalmente el de catalogación, clasificación, preparación física, almacenamiento, mantenimiento y servicio. Por este motivo, la Biblioteca aplica a las obras recibidas en canje y donativo, aunque con mayor flexibilidad, los mismos criterios de selección que operan en las adquisiciones de compra. En este sentido, el canje al igual que la compra es eje central en el desarrollo de nuestras colecciones. La Biblioteca se reserva las facultades de:

1. Integrar a sus colecciones, con los sistemas generales de clasificación que usa, las obras que recibe en canje y donativo
2. No integrar a sus colecciones dichas obras cuando carecen de utilidad para los lectores usuales de la Biblioteca
3. Dar de baja las obras, integradas previamente a las colecciones.

Descarte

La Biblioteca dispone libremente, para efectos de canje y donativo a otras instituciones, de las obras a que no le son de utilidad. En estos casos, la institución beneficiaria asume la responsabilidad de la selección de cada volumen, y nuestra Biblioteca asume los gastos de traslado.

El intercambio de publicaciones entre bibliotecas del país se facilita porque no hay que cubrir los gastos de envío si se invoca la franquicia postal concedida por el gobierno federal para las obras que se intercambian entre bibliotecas.

Procedimiento

La Biblioteca establece convenios con las instituciones afines a sus áreas de especialización a través de cartas de convenio en las cuales se manifiesta el interés en mantener esta relación.

En el caso de las propuestas de otras instituciones, se evalúa el fondo editorial que ofrecen, en cuanto a cantidad, calidad y temática de las publicaciones que tienen disponibles y en función de esto se decide o no aceptar el canje.

La evaluación de los títulos de revistas que nos ofrecen en canje se lleva a cabo en consulta con los profesores investigadores del área en que se especialice la publicación. Una vez establecido el canje se envía comunicación al Departamento de Publicaciones a fin de que incluya en la lista de distribución de la revista correspondiente a la nueva institución con que se estableció el canje. De manera general hemos tratado de que el canje de revistas se haga título por título.

En el caso de monografías éstas se solicitan al Departamento de Publicaciones a medida en que nos son requeridas por las instituciones. En todo momento tratamos de mantener un balance entre lo que enviamos y lo que recibimos.

En algunos casos el canje no resulta del todo equilibrado pero hemos tomado en cuenta la opinión de los encargados de la edición de las revistas y de algunos autores sobre el hecho de que es importante que nuestras publicaciones estén por lo menos en una biblioteca de cada uno de los países de América Latina y en las instituciones americanas y europeas que cuentan con colecciones latinoamericanas.

Convenios celebrados

La Biblioteca Daniel Cosío Villegas mantiene actualmente 511 convenios de canje con instituciones de enseñanza superior e investigación nacionales y extranjeras. La distribución de convenios por país, es la siguiente:

País	Núm. de Instituciones	País	Núm. de Instituciones
México	168	Panamá	3
Estados Unidos	49	Paraguay	3
Argentina	28	Rumanía	2
Alemania	20	Bélgica	2
Francia	18	Checoslovaquia	2
Brasil	14	Hungría	2
Colombia	14	Nicaragua	2
Japón	13	Portugal	2
Cuba	12	Suecia	2
Chile	12	Australia	1
Italia	12	Croacia	1
Inglaterra	10	Dinamarca	1
Ecuador	9	El Salvador	1
Venezuela	9	Escocia	1
Suiza	7	Honduras	1
Canadá	6	India	1
Comunidad de Estados Independientes	6	Israel	1
Perú	5	Nueva Zelanda	1
Costa Rica	4	Pakistán	1
Guatemala	4	Polonia	1
Puerto Rico	4	República Dominicana	1
Uruguay	4	Senegal	1
China	3	Sudáfrica	1
Holanda	34	Yugoslavia	1

Envíos

La Biblioteca envía actualmente, de manera regular, 337 ejemplares de sus publicaciones periódicas. A continuación se desglosan estos envíos:

Nueva Revista de Filología Hispánica	99
Foro Internacional	71
Historia Mexicana	63
Estudios de Asia y Africa	43
Estudios Demográficos y Urbanos	35
Estudios Sociológicos	10
Estudios Económicos	9
Boletín de Fuentes para la Historia Económica de México	7

Beneficios

Actualmente, la Biblioteca recibe 1,100 títulos de publicaciones periódicas, de los cuales casi el 30% (322 títulos) se reciben a través del canje. En los últimos dos años la Biblioteca ha ingresado en su acervo alrededor de 4,000 títulos de monografías recibidos en canje. Una sóla institución americana, la New York Public Library, estimó en 6,600 dlls. el costo total de los duplicados de libros que nos envió durante 1992.

El canje con la Biblioteca del Congreso de Washington nos ha reportado muchos beneficios que van desde la recepción de duplicados hasta el recibo de los discos compactos de su catálogo (CDMARC).

A través de los convenios establecidos con los Institutos de Cultura de los Estados de la República Mexicana nos ha sido posible obtener publicaciones que de otro modo hubiera sido muy difícil por los problemas que existen en la localización y adquisición de obras gubernamentales mexicanas.

Tenemos celebrados algunos convenios "amplios" con las instituciones que han aceptado esta modalidad y que consisten en que cada una de las instituciones envía un ejemplar de todo su acervo editorial sin esperar solicitud expresa de nuestra parte y nosotros les remitimos todos nuestros nuevos títulos. Entre estas instituciones podemos mencionar: Archivo General de la Nación, Centro de Estudios Latinoamericanas, El Colegio de la Frontera Norte, El Colegio Mexiquense, El Colegio de Jalisco, El Colegio de Michoacán, Instituto de Cooperación Iberoamericana, Instituto José María Luis Mora, Instituto de Investigaciones Históricas de la UNAM, y las distintas unidades de la Universidad Autónoma Metropolitana.

Es importante mencionar que una condición fundamental para que el canje sea exitoso es que sea manejado directamente por la Biblioteca, quien es la única que puede establecer los controles adecuados, hacer la selección de acuerdo con las características de su colección y mantener el balance entre lo que se envía y lo que se recibe.

Dificultades

Existe poca coordinación entre los departamentos de publicaciones y las bibliotecas de las instituciones con las que se establece el canje.

La tendencia de las instituciones a realizar co-ediciones con editoriales comerciales dificulta el intercambio de estas publicaciones que ya no son incluidas dentro de los convenios de canje.

En el caso de la UNAM no ha sido posible conseguir toda su producción editorial a través de la Dirección de Fomento Editorial, por lo que se ha recurrido a convenios con cada dependencia.

Dado que las universidades americanas no tienen disponible para canje las publicaciones de las prensas universitarias, sólo canjean duplicados, lo que hace bastante desigual el canje ya que están enviando duplicados a cambio de originales.

A los países sudamericanos cada vez les es más difícil cubrir los gastos de envío. En el caso nuestro se han comprometido a pagarlos, atendiendo al volumen de material que les enviamos pero el problema aumenta cada día.

Son pocas las instituciones mexicanas que envían listas de duplicados para canje o que se muestran interesadas en la revisión de estas listas, lo que aumenta nuestro depósito de duplicados con todos los problemas de almacenamiento que esto implica. En distintos momentos se ha tratado de establecer en México un centro nacional de canje que concentrara los materiales duplicados de las bibliotecas mexicanas en un sólo sitio, pero esta iniciativa no ha tenido el apoyo suficiente.

Existe poca información de las instituciones en lo que se refiere a sus nuevos títulos. Es necesario hacer peticiones constantes para recibir información sobre nuevos títulos.

En las instituciones mexicanas se ha descuidado este medio de adquisición por las necesidades de organización y personal que conlleva.

Las bibliotecas de universidades de provincia no han dado suficiente importancia al canje. La respuesta es escasa, por lo menos, de parte de los miembros de la Asociación Nacional de Universidades e Institutos de Enseñanza Superior a quienes enviamos nuestras listas de publicaciones y duplicados.

41. Canje dirigido: Una nueva modalidad de intercambio

Ana María Fernández Vignolo

Introducción

En el Congreso Mundial de la IFLA de 1978, Frans Vanwijngaerden, Secretario de esa Asociación de la Sección de Intercambio de Publicaciones y Director del Servicio Belga de Intercambio Internacional, consideró relevante incluir la siguiente cita:

Every day in academies, scientific institutes, learned societies, special committees, literary societies, editorial committees, joint effort is creating new sources and inexhaustible manifestations of the human brain. In our own times, one of the quickest ways of hastening the development of science and the onward march of progress is surely to collect these products of the human brain, centralize all the various efforts, draw up in each country an inventory of the general progress of intellectual work, place at the disposal of inquiring minds what might be called the dossier on each subject, prepared and supplemented by the specialists and the scientists from the new and the old worlds, bring them into association and, so to speak, into collaboration with each other. . . . [1]

La referencia es antigua. Se remonta al año 1887 y a la época de la ratificación de la convención de Bruselas, pero el autor citado ve en ella la expresión de la regla básica de todo intercambio de publicaciones, que se debe basar en "un código de ética", en una "mútua generosidad".

Es posible que olvidemos con frecuencia esta dimensión ética al concebir un programa de intercambio, que estoy de acuerdo en señalar como uno de los valores principales de esta actividad tan corriente en nuestras bibliotecas. Hoy más que nunca es imperativa la dispersión del conocimiento y de la información. La realidad mundial ha cambiado mucho desde entonces, y a través del gran desarrollo de las redes bibliotecarias se han establecido vínculos que destruyen fronteras en el tiempo y en el espacio.

Paradójicamente esta concepción global del acceso al quehacer de la cultura, no siempre va acompañada por parte de los gobiernos de disposiciones que garanticen los recursos económicos necesarios para su desarrollo. Conocemos demasiado bien la falta de atención al sector cultural, ya no solo en los países llamados en vías de desarrollo, sino también en los países industrializados, en los países del primer mundo. A la dimensión ética del intercambio de publicaciones se le suma entonces el aspecto mercantilista, es decir, la necesidad de subsanar las limitaciones impuestas por una distribución no equitativa de los presupuestos nacionales.

Programas de canje

La Biblioteca Nacional de Venezuela ha acusado desde hace varios años la urgencia de impulsar sus planes de adquisición a través del canje nacional e internacional. En la actualidad cuenta con 3,000 copartícipes y se elaboran 6 listas anuales de distribución bimensual, de material bibliográfico y no bibliográfico. Las áreas de oferta son principalmente las ciencias sociales y las humanidades, con eventuales inclusiones de material de carácter tecnológico y/o científico. Se destinan para este intercambio los sobrantes de donaciones de importantes instituciones y editoriales, de entidades gubernamentales que cumplen con el depósito obligado por ley, y las publicaciones de la Biblioteca Nacional (*Bibliografía Venezolana, Boletín Bibliotécnico*, catálogos de exposiciones y publicaciones en coedición). En el campo no bibliográfico se inició también hace tiempo un intercambio con duplicados de carteles nacionales, y más recientemente este programa se amplió con un proyecto muy interesante con The Library of Congress. Se solicitó a los diseñadores más importantes del país una donación de su producción personal para intercambiar por productos similares de diseñadores norteamericanos. Esto significó el antecedente de una modalidad de canje no convencional, que abrió el camino para propuestas de un canje dirigido, del que hablaré más adelante.

En la actualidad la División de Canje y Donaciones sufre un proceso de reestructuración, con el propósito de formar el Servicio Nacional de Canje. Los primeros pasos en tal sentido se han dado en la paulatina eliminación de un control manual y la automatización del cúmulo de información con que se cuenta. Los objetivos son la elaboración de directorios de copartícipes nacionales e internacionales. Contamos en la actualidad con el Directorio de Copartícipes Nacionales y se comenzó el de Copartícipes de América Latina y el Caribe. Estos directorios internacionales se producirán por área geográfica:

1. Iberoamérica y el Caribe
2. Estados Unidos y Canadá
3. Europa
4. Resto del mundo

Asimismo, se han registrado ya en un Directorio las Bibliotecas Nacionales mundiales.

Es amplia la actividad de intercambio de la Biblioteca Nacional de Venezuela. Se cubren las más importantes bibliotecas nacionales, incluso las de las recientemente formadas repúblicas de la antigua U.R.S.S., las instituciones gubernamentales y no gubernamentales, las principales bibliotecas universitarias internacionales y centros de investigación de Iberoamérica y el Caribe.

Canje dirigido

Antecedentes y justificación

El intercambio mencionada con anterioridad con The Library of Congress, dc material de características similares, abrió un campo de posibilidades para conseguir material que no siempre se obtiene a través de un programa de canje tradicional. Ya la Bibliotcca Nacional de Venezuela había realizado esfuerzos esporádicos en el campo de intercambio de material antiguo, pero a partir de la experiencia señalada se comenzó a estudiar la posibilidad de obtener a través de lo que llamamos un "canje dirigido", material que no es de fácil adquisición ni por canje ni por compra, como por ejemplo material agotado, tomos de enciclopedias, primeras ediciones de publicaciones venezolanas, manuscritos microfilmados, números de revistas antiguas faltantes, así como publicaciones de precios altos cuyo envío podíamos reciprocar con material valioso en nuestras colecciones.

Objetivo

Completar las colecciones bibliográficas y no bibliográficas de la Biblioteca Nacional, una vez detectados los vacíos existentes, con el material relevante que no es de fácil adquisición por medio de un canje normal.

Procedimientos

El programa de canje dirigido generó actividades especiales en la División de Canje y Donaciones, en conjunto con los directores de las diversas colecciones: Referencia Bibliografía General, Publicaciones Oficiales, Libros Raros y Manuscritos, el Centro de Documentación e Información Bibliotecológica (CEDINBI) y el Archivo Audiovisual. El primer paso fue la identificación y selección de instituciones en base al material que se quería recuperar, según las áreas deficitarias detectadas. En una primera etapa el espectro de instituciones con las que se hizo contacto fue muy amplio, y nuestra determinación de carencias tal vez no lo suficientemente específica. La experiencia nos enseñó, que estábamos trabajando con temas y materias generales, y que debíamos limitar tanto nuestro espectro de instituciones como concretar nuestras solicitudes a títulos u obras determinadas. Así mismo entendimos que el contacto más fructífero sería el establecido con bibliotecas nacionales, las que, como quedó demostrado, podían referirnos a las instituciones que publicaban el material de nuestro interés.

Igualmente, fue necesario consolidar por nuestra parte el tipo de material que estábamos en condiciones de ofertar. Se destinó para canje dirigido importante material no bibliográfico, como partituras, mapas, carteles, discos, postales, material en cassettes y diapositivas sobre distintas etnias americanas y otros, y se elaboraron por materia tres listas de material monográfico en Ciencias Sociales, Economía, Gerencia y Administración Pública y Literatura. Para esto contamos con sobrantes de nuestras colecciones, con obras solicitadas en donación a terceros (particulares, instituciones y editoriales) y con material microfilmado.

Resultados

El programa de canje dirigido comenzó a principio de 1992 y a seis meses de iniciado recibimos respuestas favorables. Desde entonces se ha consolidado de forma efectiva. Como ejemplos, quisiera nombrar solamente algunos de los resultados obtenidos, reseñando brevemente parte del material recibido:

Beinecke Studies in Early Manuscripts, remitido por Yale University, por referencia de The Library of Congress.

Registro de Discursos y Declaraciones de Mijail Gorbachov, enviado por la Biblioteca "All Union State Order of the Red Banner" de Moscú.

Bibliografías Nacionales de Malta y Madagascar.

La Prensa Nacional en la Epoca de Santander. La Bandera Nacional (1837-1839), Nº 1, por referencia de la Biblioteca Nacional de Colombia y enviada por la Biblioteca de la Presidencia de la República.

España 1492-1992 (Ed. Quinto Centenario), editado por la Escuela de Estudios Hispanoamericanos, del Consejo Superior de Investigaciones de Sevilla, a quien fuimos referidos por la Biblioteca Nacional de España.

Cartografía General de Plazas, Fuentes y Ciudades Españolas, Siglos XVII al XIX, de Antonio Bonat Correa, editada por el Instituto de Conservación y Restauración de Bienes Culturales del Ministerio de Cultura de España. Esta es una obra muy costosa, que también localizamos según la referencia de la Biblioteca Nacional de España.

Existe además la oferta de la Biblioteca Nacional de Argentina, de enviar el Fondo Antiguo de la Sala del Tesoro microfilmado, a cambio de material antiguo microfilmado de nuestras colecciones. Asimismo se han recibido importantes recopilaciones legislativas, números faltantes de publicaciones periódicas, anuarios estadísticos, informes anuales de diversos organismos, material de referencia y monografías de diversa índole.

Infraestructura técnica para el Programa de Canje

Para apoyar las acciones citadas hubo necesidad de formalizar una estructura técnica que asegura la operatividad de este tipo de canje.

Se consideró de vital importancia la creación de un directorio automatizado de todas las instituciones con las que se ha establecido canje, donde se indican además las publicaciones que ellas ofrecen.

Dentro del sistema automatizado para el procesamiento de la información en NOTIS (Northwestern Online Total Integrated System) —específicamente en el Módulo de Adquisiciones— se han realizado algunas aplicaciones para el control del canje dirigido. Estas consisten en la asignación de códigos a cada una de las instituciones participantes, a través de siglas que se colocan en la pantalla de existencia de la publicación, con una nota de su historia, es decir que se señala la fecha y concepto de ingreso (canje normal o canje dirigido). Con esto se logra la recuperación de listas especiales por instituciones, que nos otorgan información sobre el material en nuestro poder y nos permite controlar los reclamos.

El adelanto de los sistemas automatizados para el intercambio mundial de la información indica el progreso cumplido a través de los años y las posibilidades abiertas por los avances tecnológicos. A pesar de ello podemos afirmar que el intercambio de publicaciones es aún hoy día un acto ético y de mútua generosidad.

NOTA

1. Frans Vanwijngaerdin, "Exchange of Publications with the Developing Countries", IFLA, 44. Congress, 1978, p. 1.

42. Acquisition of Serials by Exchange in the Library of Congress

Terry C. Peet

The Library of Congress (LC) could not attain its acquisition goal of serials without the use of its extensive exchange program. Each year the Library acquires approximately 400,000 serials by exchange, and this figure does not include domestic titles which the Library receives via Copyright or on a donated basis.

Despite its comparatively large budget for serials, in excess of two million dollars—dedicated largely to foreign serial titles—the overwhelming majority of serial titles are acquired by LC through exchanges. In Latin America (exclusive of Brazil and Uruguay), the Library acquires in excess of 7,000 serial titles through exchange totaling more than 35,000 pieces annually. By purchase LC acquires no more than 1,100 (exclusive of Brazil and Uruguay, countries handled by the Library's office in Rio de Janeiro).

What are the characteristics and forces driving the Library's exchange program? First and foremost, the Library has resources at its disposal few libraries elsewhere have. These include:

1. A large editorial production of publications and bibliographic products with which to exchange.
2. Access to more than 200 federal government serial titles for exchange use.
3. Use of Copyright and Cataloging in Publication (CIP) duplicates (monographs) in return for serial subscriptions. LC often counter-offers monographs for serials.
4. An annual budget for the purchase at substantial discounts of more than 170 copies of the *Handbook of Latin American Studies* and 50 subscriptions to the *Hispanic American Historical Review* for exchange use, all for serials.
5. Bilateral treaties and multinational conventions (Brussels 1886, Buenos Aires 1936) stipulating the exchange of official publications; the predominant format for exchange in both directions is serials.
6. Access to millions of transfer materials, i.e., materials weeded out or discarded by other federal government libraries, which by law are required to be sent to LC for disposal.

Second, and very closely behind resources, is the Library's canon of collection policies which are broad and comprehensive and exclude chiefly material that is strictly technical agriculture and clinical medicine. Otherwise, the Library's interest is in any other area of human knowledge provided it is of research quality.

Third, LC has the staff and, oddly enough, at the same time does not have the staff. Compared to any institution, LC's staff dedicated to exchange—more than 50 people—is extraordinarily large. Much of the staff's efforts are dedicated to serial exchange and, more important, to claiming missing issues in order to maintain complete runs of serials being retained. Yet at the same time, the staffing is inadequate to ensuring complete runs. For Latin America (exclusive of Brazil and Uruguay) and Iberia, the Library has a staff of 12 dedicated to acquisitions, both exchange and purchase, as well as preliminary online acquisition records.

Fourth is prestige. Much comes to LC because of its stature. Many authors and publishers desire to make certain their work or journal is deposited in LC's collections; its cataloging information, which is distributed in paper, fiche, and electronically, can be a source of marketing.

Fifth, goodwill. The very concept of exchange of information implies a subfloor of goodwill which must be maintained in order to keep the exchange in good working order.

Let us take a brief look at the disadvantages and advantages to serial exchanges.

Disadvantages:

1. Exchange partners are sometimes unreliable or erratic. In Latin America, I am sorry to say, frequent changes in personnel and library and organizational reorganizations lead to interruptions of exchanges.
2. Exchange, whether monograph or serial, can be labor intensive. Exchange with a reliable source for serials is, however, wonderful to behold and not labor intensive; the number of these are relatively few, but important.

Advantages:

1. Exchange, even with salaried employees, can save money especially when dealing with large-scale acquisitions such as LC or any large research university library.
2. Exchange is eminently worthwhile if the institution has but one journal to offer. The more journals available, the greater flexibility in tailoring the exchange program.
3. The foreign partner saves precious U.S. dollars.

4. Acquisition of certain serials is not available any other way except through exchange.
5. Promotes information exchange and goodwill; the two go together and are inseparable.

If the Library of Congress were to convert its serials exchange program to a purchase program, it would need at least, for worldwide acquisitions, ten million dollars in additional appropriations. For Latin America, the Library would very conservatively require an additional quarter million dollars based on an average of $35.00 per subscription. The serials exchange program quite easily pays its way in terms of covering costs of salaried employees and accomplishing its mission of acquisitions.

Great Bibliographers of Latin America

43. Medina and the Medina Award

Laurence Hallewell

When the idea of an annual SALALM bibliography prize was discussed by the Executive Council during the mid-winter meeting in October 1981, the original proposal was to name the prize after founder member Curtis Wilgus, who had just died. This proposal did not meet with universal approval so, to resolve the impasse, I suggested what seemed to me an obvious alternative that should offend no one. José Toribio Medina y Zavala is not only the outstanding bibliographer for our own field of interest, but he has even been called "The Greatest Bibliographer in Christendom." Perhaps there are greater ones in the cultural domains of Islam, Hinduism, or the Middle Kingdom, but if so, I for one am unaware of them. As an Englishman I was naturally sympathetic toward someone who chose to be born on Trafalgar Day: thanks to Lord Cochrane, British naval traditions have always been important in Chile. I also believed I was being original.

No such luck. I wonder how many readers know of the Inter-American Bibliographical and Library Association (IAB&LA), which was created under Pan American Union auspices in 1930 and lasted into the 1970s—by which time the Union had become the O.A.S. Along with the Columbus Memorial Library and the Library of Congress, the Association was one of the midwives at SALALM's birth in 1956, and some of the earlier SALALMs were actually joint meetings with the Association. But by then its glory days were over. At the peak of its activities, however, in February 1939, the Association had announced an annual bibliography prize, open to anyone in the Western Hemisphere, to be called the José Toribio Medina Prize, and to be worth $100. That was of course quite a tidy sum in those days, when the starting annual salary for a female public library assistant in England and Wales was still only £52, or a dollar a working day—and, incidentally, barely more than Oliver Goldsmith's contented eighteenth-century country parson, "passing rich on £40 a year."

There were twenty-four entries from eleven countries for that first award, which went to Enrique Arana hijo, director of the law faculty library of the Universidad de Buenos Aires for a *Bibliografía del Patronato Nacional*, that is, church establishment in Argentina. A bibliography of Rubén Darío and one on northerners in the Mexican Revolution received honorary mentions, and the winning work was published in the proceedings of the Association's third convention in Washington D.C., February 23-24, 1941. There was no prize in 1942, nor in any later year that I can trace. It seems that James Brown Scott of the Carnegie Endowment for International Peace and an honorary life member of the IAB&LA, who had furnished the original $100, failed to repeat his generosity.

No one attending that 1981 mid-winter meeting remembered any of this, and my suggestion was seized upon and adopted. In celebration of ten years of SALALM Medina Prizes, this essay is devoted to our Patron.

Almost a year after thus displacing Curtis Wilgus from the honor of becoming the award's patron, I was invited to replace him in the flesh as editor of Scarecrow Press's Latin American historical dictionaries, starting with the reediting of the volume on Chile. One of my subsequent discoveries was that in the first edition, Medina had featured in neither the dictionary itself nor in the accompanying bibliography. The author readily agreed to remedy both of these omissions in the new edition. This strange oversight should not, however, reflect on Curtis's own estimation of the great man. Curtis was in fact the moving spirit of the IAB&LA: one gets the impression that in its final years, the Association was virtually sustained by Curtis as a one-man show. The idea to call its prize after Medina was almost certainly his. Moreover, among my discoveries in preparing this essay was the tribute paid to him by Sarah Elizabeth Roberts, who was Irene Zimmerman's predecessor as Latin American selector at the University of Florida, Gainesville. Roberts authored the first substantial biography of Medina in English, published by the IAB&LA in 1938. At the O.A.S. celebration of the centenary of Medina's birth in 1952, she paid Curtis the following tribute: "Before I begin this discusssion of . . . Medina, I wish to express the pleasure that I feel in having Professor Wilgus as a co-chairman of this session. It was his interest in Medina which led me, as one of his graduate students, to make the life and works of the Chilean the subject of my master's thesis. I have always been grateful to Professor Wilgus for instilling in me his own enthusiasm for Medina." So maybe Curtis's ghost will look down with some indulgence on SALALM's eventual decision to honor the Chilean rather than the American bibliographer!

On approaching the subject of Toribio Medina, the first thing to strike one is, of course, the sheer, almost incredible, bulk of his output. I am reminded of my old library school professor of bibliography, Ronald Benge, who confessed that he tried to enliven the rather dull task of teaching bibliography and reference works by adding details of the compilers' private lives—which rapidly led him to the conclusion that they were all mad. Now that we are increasingly coming to see most forms of madness no longer in absolute terms as manifestations of disease to be cured, but rather as an individual's rational refusal to be bound by cultural norms that are at bottom purely arbitrary, then a modicum of madness in this sense is perhaps necessary to resist societal pressures to find our satisfactions in life in whatever form the majority of our conformist fellow humans have decided to be most appropriate for our age, sex, and socioeconomic status.

Benge also referred to bibliographers and librarians as "human termites," which brings to mind a lecturer in the Spanish Department of King's College of London University when I was an undergraduate there. He opined, *apropos* of Benito Pérez Galdós, that, although the more typical Hispanic man of letters was not notable for the volume of his output, this rather dilettante majority, who, according to my teacher, tended to achieve fame on the basis of a single book, was more than made up for by a small number of workaholics, the quantity of whose output defied human comprehension. While his hyperbole unjustly slandered the mass of Iberian and Ibero-American writers, there are quite a number in his second category who stand comparison with the prolific Galdós: Lope de Vega, the Brazilians Wilson Martins and Coelho Neto, and the Colombian Vargas Villa are among those who first come to mind. But even among this group, Medina's truly enormous production makes him outstanding.

According to the bibliography by his secretary, Guillermo Feliú Cruz, Medina was responsible for 408 books and articles written, edited, or translated, but this is certainly not the real total, since other articles by him were scattered in the journals of the cities through which he traveled. I have seen totals as high as five hundred suggested, although these included reprints and new editions. Victor Chiappa's *Catálogo de las publicaciones de Don José Toribio Medina, 1873-1914* omits the last sixteen years of his life and still comes up with 317. But let me cite the apology in Maury Bromsen's brief 1945 bibliographical essay: "Naturally don José Toribio's writings suffered somewhat quantitatively as the years passed; from 1904 to 1923 he published only 38 volumes." How many other literary biographers would have felt a need to attribute to advancing years a decrease of their subject's output to only two books a year?

Of course, he did not do it all on his own. Roberts, among others, has pointed out how much he owed to his wife, Mercedes Ibáñez y Rondizzoni de Medina. In her, according to Eduardo Barrios, Chile's national librarian, Medina found a sweetheart, wife, mother, collaborator, and saint. The tribute by the Chilean Congress likened her to Marie Curie (which makes me want to speculate on a possible interchange of their respective reputations had it been Mercedes' José killed in that 1906 traffic accident instead of Marie's Pierre). Feliú Cruz calls her the anonymous heroine of her husband's books. Roberts, more to the point, details how much his output increased following his marriage, and suggests that his *Literatura femenina en Chile: Notas bibliográficas y en parte críticas* of 1923 was a tribute to her—a fortieth wedding anniversary in fact. Some of his remarks in this work may suggest a somewhat patronizing attitude to the literary products of what I am sure he would have called the "weaker sex," but such an attitude on our part is probably anachronistic. To quote Bromsen again: "No biography of her husband could overrate her contribution in making him the giant of letters he became. Señora Medina served as collaborator, proofreader, correspondent, and cataloguer, and in a thousand other ways performed the intellectual drudgeries that accompany research and publication," though a number of instances suggest to me that her contribution was somewhat more basic and academic than the mere performance of "intellectual drudgeries." Her own attitude, at least as she publicly avowed it, was the conventional one for a Hispanic woman of her generation. She felt, she said, that "the two principal duties of a wife are to help her husband when she can, and not to disturb him at other times," but perhaps this was irony at her interviewer's expense.

I am reminded of their English contemporaries, another enormously industrious but also childless couple, the pioneer social scientists Beatrice and Sydney Webb. In their case of course it was the husband who, no doubt flattered and even maybe intimidated by his wife's far superior social status, willingly accepted the lion's—or should I say the termite's?—share of the intellectual drudgeries, and the wife who got most of the credit. Which illustrates the truism that in England even sexism will lose out to classism.

And in speaking of classism, may I suggest that, in distributing credit for the work attributed to José Toribio, we should remember not only the wife but also all those humbler members of their household who made such single-minded dedication to bibliography possible? Virigina Wolf had much to say about the role of a room of one's own in the emancipation of the modern gentlewoman. The contribution of servants of one's own, someone in her position could take for granted. Something that struck me forcibly when I went to live in South America (Trinidad in the 1950s and Brazil in the 1980s) was how much the emancipation of the modern middle-class woman on that continent has been made possible by the availability of cheap servants. President Clinton's troubles in naming a woman to his cabinet showed that this factor is not without its importance in the United States, too. Nor are all such cheap servants necessarily female. Biographies of Medina usually add being his own typographer to the long list of his labors. But you have only to glance at some of the accompanying photographs to realize that the *Tipografia Elzevieriana* was by no means a one-man operation: there was clearly plenty of paid help around in his printing shop. This does not mean that the Medinas were wealthy—far from it; merely that nonprofessional labor before the wage revolution pioneered by Henry Ford in the early twentieth century was incredibly cheap.

Medina was in fact merely benefiting from a situation that has favored and largely made possible middle-class intellectual achievements since the days of Socrates and Plato, if not indeed since the very dawn of civilization, and in regard to which it is the experience of the middle classes in North America and Europe over the last fifty years or so that is the anomaly. (Just to remind you how relatively recent this change has been, I would instance Adolf Hitler's recruitment of slave labor from countries occupied by Germany in World War II; this was done only in part to provide workers for the Nazi war effort: a sizable proportion of the female conscripts went to keep up the supply of domestic help for German middle-class households.) All this, however, merely helps explain Medina's astonishing achievement; it in no way denigrates it.

In Miguel de Unamuno's famous phrase about his fellow countrymen, the Basque race has two great achievements to its credit: "La Compañía de Jesús y la República de Chile." So it should be no surprise that our subject had a double dose of Basque ancestry. His father's family was Basque and Andalusian, his mother's was Basque and Portuguese. The father was a politicized lawyer and supporter of Chile's great mid-nineteenth century president Manuel Montt Torres, whose reforms were so far-reaching as to make him a rival to Portales himself for the title of the "effective creator of the Chilean state." Unfortunately. Medina senior suffered a paralysis which left him bedridden at the age of thirty-three and he sought to achieve his own political ambitions vicariously through his son, a circumstance that embittered relations between them. A famous example was a row over the youngster's graduation thesis at law school. Already interested in natural sciences, he wrote it originally on the legal aspects of digging up fossils. The outraged father made him write a substitute thesis on a more orthodox topic. He obeyed in the end, and gave the original thesis to a friend to pass off as his own. The outcome was that he had the satisfaction of his father finding that, while *Si la donación es un acto o un contracto* was merely accepted, the examiners had graded *De los fosiles: a propósito del Artículo 591 del Código Civil* as *sobresaliente* and awarded it the honor of publication. The first things published under his own name, during his brief career as a lawyer, were a review of Jorge Isaac's *María* and a translation of Longfellow's *Evangeline*. When his father finally despaired of persuading him into politics, he used his political connections, namely, with foreign minister Adolfo Ibáñez, to get him the post of secretary at the Chilean legation in Lima. Medina's two years there gave him a chance to use the resources of Peru's Biblioteca Nacional—then the premier national library in Spanish America, before its sacking by the Chilean army in 1881 and the loss of what was left in the fire of 1943.

Although he had not found his brief experience in the legal profession congenial, it had been modestly profitable, and after two years as a diplomat, he was able to accept an invitation from a Mr. Thorndike, an Englishman, and his Chilean wife, not to mention a daughter with whom Medina is said to have been smitten, to accompany them on a visit to the 1876 Centenary Exhibition in Philadelphia. An alternative explanation for his acceptance is that he hoped to visit Washington where Ibáñez was now Chilean minister—the elder Ibáñez daughter was the eventual Sra. Medina.

From the United States he traveled on to Europe. At the British Museum he met Gaspar del Rio, then working on his monumental *Historia de la Inquisición en los países bajos*, which inspired Medina to a whole series of similar works, on the Holy Office in Lima, in Santiago de Chile, in Cartagena de las Indias, in the Philippines, and in the River Plate. He then went on to the Bibliothèque Nationale, El Escorial, and the Archivo de Indias, and also made brief excursions to Germany, Austria, Italy, and the Low Countries. He returned in 1877 to work on his first major work, the three-volume *Historia de la literatura colonial en Chile*. This won a competitive award from the Universidad de Chile and impressed on him the lack of reliable bibliographies on things Chilean. A growing interest in Alonso de Ercilla (the author of Chile's great sixteenth-century national epic on the conquest, *La Araucana*) took him into Mapuche country to study Chile's sturdy native Americans, whence his *Los aborígenes de Chile* of 1882.

In April 1879 his research was interrupted by the War of the Pacific (also known, rather more aptly, as the Nitrate War) when Chile invaded and defeated both her northern neighbors. He became a *juez de letras* in occupied territory and came to the notice of Patricio Lynch, Chile's "Red Prince," the vice-admiral who was in charge of the army of occupation. In 1883 interior minister (and inheritor of Montt Torres' mantle) Balmaceda appointed him to index Chile's colonial archives. He finished this just as Spain finally recognized Chilean independence and opened diplomatic relations. Admiral-turned-general Lynch now turned yet again, to become minister plenipotentiary and envoy extraordinary in charge of the new legation in Madrid, and he asked specifically for Medina to be secretary of the mission. This request was granted with the express instruction that the young man (he was just thirty-one) use the opportunity to search out documents of Chilean interest in the Spanish archives. The appointment also gave him the opportunity to make the acquaintance of the papal nuncio in Spain, the future Pope Benedict XV, which was later to be instrumental in affording him access to the documetnary treasures of the Vatican Library.

Back in Chile in 1886 he finally married Mercedes. The tranquillity of their very productive conjugal existence was interrupted by the Civil War of

1891 and subsequent overthrow of the government led by now President Balmaceda. The parallels with 1973 are notable. In both cases the progressive nationalism of a radical president proved intolerable to the right, which had ties to foreign investors apprehensive about nationalist expropriation of their assets—British nitrate interests in 1891, American copper (and telecommunication) interests in 1973. A bloody civil conflict resulted in the president's suicide and the imposition of a totally new economic policy based on ultra-orthodox finance (the gold standard in 1891, Chicago-school monetarism in 1973) and free trade (and the collapse of much of the national manufacturing sector on both occasions), accompanied by a vicious witch-hunt of supporters of the ousted regime. Medina had to flee for his life to Argentina (and only the direct physical intervention of a personal friend, British consul B. Calvert, saved his house and 3,000-volume library from being sacked and burned). The exile, however, afforded him the chance to make friends with Argentine scholars and do research on the River Plate region. The fourth centenary of Columbus's arrival had him back in Spain.

Only in late 1896 was it safe for him to return to Chile. The following year he was elected to the faculty of the Universidad de Chile, but he resigned on finding how little interest the Chilean students of his day had in serious historical research. Meanwhile he was publishing on the Philippines, one Hispanic country he never visited, then just two years away from its conquest by the United States: *La imprenta en Manila desde sus orígines hasta 1810*, *El Tribunal del Santo Oficio de la Inquisición en las Islas Filipinas*, and *Bibliografía española en las Islas Filipinas*. His interest derived, it seems, from his having done work on Magellan as the first explorer of southern Chile.

In 1902 Chile's education minister charged Medina to study the organization of public archives and libraries in Europe. He traveled first to Lima, then on through Guatemala to Mexico (where the Medinas visited all the cities which had had a colonial printing press—by rail, stage coach and, where need be, on muleback), taking ship thence to Europe, where he visited the Vatican, Turin (to track down a 1777 work on the Mapuche language), Switzerland, France, and Spain once more (to work further on the archives of Simancas and Seville).

Back in Chile again in 1904, his output—*their* output—continued: the long series of bibliographies of each colonial printing press, and, from 1908, the monographs on the early navigation of the Atlantic.

In 1910 he led the Chilean delegation to Argentina's independence centenary, and the following year he visited Spain again to do research on the conquistador-poet Ercilla, and then journeyed on to London for the

Eighteenth International Congress of Americanists, returning to Chile in 1913.

In 1919 he finally gave up printing his own books, but his writing went on. He had been making regular donations of his books to the National Library of Chile from about 1915, and in November 1925 he made a formal commitment to give all his 22,000 books (in 60,000 volumes) and 500 manuscripts to the Library of Chile, despite tempting ($50,000 plus)[1] offers to buy them (as a collection) from the Huntington, Harvard, the Hispanic Society of America, and the John Carter Brown Library. They now reside in a specially dedicated Sala de Medina.

Two and a half years later, in August 1928, he made his last overseas voyage, visiting Lima, New York (for the Twenty-third International Congress of Americanists), and Seville (for the Exposición Iberoamericana), returning in 1929. He died at the end of the following year, of pneumonia, in his seventy-ninth year. Doña Mercedes followed five years later.

Medina's work has been criticized for tending, in general, to be enumerative rather than evaluative. This, however, may well have been a conscious choice. With so vast a bibliographic area to be mapped, it was far more necessary to complete an adequate description of the totality than spend valuable time and energy in discussing necessarily restricted portions in more detail: that could always come later from other pens when the whole extent of so vast a universe had been made known. Indeed I fear I am committing a like fault (if fault it be), for I have said almost nothing about the content of his publications. But when one's subject is not only a bibliographer, but also a historian, anthropologist, numismatist, cartographer, geographer, literary critic, biographer, naturalist, philologist, linguist, printer, translator and editor, and, like so many of the great bibliographers, a bookdealer too, what can one say in a brief essay?

NOTE

1. In 1925 dollars, with a purchasing power at least ten times as much in 1994 money!

BIBLIOGRAPHY

Bromsen, Maury A. "José Toribio Medina." *South Atlantic Quarterly* 44:3 (July 1945), 316-326.

Chiappa, Víctor Manuel. *Catálogo de las publicaciones de José Toribio Medina, 1873-1914, continuado hasta el día y seguido de una bibliografía por Guillermo Feliú Cruz.* Santiago de Chile, 1924.

Donoso, Armando. *José Toribio Medina, 1852-1930.* [Santiago de Chile:] Imprensa Universitaria, 1952.

———. *Vida y viajes de un erudito: Recuerdos de don José Toribio Medina*. Santiago de Chile: Zig-Zag, 1915.

Feliú Cruz, Guillermo. *José Toribio Medina, historiador y bibliógrafo de América*. Santiago de Chile: Nascimento, 1952.

———. *Labor literaria y científica de José Toribio Medina en 1910: Homenaje a Medina en el sesquicentenario de la independencia nacional*. Santiago de Chile: Editorial Universitaria, 1961. 64 p.

Inter-American Bibliographical and Library Association. *Proceedings of the 1st-3rd conventions*. 3 vols. New York: H. W. Wilson Co., 1938–1941.

Pan American Union. *José Toribio Medina, Humanist of the Americas: An Appraisal*. Edited by Maury A. Bromsen. Washington, DC, 1960.

Roberts, Sarah Elizabeth. *José Toribio Medina, His Life and Works*. Washington, DC: Inter-American Bibliographical and Library Association, 1941.

Villalobos R., Sergio. *Medina, su vida y sus obras, 1852-1930*. Santiago de Chile: Imprensa Universitaria para la Comisión Nacional de Conmemoración del Centenario del Nacimiento de Medina, 1952.

Zamudio Z., José. *Medina y la bibliografía*. Santiago de Chile: Nascimento, 1952.

Contributors, Conference Program, and SALALM Committees

Contributors

CARMEN ALMODÓVAR MUÑOZ, Universidad de La Habana

SAÚL ARMENDÁRIZ SÁNCHEZ, Biblioteca del Centro de Información Científica y Humanística de la Universidad Nacional Autónoma de México, UNAM

JAMES C. ARMSTRONG, Library of Congress Office, Rio de Janeiro

ENRIQUE BARRETO PASTRANA, Centro de Información Científica y Humanística de la Universidad Nacional Autónoma de México, UNAM

EMMANUELLE BERVAS-RODRÍGUEZ, Biblioteca Dr. Manuel Gallardo, El Salvador

ANGELA CARREÑO, New York University Library

MICAELA CHÁVEZ VILLA, Departamento de Desarrollo de Colecciones, El Colegio de México

ARTURO CURIEL BALLESTEROS, Programa Ecología y Educación Ambiental, Universidad de Guadalajara

MARTA DOMÍNGUEZ DÍAZ, SEREC Chile, Libreros

GEORGETTE MAGASSY DORN, Hispanic Division, Library of Congress

GEORGE ELMENDORF, México Norte Booksellers

GLADYS FABA BEAUMONT, Centro Nacional de Información y Documentación sobre Salud, Ministerio de Salud, México

ANA MARÍA FERNÁNDEZ VIGNOLO, Biblioteca Nacional de Venezuela

EDMUNDO FLORES, Hispanic Division, Library of Congress

ARACELI GARCÍA-CARRANZA, Biblioteca Nacional José Martí, Cuba

NELLY S. GONZÁLEZ, University of Illinois Library, Urbana-Champaign

MINA JANE GROTHEY, Zimmerman Library, University of New Mexico

LAURENCE HALLEWELL, Columbia University Libraries

DOLORES MOYANO MARTIN, Hispanic Division, Library of Congress

FELIPE MARTÍNEZ ARELLANO, Centro Universitario de Investigaciones Bibliotecológicas, Universidad Nacional Autónoma de México, UNAM

ROBERT A. MCNEIL, Bodleian Library, University of Oxford

ROSA Q. MESA, University of Florida Libraries

LEONARDO MEZA AGUILAR, Area Ecología, Universidad de Guadalajara

BARBARA A. MILLER, Graduate School of Education and Information Studies, University of California, Los Angeles

MOLLY MOLLOY, New Mexico State University Library

CARMEN M. MURICY, Library of Congress Office, Rio de Janeiro

GRETE PASCH, Biblioteca Ludwig von Mises, Universidad Francisco Marroquín, Guatemala

TERRY C. PEET, Hispanic Acquisitions Program (Exchange and Gift), Library of Congress, Washington, D.C.

KAREN RANUCCI, Independent Media Resource Exchange

JON PAUL RODRÍGUEZ, Pro-Vita, Venezuela

ADOLFO RODRÍGUEZ GALLARDO, Dirección General de Bibliotecas, Universidad Nacional Autónoma de México, UNAM

GABRIEL SANHUEZA SUÁREZ, Universidad de Concepción, Chile

LUIS HIPÓLITO SERRANO PÉREZ, Instituto de Historia de Cuba

PETER A. STERN, Alexander Library, Rutgers University

PAULA SULLENGER, Ralph Brown Draughton Library, Auburn University

RAFAEL E. TARRAGÓ, Hesburgh Library, University of Notre Dame

LESBIA ORTA VARONA, University of Miami Library

KINLOCH WALPOLE, Latin American Information Base Project

KAREN T. WEI, Asian Library, University of Illinois at Urbana-Champaign

JOYCE C. WRIGHT, University of Illinois at Urbana-Champaign

Conference Program

Monday, May 17, 1993

9:00 - 10:00 Opening Session

Chair: *Pat Noble*, President, SALALM, University of London

Rapporteur General: *Charles Fineman*, Northwestern University

Lic. *Raúl Padilla López*, Rector, Universidad de Guadalajara

Maricarmen Canales, Feria Internacional del Libro, Universidad de Guadalajara

Lic. *Irma Pellicer*, Instituto de Bibliotecas, Universidad de Guadalajara

Laurence Hallewell, Columbia University Libraries: "Medina and the Medina Award"

11:00 - 12:30 **Panel: Popular Campaigns against Environmental Damage**

Chair: *Ana Maria Cobos*, Saddleback College

Commentator: *Peter Johnson*, Princeton University

Rapporteur: *Gabriela Sonntag-Grigera*, California State University, San Marcos

Jon Paul Rodríguez, Pro-Vita, Venezuela: "Investigación y conservación de la cotorra margariteña"

Gabriel Sanhueza, CODEFF, Chile: "Las comunidades peguenches en la defensa de sus recursos naturales"

Leonardo Meza, Area Ecología, Universidad de Guadalajara

Arturo Curiel Ballesteros, Programa Ecología y Educación Ambiental, Universidad de Guadalajara

15:00 - 16:30 **Panel: The Luso-Hispanic Collections of the Library of Congress**

Chair: *Georgette Dorn*, Library of Congress

Rapporteur: *Paula Sullenger*, Auburn University

All panelists from the Hispanic Division of the Library of Congress, unless otherwise noted

Iêda Siqueira Wiarda: "Brazil and Portugal in LC's Collections"

Dolores Moyano Martin, Editor *HLAS:* "The *Handbook of Latin American Studies*"

Edmundo Flores: "Hispanic Acquisitions Trends and Arrearage Reductions at LC since 1990"

James Armstrong, Director, LC Rio Office: "The Rio Office"

Georgette Dorn, Acting Chief, Hispanic Division: "The Archive of Hispanic Literature on Tape"

15:00 - 16:30 **Panel: Cuban Historical and Contemporary Bibliography: Problematic of Collections, Research, and Preservation**

Chair: *Rhonda Neugebauer*, Arizona State University

Rapporteur: *Tony A. Harvell* (University of San Diego)

Araceli García Carranza, Biblioteca Nacional José Martí, Cuba: "Cuban Bibliography: Inventory of Cuban Cultures"

Luis Serrano Pérez, Instituto de Historia de Cuba: "Instituto de Historia: Preserving the Historical Record"

Carmen Almodóvar, Universidad de La Habana: "Historiography of Colonial History Sources"

Lesbia Varona, University of Miami Library: "Building a Cuban Collection Abroad"

17:00 - 18:30 **Roundtable: ¿Una América Latina o una América Sajona?**

Chair: *Fernando del Paso*, Biblioteca Iberoamericana, Universidad de Guadalajara

Commentator: *Georgette Dorn*, Library of Congress

Georgette Dorn

Heracelio Cepeda

Dante Medina

Juan José Arreola

19:00 - 20:30 **Reception** in the Biblioteca Iberoamericana, Universidad de Guadalajara

Tuesday, May 18, 1993

9:00 - 10:30 **Panel: New Directions in National Cooperation**

Moderator: *Deborah L. Jakubs*, Duke University
Rapporteur: *Nancy L. Hallock*, University of Pittsburgh
Scott Van Jacob, Dickinson College
Mark L. Grover, Brigham Young University
Carl W. Deal, University of Illinois: "The Mexican Pilot Project"
Peter T. Johnson, Princeton University: "Primary Sources from Marginalized Groups"
Ann Wade, British Library: "The Review of Collecting Priorities in the British Library"

9:00 - 10:30 **Panel: Highways of the 90s: Latin American Resources and Electronic Information Networks**

Chair: *Eudora Loh*, University of California, Los Angeles
Rapporteur: *Fehl M. Cannon*, Library of Congress
Harold Colson, University of California, San Diego: "A Terrific Beauty Is Born: Latin Americana and the Virtual Library"
Barbara Stewart, Coordinadora Regional de Investigaciones Económicas y Sociales (CRIES): "Beating the Odds: An Experience in the Development of Specialized Information Networks in Central America"
Saúl Armendáriz Sánchez, Biblioteca del CICH; Enrique Barreto, CICH: "La recuperación de información en línea por medio de la Red UNAM: El caso del Centro de Información Científica y Humanística"
Gladys Faba Beaumont, Centro Nacional de Información y Documentación sobre Salud: "Networks: An Instrument of Health Information and Documentation Services Improvement in Mexico"

9:00 - 10:30 **Workshop: Creative Cataloging Techniques**

Chair: *Richard Phillips*, University of Florida
Cecilia Sercan, Cornell University
Steve Kiczek, Princeton University

11:00 - 12:30 **Town Meeting**

Chair: *David Block*, Cornell University

15:00 - 16:30 **Panel: El libro en el occidente de México**

Chair: *Henry C. Schmidt*, Texas A&M University
Commentator: *Carmen Ramos Escandón*, Occidental College
Rapporteur: *Lynn K. Shirey*, Harvard Law School
Carmen Castañeda, CIESAS - Occidente: "El libro en Jalisco"
Luis González, El Colegio de Michoacán: "El libro en Michoacán"

15:00 - 16:30 **Panel: Latin American Databases**

Chair: *Grete Pasch*, Universidad Francisco Marroquín, Guatemala
Rapporteur: *Iván E. Calimano*, University of Southern California
Grete Pasch: "On Building Database Directories: New Opportunities and a Proposal"
Emmanuelle Bervas, Biblioteca Dr. Manuel Gallardo, El Salvador: "Creación de una bibliografía salvadoreña"
Alma Rivera, Universidad Centroamericana, El Salvador: "Creación de bases de datos: Proyectos y productos"
Kinloch Walpole, Latin American Database Group: "The Database Directory"
Elsa Barbarena, UNAM, Mexico: "The *Directorio de Bases de Datos*"

15:00 - 16:30 **Workshop: Workshop of Subcommittee on Marginalized Peoples and Ideas on Environmental Organizations**

Moderator: *Peter T. Johnson*, Princeton University
Marta Domínguez, SEREC, Santiago de Chile
Carmen Muricy, Library of Congress, Rio de Janeiro Office
George Elmendorff, México Norte

Wednesday, May 19, 1993

9:00 - 10:30 **Panel: An Object of Curiosity: Latin America and "Science" from the Eighteenth Century to the Twenty-First**

Chair: *Susan Shaw*, South Dakota State University
Rapporteur: *Darlene Waller*, University of Connecticut

Rafael E. Tarragó, Hesburgh Library, University of Notre Dame: "Scientific Expeditions in Spanish America Under the Bourbons"

Robert McNeil, Bodleian Library, University of Oxford: "The Humboldt Current: Northern European Naturalists in Latin America, 1799-1859"

William H. Beezley, Texas Christian University: "U.S. Consuls: Foreign Travelers and Scientists"

9:00 - 10:30 **Workshop and Demonstration of Latin American Databases (Part 1)**

9:00 - 10:30 **Panel: Exchange and Gift**

Moderator: *Shelley Miller*, University of Kansas

Rapporteur: *Richard F. Phillips*, University of Florida

Terry Peet, Exchange and Gift Division, Library of Congress: "Serials Exchange: Is It Worth Doing?

Paula Sullenger, Auburn University: "A Comparison of Staff Time and Tasks for Acquiring Latin American Serials through Three Methods: Paid Subscription, Exchange, and Gift"

Micaela Chávez Villa, Departamento de Desarrollo de Colecciones, El Colegio de México: "Exchange Activities at El Colegio de México"

11:00 - 12:30 **Workshop and Demonstration of Latin American Databases (Part 2)**

11:00 - 12:30 **Panel: Cultural and Biological Consequences of the Encounter**

Chair: *Peter Stern*, Rutgers University

Rapporteur: *Adán Griego*, University of California, Santa Barbara

David Block, Cornell University: "From Rainforest to Plantation: The History of Chinchona (Quinine) as a Cross-Disciplinary Project and as a Challenge to Research Libraries"

Barbara Miller, University of California, Los Angeles: "Indigenous Visions of the Book"

Peter Stern, "Beyond Crosby: Recent Historiography on the Columbian Exchange"

11:00 - 12:30 **Panel: Publishing in the Sciences and the Cuban Diaspora**

Chair: *Maria Luisa Pérez*, Miami Public Library
Moderator: *Esperanza B. de Varona*
Rapporteur: *Barbara Stewart*, University of Pittsburgh

Juan Clark, Miami-Dade Community College: "Los derechos humanos como factor determinante de la diáspora cubana"

César Mena, University of Miami: "Historia de la odontología en Cuba, 1492-1984"

Juan M. Portuondo, University of Miami: "La medicina en Cuba antes y después de Castro"

Agustín A. Recio, University of Miami: "Arquitectura e ingeniería de los cubanos antes de 1959 y de la diáspora cubana hasta el presente"

15:00 - 16:30 **Panel: Independent Video in Latin America and the Caribbean**

Chair: *Angela Carreño*, New York University
Rapporteur: *Peter S. Bushnell*, University of Florida

Carmen Muricy, Library of Congress, Rio de Janeiro Office: "Recent Trends in Brazilian Social Documentary"

Karen Ranucci, International Media Resource Exchange: "Democracy in Communication: Latin American Video Resources"

15:00 - 18:30 **LASPAU Seminar: Information Resources and Computer Networks**

David Policar, Latin American Scholarship, Program of American Universities, LASPAU

15:00 - 16:30 **Roundtable: Afternoon of the Documents Acquisitions Librarian**

Chair: *Andrew Makuch*

Alfredo Montalvo, Editorial El Inca, Cochabamba, Bolivia: "The Acquisition and Distribution of Latin American Documents: A Dealer's Point of View"

Rosa María Fernández de Zamora, Biblioteca del Congreso, México: "Publicaciones oficiales latinoamericanas desde el punto de vista de una biblioteca mexicana"

Sabine Zehrer, Ibero-Amerikanisches Institut, Berlin, Germany: "Collection Development Issues of National and Subnational State Documents: Mexico, Brazil, and Argentina"

17:00 - 18:30 **Panel: The Electronic Library Environment**

Moderator: *Tony Harvell*, University of San Diego

Rapporteur: *Carlos R. Delgado*, University of California, Berkeley

Adolfo Rodríguez Gallardo, UNAM

Felipe Martínez Arellano, UNAM: "La automatización en las bibliotecas de la UNAM y su influencia en las bibliotecas mexicanas y en la conducta del usuario"

Molly Molloy, New Mexico State University: "Groping for Our Piece of the Elephant: Latin American Information on the Internet"

Mina Jane Grothey, University of New Mexico: "The Impact of Electronic Resources on Bibliographic Instruction"

Thursday, May 20, 1993

9:00 - 10:30 **Panel: The Chinese Contribution to Colonial Spanish America and the Caribbean**

Chair: *Joyce Wright*, University of Illinois at Urbana-Champaign

Rapporteur: *Sara M. Sánchez*, University of Miami

Joyce Wright, "Chinese Immigration to the Caribbean"

Rosa Mesa, University of Florida: "Chinese Immigration to Cuba: 1840-1910"

Karen Wei, University of Illinois at Urbana-Champaign: "Chinese Immigration to Mexico"

Nelly S. González, University of Illinois at Urbana-Champaign: "Connecting East and West: The Chinese in Panama, 1850-1914"

9:00 - 10:30 **SALALM Task Force on Electronic Resources**

Chair: *Harold Colson*, University of California, San Diego

No Host Lunch/Dinner Schedule

Monday, May 17, 1993

Lunch

1. Library Automation in El Salvador (Alma Rivera, Universidad Centroamericana, El Salvador)
2. New Directions in Cuban Historiography (Luis Serrano Pérez, Instituto de Historia, Cuba)
3. Cataloging of Latin Americana: Resolving Problems (Cecilia Sercan, Cornell University)
4. Official Publications: Confronting Collecting Challenges (Andrew Makuch, University of Arizona)

Tuesday, May 18, 1993

Lunch

1. Recent Developments in Cuban Bibliography (Araceli García Carranza, Biblioteca Nacional, Cuba)
2. Honduras: Libraries and Archives (Georgette M. Dorn, Library of Congress)
3. Collecting Material of Brazilian Popular Sector Groups (Carmen Muricy, Library of Congress, Rio de Janeiro Office)
4. Permanent Paper Initiatives for Mexican Publishing (Sharlane Grant, Arizona State University)

Dinner

1. New Member Orientation (Laura Shedenhelm, Membership Committee, SALALM)
2. Update on Developments at the Library of Congress (Terry Peet, Library of Congress)
3. Intensive Peruvian Collecting Group: Organizational Meeting (Dan Hazen, Harvard University; César Rodríguez, Yale University)

Wednesday, May 19, 1993

Lunch

1. New Developments in El Salvador's Bibliography and University Libraries (Emmanuelle Bervas, Biblioteca Gallardo and Bibliografía Nacional Salvadoreña)
2. Venezuelan Environmental Movement (Jon Paul Rodríguez, Pro-Vita, Venezuela)
3. University-Level Teaching and Research in Cuba, with Particular Reference to Cuban History (Carmen Almodóvar, Universidad de La Habana)

SALALM Committees, 1992-1993

Executive Board Committees

Constitution and Bylaws Committee
Policy, Research, and Investigation Committee
Editorial Board
Membership Committee
Finance Committee
Nominating Committee
Conference Planning Committee

Substantive Committees and Subcommittees

Acquisitions Committee
- Library/Bookdealer/Publisher Relations Subcommittee
- Subcommittee on Gifts and Exchanges
- Subcommittee on Serials
- Subcommittee on Marginalized Peoples and Ideas

Bibliography Committee
- Subcommittee on Cuban Bibliography
- Subcommittee on Special Bibliographical Projects

Committee on Library Operations and Services
- Subcommittee on Cataloging and Bibliographic Technology
- Subcommittee on Reference Services
- Subcommittee on Bibliographic Instruction

Committee on Interlibrary Cooperation
- Subcommittee of OCLC Users
- Subcommittee on National-Level Cooperation

Committee on Official Publications

Outreach/Enlace Committee

Affinity Groups

HAPI Indexers
Latin American Microfilming Project (LAMP)
Electronic Resources Interest Group
Task Force on Standards for Latin American Collections